Notable Scottish Trials

City of Glasgow Bank Directors

Portraits of the Prisoners William Taylor, Henry Inglis, John Innes Wright, and
Robert S. Stronach.

(From a Contemporary Print.)

Trial of the
City of Glasgow Bank
Directors

EDITED BY

William Wallace, M.A.
Advocate

GLASGOW AND EDINBURGH

WILLIAM HODGE & COMPANY

PRINTED BY
WILLIAM HODGE AND COMPANY,
GLASGOW AND EDINBURGH.
1905.

CONTENTS.

CONTENTS.

LIST OF ILLUSTRATIONS.

THE CITY OF GLASGOW BANK TRIAL:

JANUARY, 1879.

CHAPTER I.

The Stoppage of the Bank.

THE trial of the City Bank Directors ranks, in the estimation at least of the layman, if not of the professional lawyer, as probably the most important which has taken place in Scotland. The magnitude of the financial crisis brought about by the collapse of the Bank, the social standing of the Directors to whose hands the management of it was entrusted and who so shamefully abused the confidence reposed in them, the unparalleled disclosures of financial turpitude and recklessness revealed in the report of the professional gentlemen who conducted the preliminary investigation of its affairs immediately after the stoppage, and the startling nature of the evidence adduced by the prosecution, all combined to invest the trial with an interest which is not surpassed in the annals of our criminal jurisprudence. That this financial disaster, which brought ruin to so many homes, depriving in many instances the widow and the orphan of their sole means of maintenance, was brought about, not by innocent misfortune, but by the criminal recklessness of men whose commercial probity, high social standing, and professed religious belief had induced thousands of their fellow-countrymen to place implicit trust in their honesty and integrity only serves to intensify the interest felt in their trial. How these men abused the confidence reposed in them—how, by insidious steps, they converted a once-sound and prosperous banking concern into a mere machine for the abstraction of the hard-won savings of the small and all-too-confiding investor, only to throw them into the lap of wealthy and unscrupulous speculators, who were

The City of Glasgow Bank Trial.

thus enabled to dissipate them in schemes of reckless folly and insensate gambling—how, while posing as pillars of commercial integrity, they were in reality the rotten props of a decaying and worthless concern—may be seen from a perusal of the evidence adduced for the prosecution, of the brilliant and incisive speech of the Lord Advocate, and of the no less luminous and weighty charge to the jury of the learned Lord Justice-Clerk.

The City of Glasgow Bank commenced business as a banking company in the year 1839, having its head office in Glasgow and numerous branches throughout Scotland. It continued to carry on business until the end of the year 1857, about the time at which the Western Bank of Scotland closed its doors, when it also suspended payment. But at the instance of a number of influential men in the West it was resuscitated, and again resumed business in the beginning of the year 1858. It was registered under the Joint Stock Companies Act of 1862 in November of that year, and continued its operations until it finally ceased to do business and closed its doors on 2nd October, 1878. There were in all 1249 partners connected with it, and the paid-up capital amounted to £1,000,000. At the beginning of 1878 the reserve fund was stated at £450,000, the dividends and surplus profits in hand at £148,501, the deposits at £8,382,712, and the "circulation, acceptances, etc.," at £2,114,229. A noteworthy fact in connection with the bank was that it had more branches than any other Scottish establishment, the total number of these being 133. Taken at the quotations made in the course of December, the price per £100 of stock for the last three years was—1875, £228 ; 1876, £228 ; and 1877, £243.

Notwithstanding its apparent prosperity, the Bank had, however, begun to experience some difficulty in carrying on its business. For a week or two before the final crash it had been pretty generally hinted in banking circles that calamity in a certain quarter could not long be delayed. It had begun to be bruited in banking circles that the unusually large number of acceptances which the City of Glasgow Bank had floating in the London market had latterly lent colour to the belief that the Directors were not so careful in their dealings and financial operations as prudent men of business should have been.

2

The Stoppage of the Bank.

There was, it was rumoured, a disposition on the part of the Directors to lend countenance to unsound speculations, and to give credit where it could not be given without considerable risk, and that, as a consequence, the influential position of the Bank had itself in the long run become jeopardised. Against this suspicion there was, at the same time, the share list to point to, in which the stock of the Bank was to be found keeping its place well alongside its neighbours'.

To the general public, however, the intelligence came no further back than a week before the stoppage, and even then, of course, the gossip was altogether indefinite, as no one cared to overstep caution by publicly naming the bank suspected. In what manner the unhealthiness of the concern was for so long kept a secret cannot even yet be explained. But the fact that in August, 1878, a dividend at the rate of 12 per cent. had been declared, and that up till the day before the crash the stock remained steady at £236, proves that the actual state of matters was not before the minds of the shareholders, and could not, it was at first believed, have been known to the Directors. So soon, however, as the rumours began to assume a shape, the topic, notwithstanding its vagueness, engrossed a great part of the business talk up till the Friday previous; but as there was no appearance in the state of the Bank stocks to bear out suspicion, the story was, at the end of the week, believed by most outsiders to be merely an Exchange hoax.

Just as the public were beginning to believe that the disquieting rumours would, after all, prove false, the worst forebodings were realised by the stoppage of the Bank. The sudden fulfilment of the evil rumours, therefore, found the commercial community all but unprepared. The resolution of the Directors to take the step was made known at a comparatively late hour on the forenoon of Tuesday, the 1st of October, 1878, and, meeting immediately afterwards, the managers of the other banks agreed to issue an announcement to the effect that, to lessen the inconvenience of the stoppage of the Bank and its ceasing to issue notes, they would receive, in the ordinary course of business, the notes of the City of Glasgow Bank then in circulation.

Though nothing publicly transpired as to the causes which had brought about the failure, the significance of the occurrence was, happily, not misunderstood by the public, and any panic in

3

The City of Glasgow Bank Trial.

the circumstances was felt to be unreasonable. To the general public the occurrence, it was at first thought, might even prove beneficial. The complications of the Bank, it was feared, would prove fatal to the concern itself, and the failure, it was believed, might be more disastrous to those directly concerned than even the failure of the Western Bank was, but depositors, on the other hand, would, it was expected, be fully provided for. The action of the other banks in accepting City of Glasgow Bank notes prevented a repetition of the panic which occurred at the stoppage of the Western Bank, when its notes were refused by the other banks. Indeed, no better testimony of the public confidence in the soundness of the Scottish banking system could have been given than the calmness with which the announcement of the stoppage was received. Though the announcement that the City of Glasgow Bank had closed its doors came upon the public like a bolt from the blue, the common sense of the public asserted itself, and, profiting by the lesson taught by the failure of the Western Bank, there was, fortunately, no run upon the banks. It is not too much to say that, deeply as the stoppage was regretted because of the loss and inconvenience which it must necessarily occasion, there was a pretty general feeling of relief—a rotten branch had been cut away, and the good tree of Scottish banking, it was felt, would brave all storms the better for its absence.

The subject of the stoppage was, of course, the chief topic of conversation among business men throughout the day, and a good deal of uneasiness was manifested in many quarters as to the effect it was likely to have, especially on the smaller class of tradesmen. The rapid recovery of the Bank from its last crisis, and the consequent rise in the value of its stock under the impulse of improving dividends, seems to have rendered City Bank shares a favourite investment with small capitalists, and more especially with widows and persons retired from business on a moderate competency, and it was feared that a considerable number of this class might be seriously affected, more especially as, besides holding shares, many had also their deposits chiefly lodged in this Bank. The more the list of shareholders was scanned the less confidence did it inspire among commercial men. It was seen to be one of the most unsubstantial of share lists for an undertaking of such an extensive character that could possibly be imagined. A considerable number of the shareholders were alleged to have had advances made to them by the Bank to the extent of their holdings, and altogether it was believed there were so many who might not be able to respond to any call made on them that the whole of the deficiency would have to be made up by a comparatively limited section of the copartnery. When business opened on the Exchange, brokers, under instructions, pressed large quantities of stock upon the market, with the natural result of a fall. Very little bank stock changed hands, but other stock started at a reduction of from £1 to £4 per share. Several million pounds worth of stock are said to have been offered, and the losses arising from forced sales must have reached an enormous amount.

On the day following the stoppage the Directors placed the books of the Bank in the hands of Alexander Bennet M'Grigor, LL.D., of the firm of Messrs. M'Grigor, Donald & Co., writers in Glasgow, and William Anderson, C.A., of the firm of Messrs. Kerr, Andersons, Muir & Main, accountants there, with instructions to investigate into and prepare a report of the state of the affairs of the Bank, to be laid before a meeting of the shareholders, to be subsequently convened. At a meeting of the Directors of the Bank held in Glasgow on 5th October, Messrs. Anderson and M'Grigor reported that, though they had, as yet, been able only in the most cursory manner to examine into the condition of the Bank, they were satisfied it was impossible for it to continue its business, and that it would be advisable for it to wind up its affairs. They therefore recommended that in the interests of the shareholders no time should be lost in having it put into liquidation, and that with this view a meeting of the shareholders should be convened under the provisions of the Companies Acts. It was accordingly resolved to call an extraordinary general meeting of the shareholders for the 22nd October, to resolve as to whether the Bank should be wound up, and, if so resolved, to appoint liquidators. The date named was the earliest for which, legally, under the contract of copartnery, the meeting could be called. The investigation into the affairs of the Bank by Messrs. Anderson and M'Grigor was meanwhile proceeded with as rapidly as possible, but the work proved so complicated and difficult that no official statement could be placed in the hands of the shareholders for several days. Enough was, however, then known to place the magnitude of the failure beyond doubt, though it was still hoped that, when all the assets

5

were realised, the sum to be made good by the shareholders might not be quite so large as had been indicated.

The report* by Dr. M'Grigor and Mr. Anderson was issued shortly before nine o'clock on the evening of Friday, 18th October, and it revealed a state of matters which far exceeded the anticipations of the most despondent shareholder. The rumour had, indeed, got bruited about before the issue of the report that the deficiency amounted to upwards of £5,000,000, but it was at first discredited, and it only received credence at all owing to its persistent repetition by those who were supposed to have good information on the subject. Only a few copies of the report were at first issued for the use of the press, and consequently some time elapsed before the details oozed out. When they were ultimately sufficiently confirmed, there was something like consternation amongst the anxious crowds who besieged the offices of the various newspapers. Men were taken aghast, and could not realise the astounding facts disclosed. Nothing like it had been anticipated even by the most pessimistic, and groups of haggard and anxious people lounged about the streets until a late hour talking over the dreadful disclosures, while general gloom and an uneasy feeling prevailed. With the issue of the report the shareholders had at least some light thrown upon the condition of the Bank's affairs, and a most sombre light it was, unfortunately. The sum of the whole matter was seen to be that the Bank had lost, on a moderate and probably favourable estimate, £6,200,000—*i.e.*, the whole of the paid-up capital and reserve fund, together with fully £5,000,000 besides. That was a most disastrous statement for the unhappy shareholders, and it was apparent that a loss of such magnitude could never have fallen on them but for reckless mismanagement to begin with, and deliberate and long-continued fraud practised to hide that mismanagement. The story set forth in the report was one of the most disgraceful in the history of banking. Accounts had been deliberately falsified, securities entered at fictitious values, bad debts taken as good assets, and the very gold which ought to have been held under the Act of 1845 against the note issue deliberately squandered to the extent of over £300,000. The Government had been deceived by false returns, the shareholders by "cooked" balance sheets, and everything done, in short, that a perverse ingenuity could think of to conceal the bankrupt

* See Appendix.

6

The Stoppage of the Bank.

condition of the Bank until it became a national calamity. The revelations of the investigators startled the mercantile community almost as much as the news of the failure, and were felt to be the signal for many and needed reforms.   Here was a bank professedly occupied with the commerce of Scotland, a bank notable among Scots banks for its pushing endeavours to establish branches all over the northern half of the kingdom, throwing away millions of the money of its depositors to support hopelessly rotten firms in the East India trade, investing in doubtful or altogether speculative securities, such as Erie shares and other American railway stocks, buying land in Australia and New Zealand, and generally behaving like an insane gambler mad to be rid of his fortune.   This, too, was a position into which the managers of this Bank had obviously drifted at first by following the ordinary recognised course of banking business. They had lent rather freely on a bad security, or had puffed up some possibly shrewd and rich but over-eager speculator, to the loss of the concern.   Then courage failed them ; they dared not tell the truth.   It was easier to hide losses in ambiguous balance sheets, good only for deception, and the first losses were thus concealed.   Then worse came, and it became necessary to go from one criminal act to another in order to keep the ever-increasing losses out of sight, until at last the criminality reached the point of paying a splendid dividend and issuing a balance sheet showing a large surplus, at the very time when the funds of the Bank were so utterly exhausted that the managers had to abstract the gold held against the notes in order to keep the concern above water for a few more days.   Recklessness led to difficulties, and difficulties led to fraud in order that the true state of matters might be kept from the shareholders and the public.   As the deposits of honest men came in they were handed over to speculators whose losses daily demanded more and more.   One evil step led to another.   The utter, almost inconceivable rottenness of the concern had to be cloaked with a fair seeming, and to that end dividends were paid, and when people, perhaps with some suspicion that all was not right, took their stock into the market, it was bought by the Bank itself, in order to keep up the quoted price.   From first to last there was not one redeeming feature.

Paradoxical as it might seem, the case was so bad that it was even hoped that it might strengthen the confidence which the

7

The City of Glasgow Bank Trial.

country had in its banking system. It was impossible to imagine that there could be, in the management of any other bank, men so bereft of honour and honesty as to be carrying on a system so base as that which had prevailed in the City of Glasgow Bank, and if that was true, as who can doubt, the soundness of Scottish banking might be considered as fairly proved. Some critics in England had at once been ready with their assurance that the Scottish system was to blame. The truth was that the cause of the failure was the gross and criminal departure of the Directors from the Scottish system. It must, however, be remembered that among the Scottish banks the City of Glasgow had always occupied a somewhat exceptional place. The stoppage in 1857 brought to light the damaging fact that, with numerous branches, extensive deposits, and a large circulation of notes, this unwieldy and widely ramified concern had yet attempted to carry on its business without either the aid or the protection of Government stocks or other convertible securities. At that time it had been pointed out by competent financial authorities that the true safety of both public and shareholders was to be found in allowing the Bank to be wound up. Much indignation was expressed in Glasgow commercial circles at this opinion, but the result seemed to show that enormous suffering would have been saved had that advice been taken. What the Bank then was it had apparently continued to be—a bank merely in name, in truth a simple channel to convey the money of depositors from the country districts to Glasgow, in order that it might be squandered in India, the Western States of America, Canada, and New Zealand. By such operations the home trade was impoverished, foreign and colonial business inflated, and even the price of land in New Zealand raised to a point hurtful to emigrants as well as prejudicial to the ultimate interests of permanent settlers.

Upon a good many of the points that have been mentioned the list of shareholders casts a lurid light. Take, for instance, the position of the Directors. Several of them had had, beyond all doubt, large advances out of the funds of the Bank. Many hundreds of thousands of pounds had been thus applied; and the meaning of it was that these Directors had been able to use their position to get advances which no prudent manager would have made. It might have been expected that the Directors would at least have a substantial interest in the concern which

The Stoppage of the Bank.

they managed, or mismanaged.   Here is an account of their holdings:—

John Stewart,	£1,000
Robert Salmond,	1,200
Lewis Potter,	1,200
John Innes Wright,	1,200
William Taylor,	1,800
R. S. Stronach,	900
*Henry Inglis,	1,700
*John Gillespie,	2,000
*Robert Craig,	20,467
*A. F. Sommerville,	11,000

The asterisks show those Directors who constituted what was called the Edinburgh Board.   They were, it is understood, entrusted with the Edinburgh business, but had little or nothing to do with the management of the general affairs of the Bank. That was left to the Glasgow Board, and it will be seen that the stock held by all the Glasgow Directors only amounted to £7300, or less than half that of one of the Edinburgh Directors alone. A man's holding may not be a fair measure of his ability as a Director, but shareholders as a rule prefer that those who manage their affairs have a really substantial interest in the concern.   The list of the shareholders as at the date of the crisis presents features of no less interest.   The power of the shareholders to meet the demands which were likely to be made upon them became a question of much importance in view of liquidation.   An analysis of the list of shareholders may not be amiss.   The list shows that the shareholders were divided as follows:—Those holding

Under £100,					95
At £100,					183
Exceeding £100 and under £200,					55
„	200	„	500,		455
„	500	„	1,000,		240
„	1,000	„	2,000,		156
„	2,000	„	5,000,		72
„	5,000	„	10,000,		12
„	10,000				4
Total shareholders,					1272

This analysis brings out some noteworthy facts.   Thus, it will be seen that more than a fifth of the whole number of stock-holders held amounts of £100 or under.   They represented, for

9

The City of Glasgow Bank Trial.

the most part, people with small savings, the accumulations, perhaps, of years of toil, which at one fell swoop were swept away. More than a half of the whole number had less than £500 of stock, and they were largely people not able to bear any great pressure. Most prominent of all is the fact that there were only eighty-eight stockholders who held amounts of £2000 and upwards, and even in these eighty-eight were included the Bank itself, which held no less than £153,536 of stock. We have, then, this startling fact, that the quantity of stock held by the Bank reduced the actual paid-up capital of the Company to below £847,000, and it was consequently upon the holders of this sum, and not upon the holders of a full million, that the loss ultimately fell.

The Crown authorities acted with commendable vigour and promptitude in the case of the Directors. No sooner was the report of the investigators made known than the first steps were taken towards the prosecution of those who had taken part in the frauds which that report revealed. Warrants were issued, and on Saturday evening, the 19th October, Robert Salmond, Lewis Potter, John Innes Wright, William Taylor, Directors; R. S. Stronach, Director and Manager; and Charles Leresche, Secretary, were arrested in Glasgow; while John Stewart and Henry Inglis, Directors, were arrested in Edinburgh. The first-named formed the Glasgow Board, which managed all the general affairs of the Bank. They were apprehended by order of the Lord Advocate, and taken before the Sheriff of Lanarkshire, when they were remanded for forty-eight hours. A petition and complaint at the instance of William Alexander Brown, advocate, the Procurator-Fiscal of Lanarkshire, was thereupon prepared and presented to the Sheriff on the 21st October, charging them with falsehood, fraud, and wilful imposition; and declarations with reference thereto having been emitted by the accused, the Sheriff, after considering the same, and the evidence, so far as taken, of same date, committed them for trial. Thereafter a second petition and complaint at the instance of the Procurator-Fiscal was presented to the Sheriff on 29th October, 1878, charging the said Lewis Potter, William Taylor, Henry Inglis, and John Stewart, Directors of the Bank from and since the year 1872, and John Innes Wright and Robert Summers Stronach, the former a Director and the latter the Manager of said Bank from and since the year 1875, and Charles Samuel Leresche, the

The Stoppage of the Bank.

Secretary of said Bank from and since the year 1870, with the crime of theft; and the accused having been brought before the Sheriff, they each of them emitted a declaration having reference thereto, and were of same date, namely, 29th October, 1878, committed to the prison of Glasgow, therein to be detained until liberated in due course of law.

CHAPTER II.

The Petition for Bail.

By the Act 1701, cap. 6, which was the principal statute relating
to bail in force at the date of the arrest of the Directors, a
person accused of a crime not inferring a capital sentence might
demand his liberation on offering sufficient caution that he
" shall appear and answer to any libel that shall be offered
against him, for the crime or offence wherewith he is charged,
at any time within the space of six months." The effect
of this enactment was to make non-bailable such crimes as
forgery, *furtum grave* (*i.e.*, theft of a serious kind), or theft
by a person who was a thief by habit and repute, which at that
time were all crimes for which a capital sentence might be
exacted. In considering whether a crime was capital or not,
the magistrate was entitled to take into consideration all the
facts set forth, and to judge whether they amounted in law to
the name of the crime in the warrant of commitment. If the
magistrate or other judge to whom the application was made
considered the crime to be one not inferring a capital sentence,
and therefore bailable, he was obliged, within twenty-four hours
after the petition was presented to him, to specify the amount
of bail to be found, under pain of wrongous imprisonment. The
discretionary power as to fixing the amount of bail to be found,
which, before the Act, was vested in the magistrate or other
judge, was abolished, and it was provided that the maximum
amount of bail should be—For a nobleman, 6000 merks ; for
a landed gentleman, 3000 merks ; for any other gentleman or
burgess, 1000 merks ; and for an inferior person, 300 merks.
By the Act of 11 Geo. I. cap. 26, the magistrate was empowered
to double the former amounts ; and by 39 Geo. III. cap 49,
the maximum amount of bail was altered to sums of £1200,
£600, £300, and £60 sterling for the respective classes enumerated under the Act of 1701.

Portraits of the Prisoners John Stewart, Lewis Potter, and Robert Salmond.

(From a Contemporary Print.)

The Petition for Bail.

The High Court of Justiciary or the Lord Advocate had, however, in the exercise of their discretion, the power of granting bail for crimes which were not bailable under the Act, and could fix the amount of bail at any sum which they deemed right.

Immediately after their commitment, therefore, the Directors, Lewis Potter, Robert Salmond, John Innes Wright, William Taylor, and John Stewart, together with Robert Summers Stronach, the Manager, and Charles Samuel Leresche, the Secretary, applied to the Sheriff to be admitted to bail. From the latter bail to the extent of two sureties to the amount of £5000 each was accepted, with the consent of the Lord Advocate, and Charles Samuel Leresche was subsequently liberated. The application of the other petitioners was refused by the Sheriff upon the ground that the offence for which they had been committed amounted to *furtum grave*, and that bail could not be accepted without the consent of the Lord Advocate, which had not been obtained. They accordingly presented a petition to the High Court of Justiciary to be admitted to bail, and founded on the terms of commitment and of the complaint upon which it was pronounced.*

At the calling of the petition before the High Court,

Mr. ASHER, who appeared for Mr. Potter, said—The accused applied to the Sheriff to be liberated on bail, but his application was refused upon the ground that he was committed on a charge of *furtum grave*, and therefore it was not within the power of the Sheriff to grant it without the consent of the Crown. The accused thereupon applied to the Lord Advocate, and offered to find bail to the extent of £10,000, but the Lord Advocate refused his consent. His lordship having been asked to state whether his refusal was in consequence of the amount offered being insufficient, I understand it has been intimated that bail will not be accepted in the present case. In these circumstances the present application is made to your lordships on the two-fold ground— first, that the petition upon which the commitment has proceeded does not set forth facts inferring a crime not bailable by law ; and, secondly and alternatively, that, under the equitable power which the Court undoubtedly possesses, bail ought to be accepted in the circumstances of the present case. The commitment by the Sheriff is in the usual terms. It does not specify the charge on which the accused is committed, except by reference to the complaint ; and although theft is charged in the complaint, it does not follow, I submit, that the accused is committed for theft. He is committed merely for trial upon the facts stated

Mr. Asher.

* See Appendix.

The City of Glasgow Bank Trial.

Mr. Asher. in the complaint. The question therefore is whether the facts stated in the complaint do or do not amount to a case of *furtum grave*, and therefore to a crime which is not bailable by law. I have to ask your lordships' attention to the terms of the complaint. That charge, my lords, I think in substance amounts to this, that Mr. Potter, being a Director of this Bank, and knowing that the Bank was insolvent as the result of reckless trading on the part of most of the Directors, and having conspired with his co-Directors to continue the business of the Bank and make it appear solvent, and having certain bills in the possession of the Bank for the purpose of collection, endorsed those bills to the London Joint Stock Bank, by which bank the proceeds were placed to the credit of the City of Glasgow Bank. The bills must have been endorsed to the City of Glasgow Bank, because the charge is that they were transferred by that Bank by endorsation to the London Joint Stock Bank, which could not have been done unless they had been endorsed to the City Bank.

The Sheriff having committed the accused for trial on the *species facti* I have mentioned, the question is whether these *species facti* constitute a case of *furtum*. It is true that the line which separates breach of trust and embezzlement from theft has frequently been said to be somewhat shadowy; it is equally clear that theft and breach of trust and embezzlement are two distinct crimes in the eye of the law. Nothing could more thoroughly illustrate this than the consideration that if this crime is theft—looking to the number and amount of the charges—it is a capital offence; if it is embezzlement, it is not a capital offence. It has also been said in applications like the present that where the facts of the particular case are such as to bring it close to the margin which divides breach of trust and embezzlement from theft, the Court will not at this stage decide to which category it belongs, but leave it for decision on the indictment at the trial. On the other hand, it is quite plain that there are cases in regard to which there can be no doubt as to which category they belong to. The thief who walks into a shop and theftuously lifts an article and appropriates it to his own uses and purposes could never be said to have committed breach of trust and embezzlement. On the other hand, the mercantile agent who receives goods on consignment for sale, and, having sold them, appropriates the price to his own uses, could never be said to have committed theft. If in such a case the mercantile agent were committed for theft, and so was deprived of his right to bail, he would be entitled, I submit, to come to this Court and say, " The facts on which I have been committed have been improperly designated theft; they do not, in law, constitute theft, and I am therefore entitled to bail." On behalf of the accused in the present case I now prefer a like demand, and on the same grounds. The *species facti* in the

14

The Petition for Bail.

complaint in the present case never can be construed as amounting to the crime of theft.

There are two points which appear to be conclusive against the case being one of theft. First, it is not said that the proceeds of these bills were appropriated by the accused either for their own uses and purposes, or, through their instrumentality, for the uses and purposes of the institution of which they were the Directors. It is not said that the proceeds of these bills when collected in London were not immediately credited and ultimately paid to those who had deposited them for collection; and in the absence of any allegation to that effect I am entitled to assume that the case against the accused is merely this, that, having bills in their possession for collection, they prematurely sent them to London for that purpose, and that when collected the proceeds were credited or paid to the parties to whom the bills originally belonged.

The second point, which, I submit, is conclusive against the case being one of theft, is the nature of the accused's possession of the things said to have been stolen. What they are said to have stolen are bills—pieces of paper having that written upon them which made them bills. Documents are the things said to have been stolen. That gives rise to the question, was Mr. Potter's possession of them such as to make his appropriation of them, even assuming that he did so, to his own uses and purposes an act of theft, or was his possession not such as to make that appropriation merely breach of trust? My lords, I know of no case in which facts at all resembling those of the present case have been held to amount to theft. The Bank were endorsees of the bills in question. Now, there is no case, so far as I am aware, in which a person possessing a thing under such a title as an endorsee custody merely commits theft. But if the property so appropriated is in his lawful possession, he does not commit theft, but breach of trust. This distinction is recognised in several cases—for example, in the cases of *Hugh Climie*, High Court, 21st May, 1838, 2 Swinton, 118; and *George Brown*, High Court, 3rd July, 1839, 2 Swinton, 394. In all such cases—the case of the carrier, for example, the case of the servant having custody of his master's wine, and such similar cases, in which appropriation by the custodier is held to be theft and not breach of trust—the possession has been of the nature of custody merely, and did not exclude the owner's possession.

Applying that principle to the present case, the question arises whether the possession by the City of Glasgow Bank of the bills endorsed and delivered to them for collection was at all akin to that of the watchmaker who receives the watch for repair, under contract to return the very article he has received, or whether it was not, as in the class of cases represented by

15

The City of Glasgow Bank Trial.

Mr. Asher. *Climie,* such possession as that of the servant who received money to pay particular accounts, not under an obligation to apply the money so received *in forma specifica* in payment of the accounts, but to expend an amount equal to that which he had received in payment of the accounts. The bills here were put by the owners into the possession of the Bank for a purpose which excluded the idea of the possession of the owner continuing and the Bank being merely a custodier. It was no part of the contract under which the bills were endorsed and delivered to the Bank that the bills—the things stolen—should be returned to the owner *in forma specifica.* It is against the whole theory and practice of banking that such a thing should ever happen. The purpose of a bill being endorsed and put into the hands of a bank is that the bank may have a title to negotiate it, and when this has been done it is not the bill *in forma specifica* that comes back to the owner, but the proceeds which are realised from its negotiation. The purpose of the transaction was that the bills should be negotiated. All the bills, with the exception of two payable in Govan, were payable in London. Now, what was the duty of the Bank in such a case? Was it not part of the contract, and according to the intention of such a transaction, that the Bank should, some time prior to the date of payment, take the necessary steps for having the bill presented to the party by whom it was due, and at the place where it was payable? That, surely, does not imply that the Bank is to send an official to London carrying the bill with him, for the purpose of collecting the money and bringing the money back in a bag, and delivering it *in forma specifica* to the owner of the bill. The transaction is this—The City of Glasgow Bank, having a correspondent in London, has in due course to endorse the bill to the correspondent, by whom the money is collected, and, when received, it is placed to the credit of the Glasgow Bank, leaving the Glasgow Bank to account to the person from whom they received the bill, either by putting it to the credit of his account or paying over the money when it is wanted.

I submit that this is a case about which there is no doubt as to the category to which it belongs. The facts stated may amount to breach of trust, but clearly can never be theft, the Bank having been lawfully in possession of the bills for the purpose of negotiating them, and with a title to negotiate them. I know that this is not the stage of the case at which the relevancy of the charge falls to be determined. But, on the other hand, this Court, I submit, will not allow any one to be deprived of his legal right to bail where the facts disclosed in the petition plainly and distinctly do not constitute a non-bailable crime, merely because in the petition they are put under a *nomen juris* which belongs to that class. That is distinctly stated in

16

The Petition for Bail.

Mr. Asher. the case of *Joseph Dawson Wormald*, High Court, 3rd December, 1875, 3 Couper, 191. I ask your lordships to observe the marked distinction between that case and the present. In the case of *Wormald* the thing stolen was the money so viciously acquired; here the thing said to have been stolen is a bill admittedly endorsed and delivered to the Bank for collection. I submit it is not within the range of possibility that at the trial of this case facts can possibly come out which will establish that there was vice in the acquisition by the Bank of the bills in question at all analogous to the vice which existed in the acquisition of the money in *Wormald's* case. It would be contrary to the whole case set out in the petition that such a result should happen. That case is simply this, that the bills were endorsed and delivered to the Bank for collection. They were therefore in the lawful possession of the Bank, with no obligation to return them *in forma specifica*—on the contrary, with a duty to negotiate them, to convert them into cash, and account for the proceeds. It is impossible that a case of that nature ever could at the trial turn out to be theft. In the case of *Wormald*, which, of course, was a prosecution at the instance of the Lord Advocate, it was stated by the Lord Justice-Clerk, and concurred in by the other learned judges, that "if the charge of theft had been inserted in the petition in order to prevent the offence from being bailable, without any reasonable ground in the facts stated, we might interfere." My contention is that in the present case the *species facti* in the complaint have been misnamed—that they do not afford any reasonable ground for a charge of theft, and therefore that my client is entitled to bail.

I have further to ask attention to the Act 52 Geo. III. cap. 63, which is an Act passed to prevent bankers embezzling securities or documents which are placed in their custody. I refer to that Act for the purpose of showing that the Legislature, when dealing with a crime of that nature, and making statutory provision for its punishment at a long time subsequent to the Act 1701, attached to it a sentence which in law makes it a bailable offence. Now, the Legislature in that statute makes the act of a banker, entrusted with negotiable documents, fraudulently appropriating them to his own uses and purposes a statutory crime, and attaches to it a sentence which makes it a bailable offence. The charge in the present case is not under the statute, but at common law. Indeed, the facts in the complaint would not have warranted the statutory charge. The statute deals with the case of a banker who, being entrusted with a negotiable document, defrauds the party from whom he got it, and defrauds him for the purpose of taking the benefit to himself, whereas it is not said in the present case either that the banker, by endorsing the bill prematurely, or

The City of Glasgow Bank Trial.

Mr. Asher. sending it to London, benefited himself or the institution of which he was a servant to the extent of one single shilling, or defrauded the person from whom he got the bill to the extent of a single shilling either. I contend therefore that the more aggravated statutory crime being bailable by law, it would be a denial of justice to treat the charge in this complaint as constituting a crime not bailable by law. These are the remarks I have to make in support of the petition in so far as rested on the legal right of the accused to bail.

But I put the case, secondly and alternatively, on this ground, that, possessing, as your lordships undoubtedly do, an equitable power to grant bail when it cannot be demanded as matter of right, this is a case, looking to the circumstances, in which that equitable power should be exercised. My lords, I have a further ground to state, and it is this, that upon the *species facti* of this petition there are no less than five or six persons detained in jail upon a charge of theft which could only have been the act of one man. The theft is said to have been committed by endorsing and transmitting the bills to the London Joint Stock Bank. It is scarcely conceivable that that should have been the act of all the Directors. It was the ordinary mode of passing to the London banker the title to the bills which had to be collected in London, and would presumably be done by an official of the Bank in discharge of his ordinary duty. The power of the Court has, I think, never been doubted. It was expressly recognised in the case of *William Hamilton Thomson*, High Court, 10th July, 1871, 2 Couper, 103. I have only further to point out, in support of my appeal to the equitable power of the Court, the great importance to the accused of being at liberty for the purpose of assisting in the preparation of his defence for the trial. The case will necessarily involve much complicated detail, and the importance to the accused of having free access to those acting for him is too clear to require to be stated. The age, also, of the accused, viz., seventy-two, and his social position, are elements not to be overlooked. On the whole matter, I submit that the accused is entitled to bail as matter of right; but if your lordships should be of a different opinion, then I submit the circumstances of the case are such as to call for the exercise by the Court of its equitable power to allow liberation on bail being found to such an amount as your lordships may think proper.

Lord Advocate. The LORD ADVOCATE, who replied on behalf of the Crown, said—I have hitherto considered this as a non-bailable offence; but even if I had entertained the opposite view I would have refused the offers of bail that have been made, simply because I did not think that their acceptance would have enabled me to rely upon the attendance of the accused on the day of trial. It is very obvious that matters of this kind depend upon con-

18

The Petition for Bail.

siderations—nay, upon suspicions or surmises—which it would
be highly inexpedient, and certainly improper, to state in open
Court. There are two points raised on behalf of the prisoners.
The first is that the crime or offence described in the complaint
before the Court does not amount to theft; and the second is
that, assuming that it does, the circumstances of the case are
such that the Court ought to use their discretion and liberate
the accused on bail. As regards the first point, the Court will
not, I apprehend, deal with the question at this stage as one
purely of relevancy, but will view the crime charged as one
purely falling within the category to which the public prosecutor has assigned it, unless the contrary plainly appears on the
face of the complaint. And I would first call attention to what
is alleged in the complaint against the accused, and then advert
to the authorities cited in favour of the contention that the
charge made is not one of theft. No doubt, in the ordinary
course of dealing between the Bank and its customer, the
money received from the acceptor would be put to the credit
of the customer's account with the Bank. But my allegation
is that the Bank had no right to deal with the bills otherwise
than by collecting their amounts. They were not entitled to
negotiate the bills, and thereby rear up an entirely new set of
obligations, because the moment a bill is endorsed by the
Bank, either to a banking company or to an individual, the
result is that the depositor, who wants nothing more than that
the money shall be collected from the acceptor, and who gives
it for that purpose, becomes personally liable. The bill when
negotiated (being endorsed by the Bank) becomes a ground of
personal liability against the depositor as an endorser. The
purpose for which the bills were deposited with the Bank was
for collection, and that they might not go, according to commercial phrase, into the circle. The question raised here is
not whether, if the mandate given to the Bank had been
followed out and the money received by the Bank, that money
was the property of the customer of the Bank, and whether it
was stolen, because it is quite clear in criminal law that you
may have the theft of a document or obligation upon paper
given for the purpose of collection, even although the result of
following out instead of acting in breach of the mandate to
collect would be to make the collector accountable, and only
accountable, for the money. What is here complained of is
the appropriation of the *ipsissima corpora* of the documents of
these depositors, and in breach of the contract under which
they were delivered to the Bank, and the appropriation of the
same by the Bank. And I contend that is an act of theft, and
theft only.

The cases of *Climie* and *Brown* in 2 Swinton which have been
cited merely illustrate certain well-known principles of the

The City of Glasgow Bank Trial.

Lord Advocate. criminal law, and do not exhaust the whole principles of the law on the point. But the principle of these cases was carried a good deal further in the direction I am contending for by the case of *Robert Michie*, High Court, 28th January, 1839, 2 Swinton, 319. The second alternative charge in that case was in these terms—" The said James Laurie having, time and place above libelled, delivered to the said Robert Michie a bank or banker's note for £20 sterling in order that he might get the same changed, and return with and deliver the change thereof to the said James Laurie, the said Robert Michie did then and there, or at some other time and place to the prosecutor unknown, wickedly and feloniously steal and theftuously away take the said bank or banker's note for £20 sterling, the property or in the lawful possession of the said James Laurie." Thus the mandate given to Michie, the accused, along with the note, and the contract upon which he got it, being that he should get it changed and return with the twenty pounds in cash, it was contended that his appropriation of the note could not amount to theft because he had the authority of Laurie to change it, and that made him simply liable to account for the twenty pounds, the proceeds of the note. But the bench of three judges were clearly of opinion that the libel was relevant ; and when the case went to trial, the only defence made was an attempt to prove that Michie had changed the note, and, in point of fact, had stolen the change. That case goes this length, that the theft of a note given for the special purpose of getting change and returning the change is a relevant charge of theft, even although the theft of the change might not have amounted to that crime. There is also the case of *John Mooney*, High Court, 17th November, 1851, J. Shaw, 496. In that case the accused, of whom certain articles had been purchased, received from the purchaser a £1 note, that he might retain the price and return the balance. He appropriated the whole sum, and it was held that it was a theft of the £1 note, and not of the balance. The charge in the libel was that he took the note and appropriated it to his own use without changing it for the purpose of accounting for the balance.

This is not a case of sending the bills to the London Bank for collection. What is averred is that, instead of retaining them in their hands for the purpose of collection, they paid them into their account with the London Bank. If the bills had been sent to London for collection, the London Bank would have been directly liable to the creditors in the bills, and they would have accepted the mandate given to the City Bank, and would not have put the proceeds to the credit of the account between them and the City Bank. And I maintain that that is complete appropriation by the Bank of the *corpora* of the bills to their own purposes. The question is not one of account-

20

The Petition for Bail.

ing, but a question of what the Bank has done with the price of the moveable property which the bills represented.

The only remaining question is as to whether the Court ought, in the circumstances, to admit the accused to the privilege of bail. I do not in the least dispute that the Court has such a discretionary power, and I do not suppose that any public prosecutor would ever think of interposing himself between the discretion of the Court and the accused, if the Court felt disposed to exercise it ; but, my lords, I am bound to say, upon the authorities reported, that I can find nothing to justify bail on the arguments stated for the accused. In the case of *John Wilson*, High Court, October, 1875, 3 Couper, 169, Lord Ardmillan laid down the law upon an application to be admitted to bail thus— " I do not think this application incompetent. I do not say that the Court could not, in the exercise of their discretion, authorise the liberation on bail in this case, if they thought that the circumstances of the case really required it. But, while I think there is nothing to preclude the Court from granting the prayer of this petition, were they satisfied that it was right to do so, still I must keep in view that a large discretion rests on the Lord Advocate, and that the Court trusts him, and has every confidence that he exercises that discretion well." With reference to the suggestion that the Court should require something like proof from the public prosecutor, I shall not shrink from giving your lordships, in that inquiry, all the assistance in my power, but I must enter my protest against such a course being followed in a case like the present.

Mr. BALFOUR, who appeared for Potter, Salmond, Taylor, and Leresche, substantially repeated the arguments advanced by Mr. Asher.

The LORD JUSTICE-GENERAL delivered the leading judgment, which was acquiesced in by all the other judges, with the exception of Lord YOUNG, who dissented.

The LORD JUSTICE-GENERAL said—The petitioners have been committed for trial by warrant of the Sheriff of Lanarkshire, granted on a petition by the Procurator-Fiscal, charging the petitioners with the theft of certain valuable securities, being bills of exchange for the aggregate amount of £23,693 11s. 7d. No such warrant is ever granted by a Sheriff without full and deliberate consideration of the declarations of the prisoners, and of the precognitions of the witnesses examined for the prosecution. The Procurator-Fiscal did not content himself with stating the charge in the general terms which I have just used, which would be quite sufficient and according to practice in ordinary cases of theft, but he most properly, in so serious and important a case, has set out the *species facti* which he contends amount to an act of theft, committed by all the petitioners in

The City of Glasgow Bank Trial.

Lord Justice-General. pursuance of a wicked conspiracy. The offence thus charged, if it amount to theft, is, on the admission of the counsel for the petitioners, not bailable. But it is open to the petitioners still to demand that they shall be admitted to bail as a matter of right, if they can show clearly that the *species facti* alleged against them can in no view amount to the crime of theft charged. But we are not under such an application to deal with the question as if we were judging of the relevancy of an indictment. Unless the petitioners can satisfy the Court that the facts stated, even when cast into the more precise and detailed form of the minor proposition of an indictment, will be clearly and undoubtedly insufficient to sustain a charge of theft, they cannot demand liberation. I am not satisfied of this. It is, in my opinion, far from being clear. This being so, it seems to me that it would be quite improper to go further for the present, or to state or indicate any impression I might possibly entertain, as an individual judge, as to the future course or prospect of the prosecution, for that would be to prejudge to some extent questions which may hereafter arise as to the relevancy of indictments or criminal letters which may be served on the petitioners. Such a course would not be fair either to the prosecutor or to the accused.

The petitioners further appeal to the discretion of the Court to liberate them on such bail as may be sufficient to ensure their appearance hereafter to answer the charges made against them. That we possess such discretionary power cannot be disputed. But in prosecutions conducted by the public prosecutor the discretion is vested, in the first instance at least, in the Lord Advocate; and unless it can be alleged that the Lord Advocate has refused bail, not for the purpose of securing the ends of justice, but for some other and therefore illegitimate purpose, I think the Court ought not to interfere, because such interference would be nothing less than relieving the Lord Advocate of the responsibility attaching to his high office. He is subject to this responsibility, and vested with the corresponding discretion, because he has means and appliances for obtaining information and forming a judgment which are not within the reach of any other official and are not possessed by this Court. But it has not been suggested that the Lord Advocate is not discharging his important and responsible duties with fairness and impartiality, and with a sole view to the public interest and to secure the ends of justice. For the Court to interfere in such circumstances with his discretion would be inconsistent with the whole previous practice of the Court, and in the last degree inexpedient.

Lord Young. Lord YOUNG—The law of bail in Scotland stands on an enactment of the Act 1701 in these words—"That all crimes not inferring capital punishment shall be bailable." The peti-

22

The Petition for Bail.

tioners contend that the crime for which they stand committed does not infer capital punishment, and so demand, as matter of right, that they shall be admitted to bail ; and the demand is clearly irresistible if the contention on which it rests is sound. The question for us, then, is whether the crime for which the petitioners are in prison infers capital punishment or not, and we must judge of it on the facts as they are stated in the warrant of commitment, or, as it happens in this case, in the petition of the Procurator-Fiscal, to which the warrant refers. But the proposition which we have now to consider is, that the alleged conduct amounts to a capital offence, or, to use the language of the Act 1701, to a crime " inferring capital punishment." This proposition would be very shocking if it were taken to mean what it expresses ; but even taking it as unreal, except in so far as it may signify that an old barbarity of the criminal law had not been repealed by statute, but had disappeared under the influence of advancing civilisation, I cannot assent to it. For I am of opinion, first, that at no period of our history did such facts as are here alleged import a capital crime ; and, second, that they assuredly do not now. Down to the date of Mr. Hume's work, and probably for some short time thereafter, theft, if attended with any aggravating circumstance—and the great value of the thing stolen might be one—was by the custom of Scotland punishable with death, if the judge in his discretion saw fit. That it was customary law only, and subject in its application to the discretion of the judge, Mr. Hume announces emphatically and repeatedly. He introduces the subject with these words—" to come now to the practice of Scotland "—and treats of the whole law of punishment in cases of theft as depending on—I quote his expressions—" ancient custom," " equitable discretion," " the course of practice," " custom and practice," " the ordinary course of justice for such offences." As the conclusion of the whole matter, he leaves, as he doubtless intended, his readers with the impression that the law of punishment for theft was customary, and, to a large extent, discretionary, and that there had been, and was, " a variable course of practice in which the instances are numerous to the side of mercy," although grave thefts always brought the panel " into hazard of his life." The law on this head is still customary, but the custom has greatly changed, and it is not and has not for a long while been true that by the custom of Scotland theft infers capital punishment, or that any theft, however grave, brings the panel " into hazard of his life." In Hume's time the older custom was on the wane, but had not died out. It is now dead, not to be revived, unless, indeed, we should relapse into barbarism. Theft is not, and, indeed, never was, capital by statute ; and although the common law, which Hume refers to by the expressions which I have quoted from his book, such as " custom and practice," " the ordinary course of

23

The City of Glasgow Bank Trial.

Lord Young. justice," etc., once permitted, or, it may be, enjoined the graver sorts of it to be punished with death, these, viz., custom, practice, and the ordinary course of justice, and with them the common law, which rests on them, and is, indeed, another expression for them, are and have for a long while been changed. I am therefore of opinion that theft is a crime not "inferring capital punishment." But, further, I am of opinion that the facts alleged against these petitioners do not amount to the crime of theft. I quite understand the argument employed to bring them within that category, and, understanding it, reject it as too subtle. To constitute theft there must be a felonious taking of property out of the owner's possession, and the bills here in question were, I think, clearly not so taken. The Lord Advocate was unable to adduce any decided case more available for his argument than that of a man appropriating and running off with a sovereign or bank note which he had got to change. I will not now enter on an examination of the decisions, but content myself with saying that I think they are all inapplicable to the facts here presented to us. I have cited the enactment of the Act 1701, which embodies the whole law of bail. The expediency of it may be questionable, but it is certainly clear. And I cannot approve of any attempt to control or modify its operation by a fanciful and altogether unreal extension of capital crimes according to customs which have long ceased to be observed, and which no one would for a moment think of attempting to revive. Now, the question to which I have addressed myself, in a matter of purely customary law, is whether now in this year 1878 it can be safely and truly affirmed that the former custom of Scotland, according to which theft was punishable capitally, has been completely superseded by another custom, now as firmly established and on as good authority as ever it was, whereby (that is, without violating the custom) death may not be inflicted for that crime. This question no former decision can hinder me from answering, as I have done, in the affirmative. I think it not doubtful, and do not suppose any one does, that to punish any of the petitioners with death for the misappropriation of these bills would violate the custom of Scotland, as it would that of any other civilised country in the world. The result is that, in my opinion, the crime for which the petitioners stand committed is not a crime inferring capital punishment, and that it is, therefore, bailable. I have only to add that I think the law of bail is unsatisfactory, and requires amendment, and that if I could have dealt with this application as made to the discretion of the Court, I should have concurred with your lordships in refusing it.

The cautious and even hesitating opinion of the learned Lord Justice-General, one of the most brilliant and clear-headed lawyers who ever adorned the Scottish bench, seems to indicate that he

The Petition for Bail.

was endeavouring to find reasons for an opinion not wholly in accord with his intellectual judgment, and that had the burden of proving that the charges libelled against the accused amounted in law to a charge of theft rested with the prosecution rather than with the prisoners to prove the negative, the issue would have been different, with the not unlikely result that no trial of the Directors would ever have taken place. It can hardly be doubted that had the right of the prisoners to bail been affirmed and the accused set free, as they must have been on finding sufficient security for £300, the public sense of justice would have been most justly shocked. For, while all impartial people properly abstained from prejudging the case against the prisoners, it could not fail to have been regarded as a scandal if persons so deeply suspected of a serious crime had been afforded facilities for escaping trial. Yet, owing to the state of the law affecting bail then in existence, this certainly was uncomfortably near the case. Indeed, it is perhaps not wholly fanciful to suppose that this consideration was not altogether absent from the minds of the learned judges who formed the majority, and it is perhaps permissible to believe that the judgment of Lord Young was the only one dictated solely by a consideration of the law as it stood, untrammelled by a fear of the consequences of the verdict of public opinion.

The result of the judgment was undoubtedly to draw public attention to the state of the law affecting bail, and to institute an agitation in favour of its repeal. Yet so conservative are our methods, and so slowly does public opinion crystallise into statute law, that it was not till eight years after that any alteration in the law took place.

The law as to bail is now administered under the Criminal Procedure (Scotland) Act, 1887, and by the Bail (Scotland) Act, 1888, by the latter of which the Act of 1701 was repealed. It is provided by that Act that all crimes except murder and treason are bailable, it being in the discretion of the magistrate before whom the accused is charged to grant or refuse bail. If bail be admitted, the magistrate must fix the bail at such an amount as shall ensure the attendance of the accused at all diets to which he may be cited on the charge. Where an application for bail after commitment is refused, or where the accused is dissatisfied with the amount of caution ordered to be found, he may appeal to the High Court of Justiciary. 25

CHAPTER III.

The Trial.

On Monday, 28th January, 1879, in the presence of a crowded and expectant Court, the Manager and Directors of the Bank were placed at the bar to answer to the charges of falsehood, fraud, and theft preferred against them.

On the bench there were the Lord Justice-Clerk (Lord MONCREIFF) and Lords MURE and CRAIGHILL.

The counsel for the prosecution were the Lord Advocate (WATSON), the Solicitor-General (MACDONALD), and Messrs. BURNET, A.D., and PEARSON.

The counsel for the prisoners were—For John Stewart—Mr. TRAYNER and Mr. MACLEAN; for Lewis Potter—Mr. BALFOUR and Mr. JAMESON; for Robert Salmond—Mr. ASHER and Mr. GOUDY; for William Taylor—Mr. MACKINTOSH and Mr. OMOND; for Henry Inglis—Mr. J. P. B. ROBERTSON and Mr. MACONOCHIE; for John Innes Wright—Mr. J. GUTHRIE SMITH and Mr. DICKSON; for Robert Summers Stronach—The DEAN OF FACULTY (FRASER) and Mr. DARLING.

DISCUSSION ON THE RELEVANCY.

The LORD JUSTICE-CLERK having asked if there were any objections to the relevancy of the indictment,

Mr. Mackintosh. Mr. MACKINTOSH, who appeared on behalf of the panel, Mr. Taylor, said—I have to state certain objections to the relevancy of the libel, and I may say that these objections are concurred in by my learned friends who represent the other prisoners, it being, however, understood that any of my learned friends may supplement my observations upon any matter which they think material to their respective clients. The indictment is a somewhat extensive document,* and it will be proper that I begin by asking your lordships' attention to its general scheme. The major proposition sets out five separate charges which it affirms to be crimes severely punishable by the law of Scotland. The first three are the well-known and nominate charges of (1) falsehood, fraud, and wilful imposition; (2) theft; and (3) breach of trust

* See Appendix.

26

Mr. Mackintosh,
Counsel for William Taylor.

Discussion on Relevancy.

and embezzlement. The other two are innominate charges, falling under no recognised legal category, and they immediately follow the charges of falsehood, fraud, and wilful imposition. That is the major. The minor proposition sets out in the usual form that the accused are, all or one or more of them, guilty of the said crimes, or one or more of them, in so far as, during the period mentioned, they committed a number of acts, which are set forth under seventeen separate counts in the minor. It will, I think, be found that these seventeen counts divide themselves into three sets or series, the charges in each set of the series being substantially identical. The first set are counts one to three inclusive, the substance of which is that they charge the accused with issuing false balances of the City of Glasgow Bank during the years 1876-77-78. That is the first series of charges, and they apply to all the accused. The second series of counts or charges are those numbered four to seven inclusive, and they, in substance, charge what I may call for brevity the overdrawing of accounts by Directors, or certain of them. The charge is not common to the whole of the accused, Messrs. Potter, Salmond, and Stronach not being included. The third set of charges, those numbered eight to seventeen, are charges of stealing or otherwise embezzling certain bills which had been sent to the Bank for collection.* And this set of charges is directed against all the accused. That is the general scheme of the indictment, and that being so, I proceed to consider its relevancy. And, first, as to the major proposition, I do not know that it is necessary to enter upon any detailed discussion. Questions, of course, suggest themselves in regard to the two innominate charges to which I have referred, and I must say that, construing these charges upon their terms and according to the ordinary rules of construction, I think a very serious question suggests itself as to the relevancy of these charges. In one view, the charges in question are simply charges of uttering untruths in a particular form, and for the purpose and with the result of producing a particular state of public opinion. In another view, they are not distinct and separate charges at all, but simply charges of falsehood, fraud, and wilful imposition, with this remarkable peculiarity, that although it appears that the alleged fraud was committed for the benefit of the Company, it at the same time appears that the effect of the fraud was to injure, not merely third parties, namely, members of the public, but also members of the Company. But while these criticisms may be made, it must be kept in view that, in dealing with innominate charges, it is always possible to construe them by reference to the more detailed statement which is to be found in the minor. And therefore it will be convenient to take, at least in the first

* The second and third series of charges were withdrawn at the close of the evidence for the Crown, no evidence having been led in regard to them.

The City of Glasgow Bank Trial.

instance, the whole argument upon the relevancy of the minor, upon the construction of which I am to maintain to your lordships that from first to last it contains no relevant charge of falsehood, fraud, or wilful imposition, or breach of trust or embezzlement, or theft, or any other crime, nominate or innominate, known to the law of Scotland.

My lords, I begin with counts one, two, and three, which I have described as charges of issuing false balance sheets, and I propose to take as a specimen the first charge, which deals with the balance sheet of 1876. I take that charge as a specimen, because in substance the other two charges are substantially the same and raise substantially the same questions. The charge begins by narrating that the accused were Directors of the City of Glasgow Bank, an institution having a capital of one million, and that during certain years which are mentioned it was their duty as Directors and Manager to see that the books were properly kept and all transactions duly entered, and that it was further their duty to see that every year an abstract or statement at 1st June was prepared and submitted to the shareholders. It then sets forth that "nevertheless, on the first or one or more of the days of the month of June, 1876, or July immediately following, the time or times being unknown, in or near the head office of the City of Glasgow Bank, you, the said John Stewart," and so on, "did all, or one or more of you, wickedly and feloniously, with intent to defraud the members of the Company and the public, and for the purpose of concealing and misrepresenting the true state of the affairs of the said Company, concoct and fabricate, or cause and procure to be concocted and fabricated, a false and fictitious abstract balance sheet or statement of affairs, purporting to represent the true condition of the Bank's affairs as at 7th June, 1876, in the following or similar terms." Then follows a copy of the balance sheet, which I need not read. Then there follows an enumeration of the particular misrepresentations or falsehoods which it is said to have contained, which are set forth under eight heads or articles, it being premised that the prosecutor does not bind himself to prove that the whole of these eight misrepresentations were false and fictitious, but only, as the indictment expresses it, that the balance sheet was false in the eight particulars mentioned, "or part thereof."

These, my lords, are the averments of the falsehood of the balance sheet. Then the minor proposition goes on to aver the publication of the balance sheet, the purpose for which it was published, and the result of its publication.* . . . That is the purpose, and these are the results of the publication. That is all that it is necessary to read in connection with the charges of issuing false balance sheets. And the first question which arises on the relevancy of these charges is, whether the falsehood

* See page 86.

28

Discussion on Relevancy.

of the balance sheet or balance sheets is relevantly averred. I submit to your lordships that on this head the libel is irrelevant —(1) as wanting in specification; and (2) as being contradictory and unintelligible.

My lords, as I have already pointed out, the balance sheet in question is said to have been false in eight several particulars, that is to say, it is said to have contained eight several false statements. The first observation which occurs is that we are here left altogether in doubt as to the sense in which the statements complained of are said to be false. Are they false in the sense of being disconform to the books, or in the sense of being disconform to the facts? or are some of them false in the one sense and some of them in the other? and if so, which are false in the one sense and which in the other? The truth is that on the face of it this enumeration appears to have been made up on two different and inconsistent principles, without any attempt at discriminating between them. My observation is, that no information is conveyed to me as to the standard of truth in this matter—as to the sense in which the statement is false—whether it is false as disconform to the fact, or only false as disconform to the books of the Bank.

Passing, however, to the particulars, I first ask your lordships' attention to the eighth article. What I have to submit to your lordships is, that that eighth article is altogether wanting in that specification to which the accused were entitled. The statement there is that this balance sheet is false in respect that it includes, as good, bad and irrecoverable debts to an amount far exceeding the whole capital of the Bank. It is here necessary to be borne in mind, first, that the capital of the Bank thus said to have been lost amounts to £1,000,000; and, secondly, that the whole debts which are thus stated to have been overstated amount, as I read the indictment, to something like £11,000,000. There is £8,000,000 in the balance sheet, and £2,000,000 more should have been added, so that it comes to this, that out of £11,000,000 of outstanding debts, the prosecutor alleges that upwards of £1,000,000 were bad and irrecoverable; and he proposes to leave the accused to find out, as best they may, among this £11,000,000 of debts, which million he means to found upon as bad and irrecoverable. I submit that that is altogether unprecedented—that it is unjust to the accused—and that the effect of this want of specification must at least be to delete this part of the charge from the indictment. In this matter I am not speaking without authority. I do not know that this precise question has ever come up in a criminal case, but I don't suppose that the prosecutor will contend that he is entitled to greater latitude than the pursuer in an action founded on the same *media* would be entitled to in a civil cause. Now, we have a judgment of the First Division of the Court of

Mr. Mackintosh.

Session in a civil cause founded upon precisely the same *media* as those libelled here, and in that case the same point was carefully considered, and judgment pronounced upon it. I refer to the case of *Inglis* v. *The Western Bank*, 22 Dunlop, 505.

The LORD JUSTICE-CLERK—What is the specification here which you desiderate—the individual debts, or the amount?

Mr. MACKINTOSH—The individual debts; and I have not got the individual debts here, nor the amounts, nor anything else. In the case quoted, Lord Curriehill concurred with the Lord President and Lord Ivory that a suitable record should be of new made up, and that the revised condescendence lodged should be withdrawn. That was what was ultimately done. Lord Deas, I should add, also concurred with the other judges that it was impossible to require the defenders to go to trial without having the particular debts which were alleged to be bad and irrecoverable, and known to be bad and irrecoverable, set forth, so that they might prepare their defence.

Now, my lords, that being the case of *Inglis*, is there any distinction between that case and the present, except that we are here not in a civil but in a criminal case? If the defenders in that civil case were entitled to know which million of the three millions of debts there in question were to be brought against them as bad and irrecoverable, surely, *a fortiori*, we are entitled to know which million of the eleven millions of debts which are here in question are said to be bad and irrecoverable. This is a case of the Directors being charged with, both in books and balance sheets, representing a million and upwards of bad and irrecoverable debts as subsisting assets; and the question is whether, that being charged, the accused are not entitled to know what the debts are to which the charge applies, and what the accounts in the books are that are founded on, or to know in some other way what is the nature of the case to be made against them.

Without, therefore, going further, I submit to your lordships that article eight falls for want of specification, and if that is so, then the next point is, that, article eight falling, articles six and seven must fall along with it. The charges really depend on each other. If your lordships hold that article eight is bad for want of specification, articles six and seven must fall on the same ground, for it would not do for the Crown, after being shut out from proving under article eight bad debts of which they had given the accused no specification, to bring in the same evidence without notice as regards articles six and seven.

I have next, however, to submit that the averments of the falsehood of this balance sheet are irrelevant, not merely from want of specification, but in respect that they are contradictory and unintelligible. And I begin with article one of the enumeration, premising what I have already mentioned, that under this

Discussion on Relevancy.

indictment the prosecutor puts forward each of his eight particulars as being each by itself sufficient to entitle him to a conviction. Now, what is the falsehood set forth in article one? It is this—that the deposits of the Bank are said to have been understated. Now, is that intelligible as a basis for a charge of fraud? How, standing by itself, can an under-statement of the deposits in a bank tend to defraud either the shareholders, or depositors, or anybody else? Passing, however, from that, I come to article three and article eight. These articles are contradictory. The amount of bills of exchange, credit accounts, etc., it is said in article three, were understated to the extent of £2,698,000, or thereby. That is to say, the assets were understated by two millions and upwards. But, then, in article eight it is said that these same assets were overstated to the extent of over a million. How is that to be explained? The contradiction is demonstrable. For observe what it comes to. The Crown complains in article three that the accused understated the assets of the Bank, and understated a particular class of assets, namely, those under head one. But when it comes to article eight, the Crown complains that the accused overstated the assets of the Bank, and overstated that same particular class of assets, being those under head one of that balance sheet. The Crown says in one breath you have understated, and in the next breath you have overstated. It is for my learned friend to say how he explains this. I conjecture that his explanation may be something of this sort—that article three states a disconformity between the balance sheet and the books, and article eight states a disconformity between the books and the facts. But if that is so, that just brings us back to, and illustrates, the general objection with which I started, that the falsehoods here alleged are false in different senses, and that there are no means of ascertaining in what sense any particular falsehood is said to be false.

So far, my lords, I have endeavoured to show that the averments of the falsehood of this balance sheet are irrelevant. But now the next question which arises is this, whether, assuming the falsehood, it appears from the indictment that the balance sheets were issued for the purpose and with the result required to constitute the crime of falsehood, fraud, and wilful imposition, or any other cognate offence? It is here necessary to say a word or two upon a matter of principle.

We have not here, your lordships will see, to deal with documents which are said to be false in the sense in which forged documents are false. Language, no doubt, is used in the major proposition—loosely and improperly used, I think—which is only appropriate to the case of forged documents. I refer to such passages in the major proposition as that in which the Directors are accused of fabricating the balance sheets. But it is plainly not there meant, however loose may be the language, that the

31

The City of Glasgow Bank Trial.

balance sheets were other than genuine balance sheets. The alleged falsehood of the balance sheets consists simply in this, that they are said to be mendacious. In short, the balance sheet is said to be false and fraudulent simply in the sense that it purports to set out truly certain facts in regard to the assets and liabilities of this Bank, and yet sets forth those facts untruly, and is therefore a mendacious document. That being so, we are not dealing, as I have said, with a case of falsehood in the sense of forgery ; neither, again, are we dealing with another kind of case with which your lordships are familiar, the case of false statements put forward by persons holding public offices, in violation of public duty. Familiar instances of the latter kind of crime are the cases of messengers returning false executions, of notaries making false docquets, and of doctors issuing false vaccination certificates. We have nothing of that kind here. These Directors are simply managers of a trading company, and that being so, you have in these balance sheets simply certain false statements made by certain private persons to the shareholders, and it may be to the public, in regard to the state of this City of Glasgow Bank. The case would not be in the least degree different if the alleged false statements had been made in the report, or in the chairman's speech at the shareholders' meeting. Now, that being so, the question comes to be, under what conditions is simple falsehood recognised as a crime according to the law of Scotland? I submit that, upon a review of the whole authorities, it will be found that falsehood can only be a relevant basis for a criminal charge when it is used as the means of obtaining to the accused, or to some institution which the accused represents, patrimonial gain or advantage, at the expense and to the injury of some other person or persons. In other words, where you exclude forgery and breach of *munus publicum*, the only remaining category under which criminal proceedings founded upon falsehood of this sort can be brought is what Hume describes as "fraud or cheating." I may just mention one case which brings out very distinctly the necessity of the falsehood being first proved for the purpose of obtaining the resulting advantage. I refer to the case of *Wilkie*, tried before your lordship in the chair and Lord Cowan at Stirling Circuit on 13th September, 1876, and which is reported in 2 Couper, 353. The libel was there held irrelevant, in respect that it did not sufficiently appear that the false representations were made in order to obtain the patrimonial advantage which the accused was said to have obtained.

Now, my lords, if that be so, let us see here what are the advantages or results which are said to have been produced by these fraudulent balance sheets. They are three in number, and I shall take them separately. The first result said to have

Discussion on Relevancy.

been produced is this, that members of the company were
induced to retain the shares held by them therein. Now,
is it a relevant statement in a charge of this kind to say that
by means of false balance sheets made by the directors of a
joint stock company, issued to the members of the company,
the members were induced to retain their shares? It is
essential, in libelling a crime of this sort, that the indictment
shall set out some wrongful result or results as following from
the falsehood. And I am at present considering whether the
results which are set out as produced by the publication of
these balance sheets are results involving patrimonial gain
on the one hand or patrimonial loss on the other. I am not
in the least suggesting that it was defensible in any view to
issue these balance sheets. But that really brings one back
to the proposition with which one started, that the law of
Scotland does not recognise the telling of untruths as criminal;
and it does not recognise the publication of untruths as criminal
unless something follows, involving, on the one hand, injury
to the person deceived and, on the other, patrimonial gain to
the person deceiving. I therefore ask whether there is an
averment here of this fraud having been effectual to that
effect. It is quite plain that, if the truth had been told, the
shareholder must have retained his shares, as nobody would
have bought them. Therefore it is impossible to say that he
suffered any loss. He had to retain them as it was, and he
would all the more have had to retain them if the truth had
been told; and if it be necessary, in order to complete the
charge of falsehood, fraud, and wilful imposition, or any cognate
charge, that there shall have been a wrong produced to a third
party by the fraudulent act, then this averment is irrelevant
in respect that it does not involve the allegation of any wrong
as sustained by the party said to have been defrauded. And
I may say that the question thus raised is not a new one. It
arose in *Dobie* v. *The Directors of the Edinburgh and Glasgow
Bank*, 21 D. 624, where the present Lord President pronounced
the proposition now put forward by the prosecutor "as of a
startling nature." It also came up in *Cullen* v. *The Directors
of the same Bank;* but, so far as I know, there is no example
anywhere in the books of the averment being held relevant
that shareholders were induced by fraud to retain their shares,
as here alleged.

The next result said to have been produced by the issue
of these false balance sheets is this—It is said that "many
of the public, including Robert Craig," etc., "were induced
to acquire stock in the said Company." Now, my lords,
I do not dispute that this would have been quite a relevant
averment if it had borne that many of the public were
induced to purchase stock in the Company from the Com-

The City of Glasgow Bank Trial.

pany. But the averment here does not suggest that. All that it comes to is that the Directors of this Company issued certain false statements as to its affairs, with the result of inducing certain transactions between third parties. My proposition is, that no charge is relevant which does not set forth at least patrimonial gain to the Bank ; and in regard to the case of persons induced to purchase shares, which is the case I am now dealing with, I say it has never been suggested to be a crime in the law of Scotland that a person by misrepresentation induces a transaction between third parties in which the alleged offender has no interest. If that were so, it would follow that every person publishing a canard in a newspaper would be liable to be indicted for falsehood, fraud, and wilful imposition, or some similar offence. That has never been suggested ; and I say it was no interest of the Bank whether members of the public bought shares as members of the Company or not. It was all one to the Company whether transfers took place or not. If they lost the transferer, they gained the transferee ; and it was quite as likely that the transferee should be a better man than the transferer as it was that the transferer should be a better man than the transferee.

But then, my lords, we now come to the third result said to have been produced by these balance sheets, viz., that members of the public were thereby induced to deposit money in the Bank, to the great loss and prejudice of the said members of the public. There is here undoubtedly an averment of patrimonial gain to the Company—the averment that by false representations the Company obtained what I may concede to be a benefit. But two questions here arise—First, is there any averment that the depositors suffered injury ? and next, is there any averment that the false representations were made in order that depositors might make deposits, and the Company thereby benefit ? My lords, it is a remarkable fact that, from first to last of this indictment, if you except a statement in subdivision eight, which I have already submitted is bad, there is not anywhere an averment that this Company is insolvent ; there is not anywhere even an averment that it has stopped payment ; and that being so, the question arises whether the averment that by means of these false balance sheets depositors were induced to deposit money in a bank which for anything alleged is perfectly solvent is an averment which implies injury to the depositors. In regard, therefore, to the depositors, the averment, I submit, fails in respect there is no averment of patrimonial injury sustained. But apart from that, there is another point. As I have already observed, it is necessary, in order to found a criminal charge upon a false representation, that not only shall certain results be produced, but also that it shall appear that the false representations were

34

Discussion on Relevancy.

made for the purpose of producing those results. Now, where is it here averred that the Directors of the Bank published these balance sheets for the purpose of inducing depositors to deposit with them, or for the purpose of otherwise inducing any patrimonial gain to themselves or the Company? The only averment on that subject is in the middle of page 5, where it is said in general terms that the balance sheets were issued "for the purpose of concealing and misrepresenting the true state of the Company's affairs." But this is not an averment that the Directors had it as their purpose to induce depositors to make deposits. My present point is that, assuming that the falsehood is relevantly alleged, and assuming that the results which the law requires for the constitution of the crime are also relevantly alleged, yet there is no relevant averment of connection between the issuing of the fraudulent statements and the fraudulent results, for your lordship laid down, in the case of *Wilkie*, as a matter of familiar law, that you require to show that falsehood was used in order to obtain the benefit in fact obtained. A man goes into a lodging-house and makes a false statement about his affairs, and about the purpose for which he is in the place, and as a result—not the indirect but the direct result of this false statement—he gets food and lodgings; there it might be thought the offence was complete, but your lordship held that unless it could be shown that the man intended to obtain these results by the false statements it was no crime. The peculiarity of all these cases is that they cannot be other than crimes against property, and when that is once recognised, it follows as a necessary consequence, that all such cases necessarily involve the element of patrimonial loss on the one hand, and patrimonial gain on the other.

My lords, in regard to the innominate charges in the major proposition, my case is this. I said at the outset that, according to the construction put upon the language used in the major, the innominate charges might either amount to falsehood, fraud, and wilful imposition, or might resolve into no crime at all; and I explained that the question between these two constructions would depend very much on what was found in the amplified statement in the minor proposition. I now say, as the result of my examination of the minor, that the indictment throughout, both in the major and in the minor, must be construed as omitting the elements of patrimonial gain or patrimonial loss, and as therefore failing to set forth what is necessary in order to constitute an offence of the class libelled, viz., an offence against property. I have further, however, to point out in regard to the innominate charges in the major, that it is an essential part of those charges as laid that "members of the Company" are defrauded; and as the

The City of Glasgow Bank Trial.

Mr.
Mackintosh. only respect in which members of the Company are said to be defrauded is by their being induced to retain their shares, it will follow, if my argument as to the irrelevancy of the part of the minor is successful, that the innominate charges in the major must fall, upon the separate ground that in any view there is no relevant case stated of fraud committed on "members of the Company." But I pass now to the remaining charges.*

Lord
Justice-Clerk. The LORD JUSTICE-CLERK (to the Lord Advocate)—On the first of the objections, namely, the question of specification under the first head, especially as regards the eighth sub-division of that part of the indictment, we should like to have a few observations. In regard to the relevancy of the innominate offence, and in regard to the charge of theft, while we, of course, do not at all shut out any further observations that may be hereafter made on the part of the prisoners, we do not at present wish your lordship to say anything.

Lord
Advocate. The LORD ADVOCATE—After what your lordship has just said, I apprehend that my duty is a very simple and very short one, because I am no longer bound to argue against what appeared to me to be really one of the most serious contentions for the accused—serious, not as involving a difficult question of law or libel, but as involving very serious consequences to the prisoners and also the public, viz., the contention that what is set forth in the major and minor propositions of the libel in its first three counts constituted merely an exaggerated instance of moral delinquency, and not a grave commercial crime. In regard to that one point, the eighth particular, if I may call it so, I shall be glad to save the time of the Court by consenting to its being struck out. It is a question which I cannot promise your lordships you will get rid of altogether, because it may turn out that, on an examination of the books, what appears there may yet be made matter of discussion. But as constituting a separate statement I withdraw it, because I do not know, and I cannot tell at this moment precisely, *quo animo* the manipulation or fabrication of the accounts connected with this proceeded, and it may be that the £2,000,000 odds understated in stating the amount of debts due to the Bank may have been intended to include bad debts.

Mr. Guthrie Smith and Mr. Trayner both addressed the Court on the relevancy of the second charge—that of permitting overdrafts. As, however, that charge was withdrawn, the learned counsels' arguments are omitted. Mr. Balfour followed, and argued that as the eighth particular in the charge relative to the

---

* As the remaining charges were withdrawn by the Lord Advocate at the close of the evidence for the Crown, no evidence having been led with respect to them, the argument of the learned counsel bearing on them has been omitted *brevitatis causa*.

Decision on Relevancy.

falsification of the balance sheet had been withdrawn by the Lord Advocate, it followed that the sixth and seventh particulars must necessarily fall with it.

Lord Justice-Clerk.

The LORD JUSTICE-CLERK, in delivering judgment, said—The question we have to decide is whether the public prosecutor has stated in this indictment facts which are relevant to go to proof—whether the facts stated here are to be inquired into by a jury. My lords, a great many important and serious matters were raised by the counsel for the prisoners. Many of them were considerations of very great weight, which will require to be carefully dealt with when the case goes to the investigation of the facts, and for that reason I think, probably, it will be desirable not to enter at length into these considerations, which, though they had a material bearing upon the question of relevancy, will have also a material bearing upon the question of the facts when disclosed; and at a later stage of these proceedings, it may be necessary to resume them at length, but in the meantime I shall simply announce my own opinion, and, I believe, that of your lordships, on the various objections that have been taken to the different heads of this indictment in their order. The indictment itself deals substantially with three classes of offences. I forbear at present to go into them technically, but I simply state them as they appear upon the general complexion of the indictment. The first of these is the falsification of the balance sheets of this joint stock banking company, and the making of false statements to the shareholders of the Bank and the public. The second is the obtaining of advances, on the part of the Directors, of the funds committed to their care, for the purposes of the banking company, on terms and conditions not authorised by the duty which they held towards the company; and the third is the theft of certain bills of exchange which were entrusted and confided to the Directors for the purpose of collection by creditors in these bills. To the charges, under these three heads, objections have been taken in this discussion on the relevancy. In regard to the first of them, which is a charge of falsifying the statements made to the shareholders of the state of the finances of the Bank, the main objection that was taken in regard to the specification of the offence related to the eighth sub-division of the first charge, which embraces the accounts for the year 1876, the other charges for the other succeeding years being in the same terms. That eighth section charges the whole of the Directors with falsely stating the bad and irrecoverable debts to an amount far exceeding the whole capital stock of the Bank. It was admitted that the debts were not specified. The objection certainly appeared to be formidable, and the Lord Advocate has accordingly expunged that charge from his indictment. What the effect of that may be upon the evidence in

The City of Glasgow Bank Trial.

support of that charge is a question on which I do not at present give any opinion. But it was objected by Mr. Balfour that if that sub-division of the eighth charge were missed out, it would then be necessary also to omit others of the charges that are contained there, because, he says, when the figures are looked to, they will be found to be inconsistent with each other. My lords, I think it was very plain, upon Mr. Balfour's own statement, that that was a matter for proof, and not a matter of relevancy. We cannot sit here and judge without evidence of the effect of the manipulation of the figures which is here in question. It may quite well be that the affairs of the Bank have been entirely misrepresented, and yet when you come to add the misrepresentations together, the sum total may be the same, or nearly the same. For instance, it is not the same thing to say that there were eight millions of floating assets and no bad or irrecoverable debts, and to say that there were eleven millions of floating assets and a large amount of irrecoverable debts. These are two different things. I give no further opinion, but I have come to the conclusion that the objection taken by Mr. Balfour, whatever weight it may have when the facts come to be ascertained, is not truly an objection to the relevancy. Then it was said by Mr. Mackintosh, still farther on this head, that there was not a sufficient specification of injury done to the shareholders by the alleged falsehood, and that it was a falsehood without injury. My lords, I think that that was perhaps not the most forcible part of the observations of my learned friend, because it really comes to this—if a man is entrusted with the business of another, and makes false reports to him as to the amount of his finances, he suffers nothing. Mr. Mackintosh said that the shares would not have been saleable if the truth had been known. My lords, I don't think that goes far. It is quite clear that every shareholder was entitled to know how the finances stood in order that he might know how he stood himself; and what was the effect of the false statement upon the different shareholders, and of the reliance which they necessarily placed upon these false reports, it is impossible for us now to say; but it must be quite manifest that a very large and important patrimonial interest was thereby endangered; and that is alleged in the indictment. So much for the first part of these charges; and the same considerations apply to the charges as to 1877 and 1878.

Then we come to a very important part of this indictment, which has given us a great deal of anxiety. These charges are directed against individual Directors, and are contained in the sixth and seventh charges of the indictment. They are charges against individual Directors of obtaining or taking from the Bank certain large advances by way of overdrafts on their own

38

Decision on Relevancy.

individual accounts out of the moneys with which they were entrusted for the purposes of the Bank. There is no doubt that that is a most important portion of this very formidable indictment, and I am anxious not to say more upon it at present than is necessary for the discharge of the immediate duty on hand, and the decision of the question of relevancy. It is quite manifest that it embraces many topics of immense importance to the prisoners at the bar, and also of immense importance to the public. I must own that I have had a great deal of difficulty in regard to the question of relevancy here, as I believe your lordships have also had. I think I may say without speaking too strongly on the subject that perhaps the use of more precise and definite expressions might have saved some at least of the difficulties that we have felt. My general opinion upon the matters submitted for discussion yesterday is, that it is not every violation or excess of the rights of directors or persons in that position of trust which will ground a criminal prosecution. It may quite well be that directors violate the conditions on which they hold their office by doing acts which are not sanctioned by the terms of their appointment. Such cases occur every day in the civil Courts, and if directors in that position act beyond their powers, or in violation of their powers, they will be responsible in the civil consequences, and their acts will not have the validity of legal acts of directors. But before this can be raised into a criminal offence and be the subject of a criminal indictment, there must be superadded to the illegality of the act—the invalidity of the act—some element of bad faith, some corrupt motive, some guilty knowledge, some fraudulent intent, which shall raise that which, although illegal, was not a crime, into the category of a crime. These are familiar and elementary principles; and in cases of that kind the corrupt motive, the bad faith, is essential to the crime itself, and without it there is no crime. Now, here I should not have been satisfied, although the duty of the Directors had been clearly charged, and the trust reposed in them clearly expressed, and the obligation not to allow overdrafts on open account without security quite precise, and the insufficiency of the security on which these advances were made clearly alleged, unless there had appeared in the charge something beyond these elements, namely, an element of want of faith, which would give a colour and character to all the rest. I must fairly say that I could have wished that this had been more clearly and specifically expressed, nor do I altogether see why it was not so. But, my lords, upon further consideration of the whole of that argument, I am satisfied that, assuming those principles which I have now announced, and which I consider both elementary and important, such is not

39

The City of Glasgow Bank Trial.

truly the nature of the charge that is made here, because
there are some words which override all the facts alleged,
and seem to me completely to raise the element of bad faith
throughout the whole transaction, or, what is the same thing,
to exclude the good faith of the parties in the proceeding, and
that is, that these advances were obtained by taking advantage
of the position of the accused as Directors. Now, no doubt
that places upon the prosecutor a very heavy burden of proof,
but, I take it, these words signify that the Directors obtained
these advances under conditions in which, but for their character
as Directors, they could not have obtained them; in other
words, that they used their character as Directors to obtain
advantages in regard to the money entrusted to themselves
which an ordinary customer could not have obtained. That is
the element which has led me to come to be of opinion that
there is a sufficiently relevant case stated under these charges
for investigation by a jury. Doubtless the public prosecutor
has a heavy task before him, because he must not only prove
the trust, and prove the duty as he alleges it, and prove that
the security which was offered or existed was manifestly insufficient, but he must also prove what he has alleged, I think in
sufficient language, that all these things were done solely and
entirely by taking advantage of the position of a Director,
and abusing that position to the effect of a result for which
it never was conferred. If these things are proved—if it be
shown that these advances were not in the ordinary course of
business, and were not made in good faith, but were made
solely and entirely in consequence of the position which the
Directors had on that Board—if it be proved that these were
advances which no ordinary customer could have obtained,
and which therefore no Director was in good faith to accept,
I think that the logic of the indictment on this head is sufficient.

There is a minor point upon two of these charges, in relation to
Mr. Inglis and Mr. Wright, which is of this nature. It would
rather appear from the statement in the charge against Mr.
Inglis, that some part at all events of these advances had been
obtained prior to his becoming a Director of the concern. We
are of opinion that the advances to that extent are not properly or relevantly brought within the charge stated in the
indictment, and that therefore it will be necessary in Mr.
Inglis' indictment to expunge the words, " or did allow the
overdrafts on the said accounts in name of you and of your
said firm to be continued and increased "; and in the case of
Mr. Wright, the words, " or did allow the overdrafts
of your said firm to be continued and increased."
In other words, we do not hold that this charge
can apply to advances which had been already made
when the accused became a Director. Of course, any

Decision on Relevancy.

increase in the advance is another matter. That is a question that will arise upon the proof; but in the meantime we think that these words are not relevant, and therefore they must be expunged.

My lords, the only other point relates to the charge of theft of a number of bills mentioned in the indictment. The distinction between theft and breach of trust is a very fine and subtle one, and I think depends more upon words than upon substance; but I have no doubt at all that the *species facti* alleged in this particular case, if proved in its terms, amounts to theft. One can quite well see that there are elements contained in it that might come to have a very material bearing on the question whether it did or did not amount to theft. But as stated, it is nothing but this, that the Bank Directors having been entrusted with certain bills of exchange for the purpose of collecting these bills—that is to say, of obtaining payment for the creditor when due, as mandatories of the creditor—used the bills for their own purposes by endorsing them to correspondents and creditors of the Bank —viz., the London Bank. Now, that case taken by itself, on that bare statement of it, is simply the same thing as if, instead of being a bill of exchange, it had been a bond or any other document of obligation, which, having been put into the hands of a man for the purpose of making it effectual against the debtor for the benefit of the creditor, is used directly for his own purposes, to increase his own credit. It was said in the argument, and of course it will have great weight when we come to the inquiry, that what is alleged here was in truth done in the process of collection, and for no other object. But that does not appear on the indictment, nor can we assume it; and consequently at the present stage I am not prepared to say that that charge is irrelevant, although very important matters will remain for the investigation when we come to the jury. My lords, these are the views upon which, to the extent which I have now indicated, I am prepared to sustain the relevancy of this indictment.

Lord MURE and Lord CRAIGHILL concurred.

CHAPTER IV.

Evidence for the Prosecution.*

EVIDENCE OF THE INVESTIGATORS.

Dr. M'Grigor.

ALEXANDER BENNET M'GRIGOR, LL.D.

BY the LORD ADVOCATE—I am a writer, carrying on business in Glasgow, and a partner of the firm of M'Grigor, Donald & Co. My firm have acted as agents for the Royal and British Linen Company Banks. On 2nd October, 1878, I got a message asking me to meet the Directors of the City of Glasgow Bank in Mr. Potter's offices in Gordon Street. I went there. There were present—Mr. Potter, Mr. Wright, Mr. Stewart, Mr. Inglis, Mr. Taylor, Mr. Leresche, the Secretary of the Bank, and afterwards Mr. Stronach. Mr. William Anderson, C.A., was present at the commencement of the interview. I found him there. Some of the Directors mentioned that of course I understood the painful circumstances under which they were met, and a somewhat general conversation took place as to the course that should be followed, and as to the propriety of a meeting of the shareholders being called at once. I was consulted as to these, and as to the propriety of such a meeting being called, and then I was asked, in conjunction with Mr. Anderson, to prepare a balance sheet of the affairs of the Bank, in order that it might be submitted to such a meeting. That request was preferred to myself and Mr. Anderson jointly, and I cannot say that any one of the Directors more than another preferred it; it was a general request. They all took part in the conversation. Mr. Stronach came into the room apparently from a side room, I think about five minutes after I arrived. We had been conversing in regard to the state of the Bank before he arrived. I can hardly say that he took any part in the conversation. He seemed completely overpowered, and almost unable to speak. Mr. Leresche did take part, and he appeared—if one may use the expression—to have more his wits about him than any one else in the room. I at first demurred to acting in the preparation of a balance sheet, in

---

* The evidence of the purely formal witnesses and of those of minor importance has been generally omitted.

Evidence of Investigators.

consequence of my connection with those other banks; and I may say that I would almost have been glad of any excuse to get rid of what promised to be a very painful piece of business. It occurred to me that there might be some complication arising from the fact that my firm acted for those two banks; but I was very urgently pressed, and, after consulting with Mr. Anderson, I said I would communicate with those banks. I subsequently did so, and they thought there was no objection to my acting in the way proposed. I doubt if I was with the Directors on the occasion I have mentioned for more than a quarter of an hour or twenty minutes altogether. At that meeting nothing definite was said while I was there as to the state of the Bank; the conversation proceeded on a general assumption that the crisis was very serious—that there was something very far wrong. None of the Directors present at that time entered upon any explanation of the causes of the crisis. I left the meeting in company with Mr. Anderson, and having telegraphed to Edinburgh for the opinion of the cashier of the Royal Bank, and received the assurance from those banks that there was no objection on their part to my acting, I proceeded to make an investigation for the purpose of drawing up a balance sheet and report to be laid before the meeting of shareholders. I went down immediately that afternoon to the Bank, and I may say that Mr. Anderson and I were there continuously from that day until we issued our report, which was on the 18th of October. Mr. Anderson and I worked into each other's hands, doing particular parts of the work. Of course, what may be called the general accountant's part of the work devolved upon him and his partner. With respect to my portion of the work, in the first instance, having heard that a statement had been prepared as to some leading accounts, and submitted through Mr. Auldjo Jamieson (now one of the liquidators) to the Scotch banks, I telegraphed to Mr. Jamieson to send me that statement, and I received it from him that evening. I took that statement merely as a guide in my own investigation. I cannot say whether or not it was at the meeting with the Directors that I had learned Mr. Jamieson had been furnished with that information; I rather think it was at the British Linen Company's Bank. Upon receiving Mr. Jamieson's notanda, Mr. Anderson and I proceeded to investigate for ourselves. We looked over these notanda, and found that they embraced a note of four leading accounts, which had been the subject of conversation with the Bank Directors. These were the accounts of James Morton & Co., Smith, Fleming & Co., James Nicol Fleming, and John Innes Wright & Co. The statement embraced the balances at the debit of these several accounts, and the securities held against them, and as I understood that these

43

securities were put down at the valuations which the Bank itself had furnished, we took the deficit as showing the minimum deficit. We very roughly endeavoured to correct off-hand the value of the securities from such facts as were patent upon the face of the accounts, and upon that information we became satisfied next day that we must advise the Directors at once that there was no hope of the Bank continuing business. Within a day of receiving these notanda and examining them in the way I have described, I came unhesitatingly to the conclusion that the Bank could not possibly go on—that it was hopelessly insolvent. John Innes Wright & Co. is the firm of which the panel Mr. Wright is a partner, and he is a Director of the Company. There was enough in the indebtedness of these firms to make it impossible, in our judgment, for the Bank to go on.

After that we proceeded to make farther inquiry about those accounts. In conjunction with Mr. Muir I made a detailed precognition of Mr. Morison, the accountant of the Bank, and obtained from him a number of documents, in particular certain abstract balance sheets. These documents were given to me by Mr. Morison out of his custody, as an official of the Bank, and I got him to initial and mark them as he gave them. These documents are Nos. 124, 125, 127, and 128, and they were marked A, B, C, and D. From the time they were given to me by Mr. Morison, they remained in my special custody until 21st October, when I handed them over to the Procurator-Fiscal. So far as we had time between the receipt of Mr. Jamieson's notes and the issuing of our report, we proceeded to check his notes upon those accounts to the best of our ability, and likewise to check the general abstract balance sheet for 1878, which I received from Mr. Morison. When I say the general abstract balance sheet, I do not mean the balance sheet that was published. I mean the scroll abstract. That is the abstract which has just been shown to me.

The prospects of the Company did not get brighter as our examination proceeded. In the course of our examination we came upon some facts which appeared to us so peculiar and likely to lead to such consequences in the way of charges against the Directors' management, that we felt we would not be justified in putting these into print without intimating to them their nature and character, and I consequently asked the Directors individually, one by one, to meet me, and narrated to them the conclusions at which we had arrived. I communicated with Mr. Stronach on the same subject. The report was published on the evening of Friday, the 18th, and I think it would be about the Tuesday or Wednesday preceding that these communications were made. In conversation with some of the Directors previously, I had strongly urged them to

Evidence of Investigators.

employ an agent of their own, not only for their own private Dr. M'Grigor interest, but likewise an agent who could advise them in the management of the Bank, because the disposition at first was to consult Mr. Anderson and myself about a great number of questions that necessarily occurred immediately after the stoppage, and we found that we had really no time to give to these. I communicated with each Director separately in the beginning of the week which ended on 19th October. There was no joint communication made to more than one of the Directors at that time. In the case of Mr. Stronach, I said to him that I was going to put various questions to him in regard to subjects which would come up in this report, and we thought it our duty to put those before him as we had put them before the other Directors, but that it was for him to consider whether, as I knew he was then in the hands of a private agent, it would not be right that, before entering on this matter, he should consult his agent. He said he would do so, and would see me next day. I saw him next day, and he then said that he had been advised that perhaps under the circumstances the less he said the better. I said that still I would not feel myself quite clear to publish this report until I had gone over the various items of it with him, not asking him to make any remark unless he chose, and I did go over the items with him. He made no remark, but remained silent; but I am bound in justice to Mr. Stronach to say that he was thoroughly and entirely broken down during this period. I was not in the least surprised at the state in which he appeared to be; he had been confined to bed for several days. When I had those meetings with the Directors singly I did not meet Mr. Inglis, as he was in Edinburgh at the time; but after meeting the other Directors singly, I had a meeting with the whole of them collectively, including Mr. Inglis. I think that was on the morning of the day of the publication of the report— Friday, the 18th. The Board was assembled, and the object of my going up was this : we saw that we would be in a position to issue our report late that evening. We were satisfied that it was very desirable the report should be in the hands of the shareholders a day or two before the meeting, which had been summoned a week previously for Tuesday, the 22nd, and my object in going up to that meeting was to ask their permission to publish the report the moment it was ready. We had received our commission to prepare the balance sheet for them, and we felt technically that we must get their permission before we could make it public. They gave their consent. While I was there, one or other of them—I cannot remember which it was—said that I had been going over various items with them singly, and it would be better that I should go over them with the whole Board collectively. I happened

The City of Glasgow Bank Trial.

to have the rough draft of the printed report in my hand. I had not been in communication with Mr. Inglis previously upon this subject. Taking the rough draft, I went over item by item the notes on that draft which appeared to me to affect the Directors personally. I did so without, so far as I remember, any remark being made ; and the moment I had finished I was very glad to take the opportunity of leaving the room, from the unpleasant nature of the affair. No one spoke, unless there may have been an exclamation or two of astonishment. They all appeared to be very much surprised and astonished at the various items to which I referred, but there was no distinct or definite remark with which I can charge my memory. Mr. Stronach was present. He was in the same state in which he had previously been. This meeting took place in a small room in the Bank's premises.

At this time we had not checked or finally ascertained the precise amount of the deficit, according to our calculation ; the figures were not added up. Before I left the room I undertook to inform the Directors of the amount the moment we had ascertained it. We did ascertain it about half-past three the same afternoon (Friday), and I went up to the Board room with a slip of paper, on which were the words, as nearly as possible— " Deficit, upwards of five millions "—which I handed to Mr. Naismith, who was acting as agent for the Directors. And that was, in point of fact, the actual deficit, so far as I could ascertain it. That result was never challenged by any of the Directors as being an incorrect representation of the state of matters. I knew the abstract that had been published by the Directors on 5th July, 1878 ; we published that abstract as part of our report. It showed that the Bank had assets exceeding liabilities to the amount of a million and a half in round numbers. Our report brought out a balance of loss of £5,190,000, so that the difference between the two results— the one brought out in their report to the shareholders on 5th July, and the other in our report on 18th October in the same year—was something over six and a half millions. No. 576 is a copy of our report. We retained the Bank's books in our possession until we gave them over to the Crown. For convenience' sake we continued to enter the operations of the Bank in these books. We found it would have put a practical stop to the liquidation if they had started a new set of books at once ; but I arranged with Mr. Brown a stamp which should be put at the end of every entry in a book that was in use, marking the time when the liquidators began, so that the books bear evidence of that wherever there was an entry made in continuation of the Bank's own operations. I, as law agent of the liquidators, was in possession of certain of the muniments of the Bank. The contract of copartnery of the City of Glasgow

Evidence of Investigators.

Bank, No. 299, was given over by me to the Crown; and also the supplementary contract, of dates from 22nd May, 1843, to 20th June, 1844, No. 301, and the supplementary contract, of dates from 26th June, 1844, to 28th September, 1849, No. 302. No. 300 is a print which was prepared containing these three documents in full.

Cross-examined by Mr. TRAYNER—Mr. Anderson and I took sixteen days to make up the report which we issued on 18th October. During these sixteen days we were very busy the whole day, and more than the day, with the Bank's affairs. We had other accountants' assistance besides the personal labour of Mr. Anderson. All the partners of Mr. Anderson's firm were employed, I may almost say continuously, and two at least of my own partners; and we had a staff of our own. We had a large number both of Mr. Anderson's clerks and of mine employed during the whole time. I saw Mr. Stewart several times between 2nd October and the publication of our report. On 2nd October, I met him and all the other Directors, as I have already mentioned. He did not say anything on that occasion indicative of his acquaintance with the Bank's books or the entries therein.

Then the information which the Directors gave you then, that there was a crisis at hand, was information, I suppose, just as general in their minds as the expression you have mentioned to us now?—Very much so.

And no details were gone into to show you that Mr. Stewart or anybody else knew what was the exact nature of the crisis that was expected?—None.

That disposes of the 2nd of October; what was the next occasion on which you saw Mr. Stewart?—I must have seen Mr. Stewart at the first meeting or two of the Bank Directors, but no particulars with regard to these meetings dwelt upon my mind. The first time that I remember Mr. Stewart saying anything to me individually upon the subject was when I met him one day at the door of the Bank. That was before our report had been completed, and before I had spoken to the Directors privately.

What took place between you?—It was a mere shaking of hands; and he hurrying past in a state of great excitement, and saying that he was a broken-hearted man, and perfectly astounded at the state in which the Bank's affairs were found to have been.

Then, after that, you, I suppose, met him when you went over the draft report with him, as you did with each of the Directors?—I sent for him to come down to my room, and he came down alone, and I went over the various points with him. He stated then that he was entirely and totally ignorant of every fact that I brought before him. I believed him. I

47

The City of Glasgow Bank Trial.

Dr.
M'Grigor.

must say that I always looked upon him as an essentially honourable man in every respect, and not a man who, so far as I could judge, would be likely to fabricate or falsify accounts. I knew him to be a man reputed to be of large means, and one who held a position of esteem in Glasgow.

What opinion have you formed with regard to Mr. Stewart's character as an accountant?—I can only give, in the most general terms, my own impression, and that is that I should think he had a peculiarly bad head for figures.

What was Mr. Stewart's appearance when you told him at that private meeting the results of your investigation?—I should say something like horror.

Did you at all suppose him to be feigning an ignorance which was not the fact?—No ; I did not.

In short, from what he stated, and from his manner, you believed his statement that your revelations were perfectly new to him?—I did.

GEORGE AULDJO JAMIESON.

G. A.
Jamieson.

By the LORD ADVOCATE—I am a chartered accountant in Edinburgh. I am now one of the liquidators of the City of Glasgow Bank. On the 30th of September, 1878, I was sent for by the cashier of the Royal Bank, and was told that my services were required by himself and the other banks to investigate as well as I could, in a short time, the affairs of the City of Glasgow Bank, which had applied to the other Scots banks for assistance. I was informed that the state of affairs, so far as disclosed, had occasioned considerable alarm to the other banks. I met the managers of the Scots banks that evening, and next morning (Tuesday, 1st October) I went to Glasgow. Mr. Fleming, the cashier of the Royal Bank, had handed to me certain papers which had been left with him by the representatives of the City Bank. On arriving at Glasgow I went to the office of Messrs. Stewart, Pott & Co., and afterwards to the City of Glasgow Bank. I went alone to the Bank. I met there the Manager of the Bank, Mr. Stronach, and Mr. Potter, a Director. I also saw the accountant of the Bank, Mr. Morison, and the Secretary, Mr. Leresche. Mr. Potter was very strong in giving directions to the officials of the Bank that every possible information and explanation should be afforded to me ; and these directions were thoroughly carried out by the officials. Mr. Potter and Mr. Stronach were together, but Mr. Potter was spokesman. I asked for the balance sheet of the year to 5th June, 1878. [Shown No. 124.] I forget at this moment whether there were red ink figures on the balance sheet shown to me ; my impression is they were all in black; but this balance sheet was certainly shown to me. If there be a balance sheet showing these results in black figures, it was that which was shown to me. [Shown No. 125.] That is the one I saw. I asked explanations at the officials, especially as to gold. From the materials put into my hands by Mr. Fleming, I had an index by which to examine the matters in the balance sheet, and making use of that, I put the necessary questions to the officials. I also examined some of the accounts in the books. Some were large accounts. I went into the discount ledger and some of the other ledgers with the view of taking out and making notes on the largest and most important accounts I there found. In the course of the afternoon Mr. Stewart and Mr. Innes Wright, two of the Directors, came to see me, and to see what was going on. Mr. Potter had been there during a considerable part of the day, and was there when they arrived. They were anxious to know the result of my investigation, so far as it had gone. I did not communicate the result definitely to them, because I had not completed it. They asked me to communicate what would be the probable tenor of the report I should make to the banks in Edinburgh that afternoon, and I told them that I could hold out no expectation that I could recommend the banks to afford any assistance, because I had satisfied myself that the amount of probable loss greatly exceeded anything that the banks would venture to face. That conclusion was based on the rapid view which I had been enabled to take, by the information so readily supplied to me, of the position of the Bank with reference to important accounts, and to the disclosure of the affairs of the Bank contained in the balance sheets.

In speaking of important accounts, do you mean advances, and to whom? [Objected to. Objection repelled.]—I mean entries in the balance sheet itself, and advances made to specific customers of the Bank, as laid before me at that time by the officials, and in the documents then submitted to me. These specific customers of the Bank were James Morton & Co., Smith, Fleming & Co., J. Nicol Fleming, and John Innes Wright & Co. As I made them up at that hurried time, the advances shown to these four firms amounted to £5,870,000.

Was it in respect of these advances that you formed your estimate that the Bank would not be able to go on?—That, combined with some of the other elements in the balance sheet of the Bank. I intimated my opinion to Mr. Wright, Mr. Stewart, and Mr. Potter. I stated to them the advances as being about five millions. They appeared to be surprised at the amount, and I recollect Mr. Potter turned to the Manager and said, " Is it possible "—I forget whether he said " we " or " you "—"have given so much to those firms?" One of the firms was Mr. Wright's own. He did not make any observation

D

The City of Glasgow Bank Trial.

G. A.
Jamieson.

about the amount—not that I can recollect. Mr. Stronach, in answer to Mr. Potter, said he feared it was too true. I don't think Mr. Stewart said anything. He appeared to be very much distressed and disturbed by the state of matters, but I cannot recollect that he said anything.

By the LORD JUSTICE-CLERK—Distressed by your information? —By my information.

By the LORD ADVOCATE—Do you mean that he betrayed that state of mind upon receiving your information; or do you mean that he was in that state before he received it?—I should say partly both. I took it for granted that, having asked me to give an indication of the report which I was to make to the banks—on which so much depended—he was distressed at finding that I was not prepared to report favourably. I returned to Edinburgh and laid my statement before the managers of the banks, who afterwards resolved to give no assistance. I was appointed a liquidator. We have made no final estimate of the assets and liabilities. The officials of the Bank and the books have been taken up so much in connection with the investigations for this trial that it has been impossible, as yet, to complete such estimate.

James Muir.

JAMES MUIR.

By the LORD ADVOCATE—I am an accountant in Glasgow, and a member of the Institute of Accountants and Actuaries there. After the 2nd October, 1878, I aided in an investigation into the books and accounts of the City of Glasgow Bank, and more recently I have been engaged by the Crown to make certain further investigations into these books. The whole of the books at the Bank were placed at my disposal for that purpose, and I examined them in Glasgow, within the premises of the Bank. I examined the balance sheets printed and circulated among the shareholders for the years 1876, 1877, and 1878, along with the annual report. I also examined the books of the Bank as at the periods of the balances, for the purpose of ascertaining whether and how far these tallied with the books. I made out corrected balances of my own for each of these periods. I also compared these balance sheets with the book entitled "City of Glasgow Bank balance ledger, No. 3." That is a book containing the signatures of the Directors, and it is No. 12 of the inventory. I also prepared states showing the difference between the entries contained in the balance sheets as published and the books of the Bank. The credit and debit sides are differently stated in the balance ledger and in the published abstracts.

What is the difference?—In the published balance sheet the liabilities are on the left-hand side, and in the balance ledger

Evidence for Prosecution.

they are upon the right-hand side; that is a matter of no moment, but it must be kept very strictly in view to avoid confusion.

Look at No. 28, being a scroll balance sheet for 1876, and also at the published abstract as printed in the indictment, and state in detail the discrepancies?—On the debtor or liability side, head I. in the published sheet, "Deposits at the head office and branches, and balances at the credit of banking correspondents," is as published, £8,364,056; in the bank ledger it is £9,370,273. In the published sheet it is therefore understated to the extent of £1,006,216. Taking the second item on the debtor side, the "Bank notes in circulation" are properly stated on both sheets. Taking the third item, "Drafts outstanding, due, or with a currency not exceeding twenty-one days, £326,853 14s. 1d."; and item four, "Drafts accepted by the Bank and by its London agents on account of home and foreign constituents, £988,520 3s.," these are understated to the extent of £973,300 in the published sheet. The other items on the debtor side of the sheet are correctly stated.

Did you examine the books of the Bank with the view of tracing that deduction of £973,300?—I did.

What did you find?—I found an entry in the private cash book on 4th June, 1873. [Shown excerpt 2A from the City of Glasgow Bank cash book, private, No. 6.] The entry that I found in the cash book on the debtor side is "Foreign and colonial credits No. 2, for the following credits to be retired as they mature, and debited under the respective accounts to credit accounts No. 2, against which securities are now held by the Bank, and in process of realisation and payment of proceeds, £973,300"; and on the other side the entry is, "Bills payable No. 2, for the following amounts under acceptance at this date, to be retired by the Bank, under special arrangements with the parties, of date 1st June, 1873, against which certain securities are now held by the Bank, and in process of realisation and payment of the proceeds, £973,300."

What arrangement, according to your view, was indicated by these entries?—It would appear to me that if this entry were a true entry——

Assume it to be so?—Some arrangement must have been come to with certain parties who had obtained advances from the Bank, and who had lodged securities against these advances, the nature of the arrangement being that these securities were to be, and, in point of fact, were at that moment in process of realisation, and that the bills with which the advances had been financed were to be paid off at their maturity by the proceeds of the realisation.

By the LORD JUSTICE-CLERK—Are the debts enumerated which stood in that position?—They are not; there are no details.

The City of Glasgow Bank Trial.

James Muir. By the LORD ADVOCATE—They are slumped on both sides. No details are given, either of the advances or of the supposed securities.

Did you find that that sum of £973,000, according to that arrangement, was kept in the books down to the balance of 1878?—It was. We found it there in October, at the time of the investigation.

What was the effect of it?—The effect of it was, as used in the published balance sheets, to make it appear, not that the securities were to be realised, but that they had been realised, and that the bills to a corresponding amount were not to be paid off, but that they had actually been paid off.

By the LORD JUSTICE-CLERK—It is not set forth twice in the balance sheet. There is not a cross entry; it is deducted from both sides, so that it reduces the assets on the one side and the liabilities on the other.

By the LORD ADVOCATE—In other words, is the effect of it in the balance sheet not precisely the same as if these advances to the extent of £973,000 had been paid in cash?—Exactly.

Upon the day the entry was made in 1873?—And not only so, but that it was employed to retire the Bank's acceptances for an equal amount.

By the LORD JUSTICE-CLERK—And therefore that they were not to be regarded as bills payable?—Precisely.

And the amount was reduced to that extent?—Exactly.

By the LORD ADVOCATE—That was entered as an actual payment which was only an anticipated payment, and was not got during the five years afterwards?—Yes, it seems as much an anticipation at October, 1878, as it was in June, 1873.

So far as the books go?—So far as the books go.

By the LORD JUSTICE-CLERK—Do you find any trace at all in the books of what that sum of £973,000 originated in?—I did not find anything in the books, but I have seen a document which explains it. But I may say that it does not explain it to my satisfaction. I wish, my lord, to impress it very strongly upon you, that no entry in a book can possibly take a bill payable off the circle, although some people seem to have thought differently.

Can you conceive any object in a trading company dealing in money as banks do making an entry of that kind?— Yes; it is obviously very important that the acceptances of the Bank should be made to appear in the balance sheet as small as possible. A large amount of acceptances published in the balance sheet would militate against the possibility of discounting the bills of the Bank in the brokers' offices in London.

By the LORD ADVOCATE—Proceed with your examination of the other side of the abstract for 1876?—On the credit side

Evidence for Prosecution.

of the balance sheet, as published at 7th June, 1876, the first head is "Bills of exchange, local and country bills, credit accounts, and other advances upon security," £8,787,804. That is understated in the published balance sheet to the extent of £2,698,539. Then, "Cash on hand, that is to say, gold and silver coin, and notes of other banks at head office and branches," head III. of the published sheet, £862,812, is overstated £29,095. The next head, "Government stocks, exchequer bills, railway and other stocks and debentures, and balances in hands of banking correspondents," were overstated to the extent of £753,211.

Could you ascertain what that consisted of?—Yes; I have ascertained it.

In what way?—By looking at No. 128 of the inventory, which is apparently the scroll of the balance sheet.

Well, do not assume that in the meantime?—It is overstated to that amount; but without looking at this scroll, it cannot be found to be so by the books.

Then, except for the existence of scroll No. 128, the books of the Bank proper do not disclose whence came that over-statement?—No.

But, in point of fact, if you had nothing but the books to go by, they simply show an over-statement of that amount, without anything to account as to where it came from?—Quite so.

I suppose it is quite possible to conceal a good deal by making deductions on both sides of a balance sheet, leaving the result the same as it originally stood?—Yes.

In point of fact, I presume that the balance sheet of a bank ought to show their whole outstanding liabilities and their whole outstanding assets?—Undoubtedly.

Is it possible otherwise to form an accurate conception of the kind of trading they are engaged in, or what loss would result?—Quite impossible.

To take six or eight millions off each side of this account would not alter the balance?—Certainly not.

But it would alter the apparent character of the Bank's transactions?—Entirely.

Now turn to the next abstract balance sheet for 1877. I ask you in the meantime to lay out of view these scroll sheets, and to confine yourself to a comparison between this abstract and the books of the Bank, beginning again with the liabilities?—At 6th June, 1877, the published sheet disclosed under head I. of liabilities, "Deposits at the head office and branches, and balances at the credit of banking correspondents," £8,382,711. That was understated to the extent of £1,151,518.

With reference to that under-statement, leaving out of view those abstracts that I was speaking of, is there anything what-

The City of Glasgow Bank Trial.

James Muir. ever to give a clue to the particular assets that had been deducted in making up this abstract?—Yes, there is.

What is that?—There are two books specially, one of which is called, "Balances of deposit accounts," and the other, "Balances of credit accounts," which show the true balances of deposit and credit accounts which ought to have been entered in this balance sheet.

That is perfectly true; but supposing the question were put to you, which part of their assets were deducted, is there any means of telling that from the books themselves?—There is no means of comparing the books themselves with the published sheet, simply for the reason that there are no details in the published sheet.

Precisely so, and therefore you cannot, by looking at the published sheet, and then looking at the books of the Bank, tell whether the deduction was made from deposits or credits?— No, or whatever it may be, you cannot tell the precise nature of the debt which was omitted.

You may speculate as to why it was made, and how it was made, but there is no possibility of obtaining information as to that from the books?—No, in consequence of the absence of details from the published balance sheet.

Then what is the next item?—The next item on the liabilities side is head II., "Bank notes in circulation in Scotland and the Isle of Man." That is understated to the extent of £76,110. The next item, "Drafts outstanding, due, or with a currency not exceeding twenty-one days, and drafts accepted by the Bank and by its London agents on account of home and foreign constituents," £1,350,335, as published, is understated to the extent of £1,330,712, just about one-half. The other items on that side are perfectly correct as published, according to the books.

Then take the other side?—The first item on the other side, "Bills of exchange, local and country bills, credit accounts, and other advances upon security," £8,758,838, is understated to the extent of £3,227,154. Then "Cash on hand, gold and silver coin, and notes of other banks at head office and branches," is understated to the extent of £30,000. Then "Government stocks, exchequer bills, railway and other stocks and debentures, and balances in hand of banking correspondents," £2,187,896, as published, is overstated to the extent of £751,775.

I suppose that from the books themselves you have no means of tracing that over-statement? I mean from comparing the books themselves with the published sheet, you have no means of finding the items?—No, none whatever.

Now, assuming that the books are true, and that in publishing the result of the books there is a departure from them to the extent shown in this abstract, do you think it could be said

Evidence for Prosecution.

that this abstract truly sets forth the condition of the Bank?— Certainly not.

What do you think the effect would be of understating the third article on the debtor side by one-half—the bills payable— or by its own amount?—What I have already said—it would make the bills which were offered to the London brokers for discount all the more marketable.

And I presume a good deal of the effect of such an under-statement might depend upon who were known to be the customers of the Bank?—Undoubtedly.

Now, take the next abstract balance sheet for the year 1878?—On the liabilities side, head I., " Deposits at the head office and branches, and balances at the credit of banking correspondents," £8,102,001, is understated to the extent of £941,284. " Bank notes in circulation in Scotland and the Isle of Man," £710,252, as published, is under-stated to the extent of £89,031. " Drafts outstanding, due, or with a currency not exceeding twenty-one days, and drafts accepted by the Bank and by its London agents on account of home and foreign constituents," £1,488,244, ought to be £2,881,252, leaving an under-statement on that head of £1,393,008, again nearly one-half. Then, on the other side, the first item of assets, " Bills of exchange, local and country bills, credit accounts, and other advances upon security," £8,484,466, is understated £3,520,913. The " Cash on hand," £845,963, is overstated to the extent of £219,522. The " Gov-ernment stocks," etc., published at £2,296,839, are overstated to the extent of £926,764.

Do you say the same as to the impossibility of getting the details of these under the particular statements from the books? —I do.

Now, will you take the balance accounts in the " Balance ledger No. 3," or excerpt No. 12A? Take the year 1876. I wish you to contrast the entries in the balance ledger with the entries in the books, and state what, if any, discrepancies you find there?—We will take this time the credit side of this document first, being the liability side. In the first place, there is " Bills payable, £1,315,373." It ought to be £2,288,673 ; the difference is the £973,300.

Then the difference between the two entries tallies with the £973,300?—Yes ; and I find the true amount of the bills current in the " Bills payable progressive ledger," No. 40 of the inventory.

But I mean to say that the entry in the balance ledger will tally with the entries in the books if you give effect to that as a liquidating arrangement?—Yes.

If you treat unpaid debts to that extent as paid?—Yes.

Is there any other?—Yes. Four or five entries further down,

James Muir. deposit accounts are entered at £3233; that ought to be £455,444.

Will you look at No. 128? That is the scroll abstract of accounts for 1876?—It appears to be so.

Is it not titled so?—No; it does not say "scroll," it says "abstract," but it appears to be the scroll of the published abstract. I see it says "scroll" on the back; I was not aware of that.

That is a document written partly in black and partly in red ink?—Yes.

Does that appear to you to have been the scroll from which the abstract was made up?—It does.

From what does it so appear?—I find that the slump totals under the various heads correspond with the slump totals under the various heads in the published sheet.

You see there an entry of "Drafts outstanding, due, or with a currency," under head III.?—Yes; it is "Drafts outstanding, due, or with a currency, bills payable No. 1"—that is extended into a creditor column—£2,288,673 17s. 1d.

That tallies with the books?—Yes; and then, a little lower down, there is another entry, "Bills payable, No. 2," and there is a sum extended into a debtor column, £973,300, which sum is deducted from that I have just given. The difference, £1,315,373, is entered into a column called "Creditor balance," and that is the sum which is published in the balance sheet.

So that if that be correct, that would explain the way in which the sum of £973,300 has been deducted and the balance sheet made up?—Yes.

Will you refer again to the balance ledger No. 3? Is the state of deposit accounts correctly given?—No. The amount inserted in the balance ledger on the creditor side, on the left-hand side, is £3233. That ought to be £455,444.

Just explain how you come to that conclusion?—I find that that is the amount of deposits at the head office by looking at the book, "Balances of deposit accounts," which is No. 59 of inventory, and that book corresponds with the deposit ledger kept at the head office of the Bank.

That book shows in separate columns both the balances due to the Bank by overdrafts and the balances due by the Bank to depositors?—It does.

These are crossed?—Yes, and the difference alone extended.

Do you think that is a correct operation?—Not except in cases where the debtor and creditor are precisely the same.

Where there are cross accounts with the same person or firm?—Yes, and representing the same interest. The same man may be representing different interests, and it would be most improper to cross such accounts.

In the scroll abstract how is that item dealt with?—It appears

Evidence for Prosecution.

in the books as two entries, one of £455,000, and the other of £452,211.

These are made to extinguish each other, and bring out the balance ledger?—Yes, and £1346 is put in on the other side in the published sheet.

Which head would that fall under?—Head I., on the left-hand side of the published sheet. This balance ledger is not classified at all.

It appears in the book as two sums due by the Bank to depositors, and due by depositors to the Bank on overdraft?—It does.

The difference only to the extent of £3000 odds is entered in the balance ledger?—That is so.

In what account does this item appear in the scroll balance sheet?—It appears on the other side altogether, £1346 16s. 8d.

And that is the item which is given effect to in bringing out the total represented in the published sheet?—That is so.

So that it appears in three different forms—first in the books; then a different sum in the balance ledger; and thirdly, a reduced sum in the scroll abstract?—That is so; and that has arisen, I may explain, to some extent from certain entries having been made in the cash book subsequently, apparently, to this scroll having been made up.

It may be accounted for from that?—Yes, it is so; and the balance ledger is in conformity with the books after these entries have been made, but not the scroll.

There is nothing of the same kind to account for the change in the scroll?—Nothing whatever.

In the "Balance ledger No. 3" come to "credit accounts, creditor balances"?—That is omitted altogether from the balance ledger. I find on looking at a book called "Balances of credit accounts," No. 58 of the inventory, that there were such balances to the extent of £147,468. These are entirely omitted from the balance ledger.

Was that a correct omission?—Certainly not.

By the LORD JUSTICE-CLERK—What is that sum of £147,468? —These are balances standing at the credit of what are called "Credit accounts." It is a little confusing. They are at the creditor of what are called the credit accounts— a "credit account" being an account which generally has a balance at the debtor of it. A "cash credit account" is the ordinary name for it.

By the LORD ADVOCATE—But upon these balances the Bank was the debtor?—It was.

By the LORD JUSTICE-CLERK—They were balances due to customers upon their credit accounts?—Yes. Instead of overdrawing their credit accounts, they, in fact, had deposited a little.

57

The City of Glasgow Bank Trial.

James Muir. These are omitted altogether?—Yes; they are altogether omitted; they are not in the balance ledger at all.

By the LORD ADVOCATE—And, of course, they are not to be found at all in the scroll abstract?—In the scroll abstract they are not to be found.

And accordingly they did not pass into the published abstract? —They did not.

Is there any other discrepancy between the books and the balance ledger of that year?—There is another, "Adjusting account of interest," the correct state of which I find from No. 144 of process; there is an omission there to the extent of £11,405. These are all the discrepancies I find between the books and the balance ledger.

By the LORD JUSTICE-CLERK—Are these accidental errors, or do you think they were systematically done?—They were quite systematically done, but whether with an intention to defraud or not, I don't know.

But do they appear to have been accidental errors, or do they seem to have been systematically done? — Quite systematically.

By the LORD ADVOCATE—Turn to the creditor side of the scroll abstract of accounts for 1878, and point out how far it is, if it be, in disconformity with the books of the Bank? —Being the scroll of the published sheet, it is disconform to the books of the Bank precisely to the same extent as the published sheet is.

It is just the same in result?—The same in result as I have already given.

By the LORD JUSTICE-CLERK—That gives the key to these discrepancies, does it not?—Yes, it gives the actual details, and enables me to say how the thing was done.

By the LORD ADVOCATE—Go now to the debtor side of the balance ledger, and contrast it first with the entries in the books of the Bank, and then tell me how far it coincides with the debtor side of the scroll abstract?—The first item on the debtor side of the "Balance ledger No. 3" which is wrong is "Credit accounts No. 1, £1,981,934." That ought to be £2,129,403. It is understated £147,468, and it was the understated amount that went into the scroll abstract. The next item is "Foreign and colonial credits," £1,304,873, which ought to be £2,278,173, understated by the £973,300, and it was the understated sum which was carried into the abstract. That is carried also into the scroll abstract of the published sheet. The next entry is "Deposit account, debtor balances," being the indebtedness of the Bank to depositors at the head office, £452,211, which is entirely omitted from the balance ledger. It is also omitted in the scroll abstract. Then the "Adjusting

58

Evidence for Prosecution.

account of interest " is stated in the balance ledger at £19,696, James Muir.
which ought to be £31,101.   It is understated £11,405

Do these omissions appear to you to be accidental or intentional?—I cannot say that they were accidental; they seem to me to be perfectly intentional.

Do you observe any transferences in the scroll abstract No. 128 which would account for the over-statement under the third head of what appears as assets in the published sheet, and what is there represented as Government stocks?—I find that deductions are made from head I., which head is appropriated in the published sheet to the ordinary debts due to the Bank.   I find the following entries deducted from that head:—" S. F. & Co." (Smith, Fleming & Co.), £200,875; " J. N. F." (James Nicol Fleming), £100,300; " J. M. & Co." (James Morton & Co.), £450,600—together, £751,775.   I find that brought down to head III., and there represented to be " Investments in Government and other stocks," and to precisely a similar amount.

That sum, made up of these three sums, deducted from their indebtedness, when added to " Government stocks and others " as really appearing in the books, makes up the sum stated in the abstract?—It does.

Was that a correct statement?—Certainly not.

Can you conceive any object or purpose in making such an addition?—Yes.

What would the natural effect of it be?—The natural effect of it would be to make the public have greater confidence in the Bank, as possessing a large amount of easily realisable securities.

Is there at that date a " Suspense account " in the books?—There is.

Explain what a " Suspense account " means?—It may mean a great many things; but in this case it means a lot of bad debts collected into an account.

How does that appear?—It appears in the ledger of the Bank. These debts are collected under this account, apparently being in process of being wiped out at the rate of £10,000 a year, the whole sum to start with being £300,000.   It would have taken thirty years to wipe that out.

The only operation upon these debts amounting to £300,000 was that the Bank were writing them off by degrees?—By degrees, at the rate of £10,000 a year.

Is there any entry in the scroll?—In the scroll there is only £50,000, which is under the head of " Bad and doubtful debts." The reason why there is not £300,000 is that the entries in the private cash book rearing up this " Suspense account" were made subsequently to the writing of the scroll, but prior to the making up of " Balance ledger No. 3."

So that in point of fact the statement contained those?—It did.

The City of Glasgow Bank Trial.

To the amount of £250,000?—Yes; and represented as good debts to the extent of £300,000.

I thought you said that in the scroll £50,000 was taken off?—That was so. £50,000 was included in the scroll, but the remaining £250,000 was included also in the scroll, under a different title.

They appeared as good in the scroll to the extent of £250,000, and as bad and doubtful to the extent of £50,000?—But even this bad and doubtful sum was entered as a good debt in the published account.

It was carried into the summation of the assets?—It was.

Now go to the balance account for 1877. Have you got the corresponding balance ledger for 1877?—I have.

Give us the entries appearing in the ledger, beginning with the creditor side?—On the creditor side I find, in "Balance ledger No. 3," under date 6th June, 1877, "Bills payable," £1,707,748; that ought to be £2,681,048. The difference is the £973,300. The next item is "Deposit accounts," stated at £35,488. That ought to be £485,181.

By the LORD JUSTICE-CLERK—That is done just in the same way as in the previous year.

By the LORD ADVOCATE—Then I find from No. 58 of inventory, being a book entitled "Balances of credit accounts," that at 6th June, 1877, there were balances at the credit of those accounts to the extent of £220,683 entirely omitted from the "Balance ledger No. 3." Then there is a trifling sum of £59 16s., being the "Credit accounts No. 2," which is also omitted. Then there is the "Adjusting account of interest" omitted to the extent of £11,008. That is all upon that side. On the other side, "Credit accounts No. 1" are entered £1,806,987 in the balance ledger. They should be £2,027,670. The under-statement in the balance ledger is £220,683. Then there is the same trifling error of £59 16s. Then from No. 59 of inventory I find that "Deposit accounts" were due to the Bank at that time to the extent of £449,692. These are omitted. Then "Foreign and colonial credits," stated in the balance ledger at £1,710,048, ought to be £2,683,348, an under-statement of the old £973,300.

By the LORD JUSTICE-CLERK—That was in the balance ledger as well?—Yes.

By the LORD ADVOCATE—Then the "Adjusting account of interest" is in the balance ledger £19,858, and it ought to be £30,867, understated in the balance ledger £11,008. These are all the discrepancies. I have compared these with No. 127 and No. 131; there are two scroll abstracts for this year.

Are the discrepancies that occur between the books and the balance ledger carried into these drafts?—They are.

Evidence for Prosecution.

Are they all reproduced there?—They are.

Does the draft or abstract No. 127 give you any clue to the source from which these under-statements were taken?—Both No. 127 and No. 131 must be taken together, and they do show that.

By the LORD JUSTICE-CLERK—Does it occur to you that the entry in the balance ledger was made after the balance sheet had been prepared, or before? In other words, was the balance sheet made from the ledger, or the ledger from the balance sheet?—The balance sheet had evidently been made from the ledger, undoubtedly.

What you mean is that the entry of £973,000 was given effect to in the balance ledger?—Yes.

It must have been there before the balance sheet was prepared?—It appears as an open balance in the ledger, but instead of being allowed to remain at the amount at which it is in the ledger, when we come to the balance it is found deducted from another account, and the difference alone is given.

By the LORD ADVOCATE—In the abstract it appears that certain debts on open account are brought down under the head of "Government stock and other stocks"?—Yes.

By the LORD JUSTICE-CLERK—If the abstract of the balance sheet had been correctly made from the balance ledger, that sum of £973,000 could never have appeared as it is now?—No, it would not.

By the LORD ADVOCATE—Would these sums have appeared as brought down? If it had been made from the balance ledger, would these sums have appeared as brought down under the head of Government stocks?—Certainly not; there is no such entry in the books to substantiate it.

By the LORD JUSTICE-CLERK—I suppose whatever was the fact about these debts and the securities for them, they never should have come under that heading?—Most undoubtedly not. The heading was entirely reserved for absolute investments.

These were permanent investments?—Yes.

Over which the Bank had complete control?—Yes, and which they had paid for with their own money.

And not security for outstanding debts?—No.

By the LORD ADVOCATE—In the scroll abstract or draft for 1877, does the £973,300 appear as before?—No, in neither 127 nor 131 does it appear. The amount of bills payable account, after having the £973,000 deducted, is carried into this scroll, but it has been scored out, as if some new idea had occurred to them—another way of doing it; and I find in No. 131 a pencil jotting which shows the new method that was adopted of falsifying the accounts.

Of something substituted for the £973,000?—Yes.

What is substituted?—I find, opposite the words "Bills pay-

The City of Glasgow Bank Trial.

James Muir. able," entered £2,683,348. That is wrong to the extent of £2300. Then from that is deducted "Cash lodged on D/A," £94,368; "Anticipations," £527,940; "S. F. & Co.," £552,704; and "J. N. F.," £158,000—together £1,333,012 19s. 1d.; difference, £1,350,335, which was the sum stated in the published balance sheet.

Is there any trace of these deductions to be found in the books?—None.

Have you examined the balance ledger for 1878?—I have.

Is it in conformity with the books?—It is not. Taking first the creditor side, "Bills payable" are stated at £1,907,952. That ought to be £2,881,252. The difference is again the £973,300. Then "Deposit accounts" are stated at £33,959. The real liability in deposits then was £474,698. The balance ledger is understated to the extent of £440,738. Then the "Credit accounts" are omitted altogether to the extent of £346,336, and a small sum of £119 12s. The "Adjusting account of interest" is also omitted entirely, £9825. These are all the discrepancies on the credit side. Then on the debtor side, "Credit accounts, No. 1" appear in the balance ledger at £2,009,752. That ought to be £2,356,088. It is understated in the balance ledger by £346,336. "Credit accounts, No. 2" are understated by the £119 12s. Then "Deposit accounts," £440,738, are entirely omitted from the balance ledger. Then "Foreign and colonial credits," £1,907,952, ought to be £2,881,252. The difference is the £973,300. The "Adjusting account of interest" appears in the balance ledger £27,405; this should be £37,230; under-statement, £9825.

By the LORD JUSTICE-CLERK—That is contrasting the balance ledger with the books?—Yes, and these under-statements are also given effect to in the published sheet.

By the LORD ADVOCATE—Look at No. 124 of process; that is the draft or scroll abstract for 1878?—Yes.

Do the details there agree with the published abstract?—They do.

The details there given show the method by which the alterations or the discrepancies as between the published balance sheets and the books might be effected?—That is so.

In fact all these scrolls that you have seen exhibit a method by which that end might be attained?—That is so.

I suppose precisely the same results in the abstract might have been attained in a great variety of other ways?—Yes.

By the LORD JUSTICE-CLERK—Then as far as the errors in the balance ledger are concerned this is consistent with it?—Yes.

But there are additional errors?—There are additional errors

Evidence for Prosecution.

—additional falsifications. In this case they could not possibly be errors.

But the balance ledger was erroneous in the particulars you have mentioned?—Yes.

And this transcribes the errors, but adds some in addition?—Yes, to a very large amount.

That is to say, those you have gone over already—the transferences of those balances of Smith, Fleming & Co., and the others down to "Government stocks"?—Yes; and there is a very serious deduction, further than the £973,000, of £419,000 made from the "Bills payable," which is a most absurd and stupid entry. They say, "Amount of bills on the circle, and against which an equal sum is at the credit of J. M. & Co. on D/A., £419,708." That is made a deduction from the liabilities of the Bank. Now, if there was any "sum at the credit of James Morton & Co.," it was also a liability; and they would seem therefore to reduce their liabilities by deducting other liabilities from them—the most absurd and illogical thing I ever saw.

Is that the sum on the right-hand side, £419,000?—Yes.

And what do you say that is?—It is stated in this scroll, No. 134, to be "Amount of bills on the circle, and against which an equal sum is at the credit of J. M. & Co. on D/A." Now that was a liability of the Bank, and the bills payable were also a liability of the Bank, and yet they deducted the one from the other.

By the LORD ADVOCATE—That is a very easy way of getting rid of liabilities?—No doubt of it.

A man owes two sums of £1000 each, and he deducts the one from the other, and the result is he owes nothing! Is not that practically what was done?—Apparently so. Besides which, I want to state that at that time there was no such "sum at the credit of James Morton & Co." They really owed the Bank £480,000.

By the LORD JUSTICE-CLERK—And whether that was true or false, that was not the way in which it should have been dealt with?—Certainly not.

By the LORD ADVOCATE—There is also an addition of £200,000 to the gold held?—Yes.

Which is ear-marked along with another sum of £480,000, and together making up £680,000?—Yes, in branch one.

Written off to cash account?—Written off "Credit accounts No. 1."

And by that process converted into gold?—Yes. I was asked to examine into the accounts of eight debtors to the Bank, viz.: —1, James Morton & Co., and the partners; 2, Smith, Fleming & Co.; 3, James Nicol Fleming; 4, Potter, Wilson & Co., and Mr. Potter; 5, Matthew Buchanan & Co.; 6, John Innes Wright

63

The City of Glasgow Bank Trial.

& Co., and the partners; 7, W. Glen Walker; 8, The Edinburgh Pastoral Association. These parties were indebted to the Bank in various forms. I was struck with the very large amount of their debits in the various forms, as compared with the debits of the ordinary customers of the Bank.

What were the forms of indebtedness?—Cash credits, overdrawn deposits, bill credits, or foreign and colonial credits, as they were called, and discounts.

By cash credits, what do you mean?—Hard cash lent by the Bank to them.

Either with or without security?—Either with or without security.

What are "Overdrawn deposits"?—It is just another name for the same thing.

It is just a deposit account which happens to be overdrawn? —Yes.

It is a current account to which the debtor may pay in—a current account overdrawn at the time?—Yes.

There were bills accepted on what are called "Open and marginal credits"?—Yes; and which are styled in the ledger "Foreign and colonial credits."

But they were in both of these shapes?—That is so.

State the total indebtedness of Morton & Co. and James Morton to the Bank in the years from 1873 to 1878 inclusive? —James Morton & Co. :—

1873,	£1,379,400
1874,	1,399,140
1875,	1,380,000
1876,	1,855,000
1877,	1,771,000
1878,	2,173,000

In the case of Smith, Fleming & Co., the corresponding figures are—

1873,	£1,136,000
1874,	1,340,000
1875,	1,661,000
1876,	1,777,000
1877,	1,903,000
1878,	1,968,000

James Nicol Fleming—

1873,	£738,000
1874,	861,000
1875,	1,005,000
1876,	1,136,000
1877,	1,188,000
1878,	1,238,000

Evidence for Prosecution.

Potter, Wilson & Co., which includes Mr. Lewis Potter—

1873,	£78,000
1874,	109,000
1875,	76,000
1876,	75,700
1877,	64,000
1878,	108,000

Matthew Buchanan & Co.—

1873,	£31,000
1874,	7,000
1875,	17,000
1876,	7,700
1877,	17,000
1878,	17,600

John Innes Wright & Co.—

1873,	£251,000
1874,	368,000
1875,	392,000
1876,	431,000
1877,	398,000
1878,	485,000

Glen, Walker & Co., which does not appear till 1875—

1875,	£4,465
1876,	3,600
1877,	30,000
1878,	26,000

Edinburgh Pastoral Association, which appears first in the balance of 1877—

1877,	£30,000
1878,	75,200

In 1873 the amount lent to the whole customers of the Bank on cash credit or overdrawn deposits, excluding foreign and colonial credits, which form another branch, was - - - - - - - - £4,402,659

Of that there was lent to the eight firms before mentioned, excluding foreign and colonial credits, and to the Manager, Directors, and Secretary, - - - - - - - 1,339,348

Leaving the amount lent to ordinary customers, - - - - - - £3,063,311

The City of Glasgow Bank Trial.

James Muir. 1874. Total amount lent, as before, - - - £4,723,608
Lent to eight firms before mentioned, and to Manager, Directors, and Secretary, - - - - - 2,125,244

Leaving for ordinary customers, - - £2,598,363

Or little more than half.

1875. Total amount lent, as before, - - - £4,649,526
Lent to eight firms before mentioned, and to Manager, Directors, and Secretary, - - - - - 2,414,335

Leaving for ordinary customers, - - £2,235,190

Or less than one-half of the whole.

1876. Total amount lent, as before, - - - £5,507,857
Lent to eight firms before mentioned, and to Manager, Directors, and Secretary, six-elevenths of the whole, 3,044,106

Leaving for ordinary customers, - - £2,463,751

1877. Total amount lent, as before, - - - £5,436,835
Lent to eight firms before mentioned, and to Manager, Directors, and Secretary, - - - - - 2,965,424

Leaving for ordinary customers, - - £2,471,411

About the same proportion as the previous year.

1878. Total amount lent, as before, - - - £5,639,292
Lent to eight firms before mentioned, and to Manager, Directors, and Secretary, about three-fifths of the whole, - - - - - - 3,377,636

Leaving for ordinary customers, - - £2,261,656

I have made out similar details in regard to the foreign and colonial credits. These figures are taken as at the period of the balance for the year prior to that period. I have not taken the period subsequent to the balance of 1878.

Evidence for Prosecution.

In 1873 the total amount lent by the Bank upon foreign and James Muir. colonial credits—bill credits—that is to say, the Bank granted its acceptances to that extent,   -   £2,132,453
Of that, the eight firms I have already mentioned got - - - - - - - - 2,111,697

Leaving for general customers about, - £20,000

1874. Total amount lent, as before, - - - £1,897,729
Lent to the eight firms, - - - 1,866,252

Leaving for general customers, - - £31,476

1875. Total amount lent, as before, - - - £2,124,880
Lent to the eight firms, - - - 2,106,536

Leaving for general customers, - - £18,344

1876. Total amount lent, as before, - - - £2,278,173
Lent to the eight firms, - - - 2,252,071

Leaving for general customers about - £26,000

1877. Total amount lent, as before, - - - £2,683,346
Lent to the eight firms, - - - 2,589,148

Leaving for ordinary customers, - - £94,201

1878. Total amount lent, as before, - - - £2,881,252
Lent to the eight firms, - - - 2,848,839

Leaving for ordinary customers about - £32,000

If you add to the foreign and colonial credits of these eight firms in 1878 the amount which I gave as lent to these firms and to the Manager, Directors, and Secretary on cash credits and overdrawn deposits, it brings out a sum of upwards of £6,000,000. I was asked to examine and to give for 1876 the applications made for credits. So far as I can discover, there were (1) credits given upon applications which mentioned securities; (2) credits given upon applications which did not

67

The City of Glasgow Bank Trial.

mention securities; and (3) credits given for which no application appeared either in letters of application or in the minutes. Of the £2,252,071 of " foreign and colonial credits " granted to the eight firms before mentioned in 1876, I find that £1,358,431 was granted upon letters of application mentioning securities, £359,500 upon letters which did not mention securities, and £534,140 without any writing at all. As regards 1877, of the £2,589,146 lent to these firms, £1,493,936 was under the first of these classes, £323,000 under the second class, and £772,210 under the third class. In 1878, of the £2,848,839 lent to these firms, £1,808,910 was under the first class, £156,000 under the second class, and £883,928 under the third class—without any application letters at all.

By the DEAN OF FACULTY—That is, letters you did not see?— Exactly; I neither found them, nor did I see any allusion to them in the minutes.

By the LORD ADVOCATE—The debtor balance standing against Mr. John Stewart at the balancing period was—

In 1873,	£5,994
1874,	10,040
1875,	13,348
1876,	12,198
1877,	18,085
1878,	8,956

Against Stewart, Pott & Co., which begins in 1875—

1875,	£12,877
1876,	16,463
1877,	17,674
1878,	19,826

Henry Taylor & Son—in 1873 there was a balance at their credit of (if I recollect aright) £675, and the debtor balance against them was—

In 1874,	£17,673
1875,	35,945
1876,	38,829
1877,	55,295
1878,	72,266

Against John Innes Wright, whose balance begins in 1876—

1876,	£2,797
1877,	2,787
1878,	2,771

That was being gradually diminished owing to the dividend on the Bank stock being credited to a larger extent than the interest which was debited.

68

Evidence for Prosecution.

Against John Innes Wright & Co.—

1875, - - - - - - -	£217,707
1876, - - - - - - -	254,211
1877, - - - - - - -	239,496
1878, - - - - - - -	334,783

As regards this firm, they had also credits of another description, but I find these had run off by 1875.

Against Henry Inglis—

1873, - - - - - - -	£30,088
1874, - - - - - - -	37,552
1875, - - - - - - -	38,556
1876, - - - - - - -	39,598
1877, - - - - - - -	41,368
1878, - - - - - - -	44,430

Against H. & A. Inglis—

1873, - - - - - - -	£298
1874, - - - - - - -	1,799
1875, - - - - - - -	3,346
1876, - - - - - - -	2,931
1877, - - - - - - -	6,007
1878, - - - - - - -	5,455

By Mr. TRAYNER—My reason for selecting the year 1873 as that with which to commence Mr. Stewart's private account was that I had made an investigation of the books from the date when the £973,000 entry was made. I had no other reason. I cannot tell when Mr. Stewart's private account commenced. I did not think it right or necessary for my purpose that I should ascertain that. I do not know when Mr. Stewart became a Director. I did not apply myself to find whether he had had advances before he became a Director or not. I think Stewart, Pott & Co.'s account began in 1875 ; the first balance I have is in that year. I cannot tell how that account commenced. I have dealt with the accounts entirely at the balancing periods. I do not know what sort of a business Stewart, Pott & Co.'s was ; I believe they had some connection with the wine trade. I was born in Glasgow. I am thirty-nine years of age. I know Mr. Stewart personally, but I never was in his office in my life, and I know nothing whatever about the nature or extent of his business.

By Mr. BALFOUR—My evidence is given entirely as that of an accountant. At the request of the Crown, I made an examination of the books and documents of the Bank, and I deduce my results entirely from these. I had previously been engaged as the coadjutor of Mr. Anderson, one of the liquidators. There

The City of Glasgow Bank Trial.

James Muir. are a very large number of books employed in the current business of the City of Glasgow Bank—so many that I really could not approximate the number. It may be twenty, thirty, forty, or fifty. It is quite possible there are a great many more; the number is very, very large. There are a great many separate departments. I should think there must be sixty or eighty officials, including clerks, at the head office. In short, it was a very large establishment, with a very large number of books in use. In the course of our investigation we had the aid of the staff of the Bank which has remained on since the stoppage. We had also the aid of the staff of our own firm, which is a large one. We had such assistance as we desired from the clerks of Dr. M'Grigor's firm, which is a very large legal firm. They were principally engaged in looking into securities and things of that kind. We had every possible facility for making an examination. With all these facilities, we found it a very laborious one, because we went into very great detail, counted every bill in the Bank, and looked at every balance of every separate account recorded in the books. Besides, a considerable amount of time was lost in getting the returns from the branches as to the state of the accounts there. There are about 133 branches, and we got the accounts from them also. The investigation with a view to making the report was conducted in the way I have mentioned. The evidence I have given to-day has been entirely from my own checking of the books, with very little assistance from clerks at all, because I thought it very important that I should not give evidence about what I had not personally seen.

You have used the expression repeatedly in the course of your evidence that certain sums in the published abstract were understated or overstated?—That is so.

In so speaking of under-statement or over-statement, did you take as your standard the books of the Bank?—I did.

And it means under or over certain entries in the books of the Bank?—Yes, that is so.

You also said, I think, that you found what you regarded as errors in the balance ledger?—Yes, under-statements.

In using that expression, have you regard still to the other books of the Bank?—That is so.

By the LORD JUSTICE-CLERK—Under-statements and omissions? —Yes.

By Mr. BALFOUR—That is to say, things which you would have expected to be brought in from other books of the Bank?— That is so.

This balance ledger purports to set out the results brought from a very large number of accounts in other books?—Yes; the whole books of the Bank, credit and deposit ledgers, discount ledgers, and all the books of the Bank.

70

Mr. Balfour,
Counsel for Lewis Potter.

Evidence for Prosecution.

James Muir.

You would assume, I suppose, from looking at it, that the results of these different departments must have been given to some official who made up the balance ledger?—Undoubtedly. That would naturally fall under the department of the accountant in such a Bank. It was his duty to make up the balance ledger. The entry of £973,000 was raised in June, 1873, on the two sides of a book, the entries in which I have already read, and also on the two sides of the ledger.

But it was originally raised in the cash book?—The cash book entry was the subsidiary entry to what ultimately appeared in the ledger.

It was the first entry?—Yes; that entry has remained in the private cash book and in the ledger ever since it was raised there in June, 1873.

So, from 1873 down to the stoppage of the Bank, that was an entry appearing throughout the books of the Bank?—It was so; but it was omitted from the balance ledger.

But it was in the books of the Bank?—Yes. I have not seen all the weekly balances applicable to the head office, but I have generally glanced at them. I know the principle on which they are made up. The weekly balance applicable to 4th June, 1873 (No. 13), was the first weekly balance after the entry of £973,000 was raised. On the right-hand side of the sheet, in the creditor column, I find an entry of £2,128,686 11s. 9d. That is "Credit account, bills payable No. 1," as appearing in the other books. In the debtor column I find an entry of £973,000. What is carried out to the balance is the difference, being £1,155,386 11s. 9d.

Has that been the principle upon which this sum has been dealt with ever since June, 1873?—I believe it has; in fact, I know it has. It has entered every weekly abstract balance since that time, and has been regularly deducted on each of these occasions, and the balance carried out.

Have you observed whether, in the balance ledger applicable to the different years, what has been entered under "Bills payable" has been the difference between what you say is the true amount and that sum?—Exactly; in fact, this sum in the creditor column is the amount of the balance. That course has been uniformly followed since 1873.

Suppose that the principle upon which the Directors checked the balance ledger was by the Director watching the entries, and the accountant reading off the corresponding entries, what the accountant would read off and the Director would see would be the difference?—Simply.

And the Directors so checking the balance ledger would have no cognisance of that fact?—No, unless they had the sheet before them.

But assuming it was done as I have said, the Directors would

71

The City of Glasgow Bank Trial.

not see that entry, but would merely have the difference read out?—Certainly.

Do you find that—except in 1877, about which there was something special—in making out the scroll abstracts for the yearly balances, the £973,000 has been treated just as it was treated throughout the books of the Bank and the relative balance sheets?—Precisely, the relative weekly abstracts.

Is it plain that from the first scroll of these abstracts that sum has been so treated in all those different years except 1877? —I do not know whether these red-inked documents are the first scrolls or not.

But from anything you have seen?—Yes.

The earliest extant scrolls of these abstracts have this treated exactly as it is throughout the other books and papers of the Bank for those six years?—So far as I have seen them.

Then it is plain, reading these documents, that, unless it be in 1877, there has not been any change in the mode of treating that, induced by after-suggestion?—None whatever.

Are these entries simply passed into the ledger?—They are so.

So that the ledger entries applicable to that will just be the same as these?—Yes.

With no details?—With no details.

Then the way in which it is entered in the weekly balance sheet is in this form [showing]?—Yes.

And it has been so fifty-two times every year since 1873?—Precisely.

In each year from 1873, do you find that what is carried into the balance ledger is the total sum, what you think the true sum of bills, minus the £973,300?—That is so.

In short, the figuring which is in the right-hand column is what is uniformly carried into the balance ledger in those years?—The figuring which is in the right-hand column of this sheet [showing].

Exactly ; and in like manner in the abstract which ultimately becomes the published abstract, or the circulated abstract, is it treated in the same way?—Except in 1877.

In the way in which the balance ledger is framed as regards the head office, does it bring into one the results of all the accounts as appearing in the balance of the week in which it occurs?—Precisely.

Then as regards the branches, all that appears in the balance ledger is the total balance every year against the branch?—Yes.

Whereas, as regards the branches in the abstract for publication, the transactions of the Bank are brought under the different headings?—Yes, of the customers at the branch.

So that there is a different principle for that, and I suppose properly, in making up the balance of the two accounts?—Quite

Evidence for Prosecution.

properly. The details are contained in abstracts which are sent in.

You do not complain of that?—Not at all.

Then what I come to is this, if what the Directors had before them was the balance ledger, and they only heard what was read off from it, they would not know of the £973,300?—They would not.

Then I ask you again, are you perfectly satisfied, from your examination of the different scroll abstracts which you have seen, that the £973,300, except in 1877, has been treated just as it is in the books of the Bank, the original deduction?—Just as it is in the weekly balance sheets, but not as it is in the books of the Bank.

But as it is in the weekly balance sheets?—Yes.

You don't find any change in the abstracts after the first scroll had been made up?—I do not quite follow you.

What I mean is this, it appears to have been part of the original scheme?—No doubt of it.

You next gave us some answers about the balances which you disapproved of. In particular, you pointed out what appears under the head "Debtor accounts"; that is, the balance of £1346 16s. 6d. in the balance of 1876. That is the first you spoke of?—Are you talking now of the balance ledger?

No; I am speaking of the scroll balance, No. 128A. Would you also look at No. 59A, excerpts from "Balances of deposit accounts." In the right-hand column of that paper, under 7th June, 1876, does the sum of £1346 16s. 6d. appear as the difference between the debtor and creditor accounts?—That is so.

Therefore that sum of £1346 16s. 6d. is a balance, whether rightly or wrongly taken, still taken from the book of the Bank appropriate to these accounts?—Undoubtedly.

Would you also look to the balance ledger for the same time, No. 12A. In the balance for June, 1876, I observe under the head "Deposit accounts" £3233, being a different figure?—That is so.

Going back again to No. 59A, do you find how that arises?—Yes.

It has been done in this way. After apparently a summation bringing out £1346 16s. 6d. has been made, there has been an additional sum brought in?—Yes. There was an entry made in the cash book subsequently to this scroll being made up, as I have twice, I think, referred to.

And you think you can perfectly see how the sum of £4579 16s. 10d. was entered?—Yes.

Then the £3233 is the difference which appears in the balance ledger?—Yes.

And whether the principle is right or wrong, that amount is

73

The City of Glasgow Bank Trial.

a true entry brought from the book of the Bank applicable to such accounts?—That is so.

Do you find that throughout the balance ledger the principle followed as regards " Deposit accounts " has been to bring the balance only between the total of the two sides?—Yes, in the balance ledger.

Throughout?—Throughout as regards " Credit accounts " and " Deposit accounts."

As regards both?—As regards both.

Whether that is good or bad bookkeeping, what has been done has been to bring true entries from the proper books and enter them here?—To enter the mere differences.

I mean they are not fictitious entries?—Certainly not.

They are true balances brought from their appropriate books, and entered in the balance ledger?—That is so.

And that is the practice which, whether by good or bad bookkeeping, has been pursued throughout?—Yes.

How far do you find that practice to have been carried?— As far back as I have gone, 1873.

You have not gone any further?—I have not in that part of the investigation gone any further.

Then you do not find any book in which that practice has not been followed?—No.

It was nothing new in 1876?—Nothing new.

And the way in which the £973,000 was treated then was nothing new in 1876?—It was not.

You said there were some things that you disapproved of in the balance ledger; did you find that these things existed in all the balance ledgers that you examined?—From 1873.

And you examined no earlier?—No.

So that whether they were right or wrong, that has been a scheme followed so far back as your examination goes?—That is so.

There was no novelty in 1876 about these matters?—No, not as to these special matters.

Then you gave an answer to the Lord Advocate about cross accounts. You said, I think, that where the same person had more accounts than one in the same interest, the crossing of accounts was quite proper?—Yes. It is not a usual thing to be done, I believe, in a large establishment like a bank, but it is quite legitimate.

It is quite proper?—Perfectly proper.

You have nothing to say against it?—Nothing whatever.

I suppose the accountant who was responsible for and in charge of these books would know better than you would do what were proper cross accounts?—Well, I have asked him the question, and he was utterly unable to explain the entry to me.

Evidence for Prosecution.

But the accountant is the responsible official in charge of James Muir. that class of work?—Yes.

And he would be the natural person to know what were cross accounts?—He would be the natural person to know. I don't know whether he would know better than I would do.

You gave some evidence with regard to the "Suspense account." The suspense account appears, I think, in 1876 as £300,000?—Yes.

And then it gradually goes down £10,000 a year?—Yes.

Did it appear to you from your examination of the books that the suspense account had been raised between the time of the scroll abstract being prepared and the time of the balance ledger being prepared?—It undoubtedly had.

That was clear?—Quite clear to the extent of £250,000.

You told us how the £50,000 was treated?—Yes.

That being so, it would not surprise you that you found the suspense account in the balance ledger although you did not in the scroll abstract?—No.

It would suggest that it had occurred to the officials that these accounts were proper to be in suspense in the interval between the two?—Yes.

I suppose the idea of a "suspense account" is an account which contains debts which may or may not be good?—"Suspense accounts" are of a very miscellaneous kind. A "suspense account" may mean a great many things; it is a very dangerous class of account.

But is not that the natural meaning of a "suspense account," an account that is neither clearly good nor clearly bad?—No.

Is it not in "suspense"?—That is so.

And in doubt?—No, not necessarily.

But perhaps?—Perhaps; but I should say that if the suspense account is being written off at a certain rate per annum, that clears up the doubt at once.

If an account was doubtful, and not improving, it would be proper to reduce it by degrees; if it was clearly bad, it should all go at once?—Yes, it ought, and I say that £300,000 should have gone at once.

Because you think it was bad?—Yes.

But if it was only doubtful, was not the proper way to treat it to reduce it by degrees?—No.

Would you have kept it all up?—I would have been disposed to have written it off, even although it had been doubtful.

Even if it was only doubtful and not bad, you would have been disposed to have written it off?—If it had been so doubtful that I did not charge interest on it.

But is it not the case that if it were bad you would write it off, and if it were doubtful you would reduce it?—If it was doubtful I don't know if I would reduce it.

But that is a matter which it was proper for the accountant

75

to know?—Yes, or for a person who knew the facts about the account.

That would depend on extraneous knowledge, which you have not?—And which those who are in immediate contact with the account ought to have known thoroughly. They were the people who naturally ought to know.

The officials in charge?—Yes. [Shown No. 131.] There is a great deal of pencil figuring on that.

Do you also see traces of there having been previous pencil figuring which has been rubbed out?—Not on this sheet, I think.

But, at any rate, there is a great deal of pencil figuring, containing very elaborate calculations?—That is so.

It would require an accountant of some skill to make calculations like these, would it not?—It would. It caused me very great difficulty in tracing what they meant.

Even with your skill you found it difficult?—Very difficult indeed.

So that you are quite satisfied that the man who was figuring with the pencil must have been an accountant of considerable skill?—Well, I know who the accountant was, and I really must not commit myself to saying that he is an accountant of any skill.

But this is evidently the work of a skilled accountant, is it not?—It is rather the work of a bungling person who seemed to be trying to get at a result.

But evidently an accountant?—Undoubtedly.

And you see the kind of result that he got at?—Yes.

You gave an opinion about a sum of £419,000. Did you find that, with respect to Mr. Morton, there had been a system of issuing second sets of acceptances to retire the first?—That was so.

Did you identify this entry of £419,000 with the dealings with the second sets of acceptances?—I could not. I tried to do so, but I could find no details.

You merely, looking as an accountant, and without extraneous knowledge, cannot tell whether that may have been the discount money of the second set to retire the first or not?—No, I cannot.

It may have been?—It may.

Or it may not?—Yes; but I see distinctly from the books that the unreduced amount of the bills payable was on the circle at that date.

No doubt that would be so during the days before the first set were retired and after the second set were out?—Both the first and second sets were current at the same time.

No doubt that would be so if the transaction was such as I have put to you?—That would be the result.

Evidence for Prosecution.

By the LORD JUSTICE-CLERK—I suppose the system, whether it is a good one or not, implies drawing bills and putting them in the circle before the old ones are retired?—Yes, and also that the bills would have to be given to Mr. Morton to give him time to discount them, and get the proceeds into his hands before the first set became due.

So that the first set are current while the others are also current?—Yes.

By Mr. BALFOUR—And you found that that also had been put into the deposit account?—No ; I did not.

I thought you said so?—No ; I said that Mr. Morton at that time was owing the Bank £480,000 on overdrawn deposit and credit accounts.

Did you find that in any account?—No ; I could not trace that in any account.   In order to trace that I would have had to know the particulars and the amounts of each of the several bills constituting the £419,000, but I did not know.

And therefore the books of the Bank did not enable you to say what that £419,000 was?—They did not.

But you gave an opinion that that was a man really reducing his liabilities by taking one from another?—Taking one liability from another, but simply from the wording of the sheet.

But suppose that the transaction was that it was discount money got in to take up the first set of bills, it was quite proper to treat them as they are treated here?—Certainly not.

Why not?   Both sets of bills appear in the aggregate of the bills?—Yes.

So that if the aggregate stood as it was, it would have the bills for the same amounts in twice?—No doubt it would, for both sets were in the hands of the public.

And no doubt the Bank was liable to the public for both sets ; but if the Bank had got in discount money to take up the first set, was it not a perfectly proper deduction to make from the liabilities on bills?—Certainly not.

Whether it was a proper deduction to make from the liability on bills, it was a proper deduction to make, was it not, in ascertaining the Bank's aggregate liability?—Certainly not.

You did not find the cash entering the deposit account?—I could not for a single moment imagine that £419,000 was paid in to the City of Glasgow Bank without being credited to some account.

It was not treated as cash in hand?—It must have been in the cash chest at that moment.

But you do not find that sum of £419,000 carried in to reduce any other account?—It must have been.   If paid in by James Morton it must have been credited to James Morton.

Instead of saying what must have been, tell us what you

The City of Glasgow Bank Trial.

James Muir. found?—I have told you that I have been unable to trace the money, because I could not tell the amount of the bills.

Did you find that £419,000 employed to reduce any account except the bill account?—I did not specially find that sum. I could not trace the amounts that were got by the discounts of these bills.

Then your answer is that you did not?—I did not; but, in any view, I would say that it was most improper to make that deduction from the bills.

You said that you found obligations with Potter, Wilson & Co.'s name on them. Did you see that these obligations had been undertaken on behalf of the Bank by Potter, Wilson & Co.? —I did not.

You don't know whether these were obligations undertaken by them with respect to the purchase of New Zealand properties?— It was not on the face of them. The Bank had money invested in its own stock. This appears in the abstract under the first head. If it had been put under the third head, it should have appeared there under a separate line. It would have been very improper to represent it as " Government stock."

Do you read the third head as containing nothing but " Government stock "?—No, I do not. It also says " Stocks of other companies," but you could hardly call the Bank's stock the stock of another company.

Still it was an investment; it was not a debt?—Certainly not.

Nor was it security for an advance?—No.

It was an asset of the Bank, with nothing against it?— Provided the Bank was solvent.

By Mr. ASHER—You know the balance account in the balance ledger which is docqueted once a year by the Bank Directors?— Yes.

Are you acquainted with three classes of books—the " weekly balance book," the " branches book," and the " correspondents' balance book "?—I have generally examined them.

Do the balance accounts in the balance ledger for 1876, 1877, and 1878 correctly record the balances in the three subsidiary balance books I have mentioned?—The " branches balance book " contains the accounts made up on a different principle.

Does the balance account correctly record the balances for these three years in the three balance books?—It correctly records them, but on a different principle as regards the branches.

Does the balance account in the balance ledger docqueted by the Directors contain the names of the several branches?— It does.

And opposite each branch there is the sum at the debit or the credit of that branch?—Yes.

Is that sum, appearing in the balance account book opposite each branch docqueted by the Directors, the same as the sum

78

Evidence for Prosecution.

appearing in the branches balance book opposite that branch?
—I am not quite certain of the book you refer to, but if it is the branch abstract of balances, the sum that there appears is the indebtedness to the Bank of its depositors, or *vice versa*.

Do you find anything wrong in the balance account docqueted by the Directors in so far as they are entries with regard to the branches?—Nothing whatever.

And in other respects the balances appearing in that docqueted account are correct as compared with the weekly balance book and the correspondents' balance book?—That is so.

You find fault with the balance book with regard to deposits in respect there was not an entry in regard to deposits on both sides?—Yes.

Do you find in the balance account which is docqueted by the Directors any account entered on both sides?—I would not anticipate finding an account entered on both sides.

I understand you to object to the balance of the deposits being entered in this balance account instead of the sum at the debit of deposit accounts on the one side and at the credit of deposit accounts on the other?—Yes.

Is that a fault?—It is a fault unless the debtors and creditors are the same.

Is not the purpose of a balance account merely to show the balance on the whole deposits of the Bank?—No.

Do you find in this balance account any entry of an account on both sides?—What I complain of is that it does not show the balance of the deposit accounts of the Bank.

But is the balance account not made up for the special purpose of showing the balance on the several accounts there mentioned? —A balance account ought to be made up with the view of showing the debts and the liabilities of the Bank—the one on the one side and the other on the other.

The abstract of accounts is made up for that purpose?—The balance book ought to be made up for that purpose also.

But is not the balance account intended to show the balance on the whole accounts in the Bank?—It is intended to show that, but it does not show it.

You think it should show the amount at the credit of the deposit account on the one side, and at the debit of the deposit account on the other?—Undoubtedly.

Then it would not show the balance of the deposit accounts?— It would.

You would have to take the two entries on the two sides, and compare them, in order to find out the exact balance of the deposit accounts of the Bank, would you not?—No. You would have to do that in order to find out the difference between overdrafts and deposits.

And to find out the exact balance on the deposits?—Certainly

The City of Glasgow Bank Trial.

James Muir. not; the balance on deposit accounts is the balance without deducting the overdrafts.

Your view is that the balance is not the balance of deposits, but the balance of both sides?—I say it is the balance of the deposits that should appear.

The published abstract is, of course, quite a different document from the balance account?—That is so.

And it is not made up, I believe, from the balance account?—It appears to be so to a large extent.

I mean the published extract?—That appears to be so to a large extent, except as regards the branches.

Don't you require to add what appears in the large number of books connected with the branches?—No; two books.

Is not every item in the balance account varied by having incorporated with it the corresponding item from the branches?—Certainly not.

Take the deposits; do you find the deposits in the balance account the same as the deposits in the printed abstract?—Yes; I understand you are talking of the scroll abstract?

I am speaking now of the abstract which is published—the annual balance sheet of the Bank?—They are amalgamated there.

And therefore, on looking at the two documents together, you find they are utterly different; the one is not made up from the other?—No.

You cannot compare the one with the other without the aid of a large number of books?—No, three or four books; not a large number.

But books which go to disclose the whole business of the agencies?—That is so.

Are the totals of the two items necessarily different?—They are.

So that, even to look at the summation of the balance account docqueted by the Directors, you would not expect it to tally with the summation of the printed abstract?—It does not.

And it should not do it?—From the manner in which the books were kept, and as regards the branches, it should not do it.

By Mr. MACKINTOSH—Would you refer to your statement of the account of Taylor & Son with the Bank? What sum was at the debit of their account on 31st December, 1876?—I cannot tell. I directed my attention solely to the accounts at the balancing periods. I have not got the book here.

Can you tell whether it is or is not the fact that during 1877 —between 1st January, 1877, and 1st January, 1878—Taylor & Son's overdraft was considerably diminished?—No, I cannot tell. From my statements I only find that it was increased about £17,000 between the balance of 1877 and the balance of 1878.

80

Evidence for Prosecution.

But it is quite consistent with that, is it not, that it had been diminished in 1877?—Yes, temporarily.

Is it quite consistent with the account as at 1st January, 1878, having been considerably less overdrawn than it was at 1st January, 1877?—I am talking really about what I have not examined, but there is nothing inconsistent in it.

Is it not consistent with your knowledge that since 1st January, 1878, there has been no operation upon the account at all in the way of drawing out?—I cannot speak to 1st January, 1878, as I have not specially examined it.

You have not got it with you?—No.

Can you tell me whether it has fluctuated a good deal during its later period?—I did not look into it.

Can you tell me whether it was squared up during its period? —I cannot.

Did you not inquire into these matters?—No.

Were you not asked to inquire into them?—No.

Did you not think it material to inquire?—I did not. I looked at the indebtedness of Mr. Taylor when the crash came. I did not think it was material whether it was ever squared or not.

You stated the amount so as to make it appear to have continuously increased?—Oh, no! I must not have any motive imputed to me.

But its result?—Yes. The result was increased in the balance sheet at the various balancing periods, for which I am not responsible. I did not inquire or examine the books to ascertain how long Messrs. Taylor & Son had been customers of the Bank. I cannot tell whether Mr. Taylor had got accommodation from the City Bank prior to his becoming a Director, or, if so, to what extent. I was not asked to inquire into that; but I find that their overdrafts appear to have begun in 1874, because in 1873, as I said before, I think there was a little credit balance. I have not examined the account prior to 1871.

By Mr. SMITH—Mr. Innes Wright's private account begins with his being debited with the sum of about £2700. There has been no other operation upon that account, except the crediting of interest upon stock and debiting interest upon the account. That sum seems to have been the price of the shares purchased to give him a qualification as Director. He has never drawn any dividend. The dividend is placed to his credit, and he is debited with interest, the result of which would have been that, if it had gone on long enough, Mr. Innes Wright would have had his share for nothing.

Would the shares, in your opinion, be a security for the advance?—If the Bank was solvent.

You stated that at 5th June, 1875, the sum due

The City of Glasgow Bank Trial.

James Muir. by John Innes Wright & Co.—the debtor balance—was £217,707. Is that sum composed of the balances on credit accounts and deposit accounts brought together?—It is. It includes the amount standing at the debit of Innes Wright & Co. on deposit account, amounting to £133,241. The amount standing on the same account at 5th June, 1878, is £150,795.

What was the accruing interest in the interval between 2nd June, 1875, and 5th June, 1878?—I cannot tell you unless you show me the ledger.

Would it be over £20,000?—It would.

So the result is that in the interval the sum paid in was greater than the sum drawn out?—No, it could not be over £20,000. It could not be more than £5000 or £6000; but the ledger, which is in the inventory, will show it.

The sum at 5th June, 1878, was how much?—£150,000. I cannot tell, without looking at the ledger, how much of that was interest. I did not anticipate this line of examination.

Is it the case that the sum paid in in the interval between 1875 and 1878 was greater than the sum drawn out?—I cannot tell; the ledger will show that. The amount due at 5th June, 1878, in all, was £334,783. The difference between that and the £217,707 in 1875 is (roughly) £117,000. I cannot tell how much of that was interest; it will be seen from the ledger. The balance of £334,783 in 1878 includes two sums, the one of £32,233, and the other of £47,601. These two sums appear for the first time in that year.

Do you know what the £32,233 was?—Yes, it has something to do with an account called "Wool lien account."

Was that an account which had been opened on behalf of Glen, Walker & Co.?—Yes, it is so stated in the ledger, I think. That account is not closed. The £47,601 was the balance standing, at the balancing period of 1878, at the debit of Innes Wright & Co. for their short accountings upon the £100,000 of Glen, Walker & Co.'s drafts substituted for those of Holmes, White & Co.

Short accountings upon the discount account?—Not that, but short accounting of proceeds of bills which had been given to them for the purpose of discounting.

Was that an overdraft?—I would not like to characterise it.

It is not an overdraft?—I must say I would use a much stronger expression than that if I were asked what it was.

If that sum of £32,000 odds was accounted for, and the £47,000 was out of the account, and the interest taken off, would the sum standing at the debit in 1878 be greater or less than it was in 1875?—I have said I do not know the amount of the interest, so that I cannot answer the question.

But assuming that the interest was £33,000, would that be

82

Evidence for Prosecution.

sufficient to account for the difference, with the other figures? James Muir.
—Within £4000 of it.

Can you give me the details of the sum of total indebtedness that you make out against Innes Wright & Co. in 1875, £392,000?—Yes. There is, first, cash credits and overdrawn deposits, £217,707 ; then there is William Scott's indebtedness, £121,801 ; then there are bills discounted by John Innes Wright & Co. with the Bank, £40,678 ; and there are acceptances by John Innes Wright & Co., discounted with the Bank by third parties, £12,324. I think you will find that makes up the sum.

As regards the charge for " bills discounted," £40,678, and " acceptances," £12,324, do you know if that sum was reduced in 1878?—Yes, very materially reduced.

What does it stand at in 1878?—In 1878, you may take it that the bills discounted by John Innes Wright & Co. were then reduced to £24,500 ; William Scott's discounts were then £9198 ; and the acceptances of John Innes Wright & Co., discounted with the Bank by third parties, were £4304.

Mention has been made of the Edinburgh Pastoral Association ; do you know who they were?—I do not. I do not know who constituted the Association. It seemed to me to be very much an affair of the Bank's own.

Was it not simply the Bank?—Well, it has all along struck me to be the City of Glasgow Bank.

By the LORD ADVOCATE—I omitted to ask you in what way interest receivable or received by the Bank is dealt with in the profit and loss account?—It is credited to profit and loss, in a line called " Interest received."

I show you No. 146, yearly balance sheet at 5th June, 1878 ; and I also refer you to No. 2A private cash book, No. 6. It is entered there also, is it not?—That is so.

Just explain to us how it is dealt with?—The interest received or receivable by the Bank on account of the debtors to the Bank was debited once every year. The resulting sum, or rather the resulting sums, are all added together, and credited to profit and loss account through the cash book to which you have referred ; and I find it here [showing] £330,000 in this sheet as being one of the earnings of the Bank for that amount.

Refer to the cash book also, and see if the same entries pass through it?—On the debtor side of the cash book of that date there is an entry " Profit and loss account, balances transferred from the following accounts :—Interest received," and figures that I have previously given, £330,849 5s. 6d. Then there are several other items coming up to £398,743, and on the other side there is " Interest received, balance transferred to profit and loss," £338,549 5s. 6d., and so on.

83

The City of Glasgow Bank Trial.

The sum of interest received there stated ought to represent the earnings of the Bank upon its debts for the year?—That is so.

Does that sum of £330,000 include the interest upon those eight large debts that you spoke of?—It does, every penny of it.

Which were not received; at least, the books do not show that they were received, but the contrary?—Quite so.

Does that occur in each of the three years?—It does. I was very much struck, my lord, with this, that the interest upon these eight accounts in 1878 amounts to £125,875, while the total amount of the clear balance, stated of profit for that year, is £125,094, being £780 less than the interest on these balances.

And which, of course, was not made if it was not got?—No, assuredly not. Besides which, in 1878, they carried to credit of profit and loss account the sum of £12,000, which had been added to the value of City of Glasgow Bank stock beyond what they had paid for it in the market.

In 1877, what was the figure of interest that was so dealt with? —In 1877 the interest upon these eight debtors was £128,900, and the available balance of profit for that year appearing in the balance sheet was only £128,413, being less than the interest charged to the debtors by £487. Then in 1876 the amount charged to the debtors was £125,763, and the apparent available balance of profits was £125,762, a difference of about £1.

You were examined on cross with regard to retiring one set of bills by another. Suppose there are a set of bills for £200,000 acceptances of the Bank, and that a fresh set for the same amount are issued to retire those, and the proceeds are received, is it a correct thing to treat the first set of bills as paid until that money has been actually applied in extinction of them, and the bills withdrawn from the circle?—It is so utterly absurd that I can hardly conceive of any one imagining that such a thing could possibly be done.

Until the money received by discount is actually applied in payment of the bills, there are two sets of liabilities floating against the Bank?—Undoubtedly.

In regard to the scroll balance sheets, you said that these looked like the work of an accountant; what do you mean by that precisely?—They look like the work of a man who could say two and two are four, but that is about the extent of it.

Did you mean to suggest that none but an accountant could bring down these sums from the balance at the "Credit account" to the heading under "Stocks"?—Certainly not. When I used the word accountant, I did not mean a professional accountant.

Did you intend to suggest that it required an accountant to convert £200,000 of that into surplus gold in the coffers of the Bank?—Certainly not.

By the LORD JUSTICE-CLERK—Did you mean that you did not

Evidence for Prosecution.

think it looked like the hand of a professional accountant?—It simply looked like a man who understood arithmetic.

But was your impression, from the look of it, that it had been done by a professional accountant?—I knew that it was the work of the accountant of the Bank.

It was not merely the work of a man who knew that two and two made four, but the calculations were, in fact, the work of the accountant of the Bank?—There is no question of that whatever.

I asked you yesterday if you could make me out a balance sheet, as you think, on the lines of the balance abstract, as it should have been made out?—I have prepared some such statement, and my clerk is now copying it.

In the meantime, would you take the indictment, and turn to the statement of the errors on page 4. In the first place, you have been able to trace the system, rather than the principle, on which these statements proceeded?—I have, and the statement which I have prepared will bring that out.

In regard to the amount of deposits at the head office, they are understated in the balance for 1876 to the extent of a million and some odds. Now, wherein does that mis-statement consist? —There are deposit accounts omitted altogether, £455,444.

That is the balance due to customers which you told us of yesterday?—Yes. Then a debtor balance is made to appear where no such balance ought to be, amounting to £1346. That is a debtor balance appearing as if the customers owed the Bank that.

That depends upon the controversy between you and Mr. Balfour about the balances being taken instead of both sides of the account?—Quite so. These credit accounts are omitted altogether, £147,468. There are balances standing at the credit of parties who have paid in sums of money to the creditor side of their "credit accounts." They are just another name for a kind of deposit. They are omitted altogether. Then London and provincial and foreign correspondents are omitted, £14,216.

Where do you find that?—In the balance ledger. Then adjusting account of interest is omitted, £11,405. I find that in the balance sheet of profit and loss, No. 144 of inventory.

But that is nowhere correctly entered?—Not in the balance ledger.

In any of the books?—It is correctly entered in the profit and loss balance sheet.

Is there anything more?—The true amount of branch liabilities appearing in the book called abstract of branch balances is £8,163,311. In the scroll the figures representing that are in red ink, and amount to £7,786,977. The difference understated is £376,334. I cannot tell what that under-statement consists of. That brings up the amount to the sum stated in the indictment.

The City of Glasgow Bank Trial.

Then the amount of "Drafts outstanding" is the £973,000 which we have heard so much about?—Yes.

These figures make up the sum short in the first item; the second is the sum of £973,000. In regard to that, can you tell me when was the first appearance of that sum in any of the books of the Bank except the private cash book?—It never appeared anywhere till it appeared in the private cash book on 4th June, 1875.

After that, when did it first appear in the other books?—It continuously appeared in the ledger of the Bank from that date till this date, an open balance appearing there ever after.

Did it anywhere appear as deducted from the head of the "Drafts outstanding" and the other things under that head?— Not in any of the books of the Bank except the balance ledger, where it did appear so deducted.

Then, third, the "Bills of exchange" you say are understated to the extent of £698,000; where do you find that?—In the first place, credit accounts are understated to the extent of £147,468.

Does the balance which you have prepared show all these?— It does.

[The witness here handed to the Lord Justice-Clerk the documents printed on pages 88, 89, 90.]

Among other things I wanted to know was what the result of the corrections would have been upon the statement to the shareholders of the position of the Bank?—I have not yet made it up in that form, but I will be very glad to do so; I did not quite understand your object.

That was my object, because the allegation is that they made a false statement to the shareholders, and I want to know what would have been the true statement on the lines of this abstract. I can understand that you might go back on the books and make a totally different statement; but if they had stated the figures correctly in the abstract balance sheet, what would have been the result presented to the shareholders?—Perhaps I could answer the question in this way, by saying that the result of correcting the figures would have had no effect whatever upon the capital or the profit and loss or upon the reserve fund, because what was deducted from one side was also deducted from the other.

Does that apply to the whole of them?—To the whole of them.

That it would have had no effect at all?—It would have had no effect on the capital as stated.

If you assume that the bad and doubtful debts are correctly estimated there, is that so?—That is so; but the effect would

Evidence for Prosecution.

have been to impress the mind of the public with the fact that the Bank had lent so much less money.

The effect on its credit would be entirely different, but the ultimate result on the profit and loss would be the same?— Precisely the same.

I suppose the principal errors in this are the £973,000, which apparently has no foundation at all, and the £751,000, which is taken down from the credit accounts and inserted under investments?—And also the gold, £200,000, and also the deduction of the £419,000, which, as I have said, is perfectly absurd. I cannot be too strong upon that.

LIABILITIES.

LIABILITIES.	In Published Balance Sheet.	In Bank's Books.	Under-stated in Published Sheet.	Over-stated in Published Sheet.
HEAD I.				£
Deposit accounts,	Omitted	455,444	455,444	
Credit do.,	do.	147,468	147,468	
London, provincial, and foreign correspondents,	do.	14,216	14,216	
Adjusting account of interest,	do.	11,405	11,405	
Branch liabilities,	7,786,977	8,163,311	376,334	
Difference in "Deposit accounts," the published accounts showing a *Dr.* balance instead of the *Cr.* balance shown above, the amount of said *Dr.* balance being,	..	..	1,346	
Total under-statements in published sheet,	..	..	1,006,216	
HEAD III.				
Bills payable,	326,853	} 2,288,673	973,300	
Do.,	988,520			
Total under-statements in published sheet,	..	..	973,300	

ASSETS.

ASSETS.	In Published Balance Sheet.	In Bank's Books.	Under-stated in Published Sheet.	Over-stated in Published Sheet.
HEAD I.	£	£	£	£
Credit accounts No. 1.,	1,981,934	2,129,403	147,468	
Deposit do. (overdrawn),	Omitted	452,211	452,211	
Foreign and colonial credits,	1,304,873	2,278,173	973,300	
Suspense account,	50,000	300,000	250,000	
Amount deducted from Head I in published sheet in order to be carried down to Head III.,	50,000	300,000	250,000	
			751,775	
Branch assets,	2,274,381	2,683,467	409,086	
Under-statements in published sheet,			2,983,841	
Past due bills,	248,500	174,393		74,106
Contingent account,	*Dr* 10,747	*Cr.* 2,507		13,254
Credit accounts No. 2,	143,087	100,296		42,791
Heritable property account should have been included under Head II. of published balance sheet instead of Head I.,				119,541
Adjusting account of interest, viz.,	66,709	31,101		35,607
Over-statements in published sheet,				285,302
Deduct over-statements from under-statements,			285,302	
Difference, being nett under-statements in published balance-sheet,			2,698,589	
HEAD II.				
Heritable property a/c,	} 96,410	159,693	63,283	
Property a/c,				
Total under-statements in published sheet,			63,283	
HEAD III.				
Total gold and silver coin in hand,	862,812	833,717		29,095
Total over-statement in published sheet,				29,095
Government stocks, &c.:—				
Irvin & Co.'s debt,	11,995		11,995	
Sums brought down from Head I.,	751,775		751,775	
Sum in red ink in the scroll at foot of page,	3,656		3,656	
Amount overstated,				767,427
London, provincial, and foreign correspondents,	32,171	46,388	14,216	
Amount understated,			14,216	
Deduct under-statements from over-statements,			14,216	
Difference, being nett over-statement in published sheet,				753,211

1877.

LIABILITIES.

LIABILITIES.	In Published Balance Sheet.	In Bank's Books.	Under-stated in Published Sheet.	Over-stated in Published Sheet.
	£	£	£	£
HEAD I.				
Deposit accounts,	Omitted	449,692	449,692	
Credit do. No. 2,	Do.	220,683	220,683	
Do. do. No. 2,	Do.	59	59	
Branch cross accounts deducted from liabilities in published sheet, do.,	...	...	273,842	
Head office cross a/cs. do. do.,	...	...	207,240	
Total under-statements in published sheet,	...	...	1,151,518	
HEAD II.				
Circulation,	763,894	840,004	76,110	
Total under-statement in published sheet,	...	...	76,110	
HEAD III.				
Bills payable,	1,350,335	2,681,048	1,330,712	
Total under-statement in published sheet,	...	...	1,330,712	

ASSETS.

ASSETS.	In Published Balance Sheet.	In Bank's Books.	Under-stated in Balance Sheet.	Over-stated in Balance Sheet.
	£	£	£	£
HEAD I.				
Credit accounts,	1,806,987	2,027,670	220,683	
Deposit do. No. 2,	Omitted	449,692	449,692	
Credit do. No. 2,	96,617	96,677	59	
Foreign and colonial credits,	1,352,636	2,683,348	1,330,712	
Remittances between branches and branches,	86,258	132,368	46,110	
Branch cross accounts deducted from assets in published sheet,	...	...	273,842	
Head office cross a/cs. do. do.,	...	...	207,240	
Amounts carried down to Head III.,	...	...	751,775	
Understated in published sheet,	...	...	3,280,116	
Heritable property a/c included under Head I. instead of Head II. to the amount of	...	...	...	52,961
Over-statement in published sheet,	...	...	...	52,961
Deduct over-statement from under-statement,				
Difference, being total under-statement in published sheet,	...	...	3,227,154	
HEAD II.				
Heritable property a/c,	257,689	310,651	52,961	
Total under-statements in published sheet,			52,961	52,961
HEAD III.				
Cash on hand,	891,018	921,018	30,000	
Total under-statement in published sheet,	...	...	30,000	
Brought down from Head I.,	...	...	...	750,775
Total over-statement in published sheet,	...	...	...	751,775

ASSETS.

ASSETS.	In Published Balance Sheet. £	In Bank's Books. £	Under-stated in Balance Sheet. £	Over-stated in Balance Sheet. £
HEAD I.				
Credit accounts,	2,009,752	2,356,088	346,336	
Do. do., No. 2,	96,294	96,413	119	
Deposit accounts,	Omitted	440,738	440,738	
Foreign and colonial credits,	1,488,244	2,881,252	1,393,008	
Carried to Head III., viz.:—				
To gold, £200,000				
To Government and other stocks, 926,764 }			1,126,764	
Cross accounts at branches deducted from assets in published sheet,			154,090	
Remittances between branches and branches carried to Head III.,		108,553	108,553	
Total under-statements in published sheet,			3,569,609	
Less heritable property, should be included under Head II., but is put in under Head I. in published sheet,			48,696	
Nett under-statements in published sheet,			3,520,913	
HEAD II.				
Heritable property,	40,000	88,696	48,696	
Total under-statements in published sheets,			48,696	
HEAD III.				
Gold,	200,000	} 338,500		200,000
Do.	338,500			
Remittances between branches and branches, &c., brought from Head I.,		108,553		108,553
Overstated,				308,553
Head Office. Notes of other banks on hand—				
Tellers,	34,810	75,895	41,085	
Branches, Do. do.,	29,081	77,627	47,946	
Understated,			89,031	89,031
Deduct under from over,				219,522
Total over-statements,				480,614
Brought from Head I.,				148,888
				297,262
Total over-statements,				926,764

LIABILITIES.

LIABILITIES.	In Published Balance Sheet. £	In Bank's Books. £	Under-stated in Balance Sheet. £	Over-stated in Balance Sheet. £
HEAD I.				
Deposit accounts,	Omitted	440,738	440,738	
Credit do.,		346,336	346,336	
Do. do., No. 2,		119	119	
Cross accounts at branches, deducted from liabilities in published sheet,			154,090	
Total under-statements in published sheet,			941,284	
HEAD II.				
Bank notes in circulation,	710,252	799,283	89,031	
Total under-statements in published sheet,			89,031	
HEAD III.				
Bills payable,	1,488,244	2,881,252	1,393,008	
Total under-statements in published sheet,			1,393,008	

CHAPTER V.

Evidence of the Accountant, Secretary, and Superintendent of Branches.

WILLIAM MORISON.

By the LORD ADVOCATE—I was accountant of the City of Glasgow Bank from 1871 to its stoppage. I had previously been a clerk in the same department. I succeeded Mr. R. S. Stronach (afterwards manager) as accountant. I had charge of all the clerks in the accountant's department, and of the ledgers and other books in which the transactions of the Bank were entered. I had charge of the private cash-book, the general ledger, the weekly balance book, the balance ledger, and the contingent account ledger. The cash balance book was not kept by me, but I made certain entries in it, showing the amount in my general ledger. I kept a number of subsidiary books; amongst others a book titled "Credit accounts, Nos. 3 and 4." [No. 31 of inventory.] That book contains entries of cash advances to Smith, Fleming & Co. and James Nicol Fleming. There is also an account in that book under the head "New Zealand and Australian Land Co. Stock." I began to keep that book in June, 1875. The annual balance of the Bank was struck on the first Wednesday of June, in terms of the contract. The contract was followed so long as I was an officer of the Bank. The general meeting of the shareholders took place on the first Wednesday of July each year. The preparation of the balance and report of the affairs of the Company for the preceding year had to be completed between these two dates. It was my duty as accountant to take part in the preparation of the annual balance. I had to bring down balances from the general ledger, and the branches general ledger, and the correspondence general ledger, into the balance ledger. This was finished about ten days after the annual balance. When prepared, I submitted it to the Manager. [Shown No. 130.] That is a scroll abstract of the accounts at the head office for the year ending 7th June, 1876. It was prepared in the head office. No. 133 is an abstract of the accounts at the branches for the same period. It was prepared under the superintendence of Mr. Miller, superintendent of branches department. These

The City of Glasgow Bank Trial.

Wm. Morison. two abstracts showed the whole operations of the Bank of that class requiring to be brought into the balance sheet for the year; and the full balance sheet required to be made up from these. [Shown No. 128.] That is titled on the back "Scroll abstract of accounts." It was prepared in the office. The black ink figures on it bring together the two abstracts I have just spoken to. They bring together the whole operations of the Bank and their results, at the head office and branches. As originally prepared by me, the figures in red ink were not on No. 128; but No. 128 was not the first scroll. There may have been more than one scroll before it. It was the final scroll. The black and red ink figures were put on No. 128 at the same time.

You start with an abstract for the head office and an abstract for the branches; when you bring these two together you have a new scroll?—Yes.

When you had simply brought the two together on the face of the sheet, what did you do with that?—Submitted it to the Manager.

When you submitted it to the Manager, what was done?—There was an arrangement made that Mr. Potter, one of the Directors, should meet the Manager and go over the separate items.

You are speaking of the balance sheet of 1876?—Yes.

By the LORD JUSTICE-CLERK—You arranged that with the Manager?—Yes.

Did Mr. Potter meet the Manager?—Yes.

And yourself?—Yes.

By the LORD ADVOCATE—What happened at the meeting?—No. 128 was the result.

Were the red ink marks put on at that meeting, or had they been put on before?—This [No. 128] is the effect of what was done at the meeting, but I cannot say that it is the scroll that it was done on.

Were the red ink marks on before the meeting?—Not before the meeting.

The red ink marks represent the result of what was settled at that meeting?—Yes.

Added to what you had prepared?—Yes.

The black ink marks show what you have prepared?—Yes.

And the red shows what was agreed on at the meeting?—Partly so.

By the LORD JUSTICE-CLERK—The red ink marks are in my writing.

By the LORD ADVOCATE—Is the whole of it in your writing?—Yes, the whole of it.

Were the alterations made on it in red ink made out of your own head, or upon instructions?—By instructions.

Whose instructions?—Mr. Potter's and the Manager's.

Mr. J. P. B. Robertson,
Counsel for Henry Inglis.

Evidence for Prosecution.

Did these two gentlemen go over that sheet for 1876 item by **Wm. Morison.** item?—Yes.

Is that document, as it stands, giving effect to the alterations which you were instructed to make, in accordance with the books of the Bank that were under your charge?—No.

Was the abstract which you formerly spoke of [No. 130] in conformity with the books of the Bank?—Yes.

But the result of the instructions you got from Mr. Potter and Mr. Stronach was to make the balance sheet which you framed, with red figures on it, disconform to the books of the Bank?—Yes.

What did you do with the altered abstract after it was adjusted with Mr. Potter and the Manager?—It formed the annual report. The annual report was made out from it.

Did you prepare the abstract and send it to the printer?—I prepared the annual report and sent it to the printer. A proof of the report was sent to the Directors.

Was it the practice that when a final proof of the balance sheet was adjusted, it was laid before a meeting of the Directors? —I don't know as to that.

Did you not attend the meeting?—No.

Did you not attend for the purpose of having the balance ledger adjusted and docqueted?—Yes.

When was that done, and for what purpose?—For the purpose of going over the books—to compare them, and see that they were the same as the balance ledger. This took place probably on the Wednesday or Thursday before the annual meeting day.

Was there any document intermediate between the abstract No. 128 and the abstract published to the shareholders in 1876? —No.

How long were Mr. Potter and Mr. Stronach and you engaged in revising that balance sheet, resulting in the red figures being put on?—Perhaps an hour or two. On the left-hand side of No. 128 there are entries S. F. & Co. (Smith, Fleming & Co.), £200,875 ; J. N. F. (James Nicol Fleming), £100,300 ; and J. M. & Co. (James Morton & Co.), £450,600. These were credit accounts, entered in that part of the abstract which contains advances on credit.

But you bring them down and insert them among what?— Government stocks, railway stocks and debentures, and other securities.

In the abstract for 1876 there is an entry under assets, "Government stock, Exchequer bills, railway and other stocks and debentures, and balances in hands of banking correspondents, £2,218,868 13s. 7d." ; so that the effect of that change was to represent that a debt due on credit account by these firms to the amount of £751,775 was either a Government stock or a

93

The City of Glasgow Bank Trial.

Wm. Morison. security on a balance in the hands of correspondents of the Bank?—Yes.

By whose instigation were these sums brought down?—Mr. Potter's.

Was it by his directions it was done?—Yes.

Did he assign any reason or justification for it?—That the Bank held certain stocks against the debt of £751,775.

By the LORD JUSTICE-CLERK—And therefore treating them as good assets?—Yes.

By the LORD ADVOCATE—Did Mr. Potter seem to understand the different items that they were considering?—Apparently so.

Did he appear to be quite conversant with them?—Quite conversant.

Did the books of the Bank correctly show the operations of the Bank?—Yes.

Were they in conformity with the actual fact?—Yes.

How were the debts to the extent of £751,775 represented or stated in the abstract prepared by you, No. 130?—As credit accounts.

Which they were?—Which they were—in the books. In No. 130 there is an entry on the right-hand side, "Deposit accounts, £455,444 5s. 10d.," shown as due by the Bank, and on the other side there is an entry of "Deposit accounts, £1346 16s. 6d." due to the Bank. These are correctly stated in No. 130. They are not correctly stated in the revised abstract. The £1346 16s. 6d. only is put in it. The effect of this was to reduce the liabilities by the difference between £455,444 5s. 10d. and the debtor balance of £1346 16s. 6d. In No. 128, on the debtor side, under the head "Foreign and colonial credits," there is an entry of £2,278,173 5s. 10d. That is the actual amount, but £973,300 is deducted from that, leaving only £1,304,873 17s. 1d.

By the LORD JUSTICE-CLERK—It is reduced by nearly a million.

By the LORD ADVOCATE—Shown No. 39A [excerpt from progressive ledger, foreign and colonial], and asked, why was the sum of £973,300 deducted from the foreign and colonial credits? Depones—Because there was a credit account to that extent.

Did you get instructions from anybody to deduct it?—No; it was in the ledger.

Why did you put it in the ledger?—In June, 1873, there was an entry made by the instructions of the late Manager, Mr. Alexander Stronach, which appears in the book titled "City of Glasgow Bank cash book, private, No. 6," extracts from which are contained in No. 2A. I made that entry. It is in the following terms:—"Foreign and colonial credits, No. 2. The following credits to be retired as they mature, and debited under the respective accounts to 'Credit accounts No. 2,' against which securities are now held by the

Bank, and in process of realisation and payment of the proceeds, **Wm. Morison.**
£973,300." That deduction from foreign and colonial credits
was carried on in the books and in the balance-sheets from year
to year thereafter down to 1878 inclusive, without any change
being made. There was a note written by the late Manager
giving the particulars of that deduction, but I never got the
particulars.

By the LORD JUSTICE-CLERK—Was it a right deduction?—I
would not like to say so. I would not like to give an opinion
upon that.

By the LORD ADVOCATE—The entry "Foreign and colonial
credits" represents the liability side of the acceptances sent out
by the Bank—what the customer was due in respect of acceptances granted to him by the Bank.

So that, taking off £973,300 from that amount simply represented, amongst other things, that there were £973,300 less of
the Bank's acceptances afloat or in the circle than was really the
case?—Yes.

By the LORD JUSTICE-CLERK—The foreign and colonial credits
represented a sum of more than two millions?—Yes.

Then in 1873 Mr. Alexander Stronach directed that this
£973,300 should be deducted in the books from these debits to
the foreign and colonial customers?—Yes.

That represented, I presume, on the books so much security
held by the Bank against the two millions, and was therefore
deducted?—Yes.

Can you go further and say what the £973,300 was composed
of?—No.

You just took it from the notandum of Mr. Alexander
Stronach?—Yes.

By the LORD ADVOCATE—Being shown the book No. 2, from
which the excerpts No. 2A were taken, depones—There are two
entries, one on each side of this book. There is on the one
side the entry I have already read; on the other there is the
following entry:—" Bills payable No. 2. The following amounts
under acceptance at this date to be retired by the Bank under
special arrangements with the parties, of date 1st June, 1873,
against which certain securities are now held by the Bank, and
in process of realisation and payment of proceeds, £973,300."
The date of that is 4th June, 1873, and the entry has been kept
up for every successive year since that date. I am not aware
whether there has been any realisation of securities held by the
Bank against the bills; but if so, it has not been taken off this
entry. The entry has never been taken out of the books by any
other entry applicable to this or any part of it.

Therefore the floating acceptances of the Bank, whether covered
or not, have been yearly understated to the amount of £973,300?
—Yes.

The City of Glasgow Bank Trial.

By the LORD JUSTICE-CLERK—Unless there are securities for that amount?—I don't know about that. I cannot say that there are such securities, or that there are not.

By the LORD ADVOCATE—I had no charge of the securities.

Did you feel comfortable in making that entry in the books? —No.

Why not?—Because I had not the particulars of the entry in my cash book. I had no means of knowing whether it was a correct entry or not.

Had you any written authority or evidence of who had authorised you to make it?—I got a note or slip from the late Manager to make the entry.

Did you speak to him about it frequently?—At the annual balance I would speak of it.

Did you ever speak about that entry in going over abstract D with Mr. Potter and Mr. Robert Stronach in 1876?—They would see it, and I have no doubt I would speak of it. I recollect speaking of it to Mr. Potter. I recommended to Mr. Stronach that it should be taken out.

By the LORD JUSTICE-CLERK—Why?—Because there were no particulars in my cash-book of the entry. I had no particulars of it.

Was it not because you did not believe there were these securities?—No, that was not the reason.

By the LORD ADVOCATE—It was an unvouched entry so far as you were concerned?—I had a voucher for it, or rather I was aware that the late Manager had a statement of it. I have seen it. It was a memorandum, not of securities, but of the entry.

But did you ever see securities or anything of that sort that would have warranted you at your own hand in making such an entry?—No. When I spoke to Mr. Robert Stronach about having the entry taken out, I think he said it was there before he was appointed, and it would be better to leave it in the meantime. That took place in 1876.

Was that the occasion when Mr. Potter was present?—I could not say that.

On the creditor side of the abstract No. 130 (scroll abstract of accounts at head office on 7th June, 1876), at what sum are the liabilities of the Bank under credit accounts stated?—At £147,468 16s. 11d. That sum is altogether omitted from the scroll abstract No. 128, the result being to understate the liabilities to that extent. I cannot tell why it was left out. I left it out of the statement in consequence of instructions given to me by Mr. Potter and the Manager. I have no recollection whether they gave any reason for leaving it out.

On the creditor side of the abstract No. 130, what amount is there taken from the books and represented as due by the

Evidence for Prosecution.

Bank to London, provincial, and foreign correspondents?— Wm. Morison.
£378,481 8s. 5d.

Is that sum correctly transferred to the abstract No. 128?—
No. The amount there is £364,264 13s. 3d., being a difference
of £14,216 15s. 2d.

How is that managed?—The lesser amount is simply the
balance betwixt the different amounts.

Was that, in point of fact,, an under-statement of indebtedness
to that amount?—Not of indebtedness.

What then?—Well, if you look at it in that light, it was.

By the LORD JUSTICE-CLERK—Does that mean a balance due
to the London and provincial correspondents, or a balance due
by them?—The larger amount is the balance due by them.
The original sum was the correct one, and therefore the last sum
is wrong to the extent of £14,216.

By the LORD ADVOCATE—At the time you were adjusting the
balance for 1875, had you anything to do with ascertaining the
amount of bad debts?—I was sent for by the Manager—Mr.
Potter was there—and I was asked to make up a statement of the
bad debts. I told him it was not for me to make up a state
of the bad debts, but that I would make up a statement of
accounts that were not bearing interest—that is, on which no
interest was charged. That suggestion was adopted, and I made
up such a statement.

Had you any interview with the Directors about that, or any
of them?—I saw Mr. Potter repeatedly about it. I went to his
office and saw him there.

What was done as the result of that?—My figures to the extent
of £250,000 were adopted.

How much did you make it?—It was either £300,000 or
£350,000, but I think it was £300,000.

And how did you deal with them in the abstract?—They are
entered as assets.

How much was entered as assets?—There was a balance of an
old bad and doubtful debts account, and that was amalgamated
with the £250,000, making up altogether £300,000, which was
entered in my abstract under the heading of " Suspense account."

How much of that £300,000 was stated in the abstract from
which the report was made up as bad and doubtful?—You will find
under the heading of bad and doubtful debts £50,000. The
difference of £250,000 you will find entered amongst the other
accounts in the abstract as good assets. That £250,000 consisted entirely of debts on which no interest had been paid ; I
could not say exactly offhand for how long, but perhaps for five
or six years.

Did you make it known to Mr. Potter and Mr.
Stronach that these accounts had not borne interest for that
time?—Yes ; they were quite aware of it. The three sums of

The City of Glasgow Bank Trial.

Wm. Morison. £200,875, £100,300, and £450,600 already referred to as having been taken down from head I. to head III. were not taken out of the public books of the Bank in 1876.

Did Mr. Robert Stronach, in 1875, give you directions with regard to certain accounts of Smith, Fleming & Co.?—Yes; that was at 2nd June, 1875.

What were you directed to do with regard to them?—The accounts of Smith, Fleming & Co. in credit accounts were transferred to credit accounts No. 3 to the extent of £761,265 19s. 9d. The effect of that was to take them out of credit accounts where they were seen by the clerks in the cheque box, and put them into credit accounts in No. 3 ledger, which was kept by me, and was accessible only to the Manager and Directors.

Why was that transfer made?—I presume to bring all the accounts together.

Did no other reason suggest itself to you at the time?—It would have the effect of keeping the accounts quieter.

What do you mean by keeping the accounts quiet?—It would have the effect that no person would see them except myself.

And fewer people would know of the extent of the indebtedness to the Bank of Smith, Fleming & Co.?—Yes.

That was the amount in which they were indebted at that time, upon accounts kept in books to which the clerks had access?—Yes.

These accounts were closed, and the accounts transferred to a book which was patent only to you and the Manager?—Yes. They were taken out by means of a cross entry. These accounts have since been kept by me, and they are entered in the same way yet. The balance sheet for 1877 was prepared on the same principle as the other, so far as making up abstracts went. [Shown No. 129, weekly balances in general ledger, 5th June, 1878.] That was prepared in the same way from two abstracts, and then it was altered as before.

By whom was it altered, or by whose directions, in 1877?—I cannot recollect about 1877 very well.

But so far as you do recollect?—They were gone over by the Manager, but I have no recollection of meeting any other person.

By the LORD JUSTICE-CLERK—There are a number of alterations.

Did you prepare it according to the alterations of the year before?—I prepared it in the usual way—the correct way.

So the same alterations would require to be made again?—Yes.

And they were made?—Yes.

By the LORD ADVOCATE—These are shown partly in red ink and partly in pencil on this sheet.

Do I understand you to say that, so far as it is yours, it is taken from your abstract, which is correct?—Yes.

98

Evidence for Prosecution.

And that so far as it differs from those two abstracts which were brought forward by you, it is owing to the directions of others?—Yes.

But you cannot say who the others were?—With the exception of the Manager.

You cannot mention any other person than the Manager?—I have no recollection of that year. The deposit and credit accounts were dealt with on the same principle as they had been in the year before.

Was the £973,300 odds kept up again?—There is one of the sheets from which I can show that. I refer to No. 131. [Abstract of accounts at head office on 6th June, 1877.] In making up the statement the £973,300 is set aside, and certain other sums are deducted.

Instead of putting in that £973,000 as a cross entry, what did you do on both sides?—There was—cash lodged in C/A, £94,368 14s. 11d.; anticipations, £527,940; S., F. & Co., £552,704 4s. 2d.; J. N. F., £158,000; making altogether, £1,333,012 19s. 1d. "Cash lodged in credit account" would represent renewals of bills given out and the cash paid in. "Anticipations," I understand, were bills given out in the same way—anticipations of credit; that is to say, two sets of bills given out—bills upon which the Bank were debtors.

And in anticipation of credit coming in?—In anticipation of other bills to the same extent falling due; and in order to meet those bills when they did fall due, a second set of bills would be given out. "S., F. & Co." means Smith, Fleming & Co. The £552,704, I presume, would be bills payable that they would get. "J. N. F., £158,000," would represent bills given out to him.

Was there anything in your books to indicate these entries, or in any books you had access to; or were they merely suggestions?—There were no entries made for these alterations. They were not made from any entries or any heading in the books.

Are they purely fictitious?—There are no entries for them.

Then are they not fictitious entirely?—So far as I know. The £1,333,012 19s. 1d. was deducted from the amount of the bills payable by the Bank—the Bank's acceptances. The Bank's acceptances that year amounted to £2,683,348 0s. 2d., so that that took off about one-half. That was what was substituted in the year 1877 for the £973,300.

The old £973,000 disappeared, and this new invention was substituted?—Yes. In my own abstract there is a clerical error to the effect of understating the amount of bills payable. I again prepared balance sheets in 1878 with a view to the annual

The City of Glasgow Bank Trial.

Wm. Morison. public abstract as in previous years. [Shown No. 124, abstract of accounts at 5th June, 1878.] That is the result, after adjustment—the red ink draft. My own abstract was taken correctly from the books. The abstract I prepared as the basis of No. 124 was correctly made up from my own abstract and that furnished by Mr. Miller, superintendent of branches, and was in conformity with the books. Alterations were made upon that abstract of 1878. These are shown upon the document before me. They were made by directions of the Manager, Mr. Robert Stronach.

By the LORD JUSTICE-CLERK—I made them.

By the LORD ADVOCATE—There was no other person concerned in it.

By the LORD JUSTICE-CLERK—These alterations were almost on the same lines as before.

By the LORD ADVOCATE—Only you have the £973,000 back again instead of the sum in the previous year?—Yes. A clean copy of that abstract was made, by instructions of Mr. Stronach, after it was red-inked. He did not say for what purpose it was wanted. After it was made, Mr. Stewart, Mr. Potter, and the Manager met in the Manager's room, and went over it. I was present, but I did not go over it with them. I was in the room. I do not think the annual abstract issued to the shareholders had been printed at that time.

Did these three gentlemen not compare the clean document with the abstract?—They compared the clean document with the abstract published in the previous year's report. [Shown No. 125.] That is the clean copy which was made.

In the abstract balance sheet issued to the shareholders at 5th June, 1878, the first item on the debtor side is " Deposits at the head offices and branches, and balances at the credit of banking correspondents, £8,102,001 0s. 4d." That is not correctly stated as from the books of the Company. It is understated.

To what extent, and in what particulars?—Deposit accounts, £440,738 10s. 9d. [see abstract of accounts at 5th June, 1878]; credit accounts, £346,336 6s. 9d. Both these were due by the Bank.

By the LORD JUSTICE-CLERK—In other words, there were deposits to the extent of £440,000 due by the Bank which were not entered in the balance sheet?—Yes.

Is that all the deficiency?—No.

By the LORD ADVOCATE—You had entered these sums as part of the liabilities of the Bank in your abstract?—Yes.

Point out on the altered scroll balance sheet how they were got rid of?—Both sums are put into a debtor column on the creditor portion of the state.

Evidence for Prosecution.

In fact, they were taken out by a cross entry?—Not by an entry.

The amount of bank notes in circulation is stated in the published balance sheet at £710,252 ; was that correct?—There is an under-statement of £89,031.

The next item in the balance sheet is " Drafts outstanding due, or with a currency not exceeding twenty-one days, and drafts accepted by the Bank and its London agents on account of home and foreign constituents, £1,488,244 18s. 6d."; is that sum correct according to the books?—No.

To what extent is it incorrect?—There is the bills payable credit account of £973,300 deducted.

That is the old entry?—Yes; and there is also £419,708 deducted.

[Shown No. 39A.] That is an extract from the foreign and colonial credits progressive ledger No. 1?—Yes.

What was the true amount at that date?—£2,881,252 18s. 6d.

That item in the published abstract was reduced by about one-half?—Yes.

These amounts are entered in the scroll abstract No. 124?— Yes. In that abstract there is a note in red ink, " Amount of bills on the circle, and against which an equal sum is at the credit of J. M. & Co. on D/A." That note is in my handwriting. " J. M. & Co." are James Morton & Co. I was directed to make that entry by the Manager. I understood the note to mean that two sets of bills would be out for the same amount, and that the first set of bills would be discounted, and the proceeds paid in to the credit of James Morton & Co.

That is what you call anticipation?—Yes.

What was the course of dealing in the case of these anticipations?—I cannot speak personally as to that; I could only speak from hearsay. On the creditor side of the published balance sheet for 1878 the first entry is, " Bills of exchange, local and country bills, credit accounts, and other advances upon security, £8,484,466 9s. 2d."

Was that sum fully and correctly stated?—No.

What was wrongfully deducted from it?—Under the head of credit accounts there is a sum of £680,614. That is written off upon the abstract in red ink.

Then there is a sum of?—£346,336 6s. 9d.

That is written off credit accounts, creditor balances?—Yes.

Then there is the cross entry?—There is first £440,738 10s. 9d.

That same sum occurred on the other side of the account, but it was written off by being entered on both?—Yes. Then there is a sum of £973,300, which was also a cross entry; and then £419,708, also a cross entry. Then there is a sum of £148,888 deducted from credit accounts No. 3. These were

The City of Glasgow Bank Trial.

Wm. Morison. Smith, Fleming & Co.'s accounts. They stood in credit account ledgers Nos. 3 and 4. The total of their indebtedness is shown in the entry opposite, in black figures, on the left hand, as £891,762 ; and that was reduced by deducting from it that sum of £148,888. These were sums due by them on credit account. Below the last-mentioned sum there is a sum written off (in red figures) of £297,232. That is deducted from the sum (in black figures) of £512,192 12s. 6d., which was taken from credit accounts No. 4. That was the balance due by James Nicol Fleming. All these sums are deducted from head I. on the assets side of the abstract balance sheet. Referring next to head III. in the abstract sheet, there is the item, "Cash on hand, viz., gold and silver coin and notes of other banks at head office and branches, £845,963 1s."

What was stated by you as at that date as the true amount in your own figures?—£845,963 1s.

Was that correct according to the information from the books of the Bank?—With the exception of the same entry of £89,031, which was on the other side.

By the LORD JUSTICE-CLERK—Where in your own abstract, before it was altered, do you find that sum of £845,963 1s.?—Under head III.

The sum of £596,623 6s. 11d. is given there?—Yes ; that is, at the head office. Then you have to add the branches, £249,339 14s. 1d.

And that makes the £845,963 1s.?—Yes.

By the LORD ADVOCATE—Then there is a deduction made from that of £89,031 ; is that a proper deduction?—Well, I consider it so. It was Company's notes received at the exchange on the following morning before the commencement of business. I did not receive that information until after I had made up my abstract. If I had received it the night before, I would have given effect to it then.

Then there is still an over-statement, according to your statement, of £200,000 as to the gold ; is that the sum which is interlined in red ink in the scroll abstract?—Yes.

There is a cross in red ink opposite to it, and there is also a cross opposite the sum of £480,614 a short way below?—Yes.

What is the meaning of that?—It is to connect these two sums, which together make up the sum of £680,614.

Have these two sums any connection with the other sum of £680,614 deducted from credit account balances No. 1?—Yes.

So that the operation you performed there was to bring down £680,614 which was due upon credit accounts, and to enter £200,000 of it as gold in the coffers of the Bank?—Yes.

The remaining £480,614 is represented in the abstract issued to the shareholders as Government stocks, Exchequer bills, rail-

Evidence for Prosecution.

way and other stocks and debentures in the hands of the Bank and correspondents?—Yes.

These sums of £200,000 in gold, £480,614, £148,888, and £297,262 are all included in the third item of the balance sheet?—Yes.

Was that a correct statement in the published balance sheet?—So far as regards the deductions from the credit accounts, if they held absolutely the stocks that represented these amounts, I do not see much wrong in it.

Would it not have been more correct, even if they held securities, to state the amount that was due to them upon open account, and then to state also the securities held?—If they had made an entry through the books, I would have considered it quite right if they had done so.

By the LORD JUSTICE-CLERK—If they held sufficient security, you think there is not much wrong in the entry?—No.

What about the £200,000 in gold?—I cannot say anything about that; I cannot justify that.

What did it represent—anything?—Yes, the balance of the £600,000.

But was there any balance; I mean, did it represent any gold and silver?—Not that I know of.

By the LORD ADVOCATE—Just take this case. Suppose a bank to have £100,000 due to them upon open account, and that they hold securities against it, do you think it is right, instead of stating that there is a debt of £100,000 due to them, and stating the securities covering it, that they should state that they have an asset of the value of £100,000 without disclosing the debt or the security?—It would be the correct way to disclose both, but it is only figures that go into the report.

I suppose that, even according to your view, if assets to that full value were not held, that was a false entry?—Yes; but, as I said yesterday, I had no means of knowing personally whether such securities were held or not.

Was any assurance given to you when you got directions to make these entries that such securities were held?—From the conversation I understood so.

But what I want to know is whether you were simply directed to do this, and inferred from what you were told that there were securities, or were you distinctly given to understand that such things existed?—I was never told that such things existed; I was told to make the alteration.

And you fancied that it was an honest transaction, at least that it had some degree of honesty about it, and inferred that there were securities?—Exactly so. The alterations which I made upon these three abstracts prepared by me in 1876, 1877, and 1878 were all very much of the same class.

Did you receive any more explanations on any one of those

Wm. Morison. occasions than on another?—I remember the Manager stating to me that he hoped this would be the last time that he would require to do such a thing. It was in the year 1878 that he said so, and, I presume, about the time we were making up the balance sheet. I have no recollection of anything of that sort being said to me by the Manager or Mr. Potter in 1876. With regard to the clean copy of the abstract of 1878, of which I spoke in my evidence yesterday, it is not so easy on that copy to trace the under-statements and over-statements as in the red ink copy before me.

Whose duty was it to convert that clean copy of the document before you into the abstract that was published to the shareholders, and who did it?—I would take the figures after they were examined by the Directors and would get them printed; I mean get the report printed. I see the entries of "Reserve gold in cash chest," and "Gold and silver coin on hand in the cash chest," in No. 125. The reserve gold in cash chest, £200,000, was part of the sum due by Smith, Fleming & Co., from the credit ledger.

Why do you call it reserve gold?—The Bank is bound to hold a certain quantity of gold against its issue. That is what is meant by reserve gold.

Does this mean that £200,000 was held against issue, and that "gold and silver on hand" was held for other purposes?—No; they are both held against the issue.

But what is the difference between having gold on hand and having reserve gold?—I do not think there is anything in the phrase at all.

By the LORD JUSTICE-CLERK—I had no such heading as "Reserve gold" in the original abstract I prepared.

By the LORD ADVOCATE—At the foot of the left-hand page of No. 124, on the debtor side, the three sums of £480,614, £148,888, and £297,262, are entered as balances brought down from credit accounts. They are not represented as Government stocks or anything else—simply as credit account No. 1 balance, and so on.

By whose authority were these represented in the abstract as being Government stocks, or something of that kind?—It was a simple continuation of the arrangement made in 1876.

Who made the arrangement in 1876, that although these appeared as credit balances in the scroll balance, they were to be represented as Government stocks or debentures, or something of that kind in the abstract?—Mr. Potter and Mr. Robert Stronach, the Manager.

And in transferring them and calling them Government stocks, debentures, or something else, you were merely following out in 1877 and 1878 the instructions you had got in 1876?—Yes. When the clean copy, without the red ink marks, was submitted

Evidence for Prosecution.

to the Manager, Mr. Stewart, and Mr. Potter, I was in the room to give any information wanted.

Were you asked to give information about anything?—The only information I was asked for was to compare the 1877 report with the 1878 one.

Which report?—I mean the annual balance sheet. I was asked to do so, I presume, in order to compare the different sums, the one year with the other.

Simply for the purpose, I suppose, of stating what was the difference in the trading of the Bank between these two years? —Yes. I was not asked to explain any entry in this account, merely to compare results. The time occupied in that examination by the Manager and those two Directors was perhaps an hour—not so much.

Since you became the accountant of the Bank, has the Bank been in the habit of dealing in its own stock?—Yes. The entry of gold in the abstract which I prepared was taken from the cashier's ledger. [Shown No. 95.] I did not take it from there; I would get the amount from the cashier. There is a slip of paper in No. 95, which states the amount of gold at 5th June, 1878, as £338,500. It was the duty of the Directors to count the gold in the safe for the annual balance. That entry is initialed by a Director. It was usual that this should be done. I think that entry bears Mr. Stewart's initials, but I am not confident. I cannot say what the initials are.

But do you know that they are initials?—They are checked off.

By Mr. BALFOUR—The only balance signed by the Directors was the balance in the balance ledger. That balance in the balance ledger was brought out by taking the sum of all the separate heads of accounts appearing at the head office and branches.

All the separate accounts appearing at the head office had their balances brought into the balance ledger?—Yes.

And as regards the branches, the balance due by or to the Bank upon each branch was brought in separately?—As a branch, yes.

The distinction is this, is it not, that in the case of the head office you had the balances of the separate heads of account; in regard to the branches you had just the aggregate balance of the branches?—Yes.

And the sum total appearing on each side of the balance ledger was just the addition of these different items?—Yes.

And the balance ledger was the same in principle in each of the years?—Yes.

There were a large number of separate heads of accounts kept in the head office?—Yes.

The City of Glasgow Bank Trial.

Wm. Morison. You did not bring in the balances from the individual accounts, but only from the classes?—From the general accounts.

Look at the balance ledger for 1878 (12A); there appear to be about sixty separate heads on the left-hand of the debtor side?—About that.

Besides that, you have on the left-hand side also five branches, Dumfries, Dundee, etc., which appear to have been debtors at that time?—Debtors to the head office.

On the other side you have first on the creditor side somewhere about thirty-eight heads before you come to the branches?—Yes.

Then you have balances brought in from the branches: you had about 133 branches?—Yes.

What was signed by the Directors was just the addition of these two sides?—Yes.

Take an example: the second entry on the creditor side of the balance is notes issued, £7,864,500?—Yes.

That was the summation taken from the book applicable to notes, of all the notes that had been issued?—It was taken from the general ledger, which would correspond with that book.

You took it directly from the general ledger, and indirectly from the book where it was entered?—Yes. This referred to all the notes that had been issued from the beginning of the Bank. On the debtor side there is an entry of notes burned, £5,700,710. These were burned when worn out. The difference between the £7,800,000 odds and the £5,700,000 odds was the actual number of notes in existence, whether in actual use at the time or not.

That £5,000,000 swelled the total sum at the end of each side of that account?—Yes, it was summed in.

Therefore, though that was a cross entry, it swelled the total on each side?—Yes. The total on each side is £16,189,231.

There are upwards of two millions of notes shown to be in existence?—Yes.

Some of these might be in the coffers of the Bank, either at the head office or branches?—Yes.

But if you wished to show the shareholders or the public the amount of notes that were out, you would require to make a further deduction for those from the two millions?—Yes.

I suppose it would have been perfectly useless and misleading to bring into the abstract balance sheet such entries as these cross entries applicable to burned notes?—Quite so.

There may be other instances of the same kind of thing in the balance ledger?—There may; I don't know.

I suppose that was quite a correct kind of balance for the purposes for which it was made, of showing the actual results of balances standing in the books?—Yes.

If you wished to give information to the shareholders or the

Evidence for Prosecution.

public, first deducting the notes burned and no longer in use, Wm. Morison. and then the notes which were not actually out, but which were in the coffers at the head office or branches, the difference would be what ought to go into an abstract?—Yes.

And accordingly the amounts which we see in any of the published abstracts are very much smaller?—Yes.

Being what were the notes out?—What were in the hands of the public.

Deducting those burned or in the hands of the Bank?—Yes.

Still, talking of the balance ledger, look on the creditor side to the heading of deposit accounts, eight or ten entries down; do you see the entry "Deposit accounts, £33,959 14s. 8d."?—Yes.

Is that entry the balance which is brought out on the deposit account, after crossing the different entries on the two sides of that account?—Quite so.

So that this balance ledger, from its frame and the scheme on which it is made up, does not profess to show the details on the two sides, but merely to bring in a balance?—Simply the balance found in the ledger.

You see credit accounts No. 1 on the left-hand side of the same sheet, £2,009,072?—Yes.

Is that also a balance arrived at by crossing the two sides of credit account No. 1?—Yes; a balance found in the general ledger.

It does not profess to show, and does not show, the aggregates of the two sides, but merely the balance brought out by deducting the one from the other?—Yes.

When these different balances had thus been brought into the balance ledger, they were presented to the Directors?—Yes.

Assembled at a meeting?—Yes.

And was the manner in which they were treated, by an official of the Bank—I think yourself—going with the weekly balance book, so that they might check the one against the other?—Yes.

You had a weekly balance book, one applicable to the head office, another to the branches, and another to correspondents? —Yes.

And the Directors got the balance ledger placed before them, did they not, and you read off from these balance books the items which appear in it?—Yes.

The Director having his eye on the balance ledger, and you reading off from these balance books?—Yes.

That was the way in which the balance ledger was checked? —Yes.

All you read off in such cases as I gave you was, of course, the balance?—Of course the balance.

Checking by that method, the Directors did not see, and, indeed, had not the means of seeing, the details, but just the balances?—Simply balances.

The City of Glasgow Bank Trial.

Wm. Morison. Take as an instance the weekly balance of the general ledger of June, 1878. [Shown No. 129A.] Is that the weekly balance applicable to the head office, from which you read off the corresponding entries to the Directors when they checked the balance of June, 1878?—Yes.

That is the way that the balance ledger was checked, by the weekly balance applicable to the last week referring to the head office being taken?—Yes.

And the branches?—Yes; it is the head office balances with reference to branches.

But they were separate accounts?—Yes.

The head office account was one and the branches another?—I see the item about half-way down the left-hand page (129A), "Foreign and colonial credits," and the sum £2,881,252 odds. That is a debtor entry.

Against that, under the creditor column, you have the sum of £973,300?—Yes.

And you bring out as the balance of those two, deducting the latter from the former, £1,907,952?—Yes.

Then, looking to the balance ledger, the entry under foreign and colonial credits is the balance of £1,907,952?—Yes.

That was the amount you read off when the balance ledger was under the eyes of the Directors?—Yes.

So that when the balance ledger was under their eyes you did not read off the £2,881,000, or the thing you deducted from it?—No; only the £1,907,000.

By the LORD JUSTICE-CLERK—I read nothing but the £1,907,000.

By Mr. BALFOUR—The balance ledger having been checked in that way, it was signed by the Directors. I did not sign it, but I had read off the different items in the way I have explained. The docquet which the Directors signed was a docquet certifying that the whole is correctly stated, and they do hereby approve and confirm the same, being satisfied that the whole is in accordance with the Bank's books.

And it was in accordance with the Bank's books, although what it brought in were balances in such accounts as I have put to you, and not the aggregates of the two sides?—Yes. The balance ledger was the only thing the Directors signed that I am aware of, or that they examined at that time.

The abstract of accounts which was to be put before the shareholders was, I suppose, intended to show the state of the Bank's business as a going business?—Yes.

That was your understanding of its object?—Yes.

I suppose it was not intended to show obsolete entries, like those five millions of burned notes, or anything like that?—I should think not.

Was the abstract for the shareholders prepared from the

Evidence for Prosecution.

weekly states—from the states applicable to the head office, **Wm. Morison.** the branches, and the correspondents?—Yes.

Apparently to some extent that abstract, from its purpose, was upon a different principle from the balance signed by the Directors?—Yes.

And necessarily so?—Necessarily so.

It did not profess to be an abstract of what was in the balance ledger?—It corresponded with the balance ledger.

In result?—Yes, in result.

But it contained in some cases, did it not, the totals of the entries in the accounts instead of containing merely balances as they appear in the balance ledger?—Yes.

In some cases it contained balances?—In certain cases it did.

But where it contained, instead of balances as they were in the balance ledger, the aggregates of the two sides, it necessarily was on a different principle from the balance ledger?—Yes.

And properly so for its purpose?—Properly so, I think.

Which was to give information to the shareholders of the Bank as a going concern?—Yes.

[Shown No. 124A, abstract of accounts at 5th June, 1878.] Were all the figures that appear in black ink upon that balance written by you before you say you took it to the Manager?—Yes.

All of them?—All of them.

Nothing that is in red ink was put on before you took it to the Manager, you say?—This is not the first sheet that I presented to the Manager.

By the LORD JUSTICE-CLERK—This is the balance sheet of 1878.

By Mr. BALFOUR—What I want to know with regard to No. 124A is—was everything in black ink put on by you before you took it to the Manager, and was everything that appears in red ink put on after, or at the meeting?—This is not the sheet that I presented to the Manager; it may or it may not be. I may have made up five or six before I was done with it.

Is it or is it not the sheet you laid before the Manager?—I could not say.

Have you no idea?—No.

I must really ask you to try and recollect this; it is very vital. Is this—which I understood you in your evidence to represent as altered at a meeting with the Manager—is it or is it not the sheet you had with you before the Manager?—I could not say.

Do you think it was or it was not?—It is very probable it was.

But only probable?—There might have been four or five written out for all that I recollect.

I don't want to know how many were written out; I want

The City of Glasgow Bank Trial.

Wm. Morison. to know whether that is the sheet you had before the Manager, or is it not?—I could not say.

Is it so long ago that you have forgotten?—I don't recollect.

By the LORD JUSTICE-CLERK—You said before that these alterations were made by the directions of the Manager; was that so?—Yes.

By Mr. BALFOUR—Then, if these alterations and deletions were made at that meeting, this must have been the sheet that you had before the Manager?—That is the effect of the meeting.

But I want to know were they made at the meeting or not?—Do you mean did I put these red ink figures in when I was along with the Manager?

I want you to tell me, if you can recollect, whether that is the paper that you had before the Manager or not?—I cannot bring it to my memory. Would you show me the original? [Shown No. 124.]

By the LORD JUSTICE-CLERK—You prepared that abstract in 1878, on the same principles as that which you prepared in 1876?—Yes.

And it was again altered in red ink figures, on the same lines, as you expressed it yesterday?—Yes.

Had you any meeting for the purpose of going over that abstract before it was altered?—Several meetings—often.

With whom?—With the Manager.

Was the alteration made before the first of these meetings, or afterwards?—After the meetings.

Were they all made at the same time?—I should think not.

By Mr. BALFOUR—Then do you mean to say that, with regard to this important matter, which happened in June of last year, you cannot say whether that (No. 124) is the paper you had before the Manager or not?—No; I cannot say.

Have you any recollection of putting away any other paper that was before the Manager in 1878?—No.

I do not mean putting away in the sense of wilfully destroying; but have you any recollection of laying any other paper before him which was not preserved?—No; I have no recollection of it; but I might have done it.

Do you not think, when you look at that paper, and see that a great many of the black ink entries are scored out, and red ink entries substituted, that that must have been the paper that you had before the Manager?—I don't see it.

By the LORD JUSTICE-CLERK—It must have been; you would never think of making a new copy of your black ink original abstract after the red ink alterations were made?—But there might have been two or three different sheets before all these alterations were made. These (showing on paper) might have been put in after these red ink figures on the same line.

Of course they might have been put in after, but that is not the question. You made up an abstract of the Company's

Evidence for Prosecution.

affairs; did you make more than one for the Manager before
it was altered?—No; one.

Then, where is that one?—I have not got it.

Just consider for a moment. Have you any doubt that that
of which the lithograph is a copy is your original abstract?—
I have no doubt that this abstract was before the Manager,
but whether that was the first one, or the fifth, or the sixth,
I cannot tell you. But that one would be before him.

You did not make more than one, did you?—I may have made
half a dozen; I don't recollect.

But did you make more than one identical copy of your
original abstract?—Yes.

For what purpose?—Because there might have been alterations going on.

But an unaltered copy is what you were asked about. The
question is whether that is the abstract that you laid before
the Manager. Do you mean to say you made various copies
of the same abstract?—I made various copies of the abstract
with the alterations.

That is not the question. The question is whether you made
more than one copy of your original abstract unaltered?—I
cannot answer that.

By Mr. BALFOUR—Are you not satisfied that if there were
any alterations on any previous scrolls to this, you would give
effect to them in black ink when you wrote out this?—No.

Then it comes to this, you cannot say whether that (No. 124)
is the document or not?—No. It is one of them.

Can you tell me now, were all the figures that are in black
ink upon that paper written upon it by you before you took it
to the Manager?—Yes.

You are quite sure of that?—Perfectly.

With reference to the first particular in connection with the
balance sheet of 1878, mentioned on page 10 of the indictment, amounting to £941,284 13s. 5d., is that sum made up
of the following sums:—First, the sum of £440,738 10s. 9d.,
entered in red ink in the debtor column on the right-hand page
of the abstract [see abstract for 1876]; second, the sum of
£346,336 6s. 9d., entered in red ink immediately below
that, these two sums added together amounting to £787,074
17s. 6d.; third, the sum of £154,090 3s. 11d., entered in red ink
opposite "Cross accounts" in the middle of the page; and a
further sum of £119 12s. which does not appear there?—Yes.

What does the sum of £440,738 consist of?—Deposit accounts,
debtor balances.

What is the £346,336?—Credit accounts, creditor balances.

I suppose the debtor balances on deposit accounts are overdrafts—that is, sums due to the Bank by depositors on current
account who have overdrawn?—Yes.

The City of Glasgow Bank Trial.

Wm. Morison. Accordingly the £787,074 is the addition of overdrawn accounts of these two classes—the deposit accounts and the creditor balances?—Yes. The £787,074 is the sum of these two which I have explained.

Let there be no mistake. What is the £440,000?—That is in the debtor column; these are deposit accounts—debtor balances. Debtor balances are overdrafts on current accounts.

What is the £154,000?—Cross accounts at Edinburgh branches, £148,939 18s. 11d. In the business of the Bank we have instances of the same customers having different accounts with the Bank. For example, coalmasters, who have businesses in different places, or companies, have sometimes different accounts in the head office. Where that is the case, the Bank is in the way of crossing these respective accounts and bringing forward only the balance. That is when the same man is both debtor and creditor. It would be idle to bring down the particulars of a man's account in two separate columns, and so we bring down his balance in a slump.

Does that £787,000 contain a large number of cross entries of that kind?—Yes, I would say so. In 1878, I would say, about £300,000 of that sum consisted of proper cross accounts in the head office alone.

Then was it perfectly proper, in dealing with that item of the account, to cross at all events the accounts where the same person was debtor and creditor?—Yes.

And it would be absurd to do anything else?—I would say so.

You have crossed the whole of them here?—Yes.

Why did you cross the whole, and not limit that to about £300,000, which you think was at the head office, instead of the £440,000?—The crossing here has the effect of simply leaving the balance in the general ledger where it was, and takes the balance of a deposit ledger.

There is nothing wrong in that, is there?—So far as regards assets and liabilities, I should say it was.

As regards the £300,000, if the man owes money on one account to you, and you owe him money on the other, is the natural and proper thing to cross it?—So far as the cross accounts are concerned.

And there is about £300,000 in the head office alone?—Yes.

In so far as that consists of cross accounts, it is all right?—I should say so.

You cannot see anything to be said against it?—Nothing. As regards the £154,000, that is out of my personal knowledge, with the exception of £5000 at the Glasgow West End branch, which I happen to know about.

But the £148,939 was given to you as proper cross accounts by the Edinburgh officials?—By Mr. Miller, superintendent of branches. He gave me that as proper cross accounts. I know

112

Evidence for Prosecution.

that the West End branch had cross accounts to the amount of £5150.

Then, was it perfectly right that those cross accounts to the amount of £154,090 should be crossed as they are here?—That is my opinion.

And if you add that to the sum of about £300,000 of crosses at the head office, that would give you about £454,000 odds of properly crossed accounts?—Yes.

And, so far as you can see, there is no objection to the balance sheet, so far as that is concerned?—Not as regards the cross accounts.

By the Lord Justice-Clerk—Do you mean that to that extent the red ink alterations are a proper rectification of your original account?—Yes.

By Mr. Balfour—With regard to the second particular on page 10 of the indictment, that "the amount of bank notes in circulation under article two on the debtor side was understated to the extent of £89,031 or thereby," and, looking again to the abstract balance, that sum of £89,000 odds is made up of two sums, one of £41,085, and the other of £47,946, which appear on the left-hand side of the abstract in pencil, and on the right-hand side in red ink. This balance sheet professes to show the balance of gold and silver coin, notes of other banks on hand, and also your own circulation?—Yes. In the course of banking we come to be possessed of the notes of other banks, and at regular intervals we exchange these for our own notes.

Was that done, at the time this balance was prepared, between business closing on Wednesday, 5th June, and business beginning on Thursday, 6th June?—It would be.

About nine o'clock on the morning of the 6th?—Yes.

Then is it the fact that before business hours on the 6th, though after business hours on the 5th, you got back at the head office in exchange from other banks £41,085 of your own notes?—Yes.

And you got back at the branches £47,946?—Yes.

So that the £89,031 complained of by the Crown in item two of the indictment was notes of your own, which were back into the Bank in the way I have stated between the afternoon of the 5th and the beginning of business on the 6th?—Yes.

Although this abstract relates to the 5th of June, was it written up in the course of a week or so after 5th June?—After 5th June.

You could not write it up on that day, because you had not all the particulars in?—Quite so.

So before any part of the abstract was written the notes would be all back?—They would be all back.

They would be back by nine o'clock on the morning of the

H

The City of Glasgow Bank Trial.

6th, although you did not actually write up even the original edition of this bill after that?—Quite so.

Now, as these notes were back into the Bank before business began for the new year, was it not quite right to make this deduction?—I think so.

Because, before business began after the new year, they were not in circulation, but were back into the Bank?—Quite so.

Why was that entry not made at the beginning when you wrote it out?—The reason why a number of these alterations were made in red ink was simply to show that the alterations were not made in the books.

Was it merely to keep yourself in recollection?—Quite so.

Then, was it not the case that from the first time you did make up this abstract you did enter these notes?—Yes.

In pencil first?—I presume so; I cannot say. Being referred to the left-hand side of the abstract, opposite the word "branches," I see figures there in pencil to the same amount. These are just the same figures.

I suppose you would write in pencil before you wrote in ink?—Very likely. The next item in red ink, still on the left-hand side, is £41,000 odds deducted from £75,000 odds.

That is the notes at the head office; and you see again £47,000 deducted from £77,000?—Yes.

And it is the differences which make the £89,000?—Yes. These figures appear again on the right-hand side of the same page.

Were these entries about the notes not made by yourself from the very beginning?—Yes.

Before you went to the Manager at all?—Yes.

And they were quite right entries?—I consider them so.

And you merely made them in red ink as a notandum, and to keep yourself in mind that they did not go into the books?—Yes.

Then that was not an entry made to falsify the balance sheet, and the Manager had nothing to do with it?—I beg your pardon.

You have told us that these entries were made at your own instance, and that you think them right?—Yes.

And that they were made from the first in red ink merely to keep yourself in mind of what they were?—Yes; and in order to keep in my memory that there was no entry made through the books for the alteration.

Then it is not the case that everything that appears here in red ink was made at the request of the Manager?—In this instance it was not.

Was there anything else in red ink made of your own motion by yourself?—No, nothing else. I am quite sure of that.

Did you make these entries before you went in to the

Manager, or after?—I would say they would be made from the very first.

So when you took this in to the Manager it was partly black and partly red?—If this is the same sheet.

And if it was the predecessor of this sheet, it was red from the first as regards the notes?—It would be.

Does the fact of your finding these calculations about the notes jotted here in pencil not rather suggest to your mind that this was the first sheet on which these were made?—No.

Did you copy your pencil as well as your writing?—These might have been made after—long after.

I thought you said you entered the notes in red ink on the first abstract you made up?—There were so many people using these sheets that in order to show the alterations these might have been put down in pencil long after.

What was in pencil might have been long after, but what was in red ink was there from the first?—Yes.

And if this was not the original sheet, it was also in red ink on its predecessor?—I should say so.

By the LORD JUSTICE-CLERK—What I mean to say is this, that the pencil marks might have been put on the sheet after the stoppage of the Bank, because there were so many people inquiring into these sheets that they might have been put down to explain the matter.

By Mr. BALFOUR—But the red ink was there from the first?—Yes.

Then that is article two of the indictment, which, in your judgment, is all right?—Yes.

By the LORD JUSTICE-CLERK—The notes on hand of other banks represent what was actually in the Bank at the time. Then when the £41,000 of returned notes came into your hands, did you make any allowance for the notes of other banks returned at the same time?—The same amount was deducted on the one side as there was on the other side.

By Mr. BALFOUR—Is it this, that near the foot of the left-hand page you have notes of other banks on hand, £75,000?—Yes.

You deduct from that £41,000, and £34,000 is the balance?—Yes.

So with respect to notes of other banks and the branches you have £77,000, and you deduct from that £47,000, and carry across the balance?—Yes.

And so the matter was made right on both sides of the account?—I think so.

You did not make it appear that while you had called in £89,000 of your own issue you had a corresponding amount of the issue of other banks?—No.

Then that entry is all right on both sides?—Yes. The black

The City of Glasgow Bank Trial.

Wm. Morison. ink was all written first, and the red ink all written afterwards. Being referred to the creditor column, top of right-hand page, I see a summation in black ink of £1,448,453. That summation includes two sums in red ink of £440,000 odds and £346,000. It is also the case that there are black summations below which include what is written in red ink.

How is it possible that you summed up in black ink something that was only written on afterwards in red?—Because this will be simply a copy of some other sheet. I cannot tell where that is. With regard to the third particular of the indictment, "Amount of drafts outstanding," etc., understated to the extent of £1,393,008 or thereby, that amount is the summation of £973,300 and £419,708. The £973,300 is an entry which was raised in the books by Mr. Alexander Stronach's orders in 1873, and which was carried forward and received effect in the balance sheets always after that, except in 1877, when the exact amount was varied.

In preparing your balance sheet for your abstract or scroll balance for each year, did you give effect to that without anybody's instructions?—Yes.

You had it in the books?—Yes.

And if you had not given effect to it in the scroll balance, you would have been missing out something which was in the books?—Yes.

And that is the history of it, that, having been raised, and appearing in the books from 1873, it received effect ever after without your getting or needing to get anybody's instructions for it?—Yes. [Shown No. 129A, weekly balances in general ledger on 5th June, 1878.] Being referred to the foreign and colonial credits on the debit side of that weekly state, there is a sum of £2,881,000 odds, from which there is deducted the £973,000. I only read out the balance, £1,907,952, to the Directors.

Then the Directors would not know or see from what you read out that that balance was reached by deducting the £973,300?—Not from reading it.

That is the head office weekly abstract for 1878?—Yes.

Was that a correct statement of the weekly balance ending with 5th June, 1878?—A correct statement of the general ledger according to the books.

And without giving effect to anybody's alterations, for there were none?—Quite so.

By the Lord Justice-Clerk—You told us yesterday that in consequence of the directions of Mr. Potter and Mr. Stronach you made an alteration upon the original sums that you brought out in your black ink abstract in 1876. Now, was that sum of £2,800,000 consistent with your original black ink abstract, or was it consistent with the red ink alterations of 1876?—The **Wm. Morison.** £2,800,000 was quite in accordance with the books.

With the books of 1876?—Yes.

Was effect given in the weekly balance ledger to the alterations that you made in 1876?—No.

By Mr. BALFOUR—Accordingly, from 1873 onwards, with the exception of one year, was the £973,300 treated just as it is here?—Quite so.

And treated just as it is here, not only in the weekly balance for the week ending in June, but in the same way in the weekly balance of the other fifty-one weeks of the year?—Yes.

In short, for the whole fifty-two weeks of the year, that was treated just in the same way?—Yes.

And that was correct according to the books?—Yes.

Can you say that before you had the meeting with Mr. Potter and the Manager in 1876 you had given effect to the entry of £973,300 as usual, just as it had been for the three years then past?—Yes.

So they had nothing whatever to do with the mode of treating the £973,300?—No.

Neither in 1876 nor at any time?—No.

It was Mr. Alexander Stronach, and nobody else?—Just so.

You understood the reason for Alexander Stronach giving that direction to be that there was cash, or that there were securities in course of realisation, to work off those credits?—The entry in the cash book represents that. Mr. Stronach also had some slips which bore to show that.

If that was the case, was there anything wrong with the entry—if these were in the course of realisation?—It was an anticipatory entry.

And dependent upon whether the anticipations were realised or not?—Quite so.

With regard to the other item of £419,780 the Bank, as I understand, had granted acceptances which were out in the circle to a certain amount?—Yes.

These acceptances were about to mature?—Yes.

With the view of taking up these acceptances, were other acceptances issued which it was intended to discount to lift the first set?—I understand so.

Was that done within a few days before the first set of acceptances matured?—I cannot tell you that; I cannot speak personally of it.

But it would be done within a few days?—I cannot say.

So that for a time there were two sets of bills in the circle applicable to the same amounts?—Yes.

That is to say, during the time between the maturity and the retirement of the first set of bills—before that, and after the second set to lift them had been put out?—Yes.

Wm. Morison.

Now, the aggregate from which you deduct the £419,000 comprehends both of those sets of bills which were so out for a short time?—The larger amount includes both sets.

Which were out for a short time though representing the same debt?—Yes.

Would the total amount of the double set be just about £419,000?—That was the amount I got as being out.

Now, if it is the case that the second set of bills were applied to the purpose for which they were issued—that is, to be discounted and lift the first set—and if the Bank had got the money so raised, was that entry quite right?—If the money was in the cheque box.

If the discount for the second set had been got to lift the first, that entry was right?—If that money had been lodged in the cheque box.

Do you know of your own knowledge whether that money was not in the cheque box?—I do not know it was not in it. That was not a thing within my department.

Therefore you cannot say whether that entry of £419,000 odds was right or wrong, because you do not know whether the discount money had come in or not?—Yes. With regard to the fourth head of the charge, "Amount of bills of exchange, local and country bills, credit accounts and other advances under article one on creditor side, understated to the extent of £3,520,913 11s. 8d., or thereby"—and being referred to the left-hand side of the scroll 124A, the first matters that enter into that are the entries of £346,336 and £440,738. I treated these as cross entries. The very same considerations which I have already given in dealing with the same entries on the other side would again apply here. In so far as they were proper cross entries they were not understated in the one place any more than in the other.

That is, to the extent of about £445,000?—Yes. The next item complained of on that head is what is called the bringing down of the balances from the three credit accounts. The amounts as they originally appear at the top of the page contain the total amount of the overdrafts on the credit accounts there mentioned. What was done was to deduct a part of that and to bring it down under the general head where securities come.

If it was the case that to the extent of the sums so brought down there were securities held against that part of the accounts, was there anything wrong in bringing them down?—I should say not. I do not know whether or not there were securities held against these.

Were you led to suppose there were securities held against these?—In so far as that there were certain securities valued.

Was this the scheme of the alteration that the unsecured part

118

Evidence for Prosecution.

of the overdraft was left at the top, and that the part for which securities were held was taken down with its securities under the head of securities?—It does not follow.

Was that what was done?—The balance might have been covered as well.

But was that what was done—it was brought down under the head of securities?—I understood that the portion that was brought down was covered by stocks.

And if it was covered by stocks it was all right?—I consider so, in my opinion.

The other might be covered by personal obligations, cash credits, bills, or securities other than stocks?—Quite so.

The Lord Advocate put it to you once or twice that these were Government stocks and the like. I observe in the published balance issued the enumeration is not limited to Government stocks; it is Government stocks, Exchequer bills, railway and other stocks. If there were stocks held against the parts which were so brought down, was it not quite a proper denomination to put them under other stocks?—I consider so.

Did any of the alterations which you have described and explained, or any of the alterations which were made upon your scrolls, affect the profit and loss at all?—No.

They did not affect the result of the accounts or the balance of the accounts as to profit and loss?—No.

Or as to reserve?—Or as to reserve.

Or as to capital?—Or as to capital.

So from what you have said, the alterations which were made did not affect one of the amounts which entered the published balance as liabilities to partners?—Quite so.

Now, those three things which you say were not affected by the alterations, viz., the capital account, £1,000,000, the reserve fund, £450,000, and the profit and loss, £142,095, are the same in the published abstract as they are in the balance ledger signed by the Directors?—The same. They were not affected in any way by any of the things which I have explained. I signed the published balance as correct in 1877 and 1878. That balance was what I may call an abstract of the original scroll abstract.

That is to say, it epitomised further what had been already epitomised in the scroll abstract?—Just so.

Is it the case that you have lost the sheet of the balance applicable to 1877?—Yes, that is a clean copy; I cannot find it.

Are you able to give the same full explanations about 1877 that you have now given about 1878?—Not so well.

Have you any doubt that the explanations which I have now got from you as to the different entries I have asked you about would be equally applicable to 1877?—On the same lines.

By the LORD JUSTICE-CLERK—Are you quite sure that the

The City of Glasgow Bank Trial.

entries were on the same lines in 1877? You said otherwise yesterday. If the £973,000 was treated in the same way in 1877 as in 1876 you may be right?—The explanation that I made was that the first sheet was ignored, that is to say, the £973,000 was ignored, and the other sums put in.

By Mr. BALFOUR—With that exception, was there any other difference in the principle, except that the £973,000 was treated as you have explained?—Not that I recollect of; and I may add that the sums that were put in were simply following out the £973,000 entry.

Did they include it?—They must have done so.

Did it receive effect in 1877, although it received effect with something added to it? Is that it?—Quite so.

By the LORD JUSTICE-CLERK—You told us yesterday that the figures that were inserted in 1877 in order to fill the place of the £973,000 were not in the books?—Yes.

And they were not in the books?—They were not in the books.

Therefore that sum was not stated in the same way as in 1876?—Quite so.

Therefore you must qualify your answer to that effect?—Quite so.

By Mr. BALFOUR—Subject to that qualification they were on the same lines?—Yes.

By the year 1878 had you not for the first time got prepared a general printed scroll sheet to fill up the various items?—For 1877.

For the first time?—For the first time.

And it was upon that sheet that you made the entries which you have explained to us in 1878 and also in 1877?—Quite so.

By 1876 you had not, I think, got that large and complete sheet prepared?—No.

And in 1876 was your general balance got by superinducing the balances from the branches and the correspondents' books on to the head office weekly balance?—Quite so.

The principle of making out the balance was still the same?—Still the same.

The total balance of the Bank was got from, first, the weekly balance at the head office; second, the weekly balance at the branches; and third, the information from correspondents?—Yes.

But, not having the big sheet in 1876, you wrote the entries applicable to the two latter heads on to the weekly balance of the head office?—Yes; wrote them together on the one sheet.

The totals?—Yes. [Shown No. 130.] That is the head office weekly balance.

And it was the basis on which the others were superinduced?—Yes.

Evidence for Prosecution.

What is No. 133?—The branch weekly balance.

What was the paper from which you got the entries applicable to the correspondents?—That is embraced in 130.

Does it come to this, that the weekly balance applicable to branches has also upon it the information relative to correspondents?—Yes.

So that your balance of 1876 was made up from 130 and 133?—Yes.

Now, I want to know a little more particularly about 128 [abstract of accounts at head office on 7th June] and its predecessors. You said yesterday that you took the scroll abstract to a meeting at which Mr. Potter and the Manager were present?—Yes.

Was the scroll abstract which you took to that meeting, as prepared by yourself, written entirely in black ink?—It was.

You have no doubt about that?—I have no doubt about it.

That the scroll abstract that you took to those gentlemen was written entirely in black ink?—Yes.

You said that alterations were made upon it in red ink?—Not at the meeting; I did not say that.

Did the scroll abstract which you so took to the meeting, and which was written entirely in black ink, contain the entries brought from the sheet applicable to branches and to correspondents?—Yes.

So that it focussed in black ink all the entries applicable to head office, branches, and correspondents?—Yes.

Where did that meeting take place?—In the Manager's room. No one was present but Mr. Potter, the Manager, and myself. The meeting took place between the annual balance day and the annual meeting day—that is, between the first Wednesday of June and the first Wednesday of July. I cannot give the date more particularly.

Were any alterations made in writing on that document at that meeting?—I would take the different alterations and give effect to them in the balance sheet.

Were any alterations made in writing at that meeting upon the black ink scroll that you took to it?—Yes.

What alterations were made, and in what kind of ink?—The sheet is not here at all.

Do you not recollect?—It would be all in black ink or pencil.

By the LORD JUSTICE-CLERK—The alterations?—Yes.

By Mr. BALFOUR—I thought you said yesterday that the alterations were made in red ink?—No; I said the effect of the alterations.

Are you satisfied now that the alterations made on the black ink scroll were made in black ink or pencil, and not at all in red ink?—Yes.

The City of Glasgow Bank Trial.

Wm. Morison. Was it done in black ink at the meeting, or in pencil at the meeting, or do you not recollect which?—I have no recollection.

Then you don't recollect whether it was done in black ink or pencil, or partly in the one and partly in the other?—Quite so; it might have been either; I would rather say pencil.

Or both?—Or both.

Now, where is that document which you say you took to that meeting?—It would be destroyed when this one was made.

Then 128 is not the document that you had at that meeting?—Oh, no.

Do you recollect what became of that document?—I have no doubt it would be destroyed when a clean copy was made.

You have no doubt, but do you recollect?—I have no doubt I destroyed it.

Who would destroy it?—I would destroy it.

Do you recollect of that, or do you merely suppose it?—I remember I did destroy it.

By the LORD JUSTICE-CLERK—From what is the lithograph taken?—From this (128).

When was it made?—After the meeting.

Did you write out again your black ink, and then put on it the red ink alterations?—Yes.

That is what you did?—Yes.

By Mr. BALFOUR—Does it come to this, that 128 shows in black ink what you took to the meeting, and the one you say you destroyed, and what is shown in red ink on 128 shows the alterations that were made at the meeting?—I think there was a mistake made yesterday as to the red ink markings on this sheet (128). The red ink markings simply bring the two abstracts together.

Do you say, or do you not, that 128 contains in black ink what was in the abstract you took to the meeting in black ink, and that the red ink on 128 shows the alterations that you were directed to make? Do you now say that?—No.

Then, does 128 show anything in red ink which was altered in black ink at the meeting which you say you had with Mr. Potter and the Manager?—This sheet (128) is the effect of the meeting.

Do the red ink markings, or any of them, on 128 show the alterations made at the meeting?—They must have been brought together before that time.

Are not the entries applicable to the branches only brought in in red ink on 128?—Yes.

Is not this just what you explained a little ago—that the abstract of 1876 was made by taking as the basis the weekly abstract of the head office, and superinducing the entries relative to the branches and correspondents?—Quite so.

Evidence for Prosecution.

And are not those entries relative to the branches and correspondents superinduced in red ink upon 128?—Yes.

Then your evidence yesterday was not correct?—Will you allow me to explain that we were referring to the three sums of £200,000, £100,000, and £450,000?

By the LORD JUSTICE-CLERK—You told us yesterday that your original black ink abstract which you took to the meeting was a proper abstract made up from the books, and was correct. Do you still say that?—Yes; this one.

And all the red ink alterations were made upon the instructions of Mr. Potter and the Manager?—In so far as these figures are concerned—the £200,000, the £100,000, and the £450,000.

There were other alterations made in red ink which you made yourself, in order to make your original abstract entirely accurate?—In order to bring the two abstracts together.

Which two?—The branches one and the head office one.

You had done that; this original abstract was bringing them together?—Oh, no.

I understood yesterday you told us the way in which you prepared your abstract for the Directors was, first, that you prepared the abstract of the balances at the head office, and then the superintendent of branches prepared his abstract. Did you take the two and put them together in a general abstract which you took to the Directors?—Yes.

The thing you took to the Directors was the general abstract embracing both branches and head office?—Yes.

And on that the red ink alterations were made?—Yes.

By Mr. BALFOUR—Do you desire to correct anything you said yesterday or not?—I think I said yesterday that the alterations on the figures were made in red ink. If I said that these figures —£200,000, £100,000, and £450,000—were made in red ink I made a mistake.

You have told us that what you took to the Directors contained both the entries as to the branches, and the other entries in black ink?—Yes.

128 contains the entries relative to the branches in red ink; why is that?—This is not the sheet submitted.

But if you had the entries relative to the branches in black ink on the original scroll, why did you put the entries relative to the branches in red ink in the second scroll?—In order to make it more distinct.

For whom?—For myself.

Did you not know what related to the branches without putting it in red ink?—But it was clearer; it brought out where the two were put together easier.

If it was clearer to have it in red ink in the second scroll for yourself, why did you put it in black ink for the Manager and

The City of Glasgow Bank Trial.

Wm. Morison. Mr. Potter?—It was quite a different sheet altogether, the one presented in 1876.

Was not this (128) the first scroll you ever made out?—Not the one I submitted to the Directors.

Then, did you copy in red ink on 128 about the branches what you had written in black ink on the original scroll?—Yes.

Have you no further explanation of why you did that than that it was clearer for yourself?—No.

You say the thing you were told to do was to bring down £200,875, £100,300, and £450,000 from the top of the page to the bottom?—Yes.

That alteration you have shown on 128 not in red, but in black ink?—Yes.

Then does it come to this, that you have not shown anywhere in red ink the alterations which you say were made by direction of the Manager and Mr. Potter?—There is nothing here (128) in red ink that I was desired to alter.

Then upon any sheet, either the first or the second, none of the alterations were carried out in red ink?—No.

And the only thing that is in red ink is what relates to the branches, which was not an alteration?—Quite so.

Did you not say yesterday that some part at all events of the alterations had been given effect to in red ink?—On this sheet?

Upon any sheet?—Not in 1876.

I am only speaking of 1876?—There is no alteration.

But neither upon the original sheet nor upon this sheet have you given effect to any of the alterations that you were directed to make in red ink?—Quite so.

Do you adhere to the statement that this is not the first abstract you made?—Yes.

What is it that is different in black ink in 128 from what you took to the meeting in black ink on the scroll which you say you tore up?—These amounts are brought down from credit accounts.

The three sums which I have mentioned?—Yes.

By the LORD JUSTICE-CLERK—If that is not the thing you took to the meeting in 1876, what is it, and when did you make it?—This was copied after the meeting.

By Mr. BALFOUR—What led to its being made?—This was the first year that I had got it printed.

Why did you not just give effect to the alterations in red ink on the black ink scroll which you took to the meeting in the same way that you did in 1878?—It was simply for my own information that I put them in red ink at any time.

And the only thing you put in red ink here was what you had put in black at the first?—Yes.

Evidence for Prosecution.

You did not put in red anything you were told to alter?— **Wm. Morison.** Not in the 1876 one.

Were not these three amounts which appear here in black ink also written originally in that place in black ink in the scroll you took to the Directors?—No; they were not there at all in the scroll I took to the Directors.

I think you said that another particular in which this scroll differs from the scroll that you took to the Directors was in bringing out on the right-hand page only balances instead of the £455,000 on the line?—Yes.

You said you had in the original the items which the Lord Advocate put to you, and that here you brought out a balance of £1346 16s. 6d.?—Yes.

What is that balance?—The balance in general ledger on deposit accounts, and the total amount of deposit receipts.

Then is that entry of £1346 a correct balance taken from the books?—It is taken from the general ledger.

Does that correspond to the sum which I read out to you from the statements of 1878 of £33,000 odds?—Yes; it is on the same principle. It is the balance from the general ledger.

So that this is an entry brought from the books of the Bank? —Yes.

And showing correctly the balance by deducting the larger from the smaller sums of the debtor and creditor sides?—Quite so.

Then, as to the sum which you say was carried down; that, I think, is just brought down to the head of securities in the same way as the corresponding items I asked you about in 1878? —Yes.

Did you understand that there were securities held for these amounts?—From the conversation I understood so.

And if there were securities held for these amounts, was it, in your judgment, quite right so to bring them down?—Quite right.

Securities of the nature of stocks?—Securities, and held absolutely by the Bank, so that they could sell them at any time.

And if there were securities of the nature of stocks held for those sums, it would be quite proper to class them under other stocks in the printed balance sheet?—Yes.

So that whether that was right or wrong depends upon a matter that you don't know?—Yes.

On the right-hand page of the scroll abstract for 1876, Dr. No. 2, I see you have a good deal of figuring, by which you bring out a result of £860,355?—Yes.

Is that the entry which was carried into the printed balance under head II. of the debtor side—bank notes in circulation in Scotland and the Isle of Man?—Yes.

Then that is quite correct?—Quite.

125

The City of Glasgow Bank Trial.

Wm. Morison.   In the red ink figuring under Dr. No. 3, near the foot of the left-hand page, and at the right-hand side of the page, there is a sum of £29,095.   Does that sum represent your own notes which had been got in exchange for the notes of other banks between the afternoon of the Wednesday and the commencement of business on the Thursday, as you explained with reference to the £89,031?—No.

What is it?—There is a reference here to it, " Notes remitted by branches."

Was that sum remitted from the branches?—I have no doubt of it.

But were these notes then in the hands of the Bank?—They would be in transmission.

That means going from the branches to the head office?—Yes, and belonging to the head office.

But when a note is passing from a branch to the head office, it is in the hands of the Bank; it is not in circulation?—No.

Then, if these notes were in that position, was it not a perfectly proper deduction to make?—I should say so.

If you had stated these notes as in circulation you would have stated what was wrong, if they were going between a branch and the head office?—That is my opinion.

I suppose that, notwithstanding any alterations that were made upon the scroll sheet, the profit and loss, the capital, and the reserve fund are unaffected, just as you explained, as to 1878 and 1877?—Yes.

If the notes were actually in transit, they were more clearly out of circulation than those of the £89,031, which were withdrawn?—Yes.   I was a shareholder of the Bank, and continued to be so till its stoppage.

By Mr. ASHER—The books were balanced annually as at the first Wednesday in June.   The first Wednesday in June, 1876, was the 7th, in 1877 the 6th, and in 1878 the 5th.   I wrote up the entries in the balance ledger, which was docqueted by the Directors.   The balance so entered in the balance ledger showed the balances appearing in three separate books—the weekly balance book, the branches balance book, and the correspondents' balance book.   In that balance each branch was treated as a debtor to or creditor of the Bank merely.   There was only one sum entered opposite the name of each branch, representing the amount at the debit or at the credit of that particular branch. There did not appear in that balance ledger the amount of deposits at any branch, the bills discounted, or the cash in hand.

By the LORD JUSTICE-CLERK—Nor the transactions generally? —No.

It was only the result that you entered in your books?— Yes; simply the balance between the head office and the branch as a branch.

Evidence for Prosecution.

As if they had been customers of the Bank?—Yes.

By Mr. ASHER—You prepared the abstract of accounts?—Yes.

The balance ledger which I have just mentioned was the thing which was docqueted by the Directors?—Yes.

And to examine it, it was merely necessary to examine the balances in the three subordinate books I have mentioned?—Yes.

Did any one of the subordinate books show the state of accounts between the Bank and any individual customer?—No.

You were present at the examination of books by the Directors?—Yes.

Did the examination mentioned in the docquet refer merely to a comparison of the balances in the balance ledger with the balances in the weekly balance book, the agents' balance book, and the correspondents' balance book?—Quite so.

That was the only examination made?—The only one.

And with regard to 1876, 1877, and 1878, I understand you to say that the docquet is correct in saying that everything in the balance ledger is in accordance with the Bank's books?—Yes. I prepared the abstract of accounts. In 1876 I would commence the preparation of the abstract immediately after 7th June, when the books were balanced, and the abstract would be completed within perhaps a fortnight afterwards.

In making up that document did you make it from the balance ledger which had been docqueted by the Directors, or from other books?—From the weekly balance book and other books.

The balance ledger alone would not enable you to make up the abstract of accounts?—No.

You required to take the books showing the details of business at the various agencies, did you not; because in these abstracts you classed the deposits at the agencies along with the deposits at the head office, and the cash in hand at the agencies along with the cash in hand at the head office?—Yes.

And so with regard to bills and other accounts?—Yes.

Therefore the abstracts presented the state of the Bank's affairs as if the whole business at the head office, correspondents' offices, and agencies had been carried on under one roof?—Yes.

The draft abstracts were prepared in the form you have spoken to, and they were further epitomised for publication?—Yes. In 1876 the whole of the work of making up the balance and preparing the abstract balance sheet for publication was completed before the annual meeting. The annual meeting took place on the first Wednesday of July, which was the 5th.

Was the balance ledger generally docqueted by the Directors between the date down to which the books were balanced and the date of that meeting?—If I had got them to sign it.

The City of Glasgow Bank Trial.

And they generally were got to sign it at some time during that interval, were they not?—If possible.

You attended at the meeting at which the books were examined?—Yes.

If a Director happened to be absent from the meeting at which the examination of the books took place, did he generally sign the balance sheet after he came back?—Yes.

Was there any separate attendance of officials for the purpose of his making an examination if he had been absent before, or did he generally just attach his name to where the other Directors had signed?—He just signed the balance ledger at the usual place.

There was no second examination made by the Director who happened to be absent when the examination took place?—No. In 1877 also the abstract would be prepared within fourteen days after the first Wednesday of June, which was on the 6th. The annual meeting in that year was on the first Wednesday in July, which was on the 4th. In 1878, in like manner, the abstract would be prepared within a fortnight after the date when the books were balanced. The annual meeting in that year was on 3rd July. When the abstract balance which was to be published had been prepared, it was generally put into print, and I understand that a copy was sent to each Director.

But it was not the practice, I believe, to communicate the draft to the Directors?—In 1876 and in 1878 were the only times when I met the Directors for such a purpose.

You did not meet Mr. Salmond in 1876 or 1878 for that purpose?—I never met Mr. Salmond.

Or showed him the abstract balance sheet?—No.

Whom do you mean by the Directors that you met in 1876 and 1878?—In 1876 Mr. Porter, and in 1878 Mr. Stewart and Mr. Potter.

With that exception, was there ever submitted to any Director, to your knowledge, anything except the abstract printed for publication with the report?—No; not to my knowledge.

And you were the person who was engaged in the preparation of the draft, and converting it into the form in which it was published?—Yes.

And you held your position of accountant from 1871 down to the close?—Yes.

You were the custodier of the books of the Bank, except at the time when the weekly balance book, the branch balance book, and the correspondents' balance book were submitted to the Directors for comparison with the balance ledger once a year; were the Directors in the habit of examining the details of the books of the Bank?—Not that I know of.

And you were the custodier of the books?—Of the one I was.

Of which one?—Of the weekly balance book.

Photo.]   [*J. Horsburgh.*

Mr. Asher,
Counsel for Robert Salmond.

Evidence for Prosecution.

So that the weekly balance book was not submitted at the Wm. Morison. weekly meetings?—Not that I am aware of.

You spoke of a private cash book, No. 6, in which an entry of £973,300 was made; were you the custodier of that book?—Yes.

Did you ever show that book to Mr. Salmond?—No.

Did he ever see it, so far as you know?—Not that I know of.

Or any of the Directors?—No; I don't think they did.

Do you happen to know that during the years 1876, 1877, and 1878 Mr. Salmond was much in the country, and was frequently absent from the meetings of the Bank?—He was for a year or so, but I could not mention the dates.

During these years did you see him at the Bank at all, except when he was there at the weekly meetings he attended?—Very seldom.

You are aware that he resided in Ayrshire?—Yes.

Do you remember that Mr. Salmond was not at the Bank at the time the books were examined in 1878 by the other Directors?—I am quite certain he was not.

And do you remember that he did not come to the Bank until after the general meeting?—Yes.

Then, I see his name attached to the docquet in the books in 1878; was his signature put there at the same time as those of the other Directors in that year?—Mr. Potter and Mr. Salmond signed that docquet both on the same day.

When was that?—I would say it would be after the annual meeting.

Was there any examination of the books made then?—No.

I believe you cannot remember as to the years 1876 and 1877? Your memory does not enable you to say whether Mr. Salmond was there at that time or not?—No; I cannot recollect about that.

By the DEAN OF FACULTY—Mr. Robert Stronach became Manager of the Bank in 1875. I cannot give the month. I cannot recollect whether it was at the end of the year.

You mentioned yesterday the transference of an account of Smith, Fleming & Co. from one heading to another, which brought it under your jurisdiction; that took place in June, 1875?—It was of that date.

You stated certain reasons for that transference which seemed to me to be suppositions on your part?—Quite so.

Were you informed in any way of the reason of the transference?—No.

Were you aware that, about that time, an agreement had been come to between Smith, Fleming & Co. and the Bank, whereby their account was put upon a new footing, under which they were to pay a certain percentage upon the debt?—I have heard so. I know of that from having made up an account with that statement in it.

I

129

The City of Glasgow Bank Trial.

Wm. Morison. Was the entering into that agreement the ground for the change in the heading of the account, and the transference of it from the cheque box to the accountant's department?—I cannot say.

The knowledge of such agreements did not, except incidentally, come before you?—No.

[Shown No. 127, abstract of accounts in general ledger on 6th June, 1877.] In that paper you have got printed matter, figures in black ink, figures in red ink, and figures in pencil. Is the whole of the writing and the whole of the figuring in that paper in your handwriting?—Yes.

Is that paper the first scroll that was prepared of the abstract of accounts for the year 1877?—Yes.

Did you submit it to the Manager and the Directors?—Not to the Directors—to the Manager.

Did you write what we have here—the black and the red—before you had any consultation with the Manager or the Directors?—No.

What do the calculations in pencil on the right-hand side refer to?—There is a part of it apparently in connection with the heading I. of the assets in the abstract.

Can you tell me from that paper what was the amount of City Bank notes in circulation in Scotland in 1877?—Yes; £840,004.

And the amount that was published in the abstract was £763,894?—Yes.

There was thus a difference between the fact and what was stated in the abstract of £76,110?—I will take it for granted; I cannot check it here.

You prepared that abstract?—Yes.

And you inserted these figures, £763,894?—Yes.

Where did you get them?—I would require to get the other sheet before I could tell you that.

I think you will be able to get it from this sheet (No. 127, abstract for 1877), all of which contains your own figuring. About three-fourths down the right-hand page of that abstract you have the true figures, £840,004. A little above that you will find, also in your own figures, £860,355, and underneath that you put £840,004, being, as we have seen, the true circulation for 1877. The first of the figures now given, £860,355, was the circulation for the previous year; and in comparing the two you find that there is a difference of £20,355?—Yes.

Thereafter, if you refer to the black ink markings in the middle of the same page, under the heading " Circulation," you seem to have gone on to compare the four years 1874, 1875, 1876, and 1877?—Yes.

When did you make the pencil markings on that sheet?—I

130

could not well tell you that. I presume the most of them Wm. Morison. had been made when consulting with the Manager.

Was not the whole of this calculation, until you brought out the sum that is published, gone through by you before you consulted with a human being? Is it not the result of the working of your own mind?—No; certainly not.

By the Lord Justice-Clerk—When do you say you made these pencil markings?—I could not say for the whole of them.

Was it after the general meeting or before?—It would be long before the general meeting.

By the Dean of Faculty—To the left of the black ink figures, under the heading " Circulation," in the middle of the page, are certain red ink figures, 214m, etc., meaning £214,000, £176,000, £197,000, and £126,000; what are these figures?—That appears to be the difference betwixt the circulation on the Saturday and the circulation as shown on each annual balance day. The red figures under " Circulation" on the right-hand side of No. 127A indicate the Saturday issue of notes. The Wednesday issue is in black ink figures, £840,000 for 1877. I deducted the £714,000 from the £840,000, bringing out £126,000. I see the entry of £21,000 in pencil below the £714,000. I don't think that £21,000 represents the entry further up, "B of M actual issue." I cannot say what that is. It has no relation to the Bank of Mona.

Is that £21,000 the £21,000 which you have added in pencil below the £714,000?—I cannot follow it. I deducted the £735,000 from the £840,004, bringing out £105,000.

Then you say this—" Say, make it £100,000 less"; were you experimenting then?—Probably so.

What did you mean by " make it £100,000 less"?—I cannot tell you; it was not I that was experimenting.

But it is your writing?—Yes, it is.

And it is your thinking which this writing indicates?—No.

Whose thinking is it?—The Manager's.

Was the Manager looking over your shoulder and telling you to write " make it £100,000 less"?—Yes.

Then this paper was made in the Manager's presence?—Lots of it, and that amongst it.

Do you swear that, Mr. Morison?—I do.

Is there anything here your own original composition?—The black figures are taken from the books.

That is all you acknowledge to as being your own?—Yes.

Now, if you go to the right-hand side of the same page, immediately above the red ink figures £840,004, you will find an experiment of deducting the £100,000?—Yes.

And there is brought to the left £740,000?—Yes.

That was trying to see how it would look by taking off £100,000?—It must have been.

The City of Glasgow Bank Trial.

Wm. Morison. Apparently you dropped that experiment, and you took to another; for if you look down on the right-hand page, about three inches from the bottom, you will find in pencil the true figure £840,004, and there is deducted from that £46,110?—Yes.

What is that £46,110?—Notes received at exchange on Thursday morning in Glasgow.

And you deducted that from the true sum in circulation?—Yes.

And you brought out £793,894, the sum published in the abstract being £763,894. Now, how was £30,000 taken off the £793,000?—I cannot explain that.

Did you not sign the balance sheet as correct?—Yes.

On the left-hand page you will find, under head III., "gold and silver coin on hand, and notes of other banks on hand," bringing out a total of £921,018 0s. 2d.?—Yes.

And there is this pencil marking in your handwriting, "Why should this be so much?" Did that occur to your own mind, or was it suggested to you by anybody?—It was suggested to me.

And you wrote it down?—Yes.

"Why should this be so much?"—Oh! I beg your pardon; I understand what you mean now; I was astonished to see the amount of gold and silver at the branches when it should have been at head office.

Then this astonishment was your own?—It was.

You see £30,000 in pencil deducted from the £921,018?—Yes.

Bringing out £891,018?—Yes.

Where did you get that £30,000?—I got it from the Manager.

What is it?—I cannot tell.

Is it not an answer to your own question, why this should be so large?—No.

Did you not mean that it should be made less when you expressed your astonishment?—I simply did what I was told.

Did you ask the Manager where the £30,000 came from?—No.

Did you form an idea at the moment whether it was an invention of his, or whether it represented an existing sum of money?—All that I know about it is that it is taken off both sides.

Did you not ask him what the £30,000 represented which is deducted from the coin in hand?—There might have been a conversation, but I cannot recollect about it.

You certified that that £30,000 was correct when you signed this abstract?—Yes.

Then you took the £30,000 from the left-hand side to the right-hand side, and deducted it from the £793,894, and brought out the published sum of £763,000?—That is so.

Evidence for Prosecution.

And then you deduct £30,000 from the coin on hand, £921,018, and bring out £891,018 as the coin on hand?—Yes. That was published in the abstract balance sheet.

And that is less than the true amount by £30,000?—Yes.

Now, I ask again, is not the paper that I hold in my hand the working out of the operations of your own mind before a human being saw it?—No.

And were not all these experiments yours, and no other person's?—No.

The paper is without any summation; it never was presented complete to anybody?—Oh, yes, it is summed up. Both sides of it are summed up. I cannot tell when it was summed up without going over the summations.

You have said that the Manager told you to put in certain things, and that certain things were your own; why did you tell Mr. Balfour that you did not remember anything about the balance of 1877?—I did not say I did not remember anything about it.

You said there was a sheet wanting, and you could not give any explanations?—Yes.

I show you the abstract for 1878; at the left-hand you see a number of pencil figurings not obliterated yet, in the fourth column; these figures are yours?—Yes.

Was this paper covered with calculations of the same sort that we see in 1877?—I cannot tell you.

Any figuring that was here was in your handwriting?—Yes.

You recollect about 1878; do you recollect of making calculations in regard to the various items to be entered in the abstract?—Yes; I made calculations.

And they were upon this paper?—Yes.

Who obliterated the pencil markings here?—I cannot tell you.

Did you do it?—I might have done it; I cannot tell.

By the LORD ADVOCATE—I understand that in the balance abstracts furnished to you by the superintendent of branches there were entered the whole deposits at the branches, the bills floating, and all other details?—Yes.

The same as in the case of the head office?—Yes.

And you carried all these deposits, and bills, and others, into the final balance sheet?—Yes.

But in the balance ledger nothing is given except the balance at each branch?—Yes; the item of balance at each branch.

Not the details bringing it out?—Not the details.

Did you at the making up of any of these three balance sheets for 1876, 1877, or 1878, of your own accord alter the balances so as not to be in conformity with the books under your charge? —That is personally you mean?

Yes?—No.

The City of Glasgow Bank Trial.

Wm. Morison. You were responsible for keeping the books?—Yes.

But did you ever make up or complete a balance sheet without the aid and sanction of the Manager?—Never.

In bringing down to the heading No. III. the balances from credit accounts and others, I think you said that you had no knowledge which would have enabled you to say that that was a right thing to do?—I had no knowledge of the securities.

Or whether there were securities?—Or whether there were securities.

But you certified the abstract as completed, bringing these down, although you had not that knowledge?—Yes.

Upon what, then, did you rely in signing that abstract or balance sheet containing such entries?—I relied on the alterations made by the Directors.

Including the Manager?—Including the Manager, of course.

The Directors, so far as you have spoken to them?—Yes.

You have said that, in your opinion, where a debt is due in the form of an overdraft upon a current account or a bill, and there is security held by the Bank sufficient to cover that, in making out a balance sheet, the Directors, or the Manager, or yourself, would be warranted in entering that not as a debt on the one side, with security upon the other, but simply as an asset of that amount?—Simply an asset.

Do you think that would fairly inform a shareholder of the Bank of the state of the Bank?—Do you refer to the sums taken down?

Yes?—They were simply taken down from the one heading to the other; the securities, if any, would still have been there.

Suppose the Bank had lent five millions, and they held five millions of securities, would it be right to enter these as five millions lent, with securities against them, or simply as an asset of five millions?—As an asset.

Of five millions?—They are all assets; all that side are assets.

You see no difference between these two things?—No.

Suppose the security were turning out bad within a week after the publication of the balance sheet, would the balance sheet be true in that case?—It would not be true after they were bad.

You said that the alterations you made upon the accounts did not alter the balance?—They did not alter the stock account, profit and loss, and reserve.

Do you think that an entry in a balance sheet is legitimate, leaving out entries, so long as you don't affect the result?—Oh, no.

Those entries that were taken down, I understand, only appear as so taken down in that scroll balance sheet, and in the Wm. Morison. abstract which you published?—Yes.

Do they anywhere appear in the books of the Bank as so dealt with?—No.

Or in the balance ledger?—No.

You said Mr. Stronach made a remark to you in 1878 that he hoped it would not be done again, or that he would not require to do it again; what did he refer to?—I understood it to be some settlement of James Morton & Co.'s affairs.

What was it that it would not be necessary to do again?—To understate the bills payable, and, of course, the foreign and colonial credits.

Did you understand why he hoped it would not be necessary to do it again?—I understood that it was to be a settlement of James Morton & Co.'s affairs.

Did you think he was doing a right thing in so understating the bills payable and the foreign and colonial credits?—No.

Why did you think it was not right?—Because the amount in the balance sheet did not correspond with the sum in the books.

Did you believe that he held securities against it?—Yes.

Was it a wrong thing to enter the bills payable so, even if he held securities?—Yes, in so far as it did not correspond with the Bank books.

And did you understand him then to allude only to its not corresponding with the Bank books?—Quite so.

If you are right in your view, why did its non-correspondence with the Bank books make it a wrong thing to tell a share-holder?—Because the amount shown to the shareholders differed from what was in the books.

If you were right in your view, what harm did the share-holders take from not seeing what was in the books, and seeing what was in the abstract instead?—It understates their liabilities to the public.

It concealed their liabilities from the public?—It certainly concealed them.

Do you think, or do you not think, that it is of importance to the public or to shareholders to have a truthful statement of the liabilities of a bank?—A truthful statement.

According to the books?—According to the books.

Is it important to them or not?—It should be important; it must be.

Important as influencing their judgment as to the state of the Bank?—Quite so.

Does the amount of these things not affect the credit of the Bank?—I should say so.

And do you still say that it was a legitimate thing to reduce

The City of Glasgow Bank Trial.

Wm. Morison. them, although there was security held?—You mean the bills payable?

Do you still say that it was a right thing, assuming there was security, to make them disconform to the books?—I never said that it was right.

In regard to bills payable; but do you say it is a right thing in regard to these credit balances to take them down in the way that was done—as securities; is it a right thing for the public or the shareholders?—I see no reason why they should not have been taken down if they held securities.

And entered in the books?—And entered in the books.

Is it a right thing to take them down without that appearing in the books, or the security appearing in the books as against them?—The practice was not to bring them down.

But you departed from the practice. Was that departure, in your opinion, justifiable when there was no entry in the books to show it?—I should have preferred an entry.

Why should you have preferred that?—Because it would have made the amount agree with the general ledger.

Not because it was right, but only because it would make the amount agree with the general ledger?—Because the amount would then agree with the general ledger.

Who suggested that departure from the general practice?—In 1876, Mr. Potter.

And thereafter?—It was continued.

By the LORD JUSTICE-CLERK—I made up an abstract balance for the head office, and the superintendent of branches made it up for the branches. I then made up a draft of a full abstract, combining the results of these. I then submitted that to the Manager. I did so in 1876. I became accountant in 1871. In 1876, at the annual balance, I had a conversation with the Manager and Mr. Potter, and certain alterations were made at their suggestion.

Was that the first time that any such interview had taken place?—Yes.

Were these alterations consequent on an examination of the books, or how did Mr. Potter and the Manager get at the sums you have mentioned?—They got certain statements from me or some of the other gentlemen.

Had they anybody else at the meeting with them?—No.

Had they come prepared with figures?—They had no figures.

Then the figures that appear in red ink were not suggested by them?—All the alterations were suggested by them.

Had they any figures to give you?—Yes.

Your statement is that they mentioned sums to you which they instructed you to put into your abstract?—Yes.

Were these sums which they had already jotted down, or which they had in their heads, or were they derived from an

Evidence for Prosecution.

examination of the books at the time?—I got certain information Wm. Morison.
for them from certain of the clerks.

You mean that at that meeting they asked you for some information?—Yes.

And that you went and got it?—Yes.

Now, what information was that?—As to the amount of the bills payable. The full amount of them was in my abstract, but they wanted information as to the separate accounts forming the gross amount of which this sum was composed.

For what purpose?—It must have been in order to see if they could make any deductions from it.

Was it to see whether your sum total was correct or not?—Oh, no.

You understood at the time that it was to see if they could make any deduction from it?—At the time.

And you did get the details of the bills payable?—Yes.

Did they make a deduction from the bills payable?—They did. They deducted the £973,000.

What was the whole amount?—£2,288,673 17s. 1d. That was the amount appearing in my abstract, as taken from the books.

When did that £973,000 first appear, and what was the history of it up to 1876?—It was an entry or entries made in Mr. Alexander Stronach's time in June, 1873.

Where was it made?—First in the private cash book, and then in the general ledger, and then in the weekly balance book.

What was it?—I never got the particulars of it.

You said you were told to get the details of bills payable, and you understood the reason why they wanted the details to be that they might make some deduction from them. You also said that when you came back with the information they directed you to deduct £973,000. Is that right?—That is right.

Then what was that £973,000?—You cannot reconcile the figures as any portion of the £2,288,673.

But what did the £973,000 represent? What was the original of it?—It was an entry made the same as if certain bills payable had been taken out of the circle.

Who were the debtors in them?—I cannot speak to that unless I saw the memorandum, which is still to be found.

Surely you know well enough what it was?—No, I don't.

Well, the result was that they told you to strike out that £973,000 from bills payable, and you did so?—Yes.

What was the effect of that on your abstract?—To reduce the bills payable by that amount.

And the effect on the abstract was to diminish the liabilities of the Bank to that extent?—To that extent.

The City of Glasgow Bank Trial.

Now, you are quite sure that you were told to do that by the Manager and Mr. Potter?—Yes.

And did you do it in red ink?—No.

Why?—Because the amount was in the general ledger.

It was only the things that were not in the books that you put into red ink?—Yes.

Was there anything else they told you to do?—There are the three entries of Smith, Fleming & Co., etc. These stood in my abstract as credit accounts. That was the place I thought they ought to be in. They directed me to take down £751,775 of them. They were in their right place under credit accounts, and this corresponded with the books.

What was their reason for putting that under the other head? —I understood it was because they held certain stocks to that extent.

You mean that it was a good asset to the extent of the security held?—Yes.

And that they thought the £751,000 represented the security? —Yes.

Would that have been the right way of doing it if that had been the case, or were they not properly charged as in the credit accounts, whether there was security or no?—It would have been quite right; at least I don't see anything wrong in it had they made the entry.

Was the proper way of entering it as you did it at first?—The amount was in the credit accounts ledger as at 7th June.

How were you in the habit of dealing with sums appearing in the credit accounts where there was security granted for them?—The cash drawn out is simply shown.

But in your abstracts of the balances did you enter nothing under your credit account for which security was held?—We understand that all credit accounts are covered by security.

Then why should the fact of there being security for this part of the credit account alter the way of stating it?—I understood it was for stocks that were easily convertible into cash.

Is that any reason why it should not appear in the credit accounts?—None.

Was the reason not to reduce the apparent amount of the credit accounts?—It had that effect.

Was that not the object?—I cannot say.

Was that not your impression?—It increased the amount of advances which were easily convertible into cash, and reduced the amounts under the heading.

The effect was to reduce the apparent amount of the sums under credit accounts?—That was the effect of it.

So that the shareholders should not see that that £751,000 had been advanced under credit account; that is the effect of it?— That is the effect of it.

Evidence for Prosecution.

You won't say that that was the reason of it?—I could not say.

Did the Manager or Mr. Potter suggest any other reason for it?—That is the only one that I mentioned before—that it would be brought down under the heading of stocks, thereby increasing the apparent assets under that head.

Do you know of any other instance where sums advanced on credit accounts with security were placed under that head?—Not taken from credit accounts in the same way.

It is the only time you ever knew it done?—The only time.

You are quite sure that that was directed by the Manager and Potter?—Perfectly.

Did you make that alteration in red ink?—It is not made here in red ink.

Where is the alteration?—[Shown.] It is just under the heading "Railway and other stocks and debentures." It is in black ink there.

Then you say that this thing upon which the red ink marks are is not the original abstract that you made?—No.

Not the one that was altered in terms of their instructions?—No.

And you don't know where it is?—No, I do not.

What is this [No. 127]?—It is the clean copy of it. It would be made as soon after the other as I could.

You made it up, and altered it in red ink yourself in order to be ready for the ultimate abstract?—Yes. The red ink markings, you will observe, are simply bringing the head office abstract and the branches abstract together.

Were you told or did you understand that this conversation with the Manager and Potter was to be confidential?—I never was instructed so. Nothing was said to me on the subject.

You did not make any alteration on those accounts in the books that you have spoken to in consequence of what the Directors or the Manager had said to you in 1876?—No.

But in 1877 you did not repeat in your abstract the entry of the sum of £973,300?—No.

You omitted it?—Yes.

Why?—Because there were other sums adopted instead of it.

I want to know why you omitted the £973,300, and why you put in new sums? Were you told to do it?—Yes, by Mr. Stronach. I would not like to say Mr. Potter; I am not certain of that for 1877.

Had you any meeting in 1877, as you had in 1876, with the Manager or Potter?—I am not certain of 1877; I would not like to speak to it.

But that alteration in 1877 was made by the directions of Stronach?—Yes.

And no reason was given for it?—No.

The City of Glasgow Bank Trial.

Wm. Morison. Are you sure?—There was no special reason given for it.

But the effect was that these sums were entered in the book and substantially filled up the amount of the £973,300, although apparently under different heads?—Quite so.

Did these new sums represent any new transactions?—Yes; a certain amount deducted from the bills payable.

But the sums which you put in in order to deduct it from the bills payable, did they represent any real debts? You said yesterday they were not altogether fictitious?—The first amount deducted was cash lodged on credit account, £94,368 14s. 1d.

I don't want you to go through the whole of it, but the effect was that £1,333,000 was deducted from the bills payable instead of the £973,000?—Yes.

Next year the £973,000 was restored, and this sum of £1,333,000 disappeared from the abstract?—Yes.

All that was by direction of the Manager?—Yes.

With regard to the cross entries, the sum of £973,300 appears on both sides of the account?—Yes.

What is the effect of that?—It reduces the amount of the indebtedness of the Bank to that extent, and on the other hand it reduces the amount of the assets.

They balance each other?—Yes.

But if they are correct entries, you say they are rightly entered in the abstract?—They are in the abstract because they are in the general ledger.

What was the general effect of the alterations in 1876 on the position of the Bank?—By putting in the balance, or balances rather, of the deposit accounts, and the balance of the credit accounts, reducing on the one side the assets of the Bank, and on the other the liabilities. The £973,300 entry did the same on both sides.

It was to show a smaller amount of assets, and a smaller amount of liabilities than the actual fact?—Yes.

Not affecting, however, the profit and loss account?—No. Of course the £751,000 entry did not alter the liabilities at all.

With regard to securities, I suppose that sums that were fully covered are entered as assets in the credit accounts?—They are entered whether they are secured or not.

Then what notice do you take of securities in your abstracts—in your balances?—They are not referred to at all; there are simply the figures given.

When a debt is wholly unsecured, and the debtor is not supposed to be good for it, it goes into bad or doubtful debts, I suppose?—It should do.

Or suspense account?—Or suspense account.

But no notice is ever taken of securities in the abstract?—No. There is a register of securities, but I do not consult it in making up my abstract. I have no concern with it whatever.

Evidence for Prosecution.

Therefore, whether there were or were not securities for the **Wm. Morison.** sums you have been speaking to, you had no means of knowing?
—None.

Could you have ascertained from the securities book, if you had chosen, whether there was security for the £973,300?—If the law secretary had shown me the book, but I don't know that he would have shown it to me. The book was in his custody.

CHARLES SAMUEL LERESCHE.

By the SOLICITOR-GENERAL—I have been secretary of the City **C. S. Leresche.** of Glasgow Bank since 1870. I was appointed in October, 1870, and took charge in December. The Directors at the time I was appointed were Mr. Inglis, Mr. Potter, Mr. Salmond, Mr. Alexander Stronach, Mr. Lorraine, and Mr. James Nicol Fleming. Mr. Alexander Stronach resigned as a Director and also as the Manager of the Bank in 1875, and he was succeeded as Manager by his brother Robert, who was a Director *ex officio*. Mr. Lorraine died shortly after I left the Bank, in the beginning of 1871. Mr. Mackinnon had retired from the Bank a few months prior to my entering, and there were two Directors elected shortly before the next annual meeting. They were Mr. Stewart and Mr. Taylor. I could not tell from memory when James Nicol Fleming retired, but he was succeeded by Mr. Wright. My predecessor as secretary was Mr. Low, who is now dead. When I entered on my duties in 1870, Mr. Alexander Stronach spoke to me in a very marked manner, and told me that my predecessor, Mr. Low, had made himself obnoxious to the Directors by pushing himself forward, and asking for information about accounts which were in no way connected with his department, and that the feeling was so strong at the last that a letter which he had handed in to the Board in connection with these matters the Directors had refused to receive.

What effect had that on you or on your course of conduct after you became secretary?—Mr. Stronach spoke to me very plainly, and told me it was his own wish, as also the wish of the Directors, that I should just confine myself to my own department. The duties of the office of secretary were to take charge of the general correspondence of the Bank; to keep the minute book of the Directors, and to enter therein the minute of the weekly meeting of the Board; to take charge of certain properties in the Western States of America in which the Bank at that time was largely interested; and to answer inquiries from correspondents as to the financial position of local firms. The meetings of the Directors were held once a week. There was an agenda book kept, in which the business to be done

The City of Glasgow Bank Trial.

C. S. Leresche. was put on the one side, and the deliverance upon it in a rough form on the other. [Shown Nos. 554 and 556.] No. 554 is the agenda book commencing on 30th July, 1874, and No. 556 is the agenda book commencing on 7th December, 1876, and coming down to the date of the closing of the Bank. [Shown Nos. 100 and 101.] These are the minute books applicable to the period from 1st December, 1870, when the first of them commences, down to the closing of the Bank. The usual course of proceeding with regard to business to be brought before these meetings was that I went down to the Manager on the morning of each Thursday, and would ask him what business he would have to bring before the Board that day. He would tell me whether there were any letters of credit or cash credits or anything connected with the branches, whatever the business was; and he would give me the letters and any papers connected therewith. I would take these and commence entering them in the agenda book, and afterwards bring the book with them to the meeting. After the meeting, those letters that were connected with letters of credit, such as Smith, Fleming & Co.'s, I would generally take in to Mr. Morris; and sometimes I would take them back, and leave them with the Manager. Mr. Morris was the private secretary of the Manager. Where it is stated in any of the minutes that a letter was read, it was the practice when I was present really to have the letter read. That was always done. It was my duty as secretary to be present at the meetings. The names of the Directors present at the meetings were generally put down in the agenda book by the chairman for the time being. I see from the agenda book that the Directors present at the meeting on 23rd December, 1875, were Mr. Taylor, Mr. Stewart, Mr. Wright, Mr. Inglis, and Mr. Salmond. Mr. Robert Stronach, who was then Assistant Manager, was also present. Mr. Taylor was the chairman. I remember about that meeting.

What was the usual concluding part of the business at these meetings?—The reading of what was called the abstracts and statements.

Was there not the burning of notes which were to be cancelled?—That was done at any time.

When that required to be done was it not the last piece of formal business?—Yes.

On that occasion, 23rd December, 1875, were there notes which ought to have been burned?—Yes.

What happened when that item of business came on?—So far as I can remember, when these notes came forward to be burned they would say to me, "We will not take these up this week; we have some matters to talk over, and it can be postponed for another week." I would then retire from the meeting.

142

Evidence for Prosecution.

Was it at their request that you retired?—It was never said in so many words, but the usual custom was, after I had finished reading the abstracts and statements, I would say to the chairman, " That is all the business I have to bring forward," and the chairman would bow me out, and I would retire. It was an understood custom. When there was nothing else to be done, I would take the agenda book away with me ; but on other occasions they would say they had some matters to talk over, and would ask me to leave the agenda book. That was done on 23rd December, 1875. I would be called in afterwards. [Shown No. 206.] That is a letter which was handed to me when I came back, and which I was instructed to have engrossed in the minutes. It is a letter from Mr. Alexander Stronach containing his resignation on account of ill-health. At the meeting on 30th December, 1875, there were present Mr. Taylor, Mr. Potter, Mr. Stewart, Mr. Salmond, Mr. Inglis, and Mr. Wright. Mr. Alexander Stronach having retired, that was the whole Board at that time. On that occasion the burning of notes was again adjourned, and I again left the room, but I cannot say whether I left the agenda book behind me or not. The Board had a long deliberation that day. I should say it must have been two hours.

By the LORD JUSTICE-CLERK—Are you speaking from recollection alone?—I remember it, because 30th December was the occasion when the letter of the Manager was read accepting the appointment.

By the SOLICITOR-GENERAL—[Shown Nos. 208 and 209.] When I came back the letter No. 208 and the corresponding envelope No. 209 were handed to me by the chairman, who was Mr. Taylor. It is a letter from Mr. Robert Stronach to the Directors. [Letter read.]

City of Glasgow Bank,
Glasgow, 28th December, 1875.

The Chairman and Directors of the
    City of Glasgow Bank.

Gentlemen,—In thanking you for the offer of the managership of this Bank which you have kindly made to me, I beg to state my willingness to accept it. But before undertaking this responsibility, I deem it prudent to ask the Board to minute its approval of the policy which has been pursued of supporting several accounts of an unsatisfactory character since my brother discontinued personally to manage the Bank ; and, further, to appoint a committee to investigate and place on record what may be found to have been the exact position of these accounts and advances generally when my brother ceased to be Manager, and also to act and guide me in any important detail therewith connected, as I am in no wise responsible up to this date for the state of certain advances which I need not here particularise.

You will, I hope, admit the reasonableness of the precaution which this request involves ; and I feel you will the more readily

The City of Glasgow Bank Trial.

do this when you consider that whilst we are all hopeful that those advances may eventuate without loss, yet the working out of them must of necessity be a work of some time. And when you also consider that there may be changes in the Board during this time, and I should have to explain to new Directors what you know regarding my connection with the inception of these advances.— I am, gentlemen, your most obedient servant,

R. S. STRONACH.

Since that letter was read to the Board of Directors there has been no change in the directorate? The gentlemen who sat that day, with the exception of Mr. Robert Stronach, are the gentlemen at the bar?—Yes. Mr. Stronach's name is not in the agenda book that day, but I see from the minute book that he was present. [Shown No. 205.]

Is that a draft resolution which was handed to you by the chairman on the same occasion after you were recalled?—Yes. The first part of it is in Mr. Taylor's, and the last of it in Mr. Inglis's handwriting. It is—"A letter was read from Mr. Robert Summers Stronach, of date 28th December, 1875, accepting the office of Manager of the Bank, and the same having been considered and approved of, is ordered to be recorded in the minute book, and appoint all the members of the Board of Directors a committee to comply with his request. The Directors wish also to record on their own behalf the fact that the matters alluded to in the letter in question were not at any time brought before them by their late Manager." The three words "and approved of" in the first part of the document are also in Mr. Inglis's handwriting, besides the part at the end. In the agenda book, under date 18th February, 1875, there is an entry—"Appoint Messrs. Potter and Salmond a committee to assist the Manager in arranging the securities and advances connected with the late firm of James N. Fleming & Co., Calcutta, and Smith, Fleming & Co., London, with full powers."

Was that deliverance agreed to in your hearing, or after you had retired?—After I had retired.

Was it handed to you to be entered?—On this occasion I would be called up. That deliverance in the agenda book is in Mr. Taylor's handwriting. Being referred to agenda book under date 1st June, 1876—there were present that day Mr. Taylor, Mr. Potter, Mr. Salmond, Mr. Inglis, Mr. Wright, and the Manager. There is an entry on the right-hand page, near the bottom, as follows:—"The committee appointed 18th February, 1875, to look into the accounts of Smith, Fleming & Co., and J. N. Fleming & Co., reported that they had seen that these accounts had been put into shape." That entry was made by me. I was told to make it. Mr. Taylor was chairman.

Did he tell you to record it?—No; my recollection is that

Evidence for Prosecution.

Mr. Potter said the committee had looked into these accounts, and had put them into order, and he wished to have that recorded; and this minute I took down probably from what Mr. Potter said.

You heard Mr. Potter make that statement, but do you remember whether the direction was given more specially than that, or not?—It was just given verbally—"We wish to have that inserted in the minutes." It was inserted in the minutes from the agenda book. I did not ask that a draft should be made out; I just wrote it down. That deliverance is engrossed in the minute book of the Directors of the same date. In the agenda book on 22nd June, 1876, the sederunt is Mr. Taylor, chairman, Messrs. Stewart, Wright, and Potter, and the Manager. The last item of business on the left-hand page is "Appointment of committee to examine into the old accounts." The corresponding entry in the minutes of 22nd June is engrossed as follows:—"It was resolved to appoint Messrs. Taylor and Potter a committee to examine into certain old accounts of the Bank, and to assist the Manager in arranging these under one general heading, with full power." I cannot tell how that matter came up at the meeting of 22nd June; it came up after I retired. Either the book had been left, or I had brought up the book.

Do you remember the Manager saying anything while you were present on that occasion to the effect that he wished those old accounts looked into?—I do remember now. I would write this in probably just at the time when I was at the meeting. I do not recollect anything more that took place on that occasion. The Manager was desirous that certain old accounts of the Bank should be looked into.

It was on the suggestion of the Manager that the committee was appointed?—Yes.

Was any specification given of the accounts referred to, or were they just spoken of in that way?—Just in a general way. In the agenda book, under date 13th July, 1876, there were present Messrs. Inglis, Potter, Taylor, Stewart, and Wright. The sederunt is taken in pencil by myself; it had been omitted by the chairman. [Shown No. 213.] That is a letter by Mr. Scott, marked "Private," and addressed to Mr. Stronach, dated 12th July, 1876. It was read at the meeting of the 13th. Mr. Scott is a partner of John Innes Wright & Co. "J. I. W. & Co." in that letter is intended for John Innes Wright & Co. The deliverance of the Board upon that letter, in the agenda book, is in the handwriting of Mr. Inglis, and it is as follows:—"Mr. Potter and Mr. Wright appointed a committee with full powers to confer with the Manager as to the proposed re-arrangement, which is considered an advisable step; the committee to report to the Board when they consider necessary." The Mr.

The City of Glasgow Bank Trial.

C. S. Leresche. Wright there referred to, and appointed a member of the committee, is a member of the firm of John Innes Wright & Co. In the agenda book, under date 3rd August, 1876, there were present Mr. Stewart, chairman, Messrs. Potter, Wright, and Taylor, and the Manager. [Shown Nos. 214, letter, W. Glen Walker & Co. to J. Innes Wright, dated 26th July, 1876, and 215 and 216.] No. 215 is a letter from John Innes Wright & Co., dated 2nd August, 1876. I cannot say in whose handwriting it is; it appears to be in the same handwriting as the letter read at the previous meeting. That was the first piece of business that followed upon Mr. Scott's letter as to establishing a new firm. No. 216 is a letter from Mr. James Morton, dated 2nd August, produced and read at that meeting.

Was there any discussion of these letters in your hearing, or were they simply handed to you to be engrossed?—They were simply handed to me to be put up with the other letters referred to. In the agenda book, under date 17th August, 1876, there were present Mr. Stewart, chairman, Messrs. Wright, Taylor, and Potter, and the Manager. [Shown Nos. 217, 218, two letters, W. Glen Walker to R. Stronach, dated 14th August, 1876, and 219, letter, James Morton to the Bank, dated 16th August, 1876.] These are letters which are referred to in the agenda book, under the date of that meeting, at the foot of the left-hand page. I do not remember hearing those letters read at that meeting. [Shown No. 198.] That is a draft resolution, dated 21st August, 1876, in the handwriting of Mr. Robert Stronach, the Manager.

Was that handed to you by the Manager?—Yes; my recollection of it is that I was called down some days after the meeting of the 17th into the Manager's room, and I was handed this draft resolution. I was asked to bring my agenda book down, and enter it therein as under the date of the 17th. So far as I recollect, Mr. Taylor and Mr. Inglis were present when Mr. Stronach handed it to me; and my memory is confirmed by the fact that there are in Mr. Taylor's handwriting the words "Read and agreed to," and in Mr. Inglis's handwriting, "Insert in minutes deliverance of Board."

So you have no doubt that those two gentlemen were the two who were present?—That is the impression I have at present. The words at the side of the memorandum, "As referred to in the minute of 30th December, 1875," and "as referred to," are in my handwriting. The whole of the body of it is in the handwriting of Mr. Stronach, except two lines which come in, "And previously brought under the consideration of the Board by the present Manager," which is in the handwriting of Mr. Inglis. In the minutes of 17th August that memorandum is engrossed in full as I got it. There were present—Messrs. Stewart, Wright, Taylor, Potter, and Stronach. That minute was

146

Evidence for Prosecution.

approved of at next meeting, at which were present—Mr. Inglis, chairman, Messrs. Potter, Stewart, Salmond, Wright, Taylor, and Stronach. Referring to the agenda book, under date 24th August, 1876, the ordinary business of that day closed with the appointment of an agent at the Brechin branch.

How do you know that?—In this instance there are the initials of the chairman, Mr. Inglis. Then there follows:—" Report by John Innes Wright and Lewis Potter in connection with deliverance at meeting of 13th July." [Shown Nos. 192 and 193.] No. 192 is the report, and No. 193 is the envelope in which it was kept. I was not present when that report was brought before the meeting and considered; I had left after the business of the Brechin branch was over. It was afterwards handed to me to be engrossed. On 19th October there were present—Messrs. Inglis, Potter, Salmond, Stewart, Wright, and Taylor, and the Manager. There is a note in the agenda book in the following terms:—" Referred to Manager, after having heard the observations of the Board." That is in the handwriting of Mr. Inglis.

What was it about which observations had been made by the Board; you heard them?—I believe I did in this case.

Was it the credits of Smith, Fleming & Co.?—[No reply.] [Shown Nos. 194 and 195.] No. 194 is a report by Messrs. Taylor, Stewart, and Potter; it must have been handed in in a rough draft by them at that meeting.

Was the report handed to you afterwards in the form in which you see it there?—My recollection of this is that it was a rough draft report which was handed in, and I was asked to copy it fair, which I did. It is in my handwriting. After it was written out from the rough scroll it was signed by Messrs. Taylor, Stewart, and Potter. No. 195 is the envelope in which it was.

Does that recall to your recollection what was the matter that was referred to the Manager on 19th October? Look at the agenda book; does that bring it to your recollection?—I do not know it has any connection with this.

Had you to retire from that meeting?—I cannot recollect anything in regard to this particular credit of Smith, Fleming & Co. In the agenda book, under date 11th January, 1877, there were present—Messrs. Inglis, chairman, Potter, Salmond, Stewart, Wright, and Taylor, and the Manager. The ordinary business of that meeting was closed by a letter from Mr. Bain, and the initials of Mr. Inglis are after that piece of business. The Board remained in deliberation after that for a considerable time.

A long time?—Yes. I was called in, and a draft resolution was handed to me to be entered in the book. I cannot recollect

The City of Glasgow Bank Trial.

C.S. Leresche. in whose handwriting it was; probably it was in that of Mr. Inglis.

It was not preserved?—I have no knowledge of it. On the left-hand side in the agenda book is an entry—"Morton's account"—in the handwriting of Mr. Inglis. It is put in as a separate piece of business from what had been made up by me for the use of the meeting. Morton's account was never spoken of in my presence. On 18th January, 1877, Morton's account appears again. Mr. Inglis was in the chair, and there were also present—Messrs. Inglis, Potter, Taylor, Wright, and the Manager. I was not present then when Morton's account was taken up. On 8th March, 1877, there were present—Mr. Inglis, chairman, Messrs. Potter, Salmond, Stewart, Wright, and Taylor. An application of Smith, Fleming & Co. for credit was brought up that day.

Were you present when that was discussed?—I think I must have been. [After a short pause] No; the probability is, I should not have been present at that time.

Were you ever present at the discussion of credits of Smith, Fleming & Co.?—Yes; I was present at the discussion of many of those to Law, Brown & Co., and also to—— I wish to say about this, that on reconsideration I believe I would be present at this meeting when this credit was brought up.

On 8th March?—Yes; when Smith, Fleming & Co.'s was brought up.

By the LORD JUSTICE-CLERK—I was generally present when an application from Smith, Fleming & Co. for a cash credit was discussed. I never was present when there was such an application from Morton or Wright & Co., and never heard any discussion about that. That may be taken as applicable to all the minutes. I think on this occasion I must have been present, because I do not remember a credit to Law, Brown & Co. when I was not present.

By the SOLICITOR-GENERAL—I remember the meeting of 21st June, 1877, when the accounts for the year were taken up, and the dividend for 1877 was fixed. I was not present when the dividend was fixed. The dividend was increased 1 per cent. as compared with the previous year. It had been 11 per cent. in 1876, and it was raised to 12 per cent.

Was there a discussion upon that matter in private that day?—The only knowledge I have about it is that the Manager said he was going to bring up, on the morning of 21st June, the annual returns for the year to 6th June, and asked me to put that into the agenda book, but that he would not bring up the other statements as to the annual report as usual. At that meeting on 21st June Messrs. Inglis, Potter, Salmond, Stewart, Wright, and Taylor, and the Manager were present. I got from the Manager, after they had met in private, the details

148

Evidence for Prosecution.

necessary to enable me to make out the minute. [Shown Nos. 235, 236, and 237.] No. 235 is a letter from W. C. Smith to Kinross & Co., dated 18th September, 1877; No. 236, a letter from W. C. Smith to John Hunter, 20th September, 1877; and No. 237, a letter from W. C. Smith to C. Smith, 28th September, 1877. These three letters were read at the meeting of Directors on 8th November, 1877. The letters related to purchase of land in New Zealand. At the meeting on 26th July, 1877, I see from the agenda book that Mr. Stewart was chairman, and Mr. Potter, Mr. Inglis, Mr. Wright, Mr. Taylor, Mr. Salmond, and the Manager were present—a full Board. That was not the first meeting at which anything took place as to the purchase of property in New Zealand or Australia. That had been referred to as early as 17th August of the previous year. At the meeting on 26th July, 1877, there was a deliberation by the Directors, at which I was not present. There is an entry in the agenda book in the handwriting of Mr. Inglis—"Purchase of property in New Zealand and Australia." When I was called in I received a draft resolution which I would be instructed to engross in the book, and it is initialed by the chairman. It is as follows:—

"With reference to the purchase of property in New Zealand and Australia, an authority was given to Mr. Potter, Mr. Stewart, and the Manager, on the 21st June last, in the following terms:—

"'City of Glasgow Bank,
"'Glasgow, 21st June, 1877.

"'Dear Sir,—As authorised by the meeting of Directors held of this date, you will be so good as instruct Messrs. Potter and Stewart, two of our number, to purchase freehold land in New Zealand, on behalf of this Bank, to the extent of £50,000.

"'Yours truly,

"'HENRY INGLIS, Chairman.

"'Robert Stronach, Esq., Manager;'

and on more mature consideration it was resolved that the power to purchase land should be extended to Australia, and the sum to be invested in behalf of the Bank to be increased, if considered necessary, by them and by Mr. Taylor, whose name is added as formerly to this acting committee, to £100,000. These resolutions are adopted as a sequence to the Board's minute of 17th August, 1876. The usual abstracts and statements were read to the Board." [Shown No. 230.] That is a letter of 29th August, 1877, from Mr. Glen Walker to the Manager, which was read at the meeting of 30th August, 1877.

The City of Glasgow Bank Trial.

C. S. Leresehe.

Glasgow, 29th August, 1877.

The Manager of the
   City of Glasgow Bank,
      Glasgow.

Dear Sir,—A week ago I had a telegram from my partner asking that the City Bank should request the agency of the Commercial Banking Company of Sydney—address, 39 Lombard Street, London —to wire to Sydney an extension of the credits which remain in the colony, and which expire about this time.

There will be considerable sums to pay, for account of the recent purchase, and my partner's only resource is these credits.

Please, therefore, do not delay arranging that this credit be extended, or that it be allowed to lapse and a new one wired through the bank referred to.

You know my partner is not much accustomed to finance, and should be kept—strong. If a new credit be sent, I think it better be for £20,000.—I am, faithfully yours,

W. GLEN WALKER.

Mr. Stewart, chairman, Mr. Potter, Mr. Wright, and the Manager were present at that meeting. At the meeting on 6th September, 1877, Mr. Stewart, chairman, Mr. Potter, Mr. Inglis, Mr. Wright, and Mr. Taylor were present.

Was anything brought up by any one at that meeting about further investments in New Zealand or Australia?—Yes.

By whom?—By Mr. Potter. I was present.

What was suggested?—Mr. Potter just said that the committee considered it advisable to authorise a further sum of £150,000 to be invested in property in New Zealand or Australia, and requested that that should be minuted, and I took it down from their dictation.

Was there any discussion before it was agreed to?—No; the chairman just said, " I suppose that this is agreed to." That was all that passed. It was put down as agreed to. Mr. Potter dictated the minute. The minute is—" It was considered advisable to authorise the committee to invest a further sum of £150,000 in property in New Zealand or Australia. This investment, in addition to the sums already authorised, will now therefore amount to about £400,000; and this, in addition to the interest of about £100,000 already held, completes an investment to about £500,000—say, five hundred thousand pounds." On 1st November, 1877, there were present Mr. Stewart, chairman, Mr. Potter, Mr. Wright, Mr. Inglis, and the Manager. I was absent from the meeting when some deliberation took place in connection with these properties. [Shown No. 196.] That is the report signed by Messrs. Inglis, Taylor, and Salmond, which is engrossed in that minute. On 15th November, 1877, there were present—Mr. Stewart, chairman, Mr. Potter, Mr. Salmond, Mr. Inglis, Mr. Wright, Mr. Taylor, and the Manager. I was absent from the meeting during the latter part

Evidence for Prosecution.

of it, when they were deliberating on the New Zealand matters. **C.S.Leresche.** Afterwards I was called in, and recorded the deliverance.

After you had engrossed the Board's deliverance about the New Zealand and Australian advances, did the Manager say anything in your hearing to the Directors?—Yes. He said he wished that a committee of the whole Board should sit periodically to consider the various accounts of the Bank.

Did you hear what passed on that suggestion?—Yes. It was agreed to, and I then entered in this resolution—" It was resolved that a committee of the whole Board should sit periodically to consider the position of the various accounts of the Bank." A conversation then arose as to whether the Manager wished this to be done at once, and a suggestion was made that it should begin six months afterwards.

Who said that?—I cannot remember who said it.

Was it Mr. Stronach, or some one else?—It would not be Mr. Stronach. It would be one of the Directors; and afterwards it was suggested, so far as I can recollect, by Mr. Taylor that it should be four months.

What was to be done in four months?—The looking into these securities.

The sitting of this committee?—Yes.

And accordingly it was minuted—" This not to take place for four months "?—No, I think that took place afterwards.

I was referring to what appears in the agenda book, while I think you are referring to the minute book. Would you read what is written in the agenda book?—It says, " This not to take place for four months."

In whose handwriting is that entry in the agenda book—" It was resolved that a committee of the whole Board should sit periodically to consider the position of the various accounts of the Bank "?—It looks like Mr. Taylor's handwriting.

That entry is—" It was resolved that a committee of the whole Board should sit periodically to consider the position of the various accounts of the Bank. This not to take place for four months "?—Yes.

How was the entry made in the minute book?—It was entered in the minute book—" It was resolved that a committee of the whole Board should sit periodically to consider the position of the various accounts of the Bank." I put nothing more in it, and then the usual abstract and statements were read to the Board. I did not put in that part of it about the four months, but when the minute came before the Board at their meeting on the 22nd, they said it was agreed that that should not take place for four months. I gave some explanation that I thought that was more an understanding than a resolution, but they told me I had better engross it, and therefore it appears as it was entered afterwards.

The City of Glasgow Bank Trial.

C.S. Leresche. That was inserted on revisal?—Yes. It says—"The committee of inquiry above mentioned will meet not later than four months from this date."

When did that committee meet for the first time?—I have no knowledge of that committee meeting. About four months from that date I think you will find that there was another committee formed.

You don't know of your own knowledge whether that committee met or not?—No.

On 28th February, 1878, there was a discussion in private that day—I mean a discussion at which you were not present—with regard to Innes Wright & Co.'s affairs?—Yes. A draft was afterwards handed to me to be put in. It was handed to me on the Wednesday before the following meeting—after they had deliberated in private—and it was in the handwriting of the Manager. Referring to the minute of meeting of 21st March, 1878, I find there a reference to a committee appointed on Morton's account.

Had any such committee been appointed when you were present at the previous meeting, or were the instructions to write the minute given to you afterwards?—This here would be given me probably after the meeting.

But you were not present?—No; I would be called up and would engross it at the time, as it is initialed. Being referred to minute of 30th May, 1878, and shown No. 191c—That is a letter from Mr. Stronach, the Manager, to John Fleming, of London, dated 23rd May, 1878.

Was that letter brought up at the meeting while you were there on the 30th?—Yes.

Was that letter or any answer to it by Mr. John Fleming brought up while you were present?—I do not recollect that I was present then. On 6th June, 1878, the minute bears that proceedings took place in regard to Innes Wright & Co.'s accounts. I was not present when Innes Wright & Co.'s affairs were discussed that day. On 20th June what appears in the agenda book, and is recorded in the minute, took place after I had left the meeting. A rough memorandum was given to me, as had been done on former occasions. In the minute of 1st August, 1878, a resolution appears as having been formed on that date. That was done after the formal business had been brought to a close and the agenda book initialed. I was not present at what appears after the initials of the chairman; that was just given me to enter in. Since I was appointed secretary I have regularly attended the annual meetings of the shareholders, at which the election of the Directors took place. I kept the minute book containing the reports of the annual meetings. That is No. 102 of the inventory. It contains a correct record by me of what passed at the meetings up to the

Evidence for Prosecution.

date of the last annual meeting. The minute is subscribed by the chairman, and the copy of the report is subscribed by all the Directors. I never was present at any discussion that took place in regard to advances that had been made to James Nicol Fleming. I never was present at any discussion that took place in regard to advances that had been made to John Innes Wright & Co. I never was present at any discussion in regard to James Morton & Co.'s advances.

You said yesterday that you were present when Smith, Fleming & Co.'s affairs came up; were you ever present when any discussion took place in regard to their existing debts to the Company, or was it only in regard to proposed new credits? —I don't remember saying that.

I think you said you were present when Smith, Fleming & Co.'s accounts came up?—No; when the applications of Smith, Fleming & Co. for those letters of credit came up I was generally present. I never was present when any discussion or deliberation took place in reference to the state of Smith, Fleming & Co.'s account.

On those occasions when the Board deliberated in private, and you afterwards were called in or received a draft to insert, did the sederunt of the meeting remain the same during the private deliberations?—I cannot speak to that.

Do you remember on any occasion when you were recalled of the sederunt being different from what it was when you opened the meeting? I do not ask you to speak to every individual case, but was it usual that the whole Board remained for those private deliberations after you retired?—Yes, it was usual; that is, I would leave the whole of the Board there. There were some exceptions, in the case, for instance, of Mr. Taylor. He had to attend some insurance meeting on the same day, the Thursday, and he may have had to go away on many occasions. [Shown Nos. 604, 605, and 606.] These are the annual reports by the Directors of the Bank to the shareholders for the years 1876, 1877, and 1878. These are prints which were circulated by me as secretary as the annual report of the Directors. [Shown No. 95.] That is the cashier's ledger, commencing 6th June, 1866. Being referred to the slip fastened into the board of the book, stating the amount of cash under date 5th June, 1878—that slip is initialed by Mr. Stewart. The entry is dated 5th June, 1878, and is as follows:—

" Cash in cashier's hands—

" £100 notes,	-	-	-	-	£68,000
" £5 notes,	-	-	-	-	163,500
" £1 notes,	-	-	-	-	190,000
" Gold,	-	-	-	-	338,500
" Total,	-	-	-	-	£760,000 "

The City of Glasgow Bank Trial.

C. S. Leresche. Below there is a detail of the gold as follows:—

" In original safe,	-	-	-	£149,000
" In new safe below,	-	-	-	62,500
" In new safe above,	-	-	-	109,000
" In new safe top,	-	-	-	18,000
" Total,	-	-	-	£338,500 "

That memorandum is in the handwriting of Mr. Turnbull, the cashier. Mr. Stewart's initials in the first of these statements are placed to each item, so far as the notes are concerned, but apparently not to the gold; but they are placed to each item of the gold in the detailed list.

By Mr. TRAYNER—[Shown cashier's ledger]. That book is kept by Mr. Turnbull, the cashier. Being referred to page 376, I see there an entry of the money as ending 5th June, 1878. That corresponds exactly with the statement initialed by Mr. Stewart, to which I have been already referred—£338,500. The next entry beginning the account, cash in hand as at the year beginning 6th June, 1878, commences again with that exact sum.

By Mr. BALFOUR—You were asked with regard to the agenda for 18th February, 1875, and you read a note as to what was to be brought before that meeting; I should like to ask your attention to the terms of the whole of that minute?—It is as follows:—" Notice of dissolution of partnership between James Nicol Fleming and William Grant, under the firm of J. Nicol Fleming & Co., Calcutta, having been reported to the Board, it was resolved to appoint Messrs. Potter and Salmond a committee to assist the Manager in arranging the securities and advances connected with the late firm of J. Nicol Fleming & Co., Calcutta, and Smith, Fleming & Co., London, with full powers." I saw from the documents given to the Bank that there had been a dissolution at that time, which made such a re-arrangement necessary. That was the cause of this re-arrangement.

By Mr. ASHER—Being referred to the agenda book, I observe that the sederunt of 1st June, 1876, includes the name of Mr. Salmond. The date of the next meeting at which his name is entered as present is 20th July, 1876. There had been meetings in the interval on 8th, 22nd, and 28th June, and 5th and 13th July, at none of which Mr. Salmond was present. The meetings last mentioned were the meetings at which the business connected with the annual balance was dealt with. Mr. Salmond was again absent on 3rd and 17th August following. Looking at the same book for 1877, I find that Mr. Salmond was absent on 18th January, 7th and 14th June, 12th July, 30th August, 6th September, 1st and 29th November. In 1878 he was absent on 10th January and 28th March. He was present on 16th May. The next meeting after that at which he was present was 11th of July. Between 16th May and 11th July there had been meetings on 23rd and 30th May, and 6th, 20th, and 27th June, from all of which he was absent. These last-mentioned meetings were the meetings at which the business connected with the annual balance was transacted. The sederunt was noted in the agenda book by the chairman.

When business connected with your department had been transacted, you were in the habit, you told us, of withdrawing from the meeting?—Yes, after I had read the abstracts and statements.

With regard to any business in the agenda book not connected with your department, I suppose you cannot say whether all the Directors mentioned in the sederunt continued to be present when that was being done?—I cannot say that.

In short, with regard to the Directors who were present, your sole means for giving evidence here is that you find their names noted in the sederunt in the agenda book?—Yes.

To what extent they took part in the business noted in the agenda book, or whether they were present throughout the whole meeting or only a part, of course you are unable to say?—I am unable to say.

It was the custom of the Bank Board to divide the business to some extent amongst the Directors. Can you tell me which of the Directors were the committee on branches during 1876, 1877, and 1878?—There was no committee formed to my knowledge during those years.

Was there not an acting committee during those years—a standing committee?—No, I have no knowledge of that.

Perhaps that was not within your department?—There was no minute of it.

But if there had been a committee appointed before these years which continued to act, that would not fall within your knowledge, I suppose? You would have nothing to do with it, unless it was in the minutes?—Nothing to do with it except it was in the minutes.

There was no meeting of the Directors, I suppose, at some part of which you were not present? You were always present, I suppose, at some part of their meetings?—Except during my holidays.

You prepared a note of the business, I believe, which came before each meeting of the Directors?—Yes.

The Directors met weekly, on Thursdays, at twelve o'clock? —Yes.

So that you were familiar with the regular business that came before each meeting of the Directors?—Yes.

Had you any knowledge that there was anything wrong

The City of Glasgow Bank Trial.

with the Bank until its suspension?—I had no knowledge at all that there was anything wrong with the Bank until a few days before the suspension.

By Mr. MACKINTOSH—You mentioned that Mr. Taylor was in the way of leaving your meetings to attend insurance meetings? —Occasionally he was.

Was not that the case very generally?—I could not remember of it myself more than four or five times.

But it may have been oftener?—It may have been oftener; some of our meetings were short. My recollection is that his insurance meeting was held at one o'clock; our meeting was held at twelve. Our office was in Virginia Street; his insurance company was, I think, the Scottish Imperial; their office is in West George Street, about ten minutes' walk distant.

By Mr. ROBERTSON—You have been referred to the meeting of 15th November, 1877, already read. If you go on four months, that brings you to the middle of March, 1878. Look at the minute of 14th March, 1878; at the end of it you will see this—" In connection with the minute of 15th November last, it was agreed that Messrs. Stewart, Potter, and Salmond be appointed a committee, along with the Manager, to examine the advance accounts at head office weekly, and to deal in particular with the account of Messrs. James Morton & Co."? —Yes.

Were you present when that resolution was adopted?—No.

But as matter of fact, was there ever any committee of the whole Board sitting on that subject to your knowledge at this time, or did not the resolution of March, 1878, supersede so far the resolution of November, 1877?—This was given to me after the meeting to be entered. It must have been some days after the meeting. The probability is that it would be as late as—I think myself it was even on the Thursday of the next meeting.

But my question is, as matter of fact, no committee of the whole Board sat on that subject to carry out the resolution of 15th November?—Not to my knowledge.

By the DEAN OF FACULTY—You have read the minute of 18th February, 1875, where notice is taken of the dissolution of partnership between James Nicol Fleming and William Grant, and arrangements were made to appoint a committee to assist the Manager in arranging the securities and advances connected with the late firm of J. Nicol Fleming & Co., Calcutta. Do you know that an agreement was entered into during the same year—1875—in the month of August, between the Bank and Smith, Fleming & Co., of Calcutta and London, whereby their account was put on a new and distinct footing?—I have no knowledge of that, except from seeing it referred to in the minute book.

Evidence for Prosecution.

You do see it referred to in the books?—I think I have seen it in the minute book, but I have no knowledge of it myself. [Shown Nos. 188 and 189.] No. 189 is a letter dated 26th; the rest of the date is torn off. No. 188 is a letter dated 24th August, 1875, signed by Smith, Fleming & Co., John Fleming, R. M'Ilwraith, and W. Nicol, and there is a schedule of properties that follows.

The opening passage of that letter begins—" Referring to the interview which the writer had," etc. ; then there is a long agreement, consisting of no less than ten articles, whereby you see that Smith, Fleming & Co. agree to pay $3\frac{1}{2}$ per cent. for their account, and to hand over various securities, of which there is a schedule appended?—Yes, I see that under Article No. 6A they are to pay interest at the rate of $3\frac{1}{2}$ per cent. per annum upon the £100,000 as aforesaid.

Then the next item is to "pay the whole surplus interest arising from the stock, after meeting the charge for interest as above, to the credit of our account with the Bank, and in the event of a sale to apply the proceeds first in liquidation of the foresaid advance of £100,000, the whole of the surplus over and above the said advance being put to the credit of our account with the Bank "?—Yes.

I am putting these questions with reference to the transference of the account in August, 1875, from the cheque box to the accountant's office. If you will turn to the end of the letter, after the signatures of Smith, Fleming & Co. and their partners, you will find a schedule of property belonging to Smith, Fleming & Co. which was lodged as security in the City of Glasgow Bank. Did you know anything about this agreement at the time it was entered into?—No ; I never saw this letter before.

You came to a knowledge of it through the books?—I saw from some minutes that there had been some agreement entered into.

Do you know whether Smith, Fleming & Co.'s account was changed from the ordinary open credit account dealt with in the cheque box to the accountant's department after this agreement was entered into?—No ; I have no knowledge.

In the minute of 22nd June, 1876, to which you have already spoken, the concluding paragraph is—" It was resolved to appoint Messrs. Taylor and Potter a committee to examine into certain old accounts of the Bank, and to assist the Manager in arranging these under one general heading, with full powers." You told us yesterday that the Manager had required that these old accounts should be investigated into?—Yes.

Can you tell what old accounts were there referred to?—I have no knowledge.

Were you present when this resolution was come to?—I think not. I don't think I would be present then.

The City of Glasgow Bank Trial.

C.S. Leresche.   Can you tell me the meaning of these words, " in arranging them under one general heading "?—No ; this would be a draft that would probably be written out and handed to me.

Can you give me any notion of what general heading they were to be put under?—No ; I have no knowledge whatever.

Did the Manager speak to you about his anxiety to have these old accounts looked into?—No, not to me personally.

You had no conversation with Mr. Stronach about the matter? —No.   [Shown minute of 17th August, 1876] :—

Having in view the position of certain old accounts, and looking to the whole circumstances, and particularly to the fact that the contemplated arrangements for the working of the credits are largely part of transactions in existence for many years, and previously brought under consideration of the Board by the present Manager, the Board deem it expedient to come to their present decision, as referred to in minute of 30th December, 1875.

I cannot tell what are the old accounts there referred to ; I have no knowledge of that.

Can you tell me when it was that the Manager brought these old accounts under the consideration of the Board?—I would understand from this that it was on 30th December, 1875 ; but the minute reads in this way, " brought under consideration of the Board by the present Manager, the Board deemed it expedient to come to their present decision, as referred to in minute of 30th December, 1875."

You think it refers to his remonstrances of 30th December, 1875?—I cannot say whether there was any remonstrance then.

You think it refers to what took place at the meeting?—I infer so ; but I have no knowledge beyond the minute.

In the minute of 30th December, 1875, there is engrossed a letter from Mr. Stronach accepting the office of Manager ; where is that letter now?—It is produced.

Was that the first letter that Mr. Stronach submitted to the Directors with reference to his acceptance?—The first that I am aware of.

Did you see a draft of another letter?—No ; I have no knowledge of that.

Did you see a draft of any letter?—No ; I have no recollection of that.

Was this the only letter of Mr. Stronach that you knew of as having been laid before the Directors?—On that occasion?

Yes?—That was the only one.

Did any of the Directors speak to you about another having been laid before them?—On that occasion?

Yes?—No.

On any occasion do you know of any other letter by Mr. Stronach to the Directors in reference to these accounts?—No ; nothing but what is minuted.

Evidence for Prosecution.

Did Mr. Glen Walker speak to you about another letter that was given by Mr. Stronach to the Directors?—No; I have no recollection of anything.

Had you any talk with any of the officials in the Bank about this letter of Mr. Stronach's when you first saw it?—No; I have no recollection of it.

Who gave it to you to engross in the minutes?—The chairman, Mr. Taylor.

Did he make any remark when he gave it to you?—No; he merely told me that it had been handed in by the Manager; he made no remark as to the contents of the letter. I was not present at the meeting when the letter was considered.

By the LORD JUSTICE-CLERK—You have no recollection of hearing of any other letter addressed to the Directors by Stronach in regard to these accounts at that time, or about that time?— No, I have no recollection of that at all.

WILLIAM MORISON, *recalled.*

By the LORD JUSTICE-CLERK—On your first examination we were led to understand that the document No. 128, of which we have a lithograph, was the original abstract of accounts which you first submitted to the Manager and Mr. Potter; that is to say, without the red ink markings, and that the red ink markings denoted the alterations which you were instructed to make. Yesterday you corrected that, and you told us that this abstract, so far as it appears in black ink, was not the thing which you submitted to the Manager, but was another copy made after your interview with the Manager. Is that so?—Yes.

Now tell me exactly what the figures are on No. 128—go over them *seriatim*—which you were instructed to alter, and which appear as altered on the document as it now stands?— There is first the entry of Smith, Fleming & Co., £200,875 on the left-hand side; J. N. F., £100,300; J. M. & Co., £450,600.

Amounting in all to £751,000?—Yes.

That originally appeared in a larger sum; what was its amount?—£3,467,689 14s. 11d.

And that £751,000 is deducted from that on the face of this? —Yes.

And the balance of £2,715,000 is carried out?—Yes.

What becomes of the £751,000?—It is brought down under the third heading.

In what sum is it included, and under what head?—It is under the third head, Smith, Fleming & Co., stocks, £200,875; James Nicol Fleming, stocks, £100,300; James Morton & Co., stocks, £450,600.

That is included in the Government stocks, railway stocks and

The City of Glasgow Bank Trial.

debentures, London and provincial correspondents; you had originally an abstract of the accounts under that head?—Yes.

Where did you get it? From what materials did you make it up?—From the general ledger or the weekly balance book.

And these books contain all the accounts which ought to be under that head?—All the accounts.

The head "Government stocks and other securities" means investments by the Bank?—Government stocks, Nos. 1 and 2.

These are investments made by the Bank?—By the Bank.

And held by the Bank?—Held by the Bank, I understand.

They don't mean securities held for advances or open accounts? —No.

Or with credit?—I can only speak from what I have heard; I don't know personally about the securities.

But you know what the book means?—I understand they are held by the Bank.

The book from which you made up that part of head No. III. was a book which contained nothing but investments by the Bank?—I understand so.

You understood so when you made it up?—Yes.

You said yesterday that it might be right to put these accounts into that head of the abstract?—Yes.

Knowing that if they were securities, they were securities for advances upon credit?—Yes.

Why did you say that?—At the time of the alteration, from the conversation betwixt Mr. Potter and the Manager, I understood that these stocks were held by the Bank.

Did you understand that these were not advances on credit to these firms?—They were under the heading in the credit accounts ledger as advances to these firms.

And therefore they were properly, in your opinion, entered in that account?—In the credit accounts.

What difference did it make that there were securities held for them?—It made no difference so far as regarded the credit accounts.

What difference did it make in regard to the place in the abstract in which they should be entered?—By bringing them down here, it put them under the heading, or one portion of the heading, of cash held.

They were represented, in short, as being investments held by the Bank?—Yes.

Which they were not?—I cannot tell you that.

If they were credit advances, were they properly investments held by the Bank? You gave an opinion yesterday that if there were securities held for these credits, they might be properly entered under the investments of the Bank. Is that so?—With the addition, I said, that if an entry had been passed through the books.

Evidence for Prosecution.

Then you did not mean to say that that might be a right entry?—This entry here?

Yes?—Unless an entry had passed through the cash book and general ledger.

You did not mean to say it was right as it stands?—No.

What was the next alteration which the Directors directed you to make on this sheet, still dealing with the debit side?— Under the heading of heritable property account there is a sum of £30,000 deducted.

You were directed to do that?—Yes.

Is that in red ink or black ink?—Black ink.

Then that must have been done after the meeting?—Yes.

Is there not before that a sum of £430,000 struck out?—No.

Well, what next?—Under the heading of foreign and colonial credits there is a sum of £973,300 deducted from bills payable.

And that, you told us, reduced the apparent amount of bills payable?—For foreign and colonial credits in the meantime.

By nearly a million of money?—Yes; with the explanation that that £973,000 entry was in the general ledger.

Is there anything else material in that state which you were directed to alter by the Directors?—There is the same £30,000 that was deducted from the heritable property account brought down under the No. II. heading, " Advances on heritable property and value of Bank buildings and furniture."

Anything else?—There is a sum of £29,095 added to the amount of notes of other banks on hand.

Are these the material alterations which you were told to make?—Then there are the £200,875, £100,300, and £450,600 brought down that I spoke of before.

By Mr. BALFOUR—Under the first head from which these items were brought down is there not an entry " City of Glasgow Bank stock, £356,825."   Was that an investment of the Bank in its own stock?—Yes.

And yet that appeared under the first head?—Yes.

By the LORD JUSTICE-CLERK—[on the suggestion of a jury-man]—You have said that the effect of these alterations was to show a larger amount of assets and a smaller amount of liabilities than your original abstract would have shown, or than the books would have shown, and at the same time you said that the alterations did not affect the profit and loss for the year or the reserve fund. Can you explain that?—If the assets were reduced the liabilities were reduced. I did not say the liabilities were reduced and the assets enlarged. They are both reduced.

You mean that the amount of assets is reduced, and the amount of liabilities is reduced, and therefore the amount of transactions is made apparently less than in point of fact they were. Is that so?—Yes.

L

The City of Glasgow Bank Trial.

Wm. Miller.

WILLIAM MILLER.

By the LORD ADVOCATE—I was for some years, and down to the stoppage of the City of Glasgow Bank, superintendent of its branches. I was so from 1862. My duty was to conduct correspondence with the branches, and to examine the advances made at the branches, and report on them to the Manager; also to take a general oversight of the business transacted at the branches. My duties never brought me into contact with the Board of Directors.

Were you ever present at their meetings?—I have been asked to come in to answer a question occasionally, but I was not there habitually—very seldom—only when a question or explanation was asked as to something in my department. On the occasion of the annual balance being prepared there was a form prepared and given to us by Mr. Morison, on which we entered the figures from our own books, and returned the sheet to Mr. Morison. The branch balance sheets for the years 1876, 1877, and 1878 were prepared in that way under my superintendence. They contained a correct statement of the balances of the branches for these years. We got weekly returns from each branch, and the accuracy of these was checked by our inspectors. In each of these three years about £10,000 was written off for bad debts at the branches. I have made an analysis of that for the past five years, and I find that the average sum so written off for bad debts was £10,900 per annum. The business done at the branches was a very profitable one—averaging £70,000 a year, after deducting the bad debts.

By Mr. ASHER—At the annual balance Mr. Morison, the accountant, sent me a form of abstract to be filled up in connection with the branches—a form having the same heads, I believe, as there are in the balance ledger at the head office. We allocated the returns from the branches under these various heads. We gave back the form to Mr. Morison, to be incorporated in the general abstract, as I understood. I understood that the branch business and the head office business were brought together in that form only once a year.

By Mr. BALFOUR—Was it part of that return to show the cross accounts which existed at the branches?—Yes.

What did you return as the cross accounts for 1878?—I don't remember.

The amount entered in No. 124A—the abstract for 1878—under the head " Cross accounts " is, " Edinburgh branch, £148,939 18s. 11d." Have you any doubt that that was the amount you returned as the cross accounts of that branch?—I have no doubt that is correct, but I have no means here of testing it.

Evidence for Prosecution.

Did you return the amount of cross accounts for 1876?—**Wm. Miller.** I don't remember as to 1876; there was as to 1877 and 1878, but I am not sure that form was prepared before 1877.

Have you no books here that would refresh your recollection about that?—I don't think there are any. I have seen the abstracts of branches in the hands of Mr. Brown. The abstract branches account of 1876, now shown me, has been filled up by one of our inspectors of branches. I have no doubt it is quite correct. The amount of cross accounts, branches, in 1876, was £376,334 5s. 3d. No. 134 is the abstract of accounts of branches for June, 1877. There is entered there under the head of cross accounts—" Edinburgh branch, £268,692 8s. 3d."

Before you go further, will you explain to the jury what is the meaning of cross accounts as appearing in these branches abstracts?—They belong entirely to the accounts of the North British Railway. The North British Railway Company kept several accounts for their own purposes; some of them were debtor and some were creditor. The mode of bringing out these was by deducting the debtor from the creditor balance, treating it as one account. I think that is a perfectly proper book-keeping operation.

By the Lord Justice-Clerk—The amount brought out for 1876 in that way was £376,000 odds.

It is the balance of a debtor and creditor account?—You deduct the one from the other, and bring out the sum that should come in here.

By Mr. Balfour—The only instance in which we so crossed accounts was in connection with the North British Railway. We never did it anywhere but at Edinburgh, and in connection with the North British Railway.

Is there not a similar entry applicable to the West End branch, Glasgow?—Yes; that was a fictitious entry returned by me to the head office for the following purpose:—The West Calder Oil Company owed £5150. That originated at the West End branch, where they kept their account. There was also a debit account in the head office of the same kind; and it was resolved to bring up the West End balance to the head office, because I understood the head office had securities against these advances. Subsequently it was sent back to the West End branch, in order that they might make a cross entry in their books for the purpose of keeping the debt before them. Had that not been deducted the debt would have been entered twice. It was perfectly necessary and proper, having regard to the manner in which these accounts at the two offices were kept, to make that entry. The amount of cross accounts, as shown by No. 134, for the week ending Wednesday, 6th June, 1877, was—Edinburgh branch, £268,692 8s. 3d.; West End branch, Glasgow, £5150 5s. In 1878, as shown by No. 135, the cross accounts amounted to—Edinburgh branch, £148,939

The City of Glasgow Bank Trial.

Wm. Miller. 18s. 11d.; West End branch, Glasgow, £5150 5s.; total, £154,090 3s. 11d. [Shown No. 133—Abstract of accounts at branches on Thursday, 1st June, 1876.] That is the printed form which Mr. Morison supplied to us in order that we might fill in these returns.

By the DEAN OF FACULTY—I have been inspector of branches since 1862. In conducting the business of my department with the head office I dealt only with the Manager. I never came in contact with the accountant except when giving him these returns; I had no occasion to do so. Since Mr. Robert Stronach was appointed Manager I have seen him every day, and several times every day. I thought him a particularly careful Manager in all advances that we had to do with. I found him very careful, and, I would say, very strict in investigating into securities for proposed credits. I thought, up to 1st October, 1878, that he was a perfectly conscientious, honourable gentleman—a man whom I would not have suspected of doing anything wrong.

By the LORD ADVOCATE—The sum of £376,334 in 1876 was applicable entirely to the accounts of the North British Railway. I may explain that it to a large extent consisted of two accounts—the one called a general account and the other an interest and dividend account. The general account was generally creditor, because into that went all the moneys lodged, and, as these came in from day to day and week to week, they were put to that credit. Then when interest and dividends were paid, they were debited to the other account in the first place. It was really a debtor and creditor account kept in the form of two accounts—the one containing debit and the other credit entries. With regard to the two sums in each of the years 1877 and 1878, the larger of these was entirely applicable to the North British Railway, and the smaller to the West End branch relative to the West Calder Oil Company. I had nothing whatever to do with credits granted or transactions of any kind at the head office. I knew nothing that was done at the head office.

You had no means of ascertaining on what terms money was given there?—Certainly not; and I never wished to know, that was more; not that I suspected anything wrong, but I did not want to be bothered about it; I had plenty to do with my own business, and wished to keep myself entirely to that. I never asked a question about the head office.

What do you mean by saying that the Manager was very strict?—I mean to say that when any proposal, for a credit account, for instance, or an advance of any kind, came up to me and I showed it to him, he was particularly careful in seeing what he believed to be proper security lodged before it could be granted, and he was in the habit of investigating the returns of the advances himself, and looking at them.

CHAPTER VI.

Evidence of the Manager's Clerk and the Cashier.

WILLIAM MORRIS.

Wm. Morris.

By the LORD ADVOCATE—I was in the employment of the City of Glasgow Bank from the year 1864 down to the time of its stoppage, in various capacities. I was at first in the accountant's department, and in 1871 I was appointed private clerk to the Manager, Mr. Alexander Stronach. I acted in that capacity until Mr. Alexander Stronach resigned, and on the appointment of Mr. Robert Stronach I continued to act under him in the same capacity. Alexander Stronach ceased to attend the Bank about December, 1874.

Was he much about the Bank, or was he absent altogether from the Bank from that date down to December, 1875?—He was absent altogether. During that period his brother, Mr. Robert Stronach, performed the duties of Manager. My duties as private clerk to the Manager were to attend to the Manager's correspondence.

Were you employed by him to write, or did you merely write from his scroll or dictation?—Both from scroll and to dictation.

You were not employed in any other sense to conduct correspondence?—Well, there were official letters as well, such as Smith, Fleming & Co.'s.

But what I want to know is this, were you employed merely to write what was dictated or given you to copy, or were you employed to write letters from information given you?—Latterly, with Mr. Robert Stronach, from information given me. Before that date I wrote principally from scroll, with Alexander Stronach. With Robert Stronach I wrote from information given me. The official letters of the Bank were generally addressed to the City of Glasgow Bank. These letters, I understand, were opened by Mr. Leresche. When letters were addressed to the Manager by name, they were delivered to the Manager himself.

Were there any particular letters which came addressed always to the Manager?—Yes, Smith, Fleming & Co's. I wrote the replies to those letters. I had an apartment adjoining that of Mr. Alexander Stronach. Shortly after I became his private

The City of Glasgow Bank Trial.

clerk I directed a duplicate set of books to be kept by the bill clerk, Mr. Laing. The two sets of books were a little differently arranged, but the results were the same. These books included a book titled on the back, "Ledger A, Open credit, No. 3"; another book, titled "Ledger B, Open or marginal credits, No. 3"; and a third book, "Ledger C, Open or marginal credits, No. 3." The entries contained in Ledger A were the credits granted to James Morton & Co., Matthew Buchanan & Co., and Potter, Wilson & Co. Ledger B contained credits granted to Smith, Fleming & Co. and James Nicol Fleming. Ledger C contained miscellaneous credits, including credits granted to Glen Walker & Co. and John Innes Wright & Co., amongst others. In working these ledgers I kept a book, titled "Daily list of bills payable." That contained a list of the bills payable by the Bank as they matured from day to day under each of the credits in these books.

By the LORD JUSTICE-CLERK—The books were confined to the particular accounts I have mentioned. The duplicate set was applicable only to those accounts.

By the LORD ADVOCATE—These credit accounts were accounts which involved acceptances by the Bank, on which the Bank's credit was interposed. Ledger C includes acceptances by the London Joint Stock Bank on behalf of the City of Glasgow Bank.

How would you describe the character of the credits entered in Ledger A?—Running credits. By a running credit I mean a credit that has been renewed and is kept renewed, kept continuing upon the circle, renewed from day to day.

Where the Bank issue new acceptances to retire those that are in the circle when they come due?—Precisely.

Do you apply the term "open credits" also to these?—Yes, they are classed amongst the open credits.

What was the common practice of the Bank in granting such credits—how did it begin?—By a letter of application from the person requiring the credit.

And then, I believe, it was usual to issue a letter of credit?—Sometimes it was and sometimes it was not.

Was it not invariably the course pursued with the ordinary creditors of the Bank to require an application in writing?—It was.

Was that course pursued with the credits that are entered in Ledger A?—In some instances it was, in others not. Ledger B contains open and marginal credits together. A marginal credit is almost a similar document to an open credit. A marginal credit is a margin attached to a bill instead of a letter being granted; it is a set of bills, and the obligation of the Bank is attached to the bill, like a counterfoil, the obligation of the Bank being to accept the bill when presented against produce. In the case of marginal credits the bill attached to the counterfoil sets forth the sum that it is drawn for. In the case of an open

Evidence for Prosecution.

credit, where there is a letter of credit, say, for £50,000, the customer can draw for any amount that suits his purpose up to the limit of £50,000 in bills of any amount. But when a marginal credit is granted, we issue five bills of £10,000 each. There were a number of firms connected with James Nicol Fleming and Smith, Fleming & Co. who operated upon the credits given to them. These were James Nicol Fleming & Co., Calcutta; William Nicol & Co., Bombay; Todd, Findlay & Co., Rangoon; Fleming & Co., Kurrachee; and there was a Colombo credit that was operated upon by Fowlie, Richmond & Co. at one time, but that firm came to grief along with Messrs. Collie in 1875, and since then that credit has been operated upon by William Nicol & Co., Bombay. Ledger A showed that the operations of James Morton & Co. under these credits were very large. With the view of keeping up my information on the subject, I prepared folio sheets from month to month, showing James Morton & Co.'s liabilities as at the beginning of each month, on credits and discounts, past due bills, and open accounts. My object in ascertaining Morton & Co.'s liabilities at the beginning of each month was to keep the Manager supplied with information; it was such a large account that I thought that necessary. These sheets were submitted to him monthly.

Did you keep them after you had prepared them, or how did you deal with them?—The book lay with the Manager, and I was in the habit of getting it at the beginning of each month to post up. It lay with him during the intervening month, and I got it back from him. It was to Mr. Robert Stronach that I supplied that information—not to Mr. Alexander Stronach. I cannot remember whether it was his suggestion or mine that these monthly sheets should be prepared. [Shown Nos. 122, analysis of securities, James Morton & Co., commencing 20th September, 1876, and 123.] No. 123 is titled "Weekly abstract of credits, S., F. & Co. and J. N. F." It contains a weekly abstract. It is one of my own books, kept in the room I occupied. It was not patent to the other officers of the Bank. The weekly abstracts show *in cumulo* the state from week to week of the credits to those firms, as operated upon from the different places I have mentioned. The special credits granted to Smith, Fleming & Co. were not entered in that book at all. They were never put through an abstract. The sheets produced here are only a part. No. 122 goes back to 1876. I retained Smith, Fleming & Co.'s sheets—No. 123. I also kept a book (No. 120), titled "Special securities, J. N. F., S., F. & Co., J. M. & Co., and others." These initials mean James Nicol Fleming, Smith, Fleming & Co., and James Morton & Co. That book was made up by me in June, 1877. I had no special instructions to make it up. These things were recorded in loose sheets, and I

The City of Glasgow Bank Trial.

thought it proper to have them embodied in a book. It shows the amount of liabilities by these parties, and the securities supposed to be held against these liabilities.

Did you always receive from Smith, Fleming & Co. application letters for credits granted to them?—As a rule.

Do you say the same thing with regard to the credits granted to Mr. Morton?—No.

Were there, as a rule, letters there?—As a rule there were letters, but there were three or four credits without letters of application.

In some of Mr. Morton's applications he asks credit against securities annexed?—He does.

Were securities annexed in these cases?—Sometimes, and sometimes not.

How did you account for that? What occurred to you at the time as his reason for not annexing the securities?—I cannot say; I have no idea.

Did Mr. Morton deposit securities from time to time without applying for a credit at the time?—Well, probably he did, before my time; sometimes.

You kept another book, I believe, containing the entries in connection with foreign and colonial credits, and the acceptances maturing of foreign and colonial bills?—I don't remember that book.

When applications were sent in to the Manager by Morton & Co. or Smith, Fleming & Co., after the Manager opened these letters, what did he do with them—to whom did he give them?—He sent them upstairs to me, or I called for them and got them in the Manager's room.

Were they given to Mr. Leresche?—Sometimes they were.

Was that the general rule?—No.

Were applications for credits from these firms handed to Mr. Leresche?—Yes, latterly they were. The application letters for the special credits were handed to him.

But was the correspondence with regard to the credits other than special handed to Mr. Leresche?—No.

Was there any document or letter sent from your office or from the Manager with your knowledge to Mr. Leresche which could inform him of the amount of Morton's credits or liabilities? —No.

But you, as private clerk, had information upon the subject? —I had. [Shown Nos. 185 to 188 inclusive.] No. 188 is a letter, dated 24th August, 1875, from Smith, Fleming & Co. to R. S. Stronach. I am familiar with that letter; I have seen it.

You saw it at the time, didn't you?—Probably I did. Nos. 185 to 187 are letters from John Fleming to the Manager, and which were received by him. I never saw the minute books. [Shown No. 215.] That is a letter from John Innes Wright &

Lord Craighill.

Evidence for Prosecution.

Co. to the Manager, R. S. Stronach, dated 2nd August, 1876, in the following terms:—

115 St. Vincent Street, Glasgow,
2nd August, 1876.

R. S. Stronach, Esq.

Dear Sir,—Referring to the letter addressed to you by the writer on 12th ulto., we now beg to apply for marginal credits as undernoted, for one hundred thousand pounds (£100,000 stg.), to be drawn by Messrs. Glen Walker & Co., of Melbourne, the partners of which are Wm. Glen Walker, Wm. Geddes Borron, and Ferdinand Spiro.

In security for same, we engage to hold for, or lodge with you, the documents for wool and other produce sent to us by Messrs. G. W. & Co. as received (stipulating that the same represents an excess of 20 per cent. over the amounts drawn), or we shall pay you cash to the amount of your acceptances.

We beg to enclose copy of letter received from W. G. Walker, Esq., requesting the credits now applied for, and who purposes leaving this for Melbourne in a few weeks for the purpose of giving the business his personal attention.—We remain, dear sir, yours faithfully,

JOHN INNES WRIGHT & Co.

Marginal credits at 4 or 6 m/ st. Payable in London. In force for one year. In 20 bills for £5000 each, and in triplicates.

" Triplicates " means in sets of three.

You did not see the minutes, I believe?—I did not.

But you became aware, by the issuing of bills, that that credit had been granted?—Yes.

Was the security mentioned in that letter given to the Bank? —Not that I am aware of. The £100,000 marginal credit was drawn upon to the extent, I think, of £57,000. £25,000 was paid in in cash by John Innes Wright & Company, and the balance was paid by the Bank.

How did they deal with it in their books on retiring the acceptances?—It would go into the debit of John Innes Wright & Co.'s open balance.

To the extent of £32,000?—Yes. [Shown minute of Directors of 17th August, 1876, in the following terms]:—

A letter from Messrs. James Morton & Co., and two letters from Mr. W. Glen Walker, dated respectively Glasgow, the 16th and 14th instant, in regard to the drawing of credits in lieu of those now drawn by Messrs. Holmes, White & Co., and others, and one of the latter as to the acquisition of certain pastoral properties, were brought under the notice of the Board; after full consideration the Board came to the resolution that it was advisable to adopt generally the suggestions contained in these letters, and they accordingly requested the Manager, associated with Messrs. Potter, Stewart, and Taylor, to arrange with Mr. Walker as to all details. While arriving at this resolution, the Board were fully sensible of the undesirableness of such investments as the purchases proposed in the letters; but having in view the position of certain old accounts, and looking to the whole circumstances, and particularly to the fact that the contemplated arrangements for the working of the credits are largely part of transactions in

The City of Glasgow Bank Trial.

existence for many years, and previously brought under consideration of the Board by the present Manager, the Board deemed it expedient to come to their present decision, as referred to in minute of 30th December, 1875.

You were not cognisant of the terms of the minute at the time?—I was not.

But you knew the transactions to which it related?—I did.

There was a credit, No. 24/6, for £235,000?—There was.

In whose favour? Explain what you know about it?—The credit was granted to James Morton & Co., and was drawn under in favour of Holmes, White & Co., of Melbourne. The limit of the credit was £235,400, but the credit was reduced to the extent of £100,000 by the drafts of Glen Walker & Co.; and the same securities that were held against 24/6 were put up as a security against the new credit for £100,000. That was the credit 38/47.

Then was the original sum reduced?—The original sum of the credit was reduced by £100,000 by the opening of the new credit.

That had just the effect of splitting it into two, had it not? —Precisely.

I should have read you the other minute of 11th January, 1877 :—

It was proposed and agreed to that the Bank should accept drafts by Glen Walker & Co. to the extent of £20,000, in renewal of those retired for a like amount due 1st instant on a/c Glen Walker & Co., Melbourne, per minute of 30th December, 1875.

Also, that the Bank should accept drafts by Glen Walker & Co. to the extent of £100,000, to retire a like amount, drawn by Holmes, White & Co., of Melbourne, on account of James Morton & Co. The securities at present held against Holmes, White & Co.'s drafts to be placed as security against the drafts of Glen Walker & Co. Letter to be obtained from James Morton & Co. to this effect, and no drafts to be accepted until this letter is in possession of the Bank.

The original credit you say was for £235,000 to James Morton & Co.?—Yes.

It was operated upon by Holmes, White & Co.?—It was.

And that was reduced to £135,000 by taking Glen Walker & Co.'s bills for Holmes, White & Co.'s?—Precisely. Glen Walker & Co.'s acceptances were discounted by John Innes Wright & Co., and the proceeds, so far as received by the Bank, were paid into the credit of credit 38/47. That was one of the credits into which 24/6 was split.

Did Innes Wright & Co. account to the Bank for the amount of these drafts?—Not for the whole.

Who came to the Bank with regard to these drafts?—Mr. Inglis, a clerk of Potter, Wilson & Company.

Did Inglis explain to you how he was taking charge of the

Evidence for Prosecution.

matter?—He said he had a general supervision over that credit of £100,000.

But he came on behalf of Innes Wright & Co.?—On behalf of Potter, Wilson & Co.

Was it Potter, Wilson & Co. who were taking the supervision of that?—Yes.

Did you call the attention of the Manager, Mr. Robert Stronach, to these short payments on the part of Innes Wright & Co.?—I did.

Did he make any observation?—He was very much displeased.

Were you sent by him on more than one occasion to Innes Wright & Co. to inquire about it?—Yes; and I also spoke to Mr. Inglis, Potter's clerk, regarding the matter, complaining of the short payments; for example, if they got drafts for £10,000, perhaps Mr. Scott, of John Innes Wright & Co., would only pay one-half of that instead of paying in the £10,000.

Instead of paying in the proceeds that they got by discounting the bills, they only paid in a part?—Yes.

And you were sent by Mr. Stronach to remonstrate against that proceeding?—Yes.

And you did so, both to Mr. Inglis, who was supervising, or at least who was saying he was supervising, on behalf of Potter, Wilson & Co., and also to Innes Wright & Co.?—I did.

Whom did you see on these occasions when you went to Innes Wright & Co.?—Mr. Scott, as a rule; sometimes I saw Mr. Wright also.

What did Mr. Scott say when you saw him on these occasions, and you complained of him retaining these moneys?—He made excuses, and said that he was waiting telegraphic advice or such like from London.

What did Mr. Innes Wright say about it when you saw him?—He stated that Mr. Scott generally took charge of these things.

Was that all he said?—There was one occasion when Mr. Scott was from home in London, and Mr. Wright said that when the short payments were made he was waiting till he got telegraphic advice from Mr. Scott; the drafts had not been placed.

Did he seem to be aware that short payments had been made? —Oh, yes! [Shown account No. 399.] I have seen that account before. It is an account current between Glen Walker & Co. and John Innes Wright & Co. and the Bank. I think it was Mr. Inglis, Potter, Wilson & Co.'s clerk, who brought it to the Bank. It refers to the drafts on 38/47, and the payments made to the Bank against them. The last date in the series is 25th January, 1878. The accounts are signed by John Innes Wright & Co. The firm's signature there is in Mr. Scott's handwriting. The ultimate debit against the firm of short payments retained by them is £48,668 1s. 2d., being money belonging to the Bank which they had received and

The City of Glasgow Bank Trial.

Wm. Morris. failed to pay into the Bank. The date of the beginning of the account is March, 1877. [Shown minute of Directors dated 14th March, 1878, and referred to the following passage] :—

> With reference to the minute of 28th February last in regard to accounting by Messrs. John Innes Wright & Co. of proceeds of drafts in connection with the credits therein named, Messrs. Stewart and Potter, the committee appointed to deal with the matter, reported that they had had an interview with Mr. Wm. Scott, of the firm of Messrs. John Innes Wright & Co., and had arranged for a settlement by cash and securities to be completed by 21st March current, as detailed in the statement now submitted, and which was ordered to be lodged.

and also the minute of 21st March, 1878, containing the following passage :—

> Mr. Stewart reported that, as appointed by last meeting, Mr. Potter and he had had an interview with Mr. William Scott, of the firm of Messrs. John Innes Wright & Co., which resulted in his promise to send to the Bank acceptances by his London firm to the extent of £10,000 additional to those already held by the Bank; to realise forthwith sugar to the extent of from £7000 to £8000, to be paid to the Bank; and to meet the committee again on Wednesday next at twelve o'clock for further and final arrangements.

I was aware that that committee had been appointed, although I had not seen the minutes, and I was present at a meeting of the committee which was held in Mr. Potter's office in Gordon Street. There were present at that meeting Mr. Stewart, Mr. Potter, and Mr. William Scott, of John Innes Wright & Company. [Shown No. 400.] That statement was produced at the meeting. It was drawn up by me. It contains a statement of the short payments, £48,000, and a list of the payments to be made, and of the security to be lodged against the debt. The document is in the following terms :—

J. INNES WRIGHT & Co.   1st March, 1878.

Arrangement as to settlement of G. W. & Co.'s balance.

Dr.

To balance, say - - - - - - - - - - - -		£48,000

Cr.

London firm's acceptances already in Bank's possession, viz. :—

1st acceptances due 26th April, 1878, - - - - -		3,000
,, 26th July ,, - - - - -		5,000
,, 26th Oct. ,, - - - - -		7,000
,, 26th Jan., 1879, - - - - -		7,000
		£22,000
2nd Cash to Account on or before 21st March, - -		10,000
3rd ,, or other approved mercantile security, on or before 21st March, - - - - -		7,500
4th London firm's acceptances, due end of June, to be handed to Bank on or before 21st March, - -		2,500
5th Cash or securities before date above mentioned, -		6,000
		£48,000

Evidence for Prosecution.

"London firm's bills to be given to-day for £10,000. Wm. Scott to give orders for sale of sugar to-day. Mr. Scott meets us on Wednesday to arrange the remainder." There are two different handwritings on that document. The body of it, down to the summation of £48,000, was written by me. The words, "London firm's bills to be given to-day for £10,000. Wm. Scott to give orders for sale of sugar to-day. Mr. Scott meets us on Wednesday to arrange the remainder," are in Mr. Stewart's handwriting. There was considerable discussion at the meeting about this matter. Mr. Stewart took the leading part in the conversation for the Bank.

What did he say? Did he make any observation after that statement was produced?—Yes; he remarked to Mr. Scott that it was a very ugly matter indeed, and he could only characterise it by one name, and so long as he held the onerous and honourable position of the Chairman of Directors of the Bank he would not allow such a thing to be permitted.

As so dealing with the funds of the Bank?—As so dealing with the funds of the Bank.

After he said that, did Mr. Scott make any suggestion?—Mr. Scott wished evidently to make some remark, and he asked me to retire. I retired, with Mr. Stewart's permission.

Did Mr. Stewart seem to be really in earnest, and angry?—Yes, he was; he was very much heated. I remained out of the room for about ten minutes, when I was recalled, I think by Mr. Potter.

When you returned to the room, how were the three parties then engaged; what were they doing?—They were on their feet, apparently dismissing. Mr. Stewart made a remark to me. He said that I need not take any notice of what had passed.

Did he say what had passed? Did he refer to it in any other terms?—The heat of the meeting—that I need not take any notice of the heat of the meeting while I was in the room.

Were these the words he used—that you need not take any notice of the heat of the meeting?—Yes.

Did he say why?—I forget now.

Did he say that they had come to any arrangement or anything of that kind?—Yes, that the matter had been arranged satisfactorily.

Did he say with whom?—With Mr. Scott. I then left. The Bank at that time had in its possession £22,000 of the acceptances of John Innes Wright & Co.'s London firm—drafts by the Glasgow firm accepted by the London firm.

One of the things to be given in settlement was cash to account on or before 21st March, £10,000; did the Bank get that?—No.

Did they get anything instead of it?—They got an additional £10,000 of the London acceptances of John Innes Wright & Co.

The City of Glasgow Bank Trial.

Wm. Morris. More paper?—More paper.

Did the Bank get the items 3, 4, and 5, approved mercantile security, and so forth?—Not that I am aware of.

You never saw or heard of it?—No.

And it never was credited to them?—No.

Mr. Stewart says in his note, "Wm. Scott to give orders for sale of sugar to-day"; I suppose you don't know whether he gave the orders or not?—I am not aware.

But did any proceeds of such a sale come to the Bank?—No.

Has any part of that £48,000 been paid to this day, so far as you are aware, or had any part of it been paid at the stoppage of the Bank?—There was £8000 of the acceptances paid, leaving £40,000.

I believe from their failure to pay that money the Manager removed the conduct of the management of the £100,000 credit from them altogether?—Yes.

He did not entrust them with discounting any further?—No.

In what capacity were Innes Wright & Co. superintending that credit—in the interest of the Bank or whose?—The credit, of course, was a portion of James Morton & Co.'s credit.

I know, but they took charge of it?—They took charge of that portion of it.

The £100,000 being one of the portions into which the £235,000 was split?—Yes.

By the LORD JUSTICE-CLERK—For their own interest, or Morton's interest, or the Bank's interest?—I presume for Morton's interest.

By the LORD ADVOCATE—Did they charge commission?—I am not aware.

By the LORD JUSTICE-CLERK—As I understand this marginal credit, the Bank undertook to accept, within a certain margin, the drafts of the customer, which were to be discounted and the proceeds paid into the account?—Yes.

Innes Wright & Co. were employed to do that?—They were employed to discount the bills.

And they only paid part of the discount received, and retained the rest?—Precisely.

By the LORD ADVOCATE—[Shown No. 191.] That is a letter written by the Manager, Mr. Robert Stronach, and addressed to John Fleming, Esquire, dated 21st December, 1875, in the following terms:—

> City of Glasgow Bank,
> Glasgow, 21st December, 1875.

My Dear Sir,—I have your private note of yesterday, and am sorry to hear that the indulgence shown by the Directors respecting the Brown pro-note for £5000 has not been sufficient to the requirements of the case. I can, therefore, only bring the matter up again for the consideration of the Directors on Thursday, but I do

Evidence for Prosecution.

so very reluctantly, I assure you, knowing the feeling which existed among them when the matter was put before them last week, and of which you are aware.

Referring to the amount we have come under cash advance to you on the No. 2 cash account, £27m/ or thereby, and should be very glad if you could arrange to relieve us of this or part at your earliest convenience.—Yours faithfully,

R. S. STRONACH.

John Fleming, Esq., London.

P.S.—Please send me the two acceptances of Mr. Brown p. £2500 each in the meantime.

The body of the letter is in my handwriting. The *P.S.* is in the Manager's handwriting. Letter No. 191c, Mr. Stronach to John Fleming, 23rd May, 1878, read as follows:—

City of Glasgow Bank,
Glasgow, 23rd May, 1878.

My Dear Sir,—I brought up your application for a renewal of credits 38/5 p. £15,000 and 39/47 p. £25,000 at our meeting to-day; and, as I anticipated, great dissatisfaction was expressed that no tangible reduction was made upon the former, and that you should approach at all for a renewal of the latter, which was quite a temporary transaction, and only to remain in force until such time as the mails assumed their normal condition. And as we presume this difficulty has now been got over, it is very much to be regretted indeed that you should find it necessary to ask for an extension of this credit. Just to show you that the Directors have good cause for being aggrieved at the very marked manner in which your credits on the circle have been growing these few years past, I send you a comparative statement herewith of the amounts on the circle at the beginning of the Bank's financial year since 1875, which be good enough to peruse carefully and return with any comments you may think necessary to make upon the anticipated accounts and those informal in other respects.

Particularly I would call your attention to anticipations on Bombay, Rangoon, Fowlie's credit, and the two credits under consideration to-day.—Yours very truly,

R. S. STRONACH,
Manager.

John Fleming, Esq.,
London.

P.S.—Please let me have a formal application for the Mail Credit, dated Tuesday, and restrict it to £25m/.

That letter and the postscript are in my handwriting. It is signed by Mr. Stronach, the Manager. [Shown No. 186, letter, John Fleming to Mr. Stronach, 12th April, 1875.] Letter read as follows:—

17 and 18 Leadenhall Street, London, E.C.
12th April, 1875.

R. S. Stronach, Esq.,
City of Glasgow Bank, Glasgow.

Dear Sir,—Referring to the meeting I had with your Directors and yourself on Thursday, the 1st inst., respecting the state of our account with the Bank, I now beg to detail the terms of the agreement come to as I understood them.

The City of Glasgow Bank Trial.

Wm. Morris.

1. Smith, Fleming & Co., as a firm, and the partners as individuals, pledge themselves to abstain absolutely from all speculative operations unless specially sanctioned by the Bank.

2. They are to hold all property belonging to the firm, as per annexed statement, as security or cover to the Bank for its various advances to them; but inasmuch as it is of the greatest importance that the credit of the firm should not be injured, but be carefully maintained, no public transfer of the property is meanwhile to be made. The realisation of the property is to be left in S., F. & Co.'s hands, who undertake faithfully to account for and pay over to the Bank the whole proceeds of all property realised.

3. The Bank's charge for commission for all the credits issued for S., F. & Co.'s accommodation, as per list herewith, shall be at the rate of ½ per cent. per annum, and this arrangement is to be retrospective as from 1st January, 1875.

4. The Bank's charge for interest on all cash advances to S., F. & Co. shall be at the rate of 3½ per cent. per annum as from 1st January, 1875.

A statement of the balances of various accounts, as on 31st March last, is appended.

5. The Bank shall advance the sum of £100,000 at the rate of 3½ per cent. per annum, for the acquisition of £100,000 of the stock of the Canterbury and Otago Company, £7800 of which is to be provided by me, credit for the equivalent of (£7800) being given to Smith, Fleming & Co. in account with the Bank at 1st January, 1875.

6. The £100,000 of stock as above shall be held by trustees in trust for the following purposes :—

   (1) To pay interest at the rate of 3½ per cent. per annum to the Bank for the £100,000 advanced for the purchase of the stock.

   (2) To pay the whole of the surplus income arising from the stock, after meeting the charge for interest as above, to the credit of S., F. & Co.'s account with the Bank, and to continue doing so until all S., F. & Co.'s debts to the Bank have been liquidated.

   (3) Nothing was agreed as to the ultimate disposition of the stock upon the final liquidation of all S., F. & Co.'s obligations to the Bank, but I venture to suggest that in that event the trustees be directed to re-transfer the stock at cost price (viz., par) to the parties who furnished it, or their assignees or heirs.

7. A comparison of the charges on S., F. & Co.'s debt, with their probable incomings from all sources, as per memo. herewith, shows they have the command of an annual surplus amounting at present to £25,000, applicable to the reduction of their debts to the Bank. They accordingly undertake to pay £25,000 per annum in reduction of their debt to the Bank, in addition to paying punctually all charges for interest and commission.

The reduction is, in the first place, to be made on the credits, and as these involve an annual charge of 5 per cent. for commission, stamps, exchange, and discount, each reduction will be attended with a corresponding saving in future annual charges, which saving shall be applied in further reduction of the principal of the debt; and thus, starting with an annual payment of £25,000 applied to the reduction of the credits, which involve an annual charge of 5 per cent., there should be, in course of fourteen years, an aggregate reduction in the debt of half a million sterling.

The credits being duly liuqidated shall be followed by the liquidation of the cash advances.

Evidence for Prosecution.

8. Regarding the credits, W. Nicol & Co. have undertaken to pay off the Bombay credit, now amounting to about £260,000, at the rate of £20,000 per annum; and Fleming & Co. have undertaken to liquidate their credit, now amounting to £60,000, at the rate of £5000 per annum; and they have undertaken to hold the properties enumerated in the statement herewith under lien to the Bank as security for these credits.

Todd, Findlay & Co., of Rangoon and Moulmein, have undertaken to come under obligation for the Rangoon credit, amounting to £90,000, and to liquidate the same at the rate of £15,000 per annum, but I am unable to place their undertaking in your hands until arrangements now in progress for retiring certain acceptances of ours to Todd, Findlay & Co. against the debt to you as by the old firm of Todd, Findlay & Co. (*i.e.*, before Mr. Mair became a partner). I am in correspondence with Mr. Morton about this matter, which, I have not the slightest doubt, will be shortly arranged, when I shall be at liberty to place in your hands Mr. Mair's obligation, which is already in mine.

I shall be glad to learn whether I have correctly stated the understanding come to, and whether it be desired that it be reduced to a formal agreement.—I am, dear sir, yours faithfully,

JOHN FLEMING.

1.

Property belonging to Smith, Fleming & Co., pledged as security to the City of Glasgow Bank.

Tarapore Tea Gardens.
108 British India Steam Co. Shares.
150 Shares Great Eastern Telegraph Shares.
300 Shares West Calder Oil Co.
50 Shares North British and Mercantile Insurance Co.
400 Shares Universal Marine Insurance Co.
100 Shares Ocean Marine Insurance Co.
19 Shares Tuticorin Press Co. Shares.
10 Shares North China Insurance Shares.
City of Glasgow Bank Stock, £1000.
Antwerp Tool Factory.
R. Duckworth & Co.'s debt.
Gorst & Lance's debt.
T. D. Findlay & Co.'s p/notes, £80,000.

13th April, 1875.

2.

Credits issued by the City of Glasgow Bank as on Smith, Fleming & Co.'s account, 31st March, 1875.

Bombay,	-	-	-	-	£254,564	3	5
Kurrachee,	-	-	-	-	60,000	0	0
Rangoon,	-	-	-	-	87,390	15	7
Colombo,	-	-	-	-	90,500	0	0
33/50 our account,			-		60,000	0	0
36/35 Sawmill Shares,	-		-		10,000	0	0
					£562,454	19	0

Then there is No. 3—Cash advances to Smith, Fleming & Co. amounting to £771,581 18s. 2d.

Wm. Morris.

4.

Estimate of Debt Charges and Incomings.

Credits aggregating £570,000 will cost per annum for commission, stamps, exchange, and discounts, 5 per cent., - - - - -	£28,500
Cash advance, say £770,000 at 3½ per cent., -	23,485
Premium of insurance on J. Fleming's life, -	4,000
	£55,985

Incomings.

Bombay and Kurrachee, interest on partners' capital and on balances, - - - -	£13,000	
Proportion of profits, - - - - - -	28,000	
		£41,000
Home securities, - - - - - - - -		10,500
Interest on money engaged in working this business, -		3,500
Todd, Findlay & Co., - - - - - - - -		15,000
Fowlie, - - - - - - - - - -		1,000
		£71,000
Probable surplus from Canterbury and Otago stock, - -		9,000
		£80,000
Charges as above, - - - - -		55,985
		£24,015

13th April, 1875. JOHN FLEMING.

The total indebtedness of Smith, Fleming & Co., as at 31st March, 1875, was £1,334,000; and at the stoppage of the Bank £1,900,000 or thereby.

Do you see pencil marks on that document?—Yes.

In whose handwriting? Some in Mr. Stronach's?—Some in Mr. Stronach's.

What are they? Mention one or two of them?—"The power to continue the credits from time to time."

At page 6 do you see another handwriting on it, near the foot?—" Five years to hold securities, then sell if required ; £25 when due."

In whose handwriting is that addition?—Mr. Potter's.

On the next page is there not another addition in Mr. Potter's handwriting?—Yes, " Life Policies."

In the minute of the directors of date 11th January, 1877, it is said:—

It was proposed and agreed to that the Bank should accept drafts by Glen Walker & Co. to the extent of £20,000 in renewal of those retired for a like amount due 1st instant on account Glen Walker & Co., Melbourne, per minute of 30th December, 1875.

Also, that the Bank should accept drafts by Glen Walker & Co. to the extent of £100,000 to retire a like amount, drawn by Holmes, White & Co., of Melbourne, on account of James Morton & Co. The securities at present held against Holmes, White & Co.'s drafts to be placed as security against the drafts of Glen Walker & Co. Letter to be obtained from James Morton & Co. to this effect.

Evidence for Prosecution.

I also read the minute of 30th December, 1875, there referred
to :—

A letter was read from Mr. W. Glen Walker applying for an open letter of credit for £20,000 in favour of Messrs. Glen Walker & Co., Melbourne, to be drawn at or under 6 mos/st., and depositing stock of the New Zealand and Australian Land Company, Limited, in security. The application was granted on the usual terms and conditions, the details being left to the Manager to arrange.

Was that credit granted?—It was.

Was that New Zealand stock referred to in the minute of December lodged?—No.

The security stipulated was not lodged?—It was not lodged.

Was any other security lodged in lieu of it?—Not that I am aware of.

Did the Bank ultimately come under cash advance for the whole of these credits?—It did.

To whom was the cash advanced by the Bank debited?— £20,000 was debited to W. Glen Walker.

I call your attention to a minute of 28th February, 1878 :—

A letter was read from Messrs. Smith, Fleming & Co., dated London, 26th February, 1878, applying for letters of credit for £25,000 in favour of Messrs. W. Nicol & Co., Bombay, to be drawn as 3 mos./st., in terms of their letter; the application was granted on the understanding that the drafts are to be retired at maturity. The Manager reported that the Bank had recently been brought into cash advance to the extent of £48,000 from the proceeds of drafts being short accounted for by Messrs. J. Innes Wright & Co. in connection with the credit of £100,000 granted to Glen Walker & Co. per minute of 11th January, 1877, and also £18,000 in the placing of the drafts of J. Nicol Fleming in liquidation. It was resolved to appoint Messrs. Stewart and Potter a committee to deal with this matter, and to report.

Was the credit authorised by that minute carried out?—The credit of £25,000 was.

Will you explain what you know of the shortcoming of £18,000 in regard to the drafts of Nicol Fleming?—These were Calcutta drafts accepted by the Bank and discounted by John Innes Wright & Co.; £18,000 is the sum short paid from the draft they got away from the Bank.

Their duty was to pay the proceeds of the bills they got?— Yes.

Into the Bank to the account of J. Nicol Fleming?—Yes, to retire old drafts maturing.

And they failed to account for £18,000?—Yes.

What was the date of that failure? About what time did they discount these bills?—It was over a long period—throughout a considerable period.

For a considerable period prior to that report in 1878?— Precisely.

Wm. Morris. Had you been sent to remonstrate against that shortcoming of £18,000?—Yes, I had.

Sent by Mr. Stronach?—By Mr. Stronach.

And whom did you see when you went to remonstrate with Innes Wright & Co.?—Mr. Scott.

Did you see Mr. Innes Wright?—I may have seen him, but I don't recollect.

What excuse was given?—The excuse that he gave in regard to Glen Walker & Co.'s drafts was he was waiting telegraphic advice from London, or some such excuse.

I suppose the Bank had to retire the whole of these acceptances eventually?—Yes.

No. 400 is a pencil jotting by Mr. Scott of the liabilities of his firm?—Yes.

He there enters the shortcoming of £18,000 as due by the firm?—He does.

Read it.—" J. N. F. account, £18,000, securities for same will be handed to Mr. R. S. S. on or before 21st March, 1878, William Scott, 2/3/78; 21st March, 78. This has not been done."

In whose handwriting are the words "This has not been done"?—Mr. Robert Stronach, the Manager's.

By the LORD JUSTICE-CLERK—What was the date of the meeting you described with Messrs. Stewart, Stronach, and Potter about Scott's short payment?—About the beginning of March last.

By the LORD ADVOCATE—[Shown No. 120]—Where was that book kept?—As a rule, the Manager had it in his possession. It was made up by me. So far as I am aware, it was not communicated to Mr. Morison, the accountant, or to any of the other officials of the Bank. It is titled on the outside—" Special securities, J. N. F., S., F. & Co., J. M. & Co., and others." The initials are those of James Nicol Fleming, Smith, Fleming & Co., and James Morton & Co. That book was made up at the balancing period of June, 1877. It contains statements in either ink or pencil of the whole indebtedness to the Bank of James Nicol Fleming, Smith, Fleming & Co., and James Morton & Co. It includes their whole indebtedness, whether on open credits, cash advances, or past due bills. It also contains statements of the securities held against these credits in the case of each of them. James Nicol Fleming's account appears in that book as at 6th June, 1877. His total indebtedness upon cash credits, bills, and otherwise at that date was £1,142,480 11s. 7d. The summation of the securities stated to be held against that is £1,142,480 11s. 7d. The two sides balance.

By the LORD JUSTICE-CLERK—Do you mean that the securities were exactly equal in value to the debt?—Yes, it is so stated.

Evidence for Prosecution.

That is the meaning of the entry, as I read it. I made the entry myself.

By the LORD ADVOCATE—The total indebtedness of Smith, Fleming & Co. at the same date was £1,670,643, and the special securities stated to be held against that amount to £1,114,710, so that the advances were uncovered to the extent of (in round numbers) £560,000. The total indebtedness of James Morton & Co. at the same date was £1,858,294 11s. 6d., and the securities are entered at £1,018,807, leaving a deficit (in round numbers) of £840,000. Taking these three firms together, the Bank was in advance, or had given credit to them to the amount of (in round numbers) £4,670,000, and against that the Bank are stated in that book to hold securities to the amount of £3,275,000, leaving a total deficit of securities as against advances of £1,395,000. The date at which that is taken is as at the commencement of June, 1877. With regard to the securities stated to be held against James Nicol Fleming's indebtedness, the capital invested in his Manchester and Calcutta business is put down as a security granted to the Bank. The amount of that was £40,000. The Bank did not hold the capital embarked in his business, or any title to it. There is also entered a sum held in security by the British Linen Co. in course of being reduced, to the amount of £5814. The Bank had no title to that. Then there is an item of policies on Mr. Fleming's life, stated as a security for £100,000—that is, the total amount of the policies. These were only realisable to that extent on Mr. Fleming's death; there is no deduction made, and no estimate of their surrender or selling value. These are the insurances for which £4000 of premium appeared in a former account.

There is a sum of £796,000 brought out there among these securities; how do you get that out of the stocks that are stated there?—The stocks were valued at 400 per cent. premium, in order to make the two sides balance. These stocks consisted of New Zealand and Australian Land Company shares. Their par value was £62 10s. I am not aware of their ever having reached 400 per cent. premium.

But that was done for the purpose of making the two ends meet?—Yes.

The securities and the advances?—Yes.

Who directed that to be done?—Probably I did it myself.

Without directions?—Without directions.

When you say that probably you did it, do you mean you may not have done it yourself?—I did it myself; I may have got instructions from the Manager.

What were your instructions in regard to the preparation of that statement of advances and securities?—I don't think I had any particular instructions.

The City of Glasgow Bank Trial.

Wm. Morris. Had you any instructions in regard to it after you had begun the work?—No, I don't remember.

Did you show Mr. Stronach your valuation?—Yes, I think I did.

And you gave him the book?—He had the book.

In fact, he kept it after you made it up?—Yes.

How did you come to make the securities balance with the amount due in the case of James Nicol Fleming and not in the others?—I cannot remember; I don't recollect why that was done. James Nicol Fleming's account was in liquidation at the time; I mean, we were realising the securities as fast as we could.

Did you expect to get 400 per cent. premium for those stocks in realising them?—I had no idea of the value of the stocks.

Did you think at the time you made the entry that they would ever realise 400 per cent. in liquidation then?—No.

Why did you put them at 400 per cent. when making up that account as in liquidation?—I cannot tell.

In point of fact, when you made that entry, did you believe these stocks would bring that in liquidation at the time?—No, I did not.

But you thought the account would look better if the two sides balanced?—Probably. Taking next Smith, Fleming & Co.'s account, there are entered as securities policies of insurance on the life of John Fleming to the amount of £100,000. In the previous account the policies were on the life of James Nicol Fleming. The policies on the life of John Fleming are also stated at their full value as realisable at his death. Another special security stated is the estimated capital upon which Smith, Fleming & Co. were trading, £254,000. That is put as a special security held by the Bank against those advances. It was not held by the Bank. They were supposed to be trading with it.

There is another special security in that list—a debt due of £60,000; by whom was that due?—By William Nicol & Co. and Fleming & Co., of Bombay and Kurrachee respectively, to Smith, Fleming & Co. That is included in the £254,000.

In the £254,000 trading stock of those people which the Bank are stated to hold as security, how many elephants are included?—There were six elephants upon a schedule attached to the Rangoon security. With regard to Morton & Co.'s account, there are included as special securities life policies to the amount of £48,000 and £17,000; in all, £65,000. These are estimated at full value in the same way as the other policies.

Was there not £125,000 of policies?—I was not aware there was £125,000. I observe in this book an entry of £25,000,

Evidence for Prosecution.

and another of £120,000 in pencil.   That £120,000 is not included in the total summation.

By Mr. SMITH—I know that Mr. Wright has two firms—one in Glasgow and the other in London. I believe they are different firms. Mr. Scott is a partner of the Glasgow firm. As a rule, it was Mr. Scott whom I saw in my interviews about the accounts of the firm. The bills, I believe, were handed to the firm for the purpose of discounting. I am not aware how they were discounted. I know they were sent by Mr. Scott to his brother in London. I am not aware whether they received a commission for these.

But they were given to Wright & Co. in order that Mr. Scott might send them to his brother in London to be discounted?—Yes; or to some other broker.

Then Wright & Co. acted the part of bill-brokers in the matter?—Yes. [Shown No. 215, letter, J. Innes Wright & Co. to R. S. Stronach, dated Glasgow, 2nd August, 1876.] That letter is in the handwriting of Mr. Scott. It is apparently written on behalf of Glen Walker & Co., of Melbourne. The purpose of the transaction, I understood, was to enable Glen Walker & Co. to buy produce in Melbourne, which was to be shipped to this country. The proceeds were to go to pay these drafts. The application is for £100,000. Of these bills there were returned £40,000, and £3000 lapsed—that is to say, were not presented for acceptance.

By the LORD JUSTICE-CLERK—To the extent of £43,000 they were never turned into money.

By Mr. SMITH—That left £57,000 under this application which was actually used. That account was entered in the books of the Bank under the name of John Innes Wright & Co.

Was there anything else at the heading of the account?— Yes; " Wool Liens." Referring to the account, I find the drafts are favouring Glen Walker & Co., Melbourne.

That is to say, John Innes Wright & Co. were the primary debtors to the Bank under this letter, but Glen Walker & Co. were debtors also?—Yes, as being the drawers of the drafts.

So that, failing Wright & Co., the Bank would have a claim against Glen Walker & Co.?—I presume so.

Do you know if £35,000 of these drafts was used in the purchase of wool?—I cannot answer that.

Do you know that £25,000 was got upon wool liens to the value of £35,000, and paid into the Bank?—John Innes Wright paid into the Bank £25,000, but I am not aware if it was got upon wool liens.

Do you know if Glen Walker & Co. paid for some land with these drafts by instructions of the Bank?—I believe £17,000 was used by Glen Walker & Co. for the purchase of land on

The City of Glasgow Bank Trial.

Wm. Morris. behalf of the Edinburgh Pastoral Association. I was not aware at that time, but I now know that that was the Bank.

Do you know also if a further sum was used in the purchase of tin and tallow?—Yes; I have seen such a sum in Walker's statements to the amount of about £7000.

Was it not £8465?—Perhaps so. I cannot tell whether that tin and tallow was sent direct to Wright & Co., London. The undertaking in the letter is to pay in the proceeds of the produce actually shipped to account of drafts. I am not aware whether there was any loss. With regard to the original credit of £235,000, the application letter, I think, is dated in August, 1871. That credit was opened in favour of Holmes, White & Co., who, I believe, were merchants in Melbourne. Their drafts were accepted by the Bank, and were discounted by James Morton & Co. The £100,000 in favour of Glen Walker & Co. was in substitution of part of these drafts.

So it was really the substitution of Glen Walker & Co. for Holmes, White & Co. to the extent of £100,000 of the original credit opened in 1871?—Yes. These drafts were handed to Potter, Wilson & Co. for the purpose of discounting. Potter, Wilson & Co. handed them over to Innes Wright & Co. to be discounted. They were drawn by Glen Walker & Co.

Whom did they represent?—James Morton & Co., I should think.

By the Lord Justice-Clerk—It was on behalf of James Morton & Co.'s credit that Glen Walker & Co. did it.

By Mr. Smith—You understood that Glen Walker & Co. were the same as Morton & Co.—were acting on behalf of Morton & Co.?—Yes.

Was there anything on the face of the bills to show that such was their true character?—No.

Or anywhere else?—No; I think not.

By the Lord Justice-Clerk—Why were Glen Walker & Co.'s bills given to Potter?—Potter apparently was financing—was arranging. He held the drafts.

As the financial agent of Glen Walker & Co. in this country. Was that so?—I don't know, I am sure, whether they were financial agents or not.

Why did you give Glen Walker & Co.'s bills to Potter & Co.? —I cannot say why they were given; they were given for discount to replace drafts maturing under Morton's credit.

Why were they given to Potter's firm? Were they acting for the Bank, or were they acting for the customer, Glen Walker & Co.?—I cannot say who they were acting for.

But the fact is, the drafts were given to Potter's firm, and they gave them to Innes Wright & Co.?—Yes.

To discount?—To discount.

By Mr. Smith—What is the shortcoming upon these discounts

Evidence for Prosecution.

at this date? How much is it reduced to?—Upwards of £40,000 now.

There were some bills granted by the London firm in reduction of this balance?—Yes.

To what extent?—About £34,000 altogether, I think.

Supposing these London bills were paid, what would be the balance?—£26,000.

Is it not £16,000?—Yes, £16,000.

Did any one tell you if Wright & Co. had authority to retain any portion of these discounts?—Yes; I understood that they were allowed to retain £15,000.

So that it comes to this, that if the bills were paid, the sum due now would just be £1000 in excess of the sum they were allowed to retain?—Yes; but the sum they were allowed to retain was while they had the credit—while they were discounting the drafts, and not after.

How was this account entered in the Bank books?—I cannot say; the check clerk could answer that.

And you don't know how the account was closed?—The account is not closed; there is still a balance standing.

A balance at the debit of whom? Glen Walker & Co.?—I am not sure whether it is Glen Walker & Co.'s name that is the title of the account or not.

Wright & Co. had various accounts opened subsequently to June, 1875?—Yes.

If we except the wool lien credit and these discounts, are these accounts now all closed?—No.

Which of them are open?—There are a great number of accounts open of John Innes Wright & Co. still.

Are there any of the accounts which have been opened since 1875 still open?—Yes, they are still open.

The credit accounts?—The credit accounts are open—that is to say, the cash credits are still open; you are perhaps confounding them with the foreign and colonial credits.

There are no foreign and colonial credits which have been opened since 1875 now open?—No.

Do you know the indebtedness of Wright & Co. in June, 1875?—I think it is upwards of £400,000.

If you exclude the interest upon that sum, the wool lien credit, and these discounts, is the indebtedness now less or more? —Do you mean less on the present balance?

That is what I mean?—I cannot say whether it will be less on the present balance or not; that is to say, the balance at the stoppage of the Bank.

Do you know when the debt of £18,000 arose—the shortcoming in connection with J. Nicol Fleming's account?—I think it commenced about 1876. It arose from short payments of

Wm. Morris. the Bank's acceptances which they got from James Nicol Fleming to discount.

What was the form of these bills?—They were John Innes Wright's bills.

Was he drawer or acceptor?—They were drawn upon the Bank; they were all Bank's acceptances.

Were they given to Wright & Co.?—Yes; through J. Nicol Fleming.

By the LORD JUSTICE-CLERK—They were to have the bills discounted. I understood they were discounted; I believe they were sent to London.

By Mr. SMITH—Did these bills not come to Wright & Co. from Nicol Fleming?—Yes.

Then Wright & Co. will be responsible to Nicol Fleming for these bills?—Yes; I should say so.

By Mr. TRAYNER—No. 400 contains a statement of "arrangement as to settlement of G. W. & Co.'s balance," and it is headed "J. Innes Wright & Co."?—Yes.

In whose handwriting is that account down to the summation of £48,000?—In my own handwriting. It was written out by me prior to the meeting with Mr. Scott in Mr. Potter's office. It is dated 1st March, 1878. I cannot say on what day the meeting was held—perhaps the day after the preparation of this document. The portion of it "London firm's bills to be given to-day for £10,000. Wm. Scott to give orders for sale of sugar to-day. Mr. Scott meets us on Wednesday to arrange the remainder," is in Mr. Stewart's handwriting. I had that document with me at the meeting.

Was that last portion added by Mr. Stewart after he had spoken in the angry terms in which you described him as having spoken to Mr. Scott?—I cannot say. It was not on the paper when I took it to the meeting. I did not get it back from Mr. Stewart after I returned to the room. I next saw it sometime after; I may not have got it back till after the stoppage; I don't know when I got it back. When I next saw it, it had that last portion, "London firm's bills," etc., on it in Mr. Stewart's handwriting.

Had you become aware that that was the arrangement before you saw that writing by Mr. Stewart?—Yes.

Have you any doubt that that is just the embodiment by Mr. Stewart of the arrangement that took place when you were asked to retire?—No.

Along with that state there is a pencil slip, "J. N. F.'s account, £18,000. Securities for same will be handed to Mr. R. S. S. on or before 21st March, 1878"; that related to the same business, did it not?—No, it did not.

Was that given by Scott on the same date when the other arrangement was entered into?—I cannot say.

186

Evidence for Prosecution.

Had you that before you when you prepared this statement **Wm. Morris.** which was laid before the meeting?—No; I think not.

The next letter, No. 401, by Mr. Scott to Mr. Stewart, dated 21st March, 1878, says—"This is the Greenock Fast-day, so the sugar market is closed. Business will, no doubt, go on as usual on Monday or Tuesday first." Does that not enable you to come nearer the date of the meeting at which Mr. Scott undertook "to give orders for sale of sugar to-day"?—Yes; it must have been about the 20th, apparently.

From this letter you think the meeting with Mr. Stewart and Mr. Scott, to which you spoke, must have taken place about 20th March?—Evidently from this letter.

The postscript is, "The above was sent us in reply to our order to sell a cargo to-day"; so that Mr. Scott had sent to Greenock an order to sell in terms of his undertaking?—Apparently so.

And the reply comes back that it is the Fast-day, and so he excuses the non-fulfilment of it that day. That is what it comes to, is it not?—Yes.

By Mr. MACKINTOSH—Do you remember anything about the meeting referred to by Mr. Fleming in his letter to Mr. Stronach of 12th April, 1875 (No. 186), "Referring to the meeting I had with your Directors and yourself on Thursday"?—No; I remember there was such a meeting.

Look at the letter No. 78, from Mr. Stronach to John Fleming, 5th April, 1875, "In terms of the arrangement concluded at the meeting of the committee of Directors," etc. Does that refer to the same meeting?—I should think so.

You see from that letter that the meeting referred to in the letter of 12th April as a "meeting of your Directors" was a meeting with the "committee of Directors"?—Yes. I do not know who were the members of that committee. I believe that will appear from the minutes.

By the DEAN OF FACULTY—Was the arrangement in the letter of 12th April for the adjustment of Smith, Fleming & Co.'s account carried out?—I believe it was.

Was the account of Smith, Fleming & Co. taken from the current accounts on which customers were operating, and put into the accountant's department in consequence of that arrangement?—I am not aware whether it was in consequence of that arrangement or not.

But it was done at that time?—There was a sum transferred about that time.

Do you remember writing the letter of 20th April, 1875, Mr. Stronach to John Fleming, "I would suggest with reference to the accounts, and the majority of which appears to be dormant, that the inoperative should be consolidated, and that one or two having occasional operations, such as the No. 1 cash and

The City of Glasgow Bank Trial.

Wm. Morris. the No. 1 trust, to remain as they are for working purposes. This arrangement would simplify our working considerably here, and would, no doubt, I think, be equally advantageous to you"? —I remember something of that letter. The dormant accounts were those upon which there were few or no operations going on. These were put in the accountant's department. I cannot give the indebtedness of Smith, Fleming & Co., James Nicol Fleming, and Morton, as at 1st January, 1876, or at June, 1876.

What induced you to make up the indebtedness as at June, 1877?—Because previously these accounts were all kept upon sheets, and that was the date at which the book was made up; the balance was made up as at June, 1877. The sheets are still in existence; some of them may have been destroyed.

Did Morton's indebtedness arise before January, 1876?—Yes.

He was very heavily indebted, was he not, at the time you became Manager's clerk even?—Yes; even then.

But still had not Morton in Australia and New Zealand properties that were looked on as exceedingly valuable?—Yes, he had properties.

Have you not heard deliberations going on either amongst the Directors, or between the Directors and Mr. Stronach, as to the probability of these properties rising very largely in value, and clearing off the whole of his debt?—Yes; not clearing off the whole of his debt.

But clearing off a great part of it?—Yes.

Down to what date did you hear these deliberations?—The properties were always considered valuable. I heard that they were always considered valuable.

Had Smith, Fleming & Co. any Australian and New Zealand properties?—Yes; there were 1003 shares, I think.

I suppose you looked upon that property as having the same prospects as to rise as the property belonging to Morton?— Yes.

Had Smith, Fleming & Co. not pledged to the Bank properties at Bombay, Kurrachee, and in Rangoon?—Yes.

And these were only taken as security for debt after valuation made?—Yes. I believe part of these properties has been realised in Bombay. Some of it has not been realised. Their property in Rangoon was valued in the books at £86,000, I think. I am not aware that any of the Rangoon property has been sold.

At the time you made up that book in June, 1877, was the New Zealand stock quoted in the market lists?—No; I think not. I quoted it at par. I cannot at present state the indebtedness of Smith, Fleming & Co., as at 1st January, 1876.

At the end of 1875 had there been incurred by Smith, Fleming & Co. nine-tenths of that debt which they were owing to the Bank when it stopped?—I should think so. The greater **Wm. Morris.** portion of James Nicol Fleming's debt was incurred before 1876. I don't think there was any advance made to him from the beginning of 1876 onwards, except in connection with the Australian and New Zealand properties.

The Bank ordered these properties to be bought in Australia and New Zealand as a speculation of their own?—I don't know that.

But you know that they ordered these properties to be bought? —No, I did not.

Don't you know that they did buy property in Australia and New Zealand?—Not on behalf of James Nicol Fleming.

Did they buy property on their own account, in their own name, or in the name of others in trust for them?—Yes. I had no particular instructions to make up the book in June, 1877.

By the LORD ADVOCATE—I made it up for the information of the Manager, and to keep the state of accounts before him.

You said you heard some persons, in connection with the Bank, speculating as to the probable rise of Morton's securities? —Yes.

Who were these individuals?—The Manager.

Any other?—And Mr. John Hunter.

But none of the Directors of the Bank?—And Mr. Potter too, I think, was very sanguine as to the properties.

Are you making that statement from what you heard Mr. Potter say in your presence?—Yes.

What was Mr. Potter discussing at the time he made that statement as to his being sanguine, and with whom was he discussing?—He was discussing in regard to the New Zealand shares, a statement of which was before him and the Manager.

Were these the shares that the Bank themselves held?—Yes, or were supposed to have held.

Was it in regard to their own shares that he expressed that hope, or was it both in regard to their own shares and those they held in security?—I understood the observation as applying to both.

At the time he expressed a hope that the shares would rise, did he say anything as to how far they would extinguish Morton's indebtedness, or not?—No; he said nothing about that. He spoke generally about the probability of the shares rising. About 1875 certain accounts were dormant—that is, inoperative. There were debtor balances upon the whole of them.

And by dormant you mean that the debtor was not paying what was due to the Bank?—Yes.

Was the interest not accumulating?—Yes, I believe so; I am not aware whether interest was added when they were transferred or not.

The City of Glasgow Bank Trial.

You don't know whether it was entered, but I suppose you knew it was bearing interest?—Yes.

Then what you meant by dormant was that the debtor was not paying, but that interest was accumulating and the debt swelling?—Yes.

By the LORD JUSTICE-CLERK—In dormant accounts, which I suppose mean accounts where there are no operations, is interest charged generally?—It is.

Is it kept on—charged—year after year in the account?—Yes.

Or does it after a time cease to be charged?—No; I think not. It is continued to be charged.

This additional set of books—who directed you to keep them?—Mr. Alexander Stronach.

Why?—For his own convenience.

With regard to these particular debts?—Yes.

Where did you get the material that enabled you to keep the books?—I got it from the register downstairs, kept in the public office.

It was a duplicate you say?—Yes.

So I suppose the same persons had their accounts in the ordinary accounts who had their accounts in your books?—Yes; precisely.

Were they the same?—They were differently arranged—a little.

But the materials were substantially the same?—Precisely the same.

How did you come to value these securities at your own hand in the case of James Nicol Fleming?—I did not value the whole of the securities for James Nicol Fleming. It was only the stock that I extended in a pencil jotting.

I think you said that the value you attributed to the security in the book was exactly the same as the amount of indebtedness?—Yes.

Why did you do that? Had you any means of ascertaining that the value was the same, or that the securities were worth that amount?—No, I had not.

Was it a mere random thing?—Yes; a mere random thing. It was done upon the principle of making the two sides correspond.

Is that the only random sum in your book?—No.

There may be others?—Yes; there are securities that really did not exist.

And that was done entirely at your own hand?—It was done from information obtained from the Manager's sheets.

Without instructions?—Yes; from drafts made out by the late Manager.

Would you have made any of these entries without authority from the Manager?—Oh, no.

Evidence for Prosecution.

You had authority for them all?—Yes.

Including that one of the valuation of the securities?—Well, nothing was said when the book was lying with the Manager—nothing was said with regard to the extension of the value of the stock.

But you assumed that was what you were meant to do?—Yes.

When you said that you made these entries from sheets made up by the late Manager, to whom did you refer?—Mr. Alexander Stronach.

It was from these sheets you made these entries?—Yes; with respect to Smith, Fleming & Co. and James Morton & Co.

Where were these sheets when you made up the book in 1877?—They were in my possession.

Was Mr. Robert Stronach aware that you had these things?—Yes; I think so.

He had seen the sheets?—Yes.

Just explain to me a little more distinctly about these marginal credits and the bills that were granted under them. If I rightly follow the course of the transaction it was this, that in consideration of securities the Bank undertook to accept bills to a specific amount, granting a variety of bills with the precise amount of the credit attached to them?—Precisely.

These bills being granted to the drawer and accepted by the Bank, he then proceeded to discount them?—Yes; but they were not always granted to the drawer.

But sometimes with the drawer's name on them, they were given by the Bank to be discounted, and the proceeds to be paid to them?—Yes.

Was that uniform, that the proceeds of the discount were to be paid to the account of the drawer in the Bank?—Not of the drawer—to the endorser of the bill or the applicant for the credit.

But that was the mode of dealing?—It was.

In this case the bills were drawn in favour of Glen Walker & Co., of Australia?—Yes.

They were accepted by the Bank, and handed to Potter, Wilson & Co. for the purpose of discounting them, and paying in the proceeds to the Bank?—Yes.

And they again employed Innes Wright & Co. to get them discounted?—Yes.

Innes Wright & Co. sent them to their London firm. Are the London firm brokers?—Not to the London firm.

Where did they send them?—To H. C. Scott, I think, as a rule.

As a bill broker?—Yes.

In order that he might discount them in London, and transmit the proceeds here?—Yes.

And that he failed to do to a certain extent?—Yes.

The City of Glasgow Bank Trial.

JOHN TURNBULL.

By the SOLICITOR-GENERAL—I have been cashier to the City of Glasgow Bank for about eighteen years, and I was accountant before that. I have been in the service of the Bank since 1843. When I became a servant of the Bank Mr. Robert Salmond was the Manager. He ceased to be Manager about 1858, when the Bank resumed after the stoppage in 1857. I cannot tell how long Mr. Robert Stronach was in the employment of the Bank. He was there before the stoppage in 1857. It was my duty as cashier to take charge of making up the weekly returns of gold and silver coin. I kept two books—the cashier's ledger and the circulation ledger. [Shown Nos. 95 and 96.] These are the books which I kept. The cashier's ledger (No. 95) contains entries showing day by day the reserve stock of money as represented by gold and silver and bank notes; that is, the gold, silver, and bank notes which were not out in issue or in the hands of the tellers. The entries in that book are all correct. No. 96 is the circulation ledger, in which should be shown the gold and silver lying at the head office as against notes issued in excess of the authorised circulation.

In the beginning of 1878, did you find the Bank's credit being strained?—Yes.

Did you find renewals of bills being refused in London?—Yes.

Did that necessitate gold being sent to London from the Bank?—Yes. During the week ending 5th January there had been £60,000 in gold sent to London.

From whom did you get the directions to send it up?—From the Manager, through Mr. Murdoch, who is my assistant.

In making up the statement or figures of the entries for that week, was the amount correctly stated of what was in your hands?—No.

What was the incorrectness?—£60,000.

The £60,000 which was sent to London was not deducted?—No.

Explain to me how that came about?—I cannot give you any explanation further than the fact.

Who suggested it to you?—I must do it. We are bound to do it to agree with the issue of notes.

Did you speak to Mr. Stronach about that?—Not upon that particular occasion.

Did you speak to him when you had to make the return to the Commissioners of Stamps and Taxes?—Not on that occasion.

When did you speak to him?—Several times afterwards—frequently afterwards.

Had you sent several returns to the Commissioners of Stamps and Taxes, stating the sum at the full amount without taking off the £60,000, before you spoke to him?—I may have.

Evidence for Prosecution.

When did you speak to him first about it?—I cannot give the date of that.

But nearly?—I really cannot give the date. It may have been a week or a fortnight.

But a very short time after the thing was done?—Yes.

What did you say to him?—I expressed my regret that the thing should have been necessary or should have been done—that it was wrong to do it.

What did he say?—That it could not be helped.

Anything more?—I think not—not at that time. Afterwards he said of course that he was responsible for it.

Between that date in January, 1878, and down to the stoppage of the Bank, in how many weeks was the amount of gold overstated in the returns made?—I think during the whole time, except two weeks, these two weeks being the week ending 16th February and the week ending 16th March.

That was down to 28th September, which was the last, about which I will ask you more particularly. Was the amount of over-statement increasing during that time?—It varied.

But did it gradually increase? Did it gradually come up to £293,182 at the end?—Yes; about that.

Will you look at the book, and say whether under the head of the amount of gold each day during these months there is not a double entry made?—There is an interlining.

That is to say, within the space for the entry of gold for that day there is an interlining?—Yes.

Does the large figure give the amount that was returned?—No; it gives the actual cash, and the other gives the shortage.

Do those inserted figures give correctly the amount of shortage in each case?—Yes; the last return that was made was for the week ending 28th September, 1878. The amount in that return was stated correctly according to the amount in the coffers of the Bank. I did not sign that last return. I had signed all the previous ones, and sent them in.

Why did you not sign the last one?—I had various reasons. I wished that the last return should not have been sent at all.

Because it corrected the previous ones?—Not only that; but the Bank had stopped payment, and the right of issue was lost, and there was nothing to be gained by sending the return.

But the return was quite contradictory of the previous ones?—Of course it was.

Who signed it?—The Manager. I remember of a meeting of the Board on 11th October, 1878, after the Bank had stopped. I was called in before the Directors that day.

Who spoke to you?—The Chairman, I think.

Who was the Chairman?—Mr. Salmond, I think.

The City of Glasgow Bank Trial.

J. Turnbull. What did he ask you?—He asked my reasons why the return had not been made of the last week that the Bank was open. I am not sure it was Mr. Salmond that spoke to me; but I think so; he was in the chair. [Shown No. 317.] That is a letter dated the same day, and addressed by me to Mr. Cousins, Inland Revenue Office, London. It is as follows:—

City of Glasgow Bank,
11th October, 1878.

W. W. Cousins, Esq.,
    Inland Revenue, London.

Dear Sir,—I beg to acknowledge receipt of your letter of the 7th instant and to inform you that immediately on receipt I handed it to the Manager of the Bank, under whose instructions I have hitherto made the returns to your office. You may probably be aware that the Bank has stopped payment, and that its affairs are under investigation.—I am, sir, your obedient servant,

JOHN TURNBULL.

Did you lay that letter before the meeting of Directors?—I sent them a copy.

You gave them a copy of it?—Yes.

Was the statement in that letter true as to the instructions under which you had made the returns as you had made them?—Quite true.

Did anything else pass between the Directors and you after you showed them that letter?—No, nothing more.

By Mr. ASHER—I think you said that it was in January, 1878, that the gold was overstated for the first time in the return to the Inland Revenue?—Yes.

And that return was so made, you said, by the instructions of the Manager?—All the returns were.

Did you get any instructions from the Directors with regard to that matter?—None.

When did the Directors first know that the gold had been overstated in the return?—I don't think they knew at all until after the Bank had stopped. I have been cashier of the Bank for about eighteen years; and before that I was in the employment of the Bank for about seventeen years. As cashier I had charge of several of the securities.

When did you first suspect that anything was wrong with the Bank?—Never until the gold was meddled with.

Until the error was made in the return of the gold in January, 1878, you, as cashier, had no reason to suspect that there was anything wrong with the Bank?—None whatever.

And the error in the return of the gold was your only reason then for suspecting; is that so?—That is so. I am a shareholder of the Bank for £1000 of stock. I still hold that stock. I have known Mr. Salmond for a long time. He has lived in the country, in Ayrshire, for many years. I cannot give a

194

Evidence for Prosecution.

date when he went to reside there, but I should think it must be twelve or fifteen years ago—probably more. I think he has not had a house in Glasgow for a number of years.

So that he came up from the country for the weekly meetings of the Bank when he was able to attend?—Yes.

How long did the weekly meetings last?—I cannot tell that; I was never present at any of them. I should think about an hour usually, or an hour and a half.

Was it only for the weekly meetings that Mr. Salmond had been in the habit of coming to the Bank for a number of years?—I think so.

By Mr. TRAYNER—Would you look at some papers that are attached to the circulation ledger, in the inside of it? You will find there the amount of cash, as at 5th June, 1878, initialed by Mr. Stewart?—Yes.

And different sums are distinguished there as being situated in different safes?—Yes.

Was that, as initialed, a correct state of the cash in the Bank at the time?—Perfectly correct.

You were cashier, and you know that that is in point of fact the correct amount of cash that was in the different safes as there put down?—Perfectly correct.

By the SOLICITOR-GENERAL—Did Mr. Stewart take that upon your statement without counting the gold himself or turning it out at all?—He counted the notes.

But he did not count the gold?—Not in 1878.

Did he take it on trust from you?—Entirely.

And he initialed the amount that you had put down?—Yes.

Were you aware at the end of 1877 that the Directors of the Bank had advanced over five millions to three firms—James Nicol Fleming, Smith, Fleming & Co., and James Morton & Co.?—No.

You knew nothing about the internal affairs of the Bank?—No.

By the LORD JUSTICE-CLERK—Why was it on that particular occasion in 1878 that Mr. Stewart took your reason for not counting the gold?—There are a number of reasons. It was generally done at the close of the business of the year, and of the day late in the afternoon; and the safe was a very small safe, and it was a very troublesome thing to take out such a large quantity of gold as that. It cost us a great deal of trouble; that was one reason. I volunteered to turn the gold out if Mr. Stewart wished it, but he was satisfied.

You would have turned it out if he had wished it, but it was quite a correct state, you say?—Yes, quite a correct state.

When was the gold first short?—On 5th January, 1878, or about that date.

The City of Glasgow Bank Trial.

J. Turnbull. And you were aware when you made the return that it was in excess of what you had?—Yes, perfectly.

And you continued to do that until the end?—Yes.

Was there no check upon the amount of gold in the ordinary management of the Bank?—There was a check at the close of each year in the Directors counting it.

But did the Directors count the gold?—In 1877, in 1876, and previous years, it was all counted.

They did so?—Yes.

Did they do it in 1878?—They did not count it in 1878.

Why?—They took it upon my word.

But how did they come to give up the practice?—There were several reasons.

Was it your doing?—No.

Then how did they come to give up the practice?—Well, I cannot tell. It used to be taken out and laid upon the floor of the Manager's room, but in consequence of some alterations in the office the Directors came to sit in the Manager's room, and they had their large table in the middle of the room.

Was there any reason in 1878 why they should not have done the same thing that they did in 1877?—That was one reason.

Was that a reason applicable to 1878 only?—To 1878 only.

However, the fact is that they did not count it?—They did not count it.

The first short return, you say, was on 5th January, 1878?—I think so.

What had been returned the week before?—In January, 1878, the total amount of gold and silver in hand was £577,763; in the previous week it was £557,015.

What is the difference?—About £20,000.

By LORD CRAIGHILL—What was the amount of gold that was returned to the Inland Revenue office in the week before 5th June, 1878?—The amount of gold and silver returned on 1st June, 1878, was £613,642.

And the amount initialed by Mr. Stewart was what?—£338,500.

When had that gold been counted?—It was counted by the Directors the previous year.

But when had that gold been counted, the sum of which you gave to Mr. Stewart?—It was counted at various times since I took it in.

When had it been last counted?—The previous year.

Not since the previous year?—No.

On what did you proceed in making your returns to the Inland Revenue?—The returns to the Inland Revenue at that point show £200,000 of gold improperly stated.

But on what did you proceed in making your returns to the

Evidence for Prosecution.

Inland Revenue? Were the sums all the same every week?— They were altering every week.

On what did you proceed in making the alterations?—I don't understand your question.

How did you come to know what was in the coffers of the Bank?—By it being in my own possession.

When was it counted?—By me?

Yes?—I counted it every day as the gold came in and went out.

Was one of your reasons for not having the gold counted before Mr. Stewart on 5th June, 1878, that you were aware of the deficiency?—No.

By the LORD JUSTICE-CLERK—I understand that the return you made to the Inland Revenue was a thing you did yourself— the Directors had nothing to do with it?—Nothing whatever.

And you did not communicate with them before you made it?—No; never.

Then the only thing that was wrong was the return you made?—Yes.

And you returned it as if nothing had been taken out?—Yes.

By the SOLICITOR-GENERAL—The amount that was wrong stated has been entered in the space for the statement of the true figures every week in your book?—Yes.

The erroneous figure has been put into the book, and it is the adding of the true figure and the erroneous figure that made up the amount sent in the return?—Yes.

By the LORD JUSTICE-CLERK—That is the interlineation?— Yes.

By the SOLICITOR-GENERAL—What book is it in?—The circulation book.

By the LORD JUSTICE-CLERK—So, as I thought before, there is a double entry in your circulation book—one of which represents the actual gold, and the other represents the deficiency?— Yes.

By the SOLICITOR-GENERAL—For example, on 13th April, 1878, the amount put down on the blue line is £316,500, and above that there is put £120,000?—Yes.

And the return you made was the two together?—Yes; it embraced them both.

And wherever that occurs it is the same thing?—Yes.

That is in the circulation ledger?—Yes.

By Mr. TRAYNER—Is it not in the cashier's ledger?—This [No. 95] is the cashier's ledger; it contains what is right.

That is the book that Mr. Stewart initialed?—Yes.

It is right?—Yes.

And there are no interlineations?—No.

CHAPTER VII.

Evidence of the Manager of the Bank of Scotland and of Directors' Partners.

Jas. Wenley.

JAMES WENLEY.

By the SOLICITOR-GENERAL—I am manager of the Bank of Scotland in Glasgow. On the morning of Friday, 27th September last, I met Mr. Davidson, treasurer of the Bank of Scotland, to arrange with him that I should call upon Mr. Stronach. I was to refer Mr. Stronach to the conversation which Mr. Davidson had with him on 11th September, when Mr. Davidson urged upon him the necessity of taking up a large amount of the acceptances of the City of Glasgow Bank as they fell due, and further, to state to him that in consequence of the rumours——

Was there anything about the number being now greater than when that conversation took place?—No; and with reference to that conversation to say that, in consequence of the rumours affecting the City of Glasgow Bank, which had prevailed on the two previous days, Mr. Davidson thought that the necessity of taking up the acceptances of the Bank as they fell due was greater now than it had been at the interview to which I have referred. I called upon Mr. Stronach at the Bank, and communicated the message to him. He received it in silence, and said nothing for, I should think, two or three minutes.

Who spoke first?—I spoke first.

What did you say?—The pause was painful, and I referred to the cruelty of setting afloat such reports as had been prevalent for the previous two days.

And which had driven your bank to take this step?—And which had driven our bank to take this step. He said nothing, I think, for another minute or two, and then he remarked, in the possible event of the City of Glasgow Bank asking the other banks for assistance, whether I thought that assistance would be given to them. I said I had no authority to speak on behalf of the other Scotch banks, but that I had no doubt the Bank of Scotland would be quite willing to give the City of Glasgow Bank any reasonable assistance upon two conditions

Evidence for Prosecution.

—First, that they were shown to be in a sound state; and secondly, that they gave security. Just about this time Mr. Potter entered the room, and shortly afterwards Mr. Salmond. I stated to both of them what had taken place—what I had said to Mr. Stronach, and they all objected to an examination into the Bank's affairs, on the ground of the risk of publicity. I said that I thought the object might be attained if some individual in whom we all had confidence examined the books and said that he was satisfied.

Without revealing anything?—Without revealing anything. I suggested that without giving any details, if such a person examined the Bank's books, and simply said he was satisfied as to the position of the Bank, that that might be enough.

What did they say to that?—They did not assent to this suggestion.

Was anything said about how much would be needed, if they were to get assistance, to pull them through the difficulty?—At first the amount named as likely to meet the case was from £200,000 to £300,000, but afterwards a larger sum was spoken of, and £500,000 was named as likely to meet the case. I asked Mr. Stronach whether, in the event of their having such a sum as that, it would take all Morton's acceptances out of the way, and he answered "No."

Did Mr. Potter say anything about that?—No.

Was there anything else said before you parted company with them?—Mr. Potter said to me that he hoped that an examination of the Bank's affairs would be dispensed with. I immediately called on Mr. Gairdner, of the Union Bank, and told him what had taken place. Mr. Gairdner and I went to Edinburgh, and had a consultation with Mr. Davidson, of the Bank of Scotland. Mr. Fleming, of the Royal Bank, was unfortunately out of town in the afternoon, and could not be got.

As the result of your consultations, were you authorised to see Mr. Potter?—It had been arranged that Mr. Potter was to call for me at the Bank of Scotland in Glasgow next morning and hear the result.

I want to know what you conveyed to Mr. Potter when he called upon you?—I was authorised to say to Mr. Potter that, with regard to an examination of the books, if each of the Directors of the City of Glasgow Bank would give his own individual and personal assurance that the capital of the Bank was intact, we thought that possibly an examination of their affairs might be dispensed with. I told that to Mr. Potter. He said that he himself could not give that assurance.

Did he say anything about the position of the Bank?—He said he would not like to say anything with regard to the position of the Bank that he could not answer for afterwards both to God and man.

199

The City of Glasgow Bank Trial.

Jas. Wenley. Did he express any opinion about the position of the Bank? —He said that things were in such a critical state that even on that day they might have to do something. I deprecated any hasty action on their part, being extremely desirous that no hasty step should be taken by the City of Glasgow Bank without the other Scotch banks being consulted.

Did he say anything about a meeting that had been called that day?—He said that a meeting of the Directors had been called that day at twelve o'clock in Mr. Stewart's office.

Did you offer to go and see them all?—He complained with a good deal of emotion of the whole responsibility being thrown upon him, and I offered to go to this meeting of the Directors and communicate to the whole of them the message I had brought.

But they did not send for you, I believe?—They did not. Mr. Potter called on me that day, but unfortunately I was out. I saw him afterwards at his own office.

By the LORD JUSTICE-CLERK—This was on Saturday, 28th September.

By the SOLICITOR-GENERAL—I saw him about one o'clock.

And I think it was arranged that he and Mr. Stronach should meet Mr. Davidson, Mr. Fleming, and Mr. Gairdner in Edinburgh at the Bank of Scotland on the Monday?—Just so.

Did he say anything at that meeting about Morton's acceptances?—He said that the acceptances on account of Morton alone amounted to £1,200,000. I had a consultation with Mr. Gairdner, Mr. Davidson, and Mr. Fleming in Edinburgh in the afternoon; and in consequence of that meeting I called on Mr. Potter at his own house in the evening, and conveyed to him what had been arrived at at the meeting with Mr. Fleming, Mr. Gairdner, and Mr. Davidson. I told Mr. Potter that we thought that the sum of £500,000 which had been named was quite inadequate to meet the purpose in view, and I requested that he should on Monday bring with him the last detailed balance sheet of the Bank, and also information as to the total amount of their acceptances, and state what acceptances were, in the ordinary course of business, for mercantile purposes, and what were for financing purposes. On Monday at twelve o'clock a meeting took place in Edinburgh. There were present—Mr. Davidson, Mr. Fleming, of the Royal Bank; Mr. Gairdner, of the Union Bank; Mr. Stronach, Mr. Potter, and myself. At that meeting the state of the Bank was unfolded— the large accounts of Smith, Fleming & Co., James Nicol Fleming, Morton, and Innes Wright & Co., and also the large sum lent to the American railway, and other matters. It was arranged at a meeting of the Scotch banks that evening that Mr. George Auldjo Jamieson should be asked to go and look

Evidence for Prosecution.

into the books, and see if it was possible to do anything. He made a report.

By Mr. ASHER—At the meeting on 27th September I believe it was I who spoke first of a sum of £200,000 or £300,000. Mr. Stronach replied to that remark, and spoke as if it would be sufficient. After Mr. Potter and Mr. Salmond came in, the sum of £500,000 was mentioned. Mr. Stronach mentioned it as being amply sufficient to take the Bank out of its difficulties. Mr. Potter asked him, " Are you quite sure that that sum will be sufficient?" and after some consideration, Mr. Stronach said that he thought it would.

JAMES PAUL.

By the LORD ADVOCATE—I was formerly a merchant in Glasgow. I retired from the firm of John Innes Wright & Co. in 1876. I had been a partner in that firm from March or April, 1863. At that time the partners of the firm were John Innes Wright, William Scott, and myself. All three of us continued to be partners down to 1876. There were no other partners in the house during that period. While I was a partner there was a London house connected with the firm, not as partners, but as correspondents. The business of our firm, when I joined it in 1863, was that of East India merchants and commission merchants, shipping goods to the East India markets, and receiving consignments of cotton and other East India produce, which we realised in this country on behalf of clients in Bombay. Our business promised very fair for the first two or three years. We then began to lose money. I think at the close of 1865 or 1866 we were beginning to feel that we were losing money. Our first connection with the City of Glasgow Bank began, I think, about midsummer of 1866. Mr. William Scott took charge of the financial department of our firm. I took a general supervision of the export department from this side as regards goods shipped by us, conducting correspondence relating thereto, and so forth. Mr. Innes Wright, the senior partner, looked more immediately after the import department—consignments from abroad, and the realising of them. I think our first transaction with the Bank consisted in discounting a batch of mercantile bills.

I suppose you had a deposit and discount account in the ordinary form?—Quite so; it amounts to that. From 1866 down to 1870, I am sorry to say, business matters did not improve with us. They got slightly worse. I think we were getting some assistance from the Bank previous to 1870, but I cannot condescend upon the particular time.

But about 1870 you began to need advances from the Bank? —We began to get advances about that time. Mr. William

The City of Glasgow Bank Trial.

James Paul. Scott negotiated these advances; it was his special department. I was occasionally asked specially by Mr. Scott to go to the Bank about these advances, and I went at his instance. I think in almost every case in which I was sent by Mr. Scott I got the money. Mr. Alexander Stronach was Manager at that time. I made no communication to him as to the state of my affairs, or the affairs of our firm on these occasions; I simply went with my message, as it were. On almost every occasion that I remember being sent to the Bank I got a note from Mr. Scott to Mr. Alexander Stronach relating to my mission.

And your mission was for money?—Yes; and along with that I understood there was the usual cheque, as it were, for the amount, signed by the firm—Mr. Scott. Sometimes I did not get the money at that particular visit, and had to go back.

I suppose you understood that it was an advance you were getting from the Bank?—Clearly.

It was not a cheque drawing your own money out of the Bank?—Clearly. The largest sum I ever got on any of these occasions was, I think, £16,000. I got it in notes or cash slips —bank slips, as they are called; either notes or an equivalent.

And you have frequently got sums of £10,000 and £12,000? —Yes; I cannot swear to the particular sum of £16,000, but the cheque will show what it was. Personally I did not communicate to Mr. Stronach any impression that our firm was in difficulties at that time. Mr. Stronach must have known it. Mr. Scott and he had so many interviews that I always understood Mr. Stronach knew it. I never required to say anything. Mr. Stronach never asked me.

By the LORD JUSTICE-CLERK—I think he could not fail to know it.

By the LORD ADVOCATE—A balance sheet of the firm was struck in 1866. After 1866, and down to the time I left the firm in 1876, there was no balance sheet struck. The transactions with the Bank were always recorded by Mr. Scott, whose special department it was, in the cash book; but up to a certain time—subsequent to 1871, I think—I found Mr. Scott was keeping his cash on small slips or memoranda. After 1866 I never saw an account or balance of the affairs of the firm, or anything like an account of the state of the firm's liabilities.

But you knew that you were in difficulties?—Clearly.

In deep water?—In deep water.

What did you do with the money which you got from the Bank on those occasions? Did you apply it yourself?—I always returned with the money and handed it to Mr. Scott, who was the financial man—who had the conduct of the business.

Did you ever see any of the Directors on these occasions?— Never.

202

Evidence for Prosecution.

You have been speaking hitherto of Mr. Alexander Stronach? James Paul. —Yes.

After he ceased to be Manager, and his brother, Robert Stronach, took his place, did you pay visits to the Bank as before?—Occasionally—much on the same footing.

And did you get the money from him on these occasions in the same way as you got it from Alexander Stronach previously?—Yes, I got it—always with a grudge, of course.

But you did get it?—I think so; I might have been defeated in getting it once or twice, but I know I got money on several occasions.

By the LORD JUSTICE-CLERK—From Mr. Robert Stronach?—From Mr. Robert Stronach.

By the LORD ADVOCATE—But unwillingly, and with a grudge? —Mr. Stronach naturally did not give the money without expostulating as to why we needed it, and so forth.

You were not giving the Bank security as against these advances?—I did not give the Bank security.

Did you understand that your firm were giving any?—I understood that they had got certain securities; the nature of them or the true value of them I could not condescend on; and all these securities were arranged for and sent by Mr. Scott.

But you were quite cognisant that these advances were being got?—Yes; I got some of them personally.

Was your partner, Mr. Innes Wright, cognisant of these advances being got?—I believe so. We kept no cash book or finance books. The books connected with my own department and with Mr. Wright's department were all in perfect order up to the time I left the firm, but the finance books never were.

After 1870, or, say, after 1871, down to the time you ceased to be a partner, were you, or were you not, aware that the Bank was very heavily in advance to your firm?—I was aware that the Bank must be in advance, but I had no earthly idea as to the extent of it. I frequently wished to know from Mr. Scott, but never could ascertain what the amount was—not even the probable amount.

On those occasions, taking 1871 and subsequently, when you went to Mr. Alexander Stronach, and also to Mr. Robert Stronach, in order to get money, did you ever allude to the necessity of your having to stop if you did not get it?—Very likely I did.

But did you? Try to recollect that?—Oh! I must have said so.

That if you did not get the advance you must stop?—Yes.

I suppose that, having said so, it was the fact—that if you had not got it, you must stop?—Undoubtedly.

Did you ever consider or say anything about the effect that might have upon the Bank on these occasions?—Never; I never

The City of Glasgow Bank Trial.

could fancy that our indebtedness was of such a nature that it could materially affect the Bank.

From what you saw of the operations of your firm from 1870 down to 1876, was it your belief or understanding that you were getting into a better position pecuniarily, or into a worse? —I was daily growing in the belief that we were getting into a worse position. I recollect Mr. Innes Wright becoming a Director of the Bank.

Did the fact of his becoming a Director strike you at the time?—Yes; it struck me at the time.

What occurred to you at the time in reference to it?—That it was a somewhat irregular thing Mr. Wright being asked to be a Director.

Did it not occur to you that there might be an irregularity in his consenting to be a Director when asked?—Yes.

You thought so?—I thought so; Mr. Wright, however, was asked to be a Director long before that.

But he declined?—He declined positively. This was in January, 1871.

Had anything occurred since January, 1871, that made it more proper for him to accept in 1875?—Not that I know of.

Did you speak to Mr. Wright on the subject in 1875, when he became a Director?—Mr. Wright was my informant as to his having been asked to be a Director.

Did he state whether he would accept it or not?—No, he did not; evidently from the tenor of the conversation, it was under consideration by him.

Did he tell you who had asked him to be a Director?—He told me the first intimation he got on the subject—the first approach on the subject—was by Mr. Robert Stronach.

Tell us what he said?—And on a subsequent day he had, I was told—by him, I think—a visit from Mr. Salmond, following up the proposal. Mr. Wright, evidently, had doubts about accepting it.

Did you express any opinion to him at the time as to your view of his accepting it?—I said, " How far is it right—how far is it proper to accept a Directorship, Mr. Wright, in the state of our account? "

What did he say to that?—" I am alive to that, Mr. Paul; Mr. Stronach tells me that that will be no difficulty; he will arrange all that."

Mr. Robert Stronach?—Mr. Robert Stronach.

What was he to arrange, did you understand?—That the indebtedness was to remain in abeyance, I suppose, and that the fact of our indebtedness would be made no disqualification.

Had Mr. Wright any shares in the Bank at that time—when he was applied to?—Not previously, that I know of.

Had he any money to buy them with, that you knew of?—No.

Evidence for Prosecution.

In 1875, when Mr. Wright became a Director, had the character of your business remained the same as when you started the firm originally in 1863?—Not quite. At the outset, it was purely a commission business, or nearly so. About 1870 or thereby the Suez Canal and the telegraph to and from India came into operation, and consequent upon that, that description of commission business gradually subsided, and we assumed a position from that time onwards more as merchants, along with such commission business as could be got.

Had it not become very much a finance business at that time—in 1875?—There was a good deal of finance, which was becoming more a feature in the business. Under the contract of copartnery each partner had a monthly allowance of £60. That was always paid by Mr. Scott—monthly.

Did you ever speak to Mr. Wright about the position of your affairs?—Mr. Wright himself had frequent conversations about it, and more particularly about the disordered state of the books. He could not understand our position. Mr. Wright knew more about the position of the firm than I did.

Did he not know that you were in difficulties?—He knew we were in difficulties, but he had no earthly idea, I am pretty confident, about the extent of them—consequent on Mr. Scott's mode of doing business.

But he knew that you were in considerable difficulties?—Quite so.

And that the Bank were under heavy advances?—Quite so.

But he did not know the full amount?—I think not. So far as I am concerned, I did not; and I think Mr. Wright could not have known either, for we had several conversations on the point.

From 1870 downwards, while you were a partner, were you ever doing anything but making losses?—Well, it was the exception to make profit. Of course, there were individual operations that were profitable; but, on the whole, we were apparently going behind.

You knew that the result of your trading was that you were realising losses?—Quite so.

And I suppose that you knew then that the money you got to meet your liabilities must come from some other quarter than the profits upon your trade?—Yes.

And that quarter was?—The City of Glasgow Bank. Mr. Wright succeeded James Nicol Fleming in the Directorate. I was acquainted with Mr. Fleming. There were business connections between him and his firm and ours.

He was connected with various firms, I believe, under different names. With which of his firms did you trade?—With James Nicol Fleming & Co., Calcutta. He was not a partner of Smith, Fleming & Co.

The City of Glasgow Bank Trial.

James Paul.   By Mr. GUTHRIE SMITH—Who provided the capital for the firm of Wright & Co. when the firm started?—Mr. Wright. To the best of my belief we started with a capital of some £44,000 or £45,000, and Mr. Wright supplemented it afterwards with some further payments, but I cannot give the particulars of these. The capital all came from him. According to the contract of copartnery, the allowance drawn by each partner was £60 per month. That always came through Mr. Scott. I don't think Mr. Wright ever exceeded that allowance. He lived in his own house, and very plainly indeed. Mr. Scott had been a clerk in Mr. Wright's employment. He was assumed as a partner on the same day as myself, in 1863. After 1863 each of us had a special department of the business to attend to. The whole of the finance business and the relations with the Bank were managed by Mr. Scott. Mr. Wright's department was the produce department. The whole of the books connected with it were properly kept down to the time when I left.

Was the borrowing of money from the Bank always done by Mr. Scott?—It was always negotiated by Mr. Scott.

You had no knowledge of the extent of your indebtedness to the Bank?—Never at any time.

You, I believe, frequently urged Mr. Scott to give you particulars?—Frequently, and Mr. Wright also did the same thing.

But without effect?—Without effect. It brought forth no actual result.

By the DEAN OF FACULTY—You have told us that after Mr. Alexander Stronach ceased to be Manager, you had called at the Bank and had seen Mr. Robert Stronach. How often did you see him?—That goes over a period of years; I could not tell you. I was at the Bank on an average once a week at any rate on some business or other.

He became Manager in December, 1875, and you ceased to be a partner of Innes Wright & Co. in 1876?—Yes, on 19th March, 1876.

Can you tell how often you saw Robert Stronach on these occasions when you called there asking for money?—That is a very difficult question to answer.

More than twice?—Oh! more than twice or thrice.

You stated that he expostulated with you when you made your request. What was the nature of his expostulation?—Simply that he could not give the money; that he had made no arrangement with Mr. Scott to give the money, and so forth. My message was done.

Did he ask for security?—I cannot say.

Additional security?—No; I always understood he was "nagging" at Mr. Scott for securities. Whether he succeeded in getting any at the various times I could not state. I never was entrusted with any securities to give to Mr. Stronach.

No; but did he speak to you in this way that he wanted **James Paul.** more security before he would make an additional advance?— Yes.

Did you carry that message back to Mr. Scott?—Yes.

And did you get sometimes additional security from Mr. Scott to give him?—No; if securities were given, they were given by Mr. Scott, not by me.

Then you cannot tell me what the securities were which the Bank had against the indebtedness of John Innes Wright & Co.?—Yes; the securities mainly consisted in shares in joint stock companies—such as Glasgow Jute Company and Marbella Iron Ore Company.

Was the produce of imported goods sometimes assigned over to the Bank?—No, not in my day.

Were bills drawn by your firm as against cargoes coming home in favour of the Bank?—No, not in my day.

I understand you to say that you never knew the amount of your debt to the Bank?—I never knew up till the hour I left the office what our indebtedness to the Bank was.

By the LORD JUSTICE-CLERK—You saw either Mr. Alexander Stronach, when he was Manager, or Mr. Robert Stronach?— Yes.

Was Mr. Robert Stronach in the management for the most part from 1874?—Mr. Robert Stronach did not take the management at the Bank, I think, until about January or so, 1875.

But Alexander Stronach had ceased to act, had he not, before that?—Yes.

Then before the formal appointment of Robert Stronach, whom did you see when you went to the Bank?—Failing Mr. Alexander Stronach, I next fell upon Mr. Robert Stronach. I never saw a Director or was brought into contact with a Director.

You saw either one or other of the Stronachs?—Quite so.

JOHN FLEMING.

John Fleming.

By the SOLICITOR-GENERAL—I am a member of the firm of Smith, Fleming & Co., carrying on business in Leadenhall Street, London. The firm is now in liquidation on our petition. It has been in existence since 1860. The partners were then Mr. John Smith, myself, and Mr. James Nicol Fleming. I have also had to do with the firms of William Nicol & Co., of Bombay, and Fleming & Co., of Kurrachee. I am a partner of these firms. The partners of Smith, Fleming & Co. were all partners of those firms; but there were also other partners in them— Mr. Hamilton Maxwell and Mr. Gilmore Hall—who were not members of Smith, Fleming & Co.

Since about 1865 have you had intimate business relations

The City of Glasgow Bank Trial.

John Fleming. with Todd, Findlay & Co., John Innes Wright & Co., and Potter, Wilson & Co.?—With Todd, Findlay & Co. yes; less so with John Innes Wright & Co.; not at all at that date with Potter, Wilson & Co.

When did you begin to have business relations with Potter, Wilson & Co.?—Subsequent to 1870; I cannot fix the date exactly.

When with James Morton & Co.?—Shortly after 1865—about 1866 or 1867.

And with Law, Brown & Co. more recently?—Yes; in 1875.

Previous to 1866, had you many transactions with the City of Glasgow Bank, or were they quite exceptional?—They were very few, I think scarcely any, before that.

But since then your transactions have been frequent?—They have.

Your brother, James Nicol Fleming, was a member of the Directorate for a good many years?—He was.

What was the whole of your indebtedness to the Bank at the stoppage in October?—Something over £1,800,000—between £1,800,000 and £1,900,000—the exact figures I do not remember.

How much of that is on cash advances by the Bank?—About one-half of it. I have not the figures with me.

How were the cash advances obtained—I mean by what form of procedure? Were there special credits obtained from time to time?—Some of these cash advances arose in this way, that originally bill credits were granted, and these bills were paid off by the Bank, and converted from the form of bills into that of cash advanced.

The Bank had to meet their own acceptances?—They met their own acceptances.

And accordingly debited you with the cash as advanced by them?—Yes.

Were there other sums advanced directly in cash?—Yes; in some cases there were.

Which you were allowed to draw by cheque?—Yes.

What security had the Bank for that sum, which we will take at one-half—or call it £900,000, in the meantime—what security had the Bank for that? Or tell me first what was the whole amount of securities that the Bank had in its absolute control for the advances made to your firm?—There was very little in the absolute control of the Bank.

What was the total amount that was in any way secured to them?—The nominal value of the security was about £800,000 or £900,000.

As against £1,800,000 or £1,900,000?—Yes.

When you say the nominal value, I suppose the realisable value would be a very great deal less than that?—Well, the

208

Evidence for Prosecution.

circumstances at present are adverse to the realisation of a good many of the securities.

Are there a great many of them worth nothing at all?—No.

You think they are all valuable?—All more or less so.

Take it in 1876, what do you say would be the amount actually secured of the £1,900,000?—I should not like to give a definite answer to that without looking over the securities.

Would it come up to one-half?—I should say so.

About one-half?—Yes.

In whose possession were the securities?—Most of them in our own possession. Let me just modify that answer. Part of them also were in the possession of Todd, Findlay & Co.—a considerable proportion.

Was there any substantial part of those securities to which the Bank had a legal title at all?—Not a large part.

I mean such a title as gave the Bank a right to use the security without the consent of others?—There are a good many questions as to the right and title of the Bank to securities at present pending which have been raised since, and which I was ignorant of at the time.

But I want you to tell me how much they had, about which, in your view, no such question could be raised?—Well, a number of questions which were quite new to me have been raised since my stoppage, and I find with regard to things which I believed to be theirs, the title to them is now questioned.

I suppose every question has been raised that can be raised within the last three months, but you can tell me how much of the securities no question has been raised about?—A very small proportion.

Suppose the securities are all good to the Bank, how much are they worth now?—It was estimated by my trustee that there would be from £500,000 to £600,000 worth now.

That is, assuming all questions to be decided in favour of your assignee?—That I understand.

Up to July, 1870, had you any advances from the Bank which were not properly covered?—None.

All the indebtedness has arisen since then?—All the uncovered indebtedness.

How were your applications for advances generally made?— By letter addressed to the Manager.

In July, 1870, did you see Mr. Alexander Stronach, Mr. Potter, and Mr. Salmond about the state of your affairs?—I saw Mr. Alexander Stronach and Mr. Potter.

And Mr. Salmond?—I believe Mr. Salmond, but I am not quite so sure about him.

Was your brother present?—My brother was present.

Where did you meet them?—At the City of Glasgow Bank.

How many meetings had you with them at that time?—I think, at intervals of a week or ten days, two meetings.

The City of Glasgow Bank Trial.

John Fleming. You say you are not so sure of Mr. Salmond being present, but you think he was. You are not sure about the first meeting; was he present at the second meeting?—My impression is that he was present at one or other of the meetings, but I am not prepared absolutely to swear that.

At those meetings what did you say to them with regard to the state of affairs—I mean did you say anything particular to them about the state of affairs?—I told them that we were face to face with a very heavy loss through the difficulties which had arisen to our Liverpool agents, Nicol, Duckworth & Co., and that it was necessary that we should stop.

What was said in answer to that?—That it was unnecessary—that assistance would be provided.

By whom?—By the Bank.

How did you stand with the Bank at that time?—We had cash advances and credits at the moment to about £150,000, roughly—all covered.

Did you make it plain to them that you could not go on as you stood?—I desired to do so; I believe I did. My brother took part in the meeting. He was of the same opinion, I believe. There was a good deal of discussion. The discussion was as to the means of rendering us assistance.

Who proposed plans for that?—I cannot permit myself now to say who proposed them; various plans were proposed.

Did the proposals come from others at the meeting than from you?—From others, not from me. One proposal, and the proposal which ultimately in a certain shape was carried out, was the immediate formation of a new Liverpool firm, which should accept bills to be discounted and used for our relief. I said that I did not consider that such a plan would be successful; I thought it would be fatal. I expressed myself pretty strongly upon that. I said it would bring discredit upon us, and that without the maintenance of our credit there was no chance of our retrieving our position and getting out of our difficulties. The proposal was pressed upon me. This was at the first interview.

Did you get rather hot—angry—upon the subject?—I felt that it was trifling with a very big and difficult matter.

How much did you state to them was really the amount involved in the question of your failing or your being kept up?—I don't exactly understand the question; the word "involved" means something outside of us.

By the LORD JUSTICE-CLERK—We required over half a million of money to put us right.

By the SOLICITOR-GENERAL—I told them that.

When they pressed it upon you, how did you receive the pressure?—The plan as proposed by them seemed to me to be quite ineffectual, and I said there was no use discussing it

Evidence for Prosecution.

further. I then proceeded to leave the room. When I got out into the hall of the Bank, I was brought back again. It was Mr. Potter who brought me back.

What happened when you got back?—It was then promised that the Bank would assist, and if the proposed bills were not acceptable, if they were not negotiable, the Bank would discount these bills, so that we would not be forced into bankruptcy. I cannot say they said anything about what effect our stoppage would have if we did stop.

In short, did it come to this, that they undertook to pull you through if the plan proposed could not be effected as they suggested?—That was what in effect was come to.

By the LORD JUSTICE-CLERK—Do you mean the bills drawn by the new company?—Drawn on the new company.

That if these could not be discounted through the new company, the Bank would do it?—Yes.

By the SOLICITOR-GENERAL—Was that carried out by credit being given to Brown & Co. to the extent of £300,000, and about £100,000 of securities belonging to your brother, which were held for you by the Bank, being transferred to them?—Our firm in Liverpool, in accordance with that arrangement, entitled A. & A. G. Brown, was formed, and security for £300,000 was provided for them, of which about £100,000, belonging to my brother, and held by the Bank for me, was lent by the Bank. The handing over of securities to the Liverpool firm was not spoken of at the meeting I have mentioned; that was an arrangement of detail, settled afterwards.

When the acceptances of the Liverpool firm were got in order to raise money, did you find them acceptable?—To a very, very limited extent. That was exactly what I had expected. I found the attempt to negotiate them injurious to our credit. That also was what I had expected. As the result, the Bank had to make the advances on the bills themselves.

Did the Bank get back the securities which had been sent to Brown & Co.?—Ultimately those which had not been realised and applied to the reduction of the credit were returned to the Bank. Let me say this, that, as regards James Nicol Fleming, any realisations that took place during the existence of the credit were placed by the Bank to the credit of James Nicol Fleming, and not to our credit. By the end of 1870 the Bank had advanced to us, in consequence of this new arrangement, roundly, about half a million of money—nearly so, I think.

To what extent was the Bank covered for that half-million?—I cannot speak off-hand; I cannot positively say.

Would it be more than £200,000?—Certainly; I should say it would be very nearly fully covered, but I speak just now very broadly—three-fourths probably. During the years since

The City of Glasgow Bank Trial.

John Fleming. 1870, down to the stoppage of the Bank, I have kept the Bank informed of the state of our affairs from time to time.

Have you periodically submitted a balance sheet to them of your affairs?—I have submitted balance sheets of our affairs in London, Bombay, and Kurrachee. Latterly I have submitted monthly statements of bills payable. That has been going on for several years; I cannot precisely say how long. From 1870 down to the present date I have been obliged, in the course of working the business, to support the firms of Todd & Findlay, and my brother's firm of James Nicol Fleming & Co., and also the firm of Fowlie, Richmond & Co. I have kept the Bank informed that I was supporting these firms.

Were many of the credits specially applied for by you to support these firms?—They were applied for to relieve the cash advances which we were under on account of these firms.

And applied for *nominatim* for that purpose?—Certain of them were.

In regard to your affairs, have you seen Mr. Potter frequently about them?—I have seen him occasionally.

In consultation about them?—Yes; I saw him at the Bank.

Has Mr. Salmond made inquiry at you about your affairs?—Not for some years.

How long is it since he ceased to make inquiry?—I cannot precisely say.

But roughly?—For the last three or four years. Previous to that, when in London, he used to call and ask generally about our affairs.

Did you inform him?—Yes, I did.

How things stood?—That is, generally.

Did you inform him that your debt and difficulty were largely increasing?—No, I did not do so. He came to ask about our matters—just how we were getting on.

Did you tell him the truth about them?—I did.

By the LORD JUSTICE-CLERK—What did you say when you were asked about your affairs?—Sometimes I told him—as was the fact—that perhaps things were looking better; sometimes it was that matters were rather bad.

By the SOLICITOR-GENERAL—Did you gather from him whether he knew the amount of the advances of the Bank to you?—No; there was no indication of any precise knowledge of that nature.

Was there an arrangement made in March, 1875, in regard to your firm's affairs with the Bank?—Yes; although not finally concluded.

But an arrangement was discussed and gone over?—Yes.

And acted upon?—It was subsequently acted upon.

What was the arrangement of March, 1875?—To give us relief, the rate of interest charged upon our cash account was

Evidence for Prosecution.

to be reduced from 5 per cent. to $3\frac{1}{2}$; the commission upon the credits which were granted to us for our accommodation was to be reduced from 2 per cent. to $\frac{1}{2}$ per cent. per annum; and an arrangement to acquire £100,000 worth at par of the stock of the Canterbury Company, upon which we were to have an advance of £100,000 at $3\frac{1}{2}$ per cent. The effect of this was that if this Canterbury stock yielded dividend in excess of $3\frac{1}{2}$ per cent., that excess would go to the benefit of our account. These are the salient points of the arrangement.

Did you at that time lay before them a statement of your position?—I did.

Whom did you give it to?—I had been in correspondence with Mr. Alexander Stronach for some time previously. [Shown No. 186.] That is a letter from me to Mr. Robert Stronach, 12th April, 1875. The first paragraph is—

Referring to the meeting I had with your Directors on Thursday, the 1st inst., respecting the state of our account with the Bank, I now beg to detail the terms of the agreement come to as I understood them.

Who were present at the meeting you refer to in that letter?—I am unable to recall. I saw that letter this morning, but I am unable to recall who were present on that occasion. The meeting was held in Glasgow, in the Bank's premises.

Was it a meeting of Directors, though you cannot remember who were present?—I cannot remember. I have seen that letter during the last few months in going through my correspondence.

But had you a meeting—though you cannot specify the individuals who were present—with several of the Board upon this matter?—Yes, I had.

By the LORD JUSTICE-CLERK—I understand the arrangement proposed was to give you relief in three ways—(first) in regard to the interest upon your bills, (second) in regard to the amount of the Bank's commission, and (third) a new advance?—That is so.

In return for that was the Bank to receive any security or any advantage?—The object was to make it possible for us to go on.

By the SOLICITOR-GENERAL—At this time, of course, we could not go on if we were not helped; but the load was almost unbearable.

Did you explain that to those who were at the meeting?—It was well known—quite recognised.

Do you remember if Mr. Potter was present at the meeting?—I do not remember the details of that meeting at all; I cannot remember them.

Did you make any proposals for relieving your position; or

The City of Glasgow Bank Trial.

John Fleming. who made them?—I had some time previously appealed to Alexander Stronach to reduce the interest and to reduce the commission, but it was in the form of a suggestion or appeal, a considerable time previous to that.

But at the meeting were any suggestions made to you as to what should be done?—I don't remember that. I remember there was a meeting, but I don't remember the details of it.

But referring to your letter, of which I read you the first paragraph, have you any doubt now that that is a perfectly correct statement of your understanding at the time of what had been agreed to?—I feel quite certain that that is a correct statement. [Shown letters Nos. 185 to 188 from John Fleming to R. S. Stronach, dated 3rd March, 12th April, 21st April, and 24th August, 1875, the latter signed Smith, Fleming & Co.]

Taking the four letters together, they embody in writing practically what came to be agreed to?—Yes, they did.

As regards this period, did you ever come into contact with Mr. James Morton in any of the discussions with the Directors in regard to this matter?—I don't remember James Morton having been ever present with any Directors, but he was in the habit of seeing me in London.

In what capacity did you understand he came to you?—He came as the confidant of Mr. Alexander Stronach.

Has Mr. Morton not been present along with you and Mr. Potter when your affairs were discussed?—I cannot be quite sure. He may have been, but I don't remember any particular occasion.

Try to recollect?—I cannot so that I could swear to it.

But was he a medium of communication between you and the Bank when he came to see you in London?—Yes.

He conveyed messages from you, and brought messages to you?—Yes.

As part of the arrangement for relieving your position, was Mr. Morton to do anything?—I did not know absolutely that he was to do anything. I believed that he was to provide some of the stock.

Out of his superfluity, I suppose?—That was what I understood.

By the LORD JUSTICE-CLERK—You believed that—why?—It was he who originally suggested the arrangement many months previously to its being made, and he spoke to it as a means of helping us—encouraging us to face a difficult struggle.

By the SOLICITOR-GENERAL—You mean that he would provide a good handsome sum to help you?—That he would provide the stock at par.

Why was he to provide the stock at par?—The stock was supposed to be worth a great deal more than par, if not immediately, at all events prospectively. It was yielding a return

214

Mr. J. Guthrie Smith,
Counsel for John Innes Wright.

Evidence for Prosecution.

much larger than the interest which we were to pay for the advance.

You understood yourself to be under the engagements to the Bank contained in these letters, and acted upon them?—We did.

And you got the advantages which you were to get in consequence of entering into the engagement?—We did.

By the LORD JUSTICE-CLERK—Can you tell me the amount of the indebtedness of your firm to the Bank at the date of this arrangement?—About £1,300,000. I think the amount of credit was £562,000, and the cash advance £773,000.

By the SOLICITOR-GENERAL—In August, 1875, did you make a representation to Mr. Robert Stronach about the impossibility of carrying out the arrangement?—In consequence of difficulties which had arisen in connection with Collie's stoppage, I foresaw that we should be unable at the close of the year to carry out our engagements.

What did Mr. Robert Stronach reply to you about that?—I don't remember the exact reply. I remember being asked by Mr. Robert Stronach to come to Glasgow, and to have a meeting with the Directors in the month of July last year. By that time the amount of indebtedness had considerably increased.

How did you come to be able to carry on after Collie's failure till the meeting of July, 1878?—When we needed help we got it.

By the LORD JUSTICE-CLERK—From the Bank?—From the Bank.

By the SOLICITOR-GENERAL—And in consequence your indebtedness was always increasing, from that time onwards, down to the last?—It was so. In July, 1878, I was asking for an advance of £25,000. I went to Glasgow, and met Mr. Robert Stronach, Mr. Potter, and Mr. Stewart.

Was your indebtedness to the Bank referred to at that meeting—the amount of it?—No.

Was it spoken of as being very large?—The state of our account as being very unsatisfactory was spoken of. The amount was not discussed.

By the LORD JUSTICE-CLERK—What was said about the state of your account?—It was alluded to as being very unsatisfactory.

Try to remember what was said?—I cannot recall the exact expressions used, but it was spoken of as an unsatisfactory account, and that it was most unsatisfactory that the indebtedness had been increasing instead of diminishing; and I explained with reference to that, that the condition of trade for several years past had been deplorably bad.

By the SOLICITOR-GENERAL—Was anything said about adding to the indebtedness by giving you more money?—Very great reluctance to increase the debt was expressed.

The City of Glasgow Bank Trial.

How long were you with them?—Probably three-quarters of an hour or half an hour; certainly within an hour.

Did you get the money?—The credit I asked for was granted.

Did you state to them whether you could go on without the money?—I said I could not go on without the money. [Shown letters 185, 186, 187, 188.] Those are the letters I have seen. [Shown Nos. 189, letter, Smith, Fleming & Co., John Fleming, R. M'Ilwraith, and W. Nicol, to R. S. Stronach; 190, 191A, 191B, three letters, John Fleming to R. S. Stronach, dated 27th August, 1875, and 5th May and 26th November, 1877; 285, letter, John Fleming to Lewis Potter, dated 6th March, 1877; and 289, letter, John Fleming to James Morton, dated 2nd August, 1876.] I identify all these. [Shown No. 397.] That is a letter from Smith, Fleming & Co. signed by me, dated 24th January, 1876. [Shown No. 398, letter to R. S. Stronach, dated 20th December, 1875.] That is a letter from my firm, signed by me. [Shown Nos. 402 to 421 inclusive, letters, Smith, Fleming & Co. to R. S. Stronach, of various dates, between 1st September, 1875, and 4th May, 1878.] These are letters from Smith, Fleming & Co., all signed by me. [Shown No. 444.] That is a letter from Smith, Fleming & Co., signed by me. [Shown No. 191c.] That is a letter from Robert Stronach to myself.

By Mr. TRAYNER—My meeting with the Directors in July, 1878, was on a Tuesday; I think it was on the 29th, but at all events it was on the last Tuesday of the month. I had never met Mr. Stewart in my life before that meeting. He was not present at my meeting with the Directors in March, 1875. I never saw him in my life till the meeting at the end of July, 1878.

At the meeting in July, 1878, do you remember referring to some property of yours that was expected to be very productive and profitable?—I brought down some specimens of gold which had been brought home in the beginning of the year from Wynaad by an engineer—an expert—whom we had sent to India.

Specimens of gold found on a property belonging to you or your firm in India?—Yes.

And from that you expected, I believe, to realise considerable and valuable results?—What I said was, that it was the only ray of hope in our affairs.

But it was at that time a very brilliant ray in your mind?—Well, this much had occurred, that a few days previously a Californian of great experience, the agent of Messrs. Rothschild, had seen these specimens, and had heard from my partner the circumstances under which they had been collected; and he said, that if the facts were as stated to him, there was probably something very great in it.

Evidence for Prosecution.

And you communicated these facts and these hopes to the meeting that was held in July, 1878?—I did.

As also, I think, your expectation that some arrangement might be made with reference to it between you and the Messrs. Rothschild?—My partner, Mr. M'Ilwraith, had been in communication with the Messrs. Rothschild concerning these matters, and he had a hope that they might, if satisfied of the genuineness of the matter, render assistance.

And you communicated that to the meeting in July, 1878?— I did.

By Mr. Asher—I saw Mr. Salmond occasionally in London.

Did he call to ask how business was getting on generally?— Yes.

Not as an emissary of the Bank with reference to your account?—No; he called in a friendly way, and made inquiries concerning the account.

Your conversations related to business in the country generally, did they not?—The conversation generally passed into general topics.

Can you be more precise in regard to the number of years that have elapsed since you communicated with Mr. Salmond in regard to your bank matters?—I cannot say more than that several years have elapsed.

When you went to the Bank in 1870 your indebtedness, you have said, was about £150,000, fully covered by security?— Yes.

So that the reverses which came upon you then did not affect the Bank?—That is so.

For what purpose did you go to the Bank?—I was asked to go to the Bank before stopping.

Who asked you?—My brother asked me.

He was a Director of the Bank at the time?—Yes.

That is Mr. James Nicol Fleming?—Yes.

Did he explain to you why he wished you to come to the Bank before stopping?—No; he said before coming to a final decision he wished me to come to Glasgow and see the Bank Manager.

What did you understand to be his purpose in requesting you to do that before stopping?—In case the Bank might be willing to render assistance.

Did you go with the view of getting the Bank to make arrangements which would render your stoppage unnecessary? —I went with the view of laying my matters before the Bank, and of getting assistance if they were willing to give it.

Did you think that if you got assistance your matters would right themselves?—I believed it was possible; our earnings during previous years had been large.

The City of Glasgow Bank Trial.

John Fleming. The sum you said you would require to put you right would be about £500,000?—About that.

You were engaged in business to a very large extent, I believe?—Yes.

What was the largest sum which your firm had earned as profit in your various businesses in any one year?—Our profits during 1862 and 1863 were very large; they were hundreds of thousands in those days; but in the three years immediately preceding 1870 the average earnings of our three firms in London, Bombay, and Kurrachee had exceeded £90,000 per annum.

It was chiefly a commission business?—Largely.

And these facts, I presume, would be explained to the Bank?—Yes, certainly.

For the purpose of satisfying them that they would be safe to make advances to your firm?—That there was a possibility of redeeming our position.

Your commission connection at that time was still intact?—Yes.

So that if you could tide over your difficulty you had no reason to doubt that a very valuable commission business would remain with your firms?—That was what I believed.

And your brother, I presume—the Director—was fully aware of these circumstances?—Fully aware.

Was Mr. Alexander Stronach an intimate personal friend of yours?—Not at all; not beyond business.

At no time?—At no time.

You are John Fleming?—Yes.

And your place of business is Leadenhall Street, London?—It is.

You are the Mr. Fleming, I suppose, who corresponded on behalf of your firm with Mr. Alexander Stronach as representing the Bank?—Yes.

Were you in the habit of exchanging letters with Mr. Alexander Stronach, marked private, with reference to the Bank?—Yes.

To your knowledge were burdens undertaken by Alexander Stronach for you on behalf of the Bank without the knowledge of his Directors?—I was not aware of it, excepting thus far, that I was aware from his correspondence that sometimes he had done things in anticipation of obtaining the assent of the Directors.

Did you not know that the fact that he had made you advances without the knowledge of his Directors was pressing heavily on his mind?—Previously to 1875 some of the advances, I understood, were unknown to them.

At any time during Mr. Alexander Stronach's management of the Bank did you not know that it was so?—He represented

218

to me that he had made advances without the knowledge of the Directors, but required me to put matters into such a form that he might put them before the Directors.

Did you not know that the fact that he had done so was pressing heavily on his mind?—Yes; I am bound to say that I did.

When did that system begin which caused him that mental anxiety?—That I cannot tell. It was only latterly that I knew that he had not fully disclosed all my affairs to the Bank.

I show you a print for the defenders. Be kind enough to look at the first letter in that print, dated 3rd April, 1872, addressed by Alexander Stronach to you, and marked private:—

Private.

3rd April, 1872.

My Dear Sir,—I am sorry to observe by your letter of yesterday that you think you have reason to complain of my want of appreciation of your position generally, and that if I had more sympathy with you under your burden I would not have hesitated in complying with your demands in the present case. I can only appeal to the past as counterbalancing that statement, which, although you have given expression to it, I cannot believe that you seriously entertain that opinion. On the other hand, however, I fear that in looking so earnestly at your own position and burdens you are in some danger of forgetting mine. My position is, and has throughout been, an anomalous one, because, as you are aware, I could not share the burden with my Directors, and it has pressed upon me accordingly with tremendous severity, without exciting much sympathy; at least, very little has been done in any way to lighten my burden. I have borne it, however, patiently, and continue to do so uncomplainingly. The esteem and regard I have for yourself and your brothers first induced me to undertake it, and now advises me to continue, and although no other consideration on earth would induce me to bear up under the severity of the pressure.

I feel it is not quite considerate in you (however lucrative the result may appear to be in prospect) to press on me so heavy an addition to existing burdens, and on so very sudden a call, particularly at a time when I have other very heavy calls. I think you must yourself admit the difficulty of my position in the matter, and I trust that in any similar case you will either give me an opportunity of judging whether I can give it or not, or present the proposal in such a shape as I can get the Board to share the responsibility of a transaction of such magnitude, however safe it may be.

I have renewed the anticipated credits p. £30m, and send them to-night, and shall arrange a cash advance on special account p. £34m further, for which please send me a cheque to be paid into the first trust account. I note that the latter will be paid next month. I am sorry the drafts didn't mature before our balance. —Yours very truly,

ALEXANDER STRONACH.

John Fleming, Esq.,
   71 Threadneedle Street, London.

What did you understand Mr. Stronach to refer to when he mentioned the esteem and regard for you and your brothers

The City of Glasgow Bank Trial.

John Fleming. inducing him to undertake a burden which no other consideration on earth would induce him to bear up under the pressure of? —I consider that in writing that he was putting his own view of the case before me, because it was at his instigation that I went on. In the month of September, 1870, I wished to stop, and pressed my stoppage, and he came up to London and reproached me for wavering in my intention of going on.

Did you repudiate the expression of esteem and regard for you and your brothers which he there indicated?—No, I did not.

Did you reciprocate it?—I should like to see what I wrote before, and what I wrote after, before I answer that question.

Have you any reason to doubt the truth of that statement, that he could not share the burden with his Directors, and had to bear it himself?—I understood that his Directors did know, to a large extent, what was going on.

Did you challenge the accuracy of his statement?—That I don't remember. I have not got my answer. Is it here?

Look at the letter printed at the foot of page 31, and at the top of page 32, dated 30th September, 1873, and addressed by Alexander Stronach to you:—

My Dear Sir,—I wrote you a few lines yesterday, enclosing Mr. Aikman's notes and memo., and shall be glad to have your reply thereto at your early convenience. Mr. Paul, I presume, will now be due, when the financial statements will also be got ready. Yours of yesterday I received this morning, and telegraphed in reply that as this was your mail day (which I suppose you had forgotten last week in fixing Tuesday) to postpone our meeting till to-morrow at 11-15, and which I hope will be suitable for you. At same time, I feel that my time here is gliding past, and that we have made little or no progress in furtherance of the main object which brought and keeps me here. We have much to talk over and much to do in resolving on a proper basis in connection with your future business arrangements; and I feel, as I daresay you do also, that we are, up to this time, very much where we were when we met in Glasgow at the end of July or beginning of August.

I feel the distance between us is too great, as I feared it would be; and I think I must therefore revert to my former proposal to get a house of call in the city somewhere convenient and accessible, where we could meet daily, or every second or third day, as our business required, until the whole was completed, and our arrangements finally matured. I had letters recently from Mr. Potter to inquire what progress we had made, and I feel rather ashamed to answer him.

That was a proposal with a view to Mr. Stronach and you meeting daily in the city of London, to confer in regard to your affairs; Mr. Stronach was living at the south side of London at that time, I believe?—He was living at Norwood.

And it had reference to your affairs?—It was with reference to our affairs that he wished to have more intercourse with me.

Evidence for Prosecution.

He wished to have facilities for talking daily with you in regard to your affairs with the City of Glasgow Bank?—Yes.

By the LORD JUSTICE-CLERK—That is to say, when he says, "where we could meet daily, as our business requires," he meant in reference to the affairs of your firm?—Yes.

By Mr. ASHER—At page 148 there is a letter from you addressed to Mr. R. S. Stronach:—

> Western Club, Glasgow,
> Thursday Evening.
>
> My Dear Sir,—Just a line to tell you that Salmond got hold of me here and asked me what was the meaning of my being in such close consultation with Mr. Potter to-day, and I thought the best thing to say was that he had been talking of one of his sons joining us in Bombay.
>
> He rather closely questioned me on the subject, but I told him our conversation was quite general. I think it right to mention this in case he should allude to the matter to you.—Yours very truly,
>
> JOHN FLEMING.

Why did you think it right to mention that to Mr. Robert Stronach?—I never wrote such a letter to Mr. Robert Stronach.

The principal is No. 296? [Shown No. 296.]—This letter must have been written to Alexander Stronach, not to Robert Stronach.

Why did you think it right to mention the matter referred to in that letter to Mr. Stronach, in case Mr. Salmond should allude to it to him?—I wished to let him know that Mr. Salmond had questioned me about the matter.

Why did you wish to let him know that?—I conceived that Mr. Salmond was not fully informed about the matters that we were discussing—that is, the full state of our account.

And it was to put Alexander Stronach on his guard in case Mr. Salmond spoke to him on that subject; is that not so?—Yes; that I had been discussing with Mr. Potter and Mr. Alexander Stronach the question of the reconstruction of our firm with reference to the state of our accounts.

Did you intend Mr. Alexander Stronach to withhold from Mr. Salmond knowledge as to the state of your account?—No; I had no desire that he should withhold it.

Why put him on his guard?—Simply that he might know that Salmond had been inquiring.

And might judge of the expediency of telling him or not?—Truly so.

Look at the letter at foot of page 23 of the print. There is a letter there dated 14th June, 1873, addressed by you to Alexander Stronach?—There is only a little fragment of the letter here printed.

The excerpt is the postscript. The letter is dated 14th June, 1873; the postscript is—"I trust this will find you better.

The City of Glasgow Bank Trial.

John Fleming. I fear, however, it is ease of mind you need, and it is a terrible thought that it is we who keep you on the rack "?—No doubt I had that feeling, but I should prefer that the whole letter was read. The whole letter will show that there was distress of mind on both sides.

Do you wish it read?—I prefer that you should read the whole letter, though I don't know that it is material.

Witness read the letter as follows:—

Hill Hall, Epping,
14th June, 1873.

My Dear Sir,—I have your letters of Thursday and yesterday. I attempted to take up your memo. to-day, but a bursting head compelled me to give it up. I came away at two o'clock. I hope to-morrow's quiet will enable me to take it up and go through with it on Monday. With reference to your Thursday's note, I welcome the idea of any arrangement by which you can become more thoroughly and continuously informed as to our affairs. Indeed, it was in my mind to propose something of the kind, but I could not see a way through the difficulty of having some one in the office on behalf of the Bank without exposing our situation and causing great danger. I am very grieved to hear of your state, but quite understand it. If you come to the south near London, there should be no great difficulty in frequently seeing you at your house without exciting comment, and it would not be absolutely necessary to have Bell or any other intermediate. I say this not objecting to Bell, but am doubting whether James can dispense with him in Glasgow, and whether it is quite polite, at the moment at least, for James to open a separate establishment here. Findlay writes that of the £28,000 said by Meyer to be at credit of Todd, Findlay & Co., in Glasgow, £13,000 is credited merely by a cross entry, and of the balance, £9500 has been returned in various ways, and £5000 paid to us.

Will you have the kindness to return me the accounts I sent you from Mair to see how they bear out this?

I quite agree with you that the Glasgow house of Findlay's should be closed. The explanations I get seem always straight, but I don't get the money, which I know has been made.

I don't quite understand the suggestion that Mair should assume so much of the burden. When he joined Todd, Findlay & Co., it was under an express agreement, which we guaranteed, that he should be kept clear of all liability in respect of the debts of the concern before he joined.

The letter you say is so clear, showing I was all right again, was written with my head feeling as if it were bursting. It is this sort of feeling that comes on one just now when I begin to think earnestly about anything, and it paralyses me. I am quite well in body, and after my examination before the committee, which I believe is to take place on Tuesday, I shall have but the one matter to attend to, and hope I shall be out of it.—Yours very truly,

JOHN FLEMING.

Alex. Stronach, Esq.

Part of the body of that letter refers to a request by Mr. Stronach?—Yes.

The last paragraph on page 20 of the print for the defence

Evidence for Prosecution.

forms part of the letter of 12th June, 1873, that Mr. Alexander Stronach wrote you, and which is acknowledged in the beginning of the letter you have just read?—Yes.

I believe this is the statement in Mr. Stronach's letter to which you refer in your reply:—

My doctor seems determined that I shall go away for some time, and he says that the neighbourhood of London would do as well as anywhere else. I am fully alive to the non-desirability of coming to your office at all just now. But it has occurred to me that as James has been desiring to open a London office, he could transfer Bell up to an office near, and then our meetings there or at my house would not be questioned, seeing the connection that subsists between. Besides, I am desirous to have his own matters with us also put into better shape, and which, from his continued absence in Manchester, I cannot get done satisfactorily. This much, however, between ourselves.

Now, returning to the P.S., you were aware that at that time Mr. Stronach, to use your own words, was "kept on the rack" through the state of your affairs?—No doubt of it.

And didn't you know that his mental anxiety on the subject was aggravated then by the knowledge that his Directors did not know what had been done?—I was not aware that his Directors—at all events, I believe that some of his Directors were aware of the state of matters. I was not aware that they were wholly ignorant.

At that time?—At that time.

Just reflect for one moment. You were aware that Mr. Alexander Stronach was merely Manager?—I was aware of that.

If he had been acting under the orders of his Directors in what had happened, why should he be on the rack?—Because our account was a very heavy account, and an increasing account.

If he had simply obeyed the orders of his Directors why should that put him on the rack?—I should fancy that he took such an interest in the affairs of the Bank that he should be distressed about our account, a large account going bad.

If he had done it without the sanction of his Directors you have no doubt, I suppose, that he would be on the rack?—If he had done it without the sanction of the Directors I have no doubt that would aggravate his distress of mind.

I think, if you will look at the immediately succeeding letter to which this is a reply, you will find that he had been acting without the sanction of his Directors. In a letter to you of 13th June, 1873, page 23 of the same print, one of the two acknowledged by you in the one from which the excerpt is made, he says in the third last paragraph—"So soon as the terms of our arrangements are adjusted, and the whole scheme and securities are ready, I am desirous to place it before the

223

The City of Glasgow Bank Trial.

John Fleming. Board, with the view of getting their sanction to it, and my own exoneration and relief accordingly." You must have known, therefore, when you wrote the excerpt of 14th June that your affairs had not been before the Directors?—That our complete affairs had not been put before the Board—that I understood; but that they were partially before the Board, I believe.

When you made the arrangement of 1875 with the Bank did you expect to be able to carry it out?—At the time I made it? Yes?—Yes.

And did you think that through the means of that arrangement you would be able to liquidate your debt to the Bank?—I stated exactly what I expected to be able to do in my letter.

Did you state that if the Bank would assent to that arrangement you had no doubt you would be able to liquidate your debt to them?—I stated in that letter that I expected that in the course of fourteen years I should be able to pay off half a million out of our indebtedness of over £1,300,000.

I think one of the conditions of the agreement was that you should confine yourself to the extremely lucrative commission business which your firms had, and not enter on speculation at all?—Yes.

The arrangement was made in April, 1875?—Yes.

Would you look at the letter on page 85 of the same print; that is a letter from you on 24th July, 1875, to Mr. Robert Stronach, and I ask your attention to a portion of it, commencing at the third paragraph on that page. The arrangement there referred to is the arrangement of April preceding? —Yes.

You there say—

I feel very confident that we can work the arrangement through. The experience of the past year's careful non-speculative business shows me that we can depend upon an income which will enable us to carry through the arrangement with the Bank, provided we are not hampered with embarrassments arising out of old financial entanglements.

I am anxious to start clear, and shrink from the idea of raising any part of the money required for the first payment to the Bank by floating paper.

The only modification I see in the arrangement is that we be permitted to delay the first payment in reduction of the debt to the Bank until June, 1876.

Although Morton has advised me not to write, I think it very much better that I should tell you the truth as it appears to me, and I ask your kind advice.

The object of the arrangement is to repay the debt to the Bank, and if a scrambling effort to keep to the letter of the engagement as present made is calculated to impair our credit, and so diminish our ability to earn money for future payments, I submit it will be much better to postpone our first payments for a few months.

I will be guided by your kind advice.

The arrangement is a most favourable one for us, and I have no fear about being able to carry through our part of it, provided we get a fair start.

Evidence for Prosecution.

Did that letter correctly express your state of mind at the time with regard to the arrangement with the Bank?—It did.

And have you any doubt that you set out the considerations there stated to the Bank as the inducement to them to enter into that arrangement?—Which letter do you mean?

The considerations referred to in that letter?—Do you mean in the letter you have read?

Yes; that is written after the arrangement was made, you will observe?—The arrangement had not been finally concluded until 24th August.

I observe that that letter is addressed to Mr. Stronach, and is marked " confidential "?—Yes.

Amongst the securities made over to the Bank, I think there were shares in the Canterbury and Otago Company. Is that so?—There were some shares belonging to myself which I made over to the Bank.

The written arrangement between you and the Bank contains the following article———?—Is it the arrangement as finally understood, and which is dated 24th August, 1875?

Yes. In that agreement there is an article in the following terms:—" We append a statement D showing the charges on our debts and our probable income with its sources, by which it appears that we have at present the prospect of an annual surplus of about £25,000 applicable to the reduction of our debts." That statement was true?—That statement was true.

In 1875 there was £100,000 advanced as part of the arrangement. Was that advance given against a security?—Which £100,000 is that?

Part of the agreement of 1875?—If you refer to the £100,000 advanced upon the security of Canterbury stock we were debited with £100,000 by the City of Glasgow Bank in account with the City of Glasgow Bank for the acquisition of a corresponding amount of Canterbury stock.

That was to be applied in the acquisition of that stock?— Yes.

And at that time was that stock regarded as a highly lucrative investment?—It was not paying well at the time, but prospectively it would be so.

That is what I mean—it was an investment which prospectively would become highly remunerative?—Yes.

And I suppose you explained that at the time when the advance was given?—The proposal came from the other side, not from me.

As an additional security to the Bank?—As an additional security to the Bank to help my account.

In short, it was regarded as an increase of the Bank security to have £100,000 of that stock bought by you as in lieu of £100,000 of your account?—Yes; and it was also expected that

P

225

The City of Glasgow Bank Trial.

it would produce an income larger than the interest charged against me for advance.

And in that way it would lighten the burden of the accruing interest on your accounts?—Yes.

By Mr. BALFOUR—You told us there had been a proposal for the reconstruction of your firm; was that about the end of 1874 or early in 1875?—I think it was in the autumn of 1874.

Was the idea at that time to get in a young partner possessed of money?—The idea was to get one or more partners in with money.

And was it proposed that Mr. John Potter, the son of Mr. Lewis Potter, should be assumed as such a partner?—It was so suggested.

As a partner possessed of money?—Yes.

Did you think, from the state of your business at that time, that if you got one or more partners possessed of money you would be able to conduct the business to advantage and with success?—I was of opinion that if we could get one or more partners possessed of money introduced into our business, and that our business should at the same time be purged of all finance, we had a prospect of doing well; but it was an essential part of the thing that there should be a purging of finance.

And I suppose you were ready to purge it of finance if you could get in a moneyed partner?—No; I could not get a moneyed partner in without getting it first purged of finance.

But you wished first to purge it of finance, and then to get a moneyed partner in, and you believed all would be well? —I believed so.

Did you at that time see the elements of a good London business in your transactions?—Yes.

And had you particularly in view the advantage it would be to that London business of which you saw the good elements if you got a moneyed partner?—Yes.

And was it with reference to that proposal that you were talking to Mr. Lewis Potter?—It was.

I suppose that if his son was to come in with money, that money must have been got from Mr. Potter, his father?—I understood so.

That was the subject of your conversation?—That was so.

And that was, of course, a matter which nobody else had anything to do with?—No.

By Mr. MACKINTOSH—Do you know Mr. Taylor?—I have never seen Mr. Taylor to my knowledge before to-day.

Had you any communication with him, directly or indirectly, with regard to your affairs?—Never.

Or the affairs of the Bank?—Never.

By Mr. ROBERTSON—Looking back over the negotiations you had with the Bank with regard to your affairs, did you ever meet Mr. Henry Inglis on Bank business?—Never.

Evidence for Prosecution.

By the DEAN OF FACULTY—My brother, James Nicol Fleming, John Fleming. left the firm of Smith, Fleming & Co. in 1862.

You have been asked how much your firm made in the year 1870 of income, and you have told us £90,000 a year?—Not in 1870. I said the average income for the three years preceding 1870 was over £90,000. It was very nearly £93,000.

And in 1875, the year preceding the arrangement that you came to with the Bank, how much were you making in your London house and in your foreign houses?—I cannot say. In the year closing in 1875 we earned £28,000 of commission in London.

Of commissions in your London house alone?—Yes, alone.

And the foreign houses were doing well also?—Yes.

I suppose your house, Smith, Fleming & Co., had the best commission agency business in London?—Oh, no, I don't say that.

But, at all events, a most excellent commission agency business?—We had a good business.

After Alexander Stronach ceased to be Manager, and the office was taken up by Robert, did you find him more strict to deal with than his brother had been?—Yes.

You did not get advances so easily?—No.

Would you look at page 60 of the print for the defence, and read the letter addressed by Robert Stronach to you, dated 22nd January, 1875?—[Witness reads the following]:—

Private.

22nd January, 1875.

Dear Sir,—In answer to your private note of yesterday, and accompanying official, applying for an extension of part of the Bombay Saw Mill Company's credit, 31/38, for £30,000 to the extent of one-third, under the same terms and conditions as before, I regret that this application did not reach me in time for consideration at yesterday's Board meeting; and as I cannot, on my own individual responsibility, grant the extension your friends ask, it will, I fear, require to remain over for another week.

In the meantime, please let me know if you have any advice that this *is* to be done. It will be well for you to understand that all matters of this description MUST go before the Board in future.— Yours faithfully,

R. S. STRONACH,
Assistant Manager.

John Fleming, Esq.

You see there that Robert Stronach says he won't do anything upon his own responsibility?—Yes.

And that all this must go before the Board?—Yes.

In all your dealings with him, did you ever find that he made any advance upon his own responsibility?—I am not aware that he ever did.

You have told us the amount of the indebtedness of your firm at the stoppage of the Bank, and the amount of the

The City of Glasgow Bank Trial.

indebtedness at the date of the arrangement in August, 1875, there being an increase between the two periods, between 1875 and 1878. Was a portion of that increase due to the accumulation of interest, and to the adding up of the payments that you ought to have made, but did not make, in the interim upon the old debt?—To the accumulation of interest, and also to the addition of £100,000 advanced upon Otago stock.

Just so; but you have explained to us in regard to that £100,000 that the security was given at the time in August, 1875, and was then looked upon as perfectly sufficient to meet it?—Yes.

By the LORD JUSTICE-CLERK—You have not quite answered the question whether the additional amount between 1875 and 1878 was caused mainly or largely or considerably by the accumulation of interest, and the payments which you were bound to make under the arrangement on the old debt?—The payments that I was bound to make and did not make, would not add to my debt, but the accumulation of interest added to it, and there was also this £100,000 advanced, and there were also additional amounts which we had to receive to help us along.

What the Dean of Faculty wishes you to tell him, I suppose, is how much was due to the accumulation of interest and the £100,000—what proportion of the difference?—I cannot tell.

By the DEAN OF FACULTY—But it was a large sum?—Yes; a sum probably of £100,000.

By the LORD JUSTICE-CLERK—That is to say, about £200,000 out of six?—Out of five.

By the DEAN OF FACULTY—In the letter which Mr. Asher read, of 24th July, 1875, page 85 of the same print, third paragraph from the foot, you begin thus—"The object of the arrangement is to repay the debt to the Bank." That was the arrangement at that time?—Yes.

And that was to be done by paying £25,000 a year?—Yes.

Had you any doubt at that time, looking to your business, that you would have a surplus available for that purpose to that amount?—I believed that we should have.

You did get advances from the Bank subsequent to that period?—Yes.

Turn to page 103 of the same print; there is a letter there, dated 4th May, 1876, from your firm to Mr. Stronach, in the following terms:—

With reference to credit No. 37/25 for £20,000 granted in favour of Messrs. Todd, Findlay & Co. under our application of 1st September, 1875, and of which £10,000 only is now current, we would feel obliged by your accepting the enclosed drafts for £5000 under same credit; and as security for the same we engage to hold to your order the proceeds of 133 tons cutch, p. "Mandalay," value £2600; 255 b. hides, do. £3200; and to keep you free from cash advance in respect of such advance.

Evidence for Prosecution.

You got that advance, and you gave the security of the produce upon it?—Yes.

Turn next to page 107 of the same print; there is an excerpt there from a letter by you to Mr. Robert Stronach, dated 8th August, 1876, in the following terms:—

I can quite understand the disappointment felt at the absence of progress in our affairs; but if the very general and extreme badness of trade be considered, and the special difficulties we have had to contend with, through Collie's stoppage, and the subsequent derangement of credit, I do not think there is any reason to be dissatisfied with our position as compared with what it was twelve months ago, nor to be discouraged as to the future.

You entertained these hopes at that time?—I did.

You did lose something by Collie's stoppage?—Yes.

But still trade looked well for you at that time?—I hoped there might be a revival of trade.

Look at page 112 of the same print; you got another advance from the Bank under the following letter of 17th October, 1876, from your firm to Mr. Robert Stronach:—

We beg to apply for a credit to be operated under by Messrs. W. Nicol & Co. or Messrs. Todd, Findlay & Co., at six months' sight, to extent of £25,000; and as security for same we engage to hold at your order the following shipments, the proceeds of which to be applied to the retirement of your acceptances:—

Balance of teak shipments to Mauritius,	-	£5400
Do. rice p. "Cambay,"	- - -	2070
Do. do. p. "Harriet M'Gilvray,"	-	1000
Do. do. p. "Superbe Richesse,"	-	1400
Do. do. p. "Rubino,"	- - -	1200
Do. do. p. "Caterine Doge,"	-	1100
11,870 B do. p. "Rangoon,"	- - -	5500
1145 tons do. p. "Annati,"	- - -	5800
NK/10, 1 box pearls,	- - - -	2200
		£25,670

We further engage to keep you free from cash advance in respect of such credit.

You got that advance and you gave the security?—We did.

Let us pass on to page 125 of the same print. You have another letter there of the same kind, dated 10th April, 1875:—

Dear Sir,—We beg to apply for a credit in favour of Messrs. W. Nicol & Co., Bombay, at 6 m/st., to extent of £15,000, and as security for the same we engage to hold on your account the proceeds of—

And then you give the proceeds of eight different ships to that extent?—Yes.

Then on page 126, under date 5th May, 1877, you write—

I see no reason to modify the views I personally expressed to you; indeed, later advices confirming the expectation of short shipments during the next six weeks from India strengthen my belief in the certainty of a rise in the value of cotton.

The City of Glasgow Bank Trial.

John Fleming. You did entertain that belief and those hopes?—Yes.

Every day the situation is getting stronger. The stock from this time onward will be daily lightened, and as these speculative transactions are settled, the cotton passes into strong hands.

I may mention also that I know that several of the large speculators who last autumn were buyers, but turned round in January and became sellers, and have continued so until lately, are now on the buying tack again.

So that at that time trade was hopeful and good?—In the matter of cotton there was an expectation that there would be a rise in the price of cotton.

Now, look at page 127—

We beg leave to apply for a credit in favour of Messrs. W. Nicol & Co. to extent of £15,000 sterling, to be drawn under at six months' sight, and in renewal of credit No. 38/5 of a similar amount now current; and we engage to put you in funds to retire the same at maturity.

That was a renewal of an old debt—it was not a new transaction?—No; that was not.

Look at page 131—

Dear Sir,—We beg to apply for a credit in favour of Messrs. W. Nicol & Co., Bombay, to extent of £8500 in renewal of No. 36/35 for a similar amount now current, and on the security of 50 shares in the Bombay Saw Mills Company, Ltd., standing in the name of John Hunter, Esq., and 50 shares in the same company registered in the name of James Morton, Esq.

We engage to keep you free from cash advance in respect of all drafts accepted under such credit.—We are, dear sir, yours faithfully,

SMITH, FLEMING & CO.

You gave these securities?—They held these securities; that was a renewal of an old transaction.

And you got a renewal of it, and declared that the old securities should be applied to it?—Yes.

Am I right in saying that in regard to all advances that were made upon new transactions subsequent to the arrangement of August, 1875, you gave to the Bank securities of one kind or of another, generally produce and shipments then on their way?—They were not all secured.

Was the greater part of them secured in that way?—Yes.

Look at page 132, letter of 27th September, 1876, from Stronach to you—

While it is very gratifying to learn that you have been arranging most desirable connections, which you anticipate will add considerably to your emoluments in the future, it is to be regretted that you have been unable in some measure to realise the expectations of the spring, and make a tangible reduction of your debt to the Bank. The Directors are of opinion that there is still a considerable saving might be effected in the expenditure of the several

Evidence for Prosecution.

John Fleming.

drafts of your business at home and abroad. Please look into this, and let me have your report soon. I need not point out to you that even a saving of £5000 in this way would cover, at the reduced rate of interest charged, about £150m.

You had been arranging new connections?—Yes; in Ceylon.

Opening up a new trade?—At least adding to an existing trade.

Whereby you would get additional commissions to the £90,000 you had already got?—Yes.

The Bank held from your firm as security property at Rangoon?—Todd, Findlay & Co. undertook to hold certain property for the Bank at Rangoon.

What were those properties valued at at the time when an advance was made as against them?—I don't remember what figures were put down; but roughly, I believe, about £90,000. A portion of those properties, which stood in the books of Todd, Findlay & Co. at 102,000 rupees, subject to a mortgage of £5000, was sold last week for 250,000 rupees; and if you deduct the mortgage, which is equal to about 65,000 rupees, that leaves a surplus of 90,000 rupees over the valuation in the books.

By the LORD JUSTICE-CLERK—At the present rate of exchange that is not so much as £9000, but taking the rupee at 2s. it is £9000.

By the DEAN OF FACULTY—We had property also at Kurrachee which was made the subject of security.

There is a railway now being made to Kurrachee?—There is a railway now made; the Indus Valley line was completed this year. I fully expect that that will greatly increase the value of property there.

Then the sum at which the Kurrachee security was valued is not the real sum it will bring?—Well, I am not sure about that; that is a very difficult question. At the present moment it would not realise what it is valued at. The railway has just been opened, and the expectation is that there will be a large increase of trade at Kurrachee, and that consequently all landed and house property will increase in value.

By the SOLICITOR-GENERAL—Your attention has been called to some letters which were passing pretty early, the first being in April, 1872. Look at page 5, letter from Alexander Stronach, 7th October, 1872—

I am being a little troubled just now with Directors who have come on as a committee on head office advance accounts, and who, having come across your produce advance debit, wish more information than I can exactly give them. They have seen the mode it works with us, but they are not at all pleased with its size, and especially at the sudden large jump it has taken without their having been consulted beforehand; and all the more that the securities, or many of them, don't come into our hands at all, or are seen by us. I

The City of Glasgow Bank Trial.

John Fleming. have detailed to them that they are all regularly put up separately from your own securities in a box which is held in trust for us in your safe, and, like your ticketed bills, for which the account was first substituted, belongs to us exclusively against this balance. Personally, I know it will be in perfect order, and it is because I believe it to be so that I ask you now to detail the arrangements in connection with these securities, and how they are kept for us, and can easily be recognised as ours as distinct from your own. All will come right, doubtless, by the end of November as stated, when the reduction then expected takes place; but meanwhile you will require to be more specific as to what you propose to put in during the next two weeks for these gentlemen's information.

Look at page 7, 10th January, 1873, Alexander Stronach to you—

In these circumstances, I don't well see how I can substitute for these occasional drafts a permanent increase to the Bombay credits, as you seem to point at, the more especially as these latter drafts are already so largely in excess of the authorised limit, and the Directors who know of the matter are pressing to get them reduced as soon as possible, instead of increasing them.

Now, look at page 18—

Some of the Directors have already gone over this memo., and I shall be glad to have your views and criticisms, if you have any specially to offer, at your earliest convenience.

Then on page 19 there is another letter by Alexander Stronach, 11th June, 1873, in which he says—

I shall be glad how soon you can make it convenient to be in this city, in accordance with your previous arrangements for coming north, as I should like to have some further discussion on the subject-matter of our recent interviews here, along with Messrs. Potter and Fleming, and the memo. which I enclosed for your careful consideration yesterday, and remarks.

Does that refer to a meeting that had been held with Mr. Potter, Mr. Fleming, and Alexander Stronach and you?—It must be so. Look at next page, 12th June, 1873—

The impression has been growing very strongly upon me of late (and the same idea has been mooted by Mr. Potter without any communication with me), that you and I should become more intimately acquainted with, or rather communicative, as to what is doing from week to week, and that we should be more in consultation on the *financial* position and prospects of the concern generally, seeing that we have so deep an interest. I fancy I *could* be of essential service to both parties if allowed, and certainly it would be much more satisfactory to the Directors (who must have the matter in charge now) that I were able to report upon any application requiring to be made from my personal knowledge of the circumstances.

Mr. BALFOUR—Would you read the first half of the letter?

232

Evidence for Prosecution.

The SOLICITOR-GENERAL—It is as follows :—

I am sorry to hear by yours of yesterday that you are not feeling so well at present. I have also myself been much knocked up of late, and had at last, in something like desperation, to send for the doctor last night. This morning, from the application he has given me, I feel rather better, but he will not hear of my going out for some days, and insists on my going off at once for some months' rest. I fear that those heavy and unexpected demands you have been making on us (and of which I had no indication when you were here, curiously enough), although not, perhaps, the *cause*, have had their own effects in putting me in the horrors for the last week or so, and, I have no doubt, have made me write you morbidly on the subject. Now, however, that I know you are ill and unable to write for a few days, I will wait patiently till you are able to write me fully, not only as to the past, but also as to the future, and the prospects of greater ease, and being able to recoup me. You know that I am wholly in the dark, and, in present circumstances, apparently must always remain so as to what is coming, unless some change in this respect can be effected.

And later on in the letter he says—

I am far from despairing as to the future, but it is clear that the change of policy which you have lately introduced is the only sound one in present circumstances, and the only one likely to lead you out of your difficulties ultimately.

Then look on page 22, 13th June, 1873—

Meantime, I speak for the memo. I enclosed to you the other day your calm and earnest attention, as you will at once see it is based entirely upon what passed at our meetings, at which Mr. Potter and Mr. J. N. F. (Directors) were partly present, and that all I have done in embodying the substance in this form of a memo. was simply to amplify some of the details from the papers already in my hands, so as to meet the circumstances and the facts.

Look at page 25, 8th July, 1873—

Referring to our interview yesterday, Mr. Potter has been with me to-day, and we have fully gone over the ground we traversed yesterday, making him aware of all that passed between us. I have also discussed with him very fully the proposed separation of the firms (in which he takes a deep interest), and after looking carefully at the views you propounded as to the practical uselessness and inexpediency of such a change, we have failed, either of us, to see any valid objection to the proposal itself, or how you can by any other means effect the same object, and give the Bank an equally good security, which we believe that you are in earnest in trying to provide for us. At the same time we see strong and very forcible reasons why you should meet our views in perfecting the securities to the utmost of your power, notwithstanding that the mode proposed may soon be repugnant to all your prejudices and feelings, which I scarcely believe it is.

And in the same letter—

On that subject, as well as on the nature of the business which is to be done and what is to be avoided in the future, I have again read over your letter with Mr. Potter, and we are both of opinion that it would greatly strengthen our hands in presenting your

Evidence for Prosecution.

John Fleming. applications to the Board and getting them adopted, if you would write us such a letter, signed by yourself and partners, which can be read at the meeting, embodying very much what you have already written me on both these subjects, and which you are in future resolved to abide by.

These letters were all received by you from Alexander Stronach?—I believe so.

By the LORD JUSTICE-CLERK—And you assumed the statements of fact in them to be correct, and acted upon them?—I did.

By the SOLICITOR-GENERAL—From 1873 downwards were you ever able to present any substantial change that had taken place in your affairs to the Manager or Directors of the Bank?—Do you mean an improvement?

Yes?—No.

Hopes always, but nothing more?—Hopes, but nothing more.

And the only bright ray you have had for some years, I think, was the ray last year about the gold in this field?—Yes.

Did the Bank at any time from 1873 downwards decline to give you any advance that you asked?—Never; never finally declined.

Once, I think, it was temporarily declined, but granted at the following meeting?—Yes.

On all other occasions was it granted at your first application?—It was granted; I am not prepared to say on the first application, but certainly it was granted.

And without any additional security given from the time of the agreement?—No, no.

What additional security was given from the agreement of 1875?—There have been advances upon sundry securities—balances of shipments, and certain property. For instance, when the credit was given which formed the subject of the interview in July last year, there were securities specified against it.

So against some of them there were securities, and some not?—Yes.

By the LORD JUSTICE-CLERK—What was the nature generally of the securities that were granted for the fresh advances after 1875?—Generally shipments of produce, or portions of shipments, or debts due to us.

Can you tell us the proportion of unsecured advances from that date?—I think the only specific uncovered advance was one of £65,000 originally, and from the commencement uncovered.

You think the rest of the advances were covered?—At one time, when the produce of shipments was given in security, the proceeds were applied to payment of the Bank's acceptances.

234

CHAPTER VIII.

Evidence of Glasgow Merchants and of an Edinburgh Director.

WILLIAM GLEN WALKER.

By the SOLICITOR-GENERAL—I am a merchant and Australian sheep farmer, living in Surrey. I am principal partner of Glen Walker & Co., merchants, Melbourne. That is principally an agency for land and sheep farms.

There is a company called the Australian and New Zealand Land and Investment Trust, Limited, carrying on business in London. How was that company formed?—That company was formed to amalgamate certain properties that belonged to the City of Glasgow Bank and myself.

That is to say, certain properties called the Edinburgh Pastoral Association?—Properties that belonged to the Edinburgh Pastoral Association, that being another name for the Bank.

How long is it since the amalgamation was carried on?—The company is still an inchoate company. I think it was registered in February last. A good many years ago, my firm had been acting as agents in Australia for Potter, Wilson & Co.

And you were also at one time connected with the firm of Morton & Co.?—Merely as their agent, at the same time that I was agent for Potter, Wilson & Co. Mr. Alexander Stronach was my brother-in-law; we married sisters.

Do you remember his speaking to you at one time about becoming a partner of Smith, Fleming & Co.—Yes; that arrangement was once proposed. That was in 1873. I asked to see their position—how they stood. I found a very large balance sheet, which was very difficult to understand; and I found an entry which was explained to me to mean that they were behind (if I remember aright) from £150,000 to £200,000— about £170,000, I think—but I speak from recollection, and have not had an opportunity of reviving my recollection.

During these negotiations about your entering the firm of Smith, Fleming & Co., had you a meeting with Alexander Stronach and two other people about it?—Yes; the two others were Mr. Potter and Mr. Morton. The meeting took place in the Bank's office, Virginia Street. This was in 1873.

The City of Glasgow Bank Trial.

W. G. Walker. What was the nature of the conversation that took place at that meeting?—The essence of the conversation simply meant that it would be very desirable, in the interest of the Bank, if I would join that firm.

Was anything said about the position of the Bank in regard to Smith, Fleming & Co.'s deficit?—I do not recollect it at that meeting, but there was subsequently.

Had you other meetings with Potter, Morton, and Alexander Stronach?—I think I had; I certainly had with Alexander Stronach, and I think I had with the others, but I am not quite sure.

I believe at the first meeting Mr. Taylor came in about the end of the meeting?—He did not come in; he merely came to the door. He had no part whatever in the meeting. I did not know Mr. Taylor then.

What was the object of the discussion at the meeting upon the part of the others towards you? What did they want?—They wanted me to join the firm, and it was a question of terms.

What were you informed was the Bank's object in wishing you to become a partner?—To have through me a better control over the business; they believed the business to be an excellent one. They wanted me to join on the basis of adopting that deficit, and they represented, and, I believe, honestly believed, that the goodwill of the business was worth a great deal more than that deficit.

But you did not see your way to that at the time?—The negotiation broke through, not altogether on that ground, but also because I wanted an undertaking from the Bank that it would carry Smith, Fleming & Co. through, whatever the consequences might be.

When Robert Stronach became the Manager of the Bank did he communicate with you about joining anybody as a partner?—He suggested that I should join James Morton & Co. I came down from London and had an interview with him, Potter, and Morton at the Bank on that subject.

Who took the principal part in the conversation?—Almost exclusively Mr. Potter, myself, and Mr. Morton.

Had you several conversations with them?—I had several conversations—I believe I had two or three conversations with them. I had a long conversation with Morton.

And with Potter had you several conversations?—Yes; but only incidentally.

How long did this interview last at which Stronach, Potter, and Morton were present?—Probably half an hour.

What did you say to them would be necessary before you could make up your mind on the subject?—I wanted to know Morton's position, and I also wanted to know what policy

Evidence for Prosecution.

would be adopted as regards Morton's large landed interests W. G. Walker. in New Zealand.

Did the value of the shares he possessed in these companies come up?—Not at that meeting, but I was asked to meet Morton in the evening, and spend a night with him discussing these questions, and he then assured me that his position was this, that he was able to cover the Bank's account by the shares in the New Zealand companies with which he was connected at par. He told me—it was about the same time that Stronach became Manager of the Bank, either a fortnight or so before or after, I cannot quite fix the date—he asserted that he had promised Mr. Stronach to reduce his account by £400,000 as a means to induce him to become the Manager, and he had also promised him to cover his account by stock at par.

By the Lord Justice-Clerk—This was about the time that Mr. Robert Stronach became Manager. I cannot fix the date.

By the Solicitor-General—But going back to the meeting with Potter and Morton, do you remember anything being said about a premium on Morton's shares?—Yes.

By whom?—By Potter, but that premium simply meant par.

What was it he said?—He asked if I would be prepared to join the firm on the basis of taking over Morton's shares at 60 per cent. premium; and that 60 per cent. is what I now mean by par.

Would you explain that to the jury?—It was in contemplation that the two companies in which Morton was largely interested should be amalgamated, and it was believed that the basis of the amalgamation would be the watering of that stock to the extent of 60 per cent. It was supposed that the stock was very much under-valued before.

Would you explain to the jury the expression you used just now—watering the stock?—It simply meant a re-valuation of the property.

Giving it a rosy effect?—No, I don't say that; these properties we are now speaking of have been, and are, rapidly increasing in value. At the inception of these companies the properties were valued at what was supposed to be the then existing price or value. At the new arrangement they had largely increased in value, and this watering the stock was required to give them what then was supposed to be the real value.

After Robert Stronach accepted the Managership had you and he conversations about Smith, Fleming & Co.'s affairs?—Very little indeed; I don't say we never spoke about them.

I don't mean that you spoke much, but I want to know whether, from conversations with him, you learned anything about the amount in danger on James Nicol Fleming's account? —I did not directly through Mr. Stronach; I would not like

The City of Glasgow Bank Trial.

to swear that I did from Mr. Stronach, though I may have done so, but I certainly did from Mr. John Hunter.

Did you, after hearing something from Mr. Hunter, speak over the matter about J. Nicol Fleming's account with Potter and Hunter?—It was quite understood between Potter and Hunter, and, I believe, by the others, as my relations with the Bank will show, that there was a deficit upon Nicol Fleming's account. I understood that deficit to be about £200,000. I believe that deficit was covered by promissory notes which Nicol Fleming or his firms had granted, and that these promissory notes again were represented by the goodwill of his different businesses.

Was any proposal made for the purpose of overcoming that deficit?—There was.

What was it?—I was instructed to buy those properties you have already referred to as belonging to the so-called Edinburgh Pastoral Association.

For the purpose of endeavouring to cover possible losses through J. Nicol Fleming's account?—For the purpose of covering those two deficits of which I have spoken.

Did you understand from Potter as to whether there was any hope of recouping the deficit with some such scheme?—I understood from Potter that Nicol Fleming had not been a successful man, and that he did not like to rely upon the success of these businesses, and that he wanted additional security. [Shown No. 217, letter, Glen Walker & Co., to Robert Stronach, dated 14th August, 1876, as follows]:—

Glasgow, 14th August, 1876.

Pastoral Properties in Australia.

R. Stronach, Esq.

Dear Sir,—In continuation of conversations with yourself, and other gentlemen connected with the Bank, I would now place in writing the suggestions which we have been discussing towards increasing income, and recouping deficits by the judicious acquirement of pastoral properties.

More than one member of your Board are connected with New South Wales properties, which have, on an average of many years, I am assured, paid a net return upon present values exceeding 16 per cent. per annum.

The purchase price usually is paid by partly a cash deposit and the balance by bills, extending over several years. It is easy to finance against them in the colony, and if 40 per cent. of the price was provided here, the remainder could be arranged in the colony without further aid from this.

If arranged in this way, finance probably would cost for interest an average of 6 per cent. per annum, and there would remain, on the basis of the experience referred to, as net profits, 10 per cent. per annum.

The suggestion is that the Bank grant credits to the extent of from £100m to £150m towards the acquirement of pastoral interests in Australia.

Evidence for Prosecution.

For example, if a value of £250m was acquired, there should be W. G. Walker. a net profit of £25m yearly, but £25m yearly will in fourteen years repay £250m, and 5 per cent. interest, so that thus, by comparatively a very small outlay, a large amount can be recouped.

Mr. Borron and myself will be glad to be interested in the project, and to manage its detail, and finance can, in the Bank's option, be arranged either by cash advance or entirely by credit.—I am, &c.,

W. Glen Walker.

Now, was that letter written on the suggestion of any one?—That letter was written as the result of a long negotiation, the principal parties to which were Mr. Hunter, Mr. Potter, and myself.

Was it written on the suggestion of any one?—On the suggestion of some of us three, I cannot say which.

Was it your suggestion?—It was intended to place on record that which we practically then had agreed to do.

Was it on your suggestion, or on the suggestion of one of the other two?—I cannot recollect.

But it was agreed between you that such a letter should be written?—It was agreed between us that such a letter should be written.

Did you see Potter frequently at his own office on the subject before this letter was written?—My principal negotiations were with Mr. John Hunter. I sometimes called upon Mr. Potter.

By the Lord Justice-Clerk—And you embodied in that letter the result of your conference?—That is so.

By the Solicitor-General—And in consequence you or your firm bought properties for the Bank in Australia?—I did.

And subsequently to that did you also purchase for them other properties in Australia from the Australian and New Zealand Land Company?—I did.

Were these bought for the same purpose?—Partly for the same purpose, but principally for another purpose.

What other purpose?—That requires some explanation. The Bank were very largely interested indirectly in the New Zealand Company.

How?—Through Morton's account, and I suppose through Fleming's account also. I suppose two-thirds of the whole belongings of the New Zealand and Australian Company, as I now know, practically belong to the Bank. At the time I knew of their large interest, but I did not know it was so large as I now know.

How did they practically belong to the Bank?—I now find that these men are bankrupt, and that the assets of these men practically belong to the Bank.

As at that time?—No. I say the assets of these firms, James Morton & Co. and Smith, Fleming & Co., practically belong to the Bank, and these men are the owners of, I believe, from one-

239

The City of Glasgow Bank Trial.

half to three-fourths of all the shares in that company. The Bank had discovered that these stations in Australia had been very badly managed—that a drunkard had been managing them for some years. They had learnt that from their agents in Australia, and they wanted to get these properties into better management. That was the real reason for buying these properties.

And in order to cover their advances?—Well, I have already said it was for two purposes, that being the principal purpose; but also incidentally for the same purpose as the other places were bought for—that is to say, to have properties paying a high rate of interest; the difference between the rate of interest current in this country and that higher rate of interest to be used to mortise these two deficits of about £150,000 and £200,000.

These two objects—to recoup deficits and cover advances—the principal object being to recoup the deficits?—The principal object, as I have said, with regard to one of them was so; and as regards the other, to get these properties into proper management.

As regards the price of the lands, of the first lot that you bought after the arrangement of August, 1876, how was the price paid?—Partly by money, and partly by my promissory notes.

How much has the Bank paid?—I really forget without referring to the accounts. In the inception of the transaction I paid, I think, £30,000 or £40,000; but subsequently I have been converting leasehold into freehold property. A portion of that was leasehold property, and I have been converting it into freehold property; and I should fancy the advances have amounted altogether to about £130,000 or £140,000.

Were these moneys paid out by you—the £130,000 to £140,000 —for the Bank?—Certainly.

And you got the money from the Bank?—I got credits from the Bank, which I converted into money.

The advances that you made were simply as agent for the Bank?—Certainly.

How was the rest provided?—The rest was provided by my promissory notes.

They also being granted for the Bank?—Certainly.

And for which they are liable?—Certainly, I believe so. The liquidators say no.

Did you, in any way, throughout the whole proceedings, act for yourself, or did you act entirely as agent for the Bank?—The Directors intended, and I intended, that I should act as agent for the Bank.

By the LORD JUSTICE-CLERK—That seems to be a question?— The question has been raised by the liquidators as to the purchase from the New Zealand Company being *ultra vires*.

Evidence for Prosecution.

But the character in which you understood you were acting was that of agent for the Bank?—Certainly.

By the SOLICITOR-GENERAL—You were to be remunerated for what you did?—I was to charge a reasonable commission.

Which was?—It would depend upon what I would charge it.

Was it never settled?—Never settled.

Had you no interest except the commission?—None whatever. I hoped to have, but I never have had.

How much were you in advance upon acceptances or promissory notes for account of these properties?—I think at the present moment about £80,000 or £90,000.

Look at the letter No. 218, dated 14th August, 1876, the same date as the other, and addressed also to Mr. Stronach—

Glasgow, 14th August, 1876.

R. S. Stronach, Esq.

Dear Sir,—It seems right that securities should be specially held by the Bank as a basis for any drafts by my firm in substitution for others, and I suggest that you place to a special account such securities as are required fairly to cover the drafts about to be substituted, or to obtain any others for a like purpose.

I should say that, personally, I am content without this; but I will require to explain the transaction to partners, and then must justify it by explaining how the Bank is covered by securities.—I am, &c.,

W. GLEN WALKER.

Just explain in your own words the purpose of that letter?—This letter refers to a totally different transaction from what we have been speaking about, but it has some reference to the same transaction also. Mr. John Hunter had at that time the management of the liquidation of Nicol Fleming's account. That account, I was informed, as I have stated, by Mr. Hunter, showed an uncovered deficit, uncovered except by goodwill, and I think a policy of insurance, he said, to the extent of a couple of hundred thousand pounds. At the same time Nicol Fleming's name had been to some extent discredited; and Mr. Hunter suggested that it would be very desirable if my firm's name could be substituted as drawers of drafts upon the Bank in substitution of £100,000 of Nicol Fleming's. I agreed to the arrangement conditionally upon securities being placed to cover those drafts for which I was becoming responsible; and an arrangement was made by which £100,000 of stock which belonged to Morton, over which the Bank held security, should be placed as a special security against these drafts when put in circulation.

How much of paper did you agree to allow your name to be used for?—£100,000.

And were drafts signed by your partner, Mr. Brown, who was then in Glasgow?—My partner signed blank drafts, and left them with the Manager to be filled up in terms of that arrangement, and used as he wanted.

The City of Glasgow Bank Trial.

W. G. Walker. Was anybody present when the drafts were signed blank and left with the Manager except the Manager and you?—I cannot tell you that; but I was present when the Manager and Mr. Potter looked over the drafts.

Were these drafts of your firm used for that purpose?—I understand they were subsequently. By the by, I am wrong in saying I did understand they were; I have been shown a minute in which, instead of being used to reduce Nicol Fleming's account, they were used in substitution of another account, but it was quite immaterial; it did not make any matter to me. I considered they had a perfect right to use them as they pleased.

As matter of fact, were they used for the purpose of retiring the Bank's acceptances to Holmes, White & Co.?—I know nothing more excepting that Mr. Brown has shown me the minute you are now reading from. I was in Australia myself at the time.

There is a minute of the Board of Directors with regard to an application by John Innes Wright & Co. on 24th August, 1876, for marginal credits to the extent of £100,000, to be drawn by Messrs. Glen Walker & Co., Melbourne, against shipments of wool and other produce. Can you tell me anything about that?—I arranged with Mr. Scott, of Innes Wright & Co., that he should procure for my firm credits to be used in the ordinary course of business for granting advances upon wool, or for the purpose of sending produce to this country. He obtained from the Bank £100,000 of these credits, and he sent them to my firm; that was all.

How did that arrangement come to be proposed?—I don't know that.

Had it anything to do with improving John Innes Wright & Co.'s position with the Bank?—I did not know at the time if it was so. I believed Innes Wright & Co. to be a sound and solvent concern.

Was that arrangement acted upon?—It was partly acted upon and partly not. I found that the credits were of no use to me, but I required some moneys for the purposes of the Bank in connection with those land purchases that I had orders to buy, and I used a portion of the credits for that purpose, and I sent the bulk of them home. I used a few thousand pounds—I think £7000, if I remember right—in sending home produce; but I could draw from the colony on my own credit quite as well as using the Bank's credits, and consequently I returned them. [Shown No. 390, twenty-four blank drafts.] The blank drafts signed Glen Walker & Co. contained in that envelope were signed by my partner, Mr. Brown.

Were these part of the bills that were left blank at that time?—That I cannot swear to, but they are similar. The arrange-

242

Evidence for Prosecution.

ment was that if Mr. Stronach wanted some more he was to write to my partner for them.

By Mr. BALFOUR—I have been a good deal in Australia, and I am pretty familiar with that colony and its prospects and trade. As far back as twenty years ago I acted for Mr. Potter's firm in Australia.

Potter, Wilson & Co. trade with Australia as merchants and also as commission agents?—They were about the largest firm connected with Australia in those days.

And have they long been?—I presume they are still.

And also as shipowners?—They were in those days very large shipowners.

So that they had intimate relations with Australia—an intimate knowledge of it?—Certainly.

And also with New Zealand?—Certainly.

Did they also trade with New Zealand in a like capacity?—They did.

Had you also a knowledge of New Zealand from having been in the adjoining colony?—I have been in New Zealand, but I have not gone over the properties in which Mr. Potter is interested, although I have made most minute inquiries about them.

But I suppose, through having been in Australia, and your mercantile relations there, you were familiar with New Zealand and its prospects?—Yes.

You mentioned that you had had a meeting with Mr. Potter, and I think Mr. Morton and Mr. Alexander Stronach, and that the first matter you spoke of was, I think, Smith, Fleming & Co.'s debt, and the proposal that you should join them?—Yes.

On the occasion of these meetings, was the business of Smith, Fleming & Co. spoken of as one of great value?—Undoubtedly it was.

Of great earning power?—Undoubtedly.

What was the annual sum that was named as their profits?—The commissions, not their profits, were talked of as £100,000 a year easily.

These were mere commissions?—Yes.

And that is the safest of all kinds of business?—There is no doubt about it.

Was it evident to you that Mr. Potter, Mr. Morton, and Mr. Stronach believed that?—Most certainly.

And regarded it as a business of great value?—When the arrangement with me fell through, Mr. Potter intended to put his own son into the business.

Was that Mr. John Potter?—I don't know.

But you know that after the arrangement with you fell through Mr. Potter intended to put his own son in?—Yes.

It was desired at that time, was it not, to purge the business of Smith, Fleming & Co. of finance, and reduce them to the

243

The City of Glasgow Bank Trial.

W. G. Walker. safe business—to the commission business?—It was intended to purge the business of everything except commission business.

It was evidently the desire of these gentlemen to accomplish that?—That is so.

And if that was accomplished, did they appear to be satisfied that it would be greatly for the advantage of the Bank?—I think so.

You mentioned that it appeared from the statement shown to you that Smith, Fleming & Co. were a good deal behind—in debt. Did you understand that their debt to the Bank was covered by securities, or was that not gone into?—The question of their debt to the Bank never arose.

It was their total debt, was it?—No; it was their deficit.

And that was what was spoken to in the communication with you?—No; certainly not at the meeting with Mr. Potter in the Bank, but I had been with Mr. Stronach in London, and in London we had gone narrowly into these questions. Subsequently this meeting took place, and it was assumed that I knew everything.

Then the question of the deficit was not gone into with Mr. Potter and you, but had been gone into previously, apart from Mr. Potter, with Mr. Alexander Stronach in London?—I believe that is the fact.

Now, although the deficit that was spoken of by Alexander Stronach and you was considerable, was it such as a very lucrative business like that might have been expected to wipe off in a short time?—Certainly. If the business was paying £100,000 a year of commissions, £150,000 would very soon be wiped out.

The deficit was only a year and a half's income from the commissions?—Yes.

The deficit was about £150,000, and you were led to suppose that they were earning about £100,000 of commissions?—Yes. Mr. John Fleming has stated to me within the last month that during the last year his commission account came to £50,000 on his foreign businesses alone.

And therefore I suppose you were not surprised that Mr. Potter was willing to put his own son into a good thing like that?—There is no doubt that Mr. Potter at that time was perfectly sincere in his belief that it was a first-class business.

The next thing, I think, that you told us was about Mr. Morton. Is Mr. Morton a gentleman who is also well acquainted with the Australian and New Zealand colonies; has he commercial relations with them?—He has had very old relations with these colonies, but I don't think he has ever been in the colonies.

But to your knowledge has he had for long intimate commercial relations with these colonies?—Yes, undoubtedly.

Evidence for Prosecution.

And are you aware from your communications with him that he placed a very high value upon the land in these colonies and its prospects?—I know that perfectly well. He is a very sanguine man, and always spoke in the most sanguine terms of these properties.

And as if he believed it?—As if he believed it, most certainly. I believe he does believe it.

With regard to Morton and the shares he held, you used the expression "watering the stock of the two companies." Was that done on the occasion of two companies which had formerly been separate being amalgamated?—That was so.

And when these two companies were amalgamated, was the stock of each respectively put at the par value, which was then believed to be its true value?—I believe that was the intention.

And that is what you used the phrase of "watering" in respect to?—The valuations were very much too low before, and they were put more nearly the correct value.

And was that a perfectly fitting and proper thing to be done when the reorganisation was taking place, and the two being united?—Perfectly.

And has subsequent experience proved that the valuations they made were not too high, but were fair?—I can only answer that by saying that any valuation of colonial properties at the present moment would probably not exceed one-half or two-thirds of their intrinsic value; certainly not; and that these properties have recently been valued at more than these watered values.

Subsequent experience has proved that the values were not too high which were placed upon them at that time?—Certainly not.

Did you believe that the proposal embodied in the letter of 14th August, 1876, was a judicious one?—I believed that if you can get over the difficulty, or if it was determined to get over the difficulty of the Bank adopting an expedient that was not banking business, no better expedient could have been devised.

Was that the kind of thing that a prudent man managing his own affairs, and wishing to do the best for himself, would naturally have gone into?—A prudent man—certainly.

You said, with respect to the getting of the property into the hands of the Bank that there had been an unsatisfactory manager in charge?—That was so.

And with a view to unshipping him, and putting a right man in his place, the next step was taken?—The Bank at that time wanted to increase this kind of investment; they thought they had not quite enough, and I recommended them not to sell those properties which the company intended to sell, but to buy them from the company. I told them there were no better properties in Australia than these.

The City of Glasgow Bank Trial.

W. G. Walker. And when you gave them that advice you believed it to be sound?—I know it is true.

If you had been acting in your own interests and affairs, would you just have done the thing that the Bank did there?—Most certainly.

Was it the best way of getting the most value out of their securities?—Most certainly, always assuming that they were prepared to spend some money upon them.

To lay out some present expenditure as a means of getting the most out of them?—Exactly.

And was it with that view that the credits which you have described were raised and operated on?—The part of the credits which I have spoken of as representing the £130,000 or £140,000 that have been spent has been spent upon these properties.

Which are still held by the Bank, I think, or for them at all events?—They ought to be, I say ; the liquidators say no.

With respect to the next arrangement that was gone into under the letter of 14th August, 1876, did it appear to you also that that was a thing that a prudent man managing his own affairs would have done for his own advantage? You said, " I suggest that you place to a special account such securities "? —It was prudent for me to get the securities evidently. I think it was a prudent thing for the Bank to have done, seeing that they had the finance existing already. It was a prudent thing to put it in a name that was not discredited rather than in a name that was.

Does it come to this, that Nicol Fleming's name having sunk in credit rather, it was better to have them transferred to and worked in a better name?—Exactly.

By Mr. SMITH—Was the credit of £100,000, which was asked for on your behalf by Mr. Scott, on 2nd August, your first connection with Wright & Co.?—I think it was.

And was that the only credit which you got for yourself from the Bank?—I got one for £20,000. The one was for my firm, the other was for me as an individual.

You say part of the £100,000 was not used?—I sent it back.

How much was used altogether?—It is very difficult to speak accurately from memory.

Was it only £57,000?—My memory is that I sent back about £43,000.

That left £57,000 to be used in Australia?—Yes.

According to your recollection, how was that employed?—My recollection is that £25,000 and £17,000 were used on account of the Bank, speaking from memory ; £7000 or £8000 were sent home in produce ; £10,000 more was advanced upon a wool lien.

Was the £17,000 which was used for the Bank used in acquiring land for the Bank?—It was expended upon improvements, purchasing land, or making improvements upon the Bank's land.

246

Evidence for Prosecution.

Therefore of that the Bank got the benefit themselves?— **W. G. Walker.**
Altogether.

How was the £25,000 used?—It was used in the same way, or
in keeping up the Bank's properties.

Was there some employed also in the wool lien?—I have said
there was £10,000 of it; there was practically £35,000, but
£25,000 of this wool lien was for the Bank.

If the Bank then are debiting Wright & Co. with anything of
that wool lien, that is an error on the part of the Bank?—No
doubt it would be.

And there was about £7000 sent home in produce?—So far as
I remember.

Then the result of it all, I think, is that if that £7000 of ship-
ment of produce was accounted for, the whole of this advance
has been accounted for to the Bank; they got value for it?—
That I cannot tell you. I cannot answer that question. The
arrangement was that I did not get these credits from the Bank.
I got them from Innes Wright & Co. Innes Wright & Co.
instructed me to send the proceeds in the shape of produce to
Innes Wright & Co. I did so, and how they have accounted with
the Bank I do not know.

That £7000 was sent in produce, but if that were accounted
for the rest is all accounted for?—No; because I sent home produce representing the £35,000.

Which had been spent on the wool lien?—Yes; I believe the
wool lien turned out deficient.

Was there a loss on it?—Not a loss exactly. £25,000 of it
was invested upon a wool lien, of property belonging to the Bank.
After this had been done there was a very severe drought in
Australia, and a very large number of the sheep perished in
Australia; during that time ten millions of sheep died. About
50,000 of these sheep belonged to the Bank. The wool which
ought to have been shorn from these sheep did not come forward,
and consequently Innes Wright & Co. received less wool than
the wool lien represented.

That was the Bank's wool?—It was the Bank's wool.

By the DEAN OF FACULTY—When was the proposal that you
should become a partner with Morton made to you?—About the
time that Robert Stronach became the Manager.

Before he became the Manager?—I have been trying to recollect. I think it must have been before; but it was within a
fortnight before or after.

Did you find that Robert Stronach was very reluctant to take
the office of Manager?—He had been extremely reluctant.

You said something about a promise from Morton to reduce his
debt by £400,000?—Morton told me that it had been very difficult to get Stronach to accept the position, and one of his reasons
was that Morton's account was a very large one, and because he

247

The City of Glasgow Bank Trial.

had not his securities in proper order; and Morton, towards inducing him to accept the position, promised him that he would reduce his account by £400,000, and place securities which he had elsewhere with the Bank, so that his account should be fully covered at par.

It was after getting that promise from Morton that Stronach accepted the office?—Undoubtedly so.

I am going to show you a letter, print, page 107?—I know this letter quite well.

28th December, 1875, by Mr. Stronach to the Directors. Did you know that Mr. Stronach sent that letter to the Directors?—I was shown by Mr. Stronach the draft of a letter something like this, and he subsequently told me that he had sent that letter to the Board somewhat modified from what I had seen.

Can you tell me wherein the draft differs from the letter which we have here printed?

Mr. BALFOUR objected to the question.

By the DEAN OF FACULTY—Was this letter, which you call a draft letter, copied out and sent in its original shape and in its original terms to the Directors?—I was not present at the Board, and I can only speak as to what I saw. The draft which I did see contained the names of Morton and Fleming.

Mr. BALFOUR objected.

The LORD JUSTICE-CLERK (to witness)—Don't tell us what the draft contained, but tell us what you saw done.

By the DEAN OF FACULTY—Do you know what Mr. Stronach did with that letter?

By Mr. BALFOUR—From your own knowledge?—Not from my own knowledge, because I was not present at the Board.

By the DEAN OF FACULTY—What did he do with it so far as you saw?—He informed me that he intended to deliver it.

Mr. BALFOUR—Never mind "informed."

By the DEAN OF FACULTY—What did he say he intended to do with that draft?—To place it before the Board. He said he would not accept the position of Manager unless the Board relieved him of the responsibility of these accounts.

Did he mention what the accounts were?—Morton's and Fleming's—

Mr. BALFOUR objected to this.

By the DEAN OF FACULTY—Mr. Stronach wrote a draft of a letter—not this one—did he?—He wrote the draft of a letter, and he wrote a letter other than this one.

That is to say, he copied over the draft that he had made, and turned it into a letter?—Certainly.

Had that letter reference to the conditions upon which he was to accept the office of Manager?—Certainly; upon which he was willing to accept it.

Were you at the preparation of that letter?—I was not

Evidence for Prosecution.

present when the draft was written, but I was present when the letter was written, and I saw the letter.

By LORD CRAIGHILL—Was this in the Bank?—No, it was in his own house.

By the DEAN OF FACULTY—What did he do with the letter?—Took it to the Bank, I suppose.

What did he do with the letter after he had written and signed it?—I saw him a day or two afterwards.

You were present when he wrote it; what did he do with it? Did he put it in his pocket and leave the house with it?—I believe he did.

Then?—I believe he did; I did not see him actually put it in his pocket, but he certainly took it to the Bank with him.

He carried it away with him, and he was going to the Bank; is it not so?—Certainly.

Did you ever see that letter again?—Yes, I did.

Where did you see it?—I saw it in his house.

When?—That night, I believe.

What was done with that letter?—That I don't know.

Was it destroyed?—That I don't know.

Did he tell you what he had done with the letter when he took it away with him and took it to the Bank that day?

Mr. BALFOUR objected.

By the DEAN OF FACULTY—Well, he brought it back that night to his house?—That is so.

Was the second letter written then?—No, it was not.

When was the second letter written?—That I cannot tell you.

Were you present at the writing of it?—No, I was not.

Did you assist him in the preparation of it?—No, I did not—not this second letter.

Is the second letter in terms more modified than the first?

Mr. BALFOUR objected.

By the DEAN OF FACULTY—The first letter is gone, is it not?—The first letter was much more specific, and pointed to names, which this does not.

Do you know what became of the first letter?—No, nor did I see this second letter for a year or eighteen months afterwards.

Do you know if the first letter is destroyed?—I have been told so, but I do not know it of my own knowledge.

Did Mr. Stronach tell you anything as to its fate?

Mr. BALFOUR objected.

By the DEAN OF FACULTY—Did he tell you what became of the first letter?

Mr. BALFOUR objected.

By the DEAN OF FACULTY—What did he say?

Mr. BALFOUR objected.

By the DEAN OF FACULTY—You transacted a good deal of

The City of Glasgow Bank Trial.

W. G. Walker. business at this Bank of various kinds personally before you went to Australia?—Not a great deal of business; I had relations with the Bank, but not of a large character.

Did you transact business, on any occasion before you went to Australia, with the Directors without the intervention of Mr. Stronach?—The only business connected with these matters in which I had any relations with the Bank before I went to Australia was the business that I have already testified to.

Did you come in contact with the Directors before you went to Australia?—I came in contact with Mr. Potter only, I think. There are one or two of the minutes which refer to that time, from which it would appear that a committee of the Board had made various arrangements with me. Now, that minute is all nonsense; there were no such negotiations.

What minute was that?—Mr. Taylor, Mr. Stewart, and Mr. Potter are represented as a committee.

What is the date of that?—It is in 1876; it is the one in which they form themselves into a committee to arrange with me as to buying properties in Australia.

Is that the minute of 17th August, 1876, referred to on page 109?—

A letter from J. M. & Co., and two from W. Glen Walker, dated 16th and 14th inst., in regard to the drawing of credits in lieu of those now drawn by Holmes, White & Co. and others, and one of the latter as to the acquisition of certain pastoral properties, were brought under the notice of the Board; and after full consideration, the Board came to the resolution that it was advisable to adopt generally the suggestions contained in these letters, and they accordingly requested the Manager, associated with Messrs. Potter, Stewart, and Taylor, to arrange with Mr. Walker as to all details.

That is the first, and there is a subsequent letter referring to the same subject.

Then there is a report by these gentlemen stating that " in terms of the minute appointing us to arrange with Mr. Walker in regard to the acquisition of certain pastoral properties in Australia, we have to report that we then authorised an investment to the value of £120,000 or £130,000," and so on; what is wrong with that report?—I say it is untrue. I say I never met—at least, to the best of my belief—either Mr. Taylor or Mr. Stewart on that subject. There are many other minutes with which I am connected that are untrue, or at least misleading.

But I suppose this is quite true, that you were authorised to invest to the value of from £120,000 to £130,000 as stated in this report?—Yes; but not by Messrs. Stewart and Taylor. I received instructions to buy these properties after a long negotiation with John Hunter; I saw Mr. Potter once or twice, but it was principally John Hunter. I had scarcely any discussion with any one else on the subject.

Evidence for Prosecution.

But I suppose you have seen both Mr. Stewart and Mr. Taylor?—I don't believe I did. I don't think I ever met these gentlemen.

With regard to Mr. Stronach, was he a man of a yielding disposition, and one that would be easily influenced by men of a more decided character and positive views?—Yes; he was the most credulous and facile man I ever met in my life.

However, did he seem anxious to do the best he could for the interests of this Bank?—Undoubtedly.

Do you know whether the condition of some of these accounts was a source of affliction and misery to him?—Latterly, there cannot be a doubt about it; but when he became Manager he expected they would come all right.

After he got that promise of the paying up by Morton of £400,000, he thought all the rest would come right?—I think so.

Did you know that Smith, Fleming & Co.'s account had been put on a more distinct footing in August, 1875?—I knew nothing of Smith, Fleming & Co.'s account after I returned from Australia in August, 1877. I was always led to believe that the account was keeping all right. I was in Australia until August, 1877.

By Mr. BALFOUR—Let us understand about that first letter or draft; I wish to distinguish exactly what you saw from what was said to you or from your inferences about it?—I said I did not actually see it put in his pocket.

By the LORD JUSTICE-CLERK—But your firm conviction is that he did take it away with him?—Yes.

By Mr. BALFOUR—The last place you saw it was in his house? —Yes.

And what he did was not matter of observation, but matter of inference or information?—I was not in the Bank.

By the SOLICITOR-GENERAL—I think you said that you saw the letter which was laid before the Directors, about a year and a half afterwards?—No; I saw a copy of it. Mr. Stronach showed it to me in his house.

Would you tell me the names of the Directors with whom you have met in regard to the purchase of these Australian properties?—Do you mean since the purchases or before?

At any time?—I met Mr. Potter before their purchase; I believe I only met Mr. Potter. After the purchases I think I met them all.

Do you mean after the purchase of them all?—No; I mean all the Directors.

But you did not see anybody but Mr. Potter before the purchases?—To the best of my belief I did not.

Do you mean before all the purchases or before the first of them?—I mean before the first purchase.

With regard to that report of 19th October, 1876, which reports an authorisation by Mr. Taylor, Mr. Stewart, and Mr.

The City of Glasgow Bank Trial.

W. G. Walker. Potter, you say that you never met Mr. Taylor or Mr. Potter upon that subject?—To the best of my belief I never did. I am surprised to see it here, because I think I did not know them to speak to till I came home from Australia.

Did you meet any committee of the Directors upon the subject of purchase of Australian property?—Subsequent to my first purchase I met a committee with reference to the second.

Who were the committee?—Mr. Stewart, Mr. Taylor, and, if I remember right, Mr. Salmond.

Was it not Mr. Inglis?—I beg your pardon; it was Mr. Inglis instead of Mr. Stewart. I saw Mr. Stewart afterwards, but that committee consisted of Mr. Inglis, Mr. Taylor, and Mr. Salmond. I met them two or three times.

Would you consider it would be a prudent thing for a bank to do to make those purchases in Australia?—I did, considering all the circumstances.

Would you consider it would be a prudent thing for a Bank to make such purchases except for the purpose of recouping a deficit?—I think exceptional difficulties require exceptional expedients.

That is not quite an answer to my question. Would it be a prudent thing except for the purpose of recouping a deficit?—There might be other good reasons for doing so.

Of a similar kind?—Or other kinds.

What other kind except for the purpose of meeting a loss already made?—I know banks that build railways; it is quite common for banks to go into unusual transactions like this, though not a common thing for Scotch banks to do so.

John Hunter. ## JOHN HUNTER.

By the LORD ADVOCATE—I am a merchant in Glasgow, and a partner of Buchanan, Wilson & Co. I dealt at one time, from 1858, with the City of Glasgow Bank. I was acquainted with the present Manager, Robert Stronach, as well as with his predecessor, Alexander Stronach.

In the course of time you came to hold certain lands in Australia, or shares in hand in Australia, in trust for the City Bank?—Yes.

Will you explain the origin of the transaction by which you came into their possession?—The shares in my own name, or in my name along with others?

Well, both; which was first in point of time?—The first in point of time are those in my name along with others in trust. The firm of Potter, Wilson & Co., Morton & Co., and my own firm, were jointly interested in transactions in Australia and New Zealand. These properties were ultimately merged in the New Zealand and Australian Land Company.

252

Evidence for Prosecution.

These were held by Potter, Wilson & Co., Morton & Co., John Hunter. and yourself?—Yes. There was a guaranteed dividend secured when we made them over to the association. So long as that guarantee subsisted the shares were held by the three parties interested whom I have named. They were held in name of partners of the three firms. The three partners held them in trust, representing all the interests of the three firms. After the expiry of the guarantee, Potter, Wilson & Co. and my own firm got their interests into their own possession. The interest of the third, Morton & Co., remained still invested in trustees.

I believe you were asked to give a letter stating that you held these in trust for the City Bank, or part of them?—Yes.

Part of them were similarly secured to Overend & Gurney? —Yes.

I suppose your understanding was that you held these to cover advances?—I had no knowledge what they were held for.

What was the origin of your connection with Potter?—I was connected with him in these New Zealand and Australian matters, but besides that we were partners together in a coal company. He was also one of the trustees in whom the shares were originally vested for joint behoof. I had nothing to do with the financing either of Potter, Wilson & Co. or Morton & Co. At the request of the late Alexander Stronach I took over fifty shares of the Sawmill Company, Bombay, on account of Smith, Fleming & Co. The object of that was not explained to me; I was merely asked to be allowed to put them into my name.

You were asked by the Manager, Alexander Stronach, to permit them to be transferred to your name?—Yes.

Were you in any other way connected with James Nicol Fleming, or Smith, Fleming & Co.'s securities?—I never had any connection with James Nicol Fleming's securities.

Prior to November, 1874, did the Manager of the Bank ever consult you or any person else with reference to advances to Morton & Co. and Smith, Fleming & Co.?—No.

Was it known outside the Bank that these firms had advances from the Bank?—I think it was. Some time in 1874—early in the year, I think—Alexander Stronach asked me if I would, in confidence and as a friend, look into Nicol Fleming's matters, as he was not satisfied with the working of his account in the Bank. He did not say to me whether the account was bad or not. I at first told him I had no knowledge of the nature of Nicol Fleming's business, and did not feel competent to give a sufficient report, but that, if he really wished me to do so, and Fleming concurred, I had no objection to give him my opinion. Mr. Fleming invited me; and I asked him to show me one or two of his Calcutta balance sheets, the result of

The City of Glasgow Bank Trial.

John Hunter. which was that I reported to Alexander Stronach that they were doing an unsatisfactory business, and that I did not think it could be made satisfactory in the way they were doing, and I recommended him to get rid of the account as soon as possible.

All the information the Manager gave you was that the account was unsatisfactory?—Yes. I don't remember the exact date when I made my report to Alexander Stronach, but I think it must have been in the spring or early summer of 1874. From my examination of Mr. Fleming's balance sheets on that occasion—which I assumed to be correct—so far as I examined them, which was for three years, he seemed to have been going backwards.

That is to say, as time went on he was getting worse?— Well, the firm had made nothing for the three years of which I saw the balances. I had no knowledge whatever of Fleming's indebtedness at that time; I did not know that he owed anything. I had nothing to do except with the state of his business. Mr. Fleming was a Director of the Bank at that time. I made a communication to him also as to the unsatisfactory state of his balance sheets, and at the same time I spoke to him about his position as a Director.

By the LORD JUSTICE-CLERK—This was in 1874.

By the LORD ADVOCATE—I told him I considered it was not consistent with the position of his affairs that he should continue a Director of the Bank. He did not view that as I did, and seemed rather disappointed at the prospect of his not continuing a Director. I reported verbally to Alexander Stronach, in the Bank, when I advised him to get rid of this account. I don't remember that he made any particular remarks when I made that communication to him, but he did not seem to look upon the account as so bad as I made it out to be.

That is to say, he did not seem to think that Nicol Fleming was in quite so bad a state commercially as you reported?— Yes. Nothing more that occurs to my memory passed on that occasion. Alexander Stronach was in failing health about that time. Subsequently, for a considerable period, he did not attend the Bank, but lived at his house near Biggar. I saw him there upon the subject of Nicol Fleming's account. I merely confirmed what I had said before.

Repeated it?—Repeated it. He said then that he did not believe that it was so bad as I represented it to be. I said I only dealt with the figures I got from Nicol Fleming himself or his clerk, and could not make it better than I had represented. He did not say whether or not he had seen Nicol Fleming's balance sheet. He said that if he were better he was quite sure he would make the account right in a year or two. That

254

Evidence for Prosecution.

was the last occasion on which he looked at a statement of Nicol Fleming's account or went into it. I saw him again when he was rather seriously ill, when he repeated the same observation. I did not give him any details on that last occasion. I did so upon the previous occasion—I explained the grounds upon which I had come to my conclusion. On the occasion when he made the observation I have mentioned, when he was not so seriously ill, I spoke to him about Morton's account.

What led you to do so?—Nothing, except the knowledge that Morton had a large account with the Bank, and I asked him how it was working.

How did you come to know it was a large account?—It was very generally known, I think, in Glasgow, that it was a large account.

How did it come to be generally known?—It was generally known he was discounting a large amount of City of Glasgow Bank bills. I think that was perfectly well known. Morton was a great deal about the Bank at that time. When I spoke to Alexander Stronach about Morton's account, he said it was working off all right; but on that occasion he asked me if I would speak to Mr. Morton, and endeavour to get some additional security from him. I asked him to write such a letter as I could read to Morton, which he did. I read it to Morton, and the security he asked for, I believe, was given. Alexander Stronach ceased to take any active part in the management of the Bank, I believe, for a considerable time before his death. Mr. Robert Stronach acted in his room during that time.

During that time, before Robert Stronach became Manager himself, had you any conversation with him in regard to Nicol Fleming's account?—I merely stated to him what I had stated to his brother.

Did you state to him all that you had stated to his brother?— I think I did.

Did you speak to him about Nicol Fleming's continuance as a Director?—I don't quite remember whether I did or not.

Try to recollect that. You spoke about that to Alexander Stronach?—No; I spoke about it to Nicol Fleming.

Did you not speak to Alexander Stronach?—I cannot remember whether it was to Alexander Stronach or Robert Stronach; I don't remember when Alexander Stronach left the Bank.

Whether it was Alexander Stronach or Robert Stronach, did he take the same view as Nicol Fleming himself about his continuing a Director?—No; whichever it was, he quite acquiesced in the view I took that he should not be a Director.

He agreed that his position was inconsistent with his continuing a Director?—Yes.

The City of Glasgow Bank Trial.

John Hunter. By LORD CRAIGHILL—This was in the end of 1874.

By the LORD ADVOCATE—I continued to press upon Robert Stronach the state of Fleming's affairs. I advised him, as I had done his brother, that the firm should be put into liquidation and wound up. His brother did not act upon that, but Robert Stronach immediately acted upon it, and the firm was put into liquidation in the end of 1874. I do not know whether he had become Manager at that time, but he was acting as Manager. James Nicol Fleming had a partner in Calcutta. That partnership was dissolved. That was the partnership that was liquidated. He started himself, along with another party, a new firm on 1st January, 1875.

After it was resolved to liquidate, were you consulted about the realisation?—From time to time I was consulted as to the realisation.

You became cognizant of what was done?—Well, I never saw Nicol Fleming's books. I merely gave advice as to the realisation when I was consulted by his clerks.

A list of the securities was furnished to you, was it not?—Yes.

And you gave instructions for the realisation?—Yes.

By what time was the realisation practically concluded?—There were some assets in India that were a long time after 1st January, 1875, before they were concluded. It must have been some time in 1876—the end of 1876, I should think.

Or 1877?—Or 1877.

There was an exception, however, in the realisation in the case of certain Australian land shares?—Yes. So far as I am aware there are certain securities not realised yet—a part of the New Zealand shares.

Was the liquidation satisfactory in point of results?—No.

Did it leave a large balance unsecured?—Yes.

Were the times bad for realising that particular security, or how did that arise?—I don't know that it was altogether on account of the times. There were not very many securities to realise.

Did you communicate information to any of the Directors of the Bank, other than Mr. Stronach, in regard to Fleming's liquidation—I mean upon either of these points, the state of Nicol Fleming's business which led you to recommend liquidation, in regard to the fact of liquidation, or the unsatisfactory results of the liquidation? Had you any communication with any other Director than Mr. Stronach upon that point?—I think I must have named it to Mr. Potter; and, although the amount was never named, subsequently, to my knowledge, it became known to Mr. Taylor and Mr. Stewart; but I don't think, never in my presence, did they know the amount.

Just repeat that, so that the jury can hear it.—I think I

256

Evidence for Prosecution.

mentioned it to Mr. Potter, and subsequently, to my knowledge, **John Hunter.**
Mr. Taylor and Mr. Stewart became aware that there was a
balance upon the account, but the extent of it I am not aware
that they ever knew, any of them.

Nothing passed in your presence which could suggest that they
knew the extent of unsatisfactoriness?—No.

When was it that you came to know that Mr. Stewart and Mr.
Taylor did know something about the fact of there being a
balance? You say " afterwards." I want you to fix the period
a little more?—It must have been in 1876, I think.

Was it not in 1877, after the liquidation, or was it whilst
it was in progress?—It was whilst it was in progress.

What was the extent of your communication with Mr. Potter
upon the subject?—Simply that there was a large uncovered
balance. I don't know that I ever told him the exact amount.

Simply that there was a large uncovered balance upon that
account?—Yes.

How did you come to give that information to Mr. Potter?
Did you meet him casually, or upon the business of the Bank?—
No. I was in the habit of meeting him frequently; we were
connected in business.

Then it was casually mentioned?—Casually mentioned.

When were these communications with Mr. Potter that you
have just referred to now? Were they during the liquidation of
1876?—No; I think it must have been in 1875.

You became aware of the acquisition of certain lands in New
Zealand?—Yes.

That was about eighteen months or two years ago?—Yes,
about two years ago.

At that period, when that transaction was being carried
through, or after it, had you any further communication with the
Directors or any of them in regard to the state of Nicol
Fleming's account?—It was on that occasion that I understood
that Mr. Taylor and Mr. Stewart became aware of the state of the
account.

That was the occasion that you previously informed us of
about their general knowledge?—Yes.

Did you meet them on business at that time?—I was invited
to meet them.

For the purpose of giving information upon that point?—For
giving my opinion as to the value of Australian and New Zealand
property.

You were at that time, and had been previously, a director of
the New Zealand and Australian Land Company, Limited?—
Yes.

And you were conversant with that species of property?—Yes.

Were you given to understand at that time that the Bank
had in contemplation to acquire lands there?—I understood so.

The City of Glasgow Bank Trial.

John Hunter. You were given to understand that?—I was given to understand that.

And were you given to understand what purpose they had in view in buying land?—I don't know that I ever heard of the purpose they had, but I understood it was for Nicol Fleming's account—to cover it. I understood it was for the purpose of making Nicol Fleming's account right, to cover whatever discrepancy existed upon it.

That is to say, by making a profit on the Australian land they would cover any loss upon his account?—Yes.

Were you not given to understand by two of the Directors that it was for that purpose?—I quite understood it was for that purpose.

Who gave you to understand that?—I don't know that it was ever in so many words said it was for that, but I considered it was the fact of my looking into Nicol Fleming's accounts that led to my being consulted.

With whom had you communication about it chiefly?—Mr. Stronach and Mr. Potter, and Mr. Taylor and Mr. Stewart occasionally.

With whom chiefly?—There was not much difference as to that.

With all four?—With all four.

Did you see them together or separately?—I saw them together from time to time, but at long intervals. I had very few meetings with them altogether.

Where did these meetings take place?—In the Bank.

Had you not a meeting with Mr. Graham at Potter, Wilson & Co.'s office?—Yes.

What is Mr. Graham?—Mr. Graham is a member of the firm of Graham & Co., of Poverty Bay, New Zealand.

Were you told how the Bank were to work the investment they proposed to make in New Zealand and Australia, the purchase through Mr. Graham?—I understood it was to be drawn in drafts of Graham & Co. from New Zealand to a certain extent, and Potter, Wilson & Co. were to manage the rest of it.

Did any of the Directors in these conversations which you had with them refer to the large returns that were expected from these investments?—I don't remember whether they referred to that or not, but it was quite understood that they expected large returns.

When you say it was quite understood, do you mean that nobody said a thing about it, or that it was obvious from what they did say that they assumed that would be the case?—No; I mean that I may have said to them that there would be large returns from Australia and New Zealand properties if they were properly purchased.

Evidence for Prosecution.

You were asked to advise whether there would be large returns or not?—Yes.

And you said, if properly purchased, it was your opinion that there would be?—Yes.

Was nothing said by the Directors? Was no hope or expectation expressed that these large returns would be sufficient to extinguish Mr. Nicol Fleming's debt?—Yes, that was said.

By whom? Was that hope not expressed by one or other of them in presence of the whole gentlemen you have named?—I cannot remember whether it was or not in presence of the whole; but I have no doubt that it was mentioned.

By the LORD JUSTICE-CLERK—Was it by one of them or by you?—I think it would be by me.

By the LORD ADVOCATE—Did they acquiesce in your view?—Yes.

From what passed on these occasions, when you were discussing this matter, would it not have been plain to any third person who was there, that the purpose of making these investments was to wipe out that liability?—I don't know if any stranger had been present that that would have been apparent, but it was apparent to me, because I understood how matters stood.

Then probably you were advising the Bank before?—Yes.

Mr. Stronach?—Yes.

Did you meet the Directors along with Mr. Graham in Potter's office?—No.

Had you been previous to this consulted about other pastoral properties, as they are called, in Australia?—Yes; I was consulted about those which were purchased through Glen Walker.

Which, if any, of the Directors did you meet with regard to that matter?—The same as in the case of the other—Mr. Potter, Mr. Taylor, Mr. Stewart, and the Manager.

What did you understand as to the purpose for which these acquisitions were made?—I quite understood that it was in connection with Nicol Fleming's matter. I knew that they did make a purchase at that time. I frequently met Mr. Glen Walker on the subject.

Who is entitled to the credit of the name "Edinburgh Pastoral Association"?—I really don't know who originated that name. I don't know what was the object in giving it that name. I did not think of it at the time. In 1874 I was asked by Alexander Stronach to go to Bombay in connection with William Nicol & Co.'s affairs. He said he would like if I would go out and look into their matters, as they were interested in Smith, Fleming & Co.; that they were all right, but he believed that there was great extravagance going on, and he wished me to go out to try if I could put it right.

John Hunter. Would you repeat that answer so that the jury may hear it?—He asked me if I would go out to look into William Nicol & Co.'s matters, as the Bank were interested in Smith, Fleming & Co.; that there was nothing wrong with them, but he thought there was great extravagance going on, and he wished me to go out and put it right. I declined to go, and I heard nothing more of the matter.

By the LORD JUSTICE-CLERK—Who made that offer?—Mr. Alexander Stronach.

By the LORD ADVOCATE—Do you recollect of being applied to in February, 1875, by Mr. Robert Stronach in connection with some stock which he wished to be held in the name of third parties?—Yes; not in 1875. It was in 1877.

The date is not material, but you recollect of it?—I do recollect.

What was the proposal?—He told me that he wished to take in some stock, and he would be obliged if I would allow him to put it in my name for a short time. I consented. There was a transfer sent to me which I executed. I afterwards waited upon Mr. Stronach before the annual balance, and requested him to take my name out of the books, as I did not wish it to go forth to the public. That was before the annual meeting in July, 1877. He agreed to do so. I examined the list of shareholders which was issued afterwards—the published list of shareholders—and found that my name was not there. I did not examine the register of shareholders in the Bank. I never got notice after that to attend meetings or anything of that kind. I have discovered now that my name is on the stock ledger for that stock, and has been so all along. I had no intention whatever then of becoming a shareholder of the Bank.

Would you have become a shareholder at that time?—Well, I don't know. At that time I would not have become a shareholder in any bank.

I mean in 1877?—Yes; I would not have become a shareholder in any bank at that time, because my funds were otherwise taken up.

Would your knowledge of Nicol Fleming's account have affected you? [Objection taken and question withdrawn.]—I don't remember whether I read the balance sheet of 1878. The stock of the Australian and New Zealand Land Company has never been quoted on the Exchange.

Are the shares depreciated at present?—I cannot say, because there have been no sales.

I suppose you regard the intrinsic value as being as good as ever?—I do.

Is it an investment that is easily realised?—The land is

Evidence for Prosecution.

easily enough realised, but the shares are not so easily realised, because they are not upon the Stock Exchange.

By Mr. BALFOUR—Do I understand that your communications with Mr. Alexander Stronach about 1874 were as his private friend with regard to the matters you have explained?—Yes.

You had his confidence with regard to these matters, which I need not say you respected?—Yes.

You also were asked with regard to the accounts of Mr. Morton and Mr. Nicol Fleming. Were you satisfied that Mr. Alexander Stronach believed that Morton's account would come out all right?—He said so to me on more than one occasion, quite emphatically, and that it gave him no concern.

You believed him that that account was not a cause of anxiety to him?—I believed him.

With regard to Mr. Nicol Fleming's account, you have also given us some answers. I think you did not like some of the operations in which Mr. Nicol Fleming was engaged?—No, I did not. I advised him that the nature of his transactions was such that I did not think the firm could be successful.

And you communicated that view, which you arrived at by an examination of the books, to Mr. Alexander Stronach?—By an examination of Mr. Nicol Fleming's balance sheets—not the books.

You were still in these communications acting as the confidential friend of Mr. Alexander Stronach?—Yes.

You were advising him confidentially?—Yes.

Did you find that Mr. Nicol Fleming had a lucrative commission business?—Yes.

And that if he stopped speculative business and confined himself to commission business, he might do well?—He might do well. He had a good commission business.

Then in the result you advised that Nicol Fleming should be put into liquidation, which I think was done at Robert Stronach's instance about the beginning of 1875?—Yes.

Was there a new firm constituted as part of that arrangement? —There was.

It was to take up the commission business, which was regarded as good and sound?—Yes. I made out that it was worth about £20,000 a year, so far as I could judge, and the result of the first year's operations of the new firm seemed to confirm that.

That was clear profit from commissions alone?—Yes.

Was it part of the arrangement under which the liquidation was agreed to and a new firm constituted that any sum should be paid annually to the Bank?—There was an arrangement by which Mr. Nicol Fleming was to give the whole of his profits from that new firm and from a firm in Manchester with which he was connected towards the payment of his debt to the Bank. At the same time he insured his life for £100,000, and I believe

The City of Glasgow Bank Trial.

he assigned the policies. I had no knowledge of that, but I believe they were assigned. He also made over additional shares in the New Zealand Company.

What was the amount that was expected to be annually paid to the Bank in redemption of the debt if that arrangement was faithfully carried out by Nicol Fleming?—So far as I remember, I think it was expected that there would be sufficient to pay interest upon the balance due to the Bank, and over a period of years that the principal would be redeemed.

And have you any reason to doubt that if Mr. Nicol Fleming had kept clear of speculative business and stuck to his commission business that result would have been realised?—I think it was very likely to be realised.

But he did not afterwards keep clear; he resumed speculation?—Yes. After the first year he himself went out to India and went into speculative transactions.

He went into some shipping transactions?—Yes.

And in consequence of his not having done what he promised, the expectations were not realised?—No.

You were also asked with regard to the New Zealand Land Company's shares. I think you have been in the colonies, and have yourself gone over the ground belonging to the Company? —I have. I did so in 1869 and 1870—both the Australian and the New Zealand land. I am a large holder in that company; Mr. Potter is also a large holder in it.

You need not give names; but are there many others of the best-known commercial men and bankers in the country holders in it?—There are.

Are you still satisfied that these shares have a very large intrinsic value?—I am. I think there is a good prospective value in them.

From your communications with Mr. Morton, did you form any opinion as to what he thought of these prospects?—He had a very high opinion of them.

And did you believe an honest opinion on his part?—Perfectly honest on his part.

Whether it was a too sanguine opinion may be a matter as to which people may differ?—Yes.

Was Mr. Morton a man who had great force of character and power of impressing his views upon others?—Yes, he had great force of character.

From your knowledge of the value of land in the colonies, did you think that the purchases gone into through Glen Walker and Potter, Wilson & Co. would likely accomplish the ends which you have explained they were intended to achieve?—Yes; I think they would, if judiciously managed and kept for a few years.

You think they would have accomplished what they were intended to do?—Yes, to reduce Nicol Fleming's account. I

Evidence for Prosecution.

believe the value of these lands has risen, notwithstanding the prevalent depression of trade over the world. I am acquainted with Mr. Lewis Potter. I have known him for a great many years—over twenty years. He and I were fellow-directors of the New Zealand Land Company. We were also partners in the Hamilton Coal Company. I have had occasion to see a good deal of Mr. Potter in business.

What opinion have you formed with regard to his business qualities? I mean what kind of departments of a business has he made his own, and what does he leave to others?—So far as my experience of Mr. Potter goes, he never would go into details, but took a broad view of matters, and where he had confidence he was perfectly satisfied to take for granted a great deal that was put before him.

Have you found that to be the case in those companies that you have been concerned with him in?—Yes.

As regards general experience and judgment he was able and sound?—Yes.

But rather keeping off details?—Yes.

Is he a man who goes into books or any detail?—No.

Is that a kind of thing which he leaves to the officials of the companies that he is connected with, so far as you have seen? —Yes.

Is he much of a book-keeper at all, do you think?—I don't think he is.

Have you always found him honest and upright and honourable in his dealings?—Invariably.

And is that the repute that he has always enjoyed?—So far as I know, it is.

By the Dean of Faculty—I have known Mr. Robert Stronach for nearly twenty years, I think.

Before his brother's illness, what position did he hold in the Bank?—I am not quite sure. I think it was joint manager, but I am not quite sure as to that.

Before his brother's illness was he not a clerk in the Bank, an assistant?—I did not know him when he was a clerk in the Bank. I may be wrong as to the length of time I have known him, but he was in a position in the Bank then.

What kind of disposition is he of? Is he a man of a yielding disposition; would he give up his own opinion to a person of more decided views?—Yes, I think he would be influenced by people of more decided views.

Was the gradation of rank of the officers in the Bank, first the manager, then the cashier, then the accountant?—I cannot answer that; I don't know.

Did Robert Stronach hold a subordinate position in the Bank before his brother's illness?—Yes, but I don't know exactly what it was.

The City of Glasgow Bank Trial.

John Hunter.

By the LORD ADVOCATE—I suppose you don't know where Mr. Nicol Fleming got money to speculate with—whether he got it from the Bank or from any other source?—No, I don't know that.

But you know that he did speculate unprofitably?—Yes.

And you think he ought not to have done it? You think he ought not to have engaged in that speculation at all?—I think so.

You say he had a very good commission business?—Yes.

Had he a very bad other business?—Yes.

He had a big good business, but a bigger bad one?—Undoubtedly; but the bad one could be stopped at any time; it was mere speculation.

It could be wound up?—Yes, he had simply to cease the operations.

But in point of fact it was not stopped?—It was. Mr. Robert Stronach stopped it.

Do you think that there would have been a reasonable prospect of making a large profit on these Australian lands or shares except by holding them for some years to come—I mean some years from the date of the investment?—They would require to be held for some years to come to make a large profit.

They could not in any view be regarded as an immediately realisable security?—They were immediately realisable, but not to realise a large profit.

They were not realisable for the purpose for which the investment was made?—No.

Did you ever meet with Mr. Potter on business which required him to go into details of books?—Yes.

And he never did so?—He never did so.

Was he an intelligent man of business?—Yes.

Did he understand what a deficit was upon a large account due to him?—I have no doubt he did.

And I suppose he was capable of looking after the question whether he held security for it or not?—I should think so.

A. F.
Somerville.

A. F. SOMERVILLE.

By Mr. BURNET—I am a papermaker at Lasswade. I am a shareholder in the City of Glasgow Bank. I hold 110 shares—£11,000 of stock. It cost me £24,000 at any rate. I first became a shareholder about twenty-six years ago. I was made an Edinburgh Director about 1871. Mr. Inglis was on the Edinburgh Board when I joined it. He was also one of the Glasgow Board at the time. I did not know anything about the Bank purchasing property in New Zealand or Australia.

Mr. Inglis never mentioned anything of that kind to you?—No; I think not. I met him regularly once a week at the Edinburgh meetings.

Evidence for Prosecution.

Did you know whether the Bank were in the habit of purchasing their own stock to a considerable extent?—No. About the end of January, 1877, I asked Mr. Usher to join the Edinburgh Board. He agreed at first, but afterwards withdrew on account of some rumours which he had heard. In consequence of what Mr. Usher said to me, I went to the Bank office in Glasgow and saw Mr. Stronach and Mr. Potter. I spoke to them about Mr. Usher's objections. I told Mr. Stronach that one reason why Mr. Usher objected to join the Board was that he had heard they had made a loss through a person named Binning, and that he had also heard reports that the Directors had been getting advances. I said for these two reasons he would not join the Board. I had told Mr. Usher that I thought his information was wrong—as I believed it to be at the time—but that I would go to Glasgow and examine into the matter, and report to him (Mr. Usher) the result. Mr. Stronach at once acknowledged Binning's debt, but said it was all written off, and that the position of the Bank was not affected in the very smallest at that time.

What was said about the advances to the Directors?—I put the question to Mr. Potter, and he said it was not the case, and that so far as he was concerned he had never got a sixpence of advance, and he appealed to Mr. Stronach that he was correct in saying so, and Mr. Stronach said he was quite right.

Your question had reference to advances to all the Directors? —Yes, not all; it was some, Mr. Usher said.

But it was not Mr. Potter alone?—No.

By the LORD JUSTICE-CLERK—The information you had got from Mr. Usher was that some of the Directors had been getting advances?—Yes.

And Mr. Potter said that, so far as he knew, that was not the case?—Yes.

By Mr. BURNET—And Mr. Stronach confirmed it?—Yes. I returned to Edinburgh perfectly satisfied that the statements made to me in Glasgow were true, and I told Mr. Usher so, but he would not join.

Had you ever any conversation at the meetings of the Edinburgh Board with Mr. Inglis about Nicol Fleming's responsibilities to the Bank?—Yes; we spoke of that, and Mr. Inglis, I think, stated to me that they had ample security for the account, that it was being lessened, and that in the course of time it would be all right. I cannot give the exact date of that. During the whole time I sat at the Board with Mr. Inglis, from 1871 to 1878, he never indicated to me that the Bank was in difficulties; the very opposite.

By Mr. ROBERTSON—The duties of the Edinburgh Board were to attend to overdrafts or cash credits, and give an opinion upon any point that the Manager, Mr. Bain, might think it his

The City of Glasgow Bank Trial.

A. F.
Somerville.

duty to bring before us. Our duties were confined to the branch at Edinburgh. We had no concern with the general affairs of the Bank. I am aware of the declaration subscribed by the Directors under the Bank's contract, to the effect—" We pledge ourselves not only to do so," that is, to perform the duties of the office, " but also to observe strict secrecy with regard to the transactions of the Company with their customers, and the state of the accounts of individuals, and, in general, with relation to the business of the Bank." That applies to communications both to partners of the Bank and to the outside public.

There was nothing in the position or duties of the Edinburgh Directors which entitled them to more communications from the general Board of Directors than the other partners?—No. Mr. Bain held the position of Edinburgh Manager during the whole period of my directorate. We did not charge ourselves with the duty of checking or ascertaining the position of any of the accounts of customers.

Did you do more in fulfilling the duties of Director than merely to attend to such business as the Manager laid before you?—No.

And you considered that to be sufficient fulfilment of your duties?—Yes. It was arranged when the Edinburgh Board of direction was formed, that the Edinburgh Directors' accounts should be under the jurisdiction of the Glasgow Board, and not of the Edinburgh one.

When you went to Glasgow on the occasion you have mentioned, did you yourself investigate into the affairs of the Bank so far as you could in one day?—I went for a special object, and that object being attained I did nothing else. I had no documents put before me. I contented myself with the statements there made. I have met Mr. Inglis regularly during the period of our joint direction. I have never found him deficient in candour or fair dealing. As regards the performance of his duties as a Director towards myself, my opinion is that he was highly honourable in every respect. I could not conceive that Mr. Inglis would do anything—that was the opinion I always formed of him—unbecoming a gentleman ; and that is my opinion at the present moment, and after all that has happened.

By the DEAN OF FACULTY—When I went to Glasgow I made no special inquiry about advances to Nicol Fleming. His name was never spoken of.

Was it not about advances to him that you made special inquiry?—No ; I went through for the special purpose of getting information on the two points mentioned. There was no other business talked of. I was not told then that Nicol Fleming had got advances. I cannot say when I was told that. I

Evidence for Prosecution.

heard he had got some advances. Mr. Inglis mentioned that, but said that it was all right, as I said before. No Directors' names were mentioned at that interview between Mr. Potter, Mr. Stronach, and me. I put no question about who they were.

JOHN GILLESPIE.

By the SOLICITOR-GENERAL—I am a Writer to the Signet in Edinburgh. I have been a Director on the Edinburgh Board of the City of Glasgow Bank since 1862. I continued in office until the stoppage of the Bank. The other Directors were Mr. Inglis, Mr. Somerville, and Mr. Craig. Mr. Bain, who was the Manager of the Edinburgh branch, attended our meetings as such. The business brought before the Board referred exclusively to the business of the Bank in Edinburgh and the immediate neighbourhood, and the looking into the books of the Hanover Street business from time to time. The business in our branch showed a steady increase in profit. I am satisfied it was a safe and profitable banking business. Our balance sheets were transmitted to Glasgow half-yearly, for the making up of the general balance of the Bank. I think we were twice consulted about the fixing of the dividend—in 1876, and once before that. We had nothing to do with the making up of the report to the shareholders. I don't think any change was made on the dividend in 1876. I think it is about ten years since the arrangement was made of having a member of the Edinburgh Board and a member of the Glasgow Board in one person. I think that was arranged on a suggestion of my own, that we might have an opportunity of getting such information as we wished as to the general progress of matters connected with the Bank. Mr. Inglis was accordingly appointed a member of the Glasgow Board; he was the only one of our number who ever sat in Glasgow. At our Board meetings I and the other Directors present spoke now and then to Mr. Inglis about matters connected with the general business of the Bank.

Do you remember inquiries being made at Mr. Inglis about any particular accounts of firms in Glasgow or London?—I do not recollect any inquiries being made particularly. Certain accounts were now and then named—James Nicol Fleming, and Smith, Fleming & Co.—James Nicol Fleming notably.

What did Mr. Inglis tell you about the advances to Nicol Fleming?—The general impression conveyed to us was that his advances were covered by sufficient securities of various kinds. At our weekly meetings it was my custom to read out the exchanges from the clearing-house returns and the bills of the week, and latterly these exchanges were very much against us. That caused us some little anxiety, and we used to ask

J. Gillespie. information how that occurred, and why it was so constantly on our side. That was spoken about much more frequently than Nicol Fleming's account. We were told by Mr. Inglis that it was of paramount importance to maintain large reserves in London, and that it was owing to that that these exchanges were so much against us; and specially, I recollect, we were told on one occasion that there was a large shipping account kept in Glasgow, that large wages were paid in Glasgow, the price of the ships being paid in London, and that accounted so far for these exchanges being adverse to us in Scotland.

May I take it generally that any explanations made here at the Edinburgh Board regarding the general business were made by Mr. Inglis?—They must have been, because no other one had any knowledge. We heard about American securities, chiefly in connection with difficulties before the stoppage of 1857. Mr. Inglis told us that these were improving very much, and though not immediately realisable, they were now yielding a fair return, and would probably by and by be got out without loss. I recollect 6 per cent. being at one time named as the return, but I cannot tell upon what security. On the day before the stoppage of the Bank occurred, the Tuesday—that being the day of our Board meeting—there was a general feeling of anxiety, I cannot tell very well how, and I remarked that we still retained the confidence of the public, because our shares maintained their price in the market, unless, I said, the Bank are buying them in. I asked Mr. Inglis if they were doing so, and he gave me to understand they were not. In the course of making new arrangements for bringing one of my sons into the business, my partner, Mr. Paterson, and I, in the last week of July or the first week of August, 1878, purchased each £500 stock in the Bank, at, I think, £236, or within a pound of that. The purchase was made through Mr. Bain, and the transfer was signed by Mr. Tod, of Peebles. Before that I held £2000 stock, part of which I held from 1859. Besides the information I got from Mr. Inglis, I was in the habit now and then of speaking to Mr. Bain about the state of matters generally, and getting certain information from him such as he had. I had no means of getting information except from Mr. Inglis or Mr. Bain. I cannot tell whether Mr. Bain had any direct knowledge of the state of the Bank in Glasgow.

By the LORD JUSTICE-CLERK—Had you any anxiety to get further information about the Glasgow proceedings?—Now and then, in the course of the period we sat there, we had; and on one occasion Mr. Somerville went to Glasgow to make inquiry, and on his return he told us he was satisfied, or at least I understood he was satisfied.

By Mr. ROBERTSON—My inquiries were not intended to elicit

Lord Mure.

Evidence for Prosecution.

specific information from Mr. Inglis as to the accounts I mentioned; it was general conversation with regard to their position. I was quite aware it was the duty of the Directors to observe strict secrecy with regard to the transactions of the Bank with its customers and the state of accounts of individuals; but I was not aware any obligation to that effect was signed.

But you would not have desired or expected Mr. Inglis to communicate to you particular information regarding accounts which were in a critical position?—I don't know; I think the purpose of his double appointment was to keep us pretty much informed on the same questions as the Glasgow Directors. I am not aware there was any special appointment of him as holding the double office. The information he gave us was in general terms; we never heard anything of figures.

At this distance of time can you charge your memory with more than the result upon your mind that there was no reason for alarm?—No, I cannot. The subjects for the deliberation of the Board were brought before us by the Manager, who had a note of any matters he wanted to bring before us, and, after these were disposed of, it was my custom to read the bills, exchanges, and variations on deposits and cash accounts during the week. Then once a month we were in the habit of counting the cash.

But as to accounts, it is the case that the Manager took the initiative in selecting such accounts as required the attention of the Board?—Certainly. I have asked questions about certain accounts without my attention being called to them, but that was not the practice. If anything had attracted my attention, I should certainly have brought it before my colleagues or Mr. Bain. It was very rarely that anything of that kind occurred.

By the Solicitor-General—So far as I knew, we had no debtors owing large sums about which I was not sure whether they would be paid.

If you had heard of such, you would have made very careful inquiry?—I hope I would.

If you had heard of such a thing as an arrangement being required to recoup a deficit, you would have looked very carefully into it?—Well, I ought to have done so.

Alexander Sutherland.

By the Solicitor-General—I am sole partner of the firm of Reid & Co., stockbrokers, Glasgow. I have done business as a stockbroker for the City of Glasgow Bank.

What instructions had you, and from whom, about the purchase and sale of stock?—The instructions for the most part, I think, were from the Manager of the Bank.

The City of Glasgow Bank Trial.

A. Sutherland.
And for the less part?—All the instructions came from the Manager. My firm has acted for the Bank for about thirty years. I have myself acted for it for about twenty years. The Manager when I first began to act for it was Mr. Salmond, then Mr. Alexander Stronach, and then Mr. Robert Stronach. Mr. Salmond ceased to be Manager shortly after the Bank opened again after the stoppage in 1857. I have frequently bought stock for the Bank. I have done so during the whole period, I think. I bought stock for the Bank in 1876, 1877, and 1878.

When you bought stock for the Bank, how did you let them know that you had bought it?—By sending them the contract note, in the same way as to any other client.

Then if you had bought for the Bank, did you in regular course get the funds from them for the day of settlement as stated in the contract note?—Yes.

In any case, where you purchased on the instructions of the Manager during 1875, 1876, 1877, or 1878, was the name of the Bank disclosed as being the purchaser?—No, in no case.

How was it arranged that the name of the Bank should not appear?—I simply got names from the Manager, in the same way as I got them from any other client.

The Bank sent you the names into which the transfers were to be made out?—Yes. I was once or twice made a transferee myself. The transfers were sometimes made out in name of Thomas Matthew in trust. [Shown Nos. 458 and 456.] No. 458 is a bundle of seven sheets, being a transcript from my firm's ledger. The ledger itself is No. 456. These detail the purchases and sales made through my firm on the instructions of the Bank, commencing 10th February, 1875. Between 28th September and 2nd October, I negotiated the purchase of over £10,000 worth of stock for the Bank, just before the Bank stopped.

How much stock stands in the registers in name of Thomas Matthew?—I cannot give you that.

Look at the sheets (No. 462) and see if I give you the figures correctly. For 1875 was the amount £9314?—The document that I have got is simply a copy of our register, and the summation is not made in it.

Well, I will take it generally. Were the purchases of much larger amount than the sales in name of Thomas Matthew?—So far as passing through our books, they were.

On some occasions were the purchases in one year approaching to £10,000, and no sale at all?—There may have been that amount of stock transferred. In those cases where I was made a transferee myself, I did not get any certificate showing me to be the holder of the stock, nor did I receive any dividends. [Shown Nos. 463, 464, 465, 466, and 467.] The first four of these are letters or memoranda received by me from Mr. Robert

Evidence for Prosecution.

Stronach. The date of the memorandum No. 463 is about 12th May, 1875. It says—" I can take £800 of the Bank stock at £233. Please let me know the result.—Sincerely yours, R. S. Stronach." The second, No. 464, which is written on the outside of an envelop, is dated about 20th May, 1876, and is as follows:—" Sorry to get such a tremendous amount of stock. Don't take more. Who is the selling broker?—R. S. S." The third, No. 465, is a letter dated 10th November, 1876, in the following terms:—" My dear sir,—In the hurry when I saw you this forenoon, I omitted to ask you to write to Mr. Bell, Edinburgh, and ask why he was pressing the sale of the stock so much, and unduly throwing down the price to £223. Perhaps you could ascertain the names of the sellers. Kindly let me know before the close as to the amount of stock in the market, etc.—Yours sincerely, R. S. Stronach." The fourth document, No. 466, is a letter dated 2nd August, 1877, from Mr. Stronach, in the following terms:—" My dear sir,—I have your note of to-day's date, and will let you have the £400 stock for the several parties noted.—Yours sincerely, R. S. Stronach." No. 467 is a bundle of four receipts for moneys realised by me on the sale of stock, and signed " for R. S. Stronach, John Wardrop." The dates are 4th October, 1875 ; 5th October, 1875 ; 5th November, 1877 ; and 22nd July, 1878. I think these were all my transactions by way of sale for the Bank during those years.

By the Dean of Faculty—I am aware that by the contract of copartnery of the Bank the Directors had full power to purchase for behalf of the company any of the shares of the capital stock which might be offered for sale. I understood it was under that article of the contract that I so acted as directed by Mr. Stronach.

JAMES SMITH.

By Mr. Pearson—I am a partner of Messrs. James Watson & Smith, stockbrokers in Glasgow. My firm bought stock of the City of Glasgow Bank for the Bank in 1875, and also in 1878. We completed in all five transactions. These transactions were carried out by the instructions of Mr. Robert Stronach, communicated to me verbally. On 28th September, 1878, on Mr. Stronach's instructions, I purchased £2020 stock, part at £236, part at £237, and part at £238. The price of the stock rose that day from £236 to £238. These purchases have not been carried out in consequence of the stoppage of the Bank. The other transactions which I have carried out on Mr. Stronach's instructions are as follow:—In 1875 I purchased £1231 stock at a cost of £2823, and £900 stock, costing £2068—in all, £4892. Then there was nothing more till February, 1878, when I bought £500 stock at £239, costing £1207 ; in April, £1841

The City of Glasgow Bank Trial.

stock at £237, costing £4408; and 29th May, £1400 stock at £237½, costing £3360—total, £8976. The price of those stocks was paid to me in the usual way—by a cash slip handed over the counter by the teller.

By the DEAN OF FACULTY—Besides these transactions I bought and sold stock of other companies for the Bank—Chathams, Great Eastern, Caledonian, Metropolitan, East London, North British, Metropolitan District Preference, and so on. In the case of purchases they were paid for and taken by the Bank; but in the case of sales the Bank held them. It was generally from the stock clerk or transfer clerk that I got the name of the transferee for the Bank's own stock.

Dugald Bell.

DUGALD BELL.

By the LORD ADVOCATE—I am a book-keeper. Till lately I resided in London. I am now in Glasgow. I was secretary of the Australian Land and Investment Trust, Limited, till lately. I ceased to hold office in December. I was at one time clerk to James Nicol Fleming. I entered his employment when he opened his office in Glasgow in February, 1863. I remained in his employment till the end of 1877. I was in Calcutta for about a couple of years.

But till April, 1875, when you went to India on account of Mr. Fleming, you were continuously in Glasgow, as a clerk in his office?—That is so.

Were you acquainted with Mr. Fleming when you became his clerk?—No, I had only heard of him.

Did Mr. Fleming, shortly after you entered his employment, open an account with the City of Glasgow Bank?—Yes; he took me to the Bank and introduced me to Mr. Alexander Stronach, the then Manager, so that I might be known as his (Mr. Fleming's) agent, and operate on his account.

Mr. Fleming's business was not successful, I believe, eventually?—It was not. I recollect Mr. John Hunter, merchant, Glasgow, inquiring into Mr. Fleming's affairs. This was early in 1874. I never saw any report by him. No one communicated to me the result of his inquiry.

What followed on his inquiry, to your knowledge?—I understood that Mr. Fleming's affairs were put in liquidation, and I was sent out to Calcutta shortly afterwards.

By the LORD JUSTICE-CLERK—Was that in 1874 or 1875?—1875.

By the LORD ADVOCATE—Mr. Fleming traded under the firm of Nicol Fleming & Co.?—In Glasgow it was simply James Nicol Fleming.

What were his other firms?—In 1868 I think the firm of J. Nicol Fleming & Co. was started in Calcutta. [Shown book

Evidence for Prosecution.

No. 370.]   That is J. Nicol Fleming's private ledger; it was **Dugald Bell.**
kept by me down to 1877.   It is all in my handwriting down
to the end of 1877.

It was opened at the time that he started that second firm
in Calcutta in 1868?—About that time.

What is the state of Mr. Fleming's capital account as
stated in that ledger, when it begins on 31st January, 1868?—
It begins on 1st February, 1867.

At 1st February, 1867, what was the state of it?—On this
point I am in the hands of the Court.   I wish to state that,
although I have no knowledge of Mr. Fleming's movements or
intentions, yet I suppose it is quite probable that he may yet
come forward to speak for himself, and perhaps that should
be kept in view in any questions that may be asked me.   I
am quite prepared to go into it if the Court shall so rule.

The LORD JUSTICE-CLERK—I think you are bound to disclose
any knowledge that you may have.

By the LORD ADVOCATE—In February, 1867, the balance at
the credit of Mr. Fleming's capital account was £48,239.

Had there been a gain or loss upon capital account from the
time you joined him down to that date?—There had been a loss
in round numbers of about £212,000 from 1863.

So that at the time you joined there must have been about
£260,000 of capital?—Yes.

Of which about £212,000 had been lost in 1867?—Yes; the
balancing period in the book was 31st January.   At 31st
January, 1868, the balance to the credit was reduced to £25,818.
It remained very nearly the same at the balancing periods of
1869 and 1870.   At 31st January, 1871, the balance was at the
debtor of capital account to the extent of £7716.

That is to say, the capital was all lost that he had begun
with, and a debt of the amount you have mentioned was left
instead?—Yes; at the balancing period in 1872 that debit
balance was increased, and it then amounted to £35,383.   At
the balancing period in 1873 the debit balance was still
increasing; it then amounted to £84,420.   In 1874 the balance,
still on the same side, was £104,300.   In 1875 the balance was
£213,588, still to the debit.

What was that last increase of upwards of £100,000 owing
to?—It was owing to a number of old accounts having been
closed in that year before I left for Calcutta, and the debits
carried to profit and loss.

How much was the amount carried from profit and loss that
year against capital in closing these accounts?—£86,131.   Some
of those accounts had been open for a considerable time, in
the hope of making something out of them.   There was always
something expected to come in from them; but nothing came,

S

The City of Glasgow Bank Trial.

and so they were closed and carried to the debit of the capital account. I went out to India in April, 1875.

When did you bring up these balances in the book afterwards?—After I returned in 1876. In January, 1876, the balance is £248,905 to the debit. In 1877 it is £322,366, and by the end of 1877 it is £365,143.

So that in that business he had lost £365,143 *plus* the £48,000 you told us that stood at the credit during these years from 1868?—Yes.

Therefore, between 1868 and the end of 1877 he had lost £413,383?—Yes.

Does that represent the whole of Mr. Fleming's tradings and losses during that period?—No, it does not.

It was just one branch of them?—Just one branch.

On whose instruction did you proceed to Calcutta in 1875, and how long did you remain there?—Mr. Fleming spoke to me first about going, and afterwards Mr. John Hunter and the Manager, Mr. Robert Stronach, spoke to me.

You understood the estate, or part of it, was in liquidation then?—Yes, I understood the old firm of J. Nicol Fleming & Co. had gone into liquidation.

For whose behoof?—For behoof of the Bank.

And I suppose it was because of the Bank's interest in the liquidation that Mr. Stronach, the Manager, and Mr. Hunter came to you?—I understood so.

You understood so at the time?—Yes.

What was your object, or what were your duties to be in Calcutta when you went out in 1875?—I was to realise the assets of the old firm as speedily as I could without sacrificing them, and remit home the proceeds.

To whom were you to remit the proceeds?—To Mr. Hunter.

How long were you out there?—About a year.

Did you find the duty of realising an easy or a difficult one? —Well, I found matters had been going behind, and that there was very little to realise.

In fact, you found assets, but you found debts too?—I found large debts.

Bad ones?—Yes.

There were some coals, were there not?—That was the principal asset; a large claim we had upon a native firm for coals. Nothing came of that so far as I know. We could not get anything out of it.

Did you realise anything really to send home in that year?— No. After paying some of the debts of the firm, there was really nothing to send home.

Were you a good deal down at the premises of the City Bank before you went out to Calcutta?—Yes; I was frequently down at the Bank.

Evidence for Prosecution.

In relation to this matter of the liquidation?—In relation to Mr. Fleming's business generally.

Including the liquidation?—Yes.

Were you not there almost daily for a time?—I daresay I was, for some time before I went to Calcutta.

What individuals did you come in contact with on these occasions when you were at the City of Glasgow Bank?—Very seldom any one else than the Manager.

That is to say, generally you saw Robert Stronach?—Yes.

Whom did you see besides Robert Stronach upon these matters; I do not mean simply that you saw them, but who did you meet or converse with on the subject of James Nicol Fleming or his liquidation?—I saw Mr. Hunter frequently before going out, of course.

Anybody else?—Mr. Potter spoke to me about it also.

Was Mr. Robert Stronach the Manager at that time?—No, I think not. I think he was Assistant Manager only. I think his brother was absent, and he was acting as Manager, I understood.

Did you see Mr. Potter at his own office in Gordon Street about it?—His office was then in Great Clyde Street, I think. I saw him there twice, I think. He removed to Gordon Street while I was away.

When you saw Mr. Potter at his office, did you see him alone on any occasion?—Yes. Mr. Hunter came in upon one occasion.

What was the object of your conferences with Mr. Potter?—Mr. Potter impressed upon me the necessity of doing all I could to send home remittances—to realise the assets and send home remittances. I went to see Mr. Potter by arrangement, at the suggestion of Mr. Hunter. Mr. Hunter suggested that I should go to see Mr. Potter about my going out to Calcutta.

For what purpose?—He did not say for what purpose. He just suggested that I should see Mr. Potter, and I did so. Mr. Potter inculcated upon me the necessity of realisation and sending home remittances to be put to Mr. Fleming's credit and to reduce his debt.

Did he seem anxious that as much as possible should be realised?—Yes; he impressed that upon me very clearly.

That you must do your very best to get money out of the realisation?—Yes. [Shown No. 31A, excerpt from credit accounts Nos. 3 and 4.] I observe the balance of £487,906 carried over to the debit of James Nicol Fleming. I should say that is a balance due in respect of cash advances, as at June, 1876. I have no doubt it was the balance carried over after my realisations in Calcutta.

By the Lord Justice-Clerk—It was the balance at his debit after all realisations up to that time.

By the Lord Advocate—I saw that account in the ledger with

The City of Glasgow Bank Trial.

Dugald Bell. Mr. Morison. When I went down to see it I became aware it was transferred to the private book, from which No. 31A is an excerpt.

By the Lord Justice-Clerk—The date of the balance is 7th June, 1876.

By the Lord Advocate—I did not understand the reason for so transferring the account at the time. I understood that the effect of that entry would be to take it out of the cheque box. I knew Mr. Fleming had other indebtedness than represented by that balance, but I knew the details of that balance better than I knew the details of any other.

Were there any business relations during the time you were in Fleming's office between James Nicol Fleming & Co., started in 1868, and the firm of John Innes Wright & Co.?—Yes. These continued during our liquidation. There were certain credits that had been granted by the Bank to James Nicol Fleming & Co., which were continued during the liquidation. These were drawn upon by bills from Calcutta. The acceptances were by the Bank. They were discounted by various parties—some by James Morton & Co., others by Innes Wright & Co., and others I discounted myself at different banks. These bills were sent to this country from abroad. They were all sent for acceptance. Their currency was six months after acceptance.

By the Lord Justice-Clerk—These bills began shortly after the Calcutta house was opened, or perhaps about the year 1870.

Were they carried on to a larger extent during the liquidation? —Not to a larger extent; they were decreasing.

They were mere renewals?—Yes; they were renewals.

By Mr. Smith—I knew Mr. Wright. I formed a good opinion of him. His partner was Mr. Scott.

Was it Mr. Scott who conducted the affairs of the firm?—Yes. It was Mr. Scott chiefly whom I saw in regard to the matters about which I called. What brought me in contact with the firm was chiefly the discounting of bills—I handing the bills to them for discount, and they handing me the proceeds.

By Mr. Balfour—When Mr. Potter impressed on me the propriety of realising what I could, I understood it was with the view of reducing Nicol Fleming's debt to the Bank. It was quite plain that Mr. Potter was desirous to do his best for the Bank.

By the Dean of Faculty—The liquidation of the Calcutta firm began in January, 1875. The liquidation in Glasgow had been going on for some time previously. By liquidation I mean turning the securities which the Bank held into money, and applying that to the reduction of J. Nicol Fleming's debt. I don't think that process of liquidation is finished yet. The realisation account goes on after June, 1876, over 1877 and 1878. I obtained various sums of money from property belonging to

Evidence for Prosecution.

Mr. Fleming and dividends. He had New Zealand and Australian Company stock. I do not know if it is sold. My accounts during 1877 contain entries of the dividends I drew from that stock and elsewhere.

By the LORD ADVOCATE—Did you meet Mr. Innes Wright about the discounting of these bills as well as Mr. Scott?—Occasionally; chiefly when Mr. Scott was from home.

JOHN INGLIS.

By the SOLICITOR-GENERAL—I am a clerk, formerly in the employment of Potter, Wilson & Co. I was with them for about fifteen years, up till the stoppage of the Bank. I was book-keeper. There were a great number of bills between Potter, Wilson & Co. and James Morton & Co. They were accommodation bills principally.

And for a good many years had there been anything but accommodation bills between them?—For a good many years there had been nothing but that.

Were any of the bills ever paid during the time that you were there?—Rarely; but sometimes they were.

Did you ever know Morton pay a bill?—No; I never knew Morton pay a bill in his life.

The whole time?—Scarcely ever.

Where were all these bills discounted?—A large number of them were discounted by Mr. Morton. They were our acceptances to James Morton & Co.

Was there a large number of bills discounted with the City Bank?—No.

What bank did you get any of these bills discounted at?—We discounted very few of them. They were our acceptances to James Morton & Co., who discounted them, I think, principally in London.

Were Potter, Wilson & Co. correspondents of Holmes, White & Co., of Melbourne?—They were.

During the time you were with them did drafts for large amounts come home to Potter, Wilson & Co. from Holmes, White & Co.?—Yes.

Drawn in favour of James Morton & Co. and Potter, Wilson & Co.?—Yes.

On whom?—The City of Glasgow Bank.

Who got the proceeds?—In cases in which I had to do with the discounting, the City of Glasgow Bank got the proceeds.

Do you know what happened in cases that you had not to do with?—No.

Have you heard Mr. Lewis Potter saying anything about these credits?—Will you explain?

The City of Glasgow Bank Trial.

John Inglis. About the year 1870, what were the relations between Potter, Wilson & Co. and Morton & Co. and the Bank so far as you knew? —I scarcely understand the question.

You had an account in your ledger at that time called the City of Glasgow discount account?—Yes; I opened that account.

When you discounted Holmes, White & Co.'s bills, what was done with the proceeds?—When I discounted Holmes, White & Co.'s bills, I credited the City of Glasgow discount account with the amount, and I debited that account with the proceeds of the discount, which squared the transaction.

Who in your firm took the management of all these affairs?— Mr. Lewis Potter.

Had he blank forms?—He had.

From Holmes, White & Co.?—From Holmes, White & Co.

Signed by them?—Signed by them.

Were these used as required by filling them up as bills drawn by Holmes, White & Co.?—That is so.

What was on the bills written out when Mr. Potter got them? What was added in to what was printed?—The amount, the date, the currency, and the place—Melbourne.

Was all that put on in Glasgow?—It was all put on in Glasgow.

Nothing but the signature was put on in Mr. Potter's office? —Nothing but the signature and the lithographed form.

As regards the putting of the dates on these bills, were they put on of the date on which the date was written?—No; they were put on as at a mail date.

You mean a date which would correspond with their having made a journey from Melbourne?—Yes. [Shown Nos. 372 to 389; eighteen books, each containing fifty blank drafts, unstamped, by Holmes, White & Co. on the Bank, of which fifty had been used, and the counterfoils alone remained.]

Are these books of bills signed by Holmes, White & Co.?—Yes.

Blank, ready for use?—Yes.

Where were these kept?—Mr. Lewis Potter kept them.

In his own private possession?—Yes.

When they were to be handed out for use, what was done?— James Morton & Co. applied by a memorandum for certain credits. There was a memorandum book kept by me. I looked and compared these, anticipating certain bills—a bill due on such a date, perhaps eight days forward. I checked this by Mr. Potter's orders, to see that on no account was Morton to be allowed to anticipate. I then explained that it was correct to Mr. Potter, who handed out the drafts, and they were filled up and handed to James Morton & Co.

Who were they filled up by?—Sometimes by me, and sometimes by other clerks.

Do you remember, in March, 1877, of any communication

Evidence for Prosecution.

coming from Holmes, White & Co. about the protracted use of John Inglis. these bills?—I cannot speak as to the date; it must have been prior to that.

They objected to their name being so freely used?—A number of years prior to that they did.

But did they particularly object in the beginning of 1877?—Not that I am aware of.

They had been objecting prior to that?—Yes.

Who told you that?—I saw it in their letter.

Did Mr. Potter speak to you about it?—Mr. Potter at all times was very averse to these bills being given out by us at all.

Did he speak to you about Holmes, White & Co. objecting to so many bills being issued?—He did not.

By the LORD JUSTICE-CLERK—Why did he give them out?—I cannot say that.

What do you mean by objecting?—He gave them out with the greatest reluctance.

How did he show that? Was he under obligation to give them out?—Not that I am aware of.

By the SOLICITOR-GENERAL—Were you told anything by Potter about an arrangement that was made in 1877 for substituting a new credit?—Yes. Mr. Potter called me into his room in Gordon Street, I think early in January, 1877, and told me that it had been arranged that a portion of credit 24/6, presently financed by James Morton & Co., was to be transferred to another credit to be financed under the name of Glen Walker & Co., that I was to take charge of it, that it was to be apart from our firm, and that I was to call upon the Manager of the Bank, Mr. Stronach.

Was anything said as to who was to have the management of that?—The bills were to be drawn under Glen Walker & Co.'s credits in favour of Innes Wright & Co., who were to account to the Bank. I superintended the operation of that account for about ten months.

By the LORD JUSTICE-CLERK—You say they were to be drawn in favour of Innes Wright & Co. on the Bank?—Yes.

By the SOLICITOR-GENERAL—Had Mr. Potter blank forms for these bills?—Yes, in the same way as the others.

Did Innes Wright & Co. fall short in accounting for the proceeds of these bills?—They did. Mr. Potter spoke to me about that, and also Mr. Stronach frequently.

And ultimately was the discounting of bills to Innes Wright & Co. stopped?—It was stopped.

Who got the financing after that?—I think it was Mr. Morton. With regard to these shortcomings by Innes Wright & Co., I frequently saw William Scott about them—almost constantly. I

 279

The City of Glasgow Bank Trial.

John Inglis. also saw Mr. Wright in Mr. Scott's absence, and complained about it several times.

Was he quite aware of these shortcomings when you spoke to him?—He seemed to be quite aware.

By Mr. SMITH—The bills were handed to Wright & Co., as bill discounters. The business was practically managed by Mr. Scott. He rendered accounts to me, which I examined, and then submitted them to the Manager of the Bank.

Up to November, 1877, what was the shortcoming as shown in these accounts?—I am merely speaking from recollection, but there was a letter which I receivd from Mr. Scott, in which he promised to make me a payment of £38,000 during that week.

Was he to be allowed to have a margin to any extent?— At first he was not, but it was always told me by the Manager that he would be allowed a margin of £15,000 to enable him to finance such a large amount.

When you saw Mr. Wright on the subject, did he say anything about Mr. Scott managing it?—I met him as a partner of the firm, and I spoke to him concerning a subject which they were both cognizant of.

But did he say anything about Mr. Scott having charge of that business?—He did. He said that Mr. Scott took the entire charge of all these matters.

By Mr. BALFOUR—Potter, Wilson & Co. carried on a very large business both as shipowners and as commission merchants. They had intimate relations with the New Zealand and Australian colonies. They were the agents in this country for Holmes, White & Co. during all the time to which my evidence applies. The bills drawn under the credits that I have spoken to applicable to Holmes, White & Co. were sent home with Holmes, White & Co.'s name upon them as drawers to Potter, Wilson & Co., to be used as occasion_required, and they remained to be used by Potter, Wilson & Co., as the agents of Holmes, White & Co.

When the time came for using these bills, did Mr. Potter fill up the date so as to have the same effect as if it had been dated before coming from the colony?—Yes.

Did it make the least difference whether these bills drawn in the colony were sent home with authority to Mr. Potter to fill up that date, or whether the date was written in the colony?— No ; it made no difference, in my estimation.

Then were these bills treated by Potter, Wilson & Co. in accordance with the mandate or authority which they had from their constituents, Holmes, White & Co.?—They were.

Did Potter, Wilson & Co. get any sort of benefit by them?— None.

Were they merely executing their agency in the ordinary way of business?—Precisely.

Not for their own benefit?—No.

Was there anything in the least irregular in that? They

were executing it in the ordinary way, you have told us?— **John Inglis.** I would not care to pass an opinion upon that.

Does your evidence apply to the whole of the credits you have spoken to in which Holmes, White & Co. were interested? —Yes.

The City Bank were the acceptors of the bills drawn under these credits?—They were.

And the money was applied for its proper purposes?—Yes.

And before Mr. Potter gave out any bill was the application always initialed by the proper officer of the Bank?—It was invariably; he would not give them out without.

Then you spoke about certain bills to which Morton was a party, or in which Morton was interested; I believe you called them accommodation bills?—Yes; they were entirely for Morton's accommodation. Potter, Wilson & Co. got no benefit from them. They were the acceptors for Morton's accommodation, but for that alone.

You spoke about a credit which was transferred from being worked by Morton to be worked by Glen Walker & Co.; was that the credit known as 24/6?—Yes.

Do you know that the Bank held securities against that credit?—I was informed so, both by the late Manager and his brother, and also by Mr. Potter. That credit was entirely for Morton's benefit. I cannot say why it was transferred to Glen Walker & Co.; I was not informed of the reason. I was simply told that the securities for that £100,000 were transferred from 24/6 to 38/47.

You also mentioned the transaction with Innes Wright & Co. when they failed to account for the money they had raised by discount, the £48,000. When they so failed to account for that money, was Mr. Potter displeased?—Very much so.

And he expressed his displeasure at that impropriety?—Yes.

What did he do in consequence of that?—He told me frequently to call for Mr. Scott, and urge upon him the propriety of making payments.

To pay up that £48,000?—It was not always £48,000; it fluctuated.

But to pay up the balance which Scott was short of the sum he had got by discount?—Yes.

By the LORD JUSTICE-CLERK—That was a defalcation on Scott's part?—Yes.

By Mr. BALFOUR—And which Mr. Potter did his best to recover?—Yes; both Mr. Potter and Mr. Stronach.

Were there other credits which Potter, Wilson & Co. worked? —Yes.

Were they worked for behoof of the Bank?—Yes.

And that alone?—And that alone, with one exception—our own credit.

The City of Glasgow Bank Trial.

John Inglis. What was the one exception?—We had a credit. Speaking from recollection, I think we had an advance of about £9000.

How long was that ago?—Just at the time of the stoppage of Potter, Wilson & Co. 40/11 was the credit, I think.

Was that the only credit in which Potter, Wilson & Co. had any personal interest?—It was the only credit in which we had any interest. There was one credit for £10,000, a wool credit; I cannot say whether the £5000 that was running at the time of my leaving is still in existence or not.

Then these are different credits from any you have spoken to?—Yes.

Were these credits covered by securities in the regular way? —All that we had, with the exception of this wool credit and the £9000, were amply covered by securities.

So that, in the credits you were examined about by the Solicitor-General, did Mr. Potter get any sort of benefit from any one of them?—No. The regular banking business of Potter, Wilson & Co.'s firm was done with the British Linen Company, and also with the National Bank, both of Glasgow. These banks always gave Potter, Wilson & Co. any banking facilities that they required for their business. We never found any difficulty about that. I always looked upon these as our regular bankers.

By the LORD JUSTICE-CLERK—Their transactions with both of these banks were to a large amount.

J. Wardrop.   JOHN WARDROP.

By the SOLICITOR-GENERAL—I was lately transfer clerk in the City of Glasgow Bank at Glasgow. I held that situation for four years.

What was the procedure in purchases of stock for the Bank; did the broker send you in a contract note?—He sent it to the Manager. The broker who had bought the stock for the Bank, on the name day of the Stock Exchange, called at the Bank for the name of the purchaser. The Bank supplied that name. After that a letter came in from the seller's broker giving the particulars. That letter would come to Mr. Leresche, and he would hand it to me if it came in during the week before the Thursday. I would hand the whole letters to Mr. Leresche, with a list of the transfers to be laid before the Board. None of the Directors took charge of the transfer business, so far as I know.

Who were buying for the Bank, and coming to the Bank to get the names of purchasers to hold for the Bank?—Mr. Drew, Mr. Sutherland, and Watson & Smith. As a rule, since I went there, the name of the purchaser generally given was Thomas Matthew. When the names were given it was my

Evidence for Prosecution.

duty to get the parties to sign the transfers. I usually got the name signed by the person given out by the Bank as the purchaser. I never had any difficulty in getting their signature; they signed without remark.

These persons were entered in the ledger as holding in trust?—Thomas Matthew was; I don't exactly know the heading in the ledger. It would not appear in the stock ledger that that stock was held in trust for the Bank. It was entered just as " in trust " during the time I kept the stock ledger.

Did the stock thus purchased for the Bank enter the balances of the Bank?—I gave a note to the accountant of these amounts of stock on the balance day of each year. I don't know what he did with it. Mr. John Innes Wright became a partner of the concern by purchasing stock in 1875, when he became a Director. The first stage of the transfer to him was gone into on the day he was elected. There was a transfer of £1200 stock to him, the first stage of which was entered upon about one hour before the meeting. I don't think John Innes Wright held any stock previously to that. The amount of stock held by the Bank in 1876 was £140,751; Mr. Drew, £2970; Thomas Matthew, £9216; William Scott, £1300; John Innes Wright, £2681; total, £156,962. Total in 1877, £185,721; in 1878, £202,312. In January, 1878, Mr. Stewart sold £5000 stock. The Bank purchased it. Mr. Stronach gave me instructions about the transfer. Latterly the dividends upon all stock held by Drew, Matthew, and others, in trust for the Bank, were credited to an account headed " City of Glasgow Bank stock account." They were not paid over to any one. That applies to the last three half-years.

By Mr. TRAYNER—The proceeds of the stock held by Mr. Stewart were paid in to the credit of Mr. Stewart's account. No money was paid to him; it was paid in to his credit in the account he had then running with the Bank.

By Mr. SMITH—The qualification for a Director is the holding of £900 stock. I think £1200 stock was found for Mr. Wright to qualify him for a seat at the Board. Mr. Wright held £2681 stock for the Bank. I think the transfer of that stock was made shortly after he became a Director in 1875. I don't know through whom his consent was asked. I don't know if a clerk was sent from the Bank to ask his consent. I don't think there is any other Director who holds stock in trust for the company. Mr. Wright still holds that stock.

By Mr. ASHER—Mr. Salmond holds £2200 stock. Prior to 1873 he held £1800, and in 1873 he took £400 of new stock. Since then he has held £2200 down to the close. He holds also £360, as trustee for a Mr. Thomson. With regard to the purchases of stock for the Bank, it was with Mr. Stronach that I communicated. None of the Directors ever spoke to me on

The City of Glasgow Bank Trial.

J. Wardrop. the subject. None of them ever asked to see the stock ledger or the transfer ledger. So far as I recollect, Mr. Salmond has the largest holding of stock amongst the Directors. I don't think he ever sold a share all the time he was connected with the Bank.

By Mr. MACKINTOSH—Mr. Taylor at the date of the stoppage held £1800 stock ; his son and partner, Mr. Henry Taylor, £500 ; and his brother and former partner, Mr. Patrick Taylor, £500. I cannot say whether Mr. Taylor was an original shareholder of the Bank, or whether he accepted an allotment of new stock in 1864. I am aware he got £300 new stock allotted to him in 1873. The same year he bought £120 to make his holding even. Neither Mr. Taylor nor any of his family ever sold a share since they became connected with the Bank.

By Mr. DARLING—Mr. Stronach holds £900 stock. Of that he acquired £800 in August, 1876. Previously he had held only £100.

J. Hutton.
JAMES HUTTON.

By the LORD ADVOCATE—I am a chartered accountant in Glasgow. I have had submitted to me the balance abstracts published by the Directors to the shareholders of the City Bank for June, 1876, 1877, and 1878. I have also had access to all the books of the Bank, and I have examined these so far as is necessary for ascertaining how far the published abstracts coincide with the entries in the books. [Shown published abstract as at 7th June, 1876.] This document is headed "City of Glasgow Bank, Abstract Balance Sheet as at 7th June, 1876." On the assets side there is, first, "Bills of exchange, local and country bills, credit accounts, and other advances upon security," £8,787,804 17s. 9d. These assets were understated to the extent of £2,698,539 0s. 4d. The correct amount, according to the books of the Bank, is £11,486,343 18s. 1d. With regard to the details of that under-statement, I find from the scroll abstract of accounts that the bad debts are only stated at £50,000, while in the books of the Bank they appear at £300,000. I further find that the credit accounts, amounting to £147,468 16s. 11d., are entirely omitted from the abstract of the Bank. I further find that the deposit account balances, amounting to £452,211 5s. 6d., are entirely omitted from the abstract of the Bank. The sources from which I have got that information are the scroll abstracts for the year 1876, and from the general ledger. I find that foreign and colonial credits are understated—entirely omitted—to the extent of £973,300. They appear in the abstract at £1,304,873 17s. 1d. ; and the true amount was £2,278,173 17s. 1d. I find that there has been transferred from this first branch of the assets to the

Evidence for Prosecution.

third branch of the assets a sum of £751,775, consisting of three items, marked with the initials S. F. & Co., £200,875; J. N. F., £100,300; J. M. & Co., £450,600; in all, £751,775. The practical effect upon the statement of assets of bringing down that amount from head I. to head III. is to convert what might be considered a doubtful asset into what would be considered by the shareholders and the public an asset that was very assured—that is to say, to convert an asset that might be doubtful—an asset that might not have been paid at all into an asset that is beyond doubt—assured, in the nature of a Government stock or other stock—a good investment held by the Bank. The next item in error is an item deducted as cross accounts—£373,334 5s. 3d. The next item is £32,751 17s. 11d. —the balances on remittances outstanding between branches and branches and the head office.

I understand you are taking your information as to these from the scroll abstract and the books?—Yes.

And assuming the scroll abstract as the basis of the abstract published?—Yes. The gross of what I have just read out amounts to £2,983,841 5s. 7d., but there are several over-statements in the abstract balance sheet. Past due bills appear in the scroll abstract at £248,500 13s. 6d., and they appear in the books at £174,393, being a difference of £74,106. The contingent account has a credit balance of £2507, while in the books there was a debit balance of £10,747, a further error of £13,254. Credit accounts No. 2 appear in the scroll at £143,087 18s. 7d., while in the completed balance sheet from the ledger they only amounted to £100,296 5s. 2d., being a difference of £42,791. Heritable property appears in the first branch of the abstract, but should have appeared in the second —£119,541. Adjusting account of interest, £35,607 13s. 8d. That, it appeared, was only the difference between the interest due by the Bank and the interest due to the Bank. These gross over-statements amount to £285,302 5s. 3d., and deducted from the previous omissions, amounting to £298,384 5s. 7d., it shows an under-statement on the first branch of the balance of £2,698,539. Second branch—heritable property, advances on heritable property, etc., appear in the books at £319,949 5s., and in the abstract at £256,650 10s. 1d., giving a difference of £63,283 15s. Under the third head, "Cash in hand, gold and silver coin and notes of other banks at head office and branches," £862,812 4s. 4d., there is a deduction from this head of £29,095. Government stocks, exchequer bills, railway and other stocks, £2,218,868 13s. 7d.; there is the transfer I have already referred to of £751,775. There is an omission of the remittances outstanding between branches and branches of £3356 16s. 11d.; there is an item due by Irvin & Co. of £11,991 9s. 9d., which, before the balance closed, had been

J. Hutton. wiped off to suspense account, and these deductions amount to £753,211 2s. 6d., accounting for the difference of £792,306 2s. 6d., which, deducted from the former sum mentioned, leaves a balance of £197,516 12s. 10d.—the difference between the assets as published and the assets that were disclosed in the books of the Bank.

They are understated to that extent?—Yes. The amount in the balance sheet is £12,126,151 5s. 9d., and the true amount is £14,105,667 18s. 7d. The result is that about two million is taken off each side of the account, and with under and over-statements upon both sides of it. There is under-statement of certain items, over-statement of certain others, and a general deduction. Coming to the liabilities, the first branch is—"Deposits at head office and branches, and balance at credit of banking correspondents," £8,364,056 18s. 5d. That is under-stated to the extent of £1,006,216 12s. 10d., arising in the following way:—I find that the deposit account balances have been entirely omitted, amounting to £455,444 5s. 10d. I find that deposit accounts credited are deducted in error in the abstract, £1346 16s. 6d. Credit account balances have been entirely omitted, £147,468, 16s. 11d. Balance due to London and Provincial Banks, £14,216 15s. 2d. ; that has been omitted. Adjusting account of interest due by the Bank, £11,405 13s. 2d. has been omitted entirely.

You are giving us what makes up that total of £1,006,000?—Yes. I find that cross accounts have been deducted in error, amounting to £376,334 5s. 3d.—making in all £1,006,216 under the first branch. There is nothing wrong under the second branch—"Bank notes in circulation in Scotland and the Isle of Man." Third branch—"Drafts outstanding, due, or with currency not exceeding twenty-one days," etc., £1,315,373 17s. 1d., are overstated to the extent of £973,300. I find no explanation at all in the books of that £973,300. These two sums amount together to £1,979,516 12s. 10d., which are the total under-statements of the liabilities of the Bank at this balance. There is stated as at profit and loss in the balance sheet £136,365 10s. 3d.

Have you any observations to make upon that item?—In the first place, of that sum there was drawn forward from the previous balance the sum of £10,602 16s. 2d., leaving as the revenue of the year £125,762 14s. 1d. I get that from the profit and loss account in the books of the Bank, showing the earnings derived from the use of capital. I made up a memorandum of interest chargeable to the eight largest debtors of the Bank. The amount of interest is £125,763 12s. 8d., being about 18s. 7d. under what the sum declared as dividend was that year.

Did it appear from the books of the Bank that this interest

Evidence for Prosecution.

had been paid upon the accounts?—No. They were added to the debts of the parties.

In the profit and loss account, which showed the trade profits of the Bank for the year, were they entered as profits received? —They first came in under a general entry in that way as interest received, but it really was a general entry of interest added to the debts of the various parties, and transferred to the credit of profit and loss account.

So that, in point of fact, the divisible profit and loss would be payable out of capital?—It seems so.

Leaving a claim against these parties for the profit supposed to have been made?—Undoubtedly—added to their debts.

Is the interest upon the accounts of these firms dealt with in precisely the same way in the profit and loss account and in the balance sheets in the next two years?—In precisely the same way all through.

It is distributed amongst the shareholders as if it were money earned and in hand?—It is, indeed.

Although it only subsisted as a debt against these men?—It only subsisted as a debt—increasing the liability.

Are the alterations made on the balance sheets of subsequent years much the same as in 1876?—They are all entirely on the same lines, with the aggravation at the ultimate balance of heavier sums transferred in the same way.

And for the first time in that balance sheet there is a conversion—if you follow the scroll abstract—of balances on credit account into gold in the Bank's coffers?—Yes; to the amount of £200,000.

What was the reserve fund in 1876?—The amount of the reserve fund in the balance sheet published to the shareholders was £450,000. That was raised from time to time by any surplus that may have been at the credit of profit and loss transferred annually to the fund called Reserve Fund; but I am prepared to submit to you that it is an entirely fictitious entry of the amount now stated in the balance sheet for 1876 at £450,000.

On what ground do you come to that conclusion?—On the ground that there has been transferred to interest account sums of interest on assets that were yielding no return at all, and a sum equivalent to the amount said to be at the credit of this account.

You are still speaking of 1876?—Yes. In the balance ledger for 1876 there is at the credit of what they call a railway and debenture account a large sum, and of that there is a sum of £351,330 of interest debited to it that had really never been earned, but simply charged upon this account. In 1862 there has been charged to this railway and debenture account a sum

The City of Glasgow Bank Trial.

J. Hutton. of £16,046 0s. 6d.; in 1863, £20,551 10s. 10d.; in 1864, £22,492 5s. 3d.

By the LORD JUSTICE-CLERK—Are these sums carried to the reserve fund, which in reality has no existence at all?—Not directly to the reserve fund, but they are interest charged on these inoperative accounts; and, in process of time, transferred to profit and loss account, and then from profit and loss account to the reserve fund.

By the LORD ADVOCATE—There having been no receipts during the period?—None.

What is the total of them?—For the last three years there are receipts—for 1871, £45,762 15s. 11d., when there was earned £16,009 12s. 1d.; for 1872, £46,325 18s. 10d., when there was earned £17,280 14s. 11d.

When you say earned, what precisely do you mean?—The natural dividend accruing upon this stock. In 1873, £47,820 2s. 8d., when there was earned £16,744 17s. The gross receipts from 1862 to 1873 only amount to £50,090 18s. 10d., while the gross debits to interest account amount to £401,421 0s. 10d., leaving a net overcharge of £351,330 2s.

Do you mean that, in point of fact, they credit themselves as if they had £400,000 coming from that source?—That is so.

Whilst in point of fact only £50,000 came from it?—That is so. The next item is that the Bank held stock of their own, and from time to time revalued their own stock, and this revalue they transferred in the same way to interest account, then to profit and loss account, and ultimately to reserve fund. In 1864 they revalued the stock, and transferred £15,858.

You need not give the details?—Well, between 1864 and 1875 the gross is £128,854 7s. 1d.; and, added to the interest on the railway debenture account, the gross sum is £480,184 9s. 1d., entirely absorbing the reserve fund.

Look at the published balance sheet for 1877, and beginning with assets, head No. I., tell me what over or under-statement, if any, there were?—For the balance sheet of 1877 the under-statements amount to £3,227,154 12s. 8d.

That is the total under-statement of what?—Of the assets under the first branch—£3,227,154 12s. 8d., the balance sheet disclosing £8,758,838 17s. 8d., while the true amount was £11,985,993 10s. 4d. Then head II. of the assets in the balance sheet is understated to the extent of £52,961 19s. 10d. Head III., under the gold, was understated to the extent of £30,000, and the credit accounts still have a transfer from branch one to branch three of the three items formerly referred to, amounting to £751,775.

Done just as in the previous year?—Yes; making the gross under-statement of the year to be £2,558,341 12s. 6d.

Evidence for Prosecution.

About half a million more under-statement than the year J. Hutton before?—That is so.

The actual amount of their transactions was increasing by half a million, but it is brought down to about the same level?—Yes. Then the liabilities were understated to the extent of £1,151,518 13s. 5d.

That is the first head?—Yes; the balance sheet disclosing £8,382,711 12s. 10d., while the true amount was £9,534,230 6s. 3d. From the second branch there is deducted £76,110—understated to that extent; and from the third branch there is a sum of £1,330,712 19s. 1d., making the difference between the published abstract and the true. The liabilities in the published abstract are £12,095,442 6s. 5d., while the true amount was £14,653,783 18s. 11d.

How about profit and loss in this year?—The profit and loss disclosed at the credit in the published balance sheet was £148,501 12s. 6d., but of this there was brought forward from last year £19,990 10s. 3d., leaving as the natural revenue of the year £128,511 2s. 3d., and the interest on the same eight chief debtors amounts to £128,998 19s. 9d., being more by £487 17s. 6d. than the dividend declared.

Is the reserve fund in 1877 brought out in the same way as you have explained?—It was entirely absorbed in 1876, and, of course, continues to be so until now. Then in 1878, the first branch of the assets is understated to the extent of £3,520,913 11s. 8d., the balance sheet disclosing £8,484,466 9s. 2d., while the true sum is £12,005,380 0s. 10d. The second branch has an under-statement of the heritable property, amounting to £48,698 7s. 6d. The third branch this year has a transfer from the credit accounts of £200,000 as reserve gold, and the former entries of £751,000 now appear as £926,764, the gross difference being £1,146,286 5s. 10d., and the difference between the true and the published assets being, the balance sheet disclosed, £11,892,593 11s. 8d., while the true sum is £14,315,917 5s. 1d.

The two sides of the account were larger really in this than in any of the two previous years?—Yes; the transactions were all larger.

Whereas, in point of fact, they are shown on the whole to have been the same, or nearly £300,000 less?—Yes. Then on the liabilities side in 1878, the liabilities under the first branch are understated to the extent of £941,284 13s. 5d. The balance sheet discloses £8,102,001 0s. 4d., while the true sum is £9,043,285 13s. 9d., errors in the same line as those I have read out from the first balance sheet. Under the second branch there is deducted notes in error, amounting to £89,031. Under the third branch there is omitted entirely the difference between the true and the published amount of bills payable, £1,393,008,

T

The City of Glasgow Bank Trial.

J. Hutton. the actual amount being £2,881,252 18s. 6d., while the abstract only discloses £1,488,244 18s. 6d., giving the difference referred to of £1,393,008. The profit and loss for this year instructs that there was a credit entry of £142,095 12s. 10d., whereof there had been transferred from last year's account £17,001 12s., leaving only, as the natural revenue of the year, £125,094 0s. 4d.; and the interest upon the eight large debts, already referred to, for the year amounts to £125,875 9s., being an excess of the dividend declared of £781 8s. 8d.

Is that an ordinary mode of dealing with a profit or loss account?—Quite an ordinary mode.

To enter in it interests not received?—Quite a usual circumstance.

Was it a correct entry in this case?—I think it was, if it had been paid.

But that is just what I wanted to know. I asked you if it was a correct entry to insert in a profit and loss account that which had not been paid?—At this particular balance I should have said it was a correct entry; but, looking to the fact that for the previous years the interest had not been paid, it was not a correct entry. But for any one year by itself, it is quite a correct entry to transfer to interest account the interest upon any debt.

But not in a case where the interest is standing out unpaid from year to year, and simply made an addition to the debt?—I should say not, where it has been continued from year to year unpaid.

By Mr. BALFOUR—I suppose you merely examined these books and the abstracts as an accountant does, and not having that knowledge extrinsic of the books which the officials of the Bank might have?—I certainly did it as an accountant, but I got all the knowledge that the officials could give me.

But at all events you did it, merely taking the books of the Bank on the one part and the abstracts on the other?—Entirely so.

About this manner in which interest was treated, I understand you to say that if it had not been that the accounts had not been producing interest in previous years you would have thought it was quite right to charge interest upon them, and to bring that into profit and loss?—Yes; but, of course, I have the knowledge here that they were not paying the interest, and that they were not paying the principal, but both principal and interest were being accumulated to an enormous amount.

In other words, you formed the opinion that these were bad or doubtful debts?—I certainly did.

And it is upon the view that these were bad or doubtful debts that you think interest was wrongly charged upon them?—Entirely so.

Evidence for Prosecution.

Apart from that view, and but for that view, what was done would have been quite right?—I should say so. If the debt was to be paid, and the interest was to be paid, it was all in order.

And I suppose, in the books of the Bank, the interest was carried from profit and loss in the way you have described?— It is so.

Being the usual way?—The usual way.

So that, with regard to the manner of treating the interest, there is not a disconformity between the abstract and the books of the Bank?—Not in the very least. On the contrary, they agree.

And if the abstract had not treated the interest in the way you have described, it would have departed in that matter from the books of the Bank?—No doubt it would.

You said something about the American debentures, that arrears of interest were charged upon these?—Yes; all through the years that I deponed to.

Did you find from the books of the Bank that these debentures had begun to pay interest latterly?—Yes, I see that now. I saw it for the last three years. They have been producing a very fair return, but they are not producing the return by one-half that is charged in the books of the Bank against them.

That may be, but they have begun now to produce a return; and whether the whole may be paid or not is a matter, I suppose, beyond your knowledge?—I could not say.

By Mr. MACKINTOSH—I know Mr. Taylor. I have known him for a very long time—for upwards of fifteen years. I have been in the way of meeting him very frequently in business.

What opinion do you hold as to his character?—Do you mean in the light of the present case, or prior to the present case?

I mean as a man of integrity?—Well, I think a very great deal of Mr. Taylor. I always considered him to be a very honourable and a very upright gentleman, and it was a very great pleasure to me to meet Mr. Taylor at any time.

By the DEAN OF FACULTY—Has there been any interest charged upon these American bonds except the £40,000 that was remitted home from America in payment of the interest?—Yes.

During the last three years?—No, not during the last three years; but there was a number of years when there was no interest got at all, and it was charged then.

But there has been nothing charged during the last three years except what was actually got?—Oh, no. There is a regular charge in the books of the Bank for interest.

But not in excess of what was got?—It is in excess of what was got.

The City of Glasgow Bank Trial.

J. Hutton. During the last three years?—During the last three years it is in excess of what was got.

Just explain that to me. There was 7 per cent. of a return obtained. Is there anything else charged?—I am not aware that there was 7 per cent. obtained.

Is there anything more than 7 per cent. charged?—I will read each item for the last three years. In 1871 there is charged in the books of the Bank, and credited to interest account——

I am not speaking of 1871. I am speaking of the last three years, and I ask you to keep to them?—I never made a single reference to the interest of this account since 1873. I only quoted to the Lord Advocate up to 1873, because since 1873 they have been drawing a very fair return.

And there is nothing more charged in the books than what they drew?—Nothing since 1873.

By the LORD ADVOCATE—What you said was not that during the years 1876, 1877, and 1878, there was not a dividend due upon that stock from America?—No ; I did not quote anything in these years.

I understood not ; but what you stated as to the three years, as earnings that ought not fairly to have been entered in the books, was the interest upon this large account, amounting to about £125,000?—Yes ; in almost every year.

You stated that you thought that ought not to have been brought into profit and loss, because it was not in course of being received by the Bank?—Certainly not ; but that neither the debt nor the interest has been paid for some years.

By the LORD JUSTICE-CLERK—How, in your opinion, ought they to have dealt with the principal and interest?—I think there was nothing to hinder them from adding interest to the debt that was due ; but I think they should not have transferred that to a divisible account, and paid it away when they knew that they were not getting in the money. In course of time their coffers would have been empty.

Would you have carried it to bad and doubtful debts, or to a suspense account?—I would have carried it to "Suspense account, No. 2," in the special circumstances of the case.

The LORD ADVOCATE stated that this closed the evidence for the Crown, and intimated that he confined the charges against the panels to the first three charges in the indictment.

CHAPTER IX.

Evidence for Defence.

FOR MR. STEWART.

ALEXANDER MOORE.

BY MR. MACLEAN—I am a chartered accountant in Glasgow, and a partner of the firm of Moore & Brown, accountants and stockbrokers there. I know Mr. Stewart. I first became acquainted with him about twelve years ago. I was employed at that time professionally to adjust accounts—family accounts —in which his brother and he were interested. These accounts had been kept by one of his brothers, Mr. Robert Stewart, and I was called in to adjust matters between them. Mr. Stewart, up to 1874, was the leading partner in the firm of John Stewart & Co. That was a very old-standing firm in the wine trade, and one which has done a very considerable business for many years.

Were you called in at any time to deal with the accounts of that firm?—I was called in, in the year 1872-3, to adjust the partnership accounts on a dissolution. The partners up to that time were Mr. Stewart, his brother, and Mr. Stewart's own son. The dissolution of the firm was carried through in the year 1874-5. Since that date the firm, which is now Stewart, Pott & Co., has consisted of Mr. Stewart and his son. Upon a dissolution, Mr. Robert Stewart took over a portion of the business, the distillery portion, into his own hands. Since the dissolution I have audited the balance sheets of the new firm yearly. Under the old firm of John Stewart & Co., I think the book-keeping department was principally under the supervision of Mr. Robert Stewart. For the firm of Stewart, Pott & Co. I have merely audited the balance sheets since the dissolution. I have done so for the satisfaction of the partners, but chiefly, I think, from Mr. John Stewart's want of knowledge of book-keeping.

Is he deficient in his knowledge of book-keeping?—He has often expressed himself so in my hearing.

Had you any reason to doubt that?—I believe he is deficient altogether in the knowledge of figures and accounting.

The City of Glasgow Bank Trial.

Alex. Moore.   Apart from that, did he show a desire that everything should be correct and properly stated?—He was always extremely anxious that everything should be right.

You have had occasion, in consequence of the employment you have spoken of, to meet with him often?—Very often.

What opinion have you formed of him?—That he was a highly honourable man.

Upon the stoppage of the Bank Mr. Stewart and his firm, as we know, were indebted in certain sums of money to the Bank?—They were.

He had a personal account, and his firm had the firm's account, in the City of Glasgow Bank?—Yes.

Has Mr. Stewart assigned to you investments of considerable value to meet the claim?—Immediately on the stoppage of the Bank, he assigned to me investments to the amount of his liability to the Bank as a debtor, and his firm's debt as well.

So that upon these overdrafts the Bank will not lose one shilling?—I cannot say as to that. They are not realised yet.

But so far as appears?—The amount was equivalent, so far as appeared, to the debt.

Mr. Stewart remains a shareholder. Deducting what he has assigned to you in satisfaction of the overdrafts, what property remains to Mr. Stewart to meet the calls which will be made upon him as a shareholder?—I may say that Mr. Stewart executed a trust assignation in my favour. Taking his investments in the New Zealand Land Company at their par value, I estimate that Mr. Stewart's assets exceeded his liabilities by £85,000 at that date.

And is it consistent with your knowledge that Mr. Stewart has been, during all the years that you have known him, a comparatively rich man, and with his means steadily increasing?—I examined as to his means in the year 1871, and the result then was made about the same as it was at October, when the Bank stopped, £85,000.

Then he has been worth about £85,000 during all the time he has been a Director of the City of Glasgow Bank?—Yes.

By the LORD JUSTICE-CLERK—Did I understand the £85,000 to be over and above the securities assigned to you for the advance from the Bank?—No; the total value of his assets over his whole liabilities.

How much is the balance for which you had securities assigned?—£44,000.

By Mr. MACLEAN—And over and above that he has a fortune of £85,000?—No.

By the LORD JUSTICE-CLERK—No; £45,000. His fortune, I understand, was £85,000 altogether?—Yes.

But he owed £45,000 odd to the Bank?—Yes; for which he assigned security.

Evidence for Defence.

And his fortune is the balance?—Yes.

By Mr. MacLean—Let us understand about this—is it after making provision for the payment of the overdrafts that the balance of £85,000 remains?—It is.

By the Lord Justice-Clerk—You said the reverse just now. I asked you whether out of the £85,000 the amount due to the Bank must come?—After paying the Bank there is £85,000 remaining.

You have got securities for the amount of the Bank's debt, and over and above that there is a fortune of £85,000. Is that so?—The Bank is secured out of a certain portion of these assets.

Will you answer my question? You have got securities to the extent of the Bank's debt, and Mr. Stewart has over and above, when the Bank is paid, £85,000?—Yes.

By Mr. MacLean—Then it follows, from what you have just said, that his fortune in 1871, which you stated at £85,000, had been increased by the £44,000?—Not at all. Mr. Stewart's total assets in October last amounted to £120,000; his total liabilities amounted to £34,000.

By the Lord Justice-Clerk—How much did he owe to the Bank?—Of these assets he assigned to the Bank £44,000 odds, in security of his personal debt and of his firm's debt.

By Mr. MacLean—As an individual, and as representing the Company, the amount owing to the Bank was what?—It was £44,000 altogether.

Now, go back and give us the assets and liabilities as at 1871?—In 1871 Mr. Stewart's total assets amounted to £91,000, and his personal liability to the Bank at that time was £5300. Mr. Stewart had opened his account with the City of Glasgow Bank a very long time back. I don't know how long. [Shown Bank book.] I see from that book that the account was opened on 23rd July, 1868, with a sum placed to his credit of £5600. The account of Stewart, Pott & Co. with the City of Glasgow Bank was opened in June, 1874. They had previously dealt with the Commercial. The account there was closed by a payment to the Commercial of £18,008. The average value of the stock in trade of Stewart, Pott & Co. was about £10,000, and their outstanding debts £20,000. Their sales, on the average of the last three years, have exceeded £60,000.

By the Lord Advocate—You say there was £34,000 of indebtedness against £120,000 of assets. Was any part of that £34,000 Bank debt?—Yes.

To what extent?—£11,000, which is the balance of his private account.

After deducting that £34,000 of liabilities, that left about £85,000?—Yes; New Zealand land shares are what is assigned

The City of Glasgow Bank Trial.

Alex. Moore. in security of the debt which he owed to the Bank, and the debt which his firm owed to the Bank.

Covering the debt which is included in the £34,000?—Yes.

By the LORD JUSTICE-CLERK—The whole amount of Mr. Stewart's indebtedness as an individual is £34,000 odds. The debts of the firm are about £45,000, in addition to the £34,000. I do not take the assets of the firm into calculation in the £120,000; I take Mr. Stewart's capital into account.

James Hay Stewart.

JAMES HAY STEWART.

By Mr. TRAYNER—I am joint manager of the Commercial Bank at its head office in Glasgow, and have been so since February, 1865. I know Mr. John Stewart. I knew his firm of John Stewart & Co. It had an account in our bank, which was closed in 1874. That account had been in the bank from February, 1840. Throughout the whole period of my acquaintance with that account, it was a most satisfactory account to the bank.

Was it an account which in 1874 your bank would have been very glad to have retained?—Yes; I rather think we regretted the fact of its leaving us. At that date there was an overdraft of above £18,000. That overdraft was not one to cause us any uneasiness in the least, looking to the persons with whom we were dealing, and to their business. We had no security for it, except the credit and responsibility of the partners of the firm.

William M'Kinnon.

WILLIAM M'KINNON.

By Mr. TRAYNER—I am a chartered accountant in Glasgow. I was one of the liquidators of the Western Bank, and I was asked to be one of the liquidators of the City of Glasgow Bank, but I declined. I have looked at the books of the City of Glasgow Bank, with the view of giving certain information. I have seen the balance ledger which is signed and docqueted by the Directors. It is annually docqueted. I have looked at the accounts for 1876, 1877, and 1878 respectively.

Are these accounts, docqueted for these respective years in the balance ledger, correct according to the entries in the Bank's books?—They are quite conform to the books of the Bank.

And, as a balance, are they framed upon correct principles?—Yes; I believe them to be so.

By the LORD ADVOCATE—I suppose, when you say that, you mean that they correctly give effect to the entries in the books of the Bank?—Precisely.

You are not indicating any opinion as to the correctness of the entries in the books of the Bank?—No; I am giving an opinion upon the balances that appear in the balance ledger.

But it reflects what is in the books?—Quite. I have not found

Mr. Trayner,
Counsel for John Stewart.

Evidence for Defence.

any entry of £973,000 in the balance ledger. I have seen it in the cash book of 1873.

By the LORD JUSTICE-CLERK—It is quite traceable. It is very difficult to say what it is.

By the LORD ADVOCATE—But you say you can trace it?—Yes; I can trace it in the books quite well. It represents a credit entry. It represents in the books a credit entry as regards bills payable for £973,000.

On what debts?—On bills payable to the Bank, and also on foreign and colonial credits.

Is it so dealt with in the abstract of the balance?—The weekly abstract.

The abstract balance, and in the weekly abstract; how is it dealt with there?—It is dealt with there as a debit and a credit.

That is to say, it is taken out altogether?—The effect is to take it out of both sides.

Then what do you gather from that fact was the nature of this sum of £973,000?—The effect of it is to decrease the foreign and colonial credits.

But what do you gather was the nature of the transaction out of which it arose—are the bills retired?—No; it is a decrease of the bills payable. I cannot tell why it was put there. I cannot find anything in the books to account for its being there. When a debt is irrecoverably bad, it should be written off altogether; that is to say, when the Directors come to be satisfied that it is hopeless.

Where the Manager or Directors of a bank are not satisfied that a debt is hopeless, and hope it may be paid, but where there is no incoming for two or three years, what is the proper way of dealing with it?—I should say that suspense would be the proper way to deal with it.

A suspense account?—Yes.

You would not carry the interest on such debts to profit and loss in the first instance?—No; unless there was some very good reason for so treating it.

But on the whole the proper way would be not to write it off altogether?—No.

But to put it into suspense?—Yes.

EVIDENCE FOR MR. POTTER.

CUNNINGHAM SMITH.

By Mr. BALFOUR—I am a merchant in Glasgow. I am a son of the late William Smith of Carbeth-Guthrie (who was at one time Lord Provost of Glasgow) and nephew of the late Mr. James Smith of Jordanhill. I am a partner of Potter, Wilson & Co., merchants, Glasgow. Mr. Lewis Potter is the senior partner. I joined the firm in 1853, and have continued to be Mr. Lewis

The City of Glasgow Bank Trial.

Potter's partner ever since. The business we have carried on has been principally a commission business. It has been very extensive and very lucrative.

What was Mr. Lewis Potter's share of the profit of that business of late years?—£5000 or £6000 a year.

From that business alone?—Yes. He was also a partner of the separate business of Lewis Potter & Co., owners or agents for a line of steamers trading between Dublin and Liverpool. I believe that also was an extensive and lucrative business. I have been told that Mr. Lewis Potter's average income from that business was £3000, but I have no means of knowing. I know that he is possessed of a valuable landed estate—Udston. I do not know the return from it. I am aware that, besides its land rent, it is a valuable mineral estate. It is in the neighbourhood of Hamilton. There is a very valuable coal-field opening up there now.

As to Mr. Potter's business qualities, what departments of the business has he directed his attention to, and what has he left to others?—Latterly he left the details of the business very much to myself and to his son.

And in what respects has he taken part in the business?—For some years he has taken very little part in the business. He has been gradually withdrawing from an active share in the business.

And has he avoided going into details?—Very much.

As regards figures, was that a matter that he concerned himself with, or did he leave that to the subordinates?—Always to the subordinates.

As regards his style of living and expenditure, was he very moderate with reference to his means?—Very moderate indeed.

With what banks were your firm's account or accounts kept? —The British Linen Company, the National Bank of Scotland, and the City of Glasgow Bank.

How long has the firm kept an account with the British Linen? —Ever since I joined it; and, I believe, ever since it was commenced.

Did they keep an account there from 1846?—I believe so.

Down to the present time?—Yes.

Was there any particular reason why an account was kept with the British Linen?—I fancy because Mr. Patrick Brodie, agent of the Bank in Glasgow, was a brother-in-law of Mr. Wilson, the original partner of Potter, Wilson & Co.

How long has the firm kept an account with the National Bank?—When I joined there was an account kept for the Clyde and Australian Shipping Company, of which Potter, Wilson & Co. were the agents. After that company was dissolved we were requested by the Bank to continue our account on our own account.

Evidence for Defence.

Were some of the partners of the Clyde and Australian Shipping Company interested in the National Bank?—Yes.

And that led to its being kept there?—Yes.

And it has been continued ever since?—Yes.

When did it begin to be kept at the National Bank?—Before 1853; how long before I cannot tell. I recollect Mr. Potter becoming a Director of the City of Glasgow Bank. After that, as before, the accounts with the British Linen and National Banks continued to be kept.

Did the requirements of your business, or any requirements of Mr. Potter's, as far as you know, make the City Bank of importance to your firm?—Not at all.

You did not need anything of it?—No.

After he became a Director of the City Bank, did the officials express a desire to have a share of his business or of the business of the firm?—I believe so.

And was there an account opened there also?—Yes.

Kept first at the West-End City Branch?—When I first joined.

And afterwards transferred to the head office?—Yes.

Was that a drawing account or a discount account?—The West-End was entirely a drawing account, so far as I recollect.

After the Bank asked and got a share of the business, had your firm sometimes credits from them?—Sometimes.

Had you credits of the same kind from the British Linen?—At one time.

Was anything that you had in the way of credits given in the ordinary way of banking business?—Yes.

Is that a lucrative branch of a bank's business?—I believe so.

Are you aware that there were certain accounts standing unsettled between Mr. Potter, or the firm of Potter, Wilson & Co., and Morton & Co.?—Yes. They were under reference for many years. An award has been pronounced very lately by Mr. Hunter.

Upon those accounts was your firm a considerable creditor of Morton's?—Yes.

Did you ever have a conversation with Mr. Potter from which you could form an opinion as to whether he was uneasy as to Morton or his credit?—Yes. Mr. Potter seemed to believe that Morton's share in the New Zealand and Australian Land Company would more than cover all his liabilities.

Did he appear to be at all uneasy about getting all his debt paid?—No, I think not—in time. I knew that Mr. Potter himself was a large shareholder in that Land Company, and a Director.

So that he had the means of forming an opinion as to the value of its shares?—Yes.

By the LORD JUSTICE-CLERK—I do not know to what extent he was a shareholder in that company.

The City of Glasgow Bank Trial.

Cunningham
Smith.

By Mr. BALFOUR—From your intercourse with Mr. Potter, can you say whether he thought highly of the present value and future prospects of the stock of that company?—Yes.

Did the business relations which his firm had with the colonies give him good opportunities of knowledge on that subject?—Very good.

In certain business transactions on the part of your firm did you sometimes have occasion to get guarantees?—Yes.

And have you sometimes had guarantees from the City of Glasgow Bank?—We had.

Was your object in getting guarantees to have the caution of some person or body which was regarded as safe?—Exactly.

And were these taken as being so?—Yes.

From your connection with Mr. Potter in regard to these, could you form an opinion as to his view of the worth of the guarantee of the City of Glasgow Bank?—He seemed to consider that it was quite safe.

Then whenever he got the guarantee of the City Bank, he felt that he was quite safe?—Yes.

You have had twenty-five years' experience of Mr. Potter. Have you always found him an honourable, upright, and straightforward man in his dealings?—Quite so.

Not a man who would be guilty of any impropriety or fraud?—Certainly not.

By the LORD ADVOCATE—Had you any knowledge of the internal management of the City of Glasgow Bank?—None whatever. I should think Mr. Potter was a Director of it nearly the whole time of our business connection, but I am not quite sure when he joined.

Did he, or did he not, take an interest in the management of the Bank?—He attended the meetings regularly; I know no more.

You know nothing of his connection with the Bank except the fact that he went to the meetings?—Nothing.

That is all you know?—That is all I know.

Did your firm have any transactions which might be called financing on account of the City Bank?—Yes.

Did Mr. Potter know of it?—Yes.

Did he take any interest in that?—Yes.

Much?—He knew of it; it was done with his knowledge.

Who, on behalf of your firm, transacted in regard to these matters with the Bank? Was it you or Mr. Potter?—I did principally.

With whom did you transact?—With the Bank.

Can you not name anybody?—I scarcely ever had any—with Mr. Stronach, if with any one; but merely with the officials of the Bank as officials.

But who arranged the matter between your firm and the Bank?

300

Evidence for Defence.

—The matter was arranged first by Mr. Potter. I took charge of
the details after it was arranged.

You said Mr. Potter did not know much about details?—I
took all the details; he arranged the matter first.

Had he knowledge sufficient for that?—I should think so; but
he never interfered with the details.

But he had quite sufficient knowledge to arrange the transaction beforehand?—He arranged the transaction beforehand.

Do you think he understood the transaction which he arranged?
—Certainly.

But you did not think him capable of going into the details of
it; do you mean to say that?—I did not mean to say that; I
say he did not actually do so.

But do you mean to convey the impression that Mr. Potter,
though capable of arranging a transaction, was unable to understand the details of it?—No; I simply said that he practically
did not attend to the details of it.

What was the character of those financing transactions of which
you conducted the details?—The City of Glasgow Bank bought
certain shares in the New Zealand and Australian Land Company
from Potter, Wilson & Co. and Holmes, White & Co.

And it was to enable the Bank to meet their acceptances
against these shares that you financed for them?—Yes.

Tell us how that financing was carried out in detail?—The City
of Glasgow Bank accepted drafts by Holmes, White & Co., of
Melbourne, in Potter, Wilson & Co.'s favour; the bills were discounted by Potter, Wilson & Co.

Where did these bills come from?—From Melbourne.

Who signed them there?—Holmes, White & Co.

As drawers?—As drawers.

And then they were sent home?—Yes.

What became of them when they came home signed by Holmes,
White & Co.? Where were they put?—They were discounted.

Where were they kept after they came home?—They were
kept by Potter, Wilson & Co.

Where were they kept?—In their office.

Who kept them?—I kept them.

How many came home at a time?—Fifty or a hundred.

Did not Mr. Potter keep these himself?—Sometimes—partly;
they were kept in the office.

Had you a bundle apiece?—No.

What did you do with them?—After they were accepted by
the Bank, they were discounted, and the proceeds paid into the
Bank.

What was done before they were presented to the Bank for
acceptance?—I don't understand you.

By the LORD JUSTICE-CLERK—They were filled up?—They were
filled up.

The City of Glasgow Bank Trial.

By the LORD ADVOCATE—Was there a date put in?—Certainly.
By whom?—One of our clerks.

Under whose directions?—Under my direction.

What did you make him put in?—The date the mail left Melbourne.

The date about two months before?—Yes.

And then they were presented to the Bank for acceptance, and
then you discounted them?—Yes.

What did you get for all that trouble?—Nothing.

Had you no commission upon it?—None.

What was the object—there must have been some object—in
dating these bills a month or two back, so as to make it appear
that they had been drawn in Melbourne? Why did you do that?
—To save trouble; the bills came home in batches of that kind,
and we filled them up as if they had come from Melbourne by
that mail, which they would have done otherwise.

Suppose you had filled in the date when the bill was presented to the Bank, what would have been the consequence?—
I cannot say.

Do you say that seriously?—I don't understand you.

I am sorry for it, sir. Would you have had any difficulty in
discounting them if you had not put in a mail date prior to——?
—Probably.

Did you not anticipate that you would have had difficulty,
sir?—I never thought of a difficulty; it never struck me.

Why did you not put in the real date?—Because it was the
natural date at which the bills should have come forward.

Did you not wish to conceal that the bills were really filled
up in this country?—Yes.

Why did you wish to conceal that? Was it for no reason;
and if it was for a reason, be so good as to state it? Why
did you wish to conceal it?—I can hardly explain it, it seems
to be so natural. The bills were filled up at the date at which
they ought to have come from Melbourne, to save the trouble
of having them sent out and back again every mail.

But what would have gone wrong if he had known that they
had not gone out to Melbourne, for that was the thing that you
wanted to conceal?

Mr. BALFOUR—That was the Lord Advocate's expression.

The LORD ADVOCATE—The witness assented to it.

The LORD JUSTICE-CLERK—Was that what you meant to say?
—That we did not wish it to be known.

That the bills came blank, and you filled them up?—Yes.

By the LORD ADVOCATE—What was there which might have
followed, if it had been known, which led you to desire that it
should not be known?—Possibly there might have been difficulty
in discounting them.

302

Evidence for Defence

Why?—Because the bankers might have thought that they were finance bills.

They were finance bills?—They were finance bills as far as the City of Glasgow Bank was concerned.

And you did not wish any suspicion of that fact to get abroad? —No.

Now, I ask whether you do not know the fact that these bills were filled up in your office, and dated at your office, in case the clerks at the Bank should see it done, or know that it was done?—No, I do not.

You don't know that?—I do not know that.

In point of fact, they were filled up at your office?—Yes.

And not at the Bank?—Not at the Bank.

Land was purchased by the Bank in or near Poverty Bay?— Yes.

And that land was taken in the names of the individual partners of your firm?—Yes.

Was that purchase made truly on behalf of the Bank?—Yes.

And did you finance the purchase money there too?—Yes.

By Mr. BALFOUR—Were your firm of Potter, Wilson & Co. the agents in this country for Holmes, White & Co.?—They were.

And were those bills sent home by Holmes, White & Co. to your firm as their agents?—Yes.

And was what you did done as their agents?—Yes.

With their authority?—With their authority.

Did it in the least matter whether the bill sent home to be treated as you treated these had the date filled up in blank, and was then put out, or whether it was allowed to remain in Melbourne, and the date written on there, and then set home?— Certainly not.

Did it matter in the slightest degree to any human being?— Not in the slightest degree.

Mr. BALFOUR—I can give your lordship the information which you asked as to the amount of the Land Company stock in the individual name of Mr. Lewis Potter. It was, of ordinary stock, £37,608; and of A preference stock (4 per cent.), £25,073. Then there is some held by him and Hunter and Morton in trust.

By the LORD JUSTICE-CLERK—(On the suggestion of the Lord Advocate)—Is your firm sequestrated?—It is.

By Mr. BALFOUR—[Shown list of proprietors in the Land Company]—I have seen this list.

It includes the names of a number of the best mercantile men and bankers, does it not?—Yes.

Mention some of them?—Colonel Hamilton, Mr. Campbell of Camis Eskan, Mr. Davidson, of the Bank of Scotland; Mr. Ducroz, of London; Mr. Robert Ewing, the late Mr. Alexander Ewing, Mr. Gourlay, and many other names that I know.

The City of Glasgow Bank Trial.

By the LORD ADVOCATE—How many shares does Colonel Campbell hold?—Ordinary stock, £2783; four per cent. preference, £1856.

And Mr. James Morton?—I know nothing of this, except from what has been handed to me. James Morton and James Nicol Fleming, merchants, Glasgow, are put down at £23,825.

And there are a good many City Bank names—Matthew and Hunter?—Yes.

James Nicol Fleming?—Yes.

And Mr. Potter?—Yes.

By Mr. BALFOUR—Mr. Davidson, of the Bank of Scotland, is there?—Yes; he seems to be there.

For how much?—£3340 ordinary stock, and £2227 preference.

And Mr. Henry Davidson, his brother, also?—Yes, £11,805.

Mr. Gairdner, of the Union Bank, and others?—Yes.

JOHN ALEXANDER POTTER.

By Mr. BALFOUR—I am a son of Mr. Lewis Potter, and a partner of Potter, Wilson & Co. Both Potter, Wilson & Co. and Lewis Potter & Co. have been very long established firms, and successful.

What were your father's profits from Lewis Potter & Co.?—From £2500 to £3000 a year, I believe.

So that he had about £8000 a year from his business?—Yes.

Is he proprietor of the lands of Udston, Greenfield, and Burnbank, near Hamilton?—Yes; previous to his sequestration. He bought Udston in 1853, Greenfield in 1857, and Burnbank in 1859. They cost a little under £40,000 altogether. There has been a great rise in their value since he bought them. Minerals have been discovered in them, and are being worked. The properties were valued lately at £120,000. My father has been receiving a return of about £8000 a year from his land, including minerals, and, I should say, about £2000 from other investments. He was a man with an income of from £17,000 to £18,000 a year at the time the Bank stopped. His expenditure never exceeded £3000 a year, which included the expenditure of those members of his family whom he supported. He is a brother-in-law of Mr. Bain, who was the manager of the Edinburgh branch; Mr. Bain is married to his sister. Mr. Bain has been a shareholder of the Bank for some time, and to the extent, I believe, of £1200 stock. A sister of Mr. Potter, Mrs. Davidson, was also a shareholder at the time of the stoppage to the amount of £1450 stock. To both of these persons the stoppage has been ruin.

By the LORD ADVOCATE—When did your father acquire his

Evidence for Defence.

shares in the City Bank?—I understand he had some before
the stoppage of the Bank in 1857.

And then he had some when he became a Director?—I think
he had his Director's qualification at that time, because he was
made a Director shortly after the resuscitation of the Bank
in 1857.

EVIDENCE FOR MR. TAYLOR.

HENRY TAYLOR.

By Mr. MACKINTOSH—I am a son of Mr. William Taylor, and
a partner with him in the firm of Henry Taylor & Sons, grain
merchants. The firm was formed in 1835. The partners at
that time were my grandfather, Henry Taylor; my uncle,
Henry Taylor; and my father, William Taylor. I went into
the business in 1861, and I was assumed a partner on 1st
January, 1868. The partners at that time were my father and
my uncle, Patrick Taylor; my other uncle and my grandfather
having previously died. Patrick Taylor retired on 1st January,
1873, and since then my father and I have been the sole
partners. Our business has been a large one. During the last
five years the average turn-over of the firm would be about
£650,000 per annum. Our business consists in importing grain
from abroad, and selling it to our customers. Our books have
always been regularly kept from the time I first entered the
business. They have been regularly balanced at 31st December.
Bad debts have invariably been written off, and for doubtful
ones provision was made. We have had no speculative transactions in connection with our business; we have confined ourselves to the legitimate business of buying and selling. We
have never had any accommodation bills at all.

When did your firm become customers of the City of Glasgow
Bank?—We have had an account with the City of Glasgow Bank
ever since the formation of the Bank. When I went into the
business in 1861 we had a regular account current, and a No. 2
account, which was the acceptances of the City Bank or the
London Joint-Stock Bank, to our foreign correspondents. Our
ordinary current account was kept in the Argyle Street (West
End) branch. That account has continued to be kept there
ever since till the stoppage of the Bank. Considerable sums
have frequently been at our credit there. Account No. 2 has
been in operation during the last twenty years, to a greater
or less extent. In 1869 another account, No. 3, was opened.
That was an account on which we subsequently obtained overdrafts. It continued in operation until the beginning of 1878.
Prior to my father becoming a Director of the Bank we had
occasionally and repeatedly obtained large advances from it.

The City of Glasgow Bank Trial.

Henry Taylor. How much?—Sometimes we would have £50,000 or £60,000 of unsecured indebtedness to the Bank.

How long might that unsecured indebtedness last?—For several months frequently.

The Bank, having accepted drafts on your account, gave you up the documents?—Yes.

And that was under No. 2 account?—Yes; we had also had advances on No. 3 account previous to 1871. At 31st December, 1876, there was a balance at the debit of No. 3 account of £73,850, including interest. There was paid into the credit of that account during 1877 £19,000 odds, and there was drawn out £14,000, so that the debit was reduced by £5000. In 1878 nothing was drawn out of that account at all. The account frequently fluctuated from time to time. It was squared off more than once. We had a discount account with the City of Glasgow Bank, and also a discount account with one of the other Scotch banks in Glasgow. In February, 1878, we had £110,000 of bills discounted with that other bank, and, at the stoppage of the City of Glasgow Bank, we had £75,000 of bills discounted there. In the spring of 1877 we had bills discounted with the City of Glasgow Bank to the amount of about £110,000. At the time of the stoppage of the Bank that had been reduced to about £90,000.

I believe some of the officials of the Bank had suggested it had better be curtailed ?—Yes; we were asked by Mr. Stronach and Mr. Murdoch on one or two occasions to reduce our discount account. The reason they gave was just that they wished all their discount accounts reduced. We accordingly reduced our account to the amount I have stated. My father joined the Board of the City of Glasgow Bank in 1871. At that time there was standing at his credit in the books of our firm £22,085. His private estate over and above amounted to £10,100—valuing his securities at market prices. I can give the details if required. There was stock of the Glasgow and South-Western Railway, and some heritable property, and other assets. He was worth at that time about £32,000. That was exclusive of my own assets and the assets of my uncle Patrick. The business of the firm continued very profitable down to 1874. In 1874 we made heavy losses. These losses were not of an amount sufficient to exhaust our means; we had always a large surplus of assets over liabilities.

And in 1876 and 1877 did you make considerable profits?— Yes; we made good profits during those years.

At 1st January, 1878, what would be your father's total means? What was the balance at his debit in the firm's books; was it £5507?—Yes; there was at the debit of partners altogether £11,900 odds. The private estates of the partners amounted to £22,000. I have details of that if necessary.

Evidence for Defence.

For instance, there is Langbank, your father's estate; that Henry Taylor. was sold lately for £6500?—Yes; it was bonded to the extent of £4000. There was also stock of the Glasgow and South-Western Railway of the value at market price of £2600 odds. There were shares in the Glasgow Corn Exchange then worth £300. There was a life policy with the Scottish Amicable Society of old date, the surrender value of which was then £400 odds. Then there was a share in a certain ship, for which my father paid £1000, and it was worth fully that in 1878. Then there was City of Glasgow Bank stock worth £5000, taking it at its market value. There were also Scottish Imperial Insurance Company's shares, worth about £1700; and shares of the Glasgow Storage Company, Limited, £2000—that is a very good concern. There were some shares of the State Line Shipping Company in liquidation, and also some shares of the new company as well. We valued the shares of the old company at £1 each, which was about £500, my father having paid a great deal more for them, and he paid for the new shares £5000, and these were valued at their cost price. Over and above these there was furniture, etc. The total of his estate was £20,000, and there was £2000 of my own, made up of City Bank stock and my own dwelling-house.

So there was £22,000, from which the balance at the debit of the capital fell to be deducted, leaving a surplus of £10,000, according to the books?—Yes; in addition to that there was a sum of £6000 put aside in suspense account. The reason for that was that in the end of February, before our balance had been finally adjusted, there were some bad debts that seemed likely to be made in Belfast, and, as we could not at that time exactly ascertain what the amount of these might be, we put £6000 to suspense account to meet any contingencies that might arise. Our firm possessed a large property in Hope Street, Glasgow, for which they paid £40,000, and they expended £14,000 additional upon it. That was bought in 1874. It was valued in our books at £54,000, cost price. Property in that part of Glasgow rose very materially in value between 1874 and 1878, and in the beginning of 1878 we considered that property worth £16,000 more than the sum at which it stood in our books. That fell to be added to the sum I have mentioned; and, taking in the profit upon that property, the total balance in favour of my father and me would be about £32,000. Our firm lost largely, through customers becoming insolvent, directly after the stoppage of the Bank.

How did it happen that you came first to obtain this over-draft from the City of Glasgow Bank?—In 1874, or towards the beginning of 1875, there was a change in the mode of conducting the American business, in which we were largely engaged. Up to that time the drafts of our American cor-

307

The City of Glasgow Bank Trial.

Henry Taylor. respondents were invariably passed upon us free—that is to say, the documents were sent to ourselves direct, and the drafts were drawn at sixty days' sight; but owing to the commercial panic in America the system was changed, and all documents were attached to the drafts, and required to be paid for before we could get possession of any of the goods at all.

In fact, you had to pay cash instead of getting credit?—Yes; it was in connection with that change of circumstances that we got our overdraft. The advances from the Bank were got in the usual way. Either I or my father arranged them; but I generally got them—either ourselves or our cashier. In the beginning of January, 1878, we had a large stock of grain in hand—not less, I think, than from £50,000 to £60,000 worth. It was entirely unburdened. Mr. Stronach knew that we held grain largely.

Had you any debts to speak of except your debt to the Bank?—Almost nothing at all.

Your stock was free, and your assets generally were free?—Yes. My father was an original shareholder of the City of Glasgow Bank. He held at first, I think, £1080 stock. He accepted an allotment of £300 stock additional in 1866, for which he paid £390. In 1873 he accepted a further allotment of £300 stock, for which he paid £600; and, in order to square his holding, he purchased £120 stock, for which he paid £232, which altogether made up £1800 stock. He continued to hold that till the Bank stopped. He never sold a Bank share. I purchased £500 stock in 1873, for which I paid £1000. I did so on my father's recommendation. My uncle Patrick at the same time bought £500 stock, for which he paid £1000. He and I have continued to hold our stock until now. Mr. Stronach was aware we had the Hope Street property. He knew of our expenditure upon it. He never asked to have a formal conveyance of it to the Bank. If he had we would not have objected to grant a formal conveyance. My father handed to Mr. Stronach all the scrip in his possession, Glasgow and South-Western, and other scrip. My father has for a number of years past been much occupied with public matters in Glasgow. At the date of the stoppage of the Bank he was a director of the Scottish Imperial Insurance Company, and of the State Line Steam Shipping Company; he was chairman of the Glasgow Storage Company; a director of the Glasgow Corn Exchange; a trustee of the Clyde Navigation; a member of the Glasgow School Board; chairman of the High School Committee; and a member of the Mearns School Board. He had previously been preceptor of Hutchesons' Hospital for some years, and a magistrate of Glasgow. He was also a director

308

Evidence for Defence.

of several charitable and benevolent institutions. His time was Henry Taylor. very largely occupied in connection with these offices. I should think that for the last fifteen or sixteen years he must have spent not less than four or five hours every day on these matters.

PETER CLOUSTON, residing in 1 Park Terrace, Glasgow, deputy-lieutenant for the County of Lanark, Lord Provost of Glasgow from 1860 to 1863; GEORGE WILSON CLARK, merchant in Glasgow; ROBERT TOD, grain merchant and miller at the Leith Flour Mills, and also in Glasgow; and the Rev. FREDERICK LOCKHART ROBERTSON, minister of St. Andrew's Church, Glasgow; concurred in stating that they had known Mr. Taylor intimately for a great number of years, that he was in their opinion a man of thorough integrity and probity, and incapable of falsifying a balance sheet wilfully.

EVIDENCE FOR MR. WRIGHT.

PATRICK PLAYFAIR, residing at Woodside Terrace, Glasgow, retired merchant, and Lord Dean of Guild of Glasgow; and MICHAEL CONNAL, a member of the firm of William Connal & Co., merchants, Glasgow, and chairman of the School Board of Glasgow; concurred in stating that they had known Mr. Wright for many years, and that he was a man of singular simplicity of character, and in their opinion a man of honour, incapable of being a party to the issuing of a false balance sheet.

EVIDENCE FOR MR. INGLIS.

LAUDERDALE MAITLAND, proprietor of Eccles, in Dumfriesshire, stated that he had been acquainted with Mr. Henry Inglis very nearly since they were boys, that he was a man of very great cultivation and literary taste, and a man of scrupulous honour.

EVIDENCE FOR MR. STRONACH.

JOHN COWAN, a Writer to the Signet in Edinburgh, and one of the trustees under the ante-nuptial marriage-contract of Mr. and Mrs. Robert Stronach; WILLIAM BORLAND, agent in Glasgow for Mr. Robert Stronach; and SAMUEL RALEIGH, manager of the Scottish Widows' Fund, and one of the liquidators of the Western Bank; testified to the uprightness of Mr. Stronach's character, and their confidence in his moral integrity and good intention.

The City of Glasgow Bank Trial.

EVIDENCE FOR MR. SALMOND.

RICHARD HUGHES EVANS, secretary of the Netherlands Indian Steam Navigation Company, Austin Friars, London; MICHAEL CONNAL, formerly a merchant in London and in Glasgow; and ALLAN SANDILANDS, manager of the Palace Hotel, Buxton, in Derbyshire; were called to prove the special defence for Mr. Salmond intimated at the beginning of the trial, and they, along with Richard Raimes, the senior partner of the firm of Raimes, Blanchard & Co., of Leith; and David Cowan, chartered accountant in Glasgow; testified to their belief in Mr. Salmond as an upright and honourable man.

Mr. Asher put in execution of citation against Henry Hall, manager of the Burlington Hotel, London, and stated that although it had been intimated by telegraph that Mr. Hall had left London the previous evening, he had not yet appeared in Court. The facts which Mr. Hall was intended to prove were that Mr. Salmond's name appeared in the bed-book of the Burlington Hotel as having slept there on the following dates:— Every night from 5th to 11th June inclusive, 1876; every night from 3rd to 13th June inclusive, 1877; and from 6th to 13th July inclusive, 1877; and every night from 25th May to 19th June inclusive, 1878.

The Lord Advocate agreed to give an admission of these facts.

[Evidence closed.]

CHAPTER X.

Addresses to Jury.

THE LORD ADVOCATE.

MAY it please your lordships, gentlemen of the jury,—You have listened to evidence in this case in very great detail; and the time has now come when, with the aid of addresses for the Crown, whom I represent, and also for the panels at the bar, you must make up your minds, with the further assistance of the bench, as to the true result of that evidence upon the guilt or innocence of the prisoners. The charge which is brought against them in the libel before you is, I need not say, a very serious one. The only points which you have to consider are the first three in this indictment, in relation to balance sheets published in the years 1876, 1877, and 1878. But before saying a word as to the particulars of the charge, I desire to say to you, once for all, that even in this Court it is impossible to disguise the fact that the unfortunate state of the City of Glasgow Bank has been for months past the subject of private conversation and of public comment throughout the length and breadth of the land; and I say so for this reason, in order that I may call your attention to the object of this prosecution at the instance of the Crown. It is to lay before you that which those who conversed about it and wrote about it have not been thoroughly conversant with—the real facts of the case; and I shall ask you, and I trust you will make it your honest endeavour in considering the facts of this case, to dismiss entirely from your minds what may have been said or written or printed out of doors that is in the least degree calculated to prejudice in your estimation the prisoners at the bar, and to endeavour to come to a dispassionate judgment upon the facts, and nothing but the facts, which have now been for the first time put in evidence before you.

Gentlemen, the charge is based upon the fact that certain abstracts were published from year to year purporting to represent the true state of affairs of the Bank, and that the abstracts so published were in point of fact not true, but false; and, in the second place, that the falsehood of these abstracts was not mere matter of chance or accident, but the result of intention or design to conceal from the shareholders and from the public the true state of affairs of the Bank. In each of these years you will find,

The City of Glasgow Bank Trial.

Lord Advocate.

gentlemen, that there is a double charge—there is an alternative charge—and I had better explain to you precisely the effect of that. There is a charge, in the first instance, against each and all of the panels of having been art and part in fabricating these balance sheets with the intention of deceiving, concealing, and misrepresenting the true state of the Bank's affairs. If they had merely prepared a false balance sheet, and had done nothing with it but laid it aside or put it in the fire, that would not have constituted a crime according to the law of Scotland, because it would merely have been a guilty intention abandoned on second thoughts. The whole gravamen of the charge is, that, having prepared it with that purpose, the purpose was put into execution by issuing that false and fabricated balance sheet to the shareholders of the Bank. But then, under the second alternative, it is not necessary, in order to constitute the guilt of the accused, that they should have been parties to the fabrication of the balance sheet. It is quite sufficient to constitute the alternative offence if, knowing that it was a false balance sheet, and that it had been fabricated or prepared for the purpose of concealing the true state of the Bank, they lent their names and authority to the issuing of it to the shareholders and the public, with, of course, the same intention to deceive.

Now, gentlemen, I think it would be as well, in the course of the observations which I have to address to you, to consider, in the first place, whether there was falsification of all or of any of these balance sheets; and, in the second place, to consider whether that was intentional and with a design to conceal and misrepresent the true state of the Bank. I cannot deal with that second question without some inquiry into the state of the Bank, and that involves, perhaps, a still more important question for you to consider—Whether, assuming the state of the Bank, it was known to the Directors and to each of them. And, lastly, if you are satisfied that the balance sheet was prepared falsely— that the Bank was in a condition requiring, in their opinion, misrepresentation, and if they did issue these abstracts with the view of misrepresenting the position of the Bank, then you have to consider which of these persons at the bar you are to hold guilty of the crime. Now, in regard to the published balance sheets, the abstracts which you have upon pages 3, 6, and 9 of the indictment, I do not think it can for one moment be doubted, in the face of the evidence you have heard, that they are false and fabricated. I am not going into details upon this matter; I shall have a word to say upon it by and by. But just let me call your attention to the balance sheet of 1876, and point out to you the general character of the alterations that were made in order to lay a false state of affairs before the shareholders, because it humbly appears to me that the very character of those alterations is exceedingly suggestive of the object and purpose

312

The Lord Advocate (Watson)
Counsel for Prosecution.

Addresses to Jury.

for which they were made. In the first place, the general result of these is to reduce both sides of the account, and, speaking in round figures, the result of the alterations in each of the years in question is to reduce the assets of the Bank by a couple of millions or upwards, and to reduce the liabilities of the Bank by a couple of millions or upwards. A question or two was put in the course of the evidence which seemed rather to suggest that some reliance was to be placed, on the part of the accused, upon the fact that the manipulation of both sides of the balance sheet resulted in the same figures standing at balance, as capital, reserve fund, and profit and loss. That is no test whatever of the truth or falsity of a balance sheet. The purpose of such a balance sheet or abstract is to disclose honestly to the shareholders and the public the amount of business the Bank is doing, their turnover, the extent of their transactions; and it must be obvious to you that they might have altered the balance sheet by six or eight millions more, by taking that sum off both sides, with precisely the same result of leaving those figures standing at balance as information to the public. But would that have been a right or proper thing to do—to suggest that the Bank was carrying on a business of precisely half the extent with precisely half the amount of money got upon deposit with which they were entrusted? It is a question for you, and I rather think that when you come to examine into details you will find that the general purpose of representing that the Bank was doing a much smaller trade than it really was doing in money, was coupled with this, that it was also intended and calculated to represent that they were doing a much better and a much sounder trade than they actually had. Because they diminished the amount of their liabilities by cutting off large sums—in this case we are always dealing with large sums, nothing short of hundreds of thousands and millions—on both sides of the account; and thus they put out of sight an enormous quantity of bill transactions which might give a clue to the public, who knew in a general way the amount of the dealings of some whom I shall call the leading customers of the Bank—the gentlemen who absorbed a great deal of its capital from 1870 onwards, and who, at the time the Bank stopped, had had advanced to them about three-fifths of the whole money the Bank had lent. That was one object gained; but in order to keep the two sides of the account square they had to diminish the assets—that is to say, what they held in the shape of debts due to them and in the shape of investments and other securities. And how is that side of the account dealt with? Of course, at first it looks a very fair thing to reduce assets; but this is done in order to preserve the balance on the two sides of the account; and then this feature is very skilfully introduced—if you look at the top of the left hand page, Article 1, on the credit side—they frame their abstract so as to reduce

The City of Glasgow Bank Trial.

bills of exchange and so forth, and that kind of stock-in-trade is reduced in 1878 by about three millions, which is more than the deduction from the other side of the account ; but then they compensate for that by turning credit accounts—outstanding sums due them by customers—a portion of them, into Government stock, Exchequer bills, railway and other stocks, debentures and balances in the hands of foreign correspondents. In other words, while they diminish their assets upon the credit side of the account, they perform this further operation on the credit side of the account that they take off some from an inferior class of assets and add these to assets of a better class, thereby leading any one who examined the balance sheet to believe that the Bank had £700,000 or £800,000 more of good investments than they in reality held, and about two millions less of floating bills and credit accounts, which they might or might not recover.   And I need hardly suggest to you, who are conversant with mercantile affairs, that assets in the shape of outstanding securities and balances due by firms of large dealings, like Smith, Fleming & Co., James Nicol Fleming & Co., Morton & Co., and Innes Wright & Co., are not, on the whole, such good assets or reliable assets as Government stocks and balances in the hands of correspondents. So much for these two sides.   But that is not quite all.   They have a reserve fund every year of £450,000, and that seems to have been a sort of stock reserve fund that is carried along. Well, it was explained to you by the gentlemen who have examined the books of the Bank how that fund was raised.*   There were sums credited which they had not got—in other words, they professed to have received interest which they had not got.   They got a lower rate of interest or none at all, and what they had not got they carried into profit and loss account, and finally into a reserve fund—consisting of what they never had got, and what, according to all human probability, they had not the slightest chance of ever getting.   Then the next profit and loss in the balance sheet for 1876 is £136,000.   These items are made up and dealt with in precisely the same way throughout all the three years and the three balances with which we are dealing. Now, how was that profit and loss account got up?   I am certain you will accept the statements made in regard to it, because, being quite distinctly and plainly stated and explained to you by the accountants who appeared as witnesses for the Crown, not one single word was put in cross-examination by any one of my numerous friends who represent the panels at the bar tending to shake or discredit the statements which they made.   They said, "That which you are dividing as profit and loss year by year was really never earned at all."   You must know very well that the profit and loss account for a year amounts to the earnings for

* See the evidence of Dr. M'Grigor and Messrs. Jamieson and Muir.

the year; and it would not be a matter of imputation against any banker who was making up a balance sheet that, in stating his account of profit and loss, he should include in it interest which was regularly paid, although it had not come to hand. There is nothing whatever wrong in that. If their income was coming in steadily each year, they had quite a right to regard it as earnings and income, and to distribute it. But that is not what was done here. They bring into this account interest upon outstanding and unpaid balances. The principal was not paid, the interest was not paid, and they were speculating in Australian stock to recoup their deficit upon these transactions; and in that state of matters they all speak hopefully as to the ultimate profit to be obtained from that source. But how about the immediate distribution? And they actually go on dividing and paying dividends, rising from 11 per cent. in the year 1876 to 12 per cent. in 1877 and 1878; whereas, if they had struck off the sum of £125,000 odds, calculated as interest due on those debtor balances, there would not have been a sixpence to divide. If there had been any reasonable ground for so putting it, that might have been some justification; but it humbly appears to me that it was just as unjustifiable as it would be in any man who had £50,000 lent to a debtor who was unable to repay him to go on spending interest which he had not got, and which there was very little probability he would ever get, as his yearly income. The result is perfectly plain. That money was divided among the shareholders. That money was not in the Bank. It stood in the books as due upon those book balances which they were speculating to recoup, and therefore they paid it away out of some other asset; and when they were paying away those dividends they were simply eating into the capital of the Bank, and paying the shareholders dividend out of their own stock, if, indeed, there was any stock to pay it out of at all, which is very doubtful.

Now, gentlemen, there are in process, and these have been adverted to in the evidence, some very remarkable documents, which, I understand, you will be allowed to examine for yourselves at a future stage of this case. I refer to what are called the scroll abstracts for the years 1876, 1877, and 1878. Let me tell you that you must not be misled into the view that these things constitute the crime which the Crown says the panels have committed. The crime which the Crown alleges has been committed is that these abstract balances in the indictment before you, being false, were given to the public as true, with the view of misrepresenting the state of the Bank. There is no charge founded upon these scroll abstracts, but they are very important links of evidence in the present case. They show the hand of the fabricator; they are the key to his work. You can reduce these balance sheets in the way they have done, with similar

The City of Glasgow Bank Trial.

results, in millions of different ways, by taking figures of a certain
kind away here and putting figures of a certain kind on there.
But this is one way of attaining the end to be attained, to reduce
the two sides of the balance sheet, to magnify the character of
the assets by giving them a character which they had not, and to
conceal the amount and character of the liabilities by striking
them off wholesale—a practice carried so far that in 1878 the
credit account on bills outstanding and due was represented to
the extent of £200,000 as solid gold in reserve in the coffers of
the Bank. It was only that year that it occurred. That is
the end to be attained; and these scroll abstracts will show you
one way of doing it, and they show very probably, indeed almost
certainly, the way in which it was done. But it has no more
connection with the charge which is before us than the very common case which occurs in forgery, where you find A's name at a
bill written by B, in order to represent A's. The bill passes into
currency, and when A refuses to pay it because it is forged, you
find a sheet of paper in the handwriting of B, the forger, with
all sorts of signatures of A written upon it, so as to make the
forger sufficiently expert to commit the final act. There is
just the same kind of connection here. You can trace the
mind and intent of the forger in the one case because he is trying
to acquire sufficient expertness to enable him to fabricate the
signature of another. And in this case, in the same way,
you can see the steps by which the ultimate results which are
embodied in those balances have been attained—by a process of
calculation, making the two false ends fit in—a process which
is very easily performed when you come to deal with figures.

If that is so—and I think, upon the face of these balance sheets,
if I have correctly represented them, and I shall be in your judgment if I have not done so—the next question is, what was the
purpose of doing it? It could hardly be accidental. Mistakes
will often occur in matters of figures, but a mistake that goes
two millions wrong, or four millions, taking the two sides of the
transactions, and yet brings out a consistent and even sum total
on both sides, is not one of the kind of freaks generally played
by fortune or chance. I am going to take just now the effect
of the untrue balances. I shall ask your attention by and by to
the persons who are responsible for it. It is impossible to dis-
sociate the one thing from the other ; and in dealing with its
truth or falsehood, when we come to the state of the Bank, it will
be very necessary for you, in the narrative which I shall be compelled to submit to you in order to make the case intelligible, to
keep in view who are the parties that appear upon the scene,
and what is their connection with it, and what their amount of
knowledge of the state of the Bank. The charge in the libel
before you is that the balances were fabricated in order to conceal
the true state of the Bank's affairs. Of course, that is a

Addresses to Jury.

meaningless and idle proposition, unless it be the fact that the Bank's affairs are thereby concealed, or that they stood in need of concealment. You might have alterations upon a balance sheet, and it might turn out upon an examination of the affairs of the Bank that the Bank was, on the whole, better than the balance sheet showed. That would be to a jury conclusive evidence that there was no intention to misrepresent. But I am afraid that you will hardly be able to come to that lenient conclusion on the facts of the present case. Because what was the state of the Bank? I must make some observations upon the state of the Bank at the time of its stoppage, because there is some reflex light thrown by it upon the actual state during the period in question ; but I beg you to keep in view, in fairness to the panels as well as for the ends of justice—on the part of the Crown I ask you to keep in view that that is not the question as against the panels ; the question as against them is—the state of the Bank now being ascertained to be so and so, what did they know, whilst the Bank was carrying on business, as to the results which are stated in those abstract balance sheets? We know now that in July, 1876-77-78—for that is the date of the annual meetings at which those abstracts were published—this Bank was represented by those placed in the conduct of its affairs as a solvent and prosperous concern, able to pay 11 or 12 per cent. dividend to its shareholders, and with brilliant prospects for the future. These prospects, according to the representation of the balance sheet, never were fairer, never more prosperous, than as at the balance of 5th June, 1878 ; and we know that in four months from that date the Bank was bankrupt, and its losses were roughly estimated by a professional gentleman who looked into its affairs at millions sterling—I need hardly tell you the amount. You heard the evidence of Mr. Jamieson, who made an investigation on behalf of the other banks, who refused their aid, and refused it—it is not by any means unimportant to know—the moment they saw the enormous amount of the dealings of the Bank with certain firms, to whose transactions I shall have to refer you more particularly. I quite admit that the failure and stoppage of the Bank on the 2nd of October might well be a surprise to the Directors ; but it does not in the slightest degree follow that they were ignorant of the position of the Bank, or the position of its accounts, or ignorant of the fact that these balance sheets were entirely false and fabricated. It is a strange thing that when they first begged assistance, and when Mr. Wenley was in communication with them, they were exceedingly unwilling to have any examination of the books—exceedingly unwilling. Necessity drove them ultimately to show their whole hand ; it would not hide. But they declined at first even to let a neutral man in a confidential position make an inquiry in the interest of both parties ; and he was merely to state the result without giving the

The City of Glasgow Bank Trial.

figures from the books, or exposing any secret, or telling with whom they were dealing. When the Directors found that inquiry had come to be inevitable, and Mr. Wenley was taking his leave, Mr. Potter expressed, in marked terms, the hope that an examination of the books would be dispensed with, and that the banks would give assistance without it. In one point of view, if the state of the Bank was known, it is not surprising that they should be unwilling that the books should be gone into, because the books would have exposed the position of matters, and at that date—I don't want to take all the firms, but I shall take three, the worst of them, viz., Morton & Co., Smith, Fleming & Co., and James Nicol Fleming—at that moment the advances from the Bank were to the following extent:—Morton & Co., £2,173,000; Smith Fleming & Co., £1,968,000; and James Nicol Fleming, who has been liquidating for several years—that is to say, paying off his debts—at least, that is the general meaning of the word—had the modest sum of £1,238,000; making for these three firms the respectable total of indebtedness to the Bank of £5,317,000, and that was a state of matters that had been growing gradually; it was nothing new. In 1875—that is, before the period of dealings of the present Directors began, because the Board has remained constituted as at present since the accession of Mr. Wright, who came in the place of Mr. James Nicol Fleming, and Mr. Stronach, who became Manager in place of his brother in December, 1875—when the Board, as constituted at the date of the stoppage, began its operations, the state of these accounts was as follows:—Morton & Co. had £1,380,000; Smith, Fleming & Co. had £1,661,000; James Nicol Fleming had £1,005,000—in all, £4,046,000; so that the increase of their indebtedness between the time of the Directors entering on office and the stoppage of the Bank, or in three years, amounted to £1,333,000. It may have been that to a person who knew these figures the stoppage of the Bank could hardly be a surprise; on the other hand, it might be a surprise, and yet these Directors might have had quite sufficient knowledge of the state of the Bank to have made it an entirely wrong and criminal thing for them to sanction the issue of such a balance sheet as any one of these three. They may have believed that Australian land would so richly repay the investments that they had made in it as to recoup their deficits; but even on the very best of the evidence that we have had upon this point, either in cross-examination by the panel's counsel or in chief from their own witnesses, it only comes to this, that it was a matter in the future. It was a matter of hope and expectation; it was not a case of holding security, and ample security, against a present debt. The failure of the Bank may have surprised them, because they may have hoped, by more speculations of that sort, by getting another £500,000 to invest here or there, to be able, some day or other,

Addresses to Jury.

to put these accounts into what they were trying to do—a state
of order. But the mistake, and worse than mistake, committed
throughout all those years of management—and you will see who
were responsible for it, and in the knowledge of it—was this,
that they treated these as good assets, assuming that there were
good securities against them, whereas they knew—at all events,
whether they knew the full amount in £ s. d. is not a material
thing—that there were deficits so serious and so extensive that to
enable the Bank to recoup them they were obliged to enter into
transactions which they themselves recorded on the face of their
own minutes as not being legitimate banking transactions.

Now, gentlemen, I shall proceed to inquire as to the history of
these three accounts, and I shall take them because they are quite
sufficient of themselves to account for the insolvency of the Bank ;
and I shall just ask you to follow me through some details in
order to see whether it be the fact that the Directors of the
Bank did not know of them. Now, if they did know of them,
they knew the cause of the rottenness of the Bank ; because it can
hardly be suggested for one moment that all that enormous deficit,
which became apparent whenever there was an impartial investigation—ay, and a very hurried one in the month of October,
1878—it can hardly be suggested that all that enormous loss of
millions occurred between 5th June, 1878, and the 2nd October
of that year. I have not heard such a suggestion, and I can
hardly think that you will be asked to believe that it occurred in
four months, when the facts clearly show that it was not so. And
I think they also clearly show that the Directors knew very well
about these accounts, knew that they were very bad accounts,
knew that, instead of reducing these bad accounts, they were
going on increasing more and more. It may be that they were
flinging good money after bad in the hope of recouping themselves in the end ; but they knew they were sending that
money after the bad in the hope of getting it back ; and they
must have known that these accounts, so enormous as they were
in extent, must have seriously affected the state of the Bank.
At least it is for you to judge whether it would have been possible
for any man, knowing their extent, not to know at the same time
that they placed the Bank in a position, if not of ruin, at least of
the most imminent peril. It is all very well to say, and I have
no doubt it will be said, that these gentlemen did not attend to
details of business, that they managed large transactions, but did
not go into details, and therefore must not be judged hardly about
their knowledge of results and about what you discover from the
books of the Bank. Why, Mr. Jamieson only made a rough estimate after he had been four hours at work, and it took the
investigators, with the aid of a large staff of clerks, a fortnight to
work it out. But what were they doing? They were unravelling
the transactions for years back, which these gentlemen during

319

The City of Glasgow Bank Trial.

Lord
Advocate. these years were carrying on with their open eyes, from Board day to Board day, in the management of the Bank. It is one thing to spend so many hours in investigating the acts of a body of Directors from what is recorded in their minutes and ledgers, and quite another thing to be one of the body of Directors from day to day, and from week to week carrying on these transactions —refusing advances to-day and giving them to-morrow. All that an accountant can do is to try to discover from the books what the Directors had been about; and therefore it will never do to say to you, who have a general knowledge of business, that a body of Directors are to be held as justified in giving persons enormously indebted to the Bank, Board day after Board day, more credits and more money, until the advances come up to millions, and then turn round and say, "We really are very simple, quiet, honest fellows; we did not look into details; two millions are gone, but how were we to know?" Well, gentlemen, keep this other fact in view, in justice to a certain portion of the servants of the Bank. The City Bank was not all bad management. On the contrary, there was one portion of its affairs that was exceedingly well managed—I refer to the business of the Bank conducted at its branches in Scotland. You have it in evidence from the inspector of branches, Mr. Miller—against whose evidence there is no suggestion, because it is founded upon the most explicit facts—that for years past the average actual earnings of the branches of the Bank were £70,000 per annum. That was made after writing off about £10,000 a year for bad debts. But there was another cause of the prosperity of the branches. It was very well explained by more than one witness. In dealing with advances at the branches, the Manager (Mr. Miller says) was very strict about getting security. He was very strict about parting with a penny in the way of loan at the branches until it was covered by money's worth; and the result of it is, as I have stated to you, that the earnings or legitimate profits of the Bank at its branches in Scotland during many years of its trading before its stoppage, were enough to pay a dividend of 7 per cent. on its paid-up capital of one million. So that if the company had traded through its branches alone, and instead of dealing with Morton & Co., Smith, Fleming & Co., and Nicol Fleming, had simply deposited the money they had in Glasgow with another bank, and had got deposit receipt rates upon it, they would have saved their capital and their money, and would have been able to pay a dividend of 7 per cent. to their shareholders. But that illustrates and very strongly brings out this point, that if the management at the branches was good, the management at the head office, which is responsible for all the enormous losses of the Bank, was as bad as that of the branches was good. We shall see whether there was the same strictness there in parting with money. I have not the least doubt of the perfect accuracy of

Addresses to Jury.

Mr. Miller's statement that the Manager, Mr. Stronach, was exceedingly strict in getting proper security from a poor fellow in the country who wanted to get a little money in advance; and if they had only applied the same rule to some of those so-called capitalists, who indulged in those firm-names I have repeated so often, it would have been a great deal better for the Bank.

Now, gentlemen, to return to those advances, and to the period to which I will direct your attention, namely, the period of the present management. In the evidence of John Fleming there was a good deal to suggest that Alexander Stronach did not always, in giving him advances, take the Bank Directors into his confidence, and that specially applies to John Fleming's evidence about the transactions of the years 1870 and 1874. That is quite possible. But we have no question here about Alexander Stronach. The case I put to you is this, that whatever Alexander Stronach may have done, his successor, Robert Stronach, the prisoner at the bar, did not, in that respect, follow his example. On the contrary, I think you will find that he was aware of the nature of those accounts and their danger, that he was so impressed with the character of those accounts, and the deadly peril to the existence of the Bank that their continued indebtedness involved, that, like a sensible man, and acting the part of an honest man, he brought that fact clearly before the Directors before he would accept office, and accepted office only upon this condition—that the Directors would act with him and keep him right and help him with these accounts. The Directors accepted upon that condition, and I venture to say this, that it will require on the part of the Directors, other than the Manager, some much plainer testimony than any evidence in this case affords that they departed from that arrangement—that Robert Stronach, instead of enforcing fulfilment of the sole condition upon which he accepted office, took the whole responsibility of these accounts upon himself, and managed them at his own hand, concealed them from the Directors, so that these gentlemen, only having heard the note of warning in 1875, entirely forgot it, and lapsed into a state of belief that there was nothing wrong with these accounts at all. The thing is hardly credible that when a Manager comes forward and says, " I will try to help you out of this ugly position into which the Bank's affairs have got, provided you will apply yourselves to giving me efficient aid in dealing with these accounts," he should all at once have resiled from that position, and declined their aid and taken the whole responsibility upon himself, and that they should have forgotten all about it or been ignorant of it. I venture to say that, after the plain terms in which that was brought before them, it would have been the grossest breach of duty on the part of each and all of those gentlemen if they had not given the Manager the assistance he desired; still more a breach of duty if, knowing the danger of those

The City of Glasgow Bank Trial.

accounts, and knowing how they affected the position of the
Bank, they stood by for three years, knowing that there was a
mine beneath them that might explode at any moment, without
being at the trouble to inquire how those accounts were going on.
Gentlemen, that this was brought before them, and most distinctly
brought before them, very plainly appears from the letter of the
Manager, and I must ask you to permit me to read it:—

City of Glasgow Bank,
28th December, 1875.

Gentlemen,—In thanking you for the offer of the management
of this Bank which you have kindly made to me, I beg to state
my willingness to accept it. But before undertaking this responsibility, I deem it prudent to ask the Board to minute its
approval of the policy which has been pursued of supporting several
accounts of an unsatisfactory character since my brother discontinued personally to manage the Bank; and, further, to appoint a
committee to investigate and place on record what may have been
the exact position of these accounts and the advances generally
when my brother ceased to be Manager, and also to act and
guide me in any important detail therewith connected, as I am in
no wise responsible up to this date for the state of certain advances
which I need not here particularise.

You will, I hope, admit the reasonableness of the precaution
which this request involves; and I feel you will the more
readily do this when you consider that whilst we are all hopeful
that these advances may eventuate without loss, yet the working
out of them must of necessity be a work of some time. And when
you also consider that there may be changes in the Board during
this time, and I should have to explain to new Directors what you
know regarding my connection with the inception of these
advances.

Gentlemen, that was a communication surely calculated to
make the Directors consider seriously their position, whatever
may have been their knowledge of there being unsatisfactory
accounts before. It gave them distinct warning; it gave them
this warning, that although the accounts might eventuate
without loss, that was a matter which only time could decide.
And he says that he did not need to particularise them. I
don't think you will have any difficulty in making up your minds
as to the meaning of that word—saying, in other words, as
plain as language could put it, "I won't recapitulate these
accounts here, because you know them well enough." I need
not tell you this, that if the Directors had not known what
these accounts were that were indicated in that letter, it was
the gravest matter of duty to the Bank that they should
instantly require an explanation, and ask, what are those accounts
referred to in that statement—what are those accounts which
may eventuate without loss, but, of course, may eventuate in
loss—what are those accounts which will take a long time to
realise before we know whether there will be loss or not?
But it was obviously quite unnecessary for them to make any

Addresses to Jury.

such inquiry, and, accordingly, they made none, but took the Lord matter into their full consideration. Accordingly, Mr. Leresche, Advocate. at p. 75, G——

Lord Justice-Clerk—Don't you think you had better take the minute along with the letter?

Lord Advocate—I am going to take it along with the letter. Mr. Leresche's account of what took place at the meeting on the 30th December, 1875, is—"There were present Messrs. Taylor, Potter, Stewart, Salmond, Inglis, and Wright. Mr. Alexander Stronach having retired, that was the whole Board at the time. On that occasion the burning of notes was again adjourned, and I again left the room; but I cannot say whether I left the agenda book behind me or not. The Board had a long deliberation that day. I should say it must have been two hours." Your lordship in the chair put a question to Mr. Leresche, "Are you speaking from recollection alone?" and his reply was, "I remember it, because the 30th was the occasion when the letter of the Manager was read accepting the appointment." Then he is recalled after the whole of the Directors, with the exception of Mr. Stronach, had considered the matter. Mr. Leresche is recalled—because he was not permitted to be present at important deliberations upon these matters. They had a very singular way in that Bank of dealing with their Secretary. The Manager conducts his private correspondence, not through the Secretary of the Bank, who ought to be trusted officially in such a case, but through a private clerk, who communicates directly with the Manager, and conceals a lot of information in regard to these matters that would otherwise in the course of bank management have gone to the Secretary. And I must do him (the Manager) the credit to say that the Directors pursued precisely the same course in regard to Mr. Leresche, because as soon as an important question like this came up—you will see one or two instances of it by and by—again the Secretary of the Bank gets the hint that his room would be rather more desirable than his company. Out he walks, and the Directors deliberate; and then they write up their own result of the deliberations that take place in the absence of the Secretary, and hand it over to Mr. Leresche in order that it may be engrossed in the minutes. There was a book called the agenda book that was prepared by Mr. Leresche for the meeting. He noted down the business that he knew of that was to come before the meeting, and then the chairman, or some other component member of the meeting, wrote opposite that piece of business the way in which it had been disposed of. On this occasion, at the end of two hours, the doors of the council chamber are opened, and Mr. Leresche is called in, and the result of their deliberations upon the Manager's most important letter is handed to Mr.

The City of Glasgow Bank Trial.

Leresche in the form of a resolution on a slip. It is in the
handwriting of two of the Directors—the first part of it is
in Mr. Taylor's, and the last part of it in Mr. Inglis', handwriting; and that was embodied by Mr. Leresche in the minute
of the meeting of the Directors. I must ask you to attend to
its terms. This is the result of their deliberations. Mind that
Stronach was not there. They cannot say it was Stronach this
time. I have no doubt they will say it was Stronach on some
other occasions, but they cannot say it was he this time,
because he was not there. The result of their deliberations was
embodied in this document, which was under the hand of two
of themselves—Mr. Taylor, the chairman of the Board, and
Mr. Henry Inglis. The minute, which is just a copy of the
resolution, is as follows:—"A letter was read from Robert
Summers Stronach, of date 28th December, 1875, accepting the
office of Manager of the Bank, and the same having been considered and approved of, is ordered to be recorded in the minute-
book; and all the members of the Board of Directors a committee to comply with his request." And then they add—"The
Directors wish also to record, on their own behalf, the fact
that the matters alluded to in the letter in question were not
at any time brought before them by the late Manager." Does
not that resolution assume, from beginning to end of it, that
all these gentlemen knew the matters alluded to, knew the
unsatisfactory nature of these accounts? They consider this
letter, and approve of it; and the only thing they take exception
to is a statement to the effect—or rather they guard themselves against a statement—that these matters had been brought
before them by the former Manager. With the exception of
that single point they accept the letter. They do not for a
moment dispute their knowledge of the matters to which the
letter refers; and in order that these accounts may be considered with the aid of all, instead of remitting the subject
to a small committee, they appoint the whole body of the
Directors to act as a committee with Mr. Stronach. Therefore,
I think it quite impossible for any one to suggest that these
Directors had no knowledge at that time of the accounts—no
knowledge as to what was the character of those accounts,
or to deny the desire of Mr. Stronach to be aided with them.
Now, in what follows, gentlemen, I am sorry to say we are
left to evidence from the records of the Directors themselves.
It is most important in this case to know what was the state
of the Bank, what was the knowledge of the state of the Bank,
and one of the most important questions is how far, after
they had come to that resolution to aid Mr. Stronach, the
Directors continued to have knowledge of these accounts. I
shall go over what took place in the interval between that letter
and the last balance sheet and the stoppage of the Bank as

Addresses to Jury.

shortly as I can consistently with bringing the details before you, because it humbly appears to me that this is a very vital part of the case, because, as I have said before, without a knowledge that the state of the Bank required misrepresentation and concealment, I could hardly ask you to return a verdict of guilty against any one of the accused. I think, however, that a consideration of the different steps that took place after the date of that appeal made to them by the Manager will show very clearly that they did continue in the knowledge of these accounts. You already have known that these grew enormously, and you will see how they grew. Take Morton & Co. for instance. Morton stands at £1,380,000 in 1875; in 1876 (which was just the year after this point had been brought up by the Manager) he mounts up to £1,885,000; in 1877 he is reduced a little bit—to £1,771,000; and then in the year 1878 he is up a long way—to £2,173,000; or, in round numbers, he had got £900,000 more of the Bank's money than he had in 1875. Now, I don't think there will be any attempt in this case to suggest to you that these gentlemen covered their indebtedness to the Bank—that either Mr. Morton or any one of them did so. There is no suggestion of it. You might as well suggest that there ought to be no liquidation and no calls because there is no deficit, and the Bank is really a healthy concern, if they could only realise their Australian land and shares. But you have a curious insight into what was known about that in the book kept by Morris, the private secretary, who superseded the most important part of Mr. Leresche's functions—the private securities book, in which there was kept a note of the special securities held against cash credit advances and bills, and which was brought to a kind of balance in 1877. It was spoken to by Morris. There were three big accounts in it—Nicol Fleming's; Smith, Fleming & Co.'s; and Morton & Co.'s. That certainly was a very wonderful illustration of the kind of business which the Bank was doing with these people at that time. There were securities stated by Mr. Nicol Fleming equal to the amount of his indebtedness, which was very large. But when you come to look at the securities, they consisted, as they did in every case, to a large extent of this—£200,000 or £300,000 as the stock of the firm indebted; and that was dealt with as a special security available to the Bank. But the idea of taking a man's stock, with which you permit him to trade, as a special security, is a most extraordinary fallacy, and that must have been known to these men. You take the security of a man's stock in case of his failure to pay; but suppose he fails and loses his stock-in-trade, the security is also lost with the stock-in-trade. Then, again, they insure his life for £100,000; but unless they intend to poison him in the Bank parlour, and realise in that way, I don't

The City of Glasgow Bank Trial.

see how they were entitled to set that down as a cover to the extent of £100,000. And then there was what I have no doubt was done in perfect good faith, but it just exposes the inadequacy of the whole thing; it was explained by Morris that there was a quantity of shares at par value of £62 10s., and by a calculation which he made he found out that if he added 400 per cent. to the value of these shares, he brought up the total to between £700,000 or £800,000, and covered Mr. Fleming's indebtedness. It was only in that way that Fleming's indebtedness was covered. But even in that book there was not the slightest attempt to represent Morton's advances as covered, and, accordingly, his securities, which include £65,000 of insurance, bring out a deficit of £840,000 upon his account, even supposing his capital was realised as well as his life policy. That word "deficit" has a considerable deal of meaning in this case. This much must be said of Mr. Morton that, although he had enormous dealings with the Bank, he is a gentleman who keeps very much in the dark, and the way in which the Bank dealt with him was not calculated to relieve his ongoings from that obscurity. He is found in connection with all concerns and things. When you are going to make a Pastoral Association by way of a little bank speculation in Australia, when you are going to buy shares or going to Poverty Bay or elsewhere with a view to recoup the losses of the Bank, Mr. Morton is always in the neighbourhood, and is a large holder; but I am sorry to say he is a large debtor to the Bank himself. Morton's account does not appear much, but it does appear, and it was treated with very great secrecy by the Directors. You have in the minute of 11th January, 1877—"It was proposed and agreed that the Bank should accept drafts by Glen Walker & Co. to the extent of £100,000 to retire a like amount drawn by Holmes, White & Co., Melbourne, on account of James Morton & Co. The securities at present held against Holmes, White & Co.'s draft to be placed as security against the drafts of Glen Walker & Co. Letter to be obtained from James Morton & Co. to this effect, and no drafts to be accepted until this letter is in possession of the Bank." There were present at the meeting—Mr. Inglis in the chair, Mr. Potter, Mr. Salmond, Mr. Stewart, Mr. Wright, Mr. Taylor, and Mr. Stronach. Then on the 18th of the same month—"With reference to the minute of 11th January authorising the Bank to accept the drafts of Glen Walker & Co. to the extent of £100,000, so as to replace a like amount drawn by Holmes, White & Co., it was considered that the letter of Messrs. James Morton & Co., dated 16th August, 1876, and referred to in Bank's minute of 17th August, 1876, was sufficient authority to the Bank to adopt the securities which were held against Holmes, White & Co.'s drafts as applicable to the new arrange-

Addresses to Jury.

ment." The letter referred to is a letter on page 32 of the smaller print of documents, to the following effect :—

> In consideration of your arranging with Messrs. Glen Walker & Co., of Melbourne, or any other firm, for the drawing of credits to take place of a like amount at present discounted by us, we hereby authorise you to transfer to a separate account in security for same a proportionate amount of the securities held by you on our account—it being understood that our account is to be credited with the amount of the credits given out during this arrangement, and advising us of same.
>
> JAS. MORTON.   Jas. Morton & Co.

Now, gentlemen, that account was under the consideration of the Bank, and I must ask you to attend to what Mr. Leresche, in his evidence, says—"In the agenda book, under date 11th January, 1877, there were present—Mr. Inglis (chairman), Messrs. Potter, Salmond, Stewart, Wright, Taylor, and the Manager. The ordinary business of that meeting was closed by a letter from Mr. Bain, and the initials of Mr. Inglis are after that piece of business. The Board remained in deliberation after that for a considerable time—a long time. I was called in, and a draft resolution was handed to me to be entered in the book. I cannot recollect in whose handwriting it was—probably it was in that of Mr. Inglis. Q. It was not preserved? —A. I have no knowledge of it. On the left-hand side in the agenda book is an entry, 'Morton's account,' in the handwriting of Mr. Inglis. It was put in as a separate piece of business from what had been made up by me for the use of the meeting. Morton's account was never spoken of in my presence." Mr. Leresche makes up the list of subjects to come before the Board for discussion on that day. Mr. Inglis initials that as chairman, and then proceeds to enter in the agenda book that new piece of business to which I refer, which he enters under the title of "Morton's account." Out goes the Secretary as usual, and they consider that in private, and then he is called in, and the terms of the minute which I have read to you are given to him as adjusted. Then on 18th January you have the letter I have already read. Shortly after that date there follows another very important minute. The date of it is 15th November, 1877. The Directors present were Mr. Stewart (chairman), Mr. Potter, Mr. Salmond, Mr. Inglis, Mr. Innes Wright, Mr. Taylor, and Mr. Robert Stronach. At that meeting the Manager was requested to lay before the Board at their next meeting a vidimus of the securities held by the Bank in connection with the Australian and New Zealand advances, and then there is this part of the minute to which I must ask your particular attention—"It was resolved that a committee of the whole Board should sit periodically to consider the position of the various accounts of the Bank. The committee of inquiry above men-

The City of Glasgow Bank Trial.

tioned will meet not later than four months from this date." Now, gentlemen, there, upon those matters coming before them, this resolution is come to, that a committee of the whole house shall sit upon the position of the various accounts of the Bank. Can there be any doubt or hesitation as to what those accounts of the Bank were that a committee of the whole Directors were to consider? It was what they had pledged themselves to do in favour of their Manager by the minute of December when they accepted his letter. It plainly refers to the same matter; but there is a very singular addition here. The committee of inquiry, as entered in the minute, " will meet not later than four months from this date." Now, on this occasion I think you will find from Mr. Leresche's statement that the desire of the Manager was, when he brought this matter before them, that the Board should sit at once and consider these accounts. That did not seem very palatable to some of them, and one of them makes a motion not unlike in form to what occurs elsewhere. When the opponents of a disagreeable and distasteful measure object strongly to it in either House of Parliament, it is customary to move that it be read that day six months or three months; and here the motion of one of the Directors is very much equivalent to that—that these accounts be considered that day four months. Mr. Leresche says that at this meeting on 15th November, 1877, there were present Mr. Stewart (chairman), Mr. Potter, Mr. Salmond, Mr. Inglis, Mr. Wright, Mr. Taylor, and the Manager—the whole of them again. "I was absent," he says, "from the meeting during the latter part of it, when they were deliberating on the New Zealand matters. Afterwards I was called in and recorded the deliverance. Q. After you had engrossed the Board's deliverance about the New Zealand and Australian advances, did the Manager say anything in your hearing to the Directors?— A. Yes. Q. Did you hear what passed?—A. He said that he wished that a committee of the whole Board should sit periodically to consider the various accounts of the Bank. Q. Did you hear what passed on that suggestion?—A. Yes; it was agreed to, and I then entered this resolution—'It was resolved that a committee of the whole Board should sit periodically to consider the accounts of the Bank.' A conversation then arose as to whether the Manager wished this to be done at once, and a suggestion was made that it should begin six months afterwards. Q. Who said that?—A. I cannot remember who said it. Q. Was it Mr. Stronach, or some one else?—A. It would not be Mr. Stronach; it would be one of the Directors; and afterwards it was suggested, so far as I can recollect, by Mr. Taylor, that it should be four months. Q. What was to be done in four months?—A. The looking into those securities. Q. The sitting of this committee?—A. Yes." And accordingly

Addresses to Jury.

it was minuted that this should not take place for four months. In the agenda book it is entered in what appears to be Mr. Taylor's handwriting, that "it was resolved that a committee of the whole Board should sit periodically to consider the position of the various accounts of the Bank. This is not to take place for four months." Now, it is perfectly plain that the Manager again on this occasion brings these accounts before the Board, and he is met by this, "in six months," then "in four months," then "not later than four months." Now, gentlemen, is it possible to say that those men had not Morton's account in view, that they were not prepared when called upon then to fulfil the undertaking they had given to their Manager in the end of 1875, to the effect that they would lend their aid to look after these accounts? Is it not clear that the Manager then thought things were not straight with these accounts, and that they ought to be looked into; and is it not equally plain that the Directors must have known that, and must have known it even although they desired to put it aside as not a very convenient and pleasant thing? It must have interfered with dreams of 12 or 14 per cent. dividend, and probably that was not a pleasant consideration; but the thing was there, and pressed upon them; and I ask whether, in the face of that, you are to assume that in that long discussion the Manager's desire for aid was the merest sham and quibble, and that these gentlemen knew nothing of his real desire to have those matters investigated with their assistance; and investigated why? Because, according to the fact, these accounts which were unsatisfactory—the chance of putting them right merely a hope, a scintilla of hope, in December, 1875— were getting a great deal worse at the date when he made that request in 1877. Then, again, we have no trace of a meeting of that committee. In fact, it seems to have been to a considerable extent shelved by that adroit movement. But, again, on 14th March, 1878, you have the matter up. It is brought before them again; and upon that occasion "it was agreed that Messrs. Stewart, Potter, and Salmond be appointed a committee, along with the Manager, to examine the accounts at the head office weekly, and to deal in particular with the account of James Morton & Co." That is their own record of a meeting where there were present Messrs. Stewart, Salmond, Wright, Taylor, Potter, and Stronach—all except Mr. Inglis. But that comes up again at the next meeting, when Mr. Inglis is present, for this appears—"In regard to the committee appointed at the last meeting as to Morton's account, consisting of the foregoing gentlemen, along with Mr. Salmond, Mr. Stewart further reported Mr. Morton's engagement to realise as quickly as possible, consistent with prudence, his 4 per cent. preference stock of the New Zealand and Australian Land Company held

329

The City of Glasgow Bank Trial.

in security by the Bank "—and at that meeting there were
present Mr. Stewart, Mr. Salmond, Mr. Taylor, and Mr. Inglis,
the last of whom had not been at the previous meeting.

Now, gentlemen, are we to assume—and you will be asked
to assume—that these gentlemen were ignorant of Morton's
account and its state?   No matter what the Manager warns;
no matter his repeated request that they would fulfil their
pledge; no matter that a committee is appointed—they knew
nothing about it—the Manager or some inferior official of the
Bank is responsible for all that, and for the state of Morton's
account.   That you will hear that argued I have not the
slightest doubt.   It is very difficult to get into their Board-room
when Mr. Leresche was shut out; but surely you are not going
to hold that what passed in the Board-room, and the minutes
made and written in the hands of Directors at the Board, are
to be treated as a mere mockery and a delusion—that such
things never took place, that the account was not discussed,
that their deliberations were a farce, and that nothing earthly
was done about Morton or disclosed about his position?   Unless
you are prepared to accept that—to accept a suggestion coming
from counsel as an answer to a deliberately recorded resolution
at the time, you will, I venture to say, have great difficulty
in coming to the conclusion—if it is possible for you to come
to it—that these gentlemen were not one and all aware of
Morton's increasing indebtedness, and aware that the huge
account to which their attention was called in 1875 was growing like a snowball from year to year under their management.   And it was not Morton's account only.   Any one of
them was big enough to frighten a prudent man—but just
take Smith, Fleming & Co.'s; and it is very curious in itself—a
very curious specimen of the career of a mercantile man, who
makes a large fortune, and loses a large fortune, and gets pulled
through by the Bank, leaving the Bank and himself a great
deal the worse of the operation.   In 1870 Mr. John Fleming
told you his agents, Duckworth & Co., failed, and the result of
Duckworth's failure was that he became embarrassed, and, finding he could not go on, he at that time came to Glasgow to see
if arrangements could be made with the City Bank.   There
seems to have been faith everywhere in the City Bank, but
I do not know that any one had more implicit confidence in the
City Bank than those impecunious gentlemen who were constantly drawing upon its funds, and, to use language that appears
elsewhere, "absorbed"—a word very characteristic of the fact—
the greater part of the Bank's capital.   They had implicit faith
in the Bank, and their faith was justified.   He comes down
to the Bank.   He owed them then £150,000, and he says—
I have no doubt he believed it, whether it was precisely the
fact or not; we need not take him too strictly to task—he

believed it was well covered. Well, let it be so. But it is quite obvious that £150,000 did not altogether disclose the extent of Mr. John Fleming's, or rather the state of his firm's, indebtedness at that period, because the modest sum which he names as absolutely necessary to pull him through in the crisis of his fortunes in the beginning of 1870 was £500,000 cash. Well, it is said, "You may do this in various ways," but he says, "Oh, no, I object to the way proposed by the Bank; I won't hear of a new firm in Liverpool drawing upon me; it would destroy my credit." Accordingly he objected; and the Liverpool firm did not prove successful after all, and he said (I have no doubt with perfect truth), "If you do not give me £500,000, what I will do is, I'll come down; I will fail, and go into the *Gazette.*" That seems to have been a very alarming threat; why it should have been it is not very easy to see. But it seems to have given great alarm to some of the Directors of the Bank, because when Mr. Fleming was leaving the room, Mr. Potter rushed after him and brought him back. They would not let him come down, and the result was that he was as handsomely treated then as at subsequent periods. He got his £500,000 from the Bank to pull him through—at least something like it, because at the end of that year the Bank was in advance £500,000. It is right to say that Mr. Fleming thought they were covered to the extent of three-fourths of that debt. Here is a man on the verge of bankruptcy, who must come down if the Bank will not give him £500,000, and to keep him up the Bank are in advance to him at the end of that year to the extent of £125,000 of balances uncovered. That seems to have been the whole advantage the Bank got out of the transaction—that whereas they were covered at the first, they were uncovered to the extent of £125,000 at the end of the year. And that was the beginning, so far as Smith, Fleming & Co. were concerned, of that deficit which the Bank were straining every nerve to recoup at a later period of their history. Because, unfortunately, John Fleming's difficulties did not end there. They recurred in 1875, if, indeed, he was ever free from them. He never seems to have repaid the Bank; but in 1875, in the beginning of the year, he is in difficulties again, and he has been trading pretty largely on his credit with the Bank; because when these difficulties, as he was pleased to call them, overtook him in the beginning of 1875, the state of his account with the Bank stood thus—He had got upon bill credits £562,000, and he had got in cash advances £773,000, making in all £1,355,000. And then, being in difficulties, he proposes, and there is made, an arrangement. Now, gentlemen, I think you will find that at this stage the arrangement and the position of Smith, Fleming & Co. were known to the Directors. The arrangement was made—it is

The City of Glasgow Bank Trial.

Lord Advocate. called the arrangement of March, 1875, in the evidence before you, and it was embodied in a letter by Smith, Fleming & Co., part of which I shall read, written by Mr. John Fleming on the 12th April, 1875, but it was not adhered to, for this reason, that Collie's failure, of which you may have heard, took place shortly afterwards, and once more Mr. Fleming was overtaken by difficulties, and consequently the arrangement of March was modified in August of that year. That failure affected the credit and cash of Smith, Fleming & Co., and the result was that a new arrangement had to be made. The fact of this arrangement is, however, let me say, by no means so important as this other fact, that the Bank and certain of the Directors at least who are sitting at the bar, knew quite well about these things. Mr. John Fleming in his evidence undoubtedly told you that he was obtaining advances from Stronach, which were not known to the Directors; and notwithstanding the air of moral dignity with which Mr. Fleming emitted his deposition before you, I do not think it was a very straight action on his part to help to keep those facts from the Directors. He obviously did so; because when one of the Directors, Mr. Salmond, called and asked questions, he gave him at least an evasive, if not an untrue, reply, and then he wrote a warning note to Mr. Stronach, in case Mr. Stronach should give a true and therefore a different reply, and involve him with the Directors. It was not straight sailing by any means, and I do think it can be said that until 1875 these matters were really divulged to the Directors; but he stated with equal emphasis—and the correspondence to which he was referred by Mr. Stronach's counsel in cross-examination entirely bore out the statement—he stated, I say, that that was not the case when Mr. Robert Stronach came to be Manager, and that one of the first acts of Stronach in January, 1876, after he became Manager of the Bank, was to inform him (Mr. John Fleming) distinctly in writing that he would not personally give him any advances without the knowledge and sanction of his Board. And so far as Mr. Fleming knew and understood, he never from that date till the Bank closed its door got a sixpence from Mr. Stronach individually without the knowledge of the Directors.

But now about the letter of arrangement—which, of course, was Stronach again, according to one view of this case, but we shall see about that. As to the arrangement of March, 1875, Mr. Fleming wrote to Mr. Stronach on the 12th April, in the following terms:—

Referring to the meeting I had with your Directors and yourself on Thursday, 1st inst., respecting the state of our account with the Bank, I now beg to detail the terms of the agreement come to as I understood them:—(1) Smith, Fleming & Co. as a firm, and the partners as individuals, pledge themselves to abstain absolutely

332

Addresses to Jury.

from all speculative operations, unless specially sanctioned by the Bank. (2) They are to hold all property belonging to the firm as per annexed statement as security or cover to the Bank for its various advances to them; but inasmuch as it is of the greatest importance that the credit of the firm should not be injured, but be carefully maintained, no public transfer of the property is meanwhile to be made. The realisation of the property is to be left in S., F. & Co.'s hands, who undertake faithfully to account for and pay over to the Bank the whole proceeds of all property realised. (3) The Bank's charge for commission for all credits issued for S., F. & Co.'s accommodation, as per list herewith, shall be at the rate of ½ per cent. per annum, and this arrangement is to be retrospective as from 1st January, 1875. (4) The Bank's charge for interest on all cash advances to S., F. & Co. shall be at the rate of 3½ per cent. per annum, as from 1st January, 1875. A statement of the balances of various accounts as on 31st March last is appended. (5) The Bank shall advance the sum of £100,000, at the rate of 3½ per cent. per annum, for the acquisition of £100,000 of the stock of the Canterbury and Otago Company, £7800 of which is to be provided by me, credit for the equivalent of £7800 being given to Smith, Fleming & Co. in account with the Bank as at 1st January, 1875. (6) The £100,000 of stock as above shall be held by trustees in trust for the following purposes:—(1) To pay interest at the rate of 3½ per cent. per annum to the Bank for the £100,000 advanced for the purchase of the stock; (2) to pay the whole of the surplus income arising from the stock, after meeting the charge for interest as above, to the credit of S., F. & Co.'s account with the Bank, and to continue doing so until all S., F. & Co.'s debts to the Bank have been liquidated; (3) nothing was agreed as to the ultimate disposition of the stock upon the final liquidation of all S., F. & Co.'s obligations to the Bank, but I venture to suggest that in that event the trustees be directed to re-transfer the stock at cost price (viz., par) to the parties who furnish it, or their assignees or heirs.

That letter, which states the arrangement, has appended to it a statement of his indebtedness to the Bank, which is stated at the figures I gave you, namely, bill credits to the amount of £562,000 odds, and cash advances to the extent of £771,000 odds. And here you have a sort of indication, beginning even then, of the kind of way which the Bank take to recoup these losses. Such a balance is due, and here is how they try to make it up. It is a very generous course of procedure, but a very singular one. Your debtor owes you a balance which he cannot pay up, and you say to him, "Very well, you owe me £100,000, and are not able to pay it. That is perfectly true. But here I have got another £100,000 in my pocket, and I will lend it to you, and you will go and buy stock and shares in New Zealand, which will yield 8 per cent. That will enable you to pay me back 3½ per cent. on the old debt, and you will pay in the balance of the 8 per cent. towards liquidation." But then you don't even settle who is to get the balance of the capital over £100,000, if it should turn out well. The chance of gain is left in the most generous manner to your debtor instead of making a profitable investment for yourself—a very

333

The City of Glasgow Bank Trial.

handsome way of doing, but surely suggestive of this, that there was something very far wrong with a balancing requiring to be recouped by such a mode of speculation on the part of the Bank. Well, after the Collie disaster, a new arrangement is made, and the chief feature of that arrangement is the way in which they deal with the realisation of the security which is to be bought with the new loan of the Bank. The letter says—" In the event "— they had not quite settled how the surplus was to be dealt with if those shares were realised; but in this letter of August the conditions are made more tight in favour of the Bank, for this reason, that their debtor had become so much worse by reason of Collie's failure, being involved in it, and, accordingly, it is stipulated in this letter—" In the event of a sale, to apply the proceeds first in liquidation of the foresaid advance of £100,000, the whole of the surplus over and above the said advance being paid to the credit of our account with the Bank. The Bank shall have the power to direct the trustees to realise the stock at such times, and on such terms, as they (the Bank) may think proper. It is nevertheless understood and agreed that the Bank shall not exercise its power to sell or order a sale of the stock until the expiry of five years from this date, when the Bank shall have the power and option to dispose of the stock for the sum of £300,000, or to continue to hold it for two years longer, in which case the interest to be charged upon the advance shall be at the rate of 5 per cent., instead of $3\frac{1}{2}$ per cent." Now, there is a remarkable circumstance with respect to that letter, at least so far as regards one of the prisoners at the bar, to whom I shall specially refer before closing—I mean Mr. Potter—because Mr. Potter undoubtedly does appear throughout all these transactions of the Bank more prominently than any other Director. And not only so but he comes upon the stage at critical periods, and, I think, himself gives impulse to very decisive action. He disappears as fast as he appears, but not till he has set the machine in motion. In this instance you have a very singular illustration of it. I don't know whether he means to say that he knew nothing about these accounts. I don't know whether the evidence of yesterday, relating to his general incapacity for or neglect of details, is to be held as excusing him from the knowledge of the indebtedness to the Bank. But here he is in 1875 obviously a party to this arrangement, because upon the first of these letters is an important alteration, evidently made to adjust it in terms of the second. Both Mr. Stronach and he were parties to it. Mr. Morris speaks to that. He is shown the letter of April, and is asked, do you see certain marks on the document—in whose handwriting are these? He says—" Some in Mr. Stronach's." Then he is referred to another

addition—" Five years to hold securities, then sell as required;
£25 when due." This is just the substance of the alteration
made upon the agreement of March by the subsequent agreement of August. Mr. Morris is asked—" In whose handwriting
is that addition?—*A.* Mr. Potter's. *Q.* On the next page there
is another alteration in Mr. Potter's handwriting?—*A.* Yes;
life policies." He is dealing with that arrangement, and that
arrangement depends for its substance upon the advances which
had been made at that date, amounting to £1,300,000 odds.
Can it be suggested that with that information—when Mr.
Potter is told that, amongst other accounts, Smith, Fleming &
Co.'s is a source of such anxiety to Mr. Robert Stronach that
he cannot accept the responsibility of becoming Manager unless
he has the aid of the Directors in attending to that account—
can it be said that Mr. Potter did not fully understand the
effect of the appeal that was made to him by Mr. Stronach?
It is a wearisome task, and one I need not try to pursue, to
trace from that date, the agreement of 1875, down to the
final consummation, the stoppage of the Bank, the course of
this account. It is very graphically described by John Fleming
himself, who knew perfectly well the whole details of it. He
says he remembers being asked by Robert Stronach to go to
Glasgow, to meet with the Directors in July of last year.
" By that time the amount of indebtedness had considerably
increased. *Q.* How did you come to be able to carry on, after
Collie's failure, till the meeting of July, 1878?—*A.* When we
needed help we got it." Then his lordship in the chair put the
question, " From the Bank?—*A.* From the Bank." That account
went on from bad to worse. The result of it was, as Mr.
Fleming very fairly said, that, talking in round numbers—
because gentlemen like Mr. Fleming deal with large figures,
and don't content themselves with merely £5000, or anything
like that—at the date of the stoppage he was owing from
£1,800,000 to £1,900,000. " *Q.* What were your securities?
—*A.* About £450,000, if the Bank gets all, which it may not
do, as there is a dispute about them." And that is the result
of it—a result which it was pretty plain to see, because this
is a gentleman who was always liquidating and trying to pay;
and what is called, or seems to have been called, in the books
of the Bank, and according to the management of the Bank,
" liquidation," is the most extraordinary proceeding that I ever
heard of as contrasted with what is popularly understood by
liquidation. The usual process in liquidating an account is
to sell off the securities and ascertain the balance; but in the
case of Mr. John Fleming there was nothing to sell. Liquidation, if you go to the root of the word, means " melting," and
the idea is that you are to melt down the man's means and
pay off his liabilities. But in this case there were two liquida-

The City of Glasgow Bank Trial.

tions going on. They were melting down his securities when
they could, but the Bank funds were melting just as fast,
because what came from the Bank and went to Fleming flowed
a great deal faster, and in much larger quantities, than anything
that ever came from Fleming to the Bank. As showing how
they were dealing, and how true the statement of Mr. Fleming
is that the Directors, and not Mr. Stronach, or rather both
together, sanctioned his advances after 1875, let me refer to
another minute, because it shows how they dealt with Smith,
Fleming & Co., and it shows the lamentable straits to which
the fostering of these enormous credits on the part of one or
two houses had placed the Bank, when it came face to face
with a legitimate mercantile transaction. I refer to the minute
of the Directors' meeting of 11th May, 1876, at which there were
present—Mr. Taylor (in the chair), Mr. Potter, Mr. Salmond,
Mr. Stewart, Mr. Innes Wright, and Mr. Stronach—"A letter
was read from Messrs. Smith, Fleming & Co., dated London,
4th May, 1876, applying for an open letter of credit for £10,000
in favour of Messrs. W. Nicol & Co., Bombay, to be drawn
at 6 mos/st. against the security of goods and produce detailed
in said letter. The application was agreed to on the usual
terms and conditions. A letter was read from Messrs. Smith,
Fleming & Co., dated London, 4th May, 1876, for an open
letter of credit for £5000 in favour of Messrs. Todd, Findlay &
Co., Rangoon, to be drawn at 6 mos/st. against produce as
detailed in said letter. The application was agreed to on the
usual terms and conditions. A letter was read from Messrs.
Smith, Fleming & Co., dated London, 20th December, 1875,
intimating that owing to the failures that occurred during the
last crisis "—Mr. John was always getting into a crisis—" and
to general derangement of credit consequent thereon, they are
unable to fulfil their engagements to the Bank, entered into
in March, 1875, without some temporary assistance being
granted, and asking that a special credit be opened in their
favour to the extent of £45,000, to enable them to do so,
and undertaking to liquidate "—liquidation again—" the new
credit in the course of the year 1876. After explanation by
the Manager, it was agreed to grant the credit by accepting
the drafts of Messrs. W. Nicol & Co., Bombay, to be drawn
at 6 mos/st. to the extent of the credit asked, the proceeds
of the said drafts to be applied in payment of (1) the interest
amounting to '£25,033 12s. 10d., due at 31st December last,
on the Bank's cash advances to Messrs. Smith, Fleming & Co.';
and (2) the special cash advances, amounting to £20,000, made
to them during the months of October and November last, it
being understood, at the same time, that this temporary arrangement is not to interfere with or supersede the arrangement of March, 1875." Did the gentlemen who stipulated

that that was not to supersede the arrangement of March, 1875, not know what the arrangement of March, 1875, was? Did they not consider it when they expressly stipulated that it was not to be superseded, and especially when they were considering it with the view of doing what they did with their eyes open, which was simply to give the Bank's name and liability to the extent of £45,000, to enable John Fleming to pay his debt to the Bank—a sort of transaction again of the most singular character—to keep up his credit? It is just the same as if your debtor came to you and said, " I undertook to pay you £45,000 to-day, 28th January, 1879 ; I undertook to do that last November, but I cannot do it. I cannot meet my obligation ; give me £45,000 to pay you." And you give it to him, and he pays his debt, and the thing is satisfactorily squared off. Could that deceive any man sitting at the Board, even men who don't go into details, and who only deal in large and general transactions? If they choose to go into that agreement of 1875, the sums were big enough to satisfy a mind more ambitious of large transactions than even Mr. Potter's appears to have been. Then, as a contrast to that, we have instances showing what was the real effect—that they were strict at the branches, and sometimes at the head office too. They had no money except for Smith, Fleming & Co. "A letter was read from J. C. Cuninghame, applying, on behalf of Merry & Cuninghame, for an overdraft of £150,000 on the security of his estate of Foyers and the St. Vincent Street property belonging to the firm, and intimating, at the same time, that it was the intention of the firm to transfer their working account to this Bank and its branches." But £150,000 upon good heritable security in Scotland was far too big a transaction for the City of Glasgow Bank. " The Directors, after mature consideration, while feeling gratified that the proposal should have been made to them, felt that the transaction was too extensive to be entertained as a fixed loan." Then, again, as to this arrangement, and as showing the knowledge of all, there is a minute, and an important one. On 10th May, 1877, there is an application by Mr. John Fleming. There are plenty of applications by him through the minutes, but I need not weary you with them all :—" 10th May, 1877.—Present, Mr. Stewart (in the chair), Mr. Potter, Mr. Salmond, Mr. Wright, Mr. Taylor, and Mr. Stronach "—all present except Mr. Inglis. " The application by Mr. John Fleming for letters of credit for £20,000, to be used in connection with cotton purchases, which was before the Board at their last meeting, was again brought up, and an explanatory letter from Mr. Fleming, dated London, 5th May, 1877, having been read, the application was granted— this being special, but not to exceed six months ; and this not to interfere further with the terms of the original agreement,

Y

The City of Glasgow Bank Trial.

dated 24th August, 1875." Again we have the agreement
before them; recognising the agreement, they say it is not
to be departed from, and yet I fancy the suggestion will be
made—unless I mistake the line of the examination pursued
in the course of the evidence in this case—the suggestion will
be seriously made to you, that these simple gentlemen knew
nothing whatever about the arrangement, or about Smith,
Fleming & Co.'s debts. Then, again, in the minute of 1st
August you have embodied the result of Mr. John Fleming's
visit to Glasgow, as he told you. On that day their business
largely consisted again of Smith, Fleming & Co.'s credits.
They asked for a renewal of £18,500 against shipments of
shellac. The persons present were Mr. Salmond (in the chair),
Mr. Stewart Mr. Potter, Mr. Inglis, Mr. Wright, and Mr.
Stronach. Letters were read from Smith, Fleming & Co.,
dated London, 24th July, applying for £15,000 credit in favour
of W. Nicol & Co., Bombay, and £10,000 credit for the same
firm, all of which were granted on the usual terms. "In
regard to these various applications of Smith, Fleming & Co.,
the Manager reported that he had requested a meeting with
Mr. John Fleming, who came to the Bank on Tuesday last,
30th July, and had an interview with him and Mr. Stewart
and Mr. Potter. Very full explanations were given by Mr.
Fleming, and the Directors on the whole thought it proper to
agree to the advances." Mr. Taylor was absent from the
meeting, but Mr. Stewart was there, and he does not challenge
the statement and report of the Manager. And if you will
allow me to refer to the account of the meeting given by Mr.
Fleming, I think there are two important considerations that
may be derived from it, viz., that this account was represented
to be, and considered at that meeting to be, in a very unsatisfactory state, and that the cause of its being unsatisfactory was
that the indebtedness of Smith, Fleming & Co. was being constantly added to. "In July, 1878," Mr. John Fleming says—
"I was asking for an advance of £25,000. I went to Glasgow,
and met Mr. Robert Stronach, Mr. Potter, and Mr. Stewart.
Q. Was your indebtedness to the Bank referred to at that
meeting—the amount of it?—A. No. Q. Was it spoken of as
being very large?—A. The state of our account as being very
unsatisfactory was spoken of; the amount was not discussed."
Then he is examined by his lordship in the chair. "What was
said about the amount of your account?—A. It was alluded to
as being very unsatisfactory. I cannot recall the exact expressions used, but it was spoken of as an unsatisfactory account,
and that it was most unsatisfactory that the indebtedness had
been increasing instead of diminishing, and I explained, with
reference to that, that the condition of trade for several years
past had been deplorably bad." Well, that may be so. Bad

Addresses to Jury.

trade may have accounted for the want of money on the part of Smith, Fleming & Co., but it does not account for the fact that these accounts, being in the view of the Directors unsatisfactory, should have had their indebtedness added to. And if the Directors had any knowledge of these balance sheets, how did they come to deal with a bad account, which was being added to, as an account that was paying interest divisible among the shareholders? Now, gentlemen, that is another of these accounts; but Mr. Nicol Fleming's was not a whit better. The sums were hardly so large, but, on the whole, his credit was even worse than that of Smith, Fleming & Co. This account of Mr. James Nicol Fleming, or James Nicol Fleming & Co.— because it assumes two shapes in the course of these transactions with the Bank—is an important account, for this reason, that it seems more immediately to have led to the attempt to recoup deficits by means of investments in Australian and New Zealand land shares. Mr. Nicol Fleming's final indebtedness to the Bank was £1,238,000, having grown to those dimensions from £1,005,000 in 1875, and it attained that growth and magnitude notwithstanding the fact that, during that period, Mr. Fleming was practically, from first to last, if you accept the statements made as true, in liquidation. In other words, he was recognised as a bad debt, requiring to be paid off, but only likely to be paid off if the realisation of his assets went on slowly. Now, you heard no further back than yesterday the evidence of Mr. Dugald Bell, his clerk, who managed one part of his transactions in Glasgow. What Mr. Bell knew did not represent the whole of his indebtedness, but I think his evidence discloses very clearly the very rapid way in which Mr. Nicol Fleming, from 1868 onwards, was going down hill. He had started about 1863 in his Glasgow business with something like £260,000 of capital, and in 1868 the capital at his credit was £48,239, so that he had lost in the interval about £212,000. On the 31st January, 1868, the balance at his credit was reduced to £25,818. It remained very nearly the same down to 1870, but at 31st January, 1871, the balance was turned, and began with a debit of £7716. In other words, he not only lost all his capital of £260,000, but £7000 more. In 1872 the loss on capital account was £35,000; in 1873, £84,000; in 1874, £104,000; and in 1875, £213,000 upon that account alone; and I think you will not be surprised when you find that he went practically into what is called liquidation. There was another witness (Mr. Hunter) who spoke upon this matter. He was consulted about the liquidation, but Mr. Bell, the clerk, was selected to liquidate in Calcutta on behalf of the Bank, so that he went out for both interests. Any man who knew the result of that liquidation in Calcutta must have known how hopeless this balance of Nicol Fleming's had become. Just take Mr. Bell's

The City of Glasgow Bank Trial.

account of it. He was asked, "What were your duties to be
in Calcutta when you went out in 1875?" and he answered,
"I was to realise the assets of the old firm as speedily as I
could without sacrificing them, and remit home the proceeds.
Q. To whom were you to remit the proceeds?—*A.* To Mr. Hunter.
Q. How long were you out there?—*A.* About a year. *Q.* Did
you find the duty of realising an easy or a difficult one?—*A.*
Well, I found matters had been going behind, and that there
was very little to realise. *Q.* In fact, you found assets, but
you found debts too?—*A.* I found large debts. *Q.* Bad ones?
—*A.* Yes. *Q.* There were some coals, were there not?—*A.*
That was the principal asset; a large claim we had upon a
native firm for coals. Nothing came of that, so far as I know.
We could not get anything out of it. *Q.* Did you realise
anything really to send home in that year?—*A.* No. After
paying some of the debts of the firm, there was really nothing
to send home." And that gentleman, before he went, was in
communication with the Bank and in communication with Mr.
Potter about this realisation. The counsel for Mr. Potter
elicited from the witness this statement, that "when Mr. Potter
impressed upon me the propriety of realising what I could, I
understood it was with the view of reducing Nicol Fleming's
debt to the Bank. It was quite plain that Mr. Potter was
desirous to do his best for the Bank." I do not doubt for one
moment that Mr. Potter was desirous that by that liquidation
Nicol Fleming's debt to the Bank should be reduced; but that
surely infers knowledge on the part of Mr. Potter that there
was a debt to be reduced, and the more startling the amount
of that debt the greater the necessity that there should be a
good realisation. It is an ample explanation of his desire for
a good liquidation that there was a big debt, and it is absurd
to speak of his desire that it should realise a great deal if
Mr. Potter was not aware that there was a debt, and was
not aware of its magnitude and importance. But did Mr.
Potter fail to inform himself of the result of the liquidation?
Can you take it that he ever knew, or had reason to suppose
for one moment, that the liquidation of those coals or anything
else—which came to nothing, as Mr. Bell told you—satisfied in
any way that large debt he was so anxious to meet? There
is nothing to suggest that. On the contrary, there is the
clearest evidence offered by those witnesses who came in
contact with him, and by the way in which that debt is dealt
with in the minutes of the Directors, to show that there was
knowledge again on their part of the amount of the indebtedness.
Then, in the same way, Mr. Hunter supervised the liquidation
on behalf of the Bank, and he formed a bad impression of the
debt, and recommended liquidation. Whatever might be the
knowledge derived from his report, he gave a very bad account

Addresses to Jury.

of it, and recommended a liquidation, which practically ended in nothing, meaning by that, that they failed to reduce the debt, and that the realisation of assets in India turned out to be a simple farce. But what is perhaps the most important part of this is, that the Directors seem to have been, about the end of that liquidation, or even whilst it was going on, thoroughly aware not only of the extent of these accounts— unsatisfactory accounts—to which the Manager on taking office had called their attention, but had obviously come to know this, that upon these accounts there was a very serious deficit, and that unless some other means than those which had been taken up to that time were resorted to, the end would be certain loss to the Bank. They became aware of the deficit, and they resorted to means to meet it.

Now, were those means, let us consider, of a kind sufficient to warrant them, or to warrant anybody, in treating these as good debts that would bear interest—in treating these as debts covered by securities, so that they might fairly bring them down as assets held by the company, and not as debts without security against them? Very far from it. The fact of their resorting to unusual, and, in ordinary circumstances, illegitimate speculation—that is their view, gentlemen, not mine only—for the purpose of recouping or satisfying these debts, plainly shows a knowledge of the deficit, and the intention, if possible, to meet it. But how was it intended to meet it? By investing either directly or indirectly in land—not with the expectation even of immediate payment, but in the hope that, some day or other, when Australian or New Zealand property increased in value, the return from it, or the proceeds of it, would enable them to meet their obligations. With all those deficits staring them in the face, what was the plain duty of the Directors to do? which course were they to take with that knowledge before them? which was the only honest and fair course to take as regards the shareholders and the public— to treat these as debts covered by securities at that time, so well secured that the interest they were yearly adding to them was to be regarded as recoverable and divisible profit; or, on the other hand, to set them aside in a suspense account as debts which might one day be recovered and repaid, but debts which could not be recovered and repaid until a number of years had passed, and a good realisation, which was a matter of speculation, had rendered them able to meet these accounts? Well, they applied to Mr. Glen Walker, and Mr. Hunter was also employed on the subject, and he saw a number of gentlemen in connection with it, amongst others, Mr. Stronach, Mr. Potter, Mr. Taylor, and Mr. Stewart. I take Mr. Hunter's statement upon this point:—" Q. Were you given to understand what purpose they had in view in buying land?—A. I don't know that I ever heard of the purpose they had, but I understood it was for Nicol Fleming's account, to

The City of Glasgow Bank Trial.

cover it. I understood it was for the purpose of making Nicol
Fleming's account right, to cover whatever discrepancy existed
upon it. *Q.* That is to say, by making a profit on the Australian
land, they would cover any loss upon his account?—*A.* Yes.
Q. Were you not given to understand, by two of the Directors,
that it was for that purpose?—*A.* I quite understood it was
for that purpose. *Q.* Who gave you to understand that?—
A. I don't know that it was ever in so many words said it was for
that, but I considered it was the fact of my looking into Nicol
Fleming's accounts that led to my being consulted. *Q.* With
whom had you communication about it chiefly?—*A.* Mr. Stronach
and Mr. Potter, and Mr. Taylor and Mr. Stewart occasionally."
The result of these communications was an arrangement, embodied in a letter by Mr. Glen Walker, who addressed the Manager
upon 14th August, 1876, in these terms:—

Dear Sir,—In continuation of conversation with yourself and
other gentlemen connected with the Bank, I would now place in
writing the suggestions which we have been discussing towards
increasing income and recouping deficits by the judicious acquirement of pastoral properties. More than one member of your
Board are connected with New South Wales properties which have
on an average of many years, I am assured, paid a net return
upon present values exceeding 16 per cent. per annum. The
purchase price usually is paid by partly a cash deposit, and the
balance by bills extending over several years. It is easy to
finance against them in the colony; and if 40 per cent. of the price
was provided here, the remainder could be arranged in the colony
without further aid from this.

If arranged in this way, finance probably would cost for interest
an average of 6 per cent. per annum, and there would remain on
the basis of the experience referred to as net profits 10 per cent.
per annum. The suggestion is that the Bank grant credits to the
extent of from £100,000 to £150,000 towards the acquirement of
pastoral interests in Australia.

For example, if a value of £250,000 was acquired there should be
a net profit of £25,000 yearly, but £25,000 yearly will in fourteen
years repay £250,000 and 5 per cent. interest, so that thus, by
comparatively a very small outlay, a large amount can be recouped.

Mr. Borron and myself will be glad to be interested in the
project, and to manage its details; and finance can, in the Bank's
option, be arranged either by cash advance or entirely by credit.

Then that letter, which is of date the 14th August, came before
the Board upon 17th August, 1876, and this is how it was dealt
with—"A letter from Messrs. James Morton & Co., and two
letters from Mr. W. Glen Walker, dated respectively Glasgow,
the 16th and 14th inst., with regard to the drawing of credits in
lieu of those now drawn by Messrs. Holmes, White & Co., and
others, and one of the latter, as to the acquisition of certain
pastoral properties, were brought under the consideration of the
Board, and, after full consideration, the Board came to the conclusion that it was advisable to adopt generally the suggestions
contained in these letters; and they accordingly requested the

Addresses to Jury.

Manager, associated with Messrs. Potter, Stewart, and Taylor, to
arrange with Mr. Walker as to all details.   While arriving at this
resolution, the Board were fully sensible of the undesirableness of
such investments as the purchases proposed in the letters ; but
having in view the position of certain old accounts, and looking to
the whole circumstances, and particularly to the fact that the
contemplated arrangements for the working of the credits are
large part of transactions in existence for many years, and
previously brought under the consideration of the Board by the
present Manager, the Board deemed it expedient to come to their
present decision—as referred to in the minute of 30th December,
1875." Now, the persons present at that meeting were Mr.
Stewart (in the chair), Mr. Wright, Mr. Taylor, Mr. Potter, and
Mr. Stronach.   In connection with this it is important to observe
that though Mr. Inglis was not present, he not only saw that
minute, but made an alteration upon it in his own handwriting,
putting in the words " previously brought under consideration of
the Board by the present Manager."   Mr. Salmond was present
at the meeting when it was read.   Mr. Leresche, being shown a
draft resolution in the handwriting of Robert Stronach, says—
" My recollection is that I was called down some days after the
meeting of the 17th into the Manager's room, and I was handed
this draft resolution.   I was asked to bring my agenda book
down, and enter therein as under the date of the 17th.   So far as
I recollect, Mr. Taylor and Mr. Inglis were present when Mr.
Stronach handed it to me, and my memory is confirmed by the
fact that there are in Mr. Taylor's handwriting the words, ' read
and agreed to,' and in Mr. Inglis's handwriting, ' insert in
minutes, deliverance of Board.'   Q. So you have no doubt that
those two gentlemen were the two who were present?—A. That is
the impression I have at present.   The words at the side of the
memorandum, ' as referred to in the minute of 30th December,
1875,' and ' as referred to,' are in my handwriting.   The whole
body of it is in the handwriting of Mr. Stronach, except two lines
which come in, ' and previously brought under consideration of
the Board by the present Manager,' which are in the handwriting
of Mr. Inglis."   So that, when about to recoup the deficit by
Australian loans, it is done for the purpose of recouping it upon
those very accounts which are again in the hands of the Board,
and which, as recorded by them, had been brought under their
consideration by the Manager in 1875, when he took office.

Gentlemen, I do not need to say much more upon this matter
of investment in land.   It is for you to judge, not so much
whether it was a legitimate investment—that is not the question
that is before you just now—you are not here asked to say
whether the management of the Board was prudent or reckless,
was right or wrong—you are here to ascertain what were the
facts connected with that management—what was the knowledge

The City of Glasgow Bank Trial.

of the panels at the bar in regard to it—did they know the state of the Bank arising from these accounts, or did they not?—that is the question for you—not what was the cause of the Bank getting into that condition; through whose weakness or leniency towards debtors—that is not the question; the question is, did they know the state of the Bank?—the next question being, if they knew it, what did they know of the issuing of those false abstracts to the shareholders? Now, whatever may be said on the part of one of those gentlemen—I refer to Mr. Salmond—as an inference to be drawn from the circumstance that he was absent about the period when that annual balance was prepared and published, I say nothing at present, but I think it will be very obvious to you that nothing which may be said upon that point can in the least degree touch or affect his knowledge of the state of these accounts, because throughout the whole of those proceedings he is a party along with the other Directors, and shares with them the knowledge which they obviously possess; and although he does not admit it in his declaration, the words that he there uses go very far to suggest that if he did not know it at all he was shutting his eyes to the fact. The statement he makes about it—and you will bear in mind that he was an old bank manager, and tolerably well understood the way to govern the affairs of a bank—is as follows:—" I first came to know that the Bank was not in an easy condition some three or four years ago "—just when Mr. Stronach told him—" but I thought nothing of it, believing that it would all come right in a short time "; and here he states what I do not dispute—

The real cause of the unsatisfactory state of the Bank was the absorption of the capital by the foresaid advances; and though I did not know the amount of the advances, I was satisfied that the accounts must have been in a very unsatisfactory state to require such absorption. I suspected or inferred that there was something wrong with these advances, without knowing what it was.

Declares further—As regards what took place at the weekly meetings, I explain that the advances made to the parties before mentioned came up in the ordinary way, but were not specially stated. They came up just in the ordinary, general way, the same as advances to other customers.

But they were dealt with very differently; for whilst the other customers got theirs on the usual and proper terms, those other firms got theirs on very different ones. But you can hardly take from Mr. Salmond the statement that he knew these accounts were unsatisfactory because they had absorbed the capital of the Bank, and yet that he did not know that it was a wrong thing, or at least a thing involving the Bank in danger, to continue giving those firms further advances, instead of seeing that the accounts were placed on a satisfactory footing. Upon the matter of these Australian advances, you have a report by Mr. Taylor, Mr. Stewart, and Mr. Potter, and another by Mr. Inglis, Mr.

344

Addresses to Jury.

Taylor, and Mr. Salmond, which show clearly that they were employed in this matter, and were presumably conversant with it. The first is dated 19th October, 1876, and is as follows:—

> In terms of the minute of the Board of Directors, of date 17th August, 1876, appointing us to arrange with Mr. Walker with regard to the acquisition of certain pastoral properties in Australia, we have to report that we then authorised an investment to the value of £120,000 to £130,000, and have granted letters of credit in favour of Messrs. Glen Walker & Co., Melbourne, for £45,000 for the first payment, the balance to be financed by them, and the property, as acquired, to be held in trust by Messrs. Borron & Co., and by them registered in such names as the Bank may instruct. (Signed) WM. TAYLOR, J. STEWART, and LEWIS POTTER.

The next is dated 24th October, 1877—another transaction of precisely the same class for recouping the deficit:—

> The committee appointed by the Board to communicate with Mr. Glen Walker as to the purchase from the Australian and New Zealand Land Company of their Queensland properties, have had various meetings with Mr. Walker, and beg to report that they have confidence in his knowledge and discretion, and recommend the Directors to authorise him to acquire the properties in question at the price of about £150,000, on the best terms which he can accomplish, looking to his own memorandum, marked H. I., 24th October, and to the letter from Mr. Mackay similarly marked and dated. (Signed) HENRY INGLIS, WM. TAYLOR, and ROB. SALMOND.

Now, these appear to me conclusively to show this, as the result of the examination of these accounts, that their character, their unsatisfactory character, was disclosed to the Directors by Mr. Stronach when he took office in the end of 1875—so unsatisfactory that Mr. Stronach would not undertake the position of Manager unless he was to be relieved of the load of responsibility which a struggle to put such accounts into shape would necessarily involve; that they knew it; that they agreed to help him; that they went on dealing with those accounts from month to month, and from year to year; dealing with those accounts which were becoming more unsatisfactory than ever, even liquidation producing nothing, but always giving more and more; and yet I presume that, in the face of these facts recorded in their minutes and correspondence, the Directors would fain turn round now and say, "Entirely the Manager's doing. Some of us don't understand the details of business; none of us knew these details; we were innocent of that knowledge which might have led us to suspect that something was seriously wrong with the Bank." Gentlemen, that is a matter for you. If you can accept that explanation as a fair and true explanation, it would give a very different complexion to this case. I can hardly conceive that you can arrive at that result—that you will take it off the hands of gentlemen who have undertaken to aid the Manager in regard to these accounts, who deal with these accounts, who continue to

The City of Glasgow Bank Trial.

treat with these customers, that they knew nothing of the character of the debt; that they knew nothing of the increasing loss
and risk to the Bank; and that they did not know, and had
nothing to suggest to them that it was not a legitimate thing to
treat those bad and uncovered accounts as solid assets, and to
deal with those profits in the air, which never came to them,
and consisted of nothing but an entry in the books, as actual
earnings, to be paid over to the deluded shareholders in the shape
of 12 or 13 per cent. dividend.

I had hardly intended to meddle with any except these
accounts; but there is one other account which I cannot fail to
notice, because it comes very near to one of the panels—I mean
Mr. Innes Wright.   Mr. James Nicol Fleming was a Director in
1875, and when Mr. Hunter began to look into Mr. James Nicol
Fleming's affairs he came to the conclusion, which I think any
honest man would have arrived at, that a person who was getting
advances to the tune of hundreds of thousands of pounds from the
Bank, and who was constantly wanting more, was not just the
sort of person who ought to sit as a member of the Board of
Directors.   He was too good a customer of the Bank—from his
own point of view, not the Bank's—to be really in the position of
a Director, especially after he had come to occupy in reality the
position of a Director who could not pay.   Mr. Nicol Fleming
did not quite see it in that light.   I suppose he thought his
account would probably be better if he remained a Director to
look after it.   But at length he goes; and, having got rid of a
member of the Board placed in that ambiguous and very painful
position towards the Bank and its shareholders, they made a new
acquisition in the shape of Mr. Innes Wright to supply his place.
Mr. Innes Wright was asked to become a Director.   He says so,
and it does not appear to be contradicted anywhere in the
evidence.   I do not know what made the presence of Mr. Innes
Wright at the Board of Directors such a desirable thing in the
interests of the Bank.   I have gone over the evidence in this
case most carefully, and I have utterly failed to find any qualification that Mr. Innes Wright had for becoming a Director of the
Board at that time, except these three—he was not a shareholder,
he had not a penny to buy a share with, and his firm, of which he
was the leading partner, was owing the Bank about £334,000
sterling.   These were his qualifications.   How and why he
became a member of the Board is a matter of speculation.   He
knew something, at all events, about the indebtedness of one firm
to the Bank, and I think you will agree with me in holding that he
became equally acquainted with the indebtedness of these other
firms.   His admission to the Board was managed in a very snug
and comfortable way, apparently with general consent.   This is
what he says about it:—"I had not the necessary qualification
of stock when I was elected a Director.   I stated this to the

Manager, but I obtained the qualification a few days afterwards.
I also urged the condition of my firm's account as a reason against
my having any connection with the Board. Stronach was
apparently anxious that I should be a Director, and Mr. Salmond
also urged me to consent. The request to be a Director came to
me quite unexpectedly, and I am not aware what reason induced
them to make the request." The question arises here, what on
earth induced him to accede to the request when it was made?
" The stock necessary for my qualification was acquired for me by
the Bank. No cash passed, but I gave a cheque for the amount,
and that cheque stands against my account with the Bank to the
present day." He knew the state of his firm; but just let me
give it to you, because it is in more correct language than mine
would be, from the narrative given by Mr. Paul, who was a partner
of the firm, but whose functions seemed to come to an end because
the character of the firm changed from an exporting business to
a sort of financing business, in which he had little to do, and he
retired from the firm in 1876. This is the account which he
gives of that flourishing concern, the senior member of which
became a Director:—" Q. Did he tell you who asked him to
become a Director?—A. He told me the first intimation he got
on the subject, the first approach on the subject, was by Mr.
Robert Stronach, the Manager. Q. Tell us what he said?—
A. And on a subsequent day he had, I was told—by him, I think
—a visit from Mr. Salmond, following up the proposal. Mr.
Wright evidently had doubts about accepting it. Q. Did you
express any opinion at the time as to your view of his accepting?
—A. I said, ' How far is it right, how far is it proper, to accept a
Directorship, Mr. Wright, in the state of our account?' Q. What
did he say to that?—A. He said, ' I am alive to that, but Mr.
Stronach tells me that will be no difficulty; he will arrange all
that.' Q. What was he to arrange, did you understand?—
A. The indebtedness was to remain in abeyance, I suppose, and
that the fact of our indebtedness would be made no disqualification." Now, as to the state of the firm, he says:—" Q. From
1870 downwards, while you were a partner, were you ever doing
anything but making losses?—A. Well, it was the exception to
make profit. Of course, there were individual operations that
were profitable; but, on the whole, we were apparently going
behind. Q. You knew the result of your trading was that you
were realising loss?—A. Quite so. Q. And I suppose you knew
then that the money you got to meet your liabilities must have
come from some other quarter than the profits upon your trade?
—A. Quite so. Q. And that quarter was?"—the old answer—
" A. The City of Glasgow Bank." Now, what did these gentlemen want to have this impecunious shareholder as a Director for?
To aid them at the Board in putting these accounts right? And
what did that debtor want at the Board in the way of legitimate

The City of Glasgow Bank Trial.

management of the concerns of the shareholders? It is an ugly feature in the Board of Direction. That he was tolerated would be bad enough; that he was required is worse still; and that he went is bad enough too. I don't think you could expect much reduction of accounts by a man who did not want to reduce his own, who wanted to put his own account into that pleasant state that was described by his partner as in abeyance. What is abeyance? That the Bank is not to be paid till it meets their convenience, if it should ever be convenient for them to pay— that is the plain English or Scotch of it, whichever you like. And in the meantime these accounts which were elsewhere heard of in the course of evidence as dormant—a very good expression, too, because they simply slept on without either being paid or bearing any fruit—remained unpaid. And if you want a picture, there is the state of the Bank. I should like very much to know what inference can be drawn as to those who really thought that such a man, in that position, would be a useful aid in performing the task which the Directors had undertaken to their Manager in December, 1875. What was the honesty of the intention as regarded his account—ay, and as regarded those other accounts, because I think it matter of considerable doubt whether they were to be separately treated? But, gentlemen, it is matter of no small comfort to me that these are questions with which you must deal, and not I. It is my duty to lay these considerations before you, and to ask you to consider, upon the whole matter of these recorded transactions—and these accounts as I have given them to you from their proceedings and minutes from first to last, whether there was, on the part of all or any of those Directors, a knowledge of the state of the Bank which came to light so late as October, 1878? Their own books show that they had looked into the matter, that they had suspicions. If they really and truly knew that things were wrong, they were not entitled to shut their eyes and not look. A man may, through negligence or careless-ness of habit, or from want of intellectual perception, fail to see a thing, and he could not be held criminally liable for such failure; but, on the other hand, I venture to tell you that shutting your eyes against what you know to be a fact, not because you do not know it, but because you do not want to see it, and do your duty by it, infers criminal intention just as surely as if you kept your eyes open, and discredited or refused to recognise the fact.

Now, gentlemen, if the state of the Bank was, as I have repre-sented, generally known—not in precise details, but the actual fact in general terms, known to those gentlemen—I put the question to you next, are those abstracts before you, which are, as I pointed out to you, in essential particulars false, calculated or not calculated to conceal and misrepresent the true state of the Bank? If so, if you have actual misrepresentation, you have a

motive for misrepresentation, because there was something to
conceal. Do you think, if the truth had been made known as to
the real state of matters—that they had never got a penny of
these accounts ; that their reserve account was made up of unpaid
and hopelessly lost interest ; if they had told the truth as to the
actual amount of the better class of assets they had, and disclosed
the enormous amount of bad assets they had in the shape of
finance paper—if they had not concealed these facts, would not
things have taken a different course? Mr. Cunningham Smith
yesterday was very unwilling to admit that there was any distinction in the market, or according to public view, between legitimate transactions in the shape of bills coming from Australia and
drawn against produce, and bills kept in a bundle in a safe in
Mr. Potter's or his partner's room, and brought out and ante-dated
a month or two, to make it appear that they were actually drawn
by an Australian house upon their correspondents or the Bank in
Glasgow. But he partly admitted it, though he unfortunately
seemed to labour somewhat under a defect in his moral vision,
which did not enable him thoroughly to appreciate the distinction.
But, then, if that had come out, would it not have been known,
and did they not wish to conceal, that the Bank were financing at
their own hand through Mr. Morton, Mr. Potter, and others? In
other words, they were using bills to pay their debts, while all
the time they were liable under these bills, and it was not an
unuseful thing to cut off the enormous amount of indebtedness
upon such bills, because you must bear in mind that a bill is a
liability as well as an asset. If A owes £1000 and pays you,
you are £1000 the richer ; but if A gives you his bill, and you
discount it with your name upon it, and you get your £1000 in
the meantime, it does not follow you are much the richer man,
because if A does not meet the bill you will have to do it ; and
accordingly under an asset of that kind there always lurks a
liability. If the other names on the bill are good, you get the
money ; but if they are bad, you pay the money yourself.

Well, then, gentlemen, I repeat that there is a distinct connection between the state of the Bank and those misrepresentations
or falsifications that are introduced into the balance sheet. I
have not the slightest hesitation in asking you as a jury to hold
this, that whoever may have been the person or persons who
executed those fabrications, who falsified the balance sheet, and
issued it in that false and fabricated state to the public, he knew
the state of the bank, and did it because he wished that state
to be concealed. What earthly purpose could there be, if the
Bank were not in that state, in misrepresenting one single item
in this balance sheet as taken from those books? If the Bank
were really and truly doing a business so good that it had earnings sufficient to pay a dividend of 12 per cent. on its capital,
if its capital was intact, if it had a reserve fund of £450,000, and,

The City of Glasgow Bank Trial.

moreover, ample assets, and good assets, to meet all its obligations, why on earth should that state of matters have been concealed—what earthly reason not to disclose the whole assets and
the whole obligations? But it was not so, and I do not say that
you will ever get at the true balance sheet by making corrections
on the errors so plain on the face of this. The whole thing was
intended as falsification—falsification in order to make things
better than they really were—and better than they even appeared in their books by any fair interpretation—simply to still
those rumours that might arise when accounts like Morton's and
others were talked about outside the Bank, or the finance paper
was discovered, or anything arose which would disclose the
character of the investments they were going into, and which are
so carefully concealed upon the face of this abstract. There is
not a word about heritable property in Australia here—not a
syllable. They know how to describe heritable property when
they find it in Scotland, but they cannot find a name to cover
heritable property in Poverty Bay or in Australia, except by
calling it Government stock or balances in the hands of foreign
correspondents; and it is for you, gentlemen, to say why. I am
not saying one word about individuals at this moment, but it is
impossible to dissever the preparation of this false balance sheet,
made up within the walls of the Bank, from a knowledge on the
part of him who made it up of the true state of the Bank, and a
desire for the purpose, by publishing it in all its falsity, to
conceal and misrepresent—to draw a red herring across the track
of those persons outside who might otherwise have got a clue
to the utterly rotten condition of the Bank.

Well, then, who did it, and who are responsible for it, is the
serious question which, if you agree with me, so far as I have
gone into the facts of the case, it is next your duty to face. And
I here repeat that, in order to a conviction of any one of the
panels upon the charges which this indictment contains, it is not
necessary that he should have had an active hand in the preparation of that false abstract. It is not necessary that he
should either have guided the pen or directed the calculations of
the man who made up the scroll abstracts and transferred them
from that to the published balance sheets. It is not necessary,
in order to convict a panel of the alternative offence charged,
that he should have known every particular item of the arith-
metical mode by which these results were attained, so as to make
the sheet balance. It is enough if he knew and was aware that
the balance sheet was not a true, but a false balance sheet—if
he knew and was aware that, being false and untrue, it was given
out to the public for the purpose, not of honestly informing the
shareholders and the public, but of misleading them as to the true
character of the Bank's position and assets and trading. On
this part of the case I cannot help saying to you that it is wholly

a jury question. You cannot expect from the Crown evidence of all that transpired within the walls of the Bank, all that took place at the councils of these Directors, because necessarily these operations are conducted in secret. The deliberations of the Board are conducted in secret—in the present case with a privacy unusual in Boards ; because whenever you touch upon the tender and diseased parts of the Bank's trading, there is no secretary there—the Directors only. Whenever these things come up, bear in mind, the door opens, and out goes Mr. Leresche, and the door closes whilst the deliberation goes on, and until it is finished. You cannot therefore expect in this case direct testimony. The little shred that would have been left is cut away by the act of the Directors themselves, and they cannot be heard to complain of the want of it. Their act has made direct testimony impossible, and, that being so, you will judge them upon what they have done and recorded. And you are at perfect liberty, in the whole circumstances of the case, to determine, so long as you do it honestly, according to your conscientious belief, whether each or any of them was, or was not, connected with this crime, either as an active participant in the preparation of these falsified balances or as an assenting party to their being issued to the public for the purpose of deceit. It is impossible to disguise that between certain of the panels who sit at the bar there is this great distinction—Messrs. Potter and Stronach occupy the one class, and the remainder of the Directors the other, for this simple reason, that so far as the fabrication of those balance sheets is concerned the evidence against them is quite different. It is most distinctly deponed to by the witness Morison, the accountant of the Bank, who prepared these false abstracts—I fear I cannot say unknowingly—but bear this in mind, that, although Morison must at least have strongly suspected, if he was not fully aware of, their falsity, yet he had not the information in his possession which could either have induced him to fabricate them himself, or have enabled him to know where the shoe pinched, and what it was that the false representations should hide. He had not the securities book ; he had no access to the cheque box ; he had to take the statements of Mr. Potter or Mr. Stronach for the fact that there were securities standing against this or that, or that these were such utterly good securities that they might even be treated as gold. There are one or two passages of Mr. Morison's evidence which I should like to bring to your recollection upon this very matter of the preparation of those scrolls and balance sheets. Take the balance sheet of 1876, for I ought to explain that whilst Mr. Morison distinctly says that Mr. Potter was there in 1876, and advised and directed the scheme of falsification, that scheme was followed implicitly, with a small variation in regard to the £973,000 in the years 1877 and 1878. The evidence runs :—" Q. How long were Mr. Potter and you engaged

The City of Glasgow Bank Trial.

in revising that balance sheet, resulting in the red figures being
put on?—*A.* Perhaps an hour or two.   On the left hand side of
No. 128 there are entries S., F. & Co. (Smith, Fleming & Co.),
£200,875 ; J. N. F. (James Nicol Fleming), £100,300 ; and J. M.
& Co. (James Morton & Co.), £450,600.   These were credit
accounts, entered in that part of the abstract which contains
advances on credit.   *Q.* But you bring them down and insert
them among what?—*A.* Government stocks, railway stocks and
debentures, and other securities.   *Q.* In the abstract of 1876
there is an entry under assets, 'Government stocks, Exchequer
bills, railway and other stock and debentures, and balances in
the hands of banking correspondents.'   Was the effect of that to
represent debt due on credit account by those firms, to the
amount of £751,000, as either a Government stock or security?—
A. Yes.   *Q.* By whose instigation were these sums brought down?
—*A.* Mr. Potter's.   *Q.* Was it by his directions it was done?—
A. Yes.   *Q.* Did he assign any reason or justification for it?—
A. That the Bank held certain stocks against the debt of
£751,000.   By the Lord Justice-Clerk—*Q.* And therefore
treating them as good assets?—*A.* Yes."   Examination continued
—" *Q.* Did Mr. Potter seem to understand the different items they
were considering?—*A.* Apparently so.   *Q.* Did he appear to be
quite conversant with them?—*A.* Quite conversant."   Now,
gentlemen, it may be suggested—it is just possible that it may
—that Mr. Morison, the accountant of the Bank, did all that out
of his own head ; and for what purpose?   I can hardly conceive
such a suggestion seriously made as that a man in his position,
with the limited knowledge in which he was kept in regard to
the affairs and trading of the Bank, should set to work for some
purpose or other to falsify the accounts, as if he had been really
able to divine the state of the Bank.   That is something perfectly
incredible.   But if not, were Mr. Potter and Mr. Stronach not
there?   If they were, you have evidence upon which you are
entitled to rely—if you think it reliable—directly connecting
them with the fabrication ; and, if so, I think you will have little
doubt as to the result of the evidence in this case, so far as these
two gentlemen are concerned.   So far as the other panels are
concerned, you must keep in view that they had that knowledge
of the affairs of the Bank, according to the assumption of my
argument—and you will judge how far it is well founded—which
certainly should have made any man of ordinary knowledge and
common sense aware that that was not a true abstract which was
issued to the shareholders.   I do not say that the mere fact of
suspicion that it was untrue is enough to entitle you to convict
them of that alternative charge.   But if they knew that the
balance sheet had been altered so as to make it false, and if they
also knew that the purpose of doing so was to conceal the state
of the Bank, and allow that to go forth to the shareholders, I tell

Addresses to Jury.

you—under correction of his lordship—that they are guilty of that alternative charge. It is for you to consider the case of each one of these five prisoners separately and apart, to consider what they jointly knew, and to consider the extent and means of knowledge which they separately had, and to come to an independent conclusion in each case. If you can arrive at the result that they had the knowledge I have suggested, I ask you, because I am entitled to it, for a verdict against them upon the alternative charge. I ask it on behalf of the Crown and in the name of justice. But equally in the name of justice, if you are honestly unable to arrive at that conclusion, you will give the prisoners the benefit of the doubt, and a verdict which at least will have the effect of dismissing them from the bar. Gentlemen, I have only one word to say in conclusion, and I regret that that word should have been forced upon me by the enormous mass we have had in the present case of evidence of character. I don't ask you to lay aside for one moment the fact that these were gentlemen of position and of high repute. They are entitled to any fair presumption arising from their having such repute; but to press that evidence to the length to which it has been pressed by witness after witness in that box, is the most preposterous thing I ever heard in a Court of justice. If it be true that not one of them is capable of committing such an offence, nobody did it—a very singular result. Evidence of character in connection with certain offences is a valuable ingredient in determining the guilt or innocence of the accused; but I tell you, in a charge of this sort evidence of character—although it is not to be laid aside—means that you are not to treat them as if they were men of bad character; it amounts to no more; I tell you that an offence such as this is impossible except to a man of good character. If a man has not a good repute—if a man has a bad repute—you will never find him in the position of a Director of a great bank, entrusted with millions by the public, or in a position to work that wreck upon any institution which has befallen the City of Glasgow Bank.

CHAPTER XI.

Addresses on behalf of the Prisoners.

MR. TRAYNER FOR MR. STEWART.

Mr. TRAYNER said he rose to address the jury with a feeling of great anxiety, because, owing to the wide publicity and misery which had attended the stoppage of the Bank, public clamour, sometimes unreasonable, but always powerful, had at once raised its cry for immediate vengeance and execution of sentence against those who were believed to be the authors of that misfortune, without waiting to hear what might legitimately and forcibly be said in their defence. But he reminded them they were entitled to convict the prisoners at the bar only if they were satisfied upon the direct evidence submitted to them, not of their foolishness or even of their sinfulness, but only of their actual guilt of the charge laid against them. How necessary this caution was was to be seen from the fact that, although the Crown originally charged the prisoners not only with theft, fraud, and fraudulent manipulation, but with the uttering of false balance sheets, the Lord Advocate had abandoned all the graver charges, leaving only the charges connected with the balance sheets. His client was a man of honour and high personal character, a man held in universal esteem, as testified by Dr. M'Grigor, the Crown's own witness; and he reminded them of what Mr. Stewart stood to lose personally and pecuniarily, apart from the loss of his good name, by lending himself to the fabrication and utterance of false documents. The Lord Advocate had utterly failed to establish any reasonable motive to prompt Mr. Stewart to commit the crimes he was charged with. Now, gentlemen, proceeded Mr. Trayner, I am going to relieve you, so far as I am concerned, from any discussion of the question whether or not the balance sheet was true. I shall assume, for the purpose of the argument, that it was not. The Lord Advocate may make it as false as he will; I shall assume it to be false, for I knew nothing of its falsity. Upon the subject of whether it was false, or whether the alterations in it were justifiable, you will have argument from other gentlemen who are to follow; but for Mr. Stewart the defence is simply this, that, be it false or not, he knew nothing about it. There are three charges in the indictment, relating respectively

354

to the years 1876, 1877, and 1878, and you heard the evidence of Mr. Morison in regard to the manner in which these documents had been prepared, and I desire to say a word in case my silence on the subject should be misinterpreted—not because of anything the Lord Advocate said in reference to it, because I think the Lord Advocate—I was going to say with generosity, but certainly with fairness—did not press upon your consideration a circumstance relative to Mr. Stewart which does not tell against any of the other Directors except Mr. Potter and Mr. Stronach. In 1876 the balance sheet is not brought home to the knowledge of any Director except Mr. Potter and Mr. Stronach. In 1877 the same observation applies. In 1878 you undoubtedly have the balance sheet of that year laid before Mr. Stewart. I am not anxious to shirk the consideration of that subject, and let me take from the Crown the evidence in regard to what took place on that occasion. The evidence is Mr. Morison's—" A clean copy of that abstract was made by instructions of Mr. Stronach after it was red inked." [Balance sheet with red ink and pencil markings exhibited to the jury.] I do not say that these alterations are not quite justifiable. Upon that I have nothing to say. But, then, when you have seen this balance sheet in its altered condition, you see how very unlikely it was to attract Mr. Stewart's attention when it was presented, or rather how much less likely it was to attract attention when presented in the shape of a clean copy. Now, that is the document which was shown to Mr. Stewart. Mr. Morison says, that after he had made the one with the red ink alterations he got instructions from Mr. Stronach to make a clean copy. He says—" After it was made Mr. Stewart, Mr. Potter, and the Manager met in the Manager's room and went over it. I was present, but I did not go over it with them. I was in the room. I do not think the annual abstract issued to the shareholders had been printed at that time. Q. Did these three gentlemen not compare the clean document with the abstract?—A. They compared the clean document with the abstract published in the previous year's report." Then, just one other sentence from the same witness—" When the clean copy without the red ink marks was submitted to the Manager, Mr. Stewart, and Mr. Potter, I was in the room to give any information wanted. Q. Were you asked to give information about anything?—A. The only information I was asked for was to compare the 1877 report with the 1878 one. Q. Which report?—A. I mean the annual balance sheet. I was asked to do so, I presume, in order to compare the different sums, the one year with the other. Q. Simply for the purpose, I suppose, of stating what was the difference in the trading of the Bank between these two years?—A. I was not asked to explain any entry in this account, merely to compare results."

The City of Glasgow Bank Trial.

Mr. Trayner. And then he said the time occupied was not an hour. Now, in the first place, that document shown to Mr. Stewart contains on the face of it nothing whatever to attract the attention of a man who was even a better bookkeeper than Mr. Stewart was. He was not there for the purpose of testing the balance sheet, it was not his business to make up or test the balance sheet. Whatever is the duty of a Director—and I shall have a word to say upon that by and by—it was not the duty of the Directors unquestionably to make up the balance sheet for the year. Well, then, as regards 1878, I do not believe you will be disposed to think—the Lord Advocate evidently was not disposed to think—that the mere fact that Mr. Stewart was in the room, and looked at this clean copy which had been made, was in itself any indication that he was in the guilty knowledge that this was the result of manipulation and had been cooked. Gentlemen, I must say this for Mr. Stewart, that if the account of which this is the clean copy was manipulated and false, it is quite obvious that he was not a party to the falsification. He was not allowed to see the balance sheet till all the traces of the red ink marks and the alterations had been removed. He is not called in to consider whether any alteration should be made or not; and so far from being called in to consider whether those alterations were right or prudent in the circumstances of the Bank, he is excluded, then and at every other time, from the consideration of a balance sheet when that balance sheet was undergoing preparation. The Lord Advocate said that it is not in this abstract that the offence consists; the offence consists, according to his lordship, in the abstract which was published to the world. Well, I look at the abstract published to the world; I look at this which was the abstract of the affairs of the Bank shown to Mr. Stewart, and I compare them, and you will compare them for yourselves. They are identical, and if the balance that was presented to Mr. Stewart by the Manager and Mr. Potter was a true balance sheet, then the abstract published to the world was true. If it was not a true balance sheet, Mr. Stewart was deceived, and not deceiving. It will not prove that Mr. Stewart was in the guilty knowledge that this was a cooked and manipulated balance sheet to say that he was present at the meeting when it was gone over and looked at. On the contrary, you must infer that he regarded it as true and honest, because he was a party to the publication of the report which went forth to the public in 1878. I could quite understand, if the published abstract had been in any material respect different from the figures shown in the balance sheet, that it might have been said, "Mr. Stewart, how could you publish that when you had seen this?" But you cannot presume that there was anything wrong with what was published to the world so far as Mr. Stewart was concerned, so long as you find that the only means

356

Addresses to Jury.

of knowledge which Mr. Stewart had was entirely consistent
with the results and the figures published to the company and
to the public.

I come now to a question, gentlemen, which is of some
importance. The balance sheet which you see before you,
and which was subsequently epitomised and issued to the
public, is said to have been manipulated and cooked. Now,
what was Mr. Stewart's duty, or the duty of any Director, in
regard to that? The balance sheet, observe, so far as laid
before the Directors at all, is the work of the functionaries
charged with that particular duty. It is not a Director's
duty to make up a balance sheet, or to keep any of the books
of the bank; but when that balance sheet is laid before him, is
there any duty upon Mr. Stewart, or any director of any bank,
to test its accuracy by looking into the bank books? I refer
to the case of *Adie* v. *The Western Bank*, reported in III.
Macpherson. From the evidence it appeared that the pursuer
had been a partner of the Western Bank since 1848, and that
he had received the annual report from the Directors. He made
the purchases, knowing that the Bank was the seller, upon the
faith of these reports and the representation of its manager at
Coatbridge, and on the faith of the Bank being in a position
to pay a dividend at the rate of 8 per cent.; and the report
in May, 1855, contained a false statement of the position of the
bank, large debts being included in the assets, which the books
and documents showed to be bad. There was nothing in that
false statement in the report and balance sheet of the Western
Bank which, according to the statement of the Lord Advocate,
is not to be found existing in the present case. The assets were
misrepresented, the debts were misrepresented, and altogether
there could be scarcely anything nearer a parallel than what
was proved in *Adie's* case to that which is stated by the Lord
Advocate to have occurred here. In that case the Lord President, charging the jury, said—" It is not incumbent on the
Directors personally to go through the books to test their
accuracy or the results brought out from them. It is not to be
expected or supposed that the Directors had done so, and
their report is not to be taken as importing or implying that
they did so. They are entitled to rely on the information
furnished to them by the officials to whom the details of the
business is committed, and in whom confidence is placed. That
affords reasonable ground for believing in the truth of the
results and the inference reasonably deduced from them, and
if it should unfortunately turn out that the information so
furnished to the Directors was false, by reason of the negligence
or fault of those whose duty it was to furnish correct information, the Directors who honestly received it, and thus were
deceived by it, cannot be held to have practised any fraud on
the shareholders or the public." I will not detain you by reading

The City of Glasgow Bank Trial.

Mr. Trayner. further from the report of that case, because that expression of opinion by the Lord President, in charging the jury, was taken exception to by counsel, and the matter underwent discussion in the First Division of the Court of Session, and the judges of that Division, and particularly Lord Curriehill, concurred in the view which the Lord President had stated—that it is no part of the duty of Directors to look into the books of the bank to ascertain whether the balance sheet or abstract report is correct or not. They are to apply for information to the particular officials charged with the duty of making up the accounts, and when they get it, they are entitled to rely on that. If that be the duty of Directors, I ask—What is the fault of Mr. Stewart? This balance sheet is put before him, and he says— "Well, I see it brings out a profit of so much per annum, and I see it is absolutely conform to this which is published to the world." Is he to look into that account to check its accuracy? How many items does that cover? The first entry is "Local bills." Well, to satisfy himself of the figures brought out there (£766,878) involves an investigation into a number of bills which might take him a month merely to count—it may be so—or it may be that the bills are few in number, and of large amount. But all he has to do is to ask the accountant of the Bank to be *honest* and truthful in making up the ledger, and to put before him and his brethren in the direction the results of the Bank's books. And what is most remarkable in this case is, that if Mr. Stewart and his brother Directors had gone to the books to test the accuracy of the balance sheet, they would have found nothing wrong. The balance ledger which they docquet is exactly conform to the other entries in the books from which these results are taken.

Gentlemen, it would only weary you and occupy time to go into all the questions of the different accounts to which the Lord Advocate has alluded. There is only one of them further, as bearing upon Mr. Stewart's case, which I should like to say a word about. You remember that when one of the clerks in the Bank brought the attention of the Manager and the Directors of the Bank to the fact that Mr. Innes Wright's partner (Mr. Scott) was not accounting for the discounts which he ought to have accounted for, it was arranged that Mr. Stewart and Mr. Potter should go and see Mr. Scott on the subject. They met Mr. Scott, and Mr. Stewart told him that his conduct could only be designated by one name. Mr. Stewart was indignant, honestly and fairly indignant, at Mr. Scott's conduct, and he showed it both by his manner and by his language on that occasion. Does not that show you that the only time in which Mr. Stewart ever came face to face with a proper defalcation—what he knew was a defalcation—he at once resented it as an honest man would have done? And just as

Addresses to Jury.

certainly as he insisted upon an arrangement being made by which Mr. Scott should hand over the money which he had improperly retained—just as certainly would Mr. Stewart have insisted upon an arrangement with Fleming & Co., and everybody else, if he had known that things had gone the length to which we are now told they had gone. Can you say that Mr. Stewart has acted criminally here? What can lead you to that conclusion? Has anything in the whole course of his actings indicated criminal intention or criminal purpose? Has anything been brought home to him which would warrant you in branding him with the name either of thief, swindler, or liar? Do you believe that he ever put his pen "to a page that registered a lie"? Do you believe he told a lie, verbally or in writing, to the public? If he did, was it not very inconsistent with the whole of the rest of that man's conduct? He had hitherto, as far as we have seen, acted uprightly and honestly with all men; and while he may have been foolish, reckless, or ignorant in the fulfilment of his duties in the Bank parlour, you cannot say he ever acted dishonestly or falsely. Do you believe Dr. M'Grigor when he tells you that Mr. Stewart appeared astounded at the information he got from him? Do you believe that Mr. Stewart was sincere when he rushed past Dr. M'Grigor at the Bank door wringing his hands, and declaring he was a broken-hearted man? I believe Dr. M'Grigor. Have you any reason to doubt him? But if Dr. M'Grigor's evidence is worth listening to, the result of it is to prove that the revelations brought to light in the report which Dr. M'Grigor and Mr. Anderson issued were new to Mr. Stewart. And not only by the evidence of Dr. M'Grigor is that made plain, but Mr. Jamieson, one of the liquidators, tells you that a day or two before the stoppage of the Bank he went through to Glasgow to see whether any arrangement could be made by which the Bank might be carried on, and that when he told Mr. Stewart the result of his investigation Mr. Stewart was distressed by the information, and seemed to be greatly put about. Corrupt motive in Mr. Stewart's case there was none. I say emphatically there was none; and I have listened to the Lord Advocate to find wherein he imputed corrupt motive to Mr. Stewart. Guilty knowledge certainly was not brought home to him; and the suggestion that he is guilty of the crime laid to him is just about as much brought home to him as it is brought home to you. I am not going to detain you at any further length in reference to this case. You cannot convict Mr. Stewart unless you are satisfied that he issued the balance sheet of the Bank in the guilty knowledge of its being false. What does that involve? That this man, from 1876—for he is charged with this as much as with the act of 1877 and 1878—knew the Bank was in a rotten and tottering state, and might any day come down, and yet he left his fortune at

359

The City of Glasgow Bank Trial.

Mr. Trayner. its risk. He knew that Bank to be in a rotten state, hopelessly insolvent, and not paying anything, and yet he continued in its direction and allowed himself to be re-elected in the month of June, 1878, when, if he had had guilty knowledge, and had aught of intelligence above the veriest idiot, he would have hurried from the Board and saved everything he could. That was not the case with any one of them. Foolish they may have been, reckless they may have been, bad managers to the last extent they may have been, but, gentlemen, I think you will search this proof in vain for guilty knowledge, and without guilty knowledge there is no crime. Unless you are satisfied that Mr. Stewart has been guilty of criminal intent to defraud some one and to benefit himself—that he knew these falsehoods were in the balance-sheets, and that he issued them for the purpose of deceiving the public, when he had no motive to deceive the public, and no personal object in view; unless you can assert all these things as the result of the evidence, you must not find him guilty. Therefore, gentlemen, I ask you to proceed upon the evidence, and if you proceed upon the evidence in the case, you will acquit Mr. Stewart.

Mr. Balfour. Mr. BALFOUR addressed the jury on behalf of the prisoner Potter. After referring to the serious and momentous nature of the charge preferred against Mr. Potter, and to the depth and strength of public feeling that had been aroused all over the country by the failure of the Bank, which he cautioned the jury to dismiss from their minds in weighing the evidence to which they had listened, Mr. Balfour adverted to the fact that the prosecution had had to abandon the more serious charges of embezzlement and theft, which the jury would now treat as if they had never existed. He then pointed out that even at the first there had been no allegation that Mr. Potter had used his position as a Director to obtain a single sixpence of advantage for himself. The question really before the jury was, in the first instance, whether the balance sheets of the Bank in the years 1876-77-78 were false, and then whether they were false in the knowledge of the accused, and whether they were uttered by them for the purpose of perpetrating the frauds alleged. He did not go, and did not care to go, into the question whether the balance sheets were false in the sense that they were not entirely correct from a book-keeper's point of view. He was willing to assume, for the purposes of argument, that a skilled accountant would have made them up on a different principle. But he utterly denied that the prosecution had proved that Mr. Potter either fabricated them or sent them out with a knowledge that they were false. To convict the accused it would be necessary to prove something more than neglect or omission of duty, errors of book-keeping, or errors of judgment. Guilty mind and intention must also be proved;

Addresses to Jury.

and these, as he contended, the Crown had absolutely failed **Mr. Balfour.** to prove. The Lord Advocate had confessed that he could not establish his case by direct evidence, but he had argued that the Bank was in an unsound condition to the knowledge of the Directors; that the unsoundness gave a motive for concealment; that the balance sheets did, in fact, conceal that unsound condition, and therefore he asked the jury to convict the accused. That, to his (Mr. Balfour's) mind, was a very unsatisfactory process of logic. The Lord Advocate ought to have shown what part the Directors had in making up the balance sheets, and how the particulars mentioned in the indictment as false could be known by them to be false. Mr. Balfour described the way in which the weekly balances were prepared by Mr. Morison, the accountant of the Bank, and the balance ledger which he kept was checked by the Directors. That was the only book which the Directors did check, and a very large proportion of what were said to be fraudulent alterations in the balance sheet existed in the balance ledger before the abstract was made up at all. After specifying these Mr. Balfour argued that the Directors had no means of knowing them to be incorrect. They were put in the balance ledger by a responsible official of the Bank, and something must be trusted to officials. As to the allegation that entries were made of reserve fund and receipts to profit and loss which did not really exist, those entries appeared in the books of the Bank and in the weekly statements, and how could it be a fraudulent act on the part of the Directors, in that case, to admit them into the balance sheet? With respect to errors which were not in the balance ledger, but made their appearance for the first time in the balance sheets, Mr. Balfour submitted that the Directors could not have detected these by any process short of turning themselves into auditors, and stopping the business of the Bank for a week or a fortnight while they examined the books; but nobody said it was part of their duty to do any such thing. The reason why it was said to be wrong to keep up a reserve fund, and to carry certain sums of interest to the credit of profit and loss, was because there was a number of accounts which were alleged by the prosecution to have been in a very doubtful position, and upon which no interest had actually been paid for years. But, the learned counsel contended, it was surely only at the worst a matter of judgment whether these accounts were bad or not, and the accused could not be charged with fraud because they refused to treat them as irrecoverable, and continued to charge interest upon them. He denied that there had even been an error of judgment, because some investments to which interest, though charged, had not been paid for years, began after that to pay interest again. Mr. Balfour next dealt with the charge against Mr. Potter of having assisted in fabricating

The City of Glasgow Bank Trial.

Mr. Balfour. the balance sheet of 1876. The only evidence in support of this grave charge was that of Morison, the accountant. The evidence of one witness, even if trustworthy, was not enough to prove the charge without corroboration, and Morison's evidence had not received a shred of corroboration, while it was impossible to place any trust in his evidence. Mr. Balfour, at some length, subjected Mr. Morison's evidence to a most searching analysis, with the view of showing that it was inconsistent and self-contradictory, and that it would be unsafe to trust either to Mr. Morison's accuracy or to his veracity. Turning to the question of the knowledge which Mr. Potter had of the accounts of Smith, Fleming & Co., J. Nicol Fleming, and Morton & Co., Mr. Balfour said he would not dispute that Mr. Potter had some knowledge of these accounts before 1875, and that after 1875 he had generally a knowledge of their state; but he contended that Mr. Potter had also, along with the other Directors, an honest belief, not without warrant, that these accounts might in the end be wound up satisfactorily for the Bank. In support of this contention, Mr. Balfour reviewed the history of these accounts. In conclusion (said Mr. Balfour), I would ask you to consider this—What motive or inducement had Mr. Potter to be guilty of the fraud with which he is charged? In any question of crime it is of the utmost importance to see whether a man has a motive to do the thing he is said to have done. Even in crimes of violence, or sudden passion or impulse, it is always important to see whether there is a motive. Sometimes it is difficult to trace motives in cases of that kind; but where you have a crime like this, which is in the nature of a commercial fraud, you will necessarily have motive, foresight, reasoning, and scheming to gain some end. I never knew of a man who was guilty of deliberate and persistent fraud without something to gain. I ask you, what suggestion is there of any such motive on the part of Mr. Potter? I showed you at the outset that from the beginning to the end of this indictment the Crown make no charge against Mr. Potter of having overdrawn his account, or of taking advantage of his position to benefit himself. What was Mr. Potter's financial position at this time? He was a man, as you had proved to you, at the head of two leading businesses. The one was that of Potter, Wilson & Co., from which he was deriving an income of £5000 a year. The other was the great shipping firm of Lewis Potter & Son, from which he was deriving an income of about £3000. That was £8000 a year from the two businesses. But he had also valuable lands worth £120,000, from which he was getting a profit, including the minerals, of about £10,000. So that, whatever else may be said about Mr. Potter, he was not a needy speculator, or one who wanted the money of the City of Glasgow Bank or any other bank. He had an income of £17,000 or £18,000 a year. The City of

Addresses to Jury.

Glasgow Bank were not even his bankers. His bankers for many years had been the British Linen, apparently because one of his partners had been a friend of the manager, and the National Bank, because he was associated with an Australian Company, which was in some way friendly to that bank. From these two banks any accommodation that Mr. Potter needed, if he needed any, was got; and it was only at the request of the City of Glasgow Bank that it got a share of his business. There had not only been a failure to prove, but there had been no attempt to prove, that Mr. Potter had the slightest thing to gain, either by his connection with the Bank, or anything he did in regard to it. You had also proved to you that Mr. Bain, the manager of the Edinburgh branch, was his brother-in-law. His sister was Mrs. Davidson. Both of them were shareholders of the Bank, and Mr. Potter was a shareholder himself. Yet what he is accused of in this indictment is of fabricating and publishing false balance sheets to defraud the shareholders, including his brother-in-law, his sister, and himself. If you think you can by shadowy and slender inferences drawn from a perusal of the minutes, instead of looking at the solid facts in the case, examining how the balance sheets were made, examining the knowledge which the Directors had, seeing whether they were too sanguine about these accounts—if you say in the absence of all motive that Mr. Potter is guilty of all these things, I think it will be matter for great surprise. I am not going to make any appeal to your feelings on the part of Mr. Potter. From beginning to end I have gone through this matter as a matter of business, because I can confidently appeal to the facts in these documents, and I don't require to make any appeal to your feelings. I do think, however, it would be impossible for you or anyone else to witness without a certain degree of emotion a man of seventy-two years of age, after his laborious, successful, and honoured life, brought to sit there on a charge of this kind. I am sure you will not, without much clearer reason than anything we have heard, find him guilty of that crime. I don't appeal to your feelings, but I do appeal to your reason and your sense of honour in this matter— I appeal to your judgment. I have gone through the facts, and I say, treating this, not as a matter of feeling, but as a matter of judgment, that the fair inference and conclusion to be drawn from the evidence is a conclusion for innocence, and not for guilt. Therefore I ask you for a verdict of acquittal.

Mr. ASHER next addressed the jury on behalf of the prisoner Salmond. At the outset he severely censured the conduct of the Crown authorities in bringing against the accused charges which prevented their being able to claim release on bail as a matter of right, and yet abandoning those charges when the time came to prove them. The effect of this proceeding had

The City of Glasgow Bank Trial.

Mr. Asher. been to inflict on the accused three months' imprisonment before trial, and to do them a great wrong which no verdict of the jury could repair. In regard to the specific charges now urged against his client, his defence was not a denial that the balance sheets of the Bank were false and fabricated, but a simple declaration that his client had nothing to do with them in any way, and was as innocent and as ignorant of the falsification as any of the jury when they entered the box. In support of this contention, Mr. Asher pointed to the evidence adduced, which showed that on the occasion both of the preparation and of the issuing of the three balance sheets in question, Mr. Salmond was absent from Glasgow, and therefore could not possibly have had any part in the falsification. Was he connected in any way with the false balance sheets directly? He appended his name to the balances for each of the three years no doubt; but he did it as a matter of form, finding that his fellow-Directors had done it also; and from an examination of the balance book he could not possibly have detected the falsification, while it was no part of his duty to institute a general examination of the books of the Bank. Then in regard to Mr. Salmond's knowledge of the doubtful state of certain accounts, that ground of accusation had been reinforced by the prosecution by an allegation that certain items of profit said to have been earned by the Bank were not so earned, because they were made up of sums of interest on these bad accounts that had never been paid. This Mr. Asher characterised as a revival in another form of the eighth particular under the first head of the indictment, which the prosecution had been obliged to abandon, and he therefore objected to it on that ground. He admitted that Mr. Salmond had, as he averred in his declaration, some knowledge of the doubtful accounts, but it was only of a general kind; and because he, in advanced old age, allowed it to remain so, and did not of his own motion originate an investigation into the affairs of those firms which had large advances from the Bank, was he to be convicted of having had a guilty knowledge of the false entries in the balance sheets? I am sure (said Mr. Asher in concluding his address), as men of sense, you will accept no such extravagant view. It is out of the question to say that the failure to set in motion all the organisation which would have been required to clear up in the light of day the position of these large accounts in 1875—that the inability of my client, physically or mentally, to enter upon the task, is now to be imputed as evidence of guilty motive for a crime. I fear I have detained you too long, but I trust to your indulgence considering the magnitude of the issues which are involved. It is impossible to disguise the seriousness of the issues with regard to a person at the advanced age of my client, and I ask you to bear in mind, notwithstanding what

Addresses to Jury.

the Lord Advocate has said, that his long life, which is now drawing to a close, has been spent by securing to him the esteem and regard of all with whom he was associated. I ask you to bear in mind that he was a shareholder of the Bank to an extent which, if the prediction of the Crown proves true, involves ruin to himself; that he held these shares throughout, never selling a single one, and taking an additional allotment in 1873; that he has throughout the later years of his life, in respect of failing vigour, been necessarily absent from the Bank to an extent which distinguishes his case in the most marked degree from the case of the men who sit there with him. You cannot, as men of sense, look at his past position, and take these circumstances along with it, without coming to the conclusion that, whatever may be the result of this trial in regard to others, so far as he, at least, is concerned, you will in justice and fairness give him a verdict which will leave him to spend the remainder of his days, not in the squalor of a prison, but in the society of his friends; and, gentlemen, you will do more than that—you will dismiss him from this bar with his character unstained and his honour unsullied.

Mr. MACKINTOSH addressed the jury in defence of the prisoner Taylor. He pointed out that his client was put on the committee for managing the branches of the Bank as soon as he joined the Directorate, continued on that committee to the end, and was so little mixed up in what might be termed the "inner circle" of the Bank's transactions, that John Fleming did not even know him by sight. He contended that Mr. Taylor could have had no means of detecting the false statements in the balance sheets, inasmuch as they were in conformity with the books of the Bank. He evidently had faith in the balance sheets, and that being the case, the jury must acquit him, unless they were prepared to affirm one or other of two propositions—either that it was Mr. Taylor's duty personally to audit the books of the Bank, or that it had been proved that Mr. Taylor had had it brought to his knowledge that those books were falsified or manipulated. Both these propositions, the learned counsel maintained, were extravagant and untenable, and he entered at some length into argument to show that Mr. Taylor had never had before him materials for knowing that the books were falsified. In conclusion, Mr. Mackintosh said—I know that in dealing with the question whether Mr. Taylor has or has not been a party to this falsification, you will give the evidence of character which was submitted its full weight. I have said that this is an anxious case. I feel it to be a painfully anxious case. To a gentleman in Mr. Taylor's position we know what an adverse verdict means. I feel it is truly a matter of life and death. I know that if he leaves this bar branded by your verdict as guilty of this crime, time to him can bring no solace, and life

The City of Glasgow Bank Trial.

Mr. Mackintosh. for him can retain no charm. But I decline in this case to appeal to your feelings, or to demand your sympathy. Such appeals may be useful in turning the balance of a doubtful case; but here I am content to ask for simple justice. I ask you to be dispassionate, and to dismiss from your minds all prejudice. I ask you to discard all vague surmises, and all far-fetched suspicions, and to judge upon the evidence; and if you do so, I have no fear of the result.

Mr. Robertson. Mr. J. P. B. ROBERTSON next addressed the jury on behalf of the prisoner Inglis. He urged that all the evidence against his client which was of any value whatever was contained in the minute book of the Directors' proceedings, and he proceeded to discuss the part which, as revealed in that book, Mr. Inglis played in the management of the Bank, with the view of showing that, practising, as he did, his profession of the law in Edinburgh, he was really ignorant of the details about the bad accounts, and never acquired more knowledge about them than that they were unsatisfactory, but not, in the view of his co-Directors, hopeless. What Mr. Inglis had been guilty of was, as he himself said, " the most entire confidence in every statement and every figure that was laid before him." Guilty of that, guilty of remissness—the consequences of which to his friends must have been so stupendous that it must cast a shadow upon the remainder of his life—guilty of that; but of falsehood and fraud, of any crime contained in that indictment of sin against honour, or an offence against the law, not guilty.

Mr. Smith. Mr. GUTHRIE SMITH spoke in defence of the prisoner John Innes Wright. He regretted for Mr. Wright's own sake that that gentleman had not refused the invitation to join the Directorate of the Bank in 1875; but he argued that Mr. Wright was entirely ignorant of the state of the Bank when he joined it; that he remained in that ignorance throughout; that he had no personal motive in becoming a Director, as he had no overdraft on his account, and that of his firm was in fact gradually diminishing; and that the large credits advanced to his firm were arranged by Mr. Scott, and were in that gentleman's knowledge only, as he had the management of the finance department of Mr. Wright's firm. There is nothing that I can see (said Mr. Smith) from beginning to end connecting Mr. Wright in any way with the administration beyond this, that he attended Directors' meetings; and you are asked to say, upon the most shadowy evidence, that, having a seat at the Board, he had there the means of acquiring information which he failed to use. In a serious charge of this kind that, in my humble opinion, is not sufficient. It is insufficient to convict him of guilty knowledge. It certainly cannot be alleged against Mr. Wright that there was any intention to commit the serious

Addresses to Jury.

crime that is here laid to his charge. All through life his character has been entirely without reproach; and therefore, gentlemen, without fatiguing you further at this late hour of the evening, I confidently submit that, so far as Mr. Wright is concerned, the evidence wholly fails.

The DEAN OF FACULTY (Mr. FRASER) proceeded to address the jury on behalf of the prisoner Stronach, the Manager of the Bank. At the outset he complained bitterly of the conduct of the prosecution in bringing charges of embezzlement and theft against the Directors, and then withdrawing them after they had served their purpose. On these two charges he insisted on the jury pronouncing a verdict—a verdict of "not guilty." The needless imprisonment of the Directors had prevented counsel getting at the facts of the case, or learning, until they heard the figures from the accountant for the Crown, what was the misstatement of which they were accused; and if their counsel failed in satisfying the jury as to the entire innocence of these men of all intent to defraud, he begged them to make allowance for the disadvantages to which he referred. The learned Dean then proceeded to deal with the evidence as it affected Mr. Stronach, whose brother had been Manager of the Bank, and who was apparently a man of great energy and ability. He had conducted the business of the Bank from the period of Mr. Salmond's resignation down to 1875. Robert was a clerk in the Bank when his brother's illness came on—an illness caused by the anxiety of two or three large accounts. He breaks entirely down, and retires. Robert was asked to take his place, and did so apparently from fraternal affection rather than from love of office. And then he became acquainted with the position of certain accounts, which have been so often referred to. He hesitated to take the duties of a position so full of anxiety; but at last, through the entreaties of some and the remonstrances of others, he is induced to accept the appointment, after getting the promise from Morton that he would reduce his account by a payment of £400,000. But he is still in great anxiety; and he writes two letters to the Directors in answer to their offer—the second of which was preserved in the Directors' minute book. In the meantime Stronach steadfastly refused to advance a sixpence on his own responsibility; and the fact applied to the other prisoners as well as to him, that from the time of his appointment nothing was advanced to Morton, to Nicol Fleming, or to Smith, Fleming & Co., except upon good, tangible security. The Dean of Faculty therefore held that the Lord Advocate's remark about Stronach's unwillingness to advance a little money to some poor fellow in the country, while he was pouring it out like water to these firms, was unfair and unfounded. With regard to the Australian and New Zealand land speculations, it must be

The City of Glasgow Bank Trial.

Mr. Fraser. remembered that Stronach had nothing whatever to do with them; but at the same time he saw nothing in those investments that was not legitimate, and the evidence had been to the effect that they were exceedingly wise investments, and likely to prove the most valuable asset held by the liquidators of the Bank. Coming to the question of the balance sheets, the learned counsel asked if there was any evidence to show, not that they were false, but that they had been falsified by the accused for purposes of fraud. It must, in the first place, be borne in mind that these balance sheets were the work of Mr. Morison, the accountant of the Bank, and the *prima facie* responsibility for them must rest on their author. The Dean of Faculty went on to analyse Morison's evidence, and to trace from the lithographed scroll abstract of 1876 what he said was the method on which Morison had gone to work in the alterations he made. Those alterations were made by him only, and he was telling an untruth when he said that everything he did was by the direction of others. He was afraid that he might get into trouble himself, and so he laid it all on the Manager. After urging that Morison was unworthy of belief, the Dean of Faculty said the next question was whether, even if they held Stronach responsible for all these alterations, the balance sheets were actually false. The accountants called for the Crown said they were; they glibly rattled off the figures of what they called under-statements and over-statements; but what it all came to was this, that what was called a fraud was simply a system which did not commend itself to the enlightened and impartial mind of Mr. Muir. He proceeded to contend that the system followed in the Bank was simply that of entering the balance for or against the Bank under each separate head of account, instead of entering the whole amount of the assets on the one side and of the liabilities on the other. In order to establish this contention, the learned counsel quoted numerous figures from the balance sheet, and argued that the charges of under-statement were quite incorrect, because all that had been done had been to deduct the sum due to the Bank from the sum owing by it on each account, or *vice versa*, and bring out in the balance sheets simply the net result. The evidence of the Crown accountants with regard to these entries he characterised as "one of the most audacious pieces of impudence that he ever heard attempted by skilled witnesses." With regard to the item of £973,300, it had been put aside by Alexander Stronach as a sum that was absolutely secured, and all the accused did about it was to go on treating it as it had been treated for years before. They had no intention of concealing it from the public, or mis-stating it with intent to defraud. As to the bringing down of certain items from the heading of credit advances to Morton & Co., Nicol Fleming, and Smith, Fleming & Co., and placing them under the head of Government and other securi-

Addresses to Jury.

ties, they had only Mr. Morison's explanation as to how that was done; but, however it was done, Morison himself evidently regarded it as a proper thing to do, and he (the Dean of Faculty) could not for the life of him see there was anything wrong, and at all events it was perfectly capable of an innocent interpretation. Then with regard to the crediting of interest on the accounts of the three firms, he argued that the Directors were perfectly warranted in doing so—that they were hopeful that these accounts would ultimately turn out all right; and, besides, the accused could not be convicted of fraud because they were too hopeful. In conclusion the learned Dean said— Mr. Stronach was not a man like any of the other gentlemen at the bar. He was not a merchant with vast connections in every country in the globe, but he occupied the humbler position of an official with this Bank. His own fortune when he became a shareholder was, as was stated yesterday, £11,000; and he loses everything; but he must submit to that like every person involved in this vast calamity. Notwithstanding the misery caused by the collapse of this Bank, you are not entitled to intensify its horrors, as you would do by a conviction for crime where there was nothing criminal. It would not be asserting rational justice, but giving vent to the wild fury of exasperated feeling. The calamity is one which includes the largeness of national and the individuality of private interests; and certainly it would be a sad thing if one had to say that a verdict was delivered against these men, whose conduct when analysed was compatible with the purest innocence, and which, I think, is incompatible with, and cannot be construed into anything like guilt. I do not ask you to rise above the prejudices of society, not to put into your verdict the exasperated feelings that may arise from the misfortunes that have overtaken the shareholders in this Bank—the jury are men under rational influences and positive habits of thought—I do not ask you to do more than this—to give a fair consideration to what I have now laid before you, and the analysis I have made of the charges brought by the Lord Advocate in these various particulars. I do not go into the years 1877 and 1878, because they are upon the same lines, and are capable of the same explanations as the year I have treated. But I think I have done enough to show that if there is anything chargeable against me, it is not the offence of falsifying a balance sheet, but simply the offence of making up that balance sheet upon a wrong system, or according to principles not approved by the prosecution.

1 A

CHAPTER XII.

The Lord Justice-Clerk's Charge.

Gentlemen of the jury,—We are now nearing the close of this very long, painful, and important investigation. It has occupied a time, I believe, unexampled in the annals of this Court, as the occasion of it is without precedent in the history of the country. You have listened with attention, and have directed your minds and intelligence to evidence from witnesses lasting over this long time, and you have had your attention called to a great variety of documents, accounts, figures, balances, and results, which during that long period cannot fail to have perplexed you, as I must own they have perplexed me, and to leave you in considerable doubt as to what the result of the investigation was. I am glad, however, to think that, as the case went on, and with the assistance of addresses from the bar on both sides, of which I can only say that they were well worthy of the renown of the body to which those gentlemen belong, and well worthy of the occasion on which they were delivered—I am glad, I say, to think, now we have really approached the kernel of the question which is at issue before you, that I shall be able, within a reasonable compass, to winnow the case from a good deal of those surroundings which served to make it more intricate than it need have been, and to present for your consideration a few simple questions of fact which it remains for you to determine.

Something has been said by the counsel for the prisoners at the bar—not too much nor too urgently pressed—on two topics that cannot fail to be present to your minds. In the first place, the country is suffering under a great and unexampled calamity. This fabric, this joint-stock company of the City of Glasgow Bank, has met with an overwhelming catastrophe. Hundreds of families have been reduced from affluence or competence to poverty, and it is not wonderful that the feeling to which the learned counsel have alluded should have prevailed in many quarters, viz., a desire that the conduct of those in whose hands the calamity occurred, and under whose administration the institution was brought to ruin, should become the subject of judicial inquiry. That has been done. The inquiry has been full, and, as far as the Crown authorities could make it, complete. The whole facts connected with this most lamentable affair are now before you, and your verdict on it, whatever it may be, will undoubtedly

Lord Justice-Clerk (Lord Moncreiff).

The Lord Justice-Clerk's Charge.

command the respect to which it is entitled. On the other hand, gentlemen, there is no doubt that very large issues personal to the prisoners at the bar are in your hands. They are placed there—persons who have, during a long life, held a high position, enjoying the respect and confidence of their friends and the community—placed now in hazard of fame and fortune, and position, and good name, and liberty. These are the issues, no doubt, which depend upon your verdict. But, gentlemen, I have mentioned these things, as you may well suppose, for the purpose of your laying them entirely aside. What may be thought of our proceedings, what may be thought of your verdict out of doors, can be of no moment whatever either to you or to me. We are to deal with this case as if there were no such external surroundings, simply as a matter of proof and evidence, and to deal with it as we should with a case which excited no interest or sympathy in any quarter. Whether it be the one consideration or the other, they are equally foreign to the walls wherein we sit. We know of no such consideration save this, that the momentous issue which is now before you must lead you, as it will lead me, to weigh still more scrupulously the facts that have been proved in the scales of even-handed justice, and to discard from our consideration every other topic.

Now, having said so much, let me commence my remarks by referring you to the questions that are raised in this indictment. It is an indictment which substantially contains three branches of imputation against the prisoners at the bar. The prisoners are the Directors and the Manager of the City of Glasgow Bank ; and it was originally alleged against them, first, that they had fabricated and falsified on three several occasions the balance sheet for the year which they issued to the shareholders of the Bank—that they had done so in certain particulars which are specified in the indictment. The second charge which the indictment contained was one directed against certain of the individual prisoners ; and it was said that they, being Directors, had availed themselves of their position as Directors to obtain advances from the Bank in breach of their trust, and had embezzled the amount. The third charge was a charge of theft, for having improperly taken possession of bills sent to them for collection, and used them for the purpose of paying the debts of the Bank. Gentlemen, doubtless in any view which can be taken of it, these were very serious imputations indeed. However, the Lord Advocate, although we had sustained the relevancy of these two charges—and I need not go back to the views which were then expressed—after the evidence had been led, and looking to the facts at his command, and the expression of opinion which fell from us, came to the conclusion that his duty would be sufficiently discharged by abandoning the second and third charges, and confining his attention and yours to the three charges of fabri-

The City of Glasgow Bank Trial.

cating these balance sheets. Something, gentlemen, has been said regarding the course so followed by the public prosecutor. On that I have not a single remark to make. I have made it a rule from the bench never to form a judgment on the course followed by the public prosecutor in the exercise of the discretion which the law vests in him, for this simple reason, that the Court are not in possession of the information which would be necessary to form a judgment on that matter, and that the Lord Advocate exercises his discretion under a sense of his public responsibility, and may always be made responsible, although not to this Court. I cannot doubt, and I assume that the grounds on which the Lord Advocate proceeded were grounds which, to his mind, were satisfactory. He is quite able to form an opinion, and quite able to maintain it; and therefore, gentlemen, I don't make a single remark on the course which has been followed, excepting to draw your attention to the fact that these two charges of embezzlement and theft are no longer presented to you for your consideration.

Laying, therefore, that matter aside, and addressing ourselves to the questions that are raised under the three charges, viz., the charges of falsifying the balance sheets for the years 1876, 1877, and 1878, you will observe still further that the Crown have departed from the eighth head of the alleged falsification. The falsifications are alleged to have taken place in regard to eight specific sums. The last of these ran originally in this form— "Bad and irrecoverable debts to an amount far exceeding the whole capital stock of the Bank were included under article 1 on the creditor side, and so treated as subsisting and available assets of the company." That item has been struck out, and the effect of that I may have occasion to say a word upon by and by.

Now, gentlemen, you will observe that the charge which is made against these Directors and the Manager is "that you did, all and each or one or more of you, wickedly and feloniously, with intent to defraud the members of the said company and the public, for the purpose of concealing and misrepresenting the true state of affairs of the company, concoct and fabricate, or cause or procure to be concocted and fabricated, a false and fictitious abstract balance sheet or statement of affairs"; then follows the statement of affairs on page 3; and then, after the specification of the particulars, in which it is said that the balance sheet was false, it is set out farther that "the said prisoners did each, with intent to defraud, use and utter the said false and fabricated abstract balance sheet or statement of affairs as true, well knowing it to be false and fabricated, and for the purpose of concealing and misrepresenting the true state of the said company's affairs." There is a similar charge in regard to the balance sheets of 1877 and 1878, but I need not go over it in detail.

Now, gentlemen, that being the state of matters, there are three

The Lord Justice-Clerk's Charge.

questions that arise on each of these three charges, and you must keep them clearly and distinctly in mind—first, whether these balance sheets are false ; secondly, whether the prisoners, each of them or any of them, was in the knowledge that they were false ; and thirdly, whether what they did with the balance sheet— namely, the circulation and publication of the report with the balance sheet—was with the intention of deceiving the share- holders and the public.   These are three matters that will require to be very carefully kept in mind, and kept separate, during the whole course of the inquiry into which I now shortly propose to lead you.

But upon these three heads I shall make these general remarks. The prisoners at the bar are the Directors and the Manager of a joint-stock bank.   You have heard a good deal about what the duties of a Director of such an institution are ; and from the views that were quoted to you by my learned friend Mr. Trayner as having been expressed by the Court in former cases I have nothing to suggest in the way of dissent.   A Director is generally a man who has other avocations to attend to.   He is not a professional banker.   He is not expected to do the duty of a professional banker, as we all know.   He is a man selected from his position, from his character, from the influence he may bring to bear upon the welfare of the bank, and from the trust and confidence which are reposed in his integrity and in his general ability.   But I need not say that it is no part of his duty to take charge of the accounts of the bank.   He is entitled to trust the officials of the bank who are there for that purpose, and as long as he has no reason to suspect the integrity of the officials, it can be no matter of imputation to him that he trusts to the statements of the officials of the bank acting within the proper duties of the depart- ment which has been entrusted to them.   You may assume that. It will not, however, follow from that, that where special circum- stances arise to bring under the notice of the directors particular interests connected with the joint stock company there may not ensue an obligation of inquiry and an obligation of action which might not be necessarily inferred from the nature of the position which they hold.   We must look this matter plainly in the face as it actually occurs in practical life.   Remark has been made on the amounts—the extraordinary amounts—disclosed in this case —amounts that take one's breath away as applied to ordinary commercial concerns ; but we must not assume that in the incep- tion of the sad history which we have had detailed here during the last fortnight there was anything abnormal whatever.   Great mercantile success necessarily produces great mercantile transac- tions.   Where you have merchants who count their profits by a hundred thousand pounds a year they, of course, must have the same banking facilities that a man requires who only counts them by a thousand.   The proportion will be larger, but the nature of

373

The City of Glasgow Bank Trial.

them will be precisely the same ; and it cannot be doubted that a bank that secures for its customers persons in that enormous scale of business also secures for its shareholders unusually large profits. But then, gentlemen, with the magnitude of the transactions there comes a magnitude of danger also, for the merchant, although on that large scale, is subject, of course, to those fluctuations that have the effect of tying up a man's money temporarily, and depriving him of the use of it that he expected, and for these temporary occasions, of course, the millionaire, as well as the poorer merchant, requires or requests from those with whom he does his monetary transactions temporary assistance, and he gets it, with security that is reckoned to be, and is properly valued at, quite sufficient to keep the bank safe. But then, gentlemen, comes the crash. A war, a famine, a drought, a strike may make the whole of that edifice tumble down. The debt and the security go together. What is the bank to do? Then it is that the unprofessional Director finds himself face to face with an emergency which, beyond all question, it is difficult and hard to meet. The question for him then is, is he to bring the bank down by bringing down the debtor, or is he to carry on the debtor in the hope of the vessel getting into calmer water and righting herself in a smoother sea? We all know that that kind of question has been presented too often in our commercial experience. But, gentlemen, there is one rule which a Director is bound to follow. In that, as in every case, honesty is the only policy, and neither the interests of the shareholders nor the chances of recovering the debt, nor any of those considerations which doubtless, when one is in the middle of them, seem to be almost overwhelming, can for a moment justify or excuse or palliate the deliberate statement of what is known to be false. I will not say what course the Directors of this institution could or might have followed. All I can say is, that, whatever their difficulties and whatever their temptations, there is nothing in the circumstances in which they were placed which can in the least degree palliate the offence with which they are charged if in reality they are found to be guilty of it. So much, gentlemen, for the offence.

Secondly, as to the knowledge of the Directors—as to their knowledge that these balance sheets were fabricated. Now, what the prosecutor has undertaken to prove, and says that he has proved, is not that these Directors were bound to know the falsity of the statements in the balance sheets—not that they lay under obligations to know it, not that they had the means of knowledge —but that, in point of fact, they did know it ; and that is what you must find before you can convict the prisoners of any part of the offences attributed to them. You must be able to affirm in point of fact, not that they had a duty and neglected it, not that they had the means of information within their power and

374

The Lord Justice-Clerk's Charge.

failed to use them, but that, as a matter of fact, when that balance sheet was issued they knew that the statements contained in it were false. I say that, because there has been some phraseology used in the course of this trial that would seem to indicate that a constructive knowledge was all that was required for such a case. Constructive knowledge might be quite sufficient if we were dealing here simply with an action for civil debt or civil reparation ; for what a man is bound to know he shall be held to have known. But that has no place at all when a man is charged with crime. His crime is his guilty knowledge, and nothing else. He is charged with personal dishonesty, and you must be able to affirm that on the evidence before you can convict him. But while I say that, gentlemen, I by no means mean to say that the knowledge which you must find must necessarily be deduced from direct evidence of it. You are not entitled to assume it ; but you are entitled to infer that fact, as you are entitled to infer any other fact, from facts and circumstances which show and carry to your mind the conviction that the man when he circulated, or when he made that balance sheet, knew that it was false. You must be quite satisfied, however, before you can draw that conclusion, not merely that it is probable, or likely, or possible that he knew, but that he did, in point of fact, know the falsehood of which he is accused.

Then, gentlemen, lastly, on the question of intent or motive—the fraudulent use only of this document, for that is of the essence of the crime—it is said to have been issued and circulated for the purpose of deceiving the shareholders and the public as to the true state of the Bank. Of that you must also be satisfied ; for it would be of no moment that these statements were not in themselves accurate, unless they were put there for a fraudulent and dishonest purpose. It may be suggested that the end which the Directors intended to serve was not to injure any one ; that their real object was in the meantime to keep the Bank afloat, until better times should relieve their securities and their debtors, and enable them to pay their way. Gentlemen, I have to tell you that, so far from that being a sufficient defence, it is exactly the offence and the motive described in the indictment, because if they intended to give the Bank breathing time by inducing the shareholders to imagine it was more prosperous than it was, then that is precisely the intent to deceive which is libelled in the indictment, for they put in hazard exactly the same interests which would have been imperilled if they had been actuated by the strongest and most malignant motive. The men who were induced to hold on and the men who were induced to buy are just ruined precisely as they would have been if that had been the result intended by the Directors. Did they mean to deceive? If they meant to represent the Bank as being in a more prosperous condition than it was, and if they meant

375

The City of Glasgow Bank Trial.

the shareholders to believe that, then they intended to run the
risk of all the results that might follow from that deception.
And, accordingly, I could not certainly say to you that even if
you were satisfied that that was the real object which the
Directors had in view, it would tend in the slightest degree to
take off from the motive or intent that is here libelled. On
the other hand, you must be quite satisfied that there was an
intention to deceive on the part of the prisoners before you can
find them guilty. And, gentlemen, to conclude these general
remarks, I can only say that the offence with which they are
charged is not only a crime—not only comes within the compass
of the criminal law, but, if deliberately committed, is in truth a
crime of very great magnitude. I need not say that the larger
the interests committed to their charge the more they were
bound to absolutely honest administration.

And, gentlemen, having said those things, let us now turn to
the first of these balance sheets. And first, as to the falsehood.
I have endeavoured, as far as I could, by assiduous attention to
the evidence while it was being delivered, and also by devoting
such spare time as I could to the comprehension of it, to arrive
at some clear and definite result upon the figures submitted to
you, and the arguments that have been raised upon them. I am
not by any means confident that I have succeeded in that task ;
and I am the less solicitous about it because I have no doubt at
all that there are those of your number who are not unaccus-
tomed to inquiries of this kind, or at least to deal with figures of
a somewhat analogous kind. But it seems to me that the result
of the evidence which we have has now reduced this case to a
very simple issue. Mr. Muir made out some states showing
the results of his evidence in regard to the different balance
sheets, and I have requested that copies should be made for the
jury, because it will greatly shorten my exposition of the evidence
in regard to that matter, and will show you at a glance the result
of the evidence of Mr. Muir in regard to the alleged falsification
of the balance sheets. There are three of them—one applicable
to each year. I intended them, however, more to assist your
private deliberations after I have finished my remarks than
to be the subject of comment at present. [They are handed
to the jury.] These documents are simply the result of Mr.
Muir's evidence, and they show the alleged over-statements
and the alleged under-statements brought into a very clear and
intelligible form.

I shall begin with the balance sheet of 1876 ; and first let me
call your attention to what Mr. Morison described as the mode
in which these balance sheets, or abstracts rather, which are
ultimately reported to the shareholders, are made up. The
head office keeps its own books—its weekly balance book and its
general balance ledger ; and when a balance is to be struck, there

The Lord Justice-Clerk's Charge.

is obtained from the branches a statement of the balances on
their accounts, and the accountant, having received from the
inspector of branches his statement of balances, goes over the
whole and makes up a general balance sheet showing the result
of the Bank's transactions. In the balance ledger of the Bank
these transactions are entered, showing the balance on the year.
He explained to you that he took the balance as appearing upon
the last weekly balance sheet; that he read over the items to the
Directors, who had the balance ledger before them; and that
they checked how far the entries in the balance ledger corresponded with what was read to them by the accountant, Mr.
Morison, from the weekly states and other documents. And
then that balance is abstracted. Mr. Morison makes up his
abstract; he has it revised, as he explained, by the Manager; and
then it is laid before the Directors and adopted. The weekly
balance book contains the balances at the head office from week
to week—I may leave the branches out of view in the meantime
—the last weekly balance is the one taken for the entry of the
balance in the balance ledger; and then the balance ledger is
the foundation, but only the foundation, of the abstract which is
laid before the shareholders of the Bank. That is proved to be
the course of procedure.

Now, it is said that this balance sheet is defective in seven
particulars, and those seven particulars consist of sums which
are said to have been overstated or understated for the purpose
of deceiving the public. I shall, meanwhile, speak of the first
five of these sub-divisions. The first is the amount of deposits,
which is said to be understated by one million odds; the second
is the amount of drafts outstanding, which are said to be understated; third, the amount of bills of exchange said to be understated; and then you have over-statements on the other side
consisting of £29,000 cash on hand and £753,000 of investments.
Now, you have had a long and anxious inquiry, and a great deal
of most acute and powerful observation on the items contained in
these five articles of the indictment. But I am glad, for your
convenience, to think that in the view which I take of this matter
it will not be necessary for me to dwell, at all events at any
length, on any but two of these sums, which were the subject of
dispute. It was observed from the bar, and observed quite
rightly and correctly, that these alleged over-statements and
under-statements consist of two classes—one class is at variance
with the books, and the other class is in conformity with
the books. Now, in the meantime, if you please, I shall confine
myself entirely to two of these alleged mis-statements, misrepresentations, or falsifications which are not in conformity with the
books. I think you will see immediately the reason of that
observation. These two falsifications or misrepresentations are
two that you have heard a great deal about, and which it will

The City of Glasgow Bank Trial.

not be necessary for me to explain to you in any great detail. The balance sheet, it is said, contains on both sides the sum of £973,000 as a deduction from the transactions of the year. It also contains, under the head of Government securities, the sum of £751,000. £751,000 was the original sum, but it is raised to £753,000 in this particular article. It contains that sum included under Government securities and other investments, which in reality ought to have been placed in the credit accounts. And the first matter that I shall ask your attention to—and you will find it to be one of very great moment in this inquiry—is, putting aside altogether for the present the criticism on the other items contained in these specified charges, to consider these two alleged misrepresentations by themselves, and let us see how the evidence applies to them.

Gentlemen, I take the sum of £973,000 first; and it is right that you should understand what will come out still more clearly when I go to the other charges, that the charge under these heads is not so much of falsifying results as of falsifying amounts. The sides of the account will balance precisely in the same way after the operation, which was alleged to be performed, had been performed as it would before. But in regard to this £973,000, its effect is simply this—to represent the transactions of the Bank on floating debt to be just a million less than it was. Gentlemen, it is said that this sum of £973,000 was introduced into the books, and that it was to be found in the weekly balance book and in the balance ledger ; and that is quite true, and if that had been consistently followed out it would have been a very important fact. But the main thing in this sum of £973,000 for you to consider—for it is entirely in your hands—is, was there any truth or honesty in that sum ? Did it ever represent anything ? There is not a vestige or a trace of it in the general books of the Bank ; and you have the evidence of Mr. Morison, and the evidence of Mr. Muir, and the evidence of every man who has looked at the books, and the entire silence of those who could have cleared it up, which corroborate beyond all question—at least you must consider whether it does or does not—the fact that this sum of £973,000, whoever is responsible for it, is in truth an interpolation without any substance on which to rest. I shall read to you what Mr. Morison says about it. I shall have occasion to remark upon his evidence afterwards, as much comment has been made upon it ; but in the meantime I shall refer you to what he says as to what he knew about this, and if Mr. Morison can tell us no more, I think you may assume that there was no more to be told. He was asked—" Why was the sum of £973,000 deducted from the foreign and colonial credits ? —A. Because there was a credit account to that extent. Q. Did you get instructions from anybody to deduct it ?—A. No ; it was in the ledger. Q. Why did you put it in the ledger ?—A.

The Lord Justice-Clerk's Charge.

In June, 1873, there was an entry made by the instruction of the late Manager, Mr. Alexander Stronach, which appears in the book titled ' City of Glasgow Bank Cash Book, private, No. 6,' extracts from which are contained in No. 2A. I made that entry ; it is in the following terms :—' Foreign and colonial credits No. 2, the following credits to be retired as they mature, and debited under the respective accounts to credit a/c No. 2, against which securities are now held by the Bank, and in process of realisation and payment of the proceeds—£973,000.' " That entry does unquestionably occur in the private ledger which is referred to. Mr. Morison proceeds—" That deduction from foreign and colonial credits was carried on in the books and in the balance sheets from year to year thereafter down to 1878 inclusive, without any change being made. There was a note written by the late Manager giving the particulars of that deduction, but I never got the particulars." Then he is asked— " Was it a right deduction? " and he says, " I would not like to say so." Now, gentlemen, the fact unquestionably remains that that entry having been made by Alexander Stronach in 1873, there is not a trace in the books of any such sum being represented by securities or by anything else. It is for you to judge, but the question is, whether it was not a sum written off without there being anything to represent it, in consequence of the fear that the Manager then had that the transactions of the Bank would be considered too large for their position, and his anxiety to reduce the apparent amount. Gentlemen, I am not desirous at all of casting imputations on the memory of men who can no longer defend themselves, but the fact remaining that nobody can account for that sum of £973,000 is certainly one from which you are entitled to draw your own inferences. It is, unfortunately, only too true that in 1873 we have, in the correspondence under Alexander Stronach's own hand, the fact of his intense solicitude about the advances which had been given, which, it is plain from his own letters, he had not taken the Directors into counsel about, for he says so in the plainest terms. You will consider, therefore, whether it can be doubted that that sum of £973,000 was not a correct, but was a false deduction from the transactions of the Bank. You will find it in the slip that I have given you, placed on either side of the account. It makes no difference at all upon the ultimate result. The difference it does make, and the difference intended, according to the prosecutor—it is for you to say if you adopt it—was to diminish the amount of the liabilities or the contingencies of the Bank by the amount of £973,000. I say nothing at this moment as to who is responsible for that. The first question you have to consider is, whether you are satisfied that that is a false deduction.

The second question relates to the sum of £751,000, which Mr. Morison says was taken out of the amount of the credit advances,

The City of Glasgow Bank Trial.

and was inserted in the balance sheet among the Government and
other securities, the meaning of which is, according to the allegation, that it was taken out of those credit advances which were
dependent for their realisation on the debtors to whom the advances had been made, and represented that sum—amounting to
three-quarters of a million—as being invested in securities for
behoof of the Bank. Gentlemen, these are not indifferent things.
If a man borrows or obtains upon overdraft an advance of one
or two thousand pounds, that is one thing ; if the Bank invests its
surplus profits to the extent of one or two thousand pounds in
Government or other securities, that is a totally different thing.
It is not an advance ; it is a transaction of an entirely different
kind. Now, it is said, and that you must assume as true, for
there has been no evidence led on the other side to impugn that
result, although there have been strong comments made in regard
to it—I say, assuming that this ought to have been charged
against the debtors in the advances—that is to say, in their
name—as expected assets coming from debtors to whom advances
had been made, it is impossible to say that it is consistent, with
any imaginable principle of stating accounts, to take that out of
the account in which it stood in the books, and to place it where
it did not stand as a Government security, or a security of any
kind. Nor would it make the smallest difference, I think you
will be of opinion, whether security had been taken for the advance or not. The fact remained that it was not an investment.
That was not the banking term for it, nor did it express the
nature of the transaction. It was an advance—whether an
advance on security or an advance without security is of no
moment. It was under the right title in the books ; it comes
under the wrong title in the balance sheet.

Now, gentlemen, it is for you to consider that, and be satisfied
about it ; but it has this element, which is very important, that
there is no such entry in the book under the account or the
title under which it appears in the abstract, and that therefore
the alteration which was made on the abstract makes the abstract
disconform to the books. In the view which I take of this case
that is most important ; for it is one thing to say, "You made
up this abstract from the books, but the books were wrong," and
quite another thing to say, "You had the books in your hand,
and you deliberately altered what you found there, making it not
only inaccurate itself, but disconform to the accurate entry which
you had before you when you made it." And therefore, gentlemen, upon the first question, whether these two sums of £973,000
and £751,000 were entered falsely in this balance sheet for 1876,
you will consider whether the evidence has satisfied you that such
was the fact.

Gentlemen, there have been a variety of other sums called in
question in this balance sheet, and after a good deal of evidence

The Lord Justice-Clerk's Charge.

and a good deal of discussion it has at last come to this, that these sums which are called in question are accurately taken from the books—I mean from the books from which they ought to have been taken—the balance ledger and the weekly balances.   It would have saved a good deal of trouble if it had been brought out a little more clearly at first ; but the complaint really is this, that these are not balances, but differences, and that instead of giving the credit and debit balance of the accounts to which they relate, more than one account is taken, and they are set against each other, and where the Bank is debtor in one account and creditor in another, then only the difference is inserted in the balance ledger, instead of both sides of the account.   Now, that is all.   There is no controversy as to figures.   There is no controversy as to the truth of the sums in question.   There is no controversy that that is the balance of these cross accounts.   The controversy relates to this, whether it was properly entered, not so much in the balance sheet as in the balance ledger.   Gentlemen, I by no means say that if this entry in the balance ledger was an erroneous entry to the knowledge of the Directors, they are not guilty of falsifying the balance sheet if they transfer that erroneous entry to the balance sheet.   But you will at once see that it makes a very different kind of allegation from that which was the subject of my former remarks.   It may be quite true—I think we are bound to hold that it is true, because such evidence as we have from Mr. Muir and Mr. Hutton unquestionably points at that result—that these balances ought not to have been carried into the balance ledger in that way, but that both sides of the accounts should have been taken.   That may have been the correct form of book-keeping, and therefore, if that was so, then you may say that to that extent the balance sheet does not truly represent the balance which ought to have been entered in a different way in the balance ledger.   I must own, gentlemen —and I don't hesitate to tell you—that I should have been much better satisfied if the true nature of the crime alleged had been more clearly evinced in the indictment, because in those cases it must be manifest to you that the true falsification was of the books and not of the balance sheet.   But I don't think it necessary to go into that at any length, because, if it came to this question of book-keeping, the next question would be, is there evidence to show that this was done with a fraudulent intent? and in order to ascertain that it would have been necessary, in my view, to have shown, not that in this particular year the abstract balances were so carried down, but to have shown what the ordinary practice of the Bank was, and that it was departed from with an object.   I am unable to judge whether the crossing of particular accounts is or is not a proper banking operation in the balance ledger of the Bank itself.   I can conceive cases in which it might be convenient ; but, on the other hand, it might

The City of Glasgow Bank Trial.

be the instrument of great fraud, as it is said to be here. That appears to me to be doubtful, but it is entirely in your hands. You may dismiss altogether the controversy about the figures. They are there at your hand, and all I have to tell you about them is that these are the true balances, or rather the rectification of the two sides of the account. And, accordingly, it is quite unnecessary that you should pursue the investigation into the figures which has formed the subject of so much remark from the bar. The real question is whether you can say, in the first place, upon the evidence that you have, as a matter that has been demonstrated to your satisfaction, that to carry the balances of separate accounts into the balance ledger, and not the two sides of the account, is a false operation ; and in the second place, whether you think the evidence sufficient to show that that was done in these three years, with the fraudulent object of it being copied by the accountant of the Bank into the balance sheet and promulgated by the Directors. The question of how far the Directors were in the knowledge of it relates to a subsequent part of the inquiry. But on the whole matter, gentlemen, it rather seems to me—I don't withdraw it from your consideration—but it seems to me that it will lighten your labours, and really relieve you of some amount of obscurity which may still hang over this troublesome part of the case, if you dismiss it from your mind. If on the first two branches which I have referred to you shall find that the abstract balance sheet was falsified to the extent of a million and three-quarters, it does not seem to me that we need engage in book-keeping controversies, or that you need pay any great regard to these other less important items. Some of them are large beyond a doubt ; but you will consider the whole of that matter.

Before going farther, I may make a remark on the two balance sheets for 1877 and 1878. There is a very remarkable entry in the balance sheet for 1877 ; and probably you will come to be of opinion that it has a very strong bearing on some of the remarks which fell from my learned friend, the Dean of Faculty, in his very admirable address of yesterday. The £973,000 does not appear on the balance sheet of 1877 ; but instead of that there are some new entries which had never appeared before, and which made up a sum somewhat larger, amounting to £1,300,000. This is spoken to both by Mr. Morison and by Mr. Muir ; and they both say the same thing about it ; indeed, you will find it in the red ink balance sheet for 1877, on which I am going to say a word by and by. But Mr. Muir is asked, " In the scroll abstract or draft for 1877, does the £963,000 appear as before?" and he says, " No ; in neither 127 nor 131 does it appear. [131 is the red ink scroll.] The amount of bills payable to account, after having the £973,000 deducted, is carried into this ledger, but it has been scored out, as if some new idea had occurred to

The Lord Justice-Clerk's Charge.

them—another way of doing it; and I find in No. 131 a pencil
jotting which shows the new method that was adopted of
falsifying the accounts. *Q.* Of something substituted for the
£973,000?—*A.* Yes. *Q.* What is substituted?—*A.* I find opposite the words 'Bills payable' entered £2,683,348. That is
wrong to the extent of £2300. Then from that sum is deducted
cash lodged on D/A, £94,368; anticipations, £527,940; S., F.
& Co., £552,704; and J. N. F., £158,000—together, £1,333,012
19s. 1d.; difference, £1,350,335, which was the sum stated in
the published balance sheet." I should have reminded you,
under my remarks on the balance of 1876, that the £751,000
taken out of the credit advances and placed under Government
securities was a part of the debt due by these three firms,
Smith, Fleming & Co., James Nicol Fleming, and James Morton
& Co. That has a considerable bearing on some other parts of
the case, and I shall have occasion to speak of it afterwards.
Here we have the interpolation in a new form; that is to say,
the £973,000 does not appear, but these three items appear,
amounting together to £1,350,000, including cash on deposit
account, £94,000; anticipations, £527,000; brought down from
Smith, Fleming & Co., £552,000; and from Nicol Fleming,
£158,000. Gentlemen, you will consider the effect of the fact
of that alteration on the balance sheet. Morison says, "There
were no entries made for these alterations. They were not
made from any entries or any heading in the books." Then he
is asked, "Are they purely fictitious?" and he says, "There are
no entries for them. *Q.* Then are they fictitious entirely?—
A. So far as I know." So, gentlemen, whoever made that entry
or made up that balance sheet was certainly of opinion at that
time that the sum of £973,000 ought not to enter the balance
sheet, and that those other sums ought to enter the balance sheet.
You will consider what effect that fact has when you come to
consider whether the sum of £973,000 was or was not an entry
believed to be honest. I pass over the other items; they are so
analogous to those of 1876 that they don't require more observation from me, although you will keep in mind all that has been
addressed to you from both sides of the bar on that subject.
In the year 1878 the sum of £973,000 again appears—also a
fact not without its significance. But in that balance sheet
there is a sum of £200,000 added for what is called reserve gold,
which, it is said by Morison, and apparently there is no dispute
about it, was purely fictitious, and was, in fact, taken off the debt
of Smith, Fleming & Co. These are the falsifications and fabrications to which I think your attention had better be, if not
confined, at all events chiefly directed.

But then, gentlemen, I approach the much more delicate and
difficult question—who is responsible for that false statement in
the balance sheet? And in this instance, as regards those two

The City of Glasgow Bank Trial.

sums, and, indeed, as regards all that I have spoken to, we are
not without information, provided it is information on which you
can rely, in regard both to the manner in which the alteration of
falsification was made and the object of it. And this leads me
now, gentlemen, to deal with the account which Morison gives of
this matter ; and I must ask you to give to the subject, which I
am now about to enter on, your most anxious attention, because
it truly depends on the credibility of the witness, and that is so
eminently a matter for you, so entirely a matter within your
province, that you will require to make up your minds upon it
with caution, and care, and intelligence, but to come to a conclusion on that question whether you think Morison's evidence is
to be relied on or not. A great deal hangs upon it, and I must
now address myself to it. Gentlemen, it cannot fail to have
struck you—it struck me very painfully—a painful incident in a
very painful proceeding—that of all these officials of the Bank—
and I am bound in justice to the accused to say so—Mr. Leresche
was the only one who did not come here to admit that he had
committed a fraud. Of Mr. Leresche's evidence, I am bound to
say that it was given with great candour, with great sincerity,
and I think was in every way worthy of credit. I did not intend
to include Mr. Miller in my observations, but the three subordinate officials. Mr. Miller's evidence was in the highest
degree creditable to him. Nothing could have been clearer or
more explicit. But, gentlemen, Mr. Morison came here to say
that he himself was the man who perpetrated this fraud, no
doubt, as he says, at the instigation or by the direction of his
superiors, but that he did it. Morris, Stronach's confidential
clerk, admitted to you that in keeping the private ledger he
valued James Nicol Fleming's securities at par—he said, in
order to make the thing square—without any authority, and without the slightest foundation for the entry. And then you have,
I regret to say, the fact brought out that another witness, Turnbull, admitted that in his return of the gold in the Bank coffers
for 1878 he stated it at, I think, twice the amount that was
actually there. Gentlemen, I think I should not, in the discharge of my duty, avoid remarking on that matter. It is
impossible, in any inquiry of this kind, not to feel and not to
express the reprobation which acts of that kind deserve. Nor
does it make it at all better that they were the servants of a man
that they say wished them to betray their trust and falsify the
accounts. The same excuse might be open to every official in
any position of life. And therefore, gentlemen, you will take
along with you that element, and it is not without its importance
in this matter. But, gentlemen, at the same time, the prosecution can only work with the materials which are open to it. It
might have been impossible to detect this fraud without the evidence of some one who had complicity with it. And although

384

The Lord Justice-Clerk's Charge.

the observation made by some of the counsel for the prisoners is one not to be lightly treated in regard to the nature of the avowal and confession which Morison had to make, you will recollect that still it is a question for yourselves, and that which satisfies your minds on the fact is that which is evidence of the fact in the case. Now, gentlemen, I must fairly own that this evidence of Morison in some respects stands on a very insecure and unsatisfactory basis. I shall read to you a few passages from his evidence if you desire it, or probably I can state it quite accurately, unless you would rather hear his words.

A JUROR—If you state it, my lord, it will be quite sufficient.

The LORD JUSTICE-CLERK—When Mr. Morison was first in the witness-box, I certainly took up the impression, although he did not say it absolutely, and was not altogether consistent in his statement—I understood that what he said was this: He first described the mode in which the balance sheets were made up, as to getting in the balances from the branches, and then he made up a scroll abstract. That scroll abstract he wrote out in black ink, and took it to the Manager. He said it was arranged that the Manager and Mr. Potter should meet and go over that abstract, and that they did so, and that, in consequence of their instructions, he made the entry of £973,000, or rather that he made the entry of the sum of £751,000. He admitted afterwards that he had taken the figure from the balance ledger. He said he made the red ink alterations on the black ink scroll which he had taken with him, and then from that he made out the clean copy of the balance sheet for the Directors. But, gentlemen, it turned out that there was no foundation at all for that statement, as far as the particular document was concerned. I rather think the Crown originally supposed, as I certainly supposed, that the document with the red ink markings on it was the original scroll—the one which he took to the meeting with Potter and Stronach—and that the red ink marks were the alterations which Potter and Stronach directed to be made. And that would have made a very clear case of it as far as his evidence was concerned. But, gentlemen, he did not stand to that; and after a good deal of confusion—I don't think it necessary to use a stronger word, because, in my opinion, Morison was a very confused witness—I don't think he kept his presence of mind well in the witness-box; he was agitated, and, moreover, he was not by any means a willing witness for the Crown; I think there were plain indications of that; but at last it came to this, that that was not the document which he took to the meeting; that the red ink marks were not put on at that time; and at last he said he remembered that he destroyed the black ink scroll which he took to the meeting. And therefore, gentlemen, you may discard that evidence altogether, except for this purpose—you have a copy of the scroll, and it is

2 A

The City of Glasgow Bank Trial.

not difficult to see what was in the mind of the man who made up these alterations—whether he did that by direction or not by direction, you see the fact. The Dean of Faculty yesterday most ingeniously went through what he said was a demonstration that Morison was really the author of all these alterations himself. His argument was chiefly confined to the scroll of 1877, but you heard it—it was very ingenious, very powerfully put, and you will consider what effect it produced upon your own minds; but this, at all events, is certain, that the theory with which the Crown started upon Morison's evidence gave way, and that whoever made these alterations, or rather whoever instructed them to be made, the document now produced is not the original document which Morison presented, as he alleged. There is a little more, gentlemen, before I come to the main and direct question here. I asked Morison how Potter and Stronach, who he said gave these directions at that meeting, got the figures. He said they had no figures and no books, and that he had to go and get the information and the particulars of bills payable, and also to get the details of the credit advances, in order, he said, to see if any deduction could be made from them, and that he went and got information from the other officials. I suppose none was available; but it certainly would have been satisfactory if there had been some collateral evidence from these officials about this matter. There is no doubt the evidence of the abstract itself, which, as far as corroboration is concerned, is strong corroboration of the *res gestæ*—the substance of what Morison speaks to. The fact that the balance sheet was altered is a very strong circumstance in support of the allegation which Morison makes; but still, as upon his evidence a very important matter hangs, it certainly would have been to be desired, if Morison really went from the meeting to the officials, that some corroborative evidence of that should have been at hand. Now, gentlemen, I have made the observations I thought right in the direction of the defence, on Morison's testimony. But upon the main matter of fact he was clear enough, that he had a meeting with Stronach and with Potter, and that they directed him to make that alteration of the £751,000. The question is whether that carries conviction to your minds—and I need not say that in regard to Potter it is of the most vital consequence. If you believe Morison, if you think his evidence satisfactory and conclusive, if you think it is sufficient on which to find that Mr. Potter was not only cognisant of that falsification, but directed it, then I need not say that there is no alternative in this matter. And thus, on that question of the £751,000, it rests upon the evidence of Morison; but if his evidence is believed, then Stronach and Potter directed that alteration. If, on the other hand, you should think that Morison's evidence is not to be implicitly relied

The Lord Justice-Clerk's Charge.

upon, then Potter will remain in the same position as the other prisoners at the bar in relation to those two sums.

Lord
Justice-Clerk.

But, gentlemen, what are we to say of Stronach's position in regard to this particular part of the imputation? You have evidence from Morison that the £973,000 had been the subject of conversation with him. He called his attention to it standing in the book at one time, and Stronach said it was there before he came, and that it had better not be meddled with ; and that he said in 1878 that he hoped that would be the last time that he would require to make such an entry. Of course, these matters depend on the same question of credibility as the others to which I have referred ; but even if Morison had not said so—even if you had no proof that Stronach was aware of that sum of £973,000 which was there, and which he inherited from his predecessor, you could hardly fail to infer that an entry of that kind in the private cash book was known to the Manager. I don't say that the mere duty to know would convict him of knowing, but it is for you to consider whether it is or is not proof of the fact that he was cognisant of that £973,000 entry, that it stood in that private cash book, and that there was no entry of any kind or description which could be found in any of the books to justify or explain it. Gentlemen, that is a matter on which you also, painful as it is, must make up your minds. I shall say no more about it on that part of the case. It is a matter entirely in your hands. If you shall be of opinion that the evidence is not sufficient, even against Stronach, that any such meeting took place, or that he knew that the alteration had been made, then, of course, you will give him the benefit of any doubt that rests upon your minds on that subject. But it must be plain to you that the position of the Manager of the Bank is entirely different from that of the Directors, and that things that you could not infer as matters of fact as regards the Directors, it may be that you find yourselves compelled to infer in regard to the man who was professionally charged with the knowledge and the keeping of the whole accounts of the Bank.

Now, gentlemen, there is a third point. Whether Potter was or was not cognisant of this—whether the evidence is sufficient against Stronach or not, what is to be said of the other Directors as regards these sums? On that matter, gentlemen, I don't think it necessary to trouble you much. For my own part, I do not see that the knowledge of these two fabricated entries is brought home to them—at least I do not know any of the evidence which leads to the conclusion that they knew that that sum of £953,000 was a fictitious entry, or that they knew that the sum of £751,000 was transferred from the one account to the other. You had it explained by Morison that when he went over the weekly balances and read them over to the Directors, they checking the entries in the balance ledger, he only read the balances, and did not read

387

The City of Glasgow Bank Trial.

the details, and, in particular, that he did not read the sum of £973,000, and did not read the sum of £751,000, so that in their operations in making up the balance sheet there is no special knowledge traced to them of either the one entry or the other. And the same observation, if it were necessary to enlarge upon it, would apply with still more force to those entries which not only appeared in the balance ledger, but which are so far supported by the whole system of book-keeping. Even supposing it were the case that the crossing of these accounts, and the taking of their difference as representing a balance, were not true banking, or were not consistent with book-keeping—nay, even that it was done with a fraudulent intent, I do not see that in the circumstances that we have heard, the other prisoners, apart from Potter and Stronach, are necessarily involved in it. You are the judges of it, but that is the impression that I have formed upon the evidence. If you think otherwise, of course, you will give effect to your view.

Now, gentlemen, so much for the first branch of this case, which, as I have already said, I think truly resolves practically into the question whether these two sums were or were not inserted in the balance sheet falsely, and in the knowledge of the defenders that they were so inserted falsely. But then comes the question of the object or motive; and here, I think, you must keep in mind what has been explained frequently in the course of the trial, but still what it is rather difficult to apprehend, that the mode of deception is said to have been, not to make the balance false, but to make the materials for striking the balance false, so that the public and the shareholders and the London banks should believe that the amount which the Bank had out at hazard was less than in reality it was, and that their assets were better secured than in reality they were. That was the motive, or the imputed motive, of putting in the sum of £973,000, and for transferring the £751,000 from the doubtful category of advances into the certain category of investments or securities. And therefore, on that part of the question, if you are satisfied upon the falsehood, and, secondly, on the authors of the falsehood, I do not think on the last of these that there is much room for doubt. And that, gentlemen, concludes the first part of my observations on this important case. And to sum up the matter as it stands now, it appears to me that the main gravamen of the charge which is made against these two prisoners consists of their falsifying the balance sheet in the two respects that I have mentioned; and that, you will observe, applies to all the three years, for it certainly does not make it better, but makes it considerably worse that that £973,000 was missed out of the second of the three balance sheets, and a separate but equally false sum inserted. And in regard to the knowledge of the Directors and the motive, you will consider whether you think

The Lord Justice-Clerk's Charge.

that Mr. Morison's evidence is sufficient to fix Mr. Potter with
the part which he is said to have played in regard to this matter.
If it is sufficient, then there can be no question as to the object
with which the alteration was made. It is in vain to say that
it was an innocent alteration if, in point of fact, it was done in
the way that Morison suggests. If you should think his evidence
sufficient—and I cannot tell you that it is not evidence on which
you are entitled to judge, for, as I have said, it is corroborated by
the balance sheet itself, and by these scrolls very strongly—if
you should think it sufficient, then I fear that Mr. Potter is
implicated in this matter. But, on the other hand, you will
keep in mind that there have been the most serious imputations
upon that testimony; you have heard it, and I have made the
observations that I think right upon it. You will consider
whether these observations had or had not foundation, or
whether the foundation which you think they had is sufficient to
discredit his testimony. You will see it is a very serious matter,
and you will, I have no doubt, give it serious attention. Then,
as regards Stronach, that arises in different circumstances. If
you shall be of opinion that the entry of £973,000 was a fraudulent entry, you will consider whether Stronach's knowledge of it,
even without Morison's evidence, is not liable at all events to a
very strong presumption, or inference rather, arising from the
circumstances, and whether, with Morison's evidence, you can
have much doubt that he was cognisant of that entry. And as
to the other sum of £751,000, you must judge for yourselves.
You have heard the case. Stronach was the man who ought to
have checked these accounts. It is possible, if you don't believe
Morison, that the £751,000 might have escaped his observation,
charged though he was with the Bank's books. But that is all
in your hands. I don't think that I can add to the materials
that you have by any further observations on this branch of the
case.

I have now concluded the observations which I think it
necessary to address to you on the first five sub-divisions of the
charges in regard to the abstract balance sheets of 1876, 1877,
and 1878. They are substantially the same, and excepting in
the particulars that I have already mentioned, the observations
which apply to the year 1876 are equally applicable to the other
years. But there remain two charges in the indictment—two
sub-divisions of the narrative, or specification of the particulars,
in which these abstract balance sheets were falsified and fabricated. The last of them, as I have said, as to the bad and
irrecoverable debts, is no longer a subject for inquiry. That
is to say, the public prosecutor does not allege that the Directors
were in the knowledge that there were bad and irrecoverable
debts beyond those specified in the abstract. But he says in
Article VI. and Article VII. that the earnings of the Bank

389

The City of Glasgow Bank Trial.

during the year were overstated under the head of profit and
loss to the extent of £125,763, and then he says that the
reserve fund to the extent of £450,000 was also overstated.
We may dismiss the reserve fund, because the reserve
fund, as I understand it, and as was explained to
you, consists of the excess of the profit and loss
account; that is to say, whatever is not divided as dividend
is carried into the reserve fund. The real question raised here
is whether the amount stated to the credit of profit and loss
was or was not a false entry in the knowledge of the Directors
for a fraudulent object. Gentlemen, this part of the case has
given me a great deal of anxiety in relation to the proper
function that I and my colleagues have to discharge. It was
objected, and I am now taking up the observations which Mr.
Asher made, and made very powerfully, in the course of his
address—it was objected to the indictment before you were
sworn that the eighth charge was bad, because it did not
contain a specification or enumeration of the debts said to be
bad and irrecoverable, but not made allowance for in the abstract
balance sheet. On that objection no judgment was pronounced;
but the public prosecutor struck the charge out of the indictment, and the result of that was, as I have said, that he
precluded himself from alleging that bad and irrecoverable
debts to a larger extent, in the knowledge of the Directors,
were given credit for. The trial proceeded, and the objection
was also extended to Nos. 6 and 7, because, said the counsel
for the prisoners, "You cannot allow the prosecutor to go to
proof that the earnings of the Bank were less, for that is just
another way of proving that so many more debts were bad
and irrecoverable." Well, manifestly, we could not sustain
that objection, because it did not appear on the face of the
indictment that the earnings of the Bank might not have been
falsified and fabricated, although there were no bad and irrecoverable debts. We could not exclude the evidence; and,
on the other hand, we declined to exclude the evidence as to
bad and irrecoverable debts, although the charge founded upon
it was withdrawn, because it was necessary that you should
know what the true state of the Bank was, which the Directors
wished to conceal. But now it is said, and I am not quite sure
that that was the original conception when the evidence began,
that the debts to which No. 6 refers were not bad and
irrecoverable, but that they were debts which, at all events,
were temporarily unprofitable, and that, therefore, the interest
upon them ought to have been carried, not into the profit
and loss account, but the debts themselves, and the interest
charged on them should have been carried to suspense account,
and ought not to have been entered into the profit and loss
account until the debts again became profitable and advan-

The Lord Justice-Clerk's Charge.

tageous. It is said that the earnings of the Bank in that way were swelled by the amount of the interest upon these outstanding debts, whereas, in the knowledge of the Directors, not only had the interest not been paid, but in all probability it might never be paid. Now, it has been said, and I am very far from saying that there was not force in the observation, that that is in another shape reviving the question about bad and irrecoverable debts. But on the best consideration I can give to that question, with the assistance of their lordships, I have come to be of opinion, that even if the objection had been taken upon Article VI., that it did not specify the particular debts, I should not, in a question of that kind, have felt myself bound to hold the indictment irrelevant. The objection is substantially this, that profits were alleged in this abstract balance sheet and credit was taken for an amount of profit, which, in point of fact, never was earned. That is a different thing from saying that there were bad and irrecoverable debts. But if the directors of a bank allege that they have profits when they know that they have none, I am not prepared to say that it is necessary that there should be a specification of the particulars which might have led to the representation of profit. It is enough to allege that there were none, and to prove it. I must own that the indictment is not conceived in that respect in the terms in which I think it should, for clearness and distinctness, have been expressed. If the Crown meant to say that these debts, although not bad and irrecoverable, were still of so contingent a nature that they could not with propriety be carried into profit and loss, I think it would have been better if that had appeared more distinctly upon the face of the indictment.

But, gentlemen, with that observation—and the only weight it can receive, so far as you are concerned, is that you should hold the Crown very strictly to the proof of what they now undertake to establish—I must now proceed to consider how far there is any ground for the allegation that this abstract balance sheet was fabricated or falsified in respect of the entry to profit and loss which stands in Article IV. of the abstract, page 3 of the indictment. Gentlemen, this leads us into another and a larger field of inquiry. We have hitherto been considering simply the mode in which this balance sheet of 1876 and the other balance sheets were made up. The question that is now raised is of a different description. It is not denied that in the books of the Bank the profit and loss stood precisely as it is represented in the abstract balance sheet. That account of profit and loss was prepared by the proper officials of the Bank, and during these three years the same course has been followed in regard to the amount carried to it; while it is not denied that the interest on the debts I am

The City of Glasgow Bank Trial.

now going to speak of does, in point of fact, form part of the
apparent surplus which appears in the account of profit and
loss, although that could not be ascertained on the face of the
balance ledger. Now, I am going to show you shortly how,
in point of fact, those debts on which interest is so charged
and carried to profit and loss stood; and then we must go on
to inquire what was the proper mode of dealing with them,
what the intent with which they were dealt with, and what
the knowledge of the Directors themselves. Gentlemen, the
accountants spoke of eight accounts as being accounts that were
material in this investigation, but it appears to me that it
would be more accurate and quite sufficient for our purpose to
confine our attention to four of the eight, for four of the eight
absorb nine-tenths of the whole amount of the alleged deficiency.
They are the accounts of James Morton & Co., Smith, Fleming
& Co., James Nicol Fleming, and Innes Wright & Co. You
have the amounts which stood at their respective debits in the
evidence of Mr. Muir, and I shall shortly state to you what
they were. In 1878 Morton & Co. were due £2,173,000; Smith,
Fleming & Co. were due £1,900,000 in round numbers; James
Nicol Fleming was due £1,200,000; and Innes Wright & Co.
were due £485,000. So that the whole amount is as near as
may be four millions and a half. Interest was charged on these
accounts, and it is the interest charged on these accounts that
is the subject of this challenge on the part of the Crown.
Gentlemen, the history of these four accounts is undoubtedly
a very remarkable one. As I said in the outset of my observations, the mere amount of loss is not quite the test of the
character of the transactions on which the loss was created.
You must look at the extent of the operations as well as the
extent of the loss, and see what, in point of fact, was the
origin of those remarkable and extraordinary advances being
given to those four debtors.

I shall begin with Smith, Fleming & Co. Mr. Fleming was
examined, and he gave his evidence with singular clearness and
lucidity—with great candour I think you will admit—and the
story that he told had a certain flavour of romance about it,
but it was a very remarkable history of the career of a Scottish
merchant. He said that when he and his brother entered into
business, or were in business, in 1863, they were counting their
profits, as he expressed it, by hundreds of thousands a year;
and that was a business which apparently was not mere speculation, but was that solid class of business which consists in
commission agency. It seems that between 1863 and 1870
they had suffered very much by the failure of a Liverpool
correspondent; and although he was actually making £93,000
a year for the three years previous to 1870, Mr. Fleming came
to Glasgow in that year, having had some connection with the

The Lord Justice-Clerk's Charge.

City of Glasgow Bank before, and told Alexander Stronach that unless he was assisted he had resolved to stop payment. He tells us that his loss was not created at all by the debt to the Bank, which amounted to something like £150,000 ; but it was a debt created by the failure of his Liverpool correspondent, and that £500,000 would be necessary to set him afloat again. Gentlemen, Alexander Stronach, in an evil hour for himself and for the Bank, set his face against the resolution of John Fleming to stop payment, and promised that the Bank would support him. I think there is evidence that Mr. Potter was also in council in that matter, and at that time I think James Nicol Fleming was a Director of the Bank. Well, gentlemen, it was proposed to John Fleming, much against the grain, that a new firm should be created in Liverpool, and that the bills drawn by John Fleming, and accepted by the new firm, should be discounted by the Bank, and in that way credit to the amount of £500,000 should be created. John Fleming did not much like that, and he said he did not expect that it would succeed, but still he renounced the intention of suspending payment, and agreed to go into the proposal with great reluctance, for he says that he was, in fact, hurt and irritated by the proposition that was made, that he left the room, and he thinks he was brought back by Potter. Gentlemen, as to what the inducement was on the part of Alexander Stronach to take this strong step in regard to one of the Bank customers, we are left entirely in the dark. The Bank was covered, so John Fleming says ; and the mere fact of his suspension of payment would have led to no loss, or, at least, only to an insignificant loss. He said distinctly that his debt to the Bank was covered by securities, and what interest beyond that there existed on the part of Alexander Stronach to prevent the stoppage of John Fleming & Co. does not appear. But this does appear in the subsequent correspondence, that he took a great interest in the two Flemings—that he evidently was anxious to promote their interests and prevent their ruin ; and that interest he showed very clearly by his subsequent proceedings. It was arranged, therefore, on the part of the Bank at that time, that a credit of £500,000 should be raised in the way that I have described. The way is not very material to the present question. But, gentlemen, it appears quite clear that from that day forward Alexander Stronach began a course of concealed advances to John Fleming—concealed from his own Directors—for you have that alluded to over and over again in the correspondence of Alexander Stronach ; and it is possible that you may find in that the secret of the entry about which so much has been spoken ; for his letters in 1873 and 1874 are those of a man who is overwhelmed with a burden that he cannot shake off. But that these debts were not disclosed at

393

The City of Glasgow Bank Trial.

that time to the Directors is clear from his own statement.
And so the matter goes on, until in 1875 Mr. Robert Stronach
is appointed in his place. In that year Mr. Robert Stronach
was appointed Manager of the Bank. He was most reluctant
to accept the office. I don't wonder that he was. He says
in his letter to the Directors that Alexander Stronach had
withheld his confidence from him. I think that very likely,
but I think, at the same time, that he can hardly have failed
to see very good reason for the disinclination which he evinced.
He says, and there is evidence of that elsewhere, that James
Morton & Co. had promised to pay £400,000 in diminution of
their debt if he would become the Manager of the Bank, and
he did become Manager on a condition; and that is a condition
to which I shall immediately ask your attention. But such
was the state of matters in 1875, before the first of those
years when John Fleming's affairs came to a crisis. He had
still a large commission business. I think there is evidence
that he made £50,000 a year by his own personal commission
business, besides his partner's; but these old debts still hung
round him; the Bank were pressing, and accordingly he came
to an arrangement in August, 1875, which was the commencement of a career of irregular operations on the part of the
Bank, which ultimately assumed still larger dimensions. The
result of that arrangement in 1875 was this: the Bank agreed
to give up so much of their interest and commission, and to
reduce the interest from 5 to 3½ per cent., with a corresponding
reduction in the commission which they charged; they were
to advance £100,000, which was to be secured upon shares to
be purchased by the Bank in the Otago Land Company, the
rate of interest in the colony being apparently so much in
advance of that at home that it was calculated that by that
manipulation a considerable saving would be effected. When
all that was done it was calculated by John Fleming—and he
told you that he thought his calculation an accurate one—that
he would be able to pay the whole interest and commission
chargeable by the Bank, and £25,000 a year in reduction of
the principal debt. In that way, in 1875, it was calculated
that in fourteen years one-half of the debt would be entirely
extinguished. Gentlemen, that arrangement was made by
the Directors of the Bank at that time, and the shares were
purchased, the £100,000 of credit was obtained, the interest
was reduced, but, unfortunately, the £25,000 a year was not
realised, and was not paid. And in the end—for there is not
much in the interval between 1875 and 1878—it turned out
that the debt of John Fleming, instead of being diminished,
was largely increased. It was £1,300,000 in 1875 when this
arrangement was made, and, as I have told you, in 1878 it was
£1,960,000, and that is the figure at which it ultimately

The Lord Justice-Clerk's Charge.

remained. There was a meeting in 1878, after the balance sheet had been prepared and published, but apparently that was too late to be of any moment in this inquiry. And that is the history of one of these debts. The amount is about two millions.

The second of the debtors, James Nicol Fleming, had a career very similar. He was a Director of the Bank, and he resigned in 1874. He also had been a successful man in his day, but at the date which we are speaking of—between 1870 and 1875 —things had gone greatly against him, and it is proved by his own clerk that he had lost all the capital with which he started, and therefore had nothing but borrowed money to trust to. He had a large commission business, and he had very large schemes afloat. He was making, even later than that, £20,000 a year, but then these old encumbrances were still round him, and in 1875 he was owing the Bank £1,005,000. There were securities doubtless held for that, but that was the sum at which he stood in the books of the Bank. Gentlemen, it is needless to disguise that when Robert Stronach succeeded to the management of this Bank he succeeded to a very anxious and troublesome legacy. These debts were none of his creating. There were advances made by the Directors afterwards, but these were as a drop compared with the accumulation which existed; and when he succeeded, therefore, to the office of Manager, he succeeded his relative, who had been going on with a system of concealed advances until they reached that very serious and alarming amount. Mr. Hunter, who was also examined before you, and whose evidence was of the clearest and most satisfactory kind, described to you the negotiations that took place to see whether some means could not be found of enabling James Nicol Fleming, who still had a large and valuable connection, to go on. The result was that Mr. Hunter recommended Stronach to get rid of this account as soon as he could. And accordingly, in 1875, the account was put into liquidation—by which is meant that the account is no longer to go on, that there are to be no further operations upon it, but that the securities are to be realised and placed to the credit of the account. In the meantime James Nicol Fleming started a new Indian and Australian concern, by which he hoped, along with the securities which the Bank held, to be able to redress his balance. Some little time after that the Bank lighted upon a scheme which was explained to you in detail, and which I don't mean to go into at any length, but which, beyond all doubt, was beyond the pale of regular banking. But as I have said to you before, and I think it necessary to tell you again, we are not concerned here at all with the question whether the proceedings of the Directors in these matters were beyond their contract or within their con-

The City of Glasgow Bank Trial.

tract. We are dealing with the question of personal dishonesty, and not of civil liability, and although this scheme that I am now going to describe might be subject to great observation in any question in regard to civil right, or the rights of securities obtained under it, that is not a matter that can affect this case, or the charge that is now made, except as part of the history of the case. But so it is, that Mr. Potter had very large and valuable connections in Australia. Mr. Glen Walker seems to have been brought into council at this period of the Bank's history, and the result of the whole matter was this, that the Bank undertook, through Mr. Glen Walker, to make purchases in New Zealand or Australia—in New Zealand, I think—of land which was to be held in property by the Bank, or at least for them, in the hope and expectation that the rise in the value of that land, which they thought to be pretty secure, in a few years would wipe off the indebtedness of James Nicol Fleming. And in the meantime, they proposed to carry on the operations by a system of double discount—by drawing bills upon the Bank which were to be accepted by the Bank and then discounted, and before the currency of these bills expired another set of bills was put in the circle, the discount being used to retire them. Gentlemen, some questions have arisen in regard to these bills, but with these I do not think it necessary to trouble you. It was a question of accounting which Mr. Muir raised as to whether, when both sets of bills were discounted, and the proceeds paid into the Bank, it created one debt or two. In the view that I have taken it is not necessary that we should decide that matter, though undoubtedly I should have thought that Mr. Muir's view of it was right. The main matter is this, that that singular and very irregular proceeding was adopted—for a bank is incorporated not for the purpose of buying land or speculating in land, but for the proper and legitimate objects of banking—I say such was the proceeding, and such was the endeavour that the Bank made to shake themselves clear of this unfortunate encumbrance.

Now, gentlemen, the third debtor was James Morton. We have heard very little about him, and I have it not in my power —because there was not evidence to enable me to do it—to explain to you the fluctuations and vicissitudes of that account, but it was one of the largest, and it ended with a balance of £2,170,000. What the operations upon it had previously been we have had no evidence to show; and, for my own part, I should certainly have preferred that we had seen Mr. Morton or some one connected with the firm, because it is plain from the correspondence, which I don't weary you by going over, that all these firms were intimately connected, and that Potter, Wilson & Co., and Lewis Potter & Co., and Morton, and Innes Wright, and the two Flemings, had more or less business con-

The Lord Justice-Clerk's Charge.

cerns together, and were in fact, to a certain extent, in the same interest.

The fourth account stands in a singular position, and we have very little information about it also. You will recollect the evidence about it; I shall have to refer to it before I conclude. But the fourth account was the account of John Innes Wright & Co., which amounted, in 1878, to £485,000—nearly half a million. It had not increased materially since Mr. Wright became a Director in 1875, but you had his partner, Mr. Paul, who told you plainly that the other partner, Scott, managed the whole financial affairs of the company, that he never could get an account from him, that he was entirely and absolutely ignorant of the amount of the advances from the Bank, and he was not even able, at the time that he was examined, to give a clear financial history of the affairs of the firm. And I may here take the opportunity of saying that it appeared to me that Mr. Guthrie Smith succeeded in showing that the balance which comes out in 1878, which is nearly £100,000 larger than that of 1877, was truly not on a proper company account at all. £33,000 of it, he said, was the result of a wool lien—a transaction between Glen Walker & Co. under the arrangement which had been made. £46,000 of it arose in this way—in a way which, in the particular matter, can scarcely be an element against Mr. Wright, for Scott had been entrusted by the Bank, not in the way of an advance for his personal benefit, but entirely as attorney or agent for the Bank itself, to discount the Bank's acceptances and remit to them the discount. Scott did not do so, and was a defaulter to the extent of £46,000. Whatever importance may be attached to that fact now, I think it only right to say that I think it was satisfactorily established. I shall say a word upon Mr. Wright's personal interest in that matter by and by.

Now, gentlemen, there were you see four accounts, the balances on which amounted altogether to four millions and a half. And how were they secured? That is a question on which our information is imperfect, because these securities have not been realised, and their value has not been ascertained. It is but fair to the defenders to say that, although these accounts were of enormous amount, at the same time the earning power of John Fleming & Co. and James Nicol Fleming, and Morton & Co., that is to say, their business connection—their knowledge of the trade in which they were embarked, the confidence which foreign merchants had in them, still remained as a valuable asset, if it could only be made available. So say the defenders, and I think they established that. They then say that John Fleming was quite confident, in 1875, that he would be able to pay the interest, and would also in fourteen years be able to clear off the main part of the debts due to the Bank, and

397

The City of Glasgow Bank Trial.

that he had no doubt at all, if he confined himself to his proper
commission business, he could without difficulty clear off that
debt and start again without encumbrance. Nor was he alone
in that, for, if I don't mistake, some observation of the same
kind was made by Mr. Hunter. On the other hand, in regard
to the account of James Fleming & Co., Mr. Glen Walker was
very confident that in the end, if he had gone on, the New
Zealand and Australian lands would become of immense value.
And perhaps they may also say that the fact of the stoppage,
which in truth did not directly result from these debts, has
depreciated the securities, as, of course, it would, far below
what they might have been valued at if the Bank had been
going on, and their debtors consequently allowed to go on too.
Now, gentlemen, so stands that part of the case.

There are four questions which then arise for your consideration. First, did the Directors—the prisoners at the bar—
know the condition of these accounts? Second, if they did
know it, what was the proper mode of dealing with them in the
balance sheets which were to be laid before the shareholders?
Third, were the Directors personally aware of the mode in which
the accounts were dealt with in the Bank? And lastly, supposing that they didn't know these things directly, had they
such information as must have put them in bad faith to state
that amount of profit as having been earned within the year?

Gentlemen, in regard to the first of these questions, viz., the
knowledge of the Directors generally, and of Stronach., the
Manager, as to the state of these accounts, I don't think that
that is a matter which, taken as a general statement, can be
doubted. I don't say that they knew the details of accounts
in 1878; perhaps not either in 1876 or 1877; but you heard in
the course of the evidence, and there is no denial of the fact,
that Robert Stronach would not take office until he had some-
body to share with him the anxiety of this horrible legacy
that had been left him by his predecessor, and although the
accounts are not named in the letter which has been read to
you more than once, he distinctly says—" I take office on the
condition that the Directors will look into these old accounts,
and will take measures in order to their liquidation." And,
gentlemen, they did take measures. I thought the remarks of
the Dean of Faculty very well founded upon that matter. They
were not debts of their incurring. They had no responsibility
about them. They were debts which were incurred by the
former Manager, without their knowledge; but, as the Dean of
Faculty has said, they set to work manfully to devise some
means of lightening the burden for the Bank, and removing it
from the shoulders of the shareholders. Up to that point
there is nothing to say against what they did. And here I
take the opportunity of saying that I think the remarks on

The Lord Justice-Clerk's Charge.

the part of the prosecutor as to the course which they followed in their deliberations—now that we see all round this matter—were pressed somewhat more strongly than the facts altogether warranted. I don't think the Directors wanted to postpone the evil day in this matter. A postponement for four months—as appears in one of the minutes—was not an unreasonable thing, looking to the large ventures that were still unascertained. I don't think that the fact that Mr. Leresche was asked to leave the room when these matters were discussed argued anything; for what were the Directors doing but endeavouring to make arrangements by which the debt should be liquidated? I think it is no part of this case, and you may dismiss that from your minds altogether—at least I think so—that there was any hidden conspiracy on the part of the Directors to ruin the Bank for their own advantage. There was nothing of that kind. The charge of crime against the Directors is of a different description altogether, and the motive is different too. But the importance of the inquiry that I am now going into is the fact that the Directors, as a body and individually, were in cognisance of the fact that the debts were so doubtful that it was necessary to take some step for the purpose of bringing them into shape.

Gentlemen, in regard to the secretary being present at the meetings, of course every bank has its own more secret deliberations—its own more difficult and delicate accounts—and we are not going to press hardly upon gentlemen who have such a herculean task to perform as to clear off debts amounting to about four millions, which they had not incurred themselves. For my own part, as far as that is concerned, I think every one must sympathise with the difficulty of the position. But then, gentlemen, most undoubtedly in 1875 the Directors, when they set their shoulders to the task, must have been aware of the position in which these debts stood. In 1875 they made the arrangement with John Fleming. Well, John Fleming says he expected that that would enable him to pay £25,000 a year, after paying the interest and the commission. The Directors may have thought so. It is for you to consider what was the true conclusion that ought to have been derived from that position. At the same time, the arrangement was one that obliged the Bank to go out of its ordinary course, and to take shares in a trading company in Australia, which undoubtedly was not the ordinary procedure, nor an ordinary course to follow under the Bank contract. And that went on. There are a variety of meetings. I am not going to trouble you by reading the minutes over again. I will only say this, that I think the result of them all is that Mr. Stronach did do what he said he intended to do—that he brought the state of the accounts before the Directors, and they took up the accounts.

The City of Glasgow Bank Trial.

They seem to have settled the arrangement with John Fleming in 1875, and in 1876 they put James Nicol Fleming into liquidation. There he remained, and as far as that account is concerned, I don't find in the minutes that anything took place until the land speculation of Glen Walker came up. Beyond all question—it is needless to disguise it—this was not legitimate banking, although it might be the most likely way of relieving themselves of their advances. This land speculation led to further advances, to double sets of bills accepted by the Bank for that purpose—all most irregular banking unquestionably, and all most certainly foreshadowing the ruin that ultimately came. It was possible, undoubtedly, that if the commercial crisis had passed over, and a sudden rush of advance on securities had taken place, and the cloud which has been overhanging this country for so many years had dispersed—it was within the chapter of accidents that things would have come right. In short, they were precisely in the position that I have described to you in the outset of my remarks, and were brought face to face with it. They had, perhaps, the alternative of either closing the Bank doors, or doing what, in point of fact, was done. But between these two things there could be no legal choice at all. They had a deficit of four millions, though covered by securities which still remained doubtful. No doubt if they stopped and closed the Bank doors, or took away their assistance, the securities would crumble into nothing, and it might be a dead loss to the shareholders; and so it would. But, in the meantime, the question is whether they were aware of the state of these accounts at the date of the first of these balance sheets. I think, gentlemen, without holding that they were aware of all the steps and proceedings in regard to the accounts; without knowing how the arrangement of 1875, in John Fleming's instance, had succeeded; without knowing whether the New Zealand speculation was a profitable or promising one or not, they did know that these large accounts were outstanding, and that the realisation of them was still a matter of question. So much for the first of these questions. It is not of any importance to go into the question who was present at this meeting, and who was present at that. The conclusion that I think you will come to is, that there was enough known to the Bank Board to fix the general knowledge of the position of the accounts on all the Directors.

But then, gentlemen, comes the next question. It is conceded by the Crown, and the Crown have no power to withhold the concession, that they do not say that the Directors knew these debts to be bad and irrecoverable. I don't think they were bad and irrecoverable. I think that was not the category under which they should have been classed. I think they were very hazardous. But in the question whether they are to be sent

The Lord Justice-Clerk's Charge.

to the suspense account or to be carried in the ordinary way into profit and loss, there arises a question very much for you. It is, as the counsel said, to a certain extent a matter of opinion. I should have said that, looking to the position in which the accounts stood, the only safe way for the shareholders was, in the meantime, not to calculate on their being profitable. But you must keep in mind what the ordinary practice is, and it is this: when a debt is bearing interest, the interest on it when charged in the account is carried to profit and loss, whether it be paid or not, provided there is a reasonable prospect that it will be paid. And, accordingly, Mr. Hutton explained that if these large accounts had been only for a year, he would have seen nothing wrong in carrying the interest to profit and loss; but he said if the interest has not been paid for several years, then he would think it wrong to do anything but put it in the suspense account. Gentlemen, that is a matter, in the first place, as a matter of proper banking, which you must decide. It was said by the counsel for the prisoners, and said truly, that some of these accounts which are said to have been properly the subject of suspense accounts were, in point of fact, not in that position. It does appear that in 1876 James Morton & Co. paid up £80,000 of the principal debt, and that, of course, included the payment of the previous interest. It also appears, I think, that Innes Wright & Co. in one year did the same. The smaller accounts of Matthew, Buchanan & Co., and Glen Walker & Co., are liable to the same observation. They were not dormant accounts; and apparently, from John Fleming's account, the advances which he got between 1875 and 1878 were, to a certain extent, covered by securities which were actually paid in. Now, that is what the defenders say, and I have thought it right to bring it under your notice. You have heard the evidence, and you can judge for yourselves. What they substantially say is this: that in 1875 and 1876 the accounts of the two Flemings were not materially in hazard, and might have done very well if the Bank had been able to go on, and that therefore there was nothing which compelled the Directors to go out of the ordinary course, and to carry the interest upon these debts to suspense account. Now, gentlemen, if you shall think that that was clearly a matter of opinion, and that although your own opinion is the proper and true opinion as regards the administration of the Bank, if you shall yet think that the opposite course could have been followed in good faith, although wrongly—even foolishly—then you cannot find that there was any fraudulent intent in carrying this sum to the credit of profit and loss. But if you shall think that, looking to the circumstances as you have heard them detailed, no prudent man—no man in his senses—would have held out that sum of £125,000 as profit made in the year, if it truly

3 A

The City of Glasgow Bank Trial.

consisted of nothing but the interest on these debts which had never been paid, then I am afraid that will come to be a serious matter, and that is a matter that really I must leave entirely in your hands. It is right to say here that during 1878 £74,000 of profit was realised by the branches alone. That, however, applies to the next point that I am going to refer to. If you shall think that the Directors ought not to have carried this to profit and loss, but, on the contrary, must have known that they were wrong in doing so, I don't know, gentlemen, what you are to make of the fact that they actually increased the dividend that year over the year before. But, gentlemen— and this brings me to the testing and the touching point of that part of the case—this sum of £125,000 stands in the books at the credit of profit and loss ; and, of course, when the balance was made up, what the officials of the Bank were bound to do, and were wont to do, was to take the balance, transcribe it first into the balance ledger, and then pass it into the abstract balance sheet. That is the ordinary course. When the Directors saw the £125,000 at the credit of profit and loss, it did not appear, on the face of that document, how that £125,000 was entered in the books ; and it is said—and that is really the most important consideration on this head that you have— it is said it is quite true the Directors may have known all about these accounts, but they had no reason to suppose that when the books of the Bank were balanced, and £125,000 of profit was shown, any part of that or the whole of it consisted of interest on these accounts. They did not know how the accounts were dealt with in the books, but they were entitled to assume, as they could not be constantly examining the books, that the officials of the Bank had not played them false.

Gentlemen, that is the defence of the Directors on this part of the case. The observations that I have made about the Manager, I am afraid, apply to this part of the case also ; and I am afraid I must add another remark in regard to Mr. Potter, because, although the other Directors, the members of committees, and those present at Board meetings when these accounts were overhauled, might after all have a very slight and shadowy acquaintance with the details of the accounts and the details of the arrangements, I am afraid—and it is only right that I should say so, and I regret to say it—that Mr. Potter throughout, from first to last, apart altogether from his position as a Director of the Bank, was cognisant of all the proceedings that were taken for the purpose of liquidating the debts of these firms. I am far from imputing that to Mr. Potter as of itself derogatory to him. I am going to make a remark upon the personal position of all the seven prisoners at the bar before I conclude. Only I fear that it will hardly be possible for Mr. Potter to say that he was not aware of the position of the

The Lord Justice-Clerk's Charge.

accounts. It is another question—and that is for you to consider—whether, although he knew the position of the accounts intimately, he was aware that the profit and loss was struck after crediting the amount of interest on these accounts.

But, gentlemen, there is a concluding question, and with that I shall very nearly terminate the observations which I have to make. Apart from Potter and Stronach, do you think that, in 1876, 1877, and 1878, any of the Directors of this Bank thought that a dividend of 12 per cent., or a profit of £125,000, had been earned from the business? If you should come to be of opinion that the position of the accounts was such, in their knowledge, that whatever the details of the accounts might have been, that was a result which could not possibly be accurate, then I fear you have a serious duty before you. I have stated to you, as fairly as I am able, the grounds upon which I think your judgment must proceed. If you think there are the means of discrimination between the prisoners, you are quite entitled to use your own judgment on that matter. It certainly strikes one now, at the end of the day, as not a favourable fact in this case that with all the knowledge which the Directors had, and the actual fact of these liabilities before them, that knowledge found no expression whatever in their balance sheet. At the same time, I have only to repeat that what you have to find is not general suspicion or impression, but you must be satisfied that they knew that this statement, like the others, was unfounded in fact, and that it was fraudulently made.

Gentlemen, I said that before I concluded I should think it right to make an observation upon each of the prisoners at the bar, and in the first place on the case of Mr. Stewart. Now, it is quite certain that Mr. Stewart was on more than one occasion brought into direct communication with the actors in the matters that I have referred to. John Fleming said he had never seen him, but I think Mr. Hunter or Mr. Glen Walker said they had; and it is also certain that Mr. Stewart went over the draft of the report for 1878 and compared it with the abstract. Gentlemen, I don't put much stress upon that any more than I put much stress upon the fact that a man sits in the chair at a Board meeting, hears things read, and takes part in the formal business. I don't put much stress upon it, unless it had been shown that Mr. Stewart really was perfectly informed as to the matters with which they were dealing. Mr. Potter stood in a different position, for he understood the whole of the negotiations quite well. But, in the meantime, I am talking of Mr. Stewart, and as far as his personal actings are concerned, while I think you cannot relieve him of the knowledge of the general position of these accounts, probably he was not particularly conversant with their details; and as to the books of the Bank, you certainly cannot charge him with any knowledge

The City of Glasgow Bank Trial.

of them at all. I think it right to say that I don't wonder that Mr. Stewart's counsel rather protested against the allegations that were originally made in the indictment; and I think it right in justice to him to call attention to the fact, that not only could it not have been said, as the case turned out, that he had been guilty of embezzling the funds of the Bank, but, in point of fact, he was a man in such circumstances that he was able, out of his means, to have paid his obligations to the Bank twice over. I think that is a fair observation to make on the part of Mr. Stewart. On the other hand, while I bring that before you, you will not forget that if you are of opinion that all the Directors were aware generally of the position of these accounts, I have already gone over the views that occur to me as to the result of that knowledge.

As to Mr. Potter, I have made some observations upon his knowledge and proceedings already, but there are one or two remarks that I think it is only reasonable and right to make. If you believe Mr. Morison that Mr. Potter was a party to the falsification of the abstract balance of 1876, it is impossible to disguise the gravity of the offence thereby committed. In regard to the rest, I think it is quite true that Mr. Potter was very cognisant of all these matters from beginning to end, and on the whole I am not disposed to think that he was acting for any particular benefit of his own. The Bank was not in advance to him substantially; he was a man worth £16,000 a year, quite able to meet any liability that could come upon him at that time; and, moreover, it is so far in his favour, and in favour of the confidence of the Directors in these firms, that it does appear that his son, John Potter, had proposed to join the firm of Smith, Fleming & Co. just at the very crisis, and in the very middle of their embarrassments. That is a fact, and it is only due to the prisoner to say so. I have read through the correspondence very carefully, and I have not found in any portion of it any indication of a personal interest—I mean a corrupt personal interest—on the part of Mr. Potter, but, on the contrary, I have seen several indications of good feeling and friendliness.

As to the case of Mr. Salmond, I think he has established that when the negotiations about the adjustment of the balance sheets were going on in the months of June and July, in these three years he was for the most part out of Scotland for the benefit of his health. Whether he has absolutely established such an *alibi* as would have enabled him to escape in a trial of a different kind is not quite the question. But I think you may give some weight to the fact that he was not at hand for consultation. He was not there. He not only could not consult, but he could not be consulted, because he was not at home. I don't think it necessary to go into the particular

The Lord Justice-Clerk's Charge.

details which were so clearly explained by his counsel; and no very specific observations were made against that view by the Lord Advocate, who rather seemed to say that that was not the kind of plea that could be very available in an inquiry like this. Gentlemen, you must consider that. Lord Mure reminds me of an incident in the history that I gave you, where John Fleming writes to Robert Stronach to warn him that he had seen Salmond in communication with Mr. Potter, and to warn him not to be too communicative to Salmond if he should speak on the subject. That was at the time there was a proposal that John Potter should join the firm.

The DEAN OF FACULTY—That was a letter to Alexander Stronach.

The LORD JUSTICE-CLERK—The letter bears to be to Robert Stronach, but the witness Fleming corrected that, and said it was written to Alexander. It is of no moment to which of them it was written; the point is as it affects Salmond.

Gentlemen, in regard to Taylor, there was evidence led that he was quite above the world; and although his indebtedness to the Bank was considerable—to the extent of some £70,000 —he had had a large business—he had had large operations on the Bank—debits and credits—and that there was nothing in his position which should have given him any object whatever in being a party to a fraud for any possible personal advantage that he could get from it.

The account of John Innes Wright & Co. is certainly not a satisfactory element. Mr. Wright became a Director when James Nicol Fleming retired; and his partner, Mr. Paul, told him that he should not take the office. I think you must be quite satisfied, and I fear Mr. Wright must be quite satisfied, that that judgment was perfectly sound. It was not desirable that the partner of a firm indebted in over £300,000 to the Bank should be a Director. On the other hand, it does seem, as I have already said, that the financial affairs of the firm were not in his hands at all, and his personal advances from the Bank were nothing, excepting the price advanced to purchase his qualification as a Director.

Mr. Inglis states in his own vindication that he was resident in Edinburgh, and not a Glasgow man at all; that he did his best to attend the meetings of the Board, and that he neither did nor could undertake to investigate the details of any of the accounts. As to the advances which appear in the indictment, there is no allegation now made that these were improperly obtained, and his counsel chose to rest his view on this, that he was not bound to enter into Mr. Inglis' private pecuniary affairs, if no charge was made on that subject.

As regards Mr. Stronach, there is no doubt that the weight of this blow comes very heavily upon him. His position,

The City of Glasgow Bank Trial.

unquestionably, was a very painful and a difficult one; but that will not, as I have said more than once, in any degree remove the consequences of the truth of such a charge from his shoulders. Mr. Salmond was, I think, the largest shareholder amongst the Directors, and he held his shares to the end. So did Mr. Stronach, and so did Mr. Taylor. And, indeed, there is nothing in the conduct of the prisoners at the bar to indicate that they were making ready to quit a falling house, or that they were making preparations for a catastrophe that they thought was at hand. Mr. Stronach had quite means enough to meet any advances that he had received; and, indeed, it was proved that he has been able to pay the first call now due upon his shares.

Gentlemen, I have now discharged the very painful duty that has been imposed upon me, and which has now occupied our time and attention for so many days. I have never, since I had a seat on the bench, experienced so much feeling of pain, of regret—I had almost said of mortification. The circumstances that we have been inquiring into have a large significance outside these walls. I need not allude to them again. But I have only in conclusion to say, as I said at the beginning, that we have nothing but an ordinary duty to perform here, which is to weigh the evidence that has been led, and come to the conclusion that right, and justice, and conscience dictate. You will give the prisoners the benefit of every reasonable doubt, as all prisoners are entitled to have. You will take into view their character, as you would take into view the character of any prisoner accused of a crime at this bar. But if you shall be satisfied that the prosecutor has established his charge, then you will deliver the verdict which your conscience may dictate; and whether your verdict be to convict or to acquit, it will be enough for you, doubtless, that your own consciences approve; but I think I may safely say that, be it what it may, it will carry with it the respect and the approbation of the country.

The jury retired at ten minutes to four, and returned into Court at a quarter to six o'clock.

The LORD JUSTICE-CLERK—Gentlemen, what is your verdict?

The FOREMAN OF THE JURY (Mr. JAMIESON)—The jury unanimously find the panels Lewis Potter and Robert Summers Stronach guilty of the charges as libelled; and find the panels John Stewart, Robert Salmond, William Taylor, Henry Inglis, John Innes Wright, guilty of using and uttering a false abstract balance sheet or statement of the affairs of the City of Glasgow Bank.

The LORD JUSTICE-CLERK—Then, gentlemen, you will formally find the four panels who are charged with embezzlement not guilty, and the panels charged with theft not guilty, those charges having been withdrawn.

The Lord Justice-Clerk's Charge.

The VERDICT was recorded as follows:—"The jury unanimously find the panels Lewis Potter and Robert Summers Stronach guilty of the first, second, and third charges, as libelled, and find them not guilty of the remaining charges; and find the panels John Stewart, Robert Salmond, William Taylor, Henry Inglis, and John Innes Wright, guilty of using and uttering, as libelled, under the first, second, and third charges, and find them not guilty of all the remaining charges."

The LORD JUSTICE-CLERK (to the Jury)—I have to thank you for the great attention you have paid to this very important case; and to announce that in respect of your service on this occasion you will not again be required to act as jurymen for the next five years.

The LORD JUSTICE-CLERK then intimated that sentence would be pronounced next day at half-past ten o'clock.

At the meeting of the Court on the following day, the LORD JUSTICE-CLERK, addressing Lewis Potter and Robert Stronach, said—Lewis Potter, Robert Stronach, the jury, after a long investigation, and after full deliberation, have found you guilty on the first branch of the three charges of falsifying and fabricating the balance sheets of the Bank. I think it is proper to say, in explanation of the sentence which must now follow upon that verdict, that, had the other two charges contained in the indictment, or either of them, been proved to the jury, it would have imposed upon us the duty of inflicting a very severe punishment, because not only would these charges have inferred a crime of very great magnitude, but they would have brought into the case the element of personal advantage as the motive of the act which you committed; and I am desirous to say that, as the case now stands, the act which was done by both of you did not necessarily involve, and probably was not actuated by, any design or desire of personal advantage, but was a criminal act committed, as you thought, for the benefit of the Bank. That does not remove it from the category of crime—very far from it—but it does remove from the crime of which you have been convicted the element, as I have said, of corrupt personal motive for personal ends. That consideration has weighed with the Court in the sentence which I am now to pronounce, being short of one of penal servitude. The sentence of the Court on you, Lewis Potter, and on you, Robert Stronach, is that you be imprisoned for the period of eighteen calendar months.

The LORD JUSTICE-CLERK (addressing the other prisoners)— The jury have found all of you guilty, not of fabricating or falsifying the balance sheets, but of uttering and publishing them, knowing them to be false. We have considered also your case, and looking to the crime of which you have been convicted,

407

The City of Glasgow Bank Trial.

and the distinction that may be drawn between you and the
other two prisoners, and considering that you have been in jail
now since the month of October, the sentence of the Court is
that you be further imprisoned for eight calendar months.

The LORD JUSTICE-CLERK added—It has been represented to me
that, in my observations in charging the jury yesterday, I made
some remarks upon the officials of the Bank that might be
misunderstood. Some of the gentlemen who were witnesses,
at least one who was a witness at the trial—I mean Murdoch—
it has been said, might possibly feel hurt, and might be injured
if my remarks were intended to apply to him, and I wish it,
therefore, to be clearly understood that in the remarks that
I made about the officials of the Bank I referred to three of the
witnesses, viz., Morison, the accountant; Morris, the private
clerk; and Turnbull, who gave the false return to the Inland
Revenue.

APPENDIX I.

The Complaint by the Procurator-Fiscal, on which the Directors were originally arrested.

Glasgow, 29th October, 1878.

Unto the Honourable the Sheriff of Lanarkshire, or his Substitutes, the PETITION of WILLIAM ALEXANDER BROWN, Advocate, Procurator-Fiscal of Court, for the public interest,

Humbly sheweth—

THAT from information received by the petitioner, it appears, and accordingly he charges, that Robert Salmond, Lewis Potter, William Taylor, Henry Inglis, and John Stewart, all at present prisoners in the prison of Glasgow, having been Directors of the City of Glasgow Bank, incorporated under Act of Parliament from and since the year 1872, and John Innes Wright and Robert Summers Stronach, also presently prisoners in the prison of Glasgow, having been—the said John Innes Wright, a Director, and the said Robert Summers Stronach, a Director and the Manager of the said Bank, from and since the year 1875, and Charles Samuel Leresche, also presently a prisoner in the prison of Glasgow, having been Secretary of said Bank from and since the year 1870, and the said Bank having been in the years 1877 and 1878, and also during the years 1873, 1874, 1875, and 1876, or one or more of said years, by reason of the culpable, reckless, and fraudulent trading and mismanagement by the Directors thereof, in a state of hopeless insolvency and unable to meet its liabilities, and the fact of the said insolvency of the said Bank being well known during the years 1873, 1874, 1875, 1876, and 1877, and the bypast part of 1878, or one or more of said years, to the said Robert Salmond, Lewis Potter, William Taylor, Henry Inglis, John Stewart, and Charles Samuel Leresche, and to the said John Innes Wright and Robert Summers Stronach, during the years 1875, 1876, and 1877, and the bypast part of 1878, or one or more of said years, and more particularly the said Bank being—as the said Robert Salmond, Lewis Potter, John Innes Wright, William Taylor, Henry Inglis, John Stewart, Robert Summers Stronach, and Charles Samuel Leresche well knew—as at 5th June, 1878, in a state of hopeless insolvency and unable to meet its liabilities,

409

The City of Glasgow Bank Trial.

and the said Robert Salmond, Lewis Potter, John Innes Wright, William Taylor, Henry Inglis, John Stewart, Robert Summers Stronach, and Charles Samuel Leresche, or one or more of them, having, on or about the dates set forth in the first column of the schedule hereunto attached, at the offices of the said Bank described in the second column of said schedule, received from the respective persons, firms, and companies mentioned in the third column of said schedule, the several bills of exchange, specified in the fourth column of said schedule, for the special and sole purpose of collecting payment of the same when due from the debtors therein, on behalf of the said persons, firms, and companies mentioned in the third column of said schedule, none of whom were at the time indebted or under any obligation to the said Bank, and the said Robert Salmond, Lewis Potter, John Innes Wright, William Taylor, Henry Inglis, John Stewart, Robert Summers Stronach, and Charles Samuel Leresche, not being entitled to make use of the said bills of exchange for any other purpose than that of collecting payment thereof when due, yet nevertheless the said Robert Salmond, Lewis Potter, John Innes Wright, William Taylor, Henry Inglis, John Stewart, Robert Summers Stronach, and Charles Samuel Leresche, or one or more of them, did, actors or actor or art and part, in pursuance of a wicked conspiracy devised by them to continue the business of the said Bank and make it appear to the shareholders and creditors thereof and the public as a solvent concern, for accomplishing their own personal and pecuniary ends, time or times and place or places above libelled, wickedly and feloniously steal and theftuously away take the said several bills of exchange, for sums amounting in all to £23,693 11s. 7d. sterling or thereby, the property of the said several persons, firms, and companies mentioned in the said third column of said schedule, and did endorse and make over the said several bills of exchange before they had become due to the London Joint-Stock Bank, London, in order that the proceeds thereof might be credited to the City of Glasgow Bank in account between them and the said London Joint-Stock Bank, and the same were accordingly credited by the said London Joint-Stock Bank as payments made on behalf of the said City of Glasgow Bank.

> May it therefore please your Lordship to grant warrant to search for and apprehend the said Robert Salmond, Lewis Potter, John Innes Wright, William Taylor, Henry Inglis, John Stewart, Robert Summers Stronach, and Charles Samuel Leresche, and to bring them for examination, and thereafter grant warrant to imprison them within the prison of Glasgow, therein to be detained for farther examination, or

Appendix I.

till liberated in due course of law; farther, grant warrant to search the persons, repositories, and domiciles of the said delinquents, and the house or premises in which they may be found, and to secure for the purpose of precognition all articles found therein, importing guilt or participation in the crime foresaid; and to cite all persons likely to have knowledge of the premises, in order to be precognosced thereanent, and to make production for the purposes foresaid of such writs and evidents pertinent to the case as are in their possession; and recommend to the judges of other counties and jurisdictions to grant the warrants of concurrence necessary for enforcing that of your Lordship within their respective territories.

According to Justice, etc.,

W. A. BROWN, *P.F.*

SCHEDULE.

Dates when Received	Places where Received	Persons, Firms, and Companies, from whom Received	Bills of Exchange.	£	s.	d.
1878						
June 26.	At Head Office of City of Glasgow Bank, Virginia Street, Glasgow.	Wright & Brackenridge, timber merchants, Glasgow.	One accepted by Dobie & Company, shipbuilders, Govan, amounting to -	£321	4	4
July 11.	West End Branch of said Bank, Argyle Street, Glasgow.	John Ramsay, of Kildalton, distiller in Islay and Glasgow.	One accepted by Edward Young & Company, amounting to -	252	7	0
July 11.	The place last mentioned.	The said John Ramsay.	One accepted by W. & A. Gilbey, wine importers, London, amounting to -	496	12	2
September 3.	The place last mentioned.	The said John Ramsay.	One accepted by said W. & A. Gilbey, amounting to -	489	14	2
August 20.	At Anderston Branch of said Bank, Gusset House, Anderston, Glasgow.	Charles Connell & Company, shipbuilders, Scotstoun, Whiteinch.	One accepted by Alexander & Rawcliff, amounting to -	3000	0	0
,,	The place last mentioned.	The said Charles Connell & Company.	One accepted by said Alexander & Rawcliff, amounting to -	3000	0	0
,,	The place last mentioned.	The said Charles Connell & Company.	One accepted by said Alexander & Rawcliff, amounting to -	3000	0	0
,, 26.	The place last mentioned.	The said Charles Connell & Company.	One accepted by said Alexander & Rawcliff, amounting to -	3000	0	0
,, 21.	The place last mentioned.	The said Charles Connell & Company.	One accepted by said Alexander & Rawcliff, amounting to -	3000	0	0
,,	At Head Office of said Bank, as aforesaid.	The Marbella Iron Ore Company (Limited), London.	One accepted by E. J. Wait & Company, Cardiff, amounting to -	525	0	0
,,	The place last mentioned.	The Company last mentioned.	One accepted by the Panteg Steel Works Company, amounting to -	358	13	8
,, 31.	The place last mentioned.	The Company last mentioned.	One accepted by said E. J. Wait & Company, amounting to -	800	0	0
September 5.	The place last mentioned.	The Company last mentioned.	One accepted by the Ebbw Vale Steel Company (Limited), amounting to -	1187	11	3
,, 21.	The place last mentioned.	John M'Pherson & Company, engineers, Mountblue, Glasgow.	One accepted by the Chartered Bank of India, Australia, and China, amounting to -	562	10	0
,, 13.	The place last mentioned.	James Baird, merchant, Newfoundland.	One accepted by Walter Grieve, Son, & Company, Greenock, amounting to -	700	0	0
				£23,693	12	7

W. A. BROWN, *P.F.*

APPENDIX II.

The Indictment.

JOHN STEWART, now or lately residing in Moray Place, Edinburgh, and Lewis Potter, Robert Salmond, William Taylor, Henry Inglis, John Innes Wright, and Robert Summers Stronach, all now or lately prisoners in the prison of Glasgow, you are indicted and accused, at the instance of the Right Hon. William Watson, Her Majesty's advocate for Her Majesty's interest : that albeit, by the laws of this and of every other well-governed realm, falsehood, fraud, and wilful imposition ; as also the wicked and felonious fabrication and falsification, by Directors or officials of a joint-stock banking company, of any balance sheet or statement of affairs for the purpose of concealing and misrepresenting the true state of the company's affairs, with intent to defraud, and wickedly and feloniously using and uttering the same as true, for said purpose, with intent to defraud, and whereby members of the Company and of the public are deceived, imposed upon, and defrauded ; as also the wickedly and feloniously using and uttering, as true, by the Directors or officials of a joint-stock banking company, any fabricated and falsified balance sheet or statement of affairs, knowing the same to be fabricated and false, for the purpose of concealing and misrepresenting the true state of the Company's affairs, with intent to defraud, and whereby members of the Company and of the public are deceived, imposed upon, and defrauded * ; as also theft ; as also breach of trust and embezzlement, are crimes of an heinous nature and severely punishable : yet true it is and of verity, that you, the said John Stewart, Lewis Potter, Robert Salmond, William Taylor, Henry Inglis, John Innes Wright, and Robert Summers Stronach are, all and each or one or more of you, guilty of the crimes above libelled, or of one or more of them, actors or actor, or art and part.

In so far as you, the said John Stewart, Lewis Potter, Robert Salmond, William Taylor, and Henry Inglis having been, during the years 1876, 1877, and 1878, and during several previous years, Directors of a joint-stock banking company, registered under the Companies Acts, 1862 and 1867, and carrying on the business of banking in Glasgow and elsewhere throughout Scotland under the name or firm of the City of Glasgow Bank, with a paid-up capital of £1,000,000 sterling ; and you, the said John Innes Wright, having been, during the years 1875, 1876, 1877, and 1878, a Director of the said Company, and you, the said Robert Summers Stronach, having been, during the years

---

* These two are the so-called " innominate " charges and were the only charges on which evidence was led, and the prisoners ultimately convicted.

413

The City of Glasgow Bank Trial.

1876, 1877, and 1878, Manager, and also *ex officio* a Director of the said Company; and it being your duty, as Directors and Manager aforesaid respectively, to see that regular books were kept for the business of the Company, in which all its transactions, affairs, and obligations were duly entered; and it being farther your duty to see that every year a true and accurate abstract or statement of the Company's affairs, made up from the Company's books, as balanced on the first Wednesday of June in each year, was prepared and duly examined, and thereafter at each annual general meeting of the members of the Company, held on the first Wednesday of July in each year, reported for the satisfaction of all concerned:

Yet, nevertheless (I.), on one or more days in the month of June, 1876, or of May immediately preceding, or of July immediately following, the time or times being more particularly to the prosecutor unknown, in or near the head office of the City of Glasgow Bank in Virginia Street, Glasgow, or elsewhere in or near Glasgow, to the prosecutor unknown, you, the said John Stewart, Lewis Potter, Robert Salmond, William Taylor, Henry Inglis, John Innes Wright, and Robert Summers Stronach did, all and each or one or more of you, wickedly and feloniously, with intent to defraud the members of the said Company and the public, and for the purpose of concealing and misrepresenting the true state of the affairs of the said Company, concoct and fabricate, or cause or procure to be concocted and fabricated, a false and fictitious abstract balance sheet or statement of affairs, purporting to represent the true condition of the Bank's affairs as at 7th June, 1876, in the following or similar terms, videlicet:—

CITY OF GLASGOW BANK.—ABSTRACT BALANCE SHEET, AS AT 7TH JUNE, 1876.

Dr.	LIABILITIES.		
I. Deposits at the head office and branches, and balances at the credit of banking correspondents,		£8,364,056 18 5	
II. Bank notes in circulation in Scotland and the Isle of Man,		860,355 0 0	
III. Drafts outstanding, due, or with a currency not exceeding 21 days,	£326,853 14 1		
Drafts accepted by the Bank and its London agents on account of home and foreign constituents,	988,520 3 0		
		1,315,373 17 1	
Liabilities to the public,		£10,589,785 15 6	
IV. Capital account,	£1,000,000 0 0		
V. Reserve fund,	450,000 0 0		
VI. Profit and loss,	136,865 10 3		
Liabilities to partners,		1,586,365 10 3	
		£12,126,151 5 9	

Appendix II.

I. Bills of exchange, local and country bills, credit accounts, and other advances upon security, -		£8,787,804	17	9
II. Advances on heritable property, and value of Bank buildings and furniture, - - - -		256,665	10	7
III. Cash on hand—viz., gold and silver coin and notes of other banks at head office and branches, - - - -	£862,812 4 4			
IV. Government stocks, Exchequer bills, railway and other stocks and debentures, and balances in hands of banking correspondents, - - -	2,218,868 13 7	3,081,680	17	11
		£12,126,151	5	9

which abstract balance sheet or statement of affairs was false
and fictitious, and was known by you to be so, in the following
particulars or part thereof, videlicet:—(1) The amount of
deposits at the head office and branches, and balances at the
credit of banking correspondents, under Article I. on the debtor
side, was understated to the extent of £1,006,216 12s. 10d. or
thereby; (2) the amount of drafts outstanding, and drafts
accepted by the Bank and its London agents, under Article III.
on the debtor side, was understated to the extent of £973,300
or thereby; (3) the amount of bills of exchange, local and
country bills, credit accounts, and other advances under Article
I. on the creditor side, was understated to the extent of
£2,698,539 10s. 4d. or thereby; (4) the amount of cash on
hand, viz., gold and silver coin and notes of other banks, under
Article III. on the creditor side, was overstated to the extent
of £29,095 or thereby; (5) the amount of Government stocks,
Exchequer bills, railway and other stocks and debentures, and
balances in hands of banking correspondents, under Article
III. on the creditor side, was overstated to the extent of
£753,211 2s. 6d. or thereby; (6) the earnings of the Bank
during the year were overstated, under the head of profit and
loss, to the extent of £125,763 12s. 8d. or thereby; (7) a
reserve fund to the extent of £450,000 was stated to exist, while
in reality no such fund existed*; (8) bad and irrecoverable
debts to an amount far exceeding the whole capital stock of
the Bank were included under Article I. on the creditor side,
and so treated as subsisting and available assets of the Company. Farther, on or about the 5th day of July, 1876, in or
near the Chamber of Commerce, in or near West George Street,†
Glasgow, you, the said John Stewart, Lewis Potter, Robert

* Withdrawn.
† See Mr. Mackintosh's speech on the relevancy, and the Lord Advocate's
reply, when he consented to strike it out.

The City of Glasgow Bank Trial.

Salmond, William Taylor, Henry Inglis, John Innes Wright, and Robert Summers Stronach, did, all and each or one or more of you, wickedly and feloniously, and with intent to defraud, use and utter the said false and fabricated abstract balance sheet or statement of affairs as true, by then and there reporting the same to the members of the said Company at their annual general meeting, along with a report on the Bank's affairs, in which you did, wickedly and feloniously, and falsely and fraudulently, represent and pretend that the said Company was in a sound and prosperous condition, and capable of paying to its members a dividend at the rate of 11 per centum per annum, free of income tax, and of carrying forward to the credit of the next year's profit and loss account a sum of £21,365 10s. 3d., and by thereafter causing the said report and abstract balance sheet or statement of affairs to be printed and published and circulated throughout Scotland; and all this you did, well knowing the said abstract balance sheet or statement of affairs to be false and fabricated, and for the purpose of concealing and misrepresenting the true state of the said Company's affairs; by all which, or part thereof, you did, wickedly and feloniously, deceive, impose upon, and defraud members of the said Company and of the public, and induce said members of the Company to retain the stock held by them therein, and many of the public, including Robert Craig, papermaker, residing at Craigesk House, in the parish of Newbattle, and county of Edinburgh; the Rev. John Pulsford, Dalrymple Crescent, Edinburgh; James Ritchie, stationer, High Street, Edinburgh; and Thomas Brownlee, Gresham Cottage, Uddingston, Lanarkshire, to acquire stock in the said Company, and others of the public, including Thomson & Porteous, tobacco manufacturers in Edinburgh; Honeyman & Wilson, wholesale grocers in Edinburgh; Hamilton & Inches, jewellers in Edinburgh; Mossman & Watson, provision merchants in Edinburgh; Renton & Kerr, stockbrokers in Edinburgh; and Robert Christie, grocer in Edinburgh, to deposit money in the said Bank, to the great loss and prejudice of the said members of the Company and of the public.

Likeas (II.), on one or more days in the month of June, 1877, or of May immediately preceding, or of July immediately following, the time or times being more particularly to the prosecutor unknown, in or near the said office of the City of Glasgow Bank in Virginia Street, Glasgow, or elsewhere in or near Glasgow, to the prosecutor unknown, you, the said John Stewart, Lewis Potter, Robert Salmond, William Taylor, Henry Inglis, John Innes Wright, and Robert Summers Stronach, did, all and each or one or more of you, wickedly and feloniously, with intent to defraud the members of the said Company and the public, and for the purpose of concealing and misrepresenting the true state of the affairs of the said Company, concoct and fabricate,

Appendix II.

or cause or procure to be concocted and fabricated, a false and fictitious abstract balance sheet or statement of affairs, purporting to represent the true condition of the affairs of the said Bank as at 6th June, 1877, in the following or similar terms, videlicet :—

CITY OF GLASGOW BANK—ABSTRACT BALANCE SHEET, AS AT 6TH JUNE, 1877.

Dr. LIABILITIES.

I. Deposits at the head office and branches, and balances at the credit of banking correspondents,		£8,382,711 12 10
II. Bank notes in circulation in Scotland and the Isle of Man, - - - - - - -		763,894 0 0
III. Drafts outstanding, due, or with a currency not exceeding twenty-one days, and drafts accepted by the Bank and its London agents on account of home and foreign constituents, - - -		1,350,335 1 1
Liabilities to the public, - - - -		£10,496,940 13 11
IV. Capital account, - - -	£1,000,000 0 0	
V. Reserve fund, - - -	450,000 0 0	
VI. Profit and loss, - - -	148,501 12 6	
Liabilities to partners,		1,598,501 12 6
		£12,095,442 6 5

Cr. ASSETS.

I. Bills of exchange, local and country bills, credit accounts, and other advances upon security, -		£8,758,838 17 8
II. Advances on heritable property, and value of Bank buildings and furniture at head office and branches, - - - - - -		257,689 0 6
III. Cash on hand—viz., gold and silver coin and notes of other banks at the head office and branches, - - -	£891,018 0 2	
IV. Government stocks, Exchequer bills, railway and other stocks and debentures, and balances in hands of banking correspondents, - -	2,187,896 8 1	
		3,078,914 8 3
		£12,095,442 6 5

which abstract balance sheet or statement of affairs was false and fictitious, and was known by you to be so, in the following particulars, or part thereof, videlicet :—(1) The amount of deposits at the head office and branches, and balances at the credit of banking correspondents, under Article I. on the debtor side, was understated to the extent of £1,151,518 13s. 5d. or thereby; (2) the amount of bank notes in circulation under Article II. on the debtor side was understated to the extent of £76,110 or thereby; (3) the amount of drafts outstanding, and drafts accepted by the Bank and its London agents, under

The City of Glasgow Bank Trial.

Article III. on the debtor side, was understated to the extent
of £1,330,712 18s. 1d. or thereby; (4) the amount of bills
of exchange, local and country bills, credit accounts, and other
advances under Article I. on the creditor side, was understated
to the extent of £3,227,154 12s. 8d. or thereby; (5) the amount
of cash on hand, viz., gold and silver coin and notes of other
banks, under Article III. on the creditor side, was understated
to the extent of £30,000 or thereby; (6) the amount of Government stocks, Exchequer bills, railway and other stocks and
debentures, and balances in hands of banking correspondents,
under Article III. on the creditor side, was overstated to the
extent of £751,775 or thereby; (7) the earnings of the Bank
during the year were overstated, under the head of profit and
loss, to the extent of £128,998 19s. 9d. or thereby; (8) a reserve
fund to the extent of £450,000 was stated to exist, while in
reality no such fund existed; (9) bad and irrecoverable debts
to an amount far exceeding the whole capital stock of the
Bank were included under Article I. on the creditor side, and
so treated as subsisting and available assets of the Company.
Farther, on or about the 4th day of July, 1877, in or near the
Trades Hall, Glassford Street, Glasgow, you, the said John
Stewart, Lewis Potter, Robert Salmond, William Taylor, Henry
Inglis, John Innes Wright, and Robert Summers Stronach, did,
all and each or one or more of you, wickedly and feloniously,
and with intent to defraud, use and utter the said false and
fabricated abstract balance sheet or statement of affairs, last
above libelled, as true, by then and there reporting the same to
the members of the said Company at their annual general
meeting, along with a report on the Bank's affairs, in which you
did, wickedly and feloniously, and falsely and fraudulently,
represent and pretend that the said Company was in a sound
and prosperous condition, and capable of paying to its members
a dividend at the rate of 12 per centum per annum, free of
income tax, and of carrying forward to the credit of next year's
profit and loss account a sum of £18,501 12s. 6d., and by
thereafter causing the said report, and the said abstract balance
sheet or statement of affairs, last above libelled, to be printed
and published and circulated throughout Scotland; and all this
you did, well knowing the said abstract balance sheet or statement of affairs to be false and fabricated, and for the purpose
of concealing and misrepresenting the true state of the said
Company's affairs, by all which, or part thereof, you did,
wickedly and feloniously, deceive, impose upon, and defraud
members of the said Company and of the public, and induce
said members of the Company to retain the stock held by them
therein, and many of the public, including James and William
Russell, residing in Carrick Park, in or near Ayr; Peter Hume,
warehouseman, residing in Salisbury Place, Great Western

Appendix II.

Road, Glasgow; Matthew Jarvis Dick, book-keeper, residing at Glenclelland, in the parish of Shotts, Lanarkshire; Robert Dick, coalmaster, residing in Garturk Street, Govanhill, in or near Glasgow; and Edward M'Callum, residing at Plewlands House, Spylaw Road, in or near Edinburgh, to acquire stock in the said Company; and others of the public, including the said Thomson & Porteous, Honeyman & Wilson, Hamilton & Inches, Mossman & Watson, Renton & Kerr, and Robert Christie, to deposit money in the said Bank, to the great loss and prejudice of the said members of the Company and of the public.

Likeas (III.), on one or more days of the month of June, 1878, or of May immediately preceding, or of July immediately following, the time or times being more particularly to the prosecutor unknown, in or near the said office of the City of Glasgow Bank, in Virginia Street, Glasgow, or elsewhere in or near Glasgow, to the prosecutor unknown, you, the said John Stewart, Lewis Potter, Robert Salmond, William Taylor, Henry Inglis, John Innes Wright, and Robert Summers Stronach, did, all and each or one or more of you, wickedly and feloniously, with intent to defraud the members of the said Company and the public, and for the purpose of concealing and misrepresenting the true state of the affairs of the said Company, concoct and fabricate, or cause or procure to be concocted and fabricated, a false and fictitious abstract balance sheet or statement of affairs, purporting to represent the true condition of the affairs of the said Bank as at 5th June, 1878, in the following or similar terms, videlicet :—

CITY OF GLASGOW BANK—ABSTRACT BALANCE SHEET, AS AT 5TH JUNE, 1878.

Dr.	LIABILITIES.			
I. Deposits at the head office and branches, and balances at the credit of banking correspondents, - - -	£8,102,001 0 4			
II. Bank notes in circulation in Scotland and the Isle of Man,	710,252 0 0			
III. Drafts outstanding, due, or with a currency not exceeding twenty-one days, and drafts accepted by the Bank and its London agents on account of home and foreign constituents, - - -	1,488,244 18 6			
Liabilities to the public,		£10,300,497 18 10		
IV. Capital account, - - -	£1,000,000 0 0			
V. Reserve fund, - - -	450,000 0 0			
VI. Profit and loss, - - -	142,095 12 10			
Liabilities to partners, -		1,592,095 12 10		
		£11,892,593 11 8		

The City of Glasgow Bank Trial.

ASSETS.

I. Bills of exchange, local and country bills, credit accounts, and other advances upon security,	-	£8,484,466 9 2
II. Advances on heritable property, and value of Bank buildings and furniture at head office and branches,	- - - - - -	265,324 9 0

III. Cash on hand—viz., gold and
silver coin and notes of other
banks at head office and
branches, - - - £845,963 1 0
Government stocks, Exchequer
bills, railway and other
stocks and debentures, and
balances in hands of banking
correspondents, - - - 2,296,839 12 6
                                                  ―――――――― 3,142,802 13 6
                                                                        ――――――――――
                                                                        £11,892,593 11 8

which abstract balance sheet or statement of affairs was false
and fictitious, and was known by you to be so in the following
particulars, or part thereof, videlicet :—(1) The amount of
deposits at the head office and branches and balances at the
credit of banking correspondents, under Article I. on the
debtor side, was understated to the extent of £941,284 13s. 5d.
or thereby; (2) the amount of bank notes in circulation, under
Article II. on the debtor side, was understated to the extent
of £89,031 or thereby; (3) the amount of drafts outstanding,
and drafts accepted by the Bank and its London agents, under
Article III. on the debtor side, was understated to the extent
of £1,393,008 or thereby; (4) the amount of bills of exchange,
local and country bills, credit accounts, and other advances,
under Article I. on the creditor side, was understated to the
extent of £3,520,913 11s. 8d. or thereby; (5) the amount of
cash in hand, viz., gold and silver coin and notes of other banks,
under Article III. on the creditor side, was overstated to the
extent of £219,522 5s. 10d. or thereby; (6) the amount of
Government stocks, Exchequer bills, railway and other stocks
and debentures, and balances in hands of banking correspondents, under Article III. on the creditor side, was overstated to the extent of £926,764 or thereby; (7) the earnings
of the Bank were overstated, under the head of profit and loss,
to the extent of £125,875 9s. or thereby; (8) a reserve fund,
to the extent of £450,000, was stated to exist, while in reality
no such fund existed; (9) bad and irrecoverable debts to an
amount far exceeding the whole capital stock of the Bank were
included under Article I. on the creditor side, and so treated as
subsisting and available assets of the Company. Farther, on
or about the 3rd day of July, 1878, in or near the Trades Hall,
Glassford Street, Glasgow, you, the said John Stewart, Lewis
Potter, Robert Salmond, William Taylor, Henry Inglis, John

Appendix II.

Innes Wright, and Robert Summers Stronach, did, all and each or one or more of you, wickedly and feloniously, and with intent to defraud, use and utter the said false and fabricated abstract balance sheet or statement of affairs, last above libelled, as true, by then and there reporting the same to the members of the said Company at their annual general meeting, along with a report on the Bank's affairs, in which you did, wickedly and feloniously, and falsely and fraudulently represent and pretend that the said Company was in a sound and prosperous condition, and capable of paying to its members a dividend at the rate of 12 per centum per annum, free of income tax, and carrying forward to the credit of the next year's profit and loss account a sum of £13,222 12s. 10d., and by thereafter causing the said report and the said abstract balance sheet or statement of affairs, last above libelled, to be printed and published and circulated throughout Scotland, and all this you did, well knowing the said abstract balance sheet or statement of affairs to be false and fabricated, and for the purpose of concealing and misrepresenting the true state of the said Company's affairs; by all which, or part thereof, you did, wickedly and feloniously, deceive, impose upon, and defraud members of the said Company and of the public, and induce said members of the Company to retain the stock held by them therein, and many of the public, including John Gillespie, Writer to the Signet in Edinburgh; Thomas Paterson, Writer to the Signet in Edinburgh; Alexander Fergusson, treasurer to the Caledonian Railway Company, residing in Elmbank Crescent, Glasgow; William Shearer, storekeeper, residing at Chapel, in the parish of Cambusnethan, Lanarkshire; William Howe, residing at Ferndean Cottage, Uddingston, Lanarkshire; and James Drummond, residing at Mollinsburn, in the parish of Cadder, Lanarkshire; to acquire stock in the said Company, and others of the public, including the said Thomson & Porteous, Honeyman & Wilson, Hamilton & Inches, Mossman & Watson, Renton & Kerr, and Robert Christie, to deposit money in the said Bank, to the great loss and prejudice of the said members of the Company and of the public.*

Likeas (IV.), you, the said John Stewart, having been during the years 1874, 1875, 1876, 1877, and 1878 a partner of the firm of Stewart, Pott & Co., wine merchants, Glasgow, and also a Director of the said City of Glasgow Bank; and you, the said John Stewart, and the said firm of Stewart, Pott & Co. respectively, having had during the said period, or part thereof, an

---

* These three charges of fabricating and uttering false balance sheets for the years 1876, 1877, and 1878 were the only charges on which evidence for the prosecution was led, all the remaining charges being abandoned by the Lord Advocate at the close of the evidence for the prosecution.

The City of Glasgow Bank Trial.

account or accounts current, or a credit account or accounts, with the said City of Glasgow Bank, and it being your duty as Director foresaid not to allow overdrafts on such accounts to be made without any security, or upon wholly inadequate security, and in particular, not to allow any such overdraft to be made without security, or upon wholly inadequate security, as aforesaid, by you, the said John Stewart, or by any firm whereof you were at the time a partner; and you, the said John Stewart, having in your capacity as Director foresaid, along with the other Directors and officials of the said City of Glasgow Bank, received from the depositors and other creditors of the said City of Glasgow Bank, and been entrusted by them with large sums of money in order that the same might be employed in the ordinary business of banking: Yet, nevertheless, you, the said John Stewart, did, taking advantage of your official position as Director foresaid, on several or one or more occasions during the years 1874, 1875, 1876, 1877, and 1878, the time or times being more particularly to the prosecutor unknown, in or near the head office of the said City of Glasgow Bank, in or near Virginia Street foresaid, or elsewhere in or near Glasgow, to the prosecutor unknown, overdraw, or cause or procure to be overdrawn—(1) the account current or credit account standing in the books of the said City of Glasgow Bank in the name of you, the said John Stewart, to the extent of £11,521 3s. 10d. or thereby; and (2) the account current or credit account standing in the books of the said City of Glasgow Bank in the name of the said firm of Stewart, Pott & Co., to the extent of £23,717 7s. 4d. or thereby, and that without any security, or at least upon wholly inadequate security; and you, the said John Stewart, did thus, then and there, wickedly and feloniously, and in breach of the trust reposed in you as aforesaid, and in breach of your duty as Director foresaid, embezzle and appropriate to your own uses and purposes, or to the uses and purposes of the said firm of Stewart, Pott & Co., of which you were at the time a partner, the said sums of £11,521 3s. 10d. and £23,717 7s. 4d. sterling, or thereby, or part thereof, received by and entrusted to you as aforesaid, the property of the said City of Glasgow Bank, or of the depositors and other creditors of the said Bank.

Likeas (V.), you, the said William Taylor, having been during the years 1874, 1875, 1876, 1877, and 1878 a partner of the firm of Henry Taylor & Sons, grain merchants, Glasgow, and also a Director of the said City of Glasgow Bank; and the said firm of Henry Taylor & Sons having had during the said period, or part thereof, an account or accounts current, or a credit account or accounts with the said City of Glasgow Bank, and it being your duty, as Director foresaid, not to allow overdrafts

422

Appendix II.

on such accounts to be made without any security, or upon wholly inadequate security; and in particular, not to allow any such overdraft to be made without security, or upon wholly inadequate security, as aforesaid, by you, the said William Taylor, or by any firm whereof you were at the time a partner; and you, the said William Taylor, having, in your capacity as Director foresaid, along with the other Directors and officials of the said City of Glasgow Bank, received from the depositors and other creditors of the said City of Glasgow Bank, and been entrusted by them with large sums of money, in order that the same might be employed in the ordinary business of banking: Yet, nevertheless, you, the said William Taylor, did, taking advantage of your official position as Director foresaid, on several or one or more occasions during the years 1874, 1875, 1876, 1877, and 1878, the time or times being more particularly to the prosecutor unknown, in or near the head office of the said City of Glasgow Bank, in or near Virginia Street foresaid, or elsewhere in or near Glasgow, to the prosecutor unknown, overdraw, or cause or procure to be overdrawn, the account or accounts current, or credit account or accounts, standing in the books of the said City of Glasgow Bank in the name of your said firm of Henry Taylor & Sons, to the extent of £73,460 19s. 3d. or thereby, and that without any security, or at least upon wholly inadequate security; and you, the said William Taylor, did thus, then and there, wickedly and feloniously, and in breach of the trust reposed in you as aforesaid, and in breach of your duty as Director foresaid, embezzle and appropriate to your own uses and purposes, or to the uses and purposes of the said firm of Henry Taylor & Sons, of which you were at the time a partner, the said sum of £73,460 19s. 3d. sterling or thereby, or part thereof, received by and entrusted to you as aforesaid, the property of the said City of Glasgow Bank, or of the depositors and other creditors of the said Bank.

Likeas (VI.), you, the said Henry Inglis, having been during the years from 1862 to 1878, both inclusive, a partner of the firm of H. & A. Inglis, Writers to the Signet, Edinburgh, and also a Director of the said City of Glasgow Bank, and you, the said Henry Inglis, and the said firm of H. & A. Inglis respectively, having had during the said period, or part thereof, an account or accounts current, or a credit account or accounts with the said City of Glasgow Bank; and it being your duty, as Director foresaid, not to allow overdrafts on such accounts to be made or continued without any security, or upon wholly inadequate security; and in particular not to allow any such overdraft to be made or continued without security, or upon wholly inadequate security as aforesaid, by you, the said Henry Inglis, or by any firm whereof you were at the time a partner; and you,

The City of Glasgow Bank Trial.

the said Henry Inglis, having, in your capacity as Director foresaid, along with the other Directors and officials of the said City of Glasgow Bank, received from the depositors and other creditors of the said City of Glasgow Bank, and been entrusted by them with large sums of money, in order that the same might be employed in the ordinary business of banking : Yet, nevertheless, you, the said Henry Inglis, did, taking advantage of your official position as Director foresaid, on various occasions during the years from 1862 to 1878, both inclusive, the times being more particularly to the prosecutor unknown, in or near the said head office of the said City of Glasgow Bank, or elsewhere in or near Glasgow, to the prosecutor unknown, or in or near the branch office of the said City of Glasgow Bank, in or near Hanover Street, Edinburgh, overdraw, or cause or procure to be overdrawn—(1) the account or accounts current or credit account or accounts standing in the books of the said City of Glasgow Bank in the name of you, the said Henry Inglis, to the extent of £44,625 16s. 2d. or thereby ; and (2) the account or accounts current, or credit account or accounts standing in the books of the said City of Glasgow Bank in the name of the said firm of H. & A. Inglis, to the extent of £7125 3s. 10d. or thereby,* or did allow the overdrafts on the said accounts, in name of you and of your said firm, to be continued and increased to the said amounts respectively, and that without any security, or at least upon wholly inadequate security ; and you, the said Henry Inglis, did thus, then and there, wickedly and feloniously, and in breach of the trust reposed in you as aforesaid, and in breach of your duty as Director foresaid, embezzle and appropriate to your own uses and purposes, or to the uses and purposes of the said firm of H. & A. Inglis, of which you were at the time a partner, the said sums of £44,625 16s. 2d. and £7125 3s. 10d. sterling or thereby, or part thereof, received by and entrusted to you as aforesaid, the property of the said City of Glasgow Bank, or of the depositors and other creditors of said Bank.

Likeas (VII.), you, the said John Innes Wright, having been during the years 1875, 1876, 1877, and 1878 a partner of the firm of John Innes Wright & Co., merchants, Glasgow, and also a Director of the said City of Glasgow Bank ; and you, the said John Innes Wright, and the said firm of John Innes Wright & Co. respectively, having had, during the said period, or part thereof, an account or accounts current, or a credit account or accounts, with the said City of Glasgow Bank, and it being your duty, as Director foresaid, not to allow overdrafts on such accounts to be made or continued without any security, or upon wholly inadequate security ; and in particular not to allow any

* Disallowed on relevancy.

Appendix II.

such overdraft to be made or continued without security, or upon wholly inadequate security as aforesaid, by you, the said John Innes Wright, or by any firm whereof you were at the time a partner; and you, the said John Innes Wright, having, in your capacity as Director foresaid, along with the other Directors and officials of the said City of Glasgow Bank, received from the depositors and other creditors of the said City of Glasgow Bank, and been entrusted by them with large sums of money, in order that the same might be employed in the ordinary business of banking: Yet, nevertheless, you, the said John Innes Wright, did, taking advantage of your official position as Director foresaid, on several or one or more occasions, during the years 1875, 1876, 1877, and 1878, the time or times being more particularly to the prosecutor unknown, in or near the said head office of the said City of Glasgow Bank, or elsewhere in or near Glasgow, to the prosecutor unknown, overdraw, or cause or procure to be overdrawn—(1) the account current or credit account standing in the books of the said City of Glasgow Bank, in the name of you, the said John Innes Wright, to the extent of £2746 8s. 4d. or thereby; and (2) the accounts current or credit accounts standing in the books of the said City of Glasgow Bank, in the name of the said firm of John Innes Wright & Co.,* or did allow the overdrafts of your said firm to be continued and increased to the amount of £340,210 7s. 3d. or thereby, and that without any security, or at least upon wholly inadequate security; and you, the said John Innes Wright, did thus, then and there, wickedly and feloniously, and in breach of the trust reposed in you as aforesaid, and in breach of your duty as Director foresaid, embezzle and appropriate to your own uses and purposes, or to the uses and purposes of the said firm of John Innes Wright & Co., above designed, of which you were at the time a partner, the said sums of £2746 8s. 4d. and £340,210 7s. 3d. sterling or thereby, or part thereof, received by and entrusted to you as aforesaid, the property of the said City of Glasgow Bank, or of the depositors and other creditors of the said Bank.

Likeas (VIII.), you, the said John Stewart, Lewis Potter, Robert Salmond, William Taylor, Henry Inglis, John Innes Wright, and Robert Summers Stronach, or one or more of you, having, on the 11th day of July, 1878, or on one or other of the days of that month, or of June immediately preceding, or of August immediately following, in or near the branch office of the said City of Glasgow Bank, in or near Argyle Street, Glasgow, received from John Ramsay of Kildalton, Islay, distiller in Islay and Glasgow, and now or lately residing at Kildalton aforesaid,

* Disallowed on relevancy.

425

The City of Glasgow Bank Trial.

and been entrusted by him with a bill of exchange for the sum of £252 7s. sterling, dated Glasgow, 13th June, 1878, drawn by the said John Ramsay upon, and accepted by, the firm of Edward Young & Co., then and now or lately spirit merchants, Seal Street, Liverpool, and payable four months after date, at the office of Williams, Deacon & Co., bankers, London, for the special and sole purpose of retaining the said bill in your custody till due, and of collecting payment of the same when due from the debtors therein on behalf of the said John Ramsay, who was not then or afterwards indebted or under obligation to the said City of Glasgow Bank ; and you, the said John Stewart, Lewis Potter, Robert Salmond, William Taylor, Henry Inglis, John Innes Wright, and Robert Summers Stronach, not having authority to make use of the said bill of exchange above libelled for any other purpose than that of collecting payment thereof when due as aforesaid : Yet, nevertheless, you, the said John Stewart, Lewis Potter, Robert Salmond, William Taylor, Henry Inglis, John Innes Wright, and Robert Summers Stronach, did, all and each or one or more of you, on the 11th day of July, 1878, or on one or other of the days of that month, or of June immediately preceding, or of August immediately following, in or near the said branch office of the said City of Glasgow Bank, in or near Argyle Street, Glasgow, or in or near the said head office of the said City of Glasgow Bank, wickedly and feloniously steal and theftuously away take the bill of exchange for the sum of £252 7s. above libelled, the property of the said John Ramsay ; and did endorse and make over, or cause or procure to be endorsed and made over, the said bill of exchange above libelled, before it had become due, to the London Joint-Stock Bank, London, in order that the proceeds thereof might be credited to the said City of Glasgow Bank in account with the said London Joint-Stock Bank, as a payment made on behalf of the said City of Glasgow Bank, and the said proceeds were credited accordingly ; or otherwise, you, the said John Stewart, Lewis Potter, Robert Salmond, William Taylor, Henry Inglis, John Innes Wright, and Robert Summers Stronach, did, all and each or one or more of you, time and place last above libelled, wickedly and feloniously, and in breach of the trust reposed in you as aforesaid, embezzle and appropriate to your own uses and purposes, or to the uses and purposes of the said City of Glasgow Bank, the said bill of exchange last above libelled, received by and entrusted to you as aforesaid, or the proceeds of the said bill, the property of the said John Ramsay.

Likeas (IX.), you, the said John Stewart, Lewis Potter, Robert Salmond, William Taylor, Henry Inglis, John Innes Wright, and Robert Summers Stronach, or one or more of you, having, time last above libelled, in or near the said branch office of the said City of Glasgow Bank, in or near Argyle Street,

Appendix II.

Glasgow, received from John Ramsay above designed, and been entrusted by him with a bill of exchange for the sum of £496 12s. 2d. sterling, dated Glasgow, 26th June, 1878, drawn by the said John Ramsay upon, and accepted by, the firm of W. & A. Gilbey, then and now or lately wine and spirit importers, Pantheon, Oxford Street, London, and payable four months after date at the Bank of England, Western Branch, London, for the special and sole purpose of retaining the said bill in your custody till due, and of collecting payment of the same when due from the debtors therein, on behalf of the said John Ramsay, who was not then or afterwards indebted or under obligation to the said City of Glasgow Bank ; and you, the said John Stewart, Lewis Potter, Robert Salmond, William Taylor, Henry Inglis, John Innes Wright, and Robert Summers Stronach, not having authority to make use of the said bill of exchange last above libelled, for any other purpose than that of collecting payment thereof when due as aforesaid : Yet, nevertheless, you, the said John Stewart, Lewis Potter, Robert Salmond, William Taylor, Henry Inglis, John Innes Wright, and Robert Summers Stronach, did, all and each or one or more of you, on the 11th day of July, 1878, or on one or other of the days of that month, or of June immediately preceding, or of August immediately following, in or near the said branch office of the said City of Glasgow Bank, in or near Argyle Street, Glasgow, or in or near the said head office of the said City of Glasgow Bank, wickedly and feloniously steal and theftuously away take the bill of exchange for the sum of £496 12s. 2d., above libelled, the property of the said John Ramsay, and did endorse and make over, or cause or procure to be endorsed and made over, the said bill of exchange last above libelled, before it had become due, to the London Joint-Stock Bank, London, in order that the proceeds thereof might be credited to the said City of Glasgow Bank in account with the said London Joint-Stock Bank, as a payment made on behalf of the said City of Glasgow Bank, and the said proceeds were credited accordingly ; or otherwise, you, the said John Stewart, Lewis Potter, Robert Salmond, William Taylor, Henry Inglis, John Innes Wright, and Robert Summers Stronach, did, all and each or one or more of you, time and place last above libelled, wickedly and feloniously, and in breach of the trust reposed in you as aforesaid, embezzle and appropriate to your own uses and purposes, or to the uses and purposes of the said City of Glasgow Bank, the said bill of exchange last above libelled, received by and entrusted to you as aforesaid, or the proceeds of the said bill, the property of the said John Ramsay.

Likeas (X.), you, the said John Stewart, Lewis Potter, Robert Salmond, William Taylor, Henry Inglis, John Innes

Wright, and Robert Summers Stronach, or one or more of you, having, on the 3rd day of September, 1878, or on one or other of the days of that month, or of August immediately preceding, in or near the said branch office of the said City of Glasgow Bank, in or near Argyle Street, Glasgow, received from John Ramsay, above designed, and been entrusted by him with a bill of exchange for the sum of £489 14s. 2d. sterling, dated Glasgow, 24th July, 1878, drawn by the said John Ramsay upon, and accepted by, the said firm of W. & A. Gilbey, and payable four months after date, at the Bank of England, Western Branch, London, for the special and sole purpose of retaining the said bill in your custody till due, and of collecting payment of the same when due from the debtors therein, on behalf of the said John Ramsay, who was not then or afterwards indebted or under obligation to the said City of Glasgow Bank ; and you, the said John Stewart, Lewis Potter, Robert Salmond, William Taylor, Henry Inglis, John Innes Wright, and Robert Summers Stronach, not having authority to make use of the said bill of exchange last above libelled, for any other purpose than that of collecting payment thereof when due as aforesaid : Yet, nevertheless, you, the said John Stewart, Lewis Potter, Robert Salmond, William Taylor, Henry Inglis, John Innes Wright, and Robert Summers Stronach, did, all and each or one or more of you, on the 3rd day of September, 1878, or on one or other of the days of that month, or of August immediately preceding, in or near the said branch office of the said City of Glasgow Bank, in or near Argyle Street, Glasgow, or in or near the said head office of the said City of Glasgow Bank, wickedly and feloniously steal and theftuously away take the bill of exchange for the sum of £489 14s. 2d. above libelled, the property of the said John Ramsay ; and did endorse and make over, or cause and procure to be endorsed and made over, the said bill of exchange last above libelled, before it had become due, to the London Joint-Stock Bank, London, in order that the proceeds thereof might be credited to the said City of Glasgow Bank, in account with the said London Joint-Stock Bank, as a payment made on behalf of the said City of Glasgow Bank, and the said proceeds were credited accordingly ; or otherwise, you, the said John Stewart, Lewis Potter, Robert Salmond, William Taylor, Henry Inglis, John Innes Wright, and Robert Summers Stronach, did, all and each or one or more of you, time and place last above libelled, wickedly and feloniously, and in breach of the trust reposed in you as aforesaid, embezzle and appropriate to your own uses and purposes, or to the uses and purposes of the said City of Glasgow Bank, the said bill of exchange last above libelled, received by and entrusted to you as aforesaid, or the proceeds of the said bill, the property of the said John Ramsay.

Appendix II.

Likeas (XI.), you, the said John Stewart, Lewis Potter, Robert Salmond, William Taylor, Henry Inglis, John Innes Wright, and Robert Summers Stronach, or one or more of you, having, on the 20th day of August, 1878, or on one or other of the days of that month, or of July immediately preceding, or of September immediately following, in or near the Anderston branch office of the said City of Glasgow Bank, in or near Anderston, Glasgow, received from Charles Connell & Company, then and now or lately shipbuilders, Scotstoun, Whiteinch, near Glasgow, or from Charles Connell, the only partner of said firm, then and now or lately residing at Rozelle, Broomhill Drive, Partick, in the county of Lanark, and been entrusted by them, or him, with two several bills of exchange, each for the sum of £3000 sterling, and each dated Glasgow, 3rd April, 1878, drawn by the said Charles Connell & Company upon, and accepted by, the firm of Alexander & Radcliffe, then and now or lately shipowners, Liverpool and London Chambers, Exchange, Liverpool, and each payable six months after date at the office in London of Barnetts, Hoares & Company, bankers there ; and having, time and place last above libelled, received from the said Charles Connell & Company, or from the said Charles Connell, and been entrusted by them, or him, with two several bills of exchange, each for the sum of £3000 sterling, and each dated Glasgow, 28th May, 1878, drawn by the said Charles Connell & Company upon, and accepted by, the said firm of Alexander & Radcliffe above designed, and each payable six months after date at the office in London of Barnetts, Hoares & Company, above designed ; and having, on the 26th day of August, 1878, or on one or other of the days of that month, or of September immediately following, in or near the said Anderston branch office of the said City of Glasgow Bank, received from the said Charles Connell & Company, or from the said Charles Connell, and been entrusted by them, or him, with two several bills of exchange, each for the sum of £3000 sterling, and each dated Glasgow, 2nd June, 1878, drawn by the said Charles Connell & Company upon, and accepted by, the said firm of Alexander & Radcliffe, above designed, and each payable six months after date at the office in London of Barnetts, Hoares & Company, above designed, all for the special and sole purpose of retaining the said bills in your custody till due, and of collecting payment of the same when due from the debtors therein, on behalf of the said Charles Connell & Company, or of the said Charles Connell, neither of whom was, at the dates when the said six bills of exchange last above libelled were respectively received as aforesaid, or afterwards, indebted or under obligation to the said City of Glasgow Bank ; and you, the said John Stewart, Lewis Potter, Robert Salmond, William Taylor, Henry Inglis, John Innes Wright, and Robert Summers Stronach, not having authority to make use of the said six bills of exchange last above libelled, or any of them, for any other purpose than that of collecting payment thereof when due, as aforesaid: Yet, nevertheless, you, the said John Stewart, Lewis Potter, Robert Salmond, William Taylor, Henry Inglis, John Innes Wright, and Robert Summers Stronach, did, all and each or one or more of you, on the 20th day of August, 1878, or on one or other of the days of that month, or of July immediately preceding, or of September immediately following, as regards the four first above mentioned of the six bills of exchange last above libelled, and on the 26th day of August, 1878, or on one or other of the days of that month, or of September immediately following, as regards the two last above mentioned of the six bills of exchange last above libelled, in or near the said Anderston branch office of the said City of Glasgow Bank, or in or near the said head office of the said City of Glasgow Bank, wickedly and feloniously steal and theftuously away take the six bills of exchange last above libelled, or part thereof, the property of the said Charles Connell & Company, or of the said Charles Connell, and did endorse and make over, or cause or procure to be endorsed and made over, each of the said six bills of exchange last above libelled, before it had become due, to the London Joint-Stock Bank, London, in order that the proceeds thereof might be credited to the said City of Glasgow Bank, in account with the said London Joint-Stock Bank, as a payment made on behalf of the said City of Glasgow Bank, and the said proceeds were credited accordingly; or otherwise, you, the said John Stewart, Lewis Potter, Robert Salmond, William Taylor, Henry Inglis, John Innes Wright, and Robert Summers Stronach, did, all and each or one or more of you, time or times or place or places respectively above libelled, as regards the six bills of exchange last above libelled respectively, wickedly and feloniously, and in breach of the trust reposed in you as aforesaid, embezzle and appropriate to your own uses and purposes, or to the uses and purposes of the said City of Glasgow Bank, the six bills of exchange last above libelled, or part thereof, received by and entrusted to you as aforesaid, or the proceeds of the said bills, or part thereof, the property of the said Charles Connell & Company, or of the said Charles Connell.

Likeas (XII.), you, the said John Stewart, Lewis Potter, Robert Salmond, William Taylor, Henry Inglis, John Innes Wright, and Robert Summers Stronach, or one or more of you, having, on the 21st day of August, 1878, or on one or other of the days of that month, or of July immediately preceding, or of September immediately following, in or near the said head office of the said City of Glasgow Bank, received from the Marbella Iron Ore Company, Limited, having its registered office in London, and been entrusted

Appendix II.

by the said Marbella Iron Ore Company, Limited, with a bill of exchange for the sum of £525 sterling, dated London, 7th July, 1878, drawn by the said Marbella Iron Ore Company, Limited, upon, and accepted by, the firm of E. J. Waite & Company, Bute Docks, Cardiff, and payable four months after date at the office of Glyn, Mills, Currie & Company, bankers, London, for the special and sole purpose of retaining the said bill in your custody till due, and of collecting payment of the same when due from the debtors therein on behalf of the said Marbella Iron Ore Company, Limited, which was not then or afterwards indebted or under obligation to the said City of Glasgow Bank ; and you, the said John Stewart, Lewis Potter, Robert Salmond, William Taylor, Henry Inglis, John Innes Wright, and Robert Summers Stronach, not having authority to make use of the said bill of exchange last above libelled for any other purpose than that of collecting payment thereof when due as aforesaid ; yet, nevertheless, you, the said John Stewart, Lewis Potter, Robert Salmond, William Taylor, Henry Inglis, John Innes Wright, and Robert Summers Stronach, did, all and each or one or more of you, on the 21st day of August, 1878, or on one or other of the days of that month, or of July immediately preceding, or of September immediately following, in or near the said head office of the said City of Glasgow Bank, wickedly and feloniously steal and theftuously away take the bill of exchange for the sum of £525 above libelled, the property of the said Marbella Iron Ore Company, Limited, and did endorse and make over, or cause or procure to be endorsed and made over, the said bill of exchange last above libelled, before it had become due, to the London Joint-Stock Bank, London, in order that the proceeds thereof might be credited to the said City of Glasgow Bank, in account with the said London Joint-Stock Bank, as a payment made on behalf of the said City of Glasgow Bank, and the said proceeds were credited accordingly ; or otherwise, you, the said John Stewart, Lewis Potter, Robert Salmond, William Taylor, Henry Inglis, John Innes Wright, and Robert Summers Stronach, did, all and each or one or more of you, time and place last above libelled, wickedly and feloniously, and in breach of the trust reposed in you as aforesaid, embezzle and appropriate to your own uses and purposes, or to the uses and purposes of the said City of Glasgow Bank, the said bill of exchange last above libelled, received by and entrusted to you as aforesaid, or the proceeds of the said bill, the property of the said Marbella Iron Ore Company, Limited.

Likeas (XIII.), you, the said John Stewart, Lewis Potter, Robert Salmond, William Taylor, Henry Inglis, John Innes Wright, and Robert Summers Stronach, or one or more of you, having, time and place last above libelled, received from the said Marbella Iron Ore Company, Limited, and been entrusted by

The City of Glasgow Bank Trial.

them with a bill of exchange for the sum of £358 13s. 8d. sterling, dated London, 13th August, 1878, drawn by the said Marbella Iron Ore Company, Limited, upon, and accepted by, the Panteg Steel Works and Engineering Company, Limited, Panteg, near Pontypool, Monmouthshire, and payable four months after date at 77 Lombard Street, London, E.C., Messrs. Fuller, Banbury, Nix & Mathieson, for the special and sole purpose of retaining the said bill in your custody till due, and of collecting payment of the same when due from the debtors therein, on behalf of the said Marbella Iron Ore Company, Limited, which was not then or afterwards indebted or under obligation to the said City of Glasgow Bank ; and you, the said John Stewart, Lewis Potter, Robert Salmond, William Taylor, Henry Inglis, John Innes Wright, and Robert Summers Stronach, not having authority to make use of the said bill of exchange last above libelled for any other purpose than that of collecting payment thereof when due as aforesaid : Yet, nevertheless, you, the said John Stewart, Lewis Potter, Robert Salmond, William Taylor, Henry Inglis, John Innes Wright, and Robert Summers Stronach, did, all and each or one or more of you, time and place last above libelled, wickedly and feloniously steal and theftuously away take the bill of exchange for the sum of £358 13s. 8d. above libelled, the property of the said Marbella Iron Ore Company, Limited, and did endorse and make over, or cause or procure to be endorsed and made over, the said bill of exchange last above libelled, before it had become due, to the London Joint-Stock Bank, London, in order that the proceeds thereof might be credited to the said City of Glasgow Bank, in account with the said London Joint-Stock Bank, as a payment made on behalf of the said City of Glasgow Bank, and the said proceeds were credited accordingly ; or otherwise, you, the said John Stewart, Lewis Potter, Robert Salmond, William Taylor, Henry Inglis, John Innes Wright, and Robert Summers Stronach, did, all and each or one or more of you, time and place last above libelled, wickedly and feloniously, and in breach of the trust reposed in you as aforesaid, embezzle and appropriate to your own uses and purposes, or to the uses and purposes of the said City of Glasgow Bank, the said bill of exchange last above libelled, received by and entrusted to you as aforesaid, or the proceeds of the said bill, the property of the said Marbella Iron Ore Company, Limited.

Likeas (XIV.), you, the said John Stewart, Lewis Potter, Robert Salmond, William Taylor, Henry Inglis, John Innes Wright, and Robert Summers Stronach, or one or more of you, having, on the 31st day of August, 1878, or on one or other of the days of that month, or of July immediately preceding, or of September immediately following, in or near the said head office of the said City of Glasgow Bank, received from the said Marbella

Appendix II.

Iron Ore Company, Limited, and been entrusted by them with a bill of exchange for the sum of £800 sterling, dated London, 14th July, 1878, drawn by the said Marbella Iron Ore Company, Limited, upon, and accepted by, the said firm of E. J. Waite & Company above designed, and payable four months after date at the office of Glyn, Mills, Currie & Company, bankers, London, for the special and sole purpose of retaining the said bill in your custody till due, and of collecting payment of the same when due from the debtors therein, on behalf of the said Marbella Iron Ore Company, Limited, which was not then or afterwards indebted or under obligation to the said City of Glasgow Bank; and you, the said John Stewart, Lewis Potter, Robert Salmond, William Taylor, Henry Inglis, John Innes Wright, and Robert Summers Stronach, not having authority to make use of the said bill of exchange last above libelled for any other purpose than that of collecting payment thereof when due, as aforesaid: Yet, nevertheless, you, the said John Stewart, Lewis Potter, Robert Salmond, William Taylor, Henry Inglis, John Innes Wright, and Robert Summers Stronach, did, all and each or one or more of you, on the 31st day of August, 1878, or on one or other of the days of that month, or of July immediately preceding, or of September immediately following, place last above libelled, wickedly and feloniously steal and theftuously away take the bill of exchange for the sum of £800 above libelled, the property of the said Marbella Iron Ore Company, Limited, and did endorse and make over, or cause or procure to be endorsed and made over, the said bill of exchange last above libelled before it had become due to the London Joint-Stock Bank, London, in order that the proceeds thereof might be credited to the said City of Glasgow Bank, in account with the said London Joint-Stock Bank, as a payment made on behalf of the said City of Glasgow Bank, and the said proceeds were credited accordingly; or otherwise, you, the said John Stewart, Lewis Potter, Robert Salmond, William Taylor, Henry Inglis, John Innes Wright, and Robert Summers Stronach, did, all and each or one or more of you, time and place last above libelled, wickedly and feloniously, and in breach of the trust reposed in you as aforesaid, embezzle and appropriate to your own uses and purposes, or to the uses and purposes of the said City of Glasgow Bank, the said bill of exchange last above libelled, received by and entrusted to you as aforesaid, or the proceeds of the said bill, the property of the said Marbella Iron Ore Company, Limited.

Likeas (XV.), you, the said John Stewart, Lewis Potter, Robert Salmond, William Taylor, Henry Inglis, John Innes Wright, and Robert Summers Stronach, or one or more of you, having, on the 5th day of September, 1878, or on one or other of the days of that month, or of August immediately preceding,

place last above libelled, received from the said Marbella Iron
Ore Company, Limited, and been entrusted by them with a bill
of exchange for the sum of £1187 11s. 3d. sterling, dated London,
10th July, 1878, drawn by the said Marbella Iron Ore Company,
Limited, upon, and accepted by, the Ebbw Vale Steel, Iron, and
Coal Company, Limited, Ebbw Vale Works, Monmouthshire, and
payable four months after date at the office of the Consolidated
Bank, London, for the special and sole purpose of retaining the
said bill in your custody till due, and of collecting payment of
the same when due from the debtors therein, on behalf of the
said Marbella Iron Ore Company, Limited, which was not then or
afterwards indebted or under obligation to the said City of
Glasgow Bank; and you, the said John Stewart, Lewis Potter,
Robert Salmond, William Taylor, Henry Inglis, John Innes
Wright, and Robert Summers Stronach, not having authority
to make use of the said bill of exchange last above libelled for
any other purpose than that of collecting payment thereof when
due as aforesaid: Yet, nevertheless, you, the said John Stewart,
Lewis Potter, Robert Salmond, William Taylor, Henry Inglis,
John Innes Wright, and Robert Summers Stronach, did, all and
each or one or more of you, on the 5th day of September, 1878,
or on one or other of the days of that month, or of August immediately preceding, place last above libelled, wickedly and
feloniously steal and theftuously away take the bill of exchange
for the sum of £1187 11s. 3d. above libelled, the property of the
said Marbella Iron Ore Company, Limited, and did endorse and
make over, or cause or procure to be endorsed and made over,
the said bill of exchange last above libelled before it had become
due to the London Joint-Stock Bank, London, in order that the
proceeds thereof might be credited to the said City of Glasgow
Bank, in account with the said London Joint-Stock Bank, as a
payment made on behalf of the said City of Glasgow Bank, and
the said proceeds were credited accordingly; or otherwise, you,
the said John Stewart, Lewis Potter, Robert Salmond, William
Taylor, Henry Inglis, John Innes Wright, and Robert Summers
Stronach, did, all and each or one or more of you, time and
place last above libelled, wickedly and feloniously, and in breach
of the trust reposed in you as aforesaid, embezzle and appropriate
to your own uses and purposes, or to the uses and purposes of the
said City of Glasgow Bank, the said bill of exchange last above
libelled, received by and entrusted to you as aforesaid, or the
proceeds thereof, the property of the said Marbella Iron Ore
Company, Limited.

Likeas (XVI.), you, the said John Stewart, Lewis Potter,
Robert Salmond, William Taylor, Henry Inglis, John Innes
Wright, and Robert Summers Stronach, or one or more of you,

Appendix II.

having, on the 13th day of September, 1878, or on one or other of
the days of that month, or of August immediately preceding,
place last above libelled, received from James Baird, merchant
at St. John's, Newfoundland, and then residing in Glasgow, and
been entrusted by him with a bill of exchange for the sum of
£700 sterling, dated St. John's, Newfoundland, 21st August,
1878, drawn by Walter Grieve & Company, merchants at St.
John's aforesaid, upon Walter Grieve, Son & Company, merchants,
Greenock, and payable in London sixty days after sight, to the
order of the Union Bank of Newfoundland, and endorsed by the
said Union Bank of Newfoundland to the said James Baird, and
accepted by the said Walter Grieve, Son & Company, of date 2nd
September, 1878, as payable at the Union Bank of London, and
that for the special and sole purpose of retaining the said bill
in your custody till due, and of collecting payment of the same
when due from the debtors therein, on behalf of the said James
Baird, who was not then or afterwards indebted or under obligation to the said City of Glasgow Bank ; and you, the said John
Stewart, Lewis Potter, Robert Salmond, William Taylor, Henry
Inglis, John Innes Wright, and Robert Summers Stronach, not
having authority to make use of the said bill of exchange last
above libelled for any other purpose than that of collecting payment thereof when due, as aforesaid : Yet, nevertheless, you, the
said John Stewart, Lewis Potter, Robert Salmond, William Taylor,
Henry Inglis, John Innes Wright, and Robert Summers Stronach,
did, all and each or one or more of you, on the 13th day of September, 1878, or on one or other of the days of that month, or of
August immediately preceding, place last above libelled, wickedly
and feloniously steal and theftuously away take the bill of
exchange for the sum of £700 above libelled, the property of the
said James Baird, and did endorse and make over, or cause or
procure to be endorsed and made over, the said bill of exchange
last above libelled before it had become due to the London Joint-
Stock Bank, London, in order that the proceeds thereof might be
credited to the said City of Glasgow Bank, in account with the
said London Joint-Stock Bank, as a payment made on behalf of
the said City of Glasgow Bank, and the said proceeds were
credited accordingly ; or otherwise you, the said John Stewart,
Lewis Potter, Robert Salmond, William Taylor, Henry Inglis,
John Innes Wright, and Robert Summers Stronach, did, all and
each or one or more of you, time and place last above libelled,
wickedly and feloniously, and in breach of the trust reposed in
you as aforesaid, embezzle and appropriate to your own uses and
purposes, or to the uses and purposes of the said City of Glasgow
Bank, the said bill of exchange last above libelled, received by
and entrusted to you as aforesaid, or the proceeds of the said
bill, the property of the said James Baird.

The City of Glasgow Bank Trial.

Likeas (XVII.), you, the said John Stewart, Lewis Potter, Robert Salmond, William Taylor, Henry Inglis, John Innes Wright, and Robert Summers Stronach, or one or more of you, having, on the 21st day of September, 1878, or on one or other of the days of that month, or of August immediately preceding, place last above libelled, received from John M'Pherson & Company, then and now or lately engineers and ironfounders, Mount Blue Works, Camlachie, in or near Glasgow, and been entrusted by them with a bill of exchange for the sum of £562 10s. sterling, dated Hong Kong, 9th August, 1878, drawn by the Chartered Bank of India, Australia, and China, Hong Kong, upon the Chartered Bank of India, Australia, and China, Hatton Court, Threadneedle Street, London, and payable thirty days after sight to the order of, and endorsed to the said John M'Pherson & Company, and accepted by the said Chartered Bank of India, Australia, and China, Hatton Court aforesaid, of date 23rd September, 1878, as payable at the City Bank, London, and that for the special and sole purpose of retaining the said bill in your custody till due, and of collecting payment of the same when due, for the debtors therein on behalf of the said John M'Pherson & Company, which firm was not then or afterwards indebted or under obligation to the said City of Glasgow Bank; and you, the said John Stewart, Lewis Potter, Robert Salmond, William Taylor, Henry Inglis, John Innes Wright, and Robert Summers Stronach, not having authority to make use of the said bill of exchange last above libelled for any other purpose than that of collecting payment thereof when due as aforesaid: Yet, nevertheless, you, the said John Stewart, Lewis Potter, Robert Salmond, William Taylor, Henry Inglis, John Innes Wright, and Robert Summers Stronach, did, all and each or one or more of you, on the 21st day of September, 1878, or on one or other of the days of that month, or of August immediately preceding, place last above libelled, wickedly and feloniously steal and theftuously away take the bill of exchange for the sum of £562 10s., above libelled, the property of the said John M'Pherson & Company, and did endorse and make over, or cause or procure to be endorsed and made over, the said bill of exchange last above libelled, before it had become due, to the London Joint-Stock Bank, London, in order that the proceeds thereof might be credited to the said City of Glasgow Bank, in account with the said London Joint-Stock Bank, as a payment made on behalf of the said City of Glasgow Bank, and the said proceeds were credited accordingly; or otherwise, you, the said John Stewart, Lewis Potter, Robert Salmond, William Taylor, Henry Inglis, John Innes Wright, and Robert Summers Stronach, did, all and each or one or more of you, time and place last above libelled, wickedly and feloniously, and in breach of the trust reposed in you as aforesaid, embezzle and appropriate to your

436

Appendix II.

own uses and purposes, or to the uses and purposes of the said City of Glasgow Bank, the said bill of exchange last above libelled, received by and entrusted to you as aforesaid, or the proceeds of the said bill, the property of the said John M'Pherson & Company; and you, the said John Stewart, having been apprehended and taken before Francis William Clark, Esq., advocate, Sheriff of Lanarkshire, did, in his presence at Glasgow, on the 22nd and 29th days of October, 1878, respectively, emit and subscribe a declaration; and you, the said Lewis Potter, having been apprehended and taken before the said Francis William Clark, did, in his presence at Glasgow, on the 22nd, 25th, and 29th days of October, 1878, respectively, emit and subscribe a declaration; and you, the said Robert Salmond, having been apprehended and taken before the said Francis William Clark, did, in his presence at Glasgow, on the 22nd and 29th days of October, 1878, respectively, emit and subscribe a declaration; and you, the said William Taylor, having been apprehended and taken before the said Francis William Clark, did, in his presence at Glasgow, on the 22nd, and on two several occasions on the 29th days of October, 1878, respectively, emit and subscribe a declaration; and you, the said Henry Inglis, having been apprehended and taken before the said Francis William Clark, did, in his presence at Glasgow, on the 22nd, and on two several occasions on the 29th days of October, 1878, respectively, emit and subscribe a declaration; and you, the said John Innes Wright, having been apprehended and taken before the said Francis William Clark, did, in his presence at Glasgow, on the 22nd, and on two several occasions on the 29th days of October, 1878, respectively, emit and subscribe a declaration; and you, the said Robert Summers Stronach, having been apprehended and taken before the said Francis William Clark, did, in his presence at Glasgow, on the 22nd and 29th days of October, 1878, respectively, emit and subscribe a declaration, which several declarations being to be used in evidence against each of you by whom the same were respectively emitted, as also the books, letters, documents, excerpts, prints, and other articles enumerated in an inventory thereof, hereunto annexed and referred to, being to be used in evidence against all and each, or one or more of you, the said John Stewart, Lewis Potter, Robert Salmond, William Taylor, Henry Inglis, John Innes Wright, and Robert Summers Stronach, at your trial, will for that purpose be in due time lodged in the hands of the Clerk of the High Court of Justiciary, before which you are to be tried, that you may respectively have an opportunity of seeing the same, all which, or part thereof, being found proven by the verdict of an assize, or admitted by the respective judicial confessions of you, the said John Stewart, Lewis Potter, Robert Salmond, William Taylor, Henry Inglis, John Innes

The City of Glasgow Bank Trial.

Wright, and Robert Summers Stronach, before the Lord Justice-General, Lord Justice-Clerk, and Lords Commissioners of Justiciary, you, the said John Stewart, Lewis Potter, Robert Salmond, William Taylor, Henry Inglis, John Innes Wright, and Robert Summers Stronach, ought to be punished with the pains of law to deter others from committing the like crimes in all time coming.

(Signed) JOHN BURNET, A.D.

APPENDIX III.

The Declarations of the Prisoners.

First Declaration of John Stewart.

At Glasgow, the twenty-second day of October, eighteen hundred and seventy-eight, in presence of Francis William Clark, Esquire, advocate, Sheriff of Lanarkshire.

Compeared a prisoner, and the charge against him having been read over and explained to him, and he having been judicially admonished and examined, declares and says—My name is John Stewart. I am a native of Glasgow, sixty-one years of age, and I reside at 34 Moray Place, Edinburgh. I am a wine merchant.

I declare that I am not guilty of the charge of falsehood, fraud, and wilful imposition preferred against me, of having falsified the books of the City of Glasgow Bank, and prepared and issued false and fabricated balance sheets, during the years from 1873 to 1878 inclusive, while the Bank was in a state of insolvency, and well known to me to be so, so as to conceal the true state of the affairs of the Bank from the shareholders and creditors, and of declaring false dividends, in order to deceive said shareholders, creditors, and the public.

I farther declare that, as I have been advised, I decline at this stage to make any farther statements, or answer any farther questions. All which I declare to be truth. One word deleted.

Second Declaration of John Stewart.

At Glasgow, the twenty-ninth day of October, eighteen hundred and seventy-eight years, in presence of Francis William Clark, Esquire, advocate, Sheriff of Lanarkshire.

Compeared John Stewart, presently prisoner in the prison of Glasgow, and a charge of theft now preferred against him having been read over and explained to him, and he having been judicially admonished and examined, declares and says— I am not guilty of the charge made against me of stealing a number of bills, amounting to twenty-three thousand six hundred and ninety-three pounds twelve shillings and sevenpence, or thereby.

439

The City of Glasgow Bank Trial.

I am advised to make no farther statement at this stage than that I am not guilty. All which I declare to be truth. Three words deleted.

First Declaration of Lewis Potter.

At Glasgow, the twenty-second day of October, eighteen hundred and seventy-eight years, in presence of Francis William Clark, Esquire, advocate, Sheriff of Lanarkshire.

Compeared a prisoner, and the charge against him having been read over and explained to him, and he having been judicially admonished and examined, declares and says—My name is Lewis Potter. I am a native of Falkirk, seventy-one years of age; and I reside at No. 7 Claremont Terrace, Glasgow. I am a retired merchant.

I declare that I am not guilty of the charge of falsehood, fraud, and wilful imposition preferred against me, of having falsified the books of the City of Glasgow Bank, and prepared and issued false and fabricated balance sheets during the years from 1873 to 1878 inclusive, while the Bank was in a state of insolvency, and well known to me to be so, so as to conceal the true state of the affairs of the Bank from the shareholders and creditors, and of declaring false dividends in order to deceive said shareholders, creditors, and the public.

I have nothing farther to say in the meantime, and I decline to answer any questions that may be put to me. All which I declare to be truth.

Second Declaration of Lewis Potter.

At Glasgow, the twenty-fifth day of October, eighteen hundred and seventy-eight years, in presence of Francis William Clark, Esquire, advocate, Sheriff of Lanarkshire.

Compeared Lewis Potter, presently prisoner in the prison of Glasgow, and the declaration emitted by him before the said Sheriff, of date the twenty-second day of October current, having been read over to him, and he having been judicially admonished and examined, declares and says—

I am now brought before the Sheriff at my own request.

I considered that the City Bank was in a solvent state when the last balance sheet was struck. I was under the impression that all the securities were sufficient. I signed the last balance sheet. I did this under the impression that it was correct. It was done while I and the other Directors were at luncheon, and I signed it at their request. I think I had just come from Ayr at the time, where my time was spent in country quarters, and my mind was entirely off business. Before signing I had not examined any of the books or documents, so as to test

Appendix III.

the accuracy of the balance sheet. I acted on the impression that others had done so.

Shown a document, titled on the back, " City of Glasgow Bank, Abstract of Accounts at June 5, 1878, B." I cannot say whether I had seen that before I signed the balance sheet or ledger. I don't recollect of going over the foresaid document along with Mr. Stewart and Mr. Robert Stronach before signing the balance sheet. I may have seen it at the Bank. It is likely I did.

I observe that in the foresaid document the indebtedness of the Bank is stated under " Bills payable " at £2,881,252 18s. 6d., and that there is deducted from that, under " Bills payable," a sum of £973,300. I don't know why that was done, and I understand nothing about it.

On the other side of the document I see an entry showing the amount lent by the Bank on credit accounts No. 1, a sum of £2,009,752 11s. 2d., and that there is deducted from that a sum of £680,614. I do not know how that was done, and I don't understand it.

Interrogated—Did you think it was properly done? Declares —I cannot say. I am unable to give explanations regarding the said document, because, though I may have seen it, I have never thoroughly examined it.

I have been about twenty years a Director of the City Bank. I came into the direction soon after the stoppage in 1856. I did this at the urgent request of parties.

I do not think I or my firms were indebted to the Bank at that time. Ever since that time, and certainly latterly, I and my firms abstained from doing business with the Bank. What business we did was almost all transacted with the National Bank and the British Linen Company. We got some credits from the City Bank, but I think these did not exceed £30,000 at the outside. I explain that we have considerable credits from the Bank, but these are principally on its own account.

The City Bank wished to acquire certain lands in New Zealand, and they gave us credits to pay for the same, to be held on their account.

I have no doubt this proposal originated at a meeting of Directors, and was sanctioned by them, and I suppose will appear in the minutes. I know that lands were bought, but cannot say as to the form of the title. I don't think the Bank has any title to the lands. These purchases were made within the last six or nine months, and we should be glad to give up the titles to the Bank as soon as the credits are paid.

The Bank also wished my firm to acquire shares for them in the New Zealand and Australian Land Company, and they gave us credits in order to purchase these. The title was taken in name of my son, John Alexander, and Cunningham

The City of Glasgow Bank Trial.

Smith, both partners of Potter, Wilson & Co. There were also some shares taken in my own name.

Interrogated—Why were those titles not taken directly to the Bank instead of you and your partners' names? Declares—I cannot explain that. I and my partners have held these shares for about five years. We have not disposed of them or trafficked in them. They were held by us for the Bank in the hope that a large profit might be secured for the Bank in a short time.

During the time of our holding the only securities held by the Bank against us I believe to be letters which have passed between us and the Bank. These letters, if they existed, were addressed by us to the Directors or the Manager. I don't suppose such letters came before the weekly meetings of the Bank, but I am not sure. The transaction was perfectly well understood, and it was unnecessary to revert to it at the meetings. Even in the event of the stoppage of my firm, the Bank would suffer no prejudice, because I suppose the minutes would bear that such shares or property were held by us from the Bank, and my private estate remained accountable. I suppose even yet I shall have a considerable reversion.

I do not know personally of any advances made by the Bank to Smith, Fleming & Co. without the sanction of the Board. There may have been; and, if so, that was the Manager's affair.

I know nothing, even yet, about the amount of advances to James Morton & Co., but I was aware that advances had been made. The advances to that firm were never brought before us, to the best of my belief.

I never knew anything of the amount of advances to John Innes Wright & Co. till shortly before the stoppage, but I knew that some advances had been made.

It certainly was our duty as Directors to inquire into the advances which we knew were being made to the above firms, but we did not do so, from the faith we had in the Manager. For all that I knew, the Bank might have advanced £2,000,000 to James Morton & Co.

I understood they had securities, but I knew nothing of their amount.

Interrogated—Do you consider that £2,132,453 was a large or moderate sum for the Bank to be liable in on acceptances? Declares—I think moderate, considering the probability that a good part of that was for its own benefit.

Shown a book, titled on the back "City of Glasgow Bank Cash Book, Private, No. 6," and being referred to the cross entries under heads "Foreign and Colonial Credits, No. 2," and "Bills payable, No. 2"—I never saw those entries before, and was confounded when I saw a reference to them in the

Appendix III.

investigators' report. I don't think I knew that such a book existed before. I can give no explanation of how in the balance ledger of the Bank, under date 4th June, 1873, foreign and colonial credits are only entered to the amount of £1,159,153 2s. 3d. I was not aware of the fact that in the balance ledger of the Bank they were so credited.

At the date of the stoppage, I think I held about twelve shares. The shares were converted into stock about 1856. I don't think I ever held more.

I do not think, and never considered, that the Bank was in an insolvent state till its stoppage.

About a month before I thought I saw tightness in money. I was present at the meeting in Edinburgh which resolved on stoppage. The meeting in Edinburgh was composed of myself, Mr. Stewart, and the Manager, as deputed by the Board. We resolved on stoppage, for want of the usual facilities to carry on the business. It had been arranged by the Directors in Glasgow that a stoppage should take place if we failed to get facilities. The account of Smith, Fleming & Co. was talked of among the Directors before the stoppage.

The immediate want of money was the cause of the stoppage. Latterly the Manager found it difficult to negotiate the Bank's paper in the market. I do not know any reason why the Bank lost its credit, unless it were the undue amount of credit given to customers.

From 1873 to 1878 I have not taken a greater amount of interest in the Bank than the other Directors. We were all much the same in that respect.

James Nicol Fleming did not take a greater share in the management than other people.

I cannot say that during the years from 1873 downwards I have made no examination of the Bank books. I have not had conferences with the Manager in going over the books.

I don't think there is a special meeting of the Directors generally called to go over the balance sheet, but I think they should see it is correct. We had full faith in the Manager when he presented a document.

Very likely we went over it in a sort of way; but latterly I was getting old, and was not attending to business as formerly. Since I became a Director I never said to any one that I had suspicions of the Bank's stability.

The foresaid declaration, document, and private cash book No. 6, are docqueted and subscribed as relative hereto. All of which I declare to be truth. Five words deleted.

THIRD DECLARATION OF LEWIS POTTER.

At Glasgow, the twenty-ninth day of October, eighteen

The City of Glasgow Bank Trial.

hundred and seventy-eight years, in presence of Francis William Clark, Esquire, advocate, Sheriff of Lanarkshire.

Compeared Lewis Potter, presently prisoner in the prison of Glasgow, and a charge of theft, now preferred against him, having been read over and explained to him, and he having been judicially admonished and examined, declares and says— I am not guilty of the charge preferred against me of stealing a number of bills, amounting to twenty-three thousand six hundred and three pounds twelve shillings and sevenpence, or thereby.

I was not aware that the City Bank was in the habit of receiving bills for collection, and endorsing and handing them over to the London Joint-Stock Bank before they had become due.

These bills received for collection were not the property of the Bank, and therefore the Bank was not entitled to retain them, or have them discounted on their own account.

As a Director, I could not know that any such practice was followed in the Bank. We had such full confidence in the Manager that we never thought he would do such a thing. We only discovered after the stoppage that such things had been done, and we were recommended, to the best of my belief, by our law agent not to interfere.

If any such practice as that above referred to existed, and known to the Directors to exist, it would never have been sanctioned by the Directors, but would have been repudiated with indignation. All which I declare to be truth. Two words deleted.

First Declaration of Robert Salmond.

At Glasgow, the twenty-second day of October, eighteen hundred and seventy-eight years, in presence of Francis William Clark, Esquire, advocate, Sheriff of Lanarkshire.

Compeared a prisoner, and the charge against him having been read over and explained to him, and he having been judicially admonished and examined, declares and says—My name is Robert Salmond. I am a native of Inveraray, seventy-four years of age, and I reside at Rankinston, Ayrshire. I am Director of several concerns in England.

I declare that I am not guilty of the charge of falsehood, fraud, and wilful imposition preferred against me, of having falsified the books of the City of Glasgow Bank, and prepared and issued false and fabricated balance sheets during the years from 1873 to 1878 inclusive, while the Bank was in a state of insolvency, and well known to me to be so, so as to conceal the true state of the affairs of the Bank from the shareholders and creditors, and of declaring false dividends in order to deceive said shareholders, creditors, and the public.

444

Appendix III.

To the best of my recollection I was appointed Director of the Bank about 1861 or 1862.

Interrogated—Did you consider the Bank in a solvent condition when the last balance sheet was issued? Declares—Certainly I did so, to the best of my knowledge and belief. I signed it after the meeting was over, and the dividend declared twelve or fourteen days after. I had been absent from Glasgow and the Bank while the balance sheet was being prepared. Before signing the balance sheet I did not examine the accounts of the Bank to ascertain if they were correct. I signed in the full belief of the accuracy of the statements made in the balance sheets. Ever since my appointment as Director I have pursued the same course. My attendance at the examination of the books was more a matter of form than anything else. The only thing I examined specially was the branch accounts or returns, and that, I think, only on two occasions. The Manager was perfectly aware that I did not examine the books or accounts; and the other Directors acted as I did myself, confiding in our innocence and honour, and in the statements of the Manager. I think it was through my recommendation that Mr. Innes Wright became a Director. I am not aware that I ever asked any one to take shares.

I think the shareholders might have regarded my name as a guarantee for the Bank, and for its being properly conducted.

Being shown a book titled on the back " City of Glasgow Bank Cash Book, Private, No. 6," and my attention drawn to two entries, dated respectively " June 4, 1873," under the heads "Foreign and Colonial Credits, No. 2," and " Bills Payable, No. 2 "—I declare I knew nothing about these entries, and never saw them until they were in the hands of the investigators some days ago when they showed them to me.

During the years 1873, 1874, and 1875 I subscribed the balance ledger before the balance sheets were issued to the shareholders. The accounts therein appearing were all summed up by the Directors, and found to be arithmetically correct; but beyond that we made no inquiry. I now see my name at the annual balances in the current balance ledger, commencing " June 4, 1873." Shown a document titled on the back " City of Glasgow Bank Abstract of Accounts, 5th June, 1878, A.," I never saw that until I saw it in the hands of Mr. M'Grigor.

It is quite useless to ask me any questions relative to the books of the Bank, as I know nothing about them.

My present indebtedness to the Bank will range between £130,000 and £140,000, but this is entirely covered by my securities, to the extent of about £200,000, which are first-class.

I did not advise, nor was I ever consulted, in relation to the advances by the Bank to James Morton & Co., Smith, Fleming

445

The City of Glasgow Bank Trial.

& Co., James Nicol Fleming, and John Innes Wright & Co. I was not aware that such advances had been made till eighteen months ago. The names had often been before me, but I was not aware till that time that the advances had been made.

At the striking of the last balance sheet I knew that some advances had been made to these parties, but I had no doubt that ultimately they would prove quite good. There was some concealment regarding the advances to James Morton & Co., which, so far as I was concerned, was never cleared up till very recently.

Before the stoppage of the Bank I was never aware that its capital had been lost.

I was aware of the extent to which the Directors were buying their own stock, but I understood that this was done under the provisions of the contract of copartnery.

Meetings of the Directors were held once a week. I regularly attended them. At these meetings the advances made to the afore-mentioned parties were not specially stated. The statements were merely *pro forma* bills, discounts, deposits, and the like.

The first Manager of the Bank was Henry Paul. I succeeded him in 1842, and remained Manager till 1861 or 1862, when Alexander Stronach succeeded me.

I am not an annuitant of the Bank. I left the management without claiming anything.

I first came to know that the Bank was not in an easy position some three or four years ago, but I thought nothing of it, believing it would all come right in a short time. The real cause of the unsatisfactory state of the Bank was the absorption of the capital by the foresaid advances; and though I did not know the amount of the advances, I was satisfied that the accounts must have been in a very unsatisfactory state to require such absorption. I suspected or inferred that there was something wrong with these advances, without knowing what it was.

Declares farther—As regards what took place at the weekly meetings, I explain that the advances made to the parties before-mentioned came up in the ordinary way, but were not specially stated. They came up just in the ordinary general way, the same as advances to other customers.

The book, entries, and document before referred to are now docqueted and subscribed as relative hereto. All which I declare to be truth. Two words deleted.

SECOND DECLARATION OF ROBERT SALMOND.

At Glasgow, the twenty-ninth day of October, eighteen hundred and seventy-eight years, in presence of Francis William Clark, Esquire, advocate, Sheriff of Lanarkshire.

Appendix III.

Compeared Robert Salmond, presently prisoner in the prison of Glasgow, and a charge of theft now preferred against him having been read over and explained to him, and he having been judicially admonished and examined, declares and says—I am not guilty of the charge preferred against me of stealing a number of bills, amounting in the aggregate to the sum of twenty-three thousand six hundred and ninety-three pounds twelve shillings and sevenpence, or thereby.

I explain that I never even heard of the existence of such bills until the stoppage of the Bank, and even then I only heard of them from the fact that inquiries were made regarding them.

Interrogated—Were you aware that it was the practice of the City of Glasgow Bank to receive bills of exchange from customers of the Bank for the special and sole purpose of collecting payment of the same, and thereafter endorsing and making over said bills before they had become due, in order that the proceeds thereof might be credited to the City of Glasgow Bank? Declares—I knew that this was the practice of all the banks in Scotland, but I was not aware that there was any speciality in the practice of the City Bank in this respect. I cannot say whether any discrimination was made by the City Bank between bills for collection and bills for discount sent up to London. I consider that the City Bank was quite entitled to follow this practice in relation to bills received by them for collection. There was no other way by which said bills could be collected in London.

Interrogated—What, then, is the position of the creditors in these bills, now that the Bank is stopped? Declares—That is a very awkward question, insomuch that I consider the liquidators bound to pay back the money so received. I think that such moneys never were the property of the Bank. All which I declare to be truth.

First Declaration of William Taylor.

At Glasgow, the twenty-second day of October, eighteen hundred and seventy-eight years, in presence of Francis William Clark, Esquire, advocate, Sheriff of Lanarkshire.

Compeared a prisoner, and the charge against him having been read over and explained to him, and he having been judicially admonished and examined, declares and says—My name is William Taylor. I am a native of Glasgow, sixty-six years of age; and I reside at Langbank, Newton-Mearns.

I am a merchant in Glasgow.

I am not guilty of the charge of falsehood, fraud, and wilful imposition preferred against me, of having falsified the books of the City of Glasgow Bank, and prepared and issued

447

The City of Glasgow Bank Trial.

false and fabricated balance sheets during the years from 1873 to 1878 inclusive, while the Bank was in a state of insolvency, and well known to me to be so, so as to conceal the true state of the affairs of the Bank from the shareholders and creditors, and of declaring false dividends in order to deceive said shareholders, creditors, and the public.

I believed the City of Glasgow Bank to be solvent when the last balance sheet was issued, and since I became a Director I believed all the balance sheets to be correct that were issued. I always believed the statements put before us by the Bank officials to be correct. I never heard anything to the contrary.

I don't exactly know who constituted the officials, except that they included Mr. Leresche, Mr. Turnbull, and Mr. Murdoch. Mr. Aikman, the accountant, and Mr. Morris were probably conversant with the details. I have been a Director since 1872, I think.

I don't think we ever compared the balance sheets with the Bank books, so as to test their accuracy. We just took the statements of the officials on trust.

No books were ever submitted to us along with the balance sheets. We subscribed the latter on the faith of the representations made to us by the officials.

I don't think I ever examined any of the Bank books with the view of testing the accuracy of the balance sheets. I did not think it my duty as a Director to do so. Such an examination would have involved the work of an accountant. My duty as a Director, I thought, consisted in attending the weekly meetings and dealing with the questions submitted for our consideration.

I would add that shortly after my appointment as Director Mr. Stewart and I were detailed to take charge of the branches, and to visit them occasionally, and this we did. At each weekly meeting a book was brought up showing a statement of all the branch accounts, with the deposits and advances in detail. We examined these items, and if in any case a branch seemed to exceed their limit of advances we took a note of it, and their attention was called to it. At the time when we were detailed for this duty, which was in 1872, Mr. Salmond and Mr. Potter were appointed to take charge of the head office accounts.

Sometimes they made reports to the officials, which were brought up as part of the weekly business, and sometimes they drew the attention of the meeting to anything special in relation to the accounts.

My firm was indebted to the Bank at the time of the stoppage about £70,000. That represented advances made by the Bank at different times to our firm. We did not make application to the Directors for those advances. I understood they were arranged with the Manager, Mr. Stronach, and he would after-

Appendix III.

wards report them to the Directors individually, but not at a meeting of the Board.

The Bank never held any securities against those advances. Mr. Stronach knew personally that I and my firm held property in Hope Street, in relation to which we laid out part of the advances; but there was no mortgage or other security created over such property in favour of the Bank. I also gave Mr. Stronach some scrip of the South-Western Railway to the value of £2500.

Interrogated—Were you ever aware that the Bank had made heavy advances to the firms of James Morton & Co., Smith, Fleming & Co., James Nicol Fleming, and Potter, Wilson & Co.? Declares—No. On Mr. Stronach's appointment as Manager, he called the attention of the Directors to certain advances or accounts which had been gone into in his brother's time, which he said were covered by securities, but for which he did not wish to be held responsible.

These had been gone into before my time, and that was the first notice I got of them.

I think the minutes of the Directors will show what was done with those accounts when brought under the notice of the Board by Mr. Stronach.

With the exception of certain advances made to Smith, Fleming & Co. since 1876, and which in the aggregate might amount to £75,000, and against which there were special securities, I am not aware of any advances made to the above-mentioned firms since that time.

Interrogated—Can you explain how one of these firms comes to be indebted to the Bank in a sum amounting to nearly £2,000,000, and another in a sum of over £2,000,000? Declares —I am unable to explain that. The Directors never in my time authorised such advances. There were never any applications to the Board for advances such as those; and if they were got I am unable to explain how.

I was not aware of the Bank being in difficulties until, at the farthest, ten days before its stoppage. I first heard of it at a meeting of Directors called to consider a statement by Mr. Morton that the Bank's acceptances could not be discounted in London.

It was then stated that some £500,000 would tide over the difficulty.

I was quite certain that if that money could be got the Bank would go on, and I thought that but for that difficulty the Bank was in a most prosperous condition.

Until the very morning when the Bank stopped, I was not aware that a stoppage was contemplated. The very day before I directed some £700 or £800 to be deposited in the Bank. That sum belonged to my firm; and as we had an account with the Union Bank I should have deposited there if I had had any doubts of the City Bank. All the Directors were present at the meetings which took place in Glasgow before the stoppage of the Bank, with the exception of one, at which I think Mr. Inglis was not present.

From what passed at the meetings, it seemed to be the impression of the Board, as certainly it was my own, that if we had got assistance from the Edinburgh banks we should have been able to go on.

The Directors did not latterly give orders for the purchase of the Bank stock by the Bank itself. I was not aware of such a practice. I did not know who the brokers for the Bank were in such purchases till after the stoppage.

To the best of my recollection, I held stock in the Bank at its stoppage to about £2200.

I beg to explain that I have been a shareholder in the Bank since its commencement, and added to my stock in 1856.

I again took additional stock when the new stock was issued in 1874. At the same time my son and my brother, on my recommendation, took five shares each.

I have never sold a share since I was connected with the Bank.

I did not know of any gold being sent to London. All which I declare to be truth. Two words deleted.

Second Declaration of William Taylor.

At Glasgow, the twenty-ninth day of October, eighteen hundred and seventy-eight years, in presence of Francis William Clark, Esquire, advocate, Sheriff of Lanarkshire.

Compeared William Taylor, presently prisoner in the prison of Glasgow, and the declaration emitted by him before the said Sheriff, of date the twenty-second day of October, having been read over to him, and he having been again judicially admonished and examined, declares and says—I am now brought before the Sheriff at my own request, and wish to explain that when I formerly stated that I had not examined any of the books of the Bank, I should have added, what I now recollect, that I had looked over the balance ledger, but not critically, and that I took the statements in it as being substantially correct, coming as they did from the officials.

The aforesaid declaration is docqueted and subscribed as relative hereto. All which I declare to be truth.

Third Declaration of William Taylor.

At Glasgow, the twenty-ninth day of October, eighteen hundred and seventy-eight years, in presence of Francis William Clark, Esquire, advocate, Sheriff of Lanarkshire.

Compeared William Taylor, presently prisoner in the prison

Appendix III.

of Glasgow, and a charge of theft now preferred against him
having been read over and explained to him, and he having been
judicially admonished and examined, declares and says—I am not
guilty of the charge preferred against me of stealing a number
of bills amounting to twenty-three thousand six hundred and
ninety-three pounds twelve shillings and sevenpence or thereby.
I was not aware that such bills had been sent to London.   If
such bills were sent to London, it was without the authority of
the Board entirely.   Bills left for the purpose of collection were
not the property of the Bank, and the Bank had no right to
dispose of them in that manner.   I know that the London Joint-
Stock Bank were agents in London for the City of Glasgow Bank,
but beyond this I did not know of the details of the transactions
between them.   All which I declare to be truth.

First Declaration of Henry Inglis.

At Glasgow, the twenty-second day of October, eighteen
hundred and seventy-eight years, in presence of Francis William
Clark, Esquire, advocate, Sheriff of Lanarkshire.

Compeared a prisoner, and the charge against him having been
read over and explained to him, and he having been judicially
admonished and examined, declares and says—My name is Henry
Inglis.   I am a native of Edinburgh, seventy-two years of age,
and I reside at No. 1 Great Stuart Street, Edinburgh.   I am a
Writer to the Signet.

I declare that I am not guilty of the charge of falsehood, fraud,
and wilful imposition preferred against me, of having falsified
the books of the Bank, and prepared and issued false and fabricated balance sheets during the years from 1873 to 1878 inclusive, while the Bank was in a state of insolvency, and well
known to me to be so, so as to conceal the true state of the
affairs of the Bank from the shareholders and creditors, and of
declaring false dividends, in order to deceive said shareholders,
creditors, and the public.   Further, I beg to say that about nine
years ago or thereby I was requested to become a Director of the
City of Glasgow Bank.   I accepted the office, and upon taking
my seat at the Board I found that my co-Directors appeared to
me to be a body of Glasgow gentlemen irreproachable in character and in position.   I also found that the Manager of the Bank
at that period was an officer who possessed their entire confidence,
and that confidence gradually extended itself to myself without
any restriction whatsoever.   I have only to add that my crime,
if crime it be, was the possession of the most entire confidence in
every statement and in every figure which was laid before me.
Not having the minute book of the Directors before me at
present, I do not feel myself justified in saying more, and I do
not at present wish to answer any questions with reference to
the charge.   All which I declare to be truth.

451

The City of Glasgow Bank Trial.

At Glasgow, the twenty-ninth day of October, eighteen hundred and seventy-eight years, in presence of Francis William Clark, Esquire, advocate, Sheriff of Lanarkshire.

Compeared Henry Inglis, presently prisoner in the prison of Glasgow, and the declaration emitted by him before the Sheriff, of date the twenty-second day of October current, having been read over to him, and he being again judicially admonished and examined, declares and says—I am now brought before the Sheriff at my own request, as I wish to state that during one of the years embraced in the charge I was absent for many months from the Board of the Bank. The particular year I cannot specify at present, but it can be easily ascertained from the minute book of the Directors.

During that year or period I was absent in Portugal, where I was attacked by a disease called gangrenes erysipelas, and operated upon severely and dangerously by Dr. Barboza, of Lisbon. On returning home I was confined to the house. Thereafter I was further attacked by severe neuralgia in the face, and thereafter by congestion of the brain and congestion of the left lung. These circumstances will account for my absence from the Glasgow Board, and I think it right to state them. All which I declare to be truth.

The foresaid declaration is now docqueted and subscribed as relative hereto.

At Glasgow, the twenty-ninth day of October, eighteen hundred and seventy-eight years, in presence of Francis William Clark, Esquire, advocate, Sheriff of Lanarkshire.

Compeared Henry Inglis, presently prisoner in the prison of Glasgow, and a charge of theft now preferred against him having been read over and explained to him, and he having been judicially admonished and examined, declares and says—

I am not guilty of the charge preferred against me of stealing a number of bills, amounting to twenty-three thousand six hundred and ninety-three pounds twelve shillings and sevenpence or thereby, and I take the liberty of saying that I consider the charge so absurd that I am constrained to believe that it has been made for some purpose which the prosecutor deems necessary, but which is not known to me.

I was not aware of any practice in the Bank of sending bills got for collection before they became due to London, and I was only made aware of the circumstance alluded to by being told of it after the stoppage by one of the investigators, Mr. M'Grigor.

I do not know whether it is proper to send such bills to

Appendix III.

London before they become due. That and all other banking details were matters for the Manager to consider, and they never came before the Board of Directors. All which I declare to be truth. Three words deleted.

First Declaration of John Innes Wright.

At Glasgow, the twenty-second day of October, eighteen hundred and seventy-eight years, in presence of Francis William Clark, Esquire, advocate, Sheriff of Lanarkshire.

Compeared a prisoner, and the charge against him having been read over and explained to him, and he having been judicially admonished and examined, declares and says—My name is John Innes Wright. I am a native of Glasgow, sixty-eight years of age, and I reside at 10 Queen's Terrace, Glasgow. I am a merchant.

I declare that I am not guilty of the charge of falsehood, fraud, and wilful imposition preferred against me, of having falsified the books of the City of Glasgow Bank, and prepared and issued false and fabricated balance sheets during the years from 1875 to 1878 inclusive, while the Bank was in a state of insolvency, and well known to me to be so, so as to conceal the true state of the affairs of the Bank from the shareholders and creditors, and of declaring false dividends in order to deceive said shareholders, creditors, and the public.

When the last balance sheet was issued to the shareholders, I believed the Bank to be in a solvent condition. I signed that balance sheet and all balance sheets since 1876. I became a Director in 1875.

It is the duty of the Directors to make such an examination of the Bank books as to ascertain that the balance sheet is correct. With relation to all the balance sheets which I signed as a Director, I examined all the books that were laid before me. There was, I think, a special meeting always held in relation to the balance sheet. So far as my experience goes, that was the practice of the Bank. I think it was the accountant of the Bank that laid the books before us. The cashier may also have brought some.

I suppose it was the Manager, and not the Directors, who desired these books to be laid before us. I understand that the Manager would tell the accountant what were the proper books to lay before us. I cannot at present recollect what the books were, a Bank has so many kind of books. I have no recollection of seeing discount ledgers and abstracts thereof on such occasions.

I never saw the credit ledgers containing a record of the cash credits granted by the Bank.

I understood the cash credits were secured, but I did not ascertain that from the books.

The City of Glasgow Bank Trial.

When cash credits came before us, it was generally stated what were the relative securities. We learned this from the applications which were read by the secretary. I never took any means to ascertain whether the securities possessed the values put upon them. I was new to the direction, and leant very much on the older members.

The only ledger we saw, so far as I recollect, was the balance ledger. I never saw the register of securities held by the Bank, nor the circulation register, to the best of my recollection.

I do not recollect of having seen a document entitled " Abstract of Accounts."

The balance sheets were correct according to the books laid before me. Beyond that I did not think it requisite to inquire. I trusted very much to the good faith of the Manager and the Bank officials.

I did not become aware of the Bank capital having been lost till the investigators' report was drawn out. I may say that I did not know the true state of affairs till it was issued. I never suspected until then the loss of the capital.

I was not aware that the Bank was to be stopped until I read the stoppage in the morning newspapers. I believed or thought up till that time that the Scottish banks would come forward and enable the City Bank to go on.

I don't know who decided on the stoppage. It was done in Edinburgh. I was not there, and was not consulted. I was a party to the communings of the Directors which immediately preceded the stoppage. It was first intended to apply to the London Joint-Stock Bank for aid. If we did not get aid, it was quite believed that we should have to stop.

The principal or only thing that would render a stoppage necessary was, so far as I know, the difficulty of discounting the Bank's acceptances in London. I am unable to say what was the amount of those acceptances. At one of the meetings before the stoppage it was supposed that £500,000 would tide us over the difficulties. It might be a year or more before the stoppage when I became aware that the Bank's paper was not so readily taken as that of other banks.

When I became a Director in June, 1875, my firm was indebted to the Bank somewhere about £400,000. My firm was John Innes Wright & Co., and William Scott was the partner who took charge of the finance. To the best of my belief, our indebtedness to the Bank at the time of the stoppage was not more than £403,000. That indebtedness was the result of advances by the Bank to our firm. The Bank had certain securities against those advances; for example, shares in companies. I did not consider the Bank wholly secured. The stocks of all kinds for some years past had very much depreciated. I don't think the Bank was ever entirely secured for the advances made

454

Appendix III.

to us, but I cannot say to what extent they were unsecured, even approximately.

During the term of my Directorship those advances were not brought under the notice of the weekly meetings until latterly, perhaps within six or nine months of the stoppage.

Before that they might have been talked of occasionally.

I can't say whether the advances to my firm were made without the authority of the Directors. They might have been consulted privately without my knowledge; and, in point of fact, these advances were substantially made before I became a Director.

I understood that the Bank had granted open and marginal credits to Smith, Fleming & Co. and Potter, Wilson & Co., or their agents in Australia. These credits were to a certain extent brought under the notice of the Directors. I did not know the full extent of those credits. They may have exceeded what came before us. If there was any excess, it must have been granted by the Bank officials unknown to me. All those open and marginal credits ought to have proceeded on application to the Board of Directors, and, of course, the Directors would know the amounts contained in these applications.

I had no idea, at the time of the stoppage, of the extent of indebtedness of these firms as now brought out in the report by the investigators. Certain securities were held against these credits. We, the Directors, as far as we could, endeavoured to ascertain the value of these securities. We went very much on the statements of the parties themselves. Of course, we had a general idea of their value ourselves. £1200 is, as I understand, the qualification for a Director. I only held £1200 Bank stock in my own name, but I held about £2600 in trust. I never held more than £1200 stock in my own name.

Being shown a book, titled on the back "City of Glasgow Bank Cash Book, Private, No. 6," and my attention drawn to two entries, dated respectively "June 4, 1873," under the heads "Foreign and Colonial Credits, No. 2," and "Bills payable, No. 2,"

I have never seen these entries until now, and I am unable to explain their meaning.

I was not aware that these sums of £973,300 were regularly annually repeated since the year 1873, until I was told so by Mr. M'Grigor.

Shown an entry dated June 4, 1873, "By cash per cash book, £973,300," at page 87 of the volume titled on the back "City of Glasgow Bank Ledger General Accounts, 1872-3."

That entry is quite beyond my comprehension.

I make the same remarks as touching the entry June 4th, 1873, "To cash p. cash book, £973,300," at page 95 of the said last-mentioned volume. I have no recollection of ever having seen

The City of Glasgow Bank Trial.

the books at the Bank containing an abstract of the weekly balances.

The foresaid entries and volume referred to are now docqueted and subscribed as relative hereto. All which I declare to be truth. Eight words deleted.

SECOND DECLARATION OF JOHN INNES WRIGHT.

At Glasgow, the twenty-ninth day of October, eighteen hundred and seventy-eight years, in presence of Francis William Clark, Esquire, advocate, Sheriff of Lanarkshire.

Compeared John Innes Wright, presently prisoner in the prison of Glasgow, and the declaration emitted by him before the Sheriff, of date the twenty-second day of October current, having been read over to him, and he being again judicially admonished and examined, declares and says—I am now brought before the Sheriff at my own request, as I wish to state distinctly that when I became a Director in 1875 I owed the Bank nothing as an individual. I succeeded James Nicol Fleming as a Director.

Prior to my becoming a Director, my firm, John Innes Wright & Co., had had business relations with Smith, Fleming & Co., London, and Nicol, Fleming & Co., Calcutta, but to a considerable extent our relation with Smith, Fleming & Co. and their foreign correspondents had been broken off.

I had not the necessary qualification of stock when I was elected a Director. I stated this to the Manager, but I obtained the qualification a few days afterwards. I also urged the condition of my firm's account as a reason against my having any connection with the Board.

Mr. Stronach was apparently anxious that I should be a Director, and Mr. Salmond also urged me to consent.

The request to be a Director came to me quite unexpectedly, and I am not aware what reason induced them to make the request. The stock necessary for my qualification was acquired for me by the Bank. No cash passed, but I gave a cheque for the amount, and that cheque stands against my account with the Bank to the present day.

I am not aware of a similar course being followed in the case of any other Director.

The foresaid declaration is docqueted and subscribed as relative hereto. All which I declare to be truth.

THIRD DECLARATION OF JOHN INNES WRIGHT.

At Glasgow, the twenty-ninth day of October, eighteen hundred and seventy-eight years, in presence of Francis William Clark, Esquire, advocate, Sheriff of Lanarkshire.

Appendix III.

Compeared John Innes Wright, presently prisoner in the prison of Glasgow, and a charge of theft now preferred against him having been read over and explained to him, and he having been judicially admonished and examined, declares and says—

I am not guilty of the charge made against me of stealing a number of bills, amounting to twenty-three thousand six hundred and ninety-three pounds twelve shillings and seven-pence sterling, or thereby.

Bills sent in for collection, as these apparently were, never came before the Directors at all. They were received by the officials and forwarded in the usual way, as we understood, but they did not come under the cognisance of the Directors.

I was not aware, until after the stoppage of the Bank, of any bills sent in for collection having been forwarded in this irregular way. The matter came before us after the stoppage; and Mr. Stronach then informed the Board that these bills, along with various others sent in the usual way of business, had been forwarded to London without his being aware that a portion of the bills were for collection merely.

I am not aware that bills sent in for collection merely have a different marking from other bills. All which I declare to be truth.

First Declaration of Robert Summers Stronach.

At Glasgow, the twenty-second day of October, eighteen hundred and seventy-eight years, in presence of Francis William Clark, Esquire, advocate, Sheriff of Lanarkshire.

Compeared a prisoner, and the charge against him having been read over and explained to him, and he having been judicially admonished and examined, declares and says—

My name is Robert Summers Stronach. I am a native of Lonmay, Aberdeenshire, fifty-two years of age; and I reside at 13 Crown Gardens, Dowanhill, Glasgow. I am a banker in Glasgow.

I am not guilty of the charge preferred against me of false-hood, fraud, and wilful imposition, in having falsified the books of the City of Glasgow Bank, and prepared and issued false and fabricated balance sheets during the years from 1875 to 1878 inclusive, while the Bank was in a state of insolvency, and when I was well aware of that fact, so as to conceal the true state of the affairs of the said Bank from the shareholders and creditors, and in declaring false dividends in order to deceive said shareholders, creditors, and the public. I declare further that, from the state of my health, and my mind being worn out by the anxieties of the last twelve months, I do not at present feel myself in a position to make explanations or answer questions relative to the charges made against me.

457

The City of Glasgow Bank Trial.

Further, I desire to add that Mr. Leresche, Secretary to the Bank, has nothing to do with the balance sheets, but that he simply appears at the annual meetings and reads the minutes, which is simply a matter of form. All which I declare to be truth. One word deleted.

SECOND DECLARATION OF ROBERT SUMMERS STRONACH.

At Glasgow, the twenty-ninth day of October, eighteen hundred and seventy-eight years, in presence of Francis William Clark, Esquire, advocate, Sheriff of Lanarkshire.

Compeared Robert Summers Stronach, presently prisoner in the prison of Glasgow, and a charge of theft now preferred against him having been read over and explained to him, and he having been judicially admonished and examined, declares and says—I decline to make any statements or answer any questions with reference to the charge made against me of stealing a number of bills, amounting to twenty-three thousand six hundred and ninety-three pounds twelve shillings or thereby.

I am satisfied that I shall be able to clear myself of the same at the proper time. All which I declare to be truth. One word deleted.

APPENDIX IV.

REPORT by Messrs. KERR, ANDERSONS, MUIR & MAIN, Chartered
Accountants, Glasgow, and Messrs. M'GRIGOR, DONALD &
Co., Solicitors, Glasgow, in reference to BALANCE SHEET of
the CITY OF GLASGOW BANK, as at 1st October, 1878.

ON the 2nd instant we were instructed by the Directors of the
City of Glasgow Bank to prepare a balance sheet of the Bank,
as at 1st October, 1878, to be submitted to the shareholders
on the earliest possible day.

For reasons that will sufficiently appear in the course of this
report, we have felt it necessary to prefix to this balance sheet
a statement explanatory of the system adopted by us in preparing it, and of the leading points in which it contrasts with
the balance sheet issued by the Board of Directors as of 5th
June last.

On receipt of the instructions referred to, we at once proceeded to make an investigation of the books at the head office
of the Bank, and gave directions for the necessary statements
and returns being procured from the branches. For the first
few days it was extremely difficult to make any real progress.
The immediate result of the stoppage of the Bank was, as might
be expected, a temporary disorganisation of the working staff,
and, besides, the incessant demands made upon us to reply to
inquiries, and to advise as to questions calling for immediate
decision, greatly interfered with the steady prosecution of the
investigation.

By the afternoon of the 4th instant, however, we became
satisfied, from what we had even then learned of the position
of the Bank, that there was no reasonable probability of its
being able to resume business, and, with the view of protecting
the interests of the shareholders, we reported to the Directors
that it was not advisable to delay any longer calling them
together. It seemed to us to be of less importance that an
exhaustive examination of the books should take place (a matter
which would have involved weeks, if not months of delay),
than that a vidimus, however rough, showing, even approximately, the real state of matters should be laid before the
shareholders, in order that they should have the power of at
once deciding on the course to be followed, and, if they should

459

The City of Glasgow Bank Trial.

see fit, of appointing competent parties with the requisite authority to preserve and administer what remained of the Bank's property and assets. In the ordinary case, the resolutions passed at such a meeting of shareholders would have required confirmation, involving altogether a delay of four weeks, but by taking advantage, as has been done (under the advice of counsel), of the 3rd sub-section of the 129th section of the Companies Act, 1862, a fortnight will have been saved in the event of liquidation being resolved on.

The time at our disposal has thus been proportionately abridged, and we have not aimed at producing anything like an exhaustive examination of particular details, which, under the circumstances, would have proved utterly futile. We have, at the same time, been careful to indicate below the various elements of uncertainty which appear to us to attach to individual items on each side of the balance sheet. In framing this balance sheet and report, no avoidable delay has been incurred, and the work has been proceeded with as rapidly as was consistent with the circumstances, which demanded the fullest investigation possible, independent altogether of data voluntarily submitted to us.

The books which more immediately came under our cognisance, as containing a record of the transactions of the Bank, were as follows :—

1. Discount ledgers and abstracts thereof, showing, in detail, all the current bills discounted at the head office, with the exception of those having not more than seven days to run.

2. Deposit ledgers and interest registers, containing the accounts of all depositors who are creditors of the Bank on current or deposit accounts, or debtors to the Bank on cash overdrafts.

3. Credit ledgers, containing a record of the cash credits granted by the Bank, whether secured, partially secured, or wholly unsecured.

4. Returns from the various branches, 133 in number, containing, as regards these branches, the same information as the foregoing books supply with regard to the head office.

5. General ledgers and abstracts thereof, showing the results of the business of the Bank upon discounts, interests, and commission. These ledgers also contain an account raised out of profit and loss account to the amount of £450,000 as a reserve fund against losses, and a contingent account having at the credit a sum of £18,036 11s. 9d., and consisting of the accumulation of certain other sums set aside from time to time out of the profit and loss account.

6. Balance books, which contain a complete statement of the balances in the general ledgers, and which were annually docqueted by the Directors, or a majority of their number.

Appendix IV.

7. Abstract of accounts made up annually, in which the yearly result of the transactions recorded in the Bank books are brought into a focus, and from which the printed balance sheet issued to the shareholders is epitomised.

8. Registers of securities held by the Bank, of which one was kept by the law secretary, and another, containing a record of securities held against advances on certain special accounts, by the private clerk of the Manager.

9. Cashier's ledger, containing a record of notes issued, or in reserve, and of coin in possession of the Bank.

10. Circulation ledger, containing a daily record of the Bank's circulation, the coin on hand at the head office and branches, and of the monthly average, and from which the weekly returns forwarded to Government were made up.

Besides the above, we have incidentally examined, as occasion seemed to require, many of the other books necessary for the carrying on of the business of the Bank, such as tellers' cash books and jotting books, and monthly and weekly abstracts of individual accounts made up by the private clerk of the Manager, besides drafts of the more recent abstracts of accounts (No. 7 above referred to), and memoranda and jottings by the late Manager of the Bank.

We have likewise availed ourselves of all the information we could procure from the sub-officials of the Bank, which has been readily, and we believe frankly and fully, accorded to us.

At an early stage in our inquiry, it became apparent that questions seriously affecting the course of management by the Directors and Manager of the Bank were involved in the investigation, and we have felt it our duty, while soliciting from these gentlemen explanations as to certain particular items, to bring under their notice the serious nature of the questions referred to. In most instances we were told that the explanations we invited related to points which were as new and as startling to the parties interrogated as to ourselves.

We shall now proceed to refer to certain items in our detailed statement of liabilities and assets which seem to call for special explanation or remark.

I.—LIABILITIES.

(D.) Acceptances by the Bank past due or current.

In the general ledger of the Bank there is an account under the heading of "Bills payable," which, on 4th June, 1873, showed a balance at the debit of the Bank of £2,128,686 11s. 9d. In the cash book under the same date is the following entry, creating and forming the single entry in a new account entitled "Bills payable account, No. 2":—

"Bills payable account, No. 2. To the following accounts

461

The City of Glasgow Bank Trial.

under acceptance of this date to be retired by the Bank under special arrangement with the parties of date 1st June, 1873, against which certain securities are now held by the Bank and in process of realisation and payment of proceeds, £973,300."

There is likewise in the general ledger another account entitled "Foreign and colonial credits," which on 4th June showed a balance at the credit of the Bank of £2,132,452 2s. 3d. In the cash book under the same date the following entry was also made, creating and forming the single entry in a new account entitled "Foreign and colonial credits, No. 2":—

"Foreign and colonial credits, No. 2. For the following credits to be retired as they mature and debited under the respective accounts to credit accounts, No. 2, against which securities are now held by the Bank and in process of realisation and payment of the proceeds, £973,300."

No details were specified under either of these headings, and the slump sums were carried to the general ledger, and there simply entered as "to cash per cash book," and "by cash per cash book," respectively.

In the weekly balance book this £973,300 is entered and deducted from the "bills payable" account, and from the "foreign and colonial credits" account, the balances being carried to the balance book annually docqueted by the Directors.

Since 1873 this system has been regularly adhered to, the sum of £973,300 having been annually deducted from each of these accounts.

In the printed balance sheet issued by the Board for this year, the sums at the credit and debit of these accounts respectively are included, the one under the head of "Bills outstanding due or with a currency not exceeding twenty-one days, and drafts accepted by the Bank and its London agents on account of home and foreign constituents," and the other under "Bills of exchange, local and country bills, credit accounts, and other advances upon security."

The consequence of this has been that the shareholders have been led to believe—

(a) That the Bank had lent on foreign and colonial credits less than was the fact, by the amount of - - - - - £973,000

(b) That the Bank had accepted fewer bills payable than was the fact, to the amount of - - - - - £973,000

(E.) Bills parted with.

Of the £149,435 9s. of bills entered under this head, we have reason to believe that £64,595 12s. 9d., although handed to the Bank for collection or retention, have been forwarded to London, and either discounted or placed to the credit of a "No. 2 account" with the London Joint-Stock Bank, which was held by that Bank as a security for any advances under which they might come to the City of Glasgow Bank.

Appendix IV.

II.—ASSETS.

(A.) Cash.

The amount of gold and silver in the hands of the cashier at the head office on the 1st inst., as entered in the cashier's ledger, which appears to have been correctly kept, was - - - - - £231,500 0 0

To this falls to be added the amount in the hands of the tellers at that date, ascertained from their cash books and jotting books, - - - - - - 12,156 6 0

And at the branches, ascertained from the register of notes and specie in hand at branches, - - - - 49,889 0 0

Making in all, - - - - £293,545 6 0

The coin at the branches is, however, only returned once a week, and the above item of £49,889 consequently represents what was actually in hand at the 28th September.

As the authorised circulation of the Bank was only - £72,921 0 0
The addition of this - - - - - - - 293,545 6 0

Would only have justified an issue of - - - £366,466 6 0
But the circulation of the previous Saturday, as vouched by the circulation ledger, was - - - - - 604,196 0 0

The explanation of the discrepancy is to be found in the circulation ledger itself, from which it appears that since the commencement of this year it had been the habit to add to the weekly return of bullion made to Government under 8 & 9 Vict. cap. 38, an imaginary sum, less or more, according to the emergencies of the period, beginning with £60,000 under the first week in January, and fluctuating weekly until, on the 21st September, when the last return was made, it reached £300,000. The additions thus made are openly and regularly entered in the circulation ledger in smaller figures over the amount of gold really in hand at Glasgow.

The summations of the entries in this ledger, vitiated by these additions, were weekly returned to Government, and the Bank have thus, under the 14th section of the Act, become subject to very heavy penalties, which, however, under the circumstances, we have not thought it right to bring into the balance sheet.

(B.) Balances on Current Accounts for Credits and Over-drafts considered good.

We have recovered the draft of the abstract of accounts for 1878. In it there is an entry taken from the general ledger, under the heading "Credit accounts, *Dr*. balance, £2,009,752 11s. 2d." In the revision of this draft it would appear that, to lessen the apparent amount of this account, the sum of

The City of Glasgow Bank Trial.

£926,724 was deducted from its total, and transferred from the first head of the abstract, under which it was grouped, to the third head, under the new headings, " Credit accounts, Nos. 1, 3, and 4, balance." A further reduction of £200,000 was made from the same account by transferring that amount to a new entry under head No. 3 in the abstract, entitled " reserve gold."

As all accounts grouped in the abstract under head No. 1 are in the printed balance sheet included under the heading " Bills of exchange, local and country bills, credit accounts, and other advances upon security," and all accounts under head No. 3, under the heading " Cash in hand," and entered under two divisions, viz., " Gold and silver coin, and notes of other banks at head office and branches," and " Government stocks, Exchequer bills, railway and other stocks and debentures, and balances in hands of banking correspondents," the practical result of this was that the shareholders have been led to believe—

(a) That the Bank had lent upon credits less than was the fact, by
the amount of - - - - - - - - £1,126,764

(b) That the Bank had in their hands good securities belonging to themselves absolutely, more than was the fact, by - - - - - - - - - 926,764

(c) That the Bank had in their cash chest more reserve gold than was the fact, by - - - - - 200,000

(C.) Bills on Hand.

After deduction of all bills believed to be bad, amounting to £307,416 15s. 7d., a deduction of £5 per cent. has been made from the balance of bills on hand at the head office, and of £2 per cent. from the balance of country bills sent to the head office, which it is believed will cover any reasonable risk of loss. No deduction has been made from exchange bills, or bills received for collection.

(E.) Business Premises of the Bank.

The premises belonging to the Bank in Virginia Street and Glassford Street (the latter in course of erection), the Gorbals branch office, and the offices at Greenock, Paisley, and Edinburgh, have been valued for us by Mr. Thomas Binnie at £98,340. It has, of course, been impossible to overtake a detailed valuation of all the branch premises belonging to the Bank throughout the country; but from an estimate prepared by him, founded on the original cost of these, the population of the towns in which they are situated, and the fact that a considerable number will fall to be taken over by other banks as places of banking business, we have felt justified in putting down their probable value at £100,775 4s. 9d.

Appendix IV.

HERITABLE PROPERTY IN GLASGOW.

The items under this heading have been taken from a record in the books of properties practically belonging to the Bank. To a large extent we have taken these at the valuations in the books, but in many instances where sales have been effected, or satisfactory information furnished to us, we have rectified these valuations. In this case the amount brought out by us exceeds the amount in the books by £10,407 11s. 9d.

HERITABLE PROPERTY IN THE COLONIES.

These properties, consisting of lands in New Zealand (North Island) and Australia, have been entered at the price which the Bank have paid for them within the last two years.

They comprise—

(1) 40,024 acres of freehold land in the province of Poverty Bay, purchased in October, 1877, on a Government title, at 12s. 6d. per acre, and 11,808 acres of leasehold land adjoining, with the stock thereon, the lease being for eighteen years, and the price £11,628. Since the purchase of the freehold, £3433 has been expended in the purchase of stock. Since the acquisition of the leasehold, the Bank agents were in course of acquiring from the natives the freehold right thereof, and have expended towards this a further sum of £1350. The balance is in the hands of the agents, or in materials purchased for the use of the station.

We consider that we are entitled to take this at least at the cost price, as we believe it would realise that now, and, besides, it has the prospect of materially increasing in value.

(2) The property in New South Wales and Queensland, the cost of which we are informed has been £368,000, including outlay on improvements and stocking. Of this there appears to have been paid by the acceptances of the Bank, which are still current, £130,000, the balance of £238,000 being met by the promissory notes of Mr. Walker, the agent, who alleges that the Bank are bound to relieve him of this amount, but as we have not as yet been able to verify this statement, and have consequently not put this item into the liabilities, we have estimated the value of this asset at the £130,000 above referred to.

(F.) FURNITURE.

A rough estimate of the value of the furniture at the head office has been made for us by Messrs. Hutchison & Dixon. The value of furniture at the branches has been based, as far as possible, on reports from the several branches.

7 A

The City of Glasgow Bank Trial.

(G.) SHARES AND DEBENTURES IN OTHER COMPANIES, APART FROM
SHARES IN THE NEW ZEALAND AND AUSTRALIAN LAND
COMPANY, LIMITED, HELD ABSOLUTELY BY THE BANK.

Under this item we have included all the various items we
have been able to discover which are embraced under the two
following headings in the abstract of accounts from which the
balance sheet of June last was framed :—

" Railway and other stocks and debentures, - £1,023,699 7 10 "
" General securities' stocks, - - - - 67,475 16 10 "

In all, - - - - - £1,091,175 4 8

The items are as follows :—In the beginning of the year the
Bank held $2,910,000, in 7 per cent. bonds of $1000 each of
the Western Union Railway of America, which, from information
received from New York, we value at 75 per cent., representing
£436,500. On the 18th May last, bonds representing $1,500,000
were sent by the Bank to the General Credit and Discount
Company, London, for the purpose of raising money thereon,
and on these £90,000 was raised, the balance being retained
" for further instructions."

We have accordingly valued this item as follows :—

$2,910,000 at 75 per cent., - - - -	£436,500	0 0
Less advance, - - - - - -	90,000	0 0
	£346,500	0 0

Besides these the Bank hold of the stock or shares
of the Western Union Railway, $1,992,340 =
£398,468 sterling at par, but which, from the
information we have received, is only worth - 11,950 0 0
They further hold in connection with the above
railway company (who have the option of
purchasing it under arbitration), the property
of the Racine Warehouse and Dock Company,
acquired at a cost of $300,000, but which we are
advised is now worth only $30,000, or - 6,000 0 0
They also hold 3273 shares of $100 each in the
Milwaukie and St. Paul Railway, which, at
31 per cent., the present selling price, represent
$101,463, or - - - - - - - 20,292 0 0
They hold, besides, the following shares, which
we have put down at the present market
value :—

180 shares Marbella Iron Ore Company, - -	495	0 0
150 shares Glasgow Jute Company, - -	0	0 0
£85,000 Grand Trunk Railway of Canada, ordinary, - - - - - - -	5,525	0 0
430 shares Erie Railway preferred capital, 7 per cent., - - - - - -	2,279	0 0
£10,000 Grand Trunk Railway of Canada, 3rd preference, - - - - - -	1,187	10 0
18 shares Upper Assam Tea Company, - -	1,840	0 0
In all, - - - - -	£396,068	10 0

466

Appendix IV.

(H.) Government Stocks.

These in the abstract balance sheet of June last are put down as—

Government Stocks, No. 1,	-	£1,857	6	6 and
Government Stocks, No. 2,	-	7,751	15	9

In all,	- - -	£9,609	2	3

The stocks answering to this description, so far as we are aware, held by the Bank, consist of East India Government 4 per cent. promissory notes, in two lots of 10,000 and 50,000 rupees respectively, which, at 1s. 9d., give - - - - - - - - - £5,250 0 0
And £2000 British 3 per cent. annuities, worth, say, - 1,857 6 6

In all,	- - - - - -	£7,107	6	6

Estimated Value of Securities held against Bad Debts.

The total amount represented by bad debts, which we, as at 1st October, have estimated at £7,345,357 15s. 6d., the Bank have been in the habit of treating in the balance sheets as an available asset.

Among the debtors included under this head are four, of which, owing to the magnitude of the amounts, we think it right to append separate notes.

	Liabilities.		Probable Value of Securities held.		Deficit.	
I.	£2,320,591 18 9	-	£688,184 19 11	-	£1,632,406 18 10	
II.	1,864,627 2 4	-	452,582 12 9	-	1,412,044 9 7	
III.	1,142,987 18 4	-	310,532 17 7	-	832,455 0 9	
IV.	464,186 19 5	-	71,135 6 9	-	393,051 12 8	

This deficit, however, is exclusive of any return that may be received from the estates of the debtors themselves, or from the estates of parties who have suspended payment, but against whom the Bank will have a ranking in regard to these debts.

It would appear that up to the time when the books of the Bank were put into our hands, no attempt had been made to value the securities held in reference to these four assets (any more than the other securities held by the Bank), which are entered in the security ledger at sums which appear to have been indicated by the debtors themselves. It was upon a statement of these accounts, in which, as we are informed, these securities were accepted at the latter figure, that the banks consulted before the stoppage resolved that it would not be expedient to assist the City Bank. Since then, the examination we have instituted into the real value of the securities, superficial as it has necessarily been, has shown that the estimate thus put upon them was enormously exaggerated, and it is by no means improbable that our own estimate is

The City of Glasgow Bank Trial.

beyond the mark, as the Bank's title to much of what we have entered as good is of a very imperfect description.

LIFE POLICIES.

The Bank held life policies against the debts which we have dealt with as bad for an amount in all of £611,051 13s. 5d. These have been entered at the surrender value, £74,014 14s. 11d. The annual premiums due upon them amount to £17,214 14s. 8d.

SHARES IN NEW ZEALAND AND AUSTRALIAN LAND COMPANY, LIMITED.

Under this item are included all the shares of the New Zealand and Australian Land Company, Limited, to which the Bank appear to have right. The position of the Bank in regard to a large number of these shares is not so satisfactory as might be desired, many of the transfers not being completed, but it is believed that their right to the whole can be vindicated. We have dealt with the Bank as holding £219,052 of A preference stock and £912,079 of ordinary stock. The preference stock being 4 per cent. stock, we have taken it at £80 —£175,242. As to the ordinary stock we have had some difficulty. It yields at present only 3 per cent., but its main value is prospective, and we do not believe that voluntary sellers would be disposed to part with it under par. If held for a period of years, it will in all probability realise a much higher figure; but, again, were so large a quantity forced on the market at once, it is difficult to say what, on an average, it might bring. On the whole, we have thought it reasonable to value the ordinary stock, for the purpose of the present statement, at £80, like the preference, which gives £729,662, or, in all, £904,904.

It is right to mention that, besides this sum, there are a number of shares in this company belonging to parties whose liabilities to the Bank are so heavy that nearly the whole proceeds will probably fall into the funds of the Bank. The amount of such shares we make out to be £9406 preference and £76,770 ordinary—in all, £86,176, which, at £80, gives a possible additional asset of £68,941.

HERITABLE PROPERTIES HELD IN SECURITY.

To the extent of £176,320 this item is composed of the value of properties at Rangoon, Kurrachee, etc., as to which we have acted upon the best information we have been able to receive. We cannot, however, declare that in any case the title of the Bank to these securities is at all satisfactory.

Appendix IV.

It is hardly necessary for us to say that, in making this item, we have not had it in our power to avail ourselves of the assistance of professional valuators.

The various items specially above referred to will go far to explain the difference between the results brought out by the balance sheet of June last and the estimate of assets and liabilities now submitted.

We must, however, in addition explain that two items are entered in the abstract of accounts from which the June balance sheet was prepared as assets, which we have been obliged to reject *in toto*. One of these in a sum of £280,000, entered as an asset under the head of suspense account, and which we have found it necessary to include in our estimate of bad debts; the other a sum of £96,294 3s. 6d., entered as an asset under the head of " Credit Account, No. 2," but which is made up of balances so hopelessly bad that, as we are informed, they were specially removed under this heading to prevent the possibility of interest being calculated on them from year to year.

We are fully conscious of the numerous defects in the present statement, and we cannot but anticipate that many errors and omissions may become apparent from day to day. The valuations conducted, as we have been forced to conduct them, in most cases without the aid of skilled valuators, and under the urgency of continued and increasing pressure, can hardly fail to be very incomplete; but we believe that those who are most conversant with the nature and details of such a duty as has been imposed upon us, will be most ready to make allowance for, and to excuse the imperfections of, the results.

As the form in which the statement of liabilities and assets has been prepared is different from that of the printed annual balance sheets, we have thought it right to append an abstract of the results at which we have arrived under the headings adopted in the latter, and, for the convenience of comparison, we have placed above it a copy of the balance sheet which was laid before the shareholders at their meeting on 3rd July last.

(Signed)   KERR, ANDERSONS, MUIR & MAIN,
Chartered Accountants.

M'GRIGOR, DONALD & CO.,
Solicitors.

GLASGOW, 18*th October*, 1878.

The City of Glasgow Bank Trial.

ABSTRACT BALANCE SHEET AS AT 5TH JUNE, 1878.

As issued by the Bank, and submitted to Annual Meeting, 3rd July, 1878.

LIABILITIES.

I. Deposits at the head office and branches, and balances at the credit of banking correspondents,		£8,102,001	0	4		
II. Bank notes in circulation in Scotland and the Isle of Man,		710,252	0	0		
III. Drafts outstanding, due, or with a currency not exceeding 21 days, and drafts accepted by the Bank and its London agents on account of home and foreign constituents,		1,488,244	18	6		
Liabilities to the public,					£10,300,497 18 10	
IV. Capital Account,	£1,000,000 0 0					
V. Reserve Fund,	450,000 0 0					
VI. Profit and Loss,	142,095 12 10					
Liabilities to partners,					1,592,095 12 0	
					£11,892,593 11 8	

ASSETS.

I. Bills of exchange, local and country bills, credit accounts, and other advances upon security,		£8,484,466 9 2		
II. Advances on heritable property, and value of Bank buildings and furniture at head office and branches,		265,324 9 0		
III. Cash on hand—viz., gold and silver coin and notes of other banks at head office and branches,	£845,963 1 0			
Government stocks, Exchequer bills, railway and other stocks and debentures, and balances in hands of banking correspondents,	2,296,839 12 6			
		3,142,802 13 6		
		£11,892,593 11 8		

ABSTRACT BALANCE SHEET AS AT 1ST OCTOBER, 1878.

Prepared in conformity with subjoined State of Liabilities and Assets.

LIABILITIES.

I. Deposits at the head office and branches, and balances at the credit of banking correspondents,		£8,798,788 13 4		
II. Bank notes in circulation in Scotland and the Isle of Man,		863,403 0 0		
III. Drafts outstanding, due, or with a currency not exceeding 21 days, and drafts accepted by the Bank and its London agents on account of home and foreign constituents,		2,742,105 14 11		
		£12,404,297 8 3		

ASSETS.

I. Bills of exchange, local and country bills, credit accounts, and other advances upon security,		£5,996,792 3 0		
II. Advances on heritable property, and value of Bank buildings and furniture at head office and branches,		211,074 10 8		
III. Cash on hand—viz., gold and silver coin and notes of other banks at head office and branches,	£418,363 16 4			
Government stocks, Exchequer bills, railway and other stocks and debentures, and balances in hands of banking correspondents,	587,083 7 0			
		1,005,447 3 4		
Balance, being Loss,		5,190,983 11 3		
		£12,404,297 8 3		

NOTE.—To the above balance of loss,	£5,190,983 11 3	
Falls to be added the capital,	1,000,000 0 0	
Making the total loss,	£6,190,98 11 3	

Appendix IV.

BALANCE SHEET, 1st OCTOBER, 1878.

LIABILITIES.

I. ORDINARY, viz. :—

(A) Bank Notes in the Hands of the Public, - - £863,403 0 0

*(B) Current Deposit Accounts, viz. :—
1. At Head Office, - - - £361,544 19 1
2. At Branches, - - - - 2,203,525 1 11

2,565,070 1 0

*(C) Interest Receipts, viz. :—
1. At Head Office, - - - £485,132 3 8
2. At Branches, - - - - 5,345,135 15 1

5,830,267 18 9

(D) Acceptances by the Bank—Current, - - - 2,742,105 14 11

(E) Bills Lodged with the Bank and Collected
or Parted with, viz. :—
1. At Head Office, - - - £143,630 8 9
2. At Branches, - - - - 5,805 0 3

149,435 9 0

(F) Balances due to other Banks and Banking
Correspondents—
1. At Head Office, - - - £157,906 11 10
2. At Branches, - - - - 2,492 0 0

160,398 11 10

(G) Dividends past due to Shareholders, - - - 4,519 4 0

(H) Due Stamp Office for Duties—
1. At Head Office, - - - £10 11 11
2. At Branches, - - - - 24 14 8

35 6 7   £12,315,235 6 1

II. CONTINGENT :—
(I) Customers' Bills Re-discounted by the Bank and expected to
become bad in the hands of the Discounters, - - - 89,062 2 2

£12,404,297 8 3

NOTE.—*Another contingent liability is the possible cost of Re-exchange of Foreign Bills.*
* In consequence of the limited time at disposal, interest has not been credited upon the deposit accounts and interest receipts for the period between 5th June and 1st October, 1878, neither has interest been debited to the overdrafts and credit accounts for the same period.

ASSETS.

I. ESTIMATED GOOD :—

(A) Cash—
(a) Gold—
1. At Head Office, - £236,840 10 0
2. At Branches, - 38,043 10 0

£274,884 0 0

(b) Silver and copper—
1. At Head Office, - £7,679 17 11
2. At Branches, - 39,189 6 5

46,869 4 4

(c) Notes and cheques of other banks—
1. At Head Office, - £18,496 0 0
2. At Branches, - 78,114 12 0

96,610 12 0   £418,363 16 4

(B) Balances on Current Accounts for Credits and Overdrafts considered good—
1. At Head Office, - - - - - £526,825 11 4
2. At Branches, - - - - - 1,253,009 3 11

1,779,834 15 3

(C) Bills on hand—considered good—
(a) Current—Discounted by the Bank, viz. :—
1. At Head Office, - £1,073,011 2 8
2. At Branches, - 984,666 16 0

£2,057,677 18 8

(b) Past due—Discounted by the Bank, viz. :—
1. At Head Office, - £91,863 9 9
2. At Branches, - 49,422 8 1

141,285 17 10

2,198,963 16 6

(D) Balances due by other Banks and Banking Correspondents—
1. At Head Office, - - - - - £176,932 16 10
2. At Branches, - - - - - 210 2 7

177,142 19 5

Carry forward, - - - - - £4,574,305 7 6

The City of Glasgow Bank Trial.

Brought forward,				£4,574,305 7 6

(E) Heritable Property—
   (a) Business premises of the Bank—

1. At Head Office,	-	£34,500 0 0		
2. At Branches,	- -	164,615 4 9		
			£199,115 4 9	

   (b) Other Property held by the Bank—

1. In Glasgow,	- -	£98,259 8 0		
2. In the Colonies,	-	176,500 0 0		
			274,759 8 0	
				473,874 12 9

(F) Furniture—

1. At Head Office,	- - - -	£526 1 0		
2. At Branches,	- - - -	11,433 4 11		
				11,959 5 11

(G) Shares and Debentures in other Companies—apart from Shares in the New Zealand and Australian Land Company, Limited —held absolutely by the Bank,   396,068 10 0

(H) Government Stocks, - - - - - - - -   7,107 6 6

(I) Miscellaneous Assets—

1. At Head Office,	- - - -	£5,495 11 3		
2. At Branches,	- - - -	1,268 19 10		
			6,764 11 1	
				£5,470,079 13 9

NOTE.—*Between the evening of the 1st and morning of the 2nd October there would be in transit to the pay offices letters of credit purchased by customers, and on the other hand exchange and other vouchers, consisting of, for example, the cheques of other Banks honoured on 1st October at Branches of the City Bank. The full extent of these operations will, it is estimated, result in a balance in favour of the City of Glasgow Bank of about £140,000.*

II. ESTIMATED VALUE OF SECURITIES HELD AGAINST BAD DEBTS—*
  1. At Head Office—

(a) Shares in New Zealand Land Company, Limited, - - - - - -	£904,904 0 0		
(b) Shares in Companies other than New Zealand and Australian Land Company, Limited, - - - -	126,074 15 0		
(c) Heritable Securities, - - - -	378,776 6 8		
(d) Life Policies, - - - - -	74,014 14 11		
(e) Produce, - - - - -	71,750 0 0		
(f) Shipping, - - - - -	38,308 6 7		
(g) Bills and Promissory Notes, - - -	92,497 13 6		
(h) Miscellaneous, - - - - -	11,000 0 0		
	£1,697,325 16 8		

  2. At Branches—

(a) Heritable, - - - - -	£30,097 2 10		
(b) Life Policies, - - - -	13,333 2 3		
(c) Shares in other companies, - - -	1,658 12 10		
(d) Shipping, - - - - -	300 0 0		
(e) Miscellaneous, - - - -	519 8 8		
	45,908 6 7		
		1,743,234 3 3	

III. BALANCE, BEING DEFICIENCY, - - - - - - - - - - - -   5,190,983 11 3

                                  £12,404,297 8 3

---

* The above securities are held against the following debts, which are estimated bad. It is to be noted, however, that against other debts due to the Bank it holds a large quantity of securities which do not appear above, the debts against which these are held being considered good.
  1. Head Office—

(a) Current accounts for credits and overdrafts estimated bad,	£6,899,912 2 1		
(b) Discounted bills on hand, current,	do.	194,856 18 8	
(c) Do. do. past due,	do.	77,752 12 10	
		£7,172,521 13 7	

  2. At Branches—

(a) Current accounts for credits and overdrafts estimated bad,	£128,028 18 4		
(b) Discounted bills on hand, current,	do.	14,913 15 0	
(c) Do. do. past due,	do	19,893 3 7	
		162,836 1 11	

Total estimated bad debts, - - - - - - - - £7,335,357 15 6

The Assets will be increased and the loss proportionally diminished by whatever dividends are received from the estates of the debtors and obligants in respect of the above bad debts.

Thin
25 Oct. 1950.